Drug Use and Misuse

Drug Use and Misuse

Stephen A. Maisto

VA Medical Center—Brockton, Massachusetts
Brown University Medical School

Mark Galizio

University of North Carolina
at Wilmington

Gerard J. Connors

Research Institute on Alcoholism
Buffalo, New York

Holt, Rinehart and Winston, Inc.

Fort Worth   Chicago   San Francisco   Philadelphia
Montreal   Toronto   London   Sydney   Tokyo

Publisher	Ted Buchholz
Acquisitions Editor	Tina Oldham
Project Editor	Mike Hinshaw
Production Manager	Tad Gaither
Art & Design Supervisor	John Ritland
Text Designer	Ritter & Ritter, Inc.
Cover Designer	Nancy Turner
Cover Illustration	Ron Lusk

Credits and acknowledgments of permission begin on page 473.

Library of Congress Cataloging-in-Publication Data

Maisto, Stephen A.
   Drug use and misuse / Stephen A. Maisto, J. Mark Galizio, Gerard J. Connors
      p. cm.
   Includes index.
   ISBN 0-03-014973-8
   1. Psychopharmacology.   2. Neuropsychopharmacology.   3. Substance
abuse.   I. Galizio, Mark.   II. Connors, Gerard Joseph.   III. Title.
RM315.M335   1990
615′.78—dc20
                                          90-5098
                                            CIP

Address for editorial correspondence: Holt, Rinehart and Winston, Inc., 301 Commerce Street,
Suite 3700, Forth Worth, TX 76102

Address for orders: Holt, Rinehart and Winston, Inc., 6277 Sea Harbor Drive, Orlando, Florida
32887. 1-800-782-4479, or 1-800-433-0001 (in Florida)

The paper used in this book was made from recycled paper.

PRINTED IN THE UNITED STATES OF AMERICA

0 1 2 3   016   9 8 7 6 5 4 3 2 1

Holt, Rinehart and Winston, Inc.
The Dryden Press
Saunders College Publishing

Preface

Concern about alcohol and other drug use became common in the 1980s and continues into the 1990s. Television and other media have brought home all aspects of drug use—from production to stopping use—to almost everyone. Drug use has become part of the common experience of children and adults, either directly or indirectly. This powerful social force was solidified politically in the United States by creation in 1989 of a federal cabinet post devoted to the prevention and amelioration of drug use and problems. Today the informed person needs to know about psychoactive drugs, their use, and the multiple consequences of such use. This is true not only for a person's own health, but for an awareness of what citizens' drug use does to the society in which they live.

It is in this context that we wrote this book. Our aim was to provide a textbook for the college undergraduate that was scholarly yet understandable to the student who may have little background in the biological or behavioral-social sciences. We also wanted the book to reflect the complexity of psychoactive drug use on biological, psychological, and social levels. We believe that the book has achieved these goals.

The book is inclusive, in its providing, first, fundamental background information for studying psychopharmacology. Furthermore, all of the major psychoactive drugs or drug classes, including over-the-counter drugs, are covered. Each is presented by integrating biological, psychological, and social perspectives, as well as by covering historical and current patterns of use. In the final section of the book we include chapters on personality and social factors as they relate to drug use in general, and on the prevention and treatment of drug problems. In writing each chapter we used a minimum of specialized or technical language and jargon. When use of technical terms was necessary, they were defined in the running and cumulative glossaries.

Completion of projects like this book is impossible without the help of others. First, we all would like to thank the present and past editorial staff at Holt for both educating us about book publishing and for being most understanding and helpful during the almost three years that it took to finish the written product. Specifically, we thank profusely Ms. Christina Oldham, Ms. Susan Pierce, Ms. Susan Arellano, and Ms. Melissa Mashburn for all their wisdom, help and patience. All of us also would like to thank the following reviewers of earlier chapter drafts, whose comments are a major force in the strengths of this text: Sarah Myers, Jacksonville University; David Morse, State University of New York at New Paltz; Tom Elliot, East Mississippi Jr.

College; Steven Grant, University of Delaware; Stephen Hinshaw, Univ. of California—Los Angeles; Kathy Fischer, Western Illinois University; Antonio Puente, Univ. of North Carolina—Wilmington; Charles Campbell, California State—Long Beach; Mitchell J. Picker, University of North Carolina—Chapel Hill; Bill Tedford, Southern Methodist University; Robert Smith, George Mason University; Kathryne Mueller, Texas Christian University; Douglas Smith, Southern Illinois University; James Steinberg, Wright State University; James Nevitt, Mid-Plains Community College; Joe Martinez, University of California; and Thomas Moye, San Jose State University.

Each of us also would like to express our thanks to other special people who helped make this text possible. Stephen would like to thank Ms. Mary Duquette, whose sense of humor and perspective kept him on a more even keel. Ms. Ema Costa's secretarial help was excellent, fast, and always there when Stephen needed it. His written contributions to the book never would have been public without Ema. Stephen also expresses love and a thank you to Mary Jean and Eddie, who gave his personal life a great boost and made professional activities seem much more worthwhile. Mark expresses appreciation and love to Kate, whose friendship helped him survive the project. Gerard expresses his appreciation to his family and friends, all of whom have consistently provided much support and encouragement.

Stephen A. Maisto
Mark Galizio
Gerard J. Connors

Brief Contents

Detailed Contents

Contemporary Issue Boxes

To BB
SAM

To Rachel and Joey
MG

To my parents
GJC

1 DRUG USE AND MISUSE: GENERAL ISSUES

This text is about drugs and how they affect human behavior. Because our subject matter is extremely wide-ranging, this chapter spans a variety of topics. We introduce you to formal definitions throughout the chapter, beginning with terms such as pharmacology and drugs. Next, we explain the drug classification systems used in this book and then move to a discussion of psychoactive drugs: the people who use them, why they do, and some of the consequences they can expect. The final sections of the chapter cover ways to define harmful drug use. We place some emphasis on drug tolerance and withdrawal as two phenomena that influence patterns and problems associated with drug use. The chapter closes with a brief overview of the rest of the text.

PHARMACOLOGY AND DRUGS

Pharmacology
The scientific study of drugs; concerned with all information about the effects of drugs on living systems.

Psychopharmacology
The subarea of pharmacology that concerns the effects of drugs on behavior.

Psychology
The scientific study of behavior.

Drug
Broadly defined as any chemical entity or mixture of entities, not required for the maintenance of health, that alters biological function or structure when administered.

Humans have used drugs for several thousand years, but the scientific study of drugs is more recent. The scientific study of drugs is called **pharmacology,** which is concerned with all information about the effects of chemical substances (drugs) on living systems. Pharmacology is considered a part of biology and is allied with physiology and biochemistry (Blum, 1984). **Psychopharmacology** is an area within the field of pharmacology that focuses on the effects of drugs on behavior. Although psychopharmacology is a joining of the words **psychology** and pharmacology, it is now recognized that understanding how drugs affect human behavior requires knowledge about social and environmental factors. This book is about human psychopharmacology.

Drugs are easy enough to talk about, or so it seems from the numbers and variety of people who do so. However, defining ''drug'' is not so simple. Although they have run into confusion along the way, experts have arrived at a workable definition. According to a World Health Organization (WHO) report published in 1981, **drug** is defined in the broadest sense as ''any chemical entity or mixture of entities, other than those required for the maintenance of normal health (like food), the administration of which alters biological function and possibly structure'' (p. 227).

HOW ARE DRUGS CLASSIFIED?

As the WHO panel of experts understood, their definition of drug is very broad. To make the definition useful for research and practical purposes, it is necessary to order the substances that fit the definition of drug into smaller categories. Pharmacologists have done this with their many systems for classifying drugs. These classification systems have been based on the primary properties of drugs, in order to communicate the drug's nature and ways that it can be used.

Current Drug Classification Systems

The ways of classifying drugs in this text are as follows (Jacobs & Fehr, 1987, pp. 12–15):

1. By origin—An example within this system is drugs that come from plants, such as the opiates, which are derived from the opium poppy. The "pure" (nonsynthetic) opiates include compounds such as morphine and codeine. Heroin, which is a semisynthetic compound, often is called an opiate drug. As this classification distinguishes only the source of the drug, a given drug class may include many drugs with different chemical actions.

2. By action, according to similarity of **drug effects**—For example, marijuana and atrophine both increase heart rate and cause dryness in the mouth. According to this system, therefore, marijuana is called an atrophine-like drug.

> **Drug effect**
> The action of a drug on the body. Drug effects are measured in different ways.

3. By therapeutic use, or according to similarity in how a drug is used to treat or modify something in the body—For example, with this system amphetamines are called appetite suppressant drugs. Note that the reasons some drugs are used can be much different from their therapeutic effects. When amphetamines are used nonmedically it is often because of their stimulant effects. Similarly, morphine may be used medically as a powerful pain killer, but the street user takes morphine for its euphoric effects.

4. By site of drug action, which pertains to where in the body the drug is causing physical changes—For example, alcohol often is called a depressant drug because of its depressant action on the central nervous system (CNS). Conversely, because of its CNS stimulant properties, cocaine often is called a stimulant drug. The utility of this system can be limited when a drug has an effect on several different body sites. One example is the CNS stimulant cocaine, which also has local anesthetic (pain reducing) effects. Furthermore, drugs that differ widely in chemical structure or mechanisms of action may affect the same body site.

5. By chemical structure—For example, the barbiturates (such as phenobarbital, amytal, and seconal) are synthetic compounds derived from the chemical structure of barbituric acid, the synthetic compound forming the chemical base for barbiturate drugs.

6. By mechanism of action, which means how a drug produces its effects—This is a good system in principle, but we still do not know the details about how some drugs produce their effects.

7. By street name, which comes from drug "subcultures" and the street drug market—For example, amphetamines are called "speed," and drugs like the barbiturates or depressants such as methaqualone (Quaalude) are called "downers." As these latter examples show, classification by street names sometimes does reflect actual drug effects.

WHAT ARE PSYCHOACTIVE DRUGS?

Psychoactive
Pertaining to effects on mood, thinking, and behavior.

Of all the types of drugs that are known, we are most interested in what are called **psychoactive** drugs—those that affect moods, thinking, and behavior. Some substances have been designated formally as psychoactive, while others have not. That formal distinction is of less importance to us than the actual psychoactive properties of the chemicals that are taken. Psychoactive drugs are of most importance in this test because they are the ones that people are most likely to use, often in ways that create serious problems for them. This text mainly concerns the nonmedical use of psychoactive drugs, but we also discuss medical uses.

What Causes the Experiences Humans Have When They Take Drugs?

Drug dosage
Measure of the quantity of drug consumed.

Route of drug administration
The way that drugs enter the body.

Oral
As a route of drug administration, it means taken into the mouth and swallowed.

Subcutaneous
A route of drug administration, meaning introduced under the skin.

Intramuscular
A route of drug administration, meaning "in the muscle."

Intravenous
A route of drug administration, meaning "into the veins."

Mucous membranes
The moist surfaces that line the mouth, nose, eye sockets, throat, rectum, and so forth.

Psychological set
An individual's knowledge, attitudes, expectations, and other thoughts about an object or event, such as a drug.

Because nonmedical drug use occurs with some frequency among humans, people apparently like the experiences they have when they take drugs. This raises an extremely important question: What causes the "drug experience"? The drug's chemical action is part of the answer, but how much? Not too long ago, the chemical actions of drugs were viewed as the primary reason people experienced certain changes when they took different drugs. However, in the past 30 years or so research from different disciplines, such as pharmacology, psychology, and sociology, has shown that the drug experience is a product of more factors than the drug's pharmacological action.

Generally, we can look at three sets of pharmacological and nonpharmacological factors to help us understand the drug experience. The first set includes **pharmacological factors,** and three stand out. First are the chemical properties and action on the body of the drug used. Another is **drug dosage** (or dose), which is the measure of how much of the drug is consumed. The third pharmacological factor is the **route of drug administration,** or the way the drug enters the body. This is important because the route affects how much of a dosage reaches its site(s) of action and how quickly it gets there. Five major routes are explained in this text, including **oral, subcutaneous, intramuscular, intravenous,** and through the body's **mucous membranes.** Chapter 4 discusses these routes and their effects on the drug experience in greater detail.

The second set of factors is nonpharmacological and consists of the **characteristics of the drug user.** Included are such factors as the person's genetic makeup (biologically inherited differences among people govern their bodies' reaction to the ingestion of different drugs), gender, age, drug tolerance (detailed later in this chapter), and personality. An important part of personality is the person's **psychological set** about a drug, which refers to knowledge, attitudes, expectations, and thoughts about a drug. For example, sometimes the strong belief that a drug will produce a certain effect

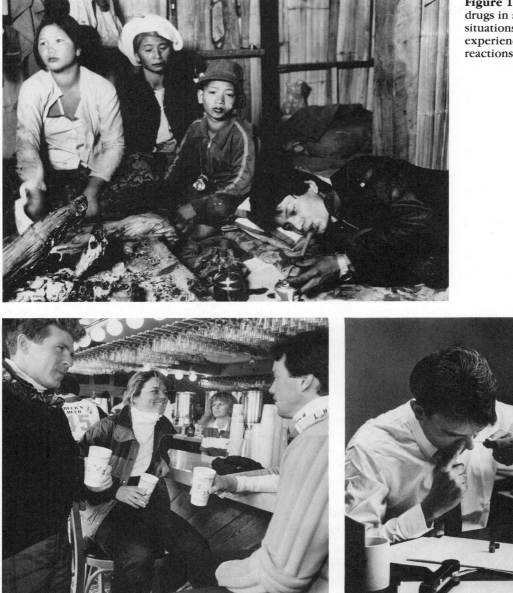

Figure 1–1 People use drugs in a variety of situations and experience different reactions to them.

will be enough to produce the effect, even though the person has ingested a chemically inactive substance **(placebo)**.

The third and last set of factors, also a nonpharmacological one, is the **setting in which a drug is used.** The factors in this group span a wide

Placebo
In pharmacology, refers to a chemically inactive substance.

range and include laws pertaining to drug use in the community where the drug is taken, the immediate physical environment where the drug is used, and whether other people are present at the time of drug use.

Together these three sets of factors influence what a person experiences when he or she takes a drug. You may have guessed that the path to a drug experience is not always easy to chart. However, many people are trying to do just that—to understand how drugs affect people. The accumulated knowledge from these efforts is the foundation of this book.

DESIRED DRUG EFFECTS AND DRUG USE

Reinforcing
Describing a consequence of a behavior that increases the likelihood that it will occur again.

When drugs are taken for "recreational" (that is, nonmedical or nonprescribed) reasons, the anticipated effect on behavior generally is, on balance, positive. Usually the effects of drugs that keep people using them are called the **reinforcing** effects of drugs. Drug users give many reasons for using drugs and, relatedly, all users do not use the same drugs for exactly the same reasons.

For example, we did an informal review of survey questionnaire items used to study drinking practices among adults (age 18 or older) in the U.S. We came up with almost fifty reasons for using alcohol! Some examples are to expand awareness and understanding, to celebrate something important, to relax, to make sex better, to be part of the group, to overcome shyness, to help forget worries, and to increase courage and self-confidence. The recorded reasons for using other drugs may not be as numerous as those reported for the ever-popular alcohol. However, other drugs are used at least partly because of what users see as positive effects. In Norman Zinberg's (1984) study of **illicit drug use**, users (135 men and women averaging about 27 years of age) reported a range of reasons for each drug class he studied. For instance, reasons opiate users reported for taking these drugs included to get a rush, to escape, to take risks, to alleviate depression, to enjoy the high, to socialize, and to relax.

Illicit drug use
Drug use not in accord with legal restrictions.

In his report, Zinberg (1984) included detailed quotes from subjects regarding their drug use. One reason for using marijuana, a "sharpening" of sensory and perceptual functions, was elaborated upon by one subject (p. 87):

> I think that most of the things I do that make me feel good, I would just as soon do stoned as straight. Chess is definitely more fun stoned. In fact, that's one of the reasons I got into chess. Once you know the rules and a couple of openings and stuff, chess is largely intuitive. And that's what getting stoned is about. It's opening the third eye, just sort of increasing that capacity, and that's why I like to play chess stoned.

Another subject discussed how marijuana enhanced his sexual pleasure (p. 88):

If I wanted to kiss a girl while I was straight there'd be too much going on in my head for me to really get into the kiss, whereas with grass I can really get into the kiss much more easily. I can really feel the kiss, more into body feelings rather than thinking, well, am I doing this right, will she like this, will I like this? Every touch, every movement, is like magnified a hundred times.

WHO USES ALCOHOL AND DRUGS?

Based on how often the substances are used, we might infer that many people in the United States feel that alcohol or drugs[1] have positive effects on them. Information about who in the United States uses what drugs in which ways is gathered through what are called survey studies. National survey studies typically involve interviewing a sample of individuals across the country. These studies generally ensure that those interviewed are as similar as possible to the United States population as a whole, regarding, for example, factors such as gender, age, race, region of the country, and rural versus urban living environment. To provide an overview of current alcohol and drug use, we use two recurring national surveys.

The first series of surveys is conducted yearly among high school seniors on their alcohol and drug use. Many of the seniors are reinterviewed over the years following the initial interview. Accordingly, the latest survey included information on that year's high school seniors and on young adults who were first interviewed as high school seniors in previous years and are now being reinterviewed. The follow-up group is divided into those who are in college and those who are not. We call the studies of current and past high school seniors the High School Seniors Survey. Full data have been published on current high school seniors through 1987, and follow-up data on the college students and young adults are available through 1986. College students are considered those who are in college and one to four years past high school, with typical ages of nineteen to twenty-two. Young adults are those one to nine years past high school ranging in age from eighteen to twenty-eight.

The second national survey is the National Household Survey on Drug Abuse, conducted every few years by the National Institute on Drug Abuse (NIDA; NIDA, 1988b). The National Household Survey is broader in the scope of persons interviewed, involving households in the contiguous forty-eight states. Most of our data are from the national household survey conducted in 1985, although we discuss preliminary findings from the 1988 survey. We also refer to data from the 1982 survey on use of more than one

---

[1]Sometimes in this book we use the term "alcohol and drugs"; at other times we use "drugs" as the inclusive term. Because alcohol is a drug, saying "alcohol and drugs" is redundant. However, we do so on occasion, when it seems useful, to distinguish alcohol from all other drugs.

drug by the same person. The year of the latest information available varies from topic to topic. Survey dates vary accordingly.

WHAT ARE THE PATTERNS OF ALCOHOL AND DRUG USE AMONG HIGH SCHOOL SENIORS, COLLEGE STUDENTS, AND OTHER YOUNG ADULTS?

Statistically different
Findings based on samples that are estimated, by use of statistical tests, to be real and not due to chance fluctuations.

Prevalence
The general occurrence of an event, usually expressed in terms of percentage of some population. Another common statistic in survey studies is incidence, or the number of first-time occurrences of an event during some time period.

The latest high school senior surveys (Johnston, O'Malley, & Bachman, 1987; NIDA, 1988a) yielded a number of findings worth highlighting. First, the decline in illicit drug use that occurred between 1981–1985 but stalled in 1985 seems to have resumed in 1986. This was true for the seniors, college students, and other young adults in the overall use of marijuana and of any illicit drugs other than marijuana. A second finding was the upward trend in cocaine use among high school seniors stopped in 1986 and resumed in 1987: high school seniors using cocaine in the thirty days before the survey rose from 4.9% in 1983 to 5.8% in 1984 to 6.7% in 1985. However, in 1986 the figure was 6.2%, not **statistically different** from 1985's data, but in 1987 the decrease was statistically different from 1986, down to 4.3%. In 1986 16.9% of seniors surveyed had tried cocaine at least once; about 40% of the 27-year-olds reinterviewed in 1986 had used cocaine at least once.

Another major finding showed three classes of illicit drugs as predominant. These were marijuana, cocaine, and major stimulants other than cocaine. The annual **prevalence** rates (in this case, the number of people who said they used the drug at least once during the last year) among the 1986 high school seniors were 38.8% for marijuana, 12.7% for cocaine, and 13.4% for stimulants. The annual prevalence rates for young adults and college students in 1986 showed some differences. College students reported use rates of 40.9%, 17.1%, and 10.3% for marijuana, cocaine, and stimulants, respectively. These same rates for other young adults were 36.9%, 19.6%, and 10.8%. Further, the 1986 survey showed that 58% of the high school seniors had used an illicit substance at least once. As you might expect, this figure increases with age: a total of 80% of the young adults (18 to 28 years old) said they had used an illicit drug at least once.

For the first time, in 1986, annual prevalence data were collected on the use of "crack," a form of cocaine that is smoked. Crack is causing grave problems of drug abuse and criminal behavior in the United States. Among the high school seniors, 4.1% said they had used crack at least once during the previous year. Use for the young adults was somewhat lower at 3.2%. The figure was lowest, at 1.3%, among the college students.

Gender and Student Status Differences in Drug Use

For most drugs, the rates of use for men were greater than those for women, with only two exceptions. Stimulant use by high school students was slightly greater among women, and tranquilizer use by both sexes in all three groups was similar. Questioning whether drug use rates were greater for the college students than for the high school students or young adults, researchers found "active" drug use rates (use at least once in the last year) were not much different among the three groups.

The Use of Alcohol and Nicotine

The use of two other psychoactive substances—alcohol and nicotine—was studied in the survey. In 1981, 70.7% of the high school seniors said they had used alcohol during the past 30 days; this dropped to 69.4% in 1983, and to 65.9% in 1985. It was 65.3% in 1986 and 66.4% in 1987. Therefore, in the 1980s alcohol use among seniors has declined, leveling off in the latter part of the decade.

The drinking data for college students, however, shows a different pattern. Although a comparable decrease is noted for daily drinking, the monthly prevalence rates did not change much from 1980 to 1986. The frequency of heavy-drinking occasions, or those times when a person has at least five drinks in a row, actually increased. The differences between these two groups—the high school seniors and the college students—are among the men. According to the survey's authors, college students are less likely than other people their age to drink daily but more likely to drink heavily when they do drink. College students tend to drink most often on weekends.

Some interesting findings on daily cigarette smoking (nicotine is the active drug in tobacco cigarettes) were reported from the 1986 survey. Daily cigarette use dropped slightly from 1980, when 21.3% of the high school seniors said they smoked cigarettes every day. The figure for 1986 seniors was 18.7%. The rate for the young adult sample was 25.9%. Despite the difference between the two groups, little difference was noted between males and females in daily smoking rates. Daily cigarette use among the college students in 1986 was much lower, at 12.7%. Somewhat unexpectedly, a difference was found in daily smoking between men and women in the college student sample. Daily smoking was more prevalent among college women (about 15%) that it was among college men (10%).

Summary

Several points from surveys of high school seniors, college students, and young adults stand out. Overall, illicit drug use among the three groups sampled is on the decline once again, after an apparent stall in 1985. The exception is the use of cocaine by high school seniors, which was up in 1987 from 1986. Another finding is that three individual classes of drug use—marijuana, cocaine, and stimulants other than cocaine—are the most popular of illicit drugs. In general, male high school seniors, college students, and young adults have a higher rate of illicit drug use than do their female counterparts. Alcohol continues as the most popular drug of all, and its use has leveled off again for high school seniors, after a decline in the early 1980s. For college students alcohol use is at the same level throughout the 1980s. Surveys show the frequency of heavy drinking among college men is up from 1986. Finally, all three groups showed lower rates of daily cigarette smoking compared to 1980, and college women reported higher rates of daily cigarette smoking than did college men.

A General Look at Findings From the 1987 High School Seniors Survey

It is instructive to take a closer look at the use of major drugs and drug classes by high school seniors today and during the past decade. Table 1-1 shows drug use by today's high school seniors. The table details the prevalence of use and recentcy of use for a number of drugs. Prevalence of use falls under the category "ever used"—that is, the percent of high school students who have ever taken a particular drug. Two categories encompass recentcy of use: "used in the past month" and "used in the past year, but not in the past month." Three substances stand out as having been used at least once by the seniors: alcohol, cigarettes, and marijuana/hashish. Alcohol has been used by over nine out of ten seniors, cigarettes by almost seven

Table 1-1

Lifetime Prevalence (Percent Ever Used) and Recency of Drug Use Among High School Seniors (1987)

Drug or Drug Class	Ever Used (%)	Used in Past Month (%)	Used in Past Year, but Not in Past Month (%)
Marijuana/Hashish	50.2	21.0	15.3
Inhalants	18.6	3.5	4.6
Hallucinogens	10.6	2.8	3.9
LSD	8.4	1.8	3.4
PCP	3.0	0.6	0.7
Cocaine	15.2	4.3	6.0
Crack	5.6	1.5	2.5
Other Cocaine	14.0	4.1	5.7
Heroin	1.2	0.2	0.3
Other Opiates	9.2	1.8	3.5
Stimulants	21.6	5.2	7.0
Sedatives	8.7	1.7	2.4
Barbiturates	7.4	1.4	2.2
Methaqualone	4.0	0.6	0.9
Tranquilizers	10.9	2.0	3.5
Alcohol	92.2	66.4	19.3
Cigarettes	67.2	29.4	Not Available

Note: Percentages in some cases include adjustments for under-reporting.
Source: National Institute on Drug Abuse (1988a).

out of ten seniors, and marijuana/hashish by slightly more than half the seniors. Other substances used at least once include stimulants (21.6 % have ever used them), inhalants (18.6%), and crack (5.6%) and other forms of cocaine (14%). Drugs ever used by about 10% of the high school seniors included hallucinogens, opiates other than heroin, sedatives, and tranquilizers. Heroin use is fairly rare: Only about one in every hundred seniors had ever used heroin.

As you might have expected, the number of seniors ever using a particular substance is markedly greater than the number using the drug recently. Alcohol (at 66.4%) was used most frequently during the month before the survey, followed by cigarettes (29.4%), marijuana/hashish (21.0%), stimulants (5.2%), and cocaine other than crack (4.1%). The rates of use for the category of "used in the past year, but not the past month" parallel the pattern for "past month" use, but generally at higher rates. Information on this category for cigarette use was not available.

The series of high school senior surveys conducted during the past decade provides us an opportunity to view trends in drug use over time. As can be seen in Figure 1-2 on lifetime prevalence rates for each senior class, alcohol,

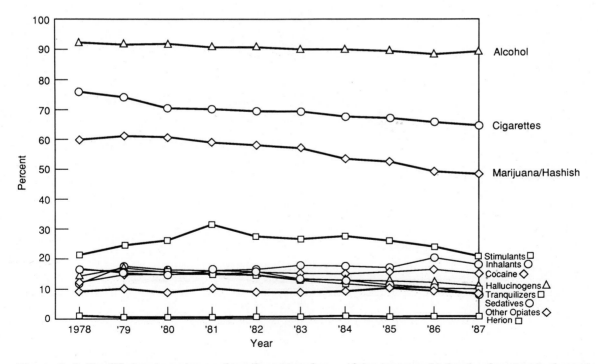

Figure 1–2 The lifetime prevalence of use for major classes of drugs among high school seniors is shown in percentages. (When available, rates that are adjusted for under-reporting are used.) Source: National Institute on Drug Abuse (1988a).

cigarettes, and marijuana/hashish have consistently remained the substances most commonly "used at least once." Since 1978 each drug has been tried by more than half the seniors surveyed each year. The next most commonly used class of drug is the stimulants, consistently tried at least once by more than 20% of the seniors each year. The remaining classes of drugs (except heroin) have reported lifetime prevalence rates of between 10 and 20 percent. The lifetime prevalence rates for heroin are lowest, and never exceeded two percent for any high school senior class since 1978.

Current drug use is shown in Figure 1-3 for the substances most often taken during the 30-day period before the survey. Alcohol is far and away the leader among the currently-used drugs, followed by cigarettes and marijuana, whose rates are fairly comparable. Stimulants, cocaine, and sedatives were further down on the list, usually taken currently by fewer than 10% of the seniors. The remaining drugs or drug classes—inhalants, hallucinogens, heroin, other opiates, and tranquilizers—rarely showed current use rates exceeding five percent in any given year and are not included on the graph.

The 1986 survey indicates some geographic variations in drug use pat-

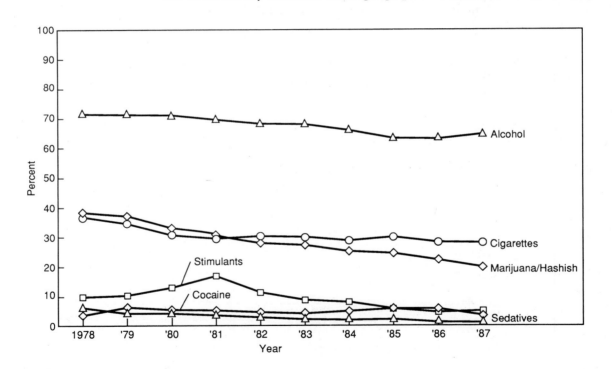

Figure 1–3 Current (past month) drug use for major classes of drugs among high school seniors is shown in percentages. (When available, rates that are adjusted for under-reporting are used.) Source: National Institute on Drug Abuse (1988a).

terns. There was a general tendency toward greater drug use in the Northeast and West sections of the United States, compared to the South and North Central sections. Perhaps the most dramatic example of this is in the use of cocaine. Figure 1-4 shows the lifetime prevalence rates for cocaine among high school seniors surveyed since 1975. As shown, cocaine use among seniors in the West and Northeast increased between 1979 and 1985 and dropped somewhat in 1986. Use among seniors in the South remained fairly stable during this period. Seniors in the North Central region showed stability, except for a decrease in 1984 and an increase again in 1985.

Summary

Among American high school seniors interviewed in 1987, alcohol (9 of 10 seniors), tobacco cigarettes (7 of 10), and marijuana/hashish (more than 5 of 10) were the drugs most frequently ever used. Moreover, trends in the lifetime use of these and other drugs seem to be fairly stable during the years 1978–1987. Note this contrasts with the decline in recent use prevalence among seniors for most drug classes since 1978. Use of drugs by seniors also varies according to where they live, as illustrated most clearly for cocaine use in 1987.

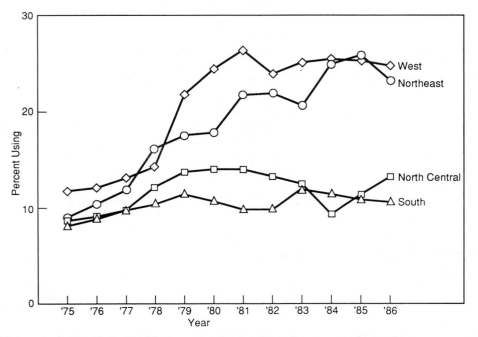

Figure 1–4 Trends in the lifetime prevalence of cocaine use are shown for different regions of the United States. Source: Johnston, O'Malley, and Bachman (1987).

CONTEMPORARY ISSUE BOX 1-1
An Update and Caution about the Seniors Surveys

Early information from the recently completed 1988 High School Seniors Survey was encouraging. Use of any illicit drug in the last year by high school seniors was at the lowest rate since the annual surveys began in 1975. This was true for all illicit drugs, including cocaine and crack. Rates of alcohol and nicotine use did not show a similar decline. Overall, the results were good news and have led some people to believe that drug and alcohol abuse prevention efforts launched in the 1980s may be having an effect.

Others, however, have not been so enthusiastic about the findings. They believe the overall survey findings may not represent certain subgroups of seniors. Two major reasons prompt a closer look at the survey findings before drawing conclusions about any trends in drug use among the nation's youth. First, the survey primarily was of high school seniors, so high school dropouts were not interviewed. Dropouts have some of the highest rates of illicit drug use among those under 21 years of age. Therefore, making valid conclusions about overall trends in drug use among youth of high school age based on the seniors survey data is impossible.

Another point about interpreting the survey findings is one we have already referred to, but one worth repeating. That is, a consistent finding shows alcohol and drug use prevalence and patterns vary according to characteristics of the user—such as sex, age, and race—and of the environment—such as area of residence and local laws and policies on drug and alcohol use. Taking these specific factors into account is essential before coming to any conclusions about a community's or person's alcohol and drug use.

WHAT ARE THE PATTERNS OF ALCOHOL AND DRUG USE AMONG AMERICANS OF ALL AGES?

Earlier we noted that the National Household Survey includes a sampling of households in the contiguous forty-eight states. This procedure allows information on alcohol and drug use to be collected from persons of all ages. The breakdown on alcohol and drug use is similar to that of the high school seniors survey, in that the major classes of drugs are covered. The age categories, however, are broader. Specifically, the household survey provides

Table 1-2
Lifetime Prevalence (in Percent) of Drug Use Among Members of American Households

Drug or Drug Class	Youth (Ages 12–17)			Young Adults (Ages 18–25)			Older Adults (Ages 26+)		
	1974	1979	1985	1974	1979	1985	1974	1979	1985
Marijuana/Hashish	23.0	30.9	23.7	52.7	68.2	60.5	9.9	19.6	27.2
Hallucinogens	6.0	7.1	3.2	16.6	25.1	11.5	1.3	4.5	6.2
Cocaine	3.6	5.4	5.2	12.7	27.5	25.2	0.9	4.3	9.5
Heroin	1.0	0.5	<.5	4.5	3.5	1.2	0.5	1.0	1.1
Stimulants	5.0	3.4	5.5	17.0	18.2	17.3	3.0	5.8	7.9
Sedatives	5.0	3.2	4.0	15.0	17.0	11.0	2.0	3.5	5.2
Tranquilizers	3.0	4.1	4.8	10.0	15.8	12.2	2.0	3.1	7.1
Alcohol	54.0	70.3	55.9	81.6	95.3	92.8	73.2	91.5	89.3
Cigarettes	52.0	54.1	45.3	68.8	82.8	76.0	65.4	83.0	80.5

Source: National Institute on Drug Abuse (1988b), on the 1985 National Household Survey on Drug Abuse.

information on three groups of people: youth (ages 12–17), young adults (ages 18–25), and older adults (ages 26 and up). The 1985 survey provides information on current alcohol and drug use patterns, and in conjunction with surveys done during previous years it is possible to see how today's use compares to usage over the past decade. We have detailed this information in Tables 1-2 and 1-3, which show the lifetime prevalence and current (last month) alcohol and drug use for three different years (1974, 1979, and 1985). Once again, for both lifetime prevalence and current use, alcohol, cigarettes, and marijuana/hashish are the substances most commonly reported in the National Household Survey for all three age categories. The lifetime prevalences for the remaining classes of drugs were much lower and fairly comparable, although among the young adults there was a greater prevalence of some substances, such as cocaine and hallucinogens in 1979,

Table 1-3
Current Drug Use (in Percent) Among Members of American Households

Drug or Drug Class	Youth (Ages 12–17)			Young Adults (Ages 18–25)			Older Adults (Ages 26+)		
	1974	1979	1985	1974	1979	1985	1974	1979	1985
Marijuana/Hashish	12.0	16.7	12.3	25.2	35.4	21.9	2.0	6.0	6.2
Hallucinogens	1.3	2.2	1.1	2.5	4.4	1.6	*	*	*
Cocaine	1.0	1.4	1.8	3.1	9.3	7.7	*	0.9	2.1
Heroin	*	*	*	0.8	0.8	0.6	*	*	*
Stimulants	1.0	1.2	1.8	3.7	3.5	4.0	*	0.5	0.7
Sedatives	1.0	1.1	1.1	1.6	2.8	1.7	*	*	0.7
Tranquilizers	1.0	0.6	0.6	1.2	2.1	1.7	*	*	1.0
Alcohol	34.0	37.2	31.5	69.3	75.9	71.5	54.5	61.3	60.7
Cigarettes	25.0	21.1(a)	15.6	48.8	42.6(a)	37.2	39.1	36.9(a)	32.8

* = Less than one-half of 1 percent.
(a) = For 1979 includes only persons who ever smoked at least 5 packs.
Source: National Institute on Drug Abuse (1988), on the 1985 National Household Survey on Drug Abuse.

cocaine, and to a lesser extent, other stimulants in 1985. The current use of the other drug classes was lower and similar, but note again the increased use of cocaine in 1979 and 1985 among the young adults. It would seem the leveling off and possible decline in the use of cocaine found in the high school seniors surveys of 1986 and 1987 would affect the trends in cocaine use discovered in the next national household survey. Indeed, information recently released suggests that cocaine use among adults that is current (last 30 days) and in the last year has declined considerably. This finding of decreasing use also occurred for other illicit drugs, alcohol, and nicotine. The only exception to this strong and general pattern was an increase since 1985 in reports of heavy cocaine, including crack, use.

Summary of the National Household Survey Data

Taken together, several general statements can be made about patterns of alcohol and drug use in the United States. First, three substances—alcohol, cigarettes, and marijuana/hashish—have consistently appeared as the most commonly tried and currently used psychoactive agents. (As you will see in Chapter 6, caffeine is the world's most commonly used drug. Caffeine use was not studied in the surveys we reviewed.) Second, a variety of other drugs are being used, but at much lower rates. Finally, a general trend of decreasing prevalence of current drug use seems to be emerging, with a few exceptions such as heavy use of cocaine, including crack.

HOW PREVALENT IS THE USE OF MORE THAN ONE DRUG AMONG ADULTS?

The person who increases the percentage of, say, marijuana users, may be the same person who increases the percentage of alcohol users. In this respect, a 1982 national survey of drug use among United States adults (Miller & Cisin, 1983) showed there were trends in the use of more than one drug. For example, the data of the 18–25–year–olds were analyzed separately to explore multiple drug use in the last month. Some findings of this analysis were that 15% of the respondents said they were currently using alcohol, marijuana, and cigarettes, and 10% said they were using marijuana and alcohol, but not cigarettes. Finally, 9% of the respondents said in the last month they had used alcohol, marijuana, and at least one of the following: cocaine, hallucinogens, heroin, or psychotherapeutic drugs nonmedically.

Polydrug use
The same person's regular use of more than one drug.

In its extreme, multiple drug use (also called **polydrug use**) can include taking drugs with different or opposite physical effects in sequence on the same occasion. In such cases, the motive for use seems to be change, positive or otherwise, from one drug experience to another. An instance of extreme polydrug use, excerpted from Goldman (1971) and cited in Mendelson and Mello (1985, pp. 200–201), illustrates how people may use one type of drug after another, without apparent rhyme or reason. The example involves famous comedian Lenny Bruce, who died in 1966 at age 40, and an associate of his:

> The night before, they ended a very successful three-week run in Chicago by traveling to the Cloisters (in New York City) and visiting the home of a show-biz druggist—a house so closely associated with drugs that show people call it the 'shooting gallery.' Terry smoked a couple of joints, dropped two blue tabs of mescaline, and skin-popped some Dilaudid; at the airport bar he also downed two double Scotches. Lenny did his usual number: 12, 1/16-**grain** Dilaudid pills counted out of a big brown bottle, dissolved in a 1-cubic centimeter (cc) ampule of Methedrine, and heated in a blackened old spoon. The resulting soup was drawn into a disposable needle and then whammed into mainline (intravenously) until you feel like you're living inside an igloo.
>
> Lenny also was into mescaline that evening: Not just Terry's two little old-maidish tabs, but a whole fistful, chewed up in his mouth and then washed down with a chocolate Yoo-Hoo.

Grain
As a measure, a unit of weight equal to .0648 of a gram.

SUMMARY: ALCOHOL AND DRUG EFFECTS AND USE

In this section on drug effects and use, we have seen that people take drugs for many varied reasons. The survey data show that alcohol or other drug use is not uncommon, especially among younger adults. Younger adults are the users who are most likely to take drugs in higher frequencies and quantities. Although the survey data have limitations (for example, the studies left out people who are in prison, known to be relatively heavy users of alcohol and drugs), the findings of the recent studies are consistent with those of the past. Americans, particularly when they are in the younger adult age range, find occasion to use alcohol or drugs.

CONTEMPORARY ISSUE BOX 1-2
U.S. Society and Drug Use

Learning about alcohol and drug use in the United States is important. One reason is the sheer number of people in the U.S. who use alcohol or other drugs. Another reason is the negative consequences associated with alcohol and drug use, which are discussed later in more detail. A third reason is the amount of controversy that drugs, especially illicit drugs, create. Despite the prevalence of drug use among Americans, as a population the U.S. attitude has been toward eradicating illicit drug use, often ranking such use as the nation's number one problem. Think of some of the major headline events that have occurred and controversies they have generated in the last few years. Some of them touch upon the basic Constitutional rights of Americans:

- The right of the federal government and other public and private employers to conduct urine screens (tests for drug taking) of employees as a way to control drug abuse in the work place

- The use of illegal drugs by professional and other athletes—some prime examples are Len Bias, the star University of Maryland basketball player who died in 1987 from an overdose of cocaine; Dwight Gooden, star pitcher for the New York Mets, who entered a drug abuse rehabilitation program before the start of the 1987 baseball season; Ben Johnson, Canadian track star, whose use of anabolic steroids nullified his gold medal in the 1988 Summer Olympics in Seoul, Korea

- The uproar resulting from the revelation that Douglas H. Ginsberg, a 1987 Supreme Court nominee, smoked marijuana at a party in the 1970s and the ensuing controversy, which revolved around Ginsberg's fitness to be a Supreme Court judge, resulting in the withdrawal of his nomination

- Some proposed legal penalties related to selling or using drugs— requirement of life sentences to drug dealers who are convicted twice of selling drugs to teenagers, and the imposition of the death penalty on dealers when a murder occurs during a drug deal

- The creation of "drug czar" as a Federal cabinet level post to coordinate and lead America's "War on Drugs"

Many Americans use alcohol or other drugs. But the country's attitudes toward such use, especially regarding illicit drugs, are far from permissive. Society's proposed and actual solutions to drug use in the United States have far reaching legal, social, and financial implications.

NEGATIVE DRUG EFFECTS AND SOCIAL CONSEQUENCES

People who use a drug regularly may experience negative effects along with whatever benefits they attribute to the drug. On the other hand, some people find the effects of a drug so negative they do not use it at all or have stopped using it. For some examples we turn again to our list of reasons from drinking practices questionnaires. This time we look at reasons given for not using alcohol. Instead of the effects of alcohol that are viewed to be positive, we are looking at effects that are perceived as negative. We uncovered more than 30 reasons that spanned a wide range. Examples include fear of having

Figure 1–5 The sometimes tragic consequences of drug use have drawn national attention and response.

a bad experience with alcohol, fear of trouble with the police, the knowledge that alcohol is addictive and interferes with playing sports, the idea that drinking seems morally wrong, the belief that an intoxicated person can be taken advantage of too easily, and the fact that alcohol can be harmful to general health. As another example of negative consequences that individuals may experience from using a drug, consider this case originally reported in an article in the *Wall Street Journal* on anabolic steroids (excerpted from the *Network News,* December, 1988):

> Aaron wanted to play football, but he felt that he wasn't big enough or fast enough. So, at thirteen, he started taking anabolic steroids. It soon seemed that his dream had come true. In his first year in high school, he was a linebacker and a nose guard on a winning St. Charles, MO, football team. As a sophomore he had bulked up to 175 pounds.

However, Aaron had become aggressive, so testy that he didn't want to be with others, and he quit playing football. He turned violent, beating his girlfriend, threatening to kill his sister, and attempting suicide. Finally, as a senior in high school, he was hospitalized for drug abuse.

Today, Aaron is off steroids, but his football dream is dead. Though he rejoined the team as a high-school senior, no college would sign him because of his abuse of steroids. "I ended up destroying my dream," he says.

What Does Alcohol and Drug Use Cost Society?

Describing the negative effects of using alcohol and drugs on one person hits home, because we can imagine having that experience ourselves. Or we may know someone who has had a bad experience. One area we seldom consider is the cost to society of the negative consequences of alcohol and drug use. Economic "cost of illness" studies estimate what different types of illnesses cost society in real resources. The emphasis in these studies is on quantifying in dollars what society "pays" for its members incurring specific illnesses. It is important to note that focusing on economic factors does not mean there are no psychological costs associated with illness. However, psychological consequences are not easily quantified and thus are much more difficult to analyze.

Two major "illness" distinctions that have been studied in detail are alcohol abuse and other drug abuse. In such research, "drug abuse" concerns the use of illegal drugs and the nonprescription use of drugs typically used for therapeutic purposes. Nicotine use has not been included. (However, this is not to understate the costs of nicotine use to United States society. The costs are devastating and are reviewed in detail in Chapter 6.)

A study by Harwood, Napolitano, Kristiansen, and Collins (1984) included estimates of the economic costs to United States society of alcohol abuse and other drug abuse. The study showed that in 1980 alcohol abuse cost United States citizens almost $90 billion, and drug abuse cost almost $50 billion (illegal drug use is considerably less common in the United States than is alcohol abuse). The $140 billion total approaches the estimated federal government **budget deficit** for 1989. Most people cannot even conceptualize what $1 billion is, never mind hundreds of billions of dollars. To help you understand how much money we are talking about, here is one illustration: A wealthy woman gives her sister $1 million to put in a drawer, telling her she can spend $1000 a day and to call when the money is spent. Three years later, the sister calls. If the original sum had been $1 billion, the sister would not have called for 3000 years. In any case, our difficulty in picturing billions of dollars does not make the cost of alcohol and drug abuse any less real.

Budget deficit
In reference to governments, the difference between the amount of money spent and the amount earned in taxes and other revenues.

Where Do These Costs Come From?

The vast majority of the cost of alcohol and drug abuse to society comes from reduced productivity of goods and services and lost employment due to injury, disability, and death. Treatment and related support also contribute to the costs. The totals: more than $79 billion for alcohol abuse and more than $29 billion for other drug abuse. For alcohol abuse almost $10 billion more comes from property loss in vehicle crashes, crime, and social welfare program expenses. These same items, with the exception of motor vehicle crashes because obtaining good estimates is impossible, totaled more than $17 billion for other drug abuse. Clearly, people individually and collectively suffer great losses from alcohol and drug abuse.

A Closing Note on Social Costs of Alcohol and Drug Abuse

Statistics on alcohol and drug use and problems are used to estimate the costs to society that are "caused" by such use. The word caused is placed in quotes because of the difficulty to say with confidence that an event or cost was a direct consequence of an individual's use of psychoactive substances. Another difficulty in making estimates is multiple diagnoses, which means that a person can be identified, for example, as having alcohol problems and a psychiatric diagnosis, such as major depression. The question becomes which is "primary," in the sense of determining the root of some damaging consequence. Often necessary is the assumption that the diagnosis listed first is of primary importance. These and other technical problems show that estimates are based in part on causality that is inferred by the researcher. Despite these problems, cost of illness studies produce extremely useful—and staggering—information.

CONTEMPORARY ISSUE BOX 1-3
Drugs, Criminal Activity, and Aggression

In 1988, New York City police recorded a record number of homicides. Other major urban centers in the U.S. also have reported a marked increase in murders, and a common explanation is that drug use, especially cocaine and its derivative crack, caused the increase. This is an illustration of a problem of tremendous cost to individuals and the society that they live in: the connection between drugs and criminal activity.

The problem is old, and much studied. First, that we are dealing with associations, or correlations, and not causes should be clear. For example, the pharmacological effects of cocaine are not known to cause a person to commit murder. Yet the high positive correlation between drugs and crime remains a fact: as drug use in a community increases so does the occurrence of certain kinds of crimes, depending on the drug.

Much of the research on drugs and crime has concerned heroin. Most of the crimes committed by heroin addicts are either violation of the drug laws or ways to get money to buy more heroin. Therefore, the addict's most commonly committed crimes are burglary, larceny, assault, and other street crimes. These crimes are indeed serious and sometimes result in injury or death to the victims. But the direct intent of the crime is not to harm the victim, but to get his or her money. This same motive probably applies to much of the violence around cocaine, as well as conflicts over money among cocaine dealers and their customers.

Surprisingly, the use of some drugs has no relationship with criminal activity, or there is negative association between use of the drug and crime. Use of the hallucinogens, for example, is not associated with crime, and marijuana seems to fall in the same category. The evidence is mixed for barbiturates and tranquilizers: some studies show no relationship, but others suggest that the relationship between use and crime is the same for barbiturates and alcohol.

Alcohol intoxication has a high correlation with criminal activity. Because alcohol is legal and very available, little violence is connected with violating drug laws or stealing to obtain alcohol. Most of the crimes associated with alcohol intoxication are assaultive. That is, they are committed with the intent to harm the victim. Alcohol is correlated with other types of crime as well, such as aggravated assault, homicides, property offenses, sexual offenses, and bad check writing.

So one point is clear: some types of drug use are associated with criminal activity. But what is the explanation? Pharmacology figures complexly in the answer but seems to be only one of many factors. Others include the person's expectations about the drug's effects, the setting where the drug is being used, and personality characteristics of the user.

The drug-crime problem is a good example of how drug use costs society money. It also illustrates that drug use and its effects on people are influenced by many factors working together.

DEFINING HARMFUL DRUG USE

Reviewing the negative correlates (associated factors or events) of alcohol and drug use raises the question, "What is drug use, and what is drug misuse?" Misuse (another, actually more commonly used term is abuse) implies that something is being used or treated in a way that is detrimental either to the individual or to others. At first glance it might seem simple to distinguish drug use and drug misuse. If a person spends $1000 a week on cocaine, and because of that loses his home, and then his family, everyone might agree that this is an instance of cocaine abuse. However, this example is more extreme than what we often face in applying a definition of misuse. For example, most adults in the United States drink alcohol and experience few or no negative consequences because of it. Another example is that many heroin users have been found to take the drug in a "controlled" fashion (called "chipping"). How do we define these different patterns of drug use? The question is important, because policy makers, clinicians, researchers, and the public need a clear and productive (leads to advancing knowledge) way to communicate among each other about drug use.

Typically, definitions of drug misuse have focused on consequences and legal restrictions. Illustrative is Blum's (1984) definition of abuse: "The use of a drug that is not legally or socially sanctioned, without proper regard for its pharmacologic actions. Such an abuse would undoubtedly result in effects that are harmful to the individual and to the society" (p. 17). Unfortunately, a major problem with this definition is that what is legally and socially sanctioned, and what harmful effects are experienced, varies widely with the social, cultural, and political context of use (Zinberg, 1984). (You can relate this idea to what we said earlier about the factors that influence drug effects and the drug experience.) A very recent example is how United States society perceives and punishes **driving while intoxicated.** Only 15 years ago such behavior generally was treated fairly casually both in the formal legal system and among the public. Today's picture is in stark contrast: Penalties even for first infractions are severe, including possible imprisonment, and the general population's attitudes are changing to match. As a result, drug-associated behavior that may not have resulted in labeling an individual an "abuser" in the past would result in such labeling today. You can see that social and culturally-bound definitions of drug misuse have limited generality and, therefore, limited value. However, we still need a way to communicate about harmful drug use patterns.

Driving while intoxicated
Operating a motor vehicle with enough alcohol or other drug in the blood to be legally defined as intoxicated.

Drug Dependence Syndrome

A current solution to this problem is the idea of a "drug dependence syndrome." This concept was developed in the World Health Organization memorandum (1981) cited at the beginning of this chapter. How this approach gives us an improved definition can be seen if we break down the term. "Dependence" implies need or reliance on. "Syndrome" means a cluster or collection of events. The need or reliance may be inferred by a person's psychological and behavioral patterns related to use of the drug. This idea coincides with the definition of the term **addiction.** Jaffe (1975) defined drug addiction as a pattern of behavior characterized by compulsive drug use as evidenced in overwhelming involvement with the use of a drug, maintaining an adequate supply of it, and a strong tendency to resume use of it after stopping for a period.

Addiction
In reference to drugs, overwhelming involvement with use of a drug, getting an adequate supply of it, and a strong tendency to resume use of it after stopping for a period.

The notion of drug dependence syndrome has become very important with the publication of the revision of the third edition of the American Psychiatric Association's (APA) Diagnostic and Statistical Manual (DSM-III-R) of Mental Disorders (APA, 1987). Since the early 1950s the APA has provided definitions and criteria for classification of different "mental disorders," including what traditionally has been called alcohol and other drug abuse. The DSM series has been highly influential, and undoubtedly its conception of substance use diagnoses will affect how health professionals, especially in the United States, think about alcohol and drug use.

The DSM-III-R Criteria

The DSM-III-R contains a set of criteria for the diagnosis of what is called "psychoactive substance use disorder." These criteria apply to all of the drugs and drug classes reviewed in this text. Consistent with the idea of drug dependence syndrome, the nine criteria (at least three must be met to diagnose a "disorder") pertain to behavioral and psychological patterns surrounding drug use. You can see this in the following annotated listing of "symptoms of dependence" (APA, 1987, pp. 166–167, cited with permission):

1. The person finds that when he or she actually takes the psychoactive substance, it often is used in larger amounts or over a longer period than originally intended. For example, the person may decide to take only one drink of alcohol, but after taking this first drink, continues to drink until extremely intoxicated.
2. The person recognizes that the substance use is excessive, and has attempted to reduce or control it, but has been unable to do so. In other instances the person may want to reduce or control his or her substance use, but has never actually made an effort to do so.
3. A great deal of time is spent in activities necessary to obtaining the substance (including theft), taking it, or recovering from its effects. In mild cases the person may spend several hours a day taking the substance, but continue to be involved in other activities. In severe cases, virtually all of the user's daily activities revolve around obtaining, using, and recuperating from the effects of the substance.
4. The person may suffer intoxication or withdrawal symptoms when he or she is expected to fulfill major role obligations (work, school, homemaking). For example, the person may be intoxicated when working outside the home or when expected to take care of his or her children. In addition, the person may be intoxicated or have withdrawal symptoms in situations in which substance use is physically hazardous, such as driving a car or operating machinery.
5. Important social, occupational, or recreational activities are given up or reduced because of substance use. The person may withdraw from family activities and hobbies in order to spend more time with substance-using friends, or to use the substance in private.
6. With heavy and prolonged substance use, a variety of social, psychological, and physical problems occur, and are exacerbated by continued use of the substance. Despite having one or more of these problems

(and recognizing that use of the substance causes or exacerbates them), the person continues to use the substance.

7. Significant **tolerance,** a markedly diminished effect with continued use of the same amount of the substance, occurs. The person will take greatly increased amounts of the substance in order to achieve intoxication or the desired effect. This is distinguished from the differences among people in their initial sensitivity to the effects of a particular substance.

8. With continued use, characteristic withdrawal symptoms develop when the person stops or reduces intake of the substance. The withdrawal symptoms vary greatly across classes of substances. Marked and generally easily measured physiologic signs of withdrawal are common with alcohol, opioids, sedatives, hypnotics, and anxiolytics (antianxiety drugs). Such signs are less obvious with amphetamines, cocaine, nicotine, and cannabis (marijuana/hashish), but intense subjective (psychological) symptoms can occur upon withdrawal from heavy use of these substances. No significant withdrawal is seen even after repeated use of hallucinogens; withdrawal from PCP and related substances has not yet been described in humans, although it has been demonstrated in animals.

9. The substance often is taken to relieve or avoid withdrawal symptoms.

Tolerance
Generally, a diminished drug effect with its continued use.

Note several features of these criteria. First, the focus is on drug use behavior. Furthermore, drug dependence may be observed in several dimensions: physical, psychological, and social. This is consistent with what has been a recurring theme in this chapter and one that is repeated throughout this text: understanding drug use and dependence requires that attention be paid simultaneously to biological, psychological, and social/environmental factors.

Conclusions about the DSM-III-R Criteria

We have discussed at some length the DSM-III-R criteria because they clearly summarize current thinking about drug use and drug dependence. In addition, the influence of this thinking should grow in the immediate future, so learning the criteria now makes reading further about alcohol and drug use easier for you. We follow the DSM-III-R definition in the remaining chapters of this text.

WHAT ARE DRUG TOLERANCE AND WITHDRAWAL?

The listing of the DSM-III-R criteria includes several new terms. The first is drug tolerance, which briefly was defined in point 7 of the criteria. A few distinctions have been made regarding tolerance to a drug. The first type, which used to be called initial tolerance, refers to an individual's sensitivity to a drug as measured the first time he or she ever takes it. People experience differences in how the first dose of a drug affects them, and this is now more aptly called a person's **initial sensitivity** to a drug.

Dispositional and Functional Tolerance

Regular use of a given drug results to some degree in **dispositional tolerance.** This refers to an increase in the rate of the metabolism of a drug, so that the user must consume greater quantities of it in order to maintain a certain level of the drug in his or her body.

Another type of tolerance is **functional tolerance.** Functional tolerance means the brain and other parts of the central nervous system become less sensitive to a drug's effects. Researchers recognize two types of functional tolerance, **acute** and **protracted.** Acute tolerance is measured within the course of action of a single dose of a drug. In this respect, when a person takes a dose of a drug, the amount of drug in his or her body—measured as the amount of drug in the blood, or blood level—rises to some peak level. For some drugs, at any point when the blood level is rising to peak, the drug effects may be greater than at that same point later when the blood level is falling. For example, people show acute tolerance to alcohol. One effect of alcohol when consumed in moderate amounts is impairment of short-term memory, or memory for events that occurred, say, in the past 30 seconds. Because of acute tolerance to alcohol, we are more likely to see impairment in short-term memory when the blood level of alcohol is rising than when it is falling.

Protracted tolerance pertains to the effects of a given dose of a drug when administered on two or more occasions. As with dispositional tolerance, the development of protracted tolerance requires that the individual consume greater amounts of a drug in order to achieve an effect that was once achieved with a lesser dose. So, in our example of alcohol and short-term memory, a person may show impairment in memory today after drinking six cans of beer, when he or she formerly showed the same degree of impairment after drinking only three beers.

Cross Tolerance and Cross Dependence

Finally, a user may develop **cross tolerance** and **cross dependence** to different drugs. In general, both may occur with drugs that have similar sites of action in the body. An example of cross tolerance is a person who has developed protracted tolerance to one drug and now has tolerance to other drugs, even though he or she may never have taken those other drugs. A practical consequence of cross tolerance commonly occurs in surgical treatment. A person who is highly tolerant to drugs that depress the central ner-

---

Initial sensitivity
The effect of a drug on a first-time user.

Dispositional tolerance
An increase in the rate of metabolizing a drug as a result of its regular use.

Functional tolerance
Decreased behavioral effects of a drug as a result of its regular use.

Acute tolerance
A type of functional tolerance that occurs within the course of action of a single drug dose.

Protracted tolerance
A type of functional tolerance that occurs over the course of two or more drug administrations.

Cross tolerance
Tolerance to a drug or drugs never taken that results from protracted tolerance to another drug or drugs.

vous system, such as alcohol or the barbiturates, creates problems for the anesthesiologist. Anesthetic drugs are useful in surgery because of their depressant effects. As a result, drugs such as alcohol or the barbiturates can cause cross tolerance to drugs used medically as anesthetics.

Cross dependence refers to taking one drug to suppress withdrawal symptoms from another. Cross dependence among drugs is used in medical treatment of drug withdrawal. Commonly, the benzodiazepine drugs, for example chlordiazepoxide (Librium), are used to treat withdrawal from alcohol. Another example is the use of clonidine (Catapres) in the treatment of heroin withdrawal. We should note that a drug could be taken to relieve its own withdrawal symptoms. However, the risk in so doing may sustain the person's reliance on the drug. We discuss the treatment of drug withdrawal in much more detail in Chapter 15.

Cross dependence
Suppression of symptoms of withdrawal from one drug by another drug.

Withdrawal Symptoms

Another important point in the listing of the DSM-III-R criteria is **withdrawal symptoms.** Withdrawal symptoms are a definable illness that occurs with a cessation or decrease in drug use, after the body has adjusted to the presence of a drug to such a degree that it cannot function without it. As noted in the DSM-III-R listing, not all drugs are associated with an identifiable withdrawal **syndrome** (also called abstinence syndrome). For any drug associated with withdrawal symptoms, the severity of those symptoms may change with the characteristics of the user and his or her history of use of that drug. So, to think of withdrawal symptoms only as being present or absent can be misleading. The better question is, can withdrawal symptoms be detected and, if so, what and how severe are they? In addition, among the various drugs associated with withdrawal symptoms, the severity of those symptoms can be considerably different. An example is the sometimes very severe and potentially fatal withdrawal syndromes associated with the barbiturates and alcohol, in contrast to the relatively minor symptoms associated with caffeine withdrawal.

Withdrawal symptoms
A definable illness that occurs with a cessation or decrease in use of a drug.

Syndrome
In medicine, a number of symptoms occurring together and characterizing a specific illness or disease.

Although the specific withdrawal symptoms for these three drugs are reviewed in later chapters, an important point is that psychological symptoms, such as anxiety, depression, and **craving** for drugs, are often part of the withdrawal syndromes. These psychological symptoms strongly influence whether the individual can stop using drugs for any length of time.

Craving
A term that has been variously defined in reference to drug use. Typically it refers to a strong or intense desire to use a drug.

Tolerance, Withdrawal, and Drug Taking Behavior

One reason we have spent a considerable amount of space on tolerance and withdrawal is because they are addressed with every drug that is evaluated or studied. More specific to psychopharmacology, tolerance and withdrawal affect patterns of drug use and their consequences. For example, if dispositional and functional tolerance to a drug develop, the individual must consume increasing amounts of it to achieve a desired drug effect. Such a trend in use may affect how much time the person may devote each day to acquiring the drug and to using it. Furthermore, with greater quantities and frequencies of drug use, the person becomes more susceptible to experiencing various physical, social, or legal negative consequences.

Similarly, drug dependence makes more likely a person's continued use of a drug or resumption of use after a period of abstaining. Many studies have shown that relief from withdrawal is a powerful reinforcing effect of drugs. In this regard, if a person is physically dependent on a drug, then when the level of drug in the blood drops he or she will start to experience withdrawal symptoms. If more of the drug is taken at this point, the symptoms are relieved. Here the reinforcement is the "turning off" of unpleasant withdrawal symptoms. Such reinforcement works to perpetuate a powerful cycle of drug use—drug withdrawal—drug use.

This discussion shows that using a drug for long period alters the patterns of use for that drug. Long-term use also relates to the DSM-III-R criteria. Tolerance and dependence may result not only in changes in drug use and preoccupation, but also in the likelihood that the person's life and the lives of those around him or her are affected by the drug in a snowballing effect, with one consequence building upon another. The outcome can reflect several of the criteria included in the DSM-III-R definition of psychoactive substance use disorder.

OVERVIEW OF THE TEXT

We close this chapter by giving you a brief overview of what is to follow. As was the goal of this chapter, the next three are designed to give you information about the history of drug-taking behavior and basic concepts in psychopharmacology. Accordingly, Chapter 2 places human drug use in a historical context, giving you a better appreciation of today's use patterns and the social and political contexts in which they occur. Chapter 3 is a basic discussion of the nervous system and how drugs affect it. This knowledge is essential to understanding drug effects because, no matter what drug effect or experience you consider, some change in the nervous system is inevitable. In Chapter 4 we review the ways scientists study drug effects and drug use, which prepares you for later chapters by showing what procedures have been followed to discover the knowledge that we now have about drugs.

Over-the-counter
Drugs that can be legally obtained without medical prescription.

Chapters 5–13 concern individual drugs and drug classes, including the major and minor stimulants, alcohol and other depressant drugs, psychiatric drugs, opiates, marijuana, hallucinogens, and **over-the-counter** drugs. These chapters broadly follow an outline of historical overview and epidemiology; mechanisms of drug action; medical and psychotherapeutic uses; and physiological, psychological, and social/environmental effects. Your study of each of the drug chapters offers good understanding of that drug (or drug class) and its use.

The last chapters of the book cover, first, the social and, second, the personality factors associated with drug use (Chapter 14). Chapter 14 explains why drug use is not the same for all people. The last two chapters concern topics often discussed in media geared to the general public. Chapter 15 is a review of treatment of the psychoactive substance use disorders, and Chapter 16 covers prevention of psychoactive substance use disorders before they occur. Prevention is a fitting topic on which to end this book because that is what all the research, politics, and discussion are about—reaching the goal of living in a society free of psychoactive substance use disorders.

SUMMARY

- Psychopharmacology, the scientific study of the effects of drugs on behavior, is the subject of this text.

- Drugs may be classified in different ways; seven of the major ones are reviewed in this chapter.

- The experience that humans have from taking drugs is influenced by three sets of factors, including pharmacological factors, characteristics of the drug user, and the setting in which the drug is used.

- Drug users give many reasons for using drugs, and all users do not use the same drugs for the same reasons.

- Survey studies have shown that American high school seniors, college students, and other young adults have used a range of psychoactive drugs.

- Overall illicit drug use, except for cocaine, was found in 1987 to be on the decline for American high school seniors, college students, and other young adults.

- Alcohol, tobacco cigarettes, and marijuana/hashish consistently have appeared as the most commonly tried and currently used psychoactive drugs.

- Reported rates of daily cigarette smoking were down from 1980 for all three groups included in the seniors survey of 1987, and college women seem to have a higher rate of daily cigarette smoking than do college men.

- The 1987 seniors survey showed lifetime prevalence rates of alcohol, tobacco cigarettes, and illicit drugs among seniors have been fairly stable over the last 10 years. This finding is in contrast to the trend of decline in recent drug use among seniors. Seniors' use of drugs seems to vary according to the region of the country.

- National surveys of Americans aged 12 and older suggest that the use of alcohol, nicotine, and illicit drugs is generally declining. An exception is heavy cocaine use, including crack.

- Some individuals use more than one drug regularly and may use different drugs together on the same occasion.

- Users often experience negative effects from drugs, some of which can be very damaging to the individual, society, or both.

- In 1980 the estimated combined cost of alcohol and illegal drug use to U.S. society was $140 billion.

- The idea of the drug dependence syndrome has helped to clarify the definitions of drug use and misuse.

- The drug dependence syndrome is one basis of the DSM-III-R criteria in defining the "psychoactive substance use disorders."

- The DSM-III-R definition includes drug tolerance and withdrawal. Drug tolerance refers to changes in how the body metabolizes a drug or to the effects of a given dose of drug as a result of using it. The two major kinds of tolerance are dispositional tolerance and functional tolerance.

· Withdrawal symptoms are a definable illness that occurs with a cessation or decrease in drug use. These symptoms occur after the body has become accustomed to the presence of a drug. Not all drugs are associated with physical withdrawal symptoms.

· This book covers basic psychopharmacology concepts, details on major drugs and drug classes and those who use them, and discussions of prevention and treatment toward a better understanding of drugs and human behavior.

References

American Psychiatric Association (1987). *Diagnostic and statistical manual of mental disorders* (Third Edition–Revised). Washington, DC: Author.

Blum, K. (1984). *Handbook of abusable drugs.* New York: Gardner Press, Inc.

Goldman, A. (1971). *Ladies and gentlemen, Lenny Bruce!* New York: Random House.

Harwood, H.J., Napolitano, D.M., Kristiansen, P.L., & Collins, J.J. (1984). *Economic costs to society of alcohol and drug abuse and mental illness: 1980.* Report submitted to the Alcohol, Drug Abuse, and Mental Health Administration (Contract No. ADM 283-83-0002), Rockville, MD.

Jacobs, M.R., & Fehr, K.O'B. (1987). *Drugs and drug abuse: A reference text* (Second Edition). Toronto, Canada: Addiction Research Foundation.

Jaffe, J.M. (1975). Drug addiction and drug abuse. In L.S. Goodman & A. Gilman (Eds.), *The pharmacological basis of therapeutics* (Fifth Edition) (pp. 284–324). New York: Macmillan Publishing Co.

Johnston, L.D., O'Malley, P.M., & Bachman, J.G. (1987). *National trends in drug use and related factors among American high school students and young adults, 1975–1986.* Rockville, MD: National Institute on Drug Abuse.

Mendelson, J.H., & Mello, N.K. (1985). *Alcohol: Use and abuse in America.* Boston: Little, Brown, & Co.

Miller, J.D., & Cisin, I.H. (1983). *Highlights from the National Survey on Drug Abuse: 1982.* Washington, DC: U.S. Government Printing Office.

National Institute on Drug Abuse (1988a). *Update on the 13th annual survey of drug abuse among high school seniors.* Rockville, MD: Author.

National Institute on Drug Abuse (1988b). *National Household Survey on Drug Abuse: Main findings, 1985.* Rockville, MD: Author.

World Health Organization (1981). Nomenclature and classification of drug- and alcohol-related problems: A WHO memorandum. *Bulletin of the World Health Organization, 59.* 225–242.

Zinberg, N.E. (1984). *Drug, set, and setting.* New Haven, CT: Yale University Press.

2 DRUG USE: YESTERDAY AND TODAY

The use of drugs dates back thousands of years. Drugs have been used for a variety of reasons in different cultures, including for religious purposes, for recreation, for altering states of consciousness, and for obtaining relief from pain or distress. In this chapter we have several objectives. One is to provide you with a historical overview of drug use, from prehistory to recent times. This is a general overview only, as more detailed histories on the specific psychoactive substances covered in this book are provided in their respective chapters. Nevertheless, this overview provides a broad perspective useful for studying the evolution of drug use and a background for considering the patterns of today's drug use described in Chapter 1. A second goal is to discuss some parallels between developments in medicine and the nonmedical use of drugs. Finally, we review the types of restrictions that have been placed on drug use historically and summarize current drug laws.

HISTORICAL OVERVIEW

Fermentation
A combustive process in which yeasts interact with the sugars in plants, such as grapes, grains, and fruits, to produce an enzyme that converts the sugar into alcohol.

Opium poppy
A plant cultivated for centuries, primarily in Eurasia, for opium, a narcotic that acts as a central nervous system depressant.

Cannabis sativa
The Indian hemp plant popularly known as marijuana; its resin, flowering tops, leaves, and stem contain the plant's psychoactive substances.

Hashish
Produced from the resin that covers the flowers of the cannabis hemp plant. This plant resin generally contains a greater concentration of the drug's psychoactive properties.

Indications of psychoactive substance use date to the beginnings of recorded history and revolve around the use of alcohol and plants with psychoactive properties. Investigations by archeologists suggest that beer and hackleberry wine were used as early as 6400 B.C. (Mellaart, 1967). Alcohol probably was discovered following accidental **fermentation.** (Grape wine, incidently, did not appear until around 300–400 B.C.) The earliest reference to use of an intoxicant appears to be Noah's drunkenness in the Book of Genesis. Also, various plants were used for the changes they produced, usually within religious or medicinal contexts. As an example, what probably was the **opium poppy** was used in Asia Minor about 5000 B.C. as a "joy plant" (Blum, 1984; O'Brien & Cohen, 1984). The use of **cannabis sativa** (brewed as a tea) dates to around 2700 B.C. in China. It was recommended by Emperor Shen Nung to his citizens for the treatment of gout and absent-mindedness, among a host of other ailments. People in the Stone Age are thought to have been familiar with opium, **hashish,** and cocaine, and to have used these drugs to produce altered states of consciousness (typically within a religious context) or to prepare themselves for battle (GPO, 1972). Chewing coca leaves (one procedure for ingesting cocaine) is recorded among Indian burial sites in Central and South America as far back as 2500 B.C. Something to keep in mind is that the use of a drug in one culture does not necessarily mean people in another culture were at the same time exposed to or using that substance. Instead, cultures (now as well as then) are characterized both by diversity and by similarity in their patterns of drug use.

Throughout history contact between distant cultures has often been forced by trade agreements or by wars or other hostilities. For example, the

Crusades and the expeditions of Marco Polo exposed Europeans to the drugs, particularly opium and hashish, that were popular in Oriental and Asian cultures. Other contacts were opened later through the travels of European explorers (particularly from England, France, Portugal, and Spain) to the Americas. The predominant psychoactive substances brought to Europe from the Americas were cocaine (from South America), various hallucinogens (from Central America), and tobacco (from North America). And according to O'Brien and Cohen (1984), the exchange was not one-sided. The trees producing the caffeine-containing coffee bean were native to Ethiopia. The coffee beverage derived from this bean was brought to Europe in the 1600s, and European seagoers were responsible for the eventual spread of coffee bean cultivation to the now world-leader supplier of coffee, South America. In addition, Europe introduced distilled alcoholic beverages to the Americas generally and cannabis to Chile in 1545 (O'Brien & Cohen, 1984).

Prior to the beginning of the twentieth century few restrictions existed on drug availability or drug use. Occasional efforts were made to decrease or eliminate certain substances, but these efforts tended to be short-lived or ineffective. For example, initial introductions to Europe of tobacco, coffee, and tea were all met with some resistance. Rodrigo de Jerez, a colleague of Columbus thought to be the first European to have smoked tobacco, was jailed in Spain because the authorities felt the devil had overtaken him (Whitaker, 1987). Also, at different times efforts were made to ban the use of coffee and tea.

Cases are also known in which governments acted not to make drugs unavailable but rather to keep drug trade open and flourishing! The best example of this involved armed conflict between China and Great Britain in the mid-nineteenth century. These conflicts, because they dealt with British traders bringing opium into China, are known now as the Opium Wars. By the mid-1800s several million Chinese men had become addicted to opium. In fact, China appears to have had the highest national use of opium by that period of time. Most of the opium being used in China was cultivated in India and brought to China by British traders. A variety of laws were passed by Chinese officials to control or eliminate opium imports, but none (including **prohibition**) had the desired effect of reducing opium use or the prevalence of addiction. Further, the British were unwilling to curtail trade of opium into China, in part for financial reasons and in part because they did not witness such a degree of addiction among users in England (where opium was widely used in medicine). Relations came to a crisis point in 1839, when the Chinese government destroyed large shipments of opium being brought into China by several British and American traders. Thus began the first Opium War between China and England. The British won the conflict, and as part of the 1842 Treaty of Nanking received rights to the port of Hong Kong as well as reimbursement for the shippers who lost their opium cargo. The opium trade continued until 1856, when the second

Prohibition
The legal forbidding of the sale of a substance, as in the alcohol Prohibition Era in the U.S., 1920–1933.

Opium War commenced. The war ended in 1858, and the Treaty of Tientsin mandated that China would continue to import opium but could impose heavy taxes. Not until the beginning of the twentieth century was this trade reduced and eventually terminated, dovetailing with a growing international recognition of **narcotic** drug abuse.

In the twentieth century, few differences existed between Europe and the United States in the types of drugs being used. What is of interest is that a large number of new or "re-discovered" drugs were first popularized in the United States, and later became popular in other countries (Brecher, 1972), making the United States something of a trend setter in drug use.

Drug Use in the United States

The use of psychoactive substances in the United States has a history as old as the country itself. Upon their arrival in the New World, Columbus and his crew were startled and amazed when they saw Indians smoking tobacco. Indeed, they described to their countrymen that these natives ate fire and belched out smoke like a dragon! The Indians inhabiting this land also introduced Columbus and the later explorers and settlers to a wide variety of psychoactive plants, including **peyote.** The Europeans, in turn, introduced to the Americas distilled spirits, a major staple on the long and arduous voyage across the Atlantic. The Pilgrims, for example, brought with them large stores of alcoholic beverages.

One of the most interesting periods of time in this country, in terms of drug use, was the nineteenth century. Into the middle 1800s, few restrictions were placed on drugs. Drugs such as opium, **morphine,** marijuana, heroin (at the end of the century), and cocaine: all were easy to obtain without prescription, and often at grocery stores or through mail order. Opium, for example, was on sale legally and at low prices; some opium poppies were grown in the United States (a national outlawing of opium cultivation did not occur until 1942). Morphine was commonly used especially during and after the Civil War, and both opium and morphine could be obtained in a variety of patent medicines readily available in stores. Examples include Godfrey's Cordial and Mrs. Wilson's Soothing Syrup. Opium was frequently taken in liquid form in mixtures such as laudanum (which contained one grain of opium to 25 drops of alcohol), and one of its more common uses was in calming and quieting crying babies!

Most narcotic use throughout this period was legal—whether through over-the-counter "tonics" or through prescription. Physicians recommended these substances widely, and referred to opium and morphine as "God's own medicine," or "G.O.M." (Morgan, 1981). And, indeed, these were effective calming agents. The list of ailments for which opium was recommended was nearly endless. A short list includes dysentery, pain, swelling, delirium tremens (associated with withdrawal from alcohol), headache, and in certain cases mental illness. Morphine, the active agent in

Narcotic
A central nervous system depressant that contains sedative and pain relieving compounds.

Peyote
(pay-yo-tea)
A cactus plant, the top of which (a "button") is dried and ingested for its hallucinogenic properties.

Morphine
A derivative of opium that is best known as a potent pain relieving medication.

the opium poppy, was isolated in 1806. It was named after Morpheus, the god of sleep and dreams, and was used widely during and after the Civil War, its administration greatly facilitated by the introduction of the hypodermic needle in the late 1840s. In fact, the widespread use of morphine during the Civil War is generally held responsible for large numbers of soldiers developing the "soldier's disease"—morphine addiction. The smoking of opium was introduced in the United States by Chinese laborers and was a widespread practice in the mid-1800s, especially on the West Coast. However, increased recognition by medical experts and others of the addictive aspects of the opium poppy products—opium, morphine, and heroin—triggered efforts to control their use and availability. We discuss some of these efforts later in this chapter.

Marijuana is another substance with a long history of use. A liquid extract of the cannabis sativa plant was used by physicians in the 1800s as a general all-purpose medication (Nahas, 1973). Its use nonmedically was noted to be much wider in the 1920s, probably in part a result of alcohol prohibition (Brecher, 1972). The use of marijuana was fairly steady in the 1930s through the 1950s but generally limited to urban areas and to the rural areas in which the marijuana was grown and harvested. In the 1960s, its popularity soared, and that popularity has remained strong. Coinciding with this popularity has been an effort to decriminalize or even legitimize marijuana sale and use. The most active organization in this effort is the National Organization to Reform the Marijuana Laws, or NORML.

A drug that has had a fluctuating popularity among drug users in this country is cocaine. Cocaine was widely used in various "tonics" and patent medicines in the late 1800s and early 1900s. Despite concerns over negative effects associated with extended use, not until 1914 was cocaine brought under strict legal controls and penalties. Its use was apparently fairly limited in the United States until into the 1960s. In the late 1960s and up to now it has been, in various forms, in much wider use. Some experts believe cocaine will be the drug of choice for many drug users in upcoming years, and that it has not yet achieved its peak in popularity.

Other psychoactive substances have had their distinct periods of popularity during this century. **Amphetamines,** for example, were quite widely used throughout the 1930s to treat depression. In addition, they were given to soldiers during World War II in the belief the drug would enhance alertness (O'Brien & Cohen, 1984). Obtaining amphetamines through medical outlets such as physician prescriptions was not particularly difficult. When concern arose about the dangers inherent in continued use of these drugs, restrictions on their availability became much tighter. At this juncture, the stage was set for a much greater production and distribution of amphetamines through illicit channels. The abuse of amphetamines remains a significant problem today, particularly when these drugs are taken intravenously.

The 1950s was the era for two central substances. During this decade the

Amphetamine
A central nervous system stimulant whose actions are similar to those of the naturally-occurring adrenaline.

Solvent
A substance, usually a liquid or gas, that contains one or more intoxicating components. Examples include glue, gasoline, and nonstick frying pan sprays.

minor tranquilizers first became popular, a trend that continues today. As we discuss in Chapter 9, minor tranquilizers are the most commonly prescribed psychiatric drugs in this country. The 1950s also are associated with the contemporary appearance of **solvent** inhaling. The first report of such abuse was in 1951 by Clinger and Johnson. They described the intentional inhalation of gasoline by two young boys. However, solvent abuse tended to be more common with other substances, such as model cements, lighter fluids, lacquer thinner, cleaning solvents, and more recently the propellant gases of aerosol products (see Hofmann, 1975). The problem was marked in the early 1960s, with solvent inhaling producing deaths and leading hobby glue producers to remove the two most toxic solvents, benzene and carbon tetrachloride, from their products (Blum, 1984). Nevertheless, solvent inhalant abuse is still a serious problem, especially among males in their teens.

CONTEMPORARY ISSUE BOX 2-1
Officially Sanctioned Use of a Hallucinogen

Did you know that the United States federal government does officially permit, as a result of court decisions, the use of one hallucinogen? The drug is *peyote,* obtained from the mescal cactus that grows in the desert areas of Northern and Central Mexico and in adjacent arid areas of the United States. The cactus is a spineless plant with a rounded head that contains disks. In these disks, more commonly called buttons, is found mescaline, which is the principal peyote hallucinogen. These buttons are moistened in the mouth and then swallowed. Following some initially unpleasant effects, including nausea and sweating, is a peyote intoxication that includes a variety of visual hallucinations characterized by an array of brilliant colors, disruptions of time and space perception, and feelings of weightlessness.

Peyote has been used for centuries by the Aztecs and other Mexican Indians for religious purposes. One description of its use today among some Mexican tribes can be found in Carlos Casteneda's 1968 book *The Teachings of Don Juan.* The use of peyote spread during the late 1800s to several American Indian tribes along the border and then northward to other tribes. Its use was almost exclusively religious and it served an important role in unifying and solidifying the individual tribes. However, its use was objected to by outsiders to the tribes, and several states, the first being Oklahoma in 1899, passed various forms of legislation to ban the use of peyote. Legal challenges to these laws were mounted successfully, and in large part because of the input provided by the Native

American Church of North America. This church, established in 1918, now includes an Indian membership of around 250,000, and its religious service includes peyote ingestion. The successful claim made by the church is that legislation attempting to curtail their use of peyote is a violation of their constitutional opportunity for freedom of religion. As a result, peyote is legally sanctioned for use in the context of their religious service, but this right is subject to periodic challenge in the courts. In 1989 the United States Supreme Court heard arguments on an Oregon case about whether the use of peyote during Indian religious ceremonies actually is a constitutional right. Future court rulings always will have the potential for modifying or eliminating the current religious freedom regarding peyote use.

A historical view of psychoactive substance use might show the 1960s as the era of lysergic acid diethylamide-25, most commonly known as LSD. The drug had been used in various tests during the 1950s (for example, as an adjunct to psychotherapy) but did not reach the zenith of its popularity (in the mid-1960s) until Dr. Timothy Leary, a Harvard psychologist, began to expound on what he found to be its mind-altering advantages. LSD eventually was banned (in 1967), and its use appears to have waned (but not ended) during the years since. The most recent psychedelic substance to appear on the scene is methylenedioxymethamphetamine, better known as MMDA or Ecstasy.

Heroin is another drug with a long history of use in the United States. Heroin was first synthesized in the late 1890s, and it has been available for use since the early 1900s. The extent of use traditionally has been greater among two populations—lower and higher socioeconomic groups (O'Brien & Cohen, 1984). During a certain period in the Vietnam War, the incidence of heroin use among United States soldiers in Vietnam was a significant concern, but soldiers who used the drug overseas did not tend to continue its use following return to the states.

This overview gives only a sample of the major drugs that have been used over the years for their psychoactive properties. Importantly, patterns of drug use and abuse are not static. The drugs more frequently used next year might include a drug used in the past that develops a renewed popularity, or they might include a newly synthesized substance, such as one of the so-called "designer drugs." What can be said with confidence is only that drugs will continue to be used, and that some drug abuse will be associated with any given psychoactive substance.

Medical Science and Drug Use

Before leaving our section on historical perspective, we should note the interesting, long-term parallel between the development and use of psychoactive substances in medicinal forms (discussed in more detail in Chapter

4) and the nonmedicinal use/misuse of these drugs. Many of the drugs described in this text were used for medicinal purposes at one time or another. Medical science only gradually became the well-respected institution that we know today. Even in the twentieth century, folk-cures, potions, and so-called "patent-medications" were freely available and widely used.

Perhaps the best examples of this are the opiates opium and morphine, which throughout most of the 1800s were used for a variety of complaints, including rheumatism, pain, fever, delirium tremens, and colds. The opiates also were used as an anesthetic for some surgeries and for setting broken bones. As we noted earlier, the opiates were widely used and prescribed by physicians, despite the lack of understanding of how they acted in the body. All that was known was that opium and morphine seemed to help alleviate pain and symptoms that simply were not understood (Morgan, 1981). Unfortunately, such widespread use contributed to a considerable number of persons becoming physically addicted to these substances. Not until the 1870s did a clear focus on the addictive properties of these drugs emerge.

Numerous other examples can be cited. Chloroform and ether were developed as anesthetics, but each also went through a period in the 1850s when their nonmedical use was quite fashionable. Cocaine went through a period in which it was used to treat a number of complaints, such as depressed mood and pain. In fact, one of its uses was as a treatment for opiate addiction! In the latter half of the nineteenth century physicians recognized an array of uses for cannabis, including treatment of insomnia and nervousness, although its prescribed use was not nearly as extensive as with the opiates. In the twentieth century, we witnessed the development of the synthetic stimulant amphetamines, some of which initially were available without prescription.

We could provide other examples similar to those noted, but the important point is that medicinal uses of psychoactive substances (whether folk medicine or more contemporary medicine), medical science, and nonmedical drug use and abuse will always be closely intertwined. In the past, folk or cultural use of a substance often became incorporated into the practice of medicine. More common today is that a substance developed for the practice of medicine will be incorporated into the array of drugs that might be used in nonmedicinal ways. In any event, keeping these processes separate is impossible.

DEVELOPMENT OF DRUG LAWS

Legislation is the main way society establishes formal guidelines regarding drugs. Further, such legislation essentially reflects society's beliefs about drugs. Laws regarding drugs generally establish restrictions or prohibit the manufacture, importation, sale, and/or possession of the substance under evaluation. Interestingly, actual use under federal law is not a crime, nor is it a crime to be a drug addict or alcoholic.

Drug laws for the most part have had limited effectiveness in reducing overall illicit drug use. In fact, the more restrictive the laws, the less effective they have tended to be in the long run (Brecher, 1972). The only circumstance in which these laws seem to have a stronger effect is during periods in which drug use or abuse is particularly unpopular (Hofmann, 1975). However, the duration of these periods, as well as the time between them is quite variable. Nevertheless, legislation remains society's central means for addressing its concerns regarding drugs.

A history of drug laws in this country does not really begin until the turn of the twentieth century. Various efforts were mounted to regulate opiates in the second half of the nineteenth century, but these were largely half-hearted and not effective. That is not to say sanctions regarding drug abuse did not exist, but rather that there were no legal penalties to speak of. However, at different times and in different locations varying degrees of social sanctions existed, such as the ostracism of citizens showing certain forms of drunkenness in Colonial times.

The San Francisco Ordinance

The only notable law regarding drug use in the nineteenth century with any effect was a city ordinance passed in San Francisco in 1875. A number of Chinese men had entered this country throughout the mid-1800s in response to labor demands in the rapidly expanding West. Most of these immigrants were working on the building of the railways. When this construction was finished, many of the laborers made their way back to San Francisco, where they often frequented "opium dens"—places where people could smoke their opium. Although little negative effect of this drug use was substantiated on the San Francisco community *per se,* some thought the practice was sinister. Rumors began to circulate that the houses were evil and that unsuspecting members of the community—frequently young women were used as examples—were at risk for unknowingly heading down dangerous paths toward disrepute and drug addiction. This concern led to the 1875 ordinance. However only opium dens were banned, not the smoking of opium. The actual impact was not great; the larger and more obvious opium dens closed, and the number of smaller dens increased. The effect was greater in the sense of setting the stage for drug regulation in other parts of the country, as a number of other cities and states passed similar ordinances in later years. Not until 1909 did Congress pass a law banishing the importation of opium for smoking.

Pure Food and Drug Act

The first federal legislative action of note occurred in 1906 with the passage of the Pure Food and Drug Act. This act, which was designed to control opiate addiction, legislated that producers of medicines indicate on the packaging of their products the amount of drug contained therein. The law was particularly focused on the opiates opium, morphine, and heroin, but also mandated the accurate labeling of products containing alcohol, marijuana, and cocaine. The overall effect of the act was mixed: it did not ban opiates in patent medicines, and thus had little impact on the addicts at the time, but the legislation may have served to decrease the number of new addicts, given the subsequent political and education efforts to describe the addictive potential of patent medicines containing opiates (Brecher, 1972).

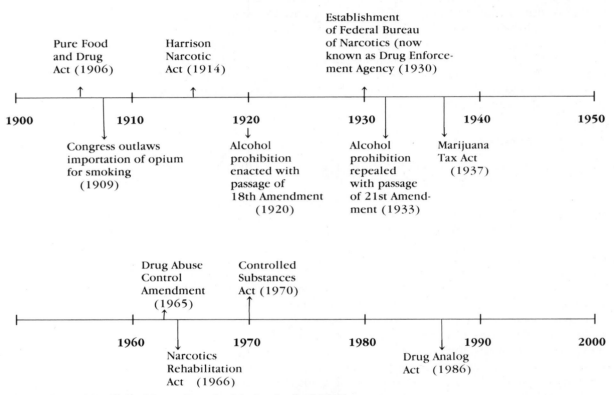

Figure 2–1 Major United States Drug Legislation in the 20th Century

Harrison Narcotic Act

Another major piece of federal legislation, the Harrison Narcotic Act, was passed in 1914. Curiously, this law was passed not in response to domestic demand, but rather as a consequence of the United States signing the Hague Convention of 1912, an international agreement that directed signing nations to regulate opium traffic within their respective countries (Brecher, 1986). The Harrison Act strictly regulated, but did not prohibit, the legal

Figure 2–2 Addicts gather outside a New York City drug clinic in 1920. (From Alexander Lambert, ''Underlying causes of the Narcotic Habit,'' *Modern Medicine, 2,* January 1920).

supply of certain drugs, particularly the opiates. The law stated that the marketing and prescribing of these drugs required licensing. Further, the physician was directed to prescribe narcotics only "in the course of his professional practice." This phrase is certainly general and open to interpretation, and controversy between law enforcement agencies and physicians ensued. The central debate was whether the prescribing of an opiate for an addict was part of a treatment plan or merely serving to maintain the addict's dependence on the drug. Although this confusion on interpretation of the act's intent led to greater restriction on the prescribing and supply of opiates, the result was little effect on opiate abuse (even when subsequent amendments through the years mandated more severe penalties for possession). In fact, Brecher (1986) argued that the ultimate outcome was actually counterproductive. Brecher maintained that the law, in the years since its passage, actually has served to shift opium and morphine addicts to heroin (which became easier to obtain on the black market) and overall to double the number of addicts in the United States. And this occurred despite more than fifty modifications to the act during the fifty years following its passage, each designed to toughen the law (Brecher, 1972).

Several other facets of the Harrison Narcotic Act should be mentioned. The first is that the act did not restrict patent medicine manufacturers, with the exception that their preparations could "not contain more than two grains of opium, or more than one-fourth of a grain of morphine, or more than one-eighth of a grain of heroin . . . in one **avoirdupois** ounce" (U.S. Pure Food and Drug Act of 1906, cited in Brecher, 1972). A second interesting aspect of this narcotic control act was its inaccurate inclusion of cocaine as a narcotic. Finally, one treatment-related result of the Harrison Act was that treatment centers for addicts began to open in some of the larger cities (Morgan, 1981). Most of these centers, however, were open for only a few years and thus had limited opportunity to help alleviate opiate addiction.

Avoirdupois
Something sold or measured by weight based on the pound of 16 ounces.

Alcohol Prohibition

Alcohol prohibition was enacted several years later, in 1920, when Congress passed the Eighteenth Amendment. The legislation was a victory for the forces that viewed alcohol as evil and destructive, notably the Anti-Saloon League and the Women's Christian Temperance Union. And the legislation was not vague about its intent: it prohibited the production, sale, transportation, and importing of alcohol in any part of the United States. The only exception was that alcoholic beverages kept in the home, such as naturally fermented hard cider, could be consumed but not offered for sale (Lender & Martin, 1982).

As you may be aware, and is discussed further in Chapter 7, Prohibition was an experiment in drug control that did not succeed and was repealed thirteen years later by the Twenty-first Amendment. Although Prohibition is

Figure 2–3 Prohibition was enacted to terminate the production, sale, and distribution of alcohol. These federal agents have just completed a raid on a Washington, DC, speakeasy in 1923.

commonly cited as a drug use control measure that failed overall, it never-theless did have substantial effect on drinking in the United States. For exam-ple, the rate of drinking in the states was reduced markedly (reasonable esti-mates in the range of by one-third to as much as one-half); other reductions included decreases in the death rates attributable to liver cirrhosis, admis-sion rates to state hospitals for alcoholism, and arrest rates for alcohol-related offenses (Aaron & Musto, 1981). The greatest degree of decrease in alcohol consumption was among the working population, which opened the legislation to widespread criticism that it was a biased law. Unfortu-nately, a variety of other undesired consequences was associated with pro-hibition, including more extensive use of marijuana, a shift in drinking hab-its to distilled spirits and away from beer, the advent of the **"speakeasy,"** and the takeover of alcohol distribution by criminal groups. (Coffee intake, incidently, according to Brecher (1972), also soared during this period.) Thus, while Prohibition was successful in achieving some of its intended effects, these outcomes were sharply tempered by other undesired results. Ultimately, however, Prohibition was repealed due to the insufficient public sentiment necessary to maintain it.

Speakeasy
A slang expression used to describe a saloon operating without a license. The term was popularly used during Prohibition.

Post-Prohibition Legislation

The 1930s, following repeal of Prohibition, marked more attention on stricter guidelines and penalties regarding drug possession and sale, particularly of marijuana. Legislative action taken in 1930 provided independent status for narcotic control agents through the establishment of the Federal Bureau of Narcotics (later to be called the Bureau of Narcotics and Dangerous Drugs and now the Drug Enforcement Agency). One of the major thrusts of the Federal Bureau of Narcotics, spearheaded by Commissioner Harry J. Anslinger, was the eradication of marijuana use. Anslinger's crusade resulted in the Marijuana Tax Act of 1937. As with the Harrison Narcotic Act, this measure did not ban marijuana, but instead required authorized producers, manufacturers, importers, and dispensers of the drug to register themselves and pay a yearly license fee. Outlawed was only the nonmedical possession or sale of marijuana (Brecher, 1972). The recognition of some medical uses for marijuana continued. Legislative actions regarding marijuana gradually grew more restrictive and provided for greater penalties until the decriminalization movement began in the latter part of the 1970s.

Additional federal legislation was passed periodically from 1940–1970. However, as with previous legislation, these actions failed to have a sustained influence on the prevalence of drug use or dependence, despite the increased severity of the penalties for drug law infractions. However, two trends are worth noting. The first is increased attention to non-narcotic drug use, whereby stimulants, depressants, and hallucinogenic substances became regulated under legislation such as the Drug Abuse Control Amendment of 1965. The second notable change in federal legislation was a shifting of some of its attention to treatment of drug abuse through such measures as the Community Mental Health Centers Act of 1963 and the Narcotic Rehabilitation Act of 1966.

The last major piece of legislative action was the Comprehensive Drug Abuse Prevention and Control Act. This measure, more commonly known as the Controlled Substances Act, was passed in 1970, and forms the basis for drug regulation in the United States today.

CURRENT DRUG LAWS

Drug classifications for law enforcement purposes are rooted in the 1970 Controlled Substances Act. Under this measure, drugs are not classified according to pharmacological action, but according to their medical use, their potential for abuse, and their likelihood for producing dependence. Almost all psychoactive substances have been placed in one of the five categories, or schedules, generated by the act. A description of each of the five schedules is shown in Table 2-2, and Table 2-3 lists examples of the drugs

Table 2-2

Schedules of Controlled Substances

Schedule I: High potential for abuse and dependence. No current medicinal use in the U.S. Not available with prescription. Available for research purposes only. Included in this category are narcotics and hallucinogens.

Schedule II: Medicinal drugs with accepted therapeutic use. High potential for abuse and dependence. Requires written prescription. No refills allowed without first being seen again by doctor for new prescription. Providers must keep these drugs in secured area. Included in this category are the opiates and some stimulants and hypnotics.

Schedule III: Medicinal drugs with accepted therapeutic use. Potential for abuse and dependence greater than for Schedule IV and V drugs but less than for drugs in Schedule I or II. Abuse can lead to moderate or low physical dependence or high levels of psychological dependence. Prescription can be written or phoned in by doctor. Prescription must be renewed every six months and can be refilled up to five times. Included in this category are the less abusable sedative-hypnotics and narcotics.

Schedule IV: Medicinal drugs with acceptable therapeutic use. Less potential for abuse and dependence than for Schedule III drugs. Abuse can lead to limited physical or psychological dependence. Same prescription guidelines as for Schedule III drugs. Included in this category are sedative-hypnotics, drugs used for weight reduction, and minor tranquilizers.

Schedule V: Medicinal drugs with accepted therapeutic use. Lowest potential for abuse or dependence. Abuse leads to only limited physical or psychological dependence. Prescription not needed for many of these drugs, which often are sold over the counter. Need to be 18 years of age. Purchaser in some cases needs to sign a dispensing log maintained by the pharmacist. Included in this category are medicines containing small amounts of a narcotic.

Adapted from Blum (1984)

in each classification. Several substances having little or no potential for abuse or dependence are not classified. These include the major tranquilizers, such as chlorpromazine (trade name Thorazine), thioridazine (Mellaril), and haloperidol (Haldol), and the antidepressants, such as imipramine (Tofranil) and amitriptyline (Elavil). (We discuss these drugs in greater detail in Chapter 9.)

The Controlled Substances Act contains provisions for adding drugs to the schedules and for rescheduling drugs. For example, diazepam (Valium) and other benzodiazepines were unscheduled when the act was passed but were classified as Schedule IV drugs in 1975. Similarly, phencyclidine (PCP, "Angel Dust") was initially unscheduled but quickly classified as a Schedule II substance in 1978 when it began to be abused. A variety of Schedule III substances were reclassified into Schedule II during the early 1970s, including amphetamine (Benzedrine), methylphenidate (Ritalin), and secobarbital (Seconal).

Consistent with its intended comprehensive character, the Controlled Substances Act also establishes the maximum penalties for criminal manu-

Table 2-3
Examples of Scheduled Drugs

	Schedule I
Heroin	Marijuana
Peyote	Lysergic acid diethylamide (LSD)
Mescaline	Dimethyltryptamine (DMT)
Psilocybin	Quaalude

	Schedule II
Opium	Cocaine
Morphine	Benzedrine
Codeine	Dexedrine
Percodan	Dilaudid
Ritalin	Demerol

	Schedule III
Empirin with codeine	Butisol
Tylenol with codeine	Fiorinal
Paregoric	

	Schedule IV
Luminal	Serax
Darvon	Dalmane
Valium	Tranxene
Librium	Miltown

	Schedule V
Cheracol with codeine	Cosadein
Robitussin A-C	

Adapted from Cohen (1981)

facture or distribution of the scheduled drugs. The maximum penalties for a first offense range from one year in jail and/or a $10,000 fine for Schedule V substances to fifteen years and/or a $25,000 fine for Schedule I and II substances. Subsequent offenses are punishable by penalties up to twice those for the first offense. The penalty for unlawful possession of a controlled substance, regardless of how it is scheduled, is the same: up to one year in jail and/or a $5,000 fine. First offense possession charges are classified as a misdemeanor.

We should note before closing that each state has the opportunity to modify these guidelines according to its own needs and preferences. Most states have adopted these guidelines but may have changed certain components of them. For example, marijuana is classified as a Schedule I substance, but the penalties for possession in most states are generally less severe than listed. In fact, eleven states have passed legislation to decriminalize marijuana possession. Also important to note is a quite recent legislative action. During

CONTEMPORARY ISSUE BOX 2-2
Drug Testing in the Workplace

One result of the growing concern over drug use and misuse has been efforts by corporations to have their workers submit to mandatory drug tests. The employers argue the tests are needed to identify those workers who, because of their drug use, may be at risk for subpar or even dangerous work performance. Further, employers often believe random drug tests serve as a deterrent to drug use. About one-third of the largest American corporations currently use drug screens as part of their hiring process. And according to a report in *U.S. News and World Report* (July 28, 1986), anywhere from 8–35% of these applicants will test positive for recent drug use (a "positive" result means the test revealed indications of drug use).

The argument put forth by employers may appear relatively straightforward: if drugs can impair work performance, then checking for drugs is a legitimate practice. But drug testing remains quite controversial, and for several reasons. Consider the three following aspects of the controversy.

First is the issue of the possible infringement on constitutional rights of privacy when tests are administered randomly (that is, without warning and independent of "probable cause"). This has led some to suggest tests should be used only if a demonstrable "reasonable cause" exists to believe a person is under the influence of a drug.

A second issue is the relationship between a positive test result and actual job performance. For example, traces of marijuana can be detected in the system for several weeks and sometimes much longer after it was smoked, even though no associated impairment in the person's functioning can be proven. Is drug use a legitimate reason for termination or other disciplinary action if no obvious effect of that drug use on the worker's job performance can be demonstrated?

A third issue is very basic, yet crucial. Unfortunately, questions abound regarding accuracy of the drug tests themselves. A study by the Center for Disease Control, a federal agency, found that many urinalysis test results were unreliable. In some cases the poor reliability was a result of primitive technology in testing for the presence of particular drugs. Sometimes the presence of a drug was missed, and in other cases a legitimate drug use (such as a prescribed medication) was identified by the test as an illicit substance. However, the biggest factor contributing to the poor test reliability was human error and carelessness on the part of the people doing the urinalysis at the laboratory!

Before the question of drug testing is resolved, these issues are going to have to be addressed. A balancing of employee rights with the perceived needs of employers, along with improvements in the drug testing process itself, still seems a distance away.

the 1980s, law enforcement agencies were having difficulties controlling the production of the so-called "designer drugs," drugs that were structurally similar but not identical to illegal substances. Each time a slight modification in the chemical structure of the drug was made, enforcement officials were forced to go through a time-consuming process of documenting the drug and having it certified as a controlled substance. In response, Congress in 1986 passed the Controlled Substances Analogue Enforcement Act, which allowed for the immediate classification of a substance as a controlled substance. In this way, drug enforcement officials were in a position to address the arrival of a new drug as soon as it appeared in circulation.

SUMMARY

· Drugs have been used for a variety of reasons in different cultures for thousands of years; earliest drug use involved ingestion of alcohol and of plants with psychoactive properties.

· Prior to the twentieth century, few restrictions were placed on drug availability or drug use.

· During the nineteenth century, drugs such as opium, morphine, marijuana, heroin, and cocaine could be easily obtained without prescription.

· Marijuana was used by physicians during the 1800s as a general all-purpose medication; its nonmedical use increased during the Prohibition-era of the 1920s.

· Various drugs have enjoyed periods of relatively greater popularity in the United States. Cocaine was widely used in medicines and tonics during the late 1800s and early 1900s, but less so thereafter until the 1960s and continuing today. Amphetamines were used relatively widely during the 1930s, minor tranquilizers and inhalants during the 1950s, LSD during the 1960s.

· A parallel exists between the development and use of psychoactive substances in medicinal forms and the nonmedical use/misuse of these drugs.

· The main mechanism through which society establishes formal guidelines regarding drugs and drug use is legislation. However, a history of drug laws in the United States does not really begin until the turn of the twentieth century.

· The first major federal legislation regarding drugs was the 1906 Pure Food and Drug Act, which mandated a listing of the types and amounts of drug contained in the medicines.

· Other major legislation of note were the 1914 Harrison Narcotic Act, which regulated the legal supply of certain drugs, and alcohol prohibition, which spanned the years 1920–1933.

· Drug classifications for law enforcement today are rooted in the 1970 Controlled Substances Act, which classifies drugs according to their legitimate medical uses and their potential for abuse and dependence.

References

Aaron, P., & Musto, D. (1981). Temperance and prohibition in America: A historical overview. In M.H. Moore & D.R. Gerstein (eds.), *Alcohol and public policy.* Washington, D.C.: Academy Press.

Blum, K. (1984). *Handbook of abusable drugs.* New York: Gardner Press.

Brecher, E.M. (1972). *Licit and illicit drugs.* Boston: Little, Brown.

Brecher, E.M. (1986). Drug laws and drug law enforcement: A review and evaluation based on 111 years of experience. *Drugs and Society, 1,* 1–27.

Clinger, O.W., & Johnson, N.A. (1951). Purposeful inhalation of gasoline vapors. *Psychiatric Quarterly, 25,* 557–567.

Cohen, S. (1981). *The substance abuse problems.* New York: Haworth Press.

Government Printing Office (GPO). (1972). *Drug abuse: Games without winners.* Washington, D.C.: Government Printing Office.

Hofmann, F.G. (1975). *A handbook on drug and alcohol abuse.* New York: Oxford University Press.

Lender, M.E., & Martin, J.K. (1982). *Drinking in America.* New York: The Free Press.

Mellaart, J. (1967). *Catal Huyuk: A neolithic town in Anatolia.* New York: McGraw-Hill.

Morgan, H.W. (1981). *Drugs in America: A social history, 1800–1980.* Syracuse: Syracuse University Press.

Nahas, G.G. (1973). *Marihuana—Deceptive weed.* New York: Raven Press.

O'Brien, R., & Cohen, S. (1984). *The encyclopedia of drug abuse.* New York: Facts on File, Inc.

Spector, I. (1985). AMP: A new form of marijuana. *Journal of Clinical Psychiatry, 46,* 498–499.

Whitaker, B. (1987). *The global connection: The crisis of drug addiction.* London: Jonathan Cade.

3 DRUGS AND THE NERVOUS SYSTEM

Every feeling or emotion you have—in fact, all psychological experience—is based on brain activity. The fact that this physical entity, the brain, is the basis of conscious experience is the key to understanding how the chemical agents we call drugs alter psychological processes.

One feature all psychoactive drugs have in common is that they produce their effects by acting in some way on nervous system tissue, and this chapter focuses on these physiological actions of drugs. Most of these actions occur at the level of the brain. As recent discoveries in the neurosciences have led to a greater understanding of how the brain works, parallel advances have taken place in our understanding of drug actions. These developments have led to some radically new ways of conceptualizing drug effects and drug problems such as addiction. However, in order to discuss how drugs act on the brain, we first must cover some of the fundamentals on just how the brain works.

THE NEURON

The basic building blocks of the nervous system are cells called **neurons.** Neurons are similar to other cells in the human body, such as blood cells or muscle cells, but they have the unique feature of being able to communicate with each other. The unique structural properties of neurons provide us with some clues as to the nature of the neural transmission process.

Notice in Figure 3-1 that the neurons depicted have cell bodies similar to those of any other cell. These cell bodies include a nucleus containing the genetic material for the neuron and other processes that control the metabolic activities of the cell. Extending from the cell body of the neuron are a number of small spine- or branch-like structures called **dendrites** and one long cylindrical structure called the **axon.** These structures are unique to the neuron and responsible for some of its remarkable properties.

Axons vary in length but are usually much longer than shown in the illustration—sometimes as many as thousands of times longer than the diameter of the cell body. The axon depicted in Figure 3-1a is enclosed within a sheath of a white, fatty substance called **myelin** (not all axons are covered by myelin sheaths, and "unmyelinated" axons are gray in color—note, for example, the axons in Figures 3-1B and C). Myelin provides insulation for the axon, similar to insulation for a wire. That comparison is fitting, for the principal function of the axon is to conduct electrical current. The axon transmits information by conducting an electrical signal from one end of the neuron to the other. The current flow is always initiated in the cell body, which sends its electrical message (called the **action potential**) to the small branches at the end of the axon. The change in potential is small (about 70 millivolts), and is said to be "all-or-none," in that, the axon is either firing—conducting its full current—or is quiescent.

Neuron (NUR-on)
The individual nerve cell that is the basic building block of the nervous system.

Dendrite (Den-drite)
Spiny branch-like structures that extend from the cell body of a neuron. Dendrites typically contain numerous receptor sites and are thus important in neural transmission.

Axon (AKS-on)
A long cylindrical extension of the cell body of the neuron. The axon conducts an electrical charge from the cell body to the axon terminals.

Myelin (MY-a-lin)
A fatty white substance that covers the axons of some neurons.

Action potential
The electrical impulse along the axon that occurs when a neuron "fires."

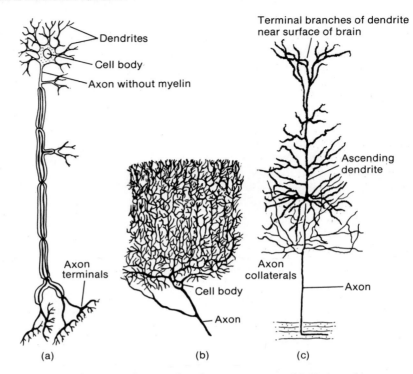

Figure 3–1 (a) Diagram of a peripheral motor neuron. (b) Neuron from cerebellum. (c) Neuron from rabbit cerebral cortex.

NEURAL TRANSMISSION

Axon terminal (or terminal button)
Enlarged button-like structures that occur at the end of axon branches.

Synapse (SIN-naps)
The junction between neurons.

Neurotransmitters
Chemical substances stored in the axon terminals that are released into the synapse when the neuron fires. Neurotransmitters then influence activity in postsynaptic neurons.

The branches at the end of the axon shown in Figure 3-1a terminate in small button-like structures known as **axon terminals** or **terminal buttons.** These axon terminals hold the key to an important puzzle: how the electrical message actually gets from one neuron to another. When advances in microscopy made possible the viewing of neurons as they are seen here, a surprising finding was that the axon terminals of one neuron do not come into direct contact with the dendrites of the neighboring neuron as had been supposed; instead they are separated by a space called the **synapse** (shown in Figure 3-2). The question, of course, is how does electrical current flow from one neuron to another without direct contact between them? It is now known that when electrical current reaches the axon terminal, chemical substances stored in the terminal button are released into the synapse and these chemical substances, called **neurotransmitters,** actually trigger activity in the adjacent neuron.

Thus, neural transmission is an electrochemical event—electrical along

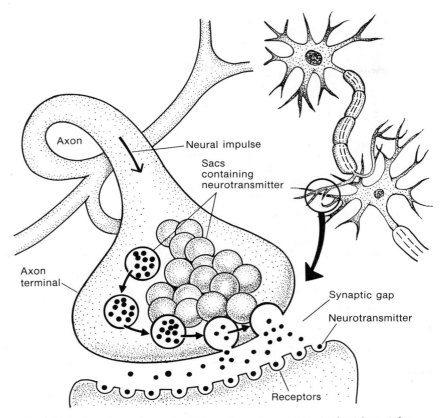

Figure 3–2 Diagram of a synapse showing enlarged axon terminal with vesicles containing neurotransmitter molecules.

Thus, neural transmission is an electrochemical event—electrical along the axon, and chemical at the synapse. This is of some importance for our purposes as it suggests that drugs may interact with the nervous system at the synapse, because that is where the chemical transmission takes place. In fact, most of the psychoactive drugs we discuss produce their important effects by action at the synapse. Therefore, more detailed analysis of the chemical processes occurring at the synapse seems justified.

The lock-and-key analogy is useful for depicting the neural transmission process. Scattered along the dendrites and cell body are special structures known as **receptor sites** or receptors. These structures may be viewed as locks that keep the neuron from firing. In order to fire, the locks must be opened, which is accomplished by the neurotransmitter substances released at the terminal button. Think of the neurotransmitters as keys. The point is illustrated in Figure 3-2. Receptor sites are depicted as circular holes in the dendrite and neurotransmitters as circles being released from the axon terminal. In fact, neurotransmitter molecules have far more complex chemical

Receptor sites
Specialized structures located on dendrites and cell bodies for neurons which are activated by neurotransmitters.

structures than illustrated, and so do receptor sites. But the basic notion is simple enough: the key must fit the lock. Indeed, these processes involve many different neurotransmitter keys—and many corresponding receptor site locks. We now understand that the brain is chemically coded with different pathways that respond to different neurotransmitter chemicals.

HOW DRUGS INFLUENCE NEURAL TRANSMISSION

Several ways that drugs can interfere with synaptic transmission may have already occurred to you. For example, suppose the chemical structure of some drug is quite similar to that of a naturally-occurring (or endogenous) neurotransmitter. If the similarity is close enough, the drug molecules might "fit" the receptor sites, thus duping the receptor into reacting as if the natural transmitter is present and stimulating the neuron. Just such a process, called mimicry, actually does occur with a number of drugs. For example, drugs such as morphine and heroin are now thought to act by mimicking a recently discovered natural neurotransmitter called endorphin.

Mimicry is an obvious mechanism of drug action, but drugs can influence neural transmission in numerous other ways. A sampling of these mechanisms is listed in Table 3-1. Neurotransmitters must be manufactured from simpler building blocks, or precursor molecules. The manufacture of transmitters usually takes place in a cell body or axon terminal, but if the substance is manufactured in the cell body it must still be transported to the terminal before it is functional. Some drugs interfere with transmitter pro-

Table 3-1
Neurochemical Mechanisms of Drug Action

Drug Effects Can Be Produced By Altering The Following Neurochemical Systems:

1. *Neurotransmitter Synthesis.* A drug may increase or decrease the synthesis of neurotransmitters.
2. *Neurotransmitter Transport.* A drug may interfere with transport of neurotransmitter molecules to the axon terminals.
3. *Neurotransmitter Storage.* A drug may interfere with the storage of neurotransmitters in the vesicles of the axon terminal.
4. *Neurotransmitter Release.* A drug may cause the axon terminals to prematurely release neurotransmitter molecules into the synapse.
5. *Neurotransmitter Degradation.* A drug may influence the breakdown of neurotransmitters by enzymes.
6. *Neurotransmitter Reuptake.* A drug may block the reuptake of neurotransmitters into the axon terminals.
7. *Receptor Activation.* A drug may activate a receptor site by mimicking a neurotransmitter.
8. *Receptor Blocking.* A drug may cause a receptor to become inactive by blocking it.

duction or transport. Neurotransmitter molecules are stored in small packages called **vesicles,** located in the terminal buttons. Some drugs affect the ability of the vesicles to store neurotransmitter substances. For example, the drug reserpine, once used to treat high blood pressure, causes certain vesicles to become leaky and the transmitters involved are not effectively released into the synapse. Alternatively, other drugs can enhance the release of neurotransmitter substances into the synapse and this is one of the ways stimulants such as amphetamine act.

Another important rule of neural transmission is that neurotransmitters, once released, must be deactivated. The neuron can be thought of as a rechargeable battery—once it fires it may be recharged and fired again. But first, we need to get those keys out of the locks so that the recharging process can take place. The deactivation of the neurotransmitter keys is accomplished in two ways: **enzyme breakdown** and **reuptake.** Certain chemicals called enzymes act both to build the complex molecules of neurotransmitters and to break down neurotransmitters to inactive form. The enzyme pathways for synthesis and breakdown of some of the major neurotransmitters are shown in Figure 3-3. As the figure shows, these pathways are complex and reveal one reason that identifying and isolating the functions of neurotransmitters in the brain is difficult. There are a number of different chemicals in the brain, and they are constantly changing form. Consider the processes involved in the production and destruction of **acetylcholine,** one of the most important neurotransmitters. The precursor molecule choline is acted on by an enzyme (choline acetyltransferase) to make acetylcholine. Acetylcholine itself is broken down by a different enzyme, acetylcholinesterase, to yield two metabolites: choline and acetate. (Enzymes are named by the stem of the chemical that they influence and always take an "-ase" ending.) A drug can alter neural transmission by affecting enzyme activity. For example, some antidepressant drugs alter the deactivation of the neurotransmitters norepinephrine, dopamine, and serotonin by inhibiting the activity of monoamine oxidase, the enzyme that breaks down these compounds.

A second mechanism for removing neurotransmitters from the synapse is called reuptake. Some neurotransmitters are taken back up into the terminal button after they have been released, thus the term reuptake. Reuptake is an economical mechanism of deactivating transmitters, because the neurotransmitter molecule is preserved intact and can be used again without the energy involved in the manufacture of new transmitters. Some drugs (notably cocaine and the amphetamines) exert some of their action by blocking the reuptake process.

A final site of drug action is directly at the receptor. Some drugs directly affect the receptor by mimicking the activity of natural neurotransmitters—similar to a duplicate key that fits into and opens the locks. But other drugs seem to act as if they fit into the lock, only to get "jammed" as if in putty and prevent the neuron from firing. Such a drug is called a blocking agent.

Vesicles (VES-ik-ulls)
Tiny sacs located in axon terminals that store neurotransmitters.

Enzyme breakdown
One process by which neurotransmitters are inactivated. Chemicals called enzymes interact with the transmitter molecule and change its structure so that it no longer is capable of occupying receptor sites.

Reuptake
Another process by which neurotransmitters are inactivated. Neurotransmitter molecules are taken back up into the axon terminal that released them.

Acetylcholine (ass-it-teel-KOLE-een)
A neurotransmitter found both in the brain and in the parasympathetic branch of the autonomic nervous system.

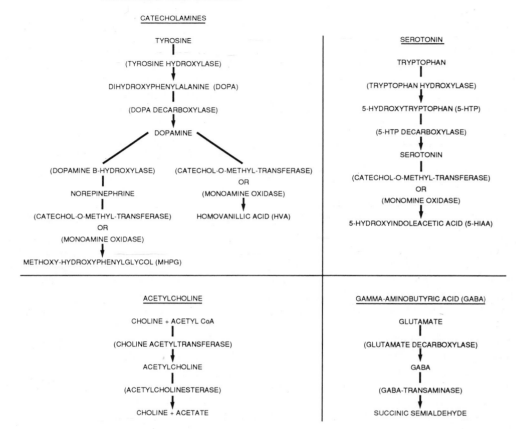

CATECHOLAMINES

TYROSINE

(TYROSINE HYDROXYLASE)

DIHYDROXYPHENYLALANINE (DOPA)

(DOPA DECARBOXYLASE)

DOPAMINE

(DOPAMINE B-HYDROXYLASE)   (CATECHOL-O-METHYL-TRANSFERASE)
                                              OR
NOREPINEPHRINE   (MONOAMINE OXIDASE)

(CATECHOL-O-METHYL-TRANSFERASE)   HOMOVANILLIC ACID (HVA)
              OR
(MONOAMINE OXIDASE)

METHOXY-HYDROXYPHENYLGLYCOL (MHPG)

SEROTONIN

TRYPTOPHAN

(TRYPTOPHAN HYDROXYLASE)

5-HYDROXYTRYPTOPHAN (5-HTP)

(5-HTP DECARBOXYLASE)

SEROTONIN

(CATECHOL-O-METHYL-TRANSFERASE)
              OR
(MONOMINE OXIDASE)

5-HYDROXYINDOLEACETIC ACID (5-HIAA)

ACETYLCHOLINE

CHOLINE + ACETYL CoA

(CHOLINE ACETYLTRANSFERASE)

ACETYLCHOLINE

(ACETYLCHOLINESTERASE)

CHOLINE + ACETATE

GAMMA-AMINOBUTYRIC ACID (GABA)

GLUTAMATE

(GLUTAMATE DECARBOXYLASE)

GABA

(GABA-TRANSAMINASE)

SUCCINIC SEMIALDEHYDE

Figure 3–3 Synthesis and breakdown pathways and products for some of the major neurotransmitter systems (from Bardo & Risner, 1985).

Agonist (AG-o-nist)
A substance that occupies a neural receptor and causes some change in the conductance of the neuron.

Antagonist
A substance that occupies a neural receptor, but blocks normal synaptic transmission.

In general, any chemical—natural or otherwise—that fits a receptor lock and activates it is said to be an **agonist** of that receptor. Any compound that occupies a receptor and does not activate it, but rather prevents other compounds from activating the receptor, is said to be an **antagonist** of the receptors on which opiate drugs such as heroin work. If naloxone is administered to a patient who has just taken a lethal dose of heroin, the patient not only does not die, but is rapidly brought to a state in which the patient acts as if the heroin had not even been taken. In fact, all of the effects of heroin and other opiates are blocked completely or reversed by naloxone. Thus, naloxone is called an opiate antagonist.

We have seen a number of ways that drugs can act to influence neural transmission (see Bardo & Risner, 1985, for a more detailed review). However, a point to remember is that although drugs can interact with the brain in many different ways, the effects of the drugs always involve naturally-occurring processes. That is, some systems in the brain or body with defined natural functions are made more or less active by the drug. The differences between the effects of various drugs are coming to be understood in terms of which transmitter systems they influence, and exactly how they influence them. Therefore, next we take a brief look at the neurotransmitter systems of the human brain and note some of their known functions.

THE MAJOR NEUROTRANSMITTER SYSTEMS

Acetylcholine

One of the first neurotransmitters to be discovered was acetylcholine, probably because it is found in the more easily studied neurons located outside the brain. Acetylcholine resides in the axon terminals of neurons that activate the skeletal muscles. At sites where nerves meet muscles there is a space similar to the synapse called the **neuromuscular junction.** When the neurons that synpase with muscle fibers are fired they release acetylcholine into the neuromuscular junction and the muscle contracts. Acetylcholine is also important in the brain, but as with most neurotransmitters, its function in the brain is not thoroughly understood. However, the body of evidence is that acetylcholine is important in the regulation of thirst. (By the way, if a neurotransmitter is to be used in the adjectival form, one simply takes the stem of the name [i.e., choline] and adds the suffix "-ergic." Thus, thirst is said to be a cholinergic function, neurons containing acetylcholine are said to be cholinergic neurons, and drugs which block acetylcholine are said to be anticholinergic drugs.) Acetylcholine is also thought to be important in memory. In fact, substantial evidence is mounting that **Alzheimer's disease,** a progressive loss of memory function that occurs in the elderly, is related to the loss of neural function in some of the brain's cholinergic pathways. Much current research on Alzheimer's disease is attempting to determine just what might be going wrong in these pathways and to develop ways of correcting or preventing the problem. The problem of Alzheimer's disease underscores an important point: when neurotransmitter systems malfunction, disease states are a likely consequence. This point is at the heart of contemporary theories of the biological basis of mental illness, which is considered in the next section.

Monoamines

Three important neurotransmitters, **norepinephrine (noradrenalin), dopamine,** and **serotonin,** are collectively known as the **monoamines** because the chemical structure for each contains a single amine group. Like acetylcholine, norepinephrine was discovered early on because it is found outside the brain. It serves as a key chemical mediating the physical changes

Neuromuscular junction
Junction between neuron and muscle fibers where release of acetylcholine by neurons causes muscles to contract.

Alzheimer's disease (ALLZ-hi-merz)
One of the most common forms of senility among the elderly, Alzheimer's disease involves a progressive loss of memory and other cognitive functions.

Norepinephrine (nor-ep-in-EFF-rin)
A neurotransmitter found in the brain and involved in activity of the sympathetic branch of the autonomic nervous system.

Dopamine (DOP-ah-meen)
A neurotransmitter found in the brain.

Serotonin (sair-o-TONE-in)
A neurotransmitter found in the brain.

Monoamine (mon-o-AM-mean)
A class of chemicals characterized by a single amine group. This class includes neurotransmitters: norepinephrine, dopamine, and serotonin.

Parkinson's disease
A disease that primarily
afflicts the elderly and
involves a progressive
deterioration of motor
control.

**L-dopa
(el-DOPE-ah)**
A chemical precursor of
dopamine used in the
treatment of Parkinson's
disease.

Blood-brain barrier
A term given to the system
that "filters" the blood
before it can enter the
brain.

that accompany emotional arousal. Norepinephrine is also found in the brain as a neurotransmitter, where it seems important in the regulation of hunger, alertness, and arousal. Serotonin is found throughout the brain and has been shown to be important in the regulation of sleep. Dopamine is a key neurotransmitter in the pathways that regulate coordinated motor movements. This discovery led to the hypothesis that dopamine-insufficiency may be the basis of **Parkinson's disease,** a disorder characterized by progressive loss of fine motor movements, muscle rigidity, and tremor primarily afflicting elderly persons. The dopamine deficiency hypothesis of Parkinson's disease led to new treatment approaches involving the administration of **L-dopa,** a precursor of dopamine (see Figure 3-3). L-dopa was administered to patients in the hopes of correcting the dopamine deficiency and proved to be dramatically effective in relieving the symptoms of this disease. Dopamine itself is not effective because it does not enter the brain from the bloodstream. The brain is protected from toxic compounds that might enter the bloodstream by a **blood-brain barrier** that screens many chemicals, including dopamine. But L-dopa does penetrate the barrier and once it reaches the brain, it is converted to dopamine (Bradford, 1986; Kruk & Pycock, 1979). The use of L-dopa in the treatment of Parkinson's disease is a dramatic example of the value of new knowledge about neurotransmitters in the treatment of disease. Although L-dopa does not cure the disease process (loss of dopaminergic neurons continues to take place and eventually even L-dopa cannot correct the loss), it has brought years of productive living to many whose lives would otherwise have been prematurely ended by Parkinsonism.

In addition to these functions, the monoamine neurotransmitters norepinephrine, dopamine, and serotonin have been closely linked to mood states and emotional disorders. In fact, drugs that influence the monoamine systems have revolutionized modern psychiatry. For example, considerable evidence shows that severe clinical depression may have a biological basis (see Chapter 9). Current theories propose that clinical depression results from a deficiency of monoamines, particularly norepinephrine and serotonin. This monoamine theory of depression originated with the finding that certain drugs that depleted monoamines seemed to produce depression. Reserpine, once used to treat high blood pressure, makes monoaminergic vesicles leaky (as we noted earlier) and the transmitters are then destroyed by enzymes, resulting in a depletion of norepinephrine, serotonin, and dopamine. This process often causes depression in persons whose mood states were normal before treatment (as you may have guessed, it also produces Parkinson's symptoms due to dopamine depletion and this side effect helped lead to the use of L-dopa previously mentioned). The drugs that are useful in the treatment of depression generally influence either norepinephrine or serotonin transmission or both, which further supports this monoamine-deficiency hypothesis (see Bradford, 1986; Cooper, Bloom, & Roth, 1986; and Lickey & Gordon, 1983).

Monoamines, particularly dopamine, appear to be important as the bio-chemical basis of another important mental illness, schizophrenia. Schizo-phrenia involves a major loss of reality contact characterized by false beliefs or delusions, hallucinations, social withdrawal, and distortions of emotion-ality. The evidence relating these symptoms to high levels of monoamine activity is strong. First, all of the drugs that are effective in the treatment of schizophrenia block monoamine transmission. In fact, a very close correla-tion exists between the clinical potency of the various drugs used and their ability to block dopamine receptors (Snyder, Burt, & Creese, 1976). More-over, compounds that fail to block dopamine receptors do not relieve schizophrenic symptoms even though such compounds possess the other neurochemical properties of the more effective drugs (see Crow & Deakin, 1979). Another interesting piece of evidence is that stimulant drugs such as cocaine and amphetamine increase dopaminergic activity of the brain. — block the reuptake Although low or moderate doses of these stimulants enhance mood, over-dose levels often lead to paranoid delusions and a loss of reality contact that strongly resembles symptoms of schizophrenia. When the drug wears off and dopamine activity returns to normal, these symptoms dissipate, a finding that provides further support for the link between abnormally high dopa-mine activity and schizophrenia.

Other Transmitters

The four neurotransmitters previously discussed (acetylcholine, norepi-nephrine, dopamine, and serotonin) have been relatively well studied, and until recently were thought to be the main chemicals involved in neural transmission. However, the development of more sophisticated research techniques has led to the recognition that many more neurotransmitters await discovery. Thorough discussion of the recent advances in neurophar-macology is beyond the scope of this text, but some of the recent advances have already caused a substantial impact on our understanding of psycho-active drug actions.

During the late 1970s, compounds were discovered in mammalian brain tissue that were functionally similar to opiate drugs such as morphine and heroin. Because these chemicals were similar to natural-occurring mor-phine, they were named **endorphins**—a contraction of the term endoge-nous morphine. We now understand the effects of opiate drugs are mediated through endorphinergic activity. The natural functions of the endorphins themselves are still far from clear but they certainly modulate pain relief. The endorphins are explained in more detail in Chapter 10.

Another important neurotransmitter is gamma-aminobutyric acid, com-monly referred to as **GABA** (see Figure 3-3). GABA is among the most abun-dant of the known neurotransmitters in brain tissue, and it acts somewhat differently from the neurotransmitters already described. The lock-and-key

Endorphins
(en-DORE-finz)
Neurotransmitters found in the brain that are mimicked by opiate drugs.

GABA
Short for gamma-amino-butyric acid, a neurotransmitter found in the brain.

analogy still holds, but when GABA occupies a receptor it seems to "turn the lock the wrong way." That is, GABA does not cause the neuron to fire; instead it impedes the neural firing. Thus, it is often referred to as an inhibitory transmitter (although the other transmitters can be inhibitory at some synapses). If a neuron has a GABA-ergic receptor site that is activated, a larger quantity of the excitatory transmitter is required in order for the neuron to fire. A number of drugs are now thought to act on the GABA system, as you might guess, they are the classic depressant drugs: barbiturates, tranquilizers such as Valium (diazepam) and Librium (chlordiazepoxide), and alcohol.

STRUCTURE OF THE NERVOUS SYSTEM

Central nervous system
The brain and the spinal cord comprise the central nervous system or CNS.

Peripheral nervous system
Sensory nerves, motor nerves, and the autonomic nervous system comprise the peripheral nervous system or PNS.

We have been focusing on a microscopic view of the nervous system as we considered how drugs might act at the level of the single neuron. We now turn to the larger picture and consider a macroscopic view of the nervous system. The basic structure of the nervous system is outlined in Figure 3-4. The major distinction is between the **central nervous system** or CNS and **peripheral nervous system** or PNS. The CNS includes the brain and spinal cord. All nervous tissue outside (or peripheral to) the CNS is part of the PNS.

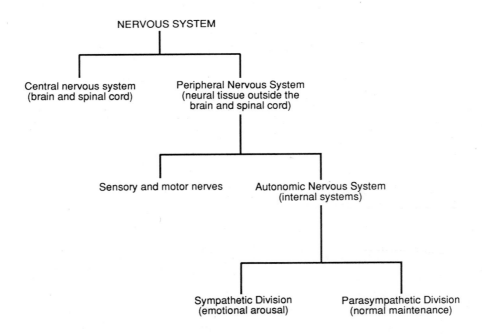

Figure 3-4 Organizational structure of the nervous system.

The PNS includes nerves (nerves are simply bundles of axons) that send input from the senses to the brain (sensory nerves) and nerves that send output from the brain to muscles (motor nerves).

The Autonomic Nervous System

Additionally, the PNS includes an important regulatory system known as the **autonomic nervous system** (ANS). The ANS regulates various non-conscious or automatic functions and is divided into two parts. The **sympathetic branch** of the autonomic nervous system is activated during emotional arousal by a release of epinephrine and norepinephrine from the adrenal glands. This branch is reponsible for the various physiological changes that characterize the "fight or flight" reaction. During sympathetic arousal, heart rate increases, blood pressure increases, respiratory rate increases, sweating increases, pupils dilate, the mouth becomes dry, and changes occur in blood flow, as blood is shunted away from the internal organs and to the brain and large muscle groups. These physiological effects are important to keep in mind because some psychoactive drugs mimic sympathetic arousal. Such drugs are said to be **sympathomimetic;** they include cocaine, amphetamines, and some hallucinogens such as LSD. Another group of drugs blocks a type of norepinephrine receptor in the sympathetic system called "beta" receptors. These beta receptors regulate blood pressure and the so-called **beta-blockers** (drugs such as propranolol) are widely used in the treatment of hypertension.

The other branch of the autonomic nervous system is the **parasympathetic branch,** which in general exerts actions opposite those of the sympathetic branch. Parasympathetic activity reduces heart rate, blood pressure, and so on. In contrast to sympathetic neurons, parasympathetic synapses are primarily cholinergic. Drugs that act directly on the parasympathetic system can be highly toxic. For example, nerve gases such as Sarin and Soman act to inhibit acetylcholinesterase, which results in excessive parasympathetic activity. The result can be death through respiratory or cardiovascular failure.

Autonomic nervous system
Part of the PNS, the autonomic nervous system or ANS has two branches: the sympathetic and parasympathetic.

Sympathetic branch
Branch of the ANS that is activated during emotional arousal and is responsible for such physiological changes as increased heart and respiratory rate, increased blood pressure, and pupil dilation.

Sympathomimetic
Term applied to drugs such as cocaine and amphetamine which produce the physiological effects of sympathetic activity.

Beta-blockers
Drugs that block beta-adrenergic receptors of the sympathetic system and thus act to relieve high blood pressure.

Parasympathetic branch
The branch of the ANS that is responsible for lowering heart rate, blood pressure. and so on.

THE BRAIN

The key organ of the nervous system is, of course, the brain (see Figure 3-5). Covered with a tough membrane called the meninges, the brain floats within the skull in a liquid known as cerebrospinal fluid. Though just a few pounds in mass, the human brain is an extremely complex structure. We have just examined the various processes involved when a single neuron fires. Now consider that the human brain contains literally billions and billions of neurons. Many of the neurons of the brain synapse with several thousand other neurons because of an elaborate branching of axons. The com-

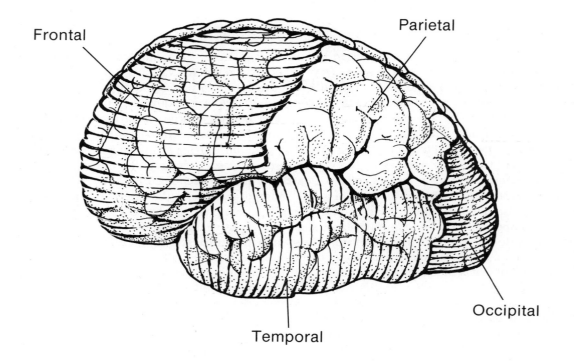

Frontal

Parietal

Occipital

Temporal

Figure 3-5 The four lobes of the human cerebral cortex.

Hindbrain
The lower part of the brain
including the medulla,
pons, and cerebellum.

Midbrain
Includes the inferior and
superior colliculi.

Forebrain
The largest part of the
human brain, the forebrain
includes the cerebral
cortex, thalamus,
hypothalamus, and the
limbic system.

plexity of billions of neurons and more billions of synapses is absolutely
staggering and a bit beyond comprehension. Despite the sheer enormity of
the task, great strides have been made in understanding how this most complex of organs works. One fruitful approach is considering the different
parts of the brain separately in an attempt to determine their individual
functions.

The major divisions of the human brain are the **hindbrain, midbrain,**
and **forebrain.** Figure 3-6 shows the relative locations of these three levels
of the brain. If a voyage through the brain began at the spinal cord and
moved up, the first part of the brain encountered would be the hindbrain.

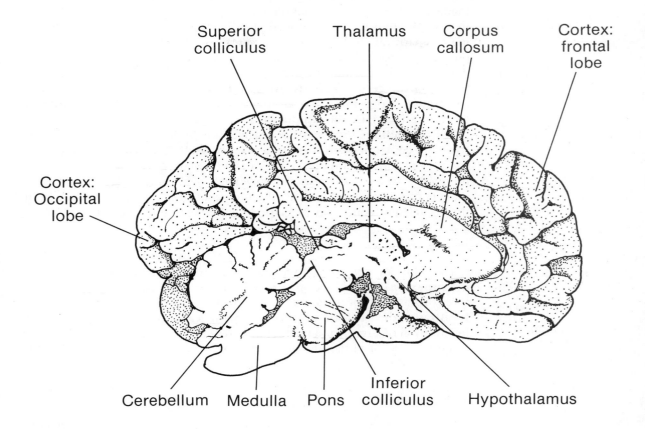

Superior colliculus   Thalamus   Corpus callosum   Cortex: frontal lobe

Cortex: Occipital lobe

Cerebellum   Medulla   Pons   Inferior colliculus   Hypothalamus

Figure 3–6 Section of the human brain showing the inside of the left hemisphere.

The Hindbrain

The hindbrain consists of three main components: the **medulla oblongata,** the **cerebellum,** and the **pons** (see Figure 3-6). The medulla is located just above, and is really a slight enlargement of, the spinal cord. A highly significant structure for the regulation of basic life functions, the medulla controls breathing, heart rate, vomiting, swallowing, blood pressure, and digestive processes. As you can see, normal functioning of the medulla is critical, and when drugs begin to affect the medulla the person is often in danger. When toxic chemicals reach high levels in this area, the vomit center is often triggered to purge the body, which may be why drink-

Medulla oblongata (meh-DULL-ah ah-blong-GOT-ah)
The lowest hindbrain structure of the brain, the medulla is important in the regulation of breathing, heart rate, and other basic life functions.

Cerebellum (sair-ah-BELL-um)
Hindbrain structure important in motor control and coordination.

Pons (pahnz)
Hindbrain structure important in the control of sleep and wakefulness.

ing large quantities of alcohol often causes nausea and vomiting. Further up the hind brain is an enlarged section called the pons. In addition to providing the pathways for input up and output down from the spinal cord, the pons plays a role in the control of sleep and wakefulness. Running along the pons and through the medulla is a pathway (not visible in Figure 3-6) known as the **reticular activating system,** which is critical for alertness and arousal. Drugs that lower arousal and induce sleep (such as barbiturates or tranquilizers) are thought to act in this region of the brain.

The cerebellum, the last major organ of the hindbrain, is a highly complex structure containing several billion neurons itself. The cerebellum is critical for motor control. Activities of the cerebellum are largely unconscious, but do involve balance, coordinated movement of all kinds, speech, and other aspects of movement. The loss of motor control and balance produced by drugs such as alcohol may be caused by their action on the cerebellum.

The Midbrain

The midbrain consists of two small structures: the **inferior colliculi** and the **superior colliculi** (see Figure 3-6). The inferior colliculi are two structures that are part of the auditory system. The superior colliculi function in localization of visual stimuli. These structures are specifically involved with localization of stimuli and mediation of reflexes. The actual recognition and interpretation of visual and auditory stimuli takes place elsewhere in the brain (see the section on cerebral cortex).

The Forebrain

The **thalamus and hypothalamus**   The most important brain regions from the perspective of interpreting drug actions are in the forebrain, which includes the **thalamus, hypothalamus,** and several other higher structures, particularly the cortex (see Figure 3-6). The thalamus is often referred to as a relay station because it receives incoming sensory stimuli and then "relays" that information to relevant centers throughout the brain. The hypothalamus is a critical structure in the motivation of behavior. The hypothalamus contains areas that appear to be central in the control of eating, drinking, control of body temperature, aggression, and sexual behavior. Worth noting is that information about the particular function of given brain regions has not been easily determined and remains somewhat controversial. The methods for analysis of brain structures involve primarily lesions and stimulation. Lesioning a structure involves performing surgery on an animal subject and causing localized damage to the structure in question. When the animal has recovered from surgery, changes in behavior are then attributed to the damaged structure. For example, lesions in one part of the hypothalamus result in an animal that will not eat and will starve to death if not fed

Reticular activating system
Pathway running through the medulla and pons that regulates alertness and arousal.

Inferior colliculi (ko-LICK-you-lie)
Midbrain structures that control sound localization.

Superior colliculi
Midbrain structures that control visual localization.

Thalamus (THAL-ah-muss)
Forebrain structure that organizes sensory input.

Hypothalamus (HIGH-poe-THAL-ah-muss)
Forebrain structure that regulates eating, drinking, and other basic biological drives.

intravenously. Damage to another part of the hypothalamus results in an animal that cannot stop eating and becomes enormously obese. Thus, the hypothalamus appears to contain two separate sites of eating control. One area seems to be the excitatory or "hunger" center, because its loss results in loss of appetite. Activity in the other site appears to inhibit eating (its loss results in overeating) and is called the "satiety" center. The effects of electrical stimulation of a brain region generally are opposite the effects of lesioning or removing that region. For example, stimulating the hunger center prompts eating and stimulating the satiety center suppresses eating.

However, a note of caution accompanies these findings. When cells in the brain are lesioned or stimulated, the effects extend beyond those specific cells, and indeed entire pathways may become damaged or stimulated. Thus, rather than speak of the hunger or satiety **centers,** more appropriate terms are hunger or satiety **pathways.** However, even this may be an oversimplification, as some researchers have noted the role of these pathways may not be as specific to hunger as we first thought. That is, these pathways could affect motor movements, the sensation of taste, or more general motivational variables, and much current research is devoted to these effects (see Carlson, 1986; Logue, 1986).

The pleasure center   Despite the difficulties of such research, electrical stimulation of brain regions was the basis of one of the most significant discoveries in the quest to understand the relationship between brain, behavior, and drugs. During the 1950s, the psychologist James Olds was trying to map the effects of stimulation on the rat brain by implanting electrodes into various regions. In some areas of the brain, the rat seemed to enjoy the electrical stimulation. Here is how Olds describes his serendipitous discovery:

> I applied a brief train of 60-cycle sine wave electrical current whenever the animal entered one corner of the enclosure. The animal did not stay away from the corner, but rather came back quickly after a brief sortie which followed the first stimulation and came back even more quickly after a briefer sortie which followed the second stimulation. By the time the third electrical stimulus had been applied the animal seemed indubitably to be "coming back for more" (Olds, cited in Carlson, 1980, p. 540–541).

Following up this finding, Olds and Milner (1954) discovered that when electrodes are implanted in some brain areas, particularly the **medial forebrain bundle,** rats could actually be trained to press a lever in order to electrically stimulate themselves. The medial forebrain bundle involves a group of neurons that travel through the lateral part of the hypothalamus. When rats have been trained to self-stimulate this area they often respond with great vigor (over 1000 responses per hour), and the potency of the reinforcement related to this center led Olds and others to refer to it as the

Medial forebrain bundle
Pathway that is rewarding when stimulated. Thus it is often referred to as the pleasure center.

"pleasure center." The notion is that the region may represent the final common pathway for pleasurable stimulation and reward. Clearly, this region is of significance in understanding the ability of some drugs to produce euphoria or intense pleasure in individuals. The preponderance of evidence suggests that two neurochemicals are important in mediating pleasurable stimulation: dopamine and endorphins (Carlson, 1986). It is probably no accident that two of the most powerful drugs of abuse, cocaine and heroin, affect these systems (heroin mimics endorphins; cocaine stimulates dopamine activity). Indeed, one recent study has shown that rats will learn to press a lever that results in the delivery of cocaine through a micropipette implanted in one of the "pleasure area" brain regions containing dopaminergic neurons (Goeders, Dworkin, & Smith, 1986). As Dakkis and Gold (1985) put it, cocaine addicts can be seen as individuals who have "tampered chemically with endogenous systems of reward and lost control of this shortcut to pleasure" (p. 476).

The forebrain also includes three complex systems: the **limbic system,** the **basal ganglia,** and the **cortex.** The aspects of behavior that are most uniquely human such as complex reasoning, memory, logic, speech, and planning, are largely derived from these structures.

The limbic system   The limbic system includes several structures in the interior of the forebrain. One limbic structure, the amygdala, is important in controlling aggression. Another important limbic system structure is the **hippocampus,** which appears to be critical in memory storage. Persons with damage to the hippocampus can remember things that occurred in their life prior to the damage, but are unable to store new memories. In other words, their long-term memories are intact but they cannot form new permanent memories. Heavy use of alcohol, coupled with malnutrition, in "skid-row" alcoholics often produces a severe psychotic state known as **Korsakoff's Syndrome.** Korsakoff's patients often show this sort of memory problem that appears due to brain damage to the hippocampus and perhaps other structures as well (also see Chapter 7).

The basal ganglia   The basal ganglia include the caudate nucleus, the putamen, and the globus pallidus. These structures are critical for motor movements. The problem of Parkinson's disease involves damage to the basal ganglia. Specifically, Parkinson's develops when a group of nerve cells known as the **substantia nigra** begin to degenerate. The substantia nigra produces dopamine, which is transported to the basal ganglia, and as the substantia nigra deteriorates, less and less dopamine is available for neurotransmission. Interestingly, Parkinson's symptoms do not appear until about 80% of the substantia nigra is destroyed.

Some of the recent controversy about designer drugs involves the substantia nigra. (see Contemporary Issue Box 3-1.)

Limbic system
Forebrain structures including the amygdala, hippocampus, and others.

Basal ganglia (BAY-sell GANG-lee-ah)
Forebrain structures important for motor control. The basal ganglia include the caudate nucleus, the putamen, and the globus pallidus.

Cortex
The cerebral cortex or cortex is the outermost and largest part of the human brain.

Hippocampus (hip-poe-KAMP-us)
A structure of the limbic system thought to be important in the formation of memories.

Korsakoff's Syndrome
A disorder characterized by memory loss and psychotic behavior and related to heavy use of alcohol and malnutrition.

Substantia nigra (sub-STAN-shah NIE-gruh)
Literally, "black substance" this basal ganglia structure is darkly pigmented. The substantia nigra produces dopamine. Damage to this area produces Parkinson's disease.

CONTEMPORARY ISSUE BOX 3-1
Designer Drugs and the Brain

Designer drugs are synthetic chemicals produced by making a small chemical change in the structure of previously known psychoactive drugs. If the change does not alter the receptor activating properties of the compound, the drug will still produce the psychoactive properties desired by the user, but not be specifically controlled by federal law. In other words, a clever chemist could make a slight change in the heroin molecule and produce a new drug with the effects of heroin, but because it was unknown, the new compound was completely legal. (The 1986 Drug Analogue Act changed that.) Thus, designer drugs placed the dealer at less risk, but not necessarily the user. Recently in California, an underground chemist began to produce a designer heroin called MPPP, but due to poor laboratory technique some of what hit the streets was a closely related but highly toxic compound called MPTP. The error was discovered when a number of young drugs users were hospitalized with complete paralysis. At first the cause of this epidemic of paralysis was a mystery. The symptoms were similar to those of advanced Parkinson's disease. But because Parkinson's is a disease of the elderly, only an inspired guess from a physician named Langston solved the puzzle. He tried to use L-dopa with these "frozen" addicts. The L-dopa was successful enough that the paralyzed patients were able to at least talk a little. Eventually they were identified as heroin addicts who had tried the mis-designed heroin, MPTP.

We now know that MPTP selectively attacks the substantia nigra and causes rapid destruction of this organ. Thus, the addicts who became victims of MPTP have sustained permanent damage, although some symptom reduction is possible with L-dopa (Markey, Castagnoli, Trevor, & Kopin, 1986).

A couple of important points: the tremendous hazard associated with designer drugs is obvious. Because these drugs are not tested in animals and screened by the FDA, the risks they pose to the user are great. An additional point is that brain damage can occur without overt symptoms. Many people who were exposed to MPTP only once or twice probably do not show any Parkinson symptoms at present. Nonetheless, some damage to the substantia nigra has occurred. As more cells are lost during the normal aging process, the 80% threshold may be reached and these individuals may yet pay the price by developing premature Parkinsonism.

The cerebral cortex Figure 3-5 shows the lobes of the cerebral cortex. The occipital lobe is at the back of the brain and is often referred to as the visual projection area. Stimulation of the eye is eventually perceived as a visual stimulus when the signal reaches the occipital cortex. The temporal lobe is similarly specialized for auditory stimulation, and also appears to be important in language. Damage to the left temporal lobe results in severe impairment of language abilities. The frontal lobe is important in the initiation of motor movement (precentral gyrus) and also is involved with emotionality, intelligence, and personality. Tactile stimuli are registered in the parietal lobe.

COMTEMPORARY ISSUE BOX 3-2
Assessment of Brain Damage

An important question that comes up whenever chronic effects of drugs are discussed is the issue of drug-induced brain damage. We discuss this problem throughout the text with each drug we consider, but now, after this lengthy discussion of the brain, a few general comments are warranted. First, detecting brain damage caused by drugs is often very difficult. Rarely do psychoactive drugs produce such dramatic destruction as is seen with MPTP, so more often we must rely on specialized methods to determine whether damage has occurred. Various tests are available that can be used to detect impairment in memory, perceptual-motor skills, language, or other functions that may be influenced by chronic drug use.

Electroencephalography (EEG)
Technique used to measure electrical activity in the brain.

More direct analysis of brain tissue may be accomplished through **electroencephalography (EEG).** This technique involves measuring the brain's electrical activity through the scalp. These brain waves change in predictable ways with sleep or various kinds of arousal, and abnormalities in EEG patterns can reveal gross brain damage.

Computerized Axial Tomography (CAT)
The CAT scan is a technique for developing a three-dimensional x-ray image of the brain.

A more recently developed and more sensitive measure of brain impairment is the technique of **Computerized Axial Tomography,** better known as the CAT scan. The CAT scan involves passing x-rays through the head in a circular pattern, resulting in a three-dimensional image of the brain. The focus can be changed to different depths of the brain so that internal tumors, enlarged spaces or ventricles, or other internal abnormalities can be detected.

Positron Emission Transaxial Tomography (PETT or PET)
The PET scan is a technique used to measure activity in selected brain regions.

CAT scans can provide a picture of the brain but reveal nothing about its functioning. However, a newly developed technique called the PETT scan may greatly increase our ability to detect brain activity. **Positron Emission Transaxial Tomography** (PETT) involves injecting weak radioisotopes into the brain. Radioactive glucose or oxygen or even radioactive neurochemicals are then measured by sensitive detectors that can determine where the isotopes are absorbed, their rate of absorption, and so on. Then changes in activity in various brain regions can be assessed. The PETT scan is just beginning to be widely used but offers promise to greatly increase our ability to detect the forms of subtle brain damage that drugs may induce. On the horizon may be an even more sophisticated and sensitive technique to image the brain called **Nuclear Magnetic Resonance** or NMR. With this technique, a strong magnetic field is passed through the person's head. Radio waves are then generated, causing the molecules of the brain to emit energy of different frequencies, depending on their properties. This technique creates a localized anddetailed brain image and eventually may greatly improve our ability to detect and understand brain dysfunction (Carlson, 1986).

Nuclear Magnetic Resonance (NMR) Increasingly referred to as Magnetic Resonance Imaging (MRI), this technique creates a high-resolution, three-dimensional image of the brain.

SUMMARY

· All psychoactive drugs produce their effects by action on the nervous system—primarily by altering normal brain function.

· The brain is composed of specialized cells called neurons. Neurons transmit information by conducting electrical currents along their axons and releasing chemical substances called neurotransmitters into the synapse. Most drugs act by altering this chemical phase of neural transmission.

· Neurotransmitters work through a "lock-and-key" mechanism. The transmitter substance is like a key, and specialized areas on the neuron, called receptor sites, are like locks. Neurotransmitter chemicals must occupy the receptor sites in order for the neuron to fire.

· Drugs alter neural transmission in several ways. For example, a drug may mimic a natural or endogenous neurotransmitter by activating receptor sites. Alternatively a drug may block a receptor site. Drugs can also affect the deactivation or release of neurotransmitters.

· Although dozens of different chemicals have been proposed to act as neurotransmitters in the human brain, six are known to be related to drug effects. These are acetylcholine,

dopamine, endorphins, GABA, norepinephrine, and serotonin.

· The nervous system is divided into two main sections. The central nervous system includes the brain and spinal cord. The peripheral nervous system includes the sensory nerves, motor nerves and the autonomic nervous system.

· The autonomic nervous system is divided into two branches. The sympathetic branch produces the physiological effects that accompany emotional arousal, and the parasympathetic controls the body when at rest.

· The brain is divided into three divisions: the hindbrain, the midbrain, and the forebrain.

· The evolutionarily primitive hindbrain includes the medulla, the pons, and the cerebellum.

· The midbrain includes the superior and inferior colliculi.

· The forebrain includes the cerebral cortex, the thalamus, the hypothalamus, the basal ganglia, and the limbic system.

References

Bardo, M.T. & Risner, M.E. (1985). Biochemical substrates of drug abuse, In M. Galizio and S.A. Maisto (eds.) *Determinants of substance abuse: Biological, psychological and environmental factors* (pp. 65–101). New York: Plenum Press.

Bradford, H.F. (1986). *Chemical neurobiology: An introduction to neurochemistry,* New York: W.H. Freeman and Company.

Carlson, N.R. (1986). *Physiology of behavior,* Third Edition, Boston: Allyn and Bacon, Inc.

Crow, T.J. & Deakin, J.F.W., (1979). Monoamines and the psychoses. In K. Brown and S.J. Cooper (Eds.) *Chemical influences on behaviour,* (pp. 503–533). London: Academic Press.

Cooper, J.R., Bloom, F.E. & Roth, R.H. (1986). *The biochemical basis of neuropharmacology,* (Fifth ed.), New York: Oxford University Press.

Dackis, C.A. & Gold, M.S. (1985). New concepts in cocaine addiction: The dopamine depletion hypothesis. *Neuroscience and Biobehavioral Reviews, 9,* 469–477.

Goeders, N.E., Dworkin, S.I. & Smith, J.E. (1986). Neuropharmacological assessment of cocaine self-administration into the medial prefrontal cortex. *Pharmacology, Biochemistry, and Behavior, 24,* 1429–1440.

Kruk, Z.L. & Pycock, C.J. (1979). *Neurotransmitters and drugs,* Baltimore: University Park Press.

Lickey, M.E. & Gordon, B. (1983). *Drugs for mental illness: A revolution in psychiatry,* New York: W.H. Freeman and Company.

Logue, A.W. (1986). *The psychology of eating and drinking,* New York: W.H. Freeman and Company.

Markey, S.P., Castagnoli, N., Trevor, A.J. & Kopin, I.J., (Eds.) (1986). *MPTP: A neurotoxin producing a parkinsonian syndrome,* Orlando, FL: Academic Press.

Olds, J. & Milner, P. (1954). Positive reinforcement produced by electrical stimulation of septal area and other regions of rat brains. *Journal of Comparative and Physiological Psychology, 47,* 419–427.

Snyder, S.H., Burt, D.R. & Creese, I. (1976). Dopamine receptor of mammalian brain: Direct demonstration of binding to agonist and antagonist states. *Neuroscience Symposia, 1,* 28–49.

4 PHARMACOLOGY PRINCIPLES AND NEW DRUG DEVELOPMENT

This wide-ranging chapter covers basic principles and methods of pharmacology and the procedures for developing and marketing new drugs. We will present the principles of pharmacology by elaborating on our previous discussion of the drug experience, which we first referred to in Chapter 1. In developing the drug experience theme, many of the basics about pharmacology and psychopharmacology in particular, will emerge. This additional knowledge about the principles and methods of pharmacology will prepare you to better understand the second part of this chapter, which focuses on the discovery, development, and distribution of new drugs in the United States.

THE DRUG EXPERIENCE

Control
In research, control means to be able to account for variables that may affect the results of a study.

Feedback
In this context, in a series of events, what happens in a later event alters those preceding it.

Absorbed
Drugs are absorbed, or entered into, the bloodstream.

To present basic principles and methods of pharmacology, the first part of this chapter details the various effects of a drug. In Chapter 1 we called such effects the "drug experience", and the term is especially applicable to the nonmedical use of drugs among humans. A series of interrelated factors contributes to a given drug effect. The importance of any one factor, or set of factors, for a given drug-taking occasion depends on the importance of the other factors. This complicated-sounding idea is even more complicated to analyze in practice. To evaluate the importance or contribution of any one factor to a drug effect or experience, the researcher must comprehend or at least somehow **control** the effects that other relevant factors are having.

We will try to walk down the path of the drug experience from beginning to end as if it were always a logical and linear route. However, that analogy is not fully accurate, because not only are the contributory factors of a drug effect interdependent, but also **"feedback"** relationships may occur among those factors. For example, a large quantity of some drugs may be taken and then **absorbed** into the blood. Then the drug is carried to its site of action

Table 4-1
"Steps" to the Drug Experience

1. A drug of specified chemical structure is
2. Measured in a certain quantity. It is then
3. Administered in one of a number of possible ways and
4. Absorbed into the blood and distributed to site(s) of action
5. To achieve a desired drug effect.
6. But in humans, the drug effect depends not only on the chemical properties of the drug and its physiological consequences,
7. But also on characteristics of the person, such as genetic constitution, gender, age, personality, and drug tolerance.
8. The setting or context of drug use may also affect the drug experience.
9. Steps 1-4 and 6-8 combine to produce the drug experience.

(distributed). But, in some cases a large quantity of a drug may cause the body to slow absorption or quicken **metabolism** of the drug in order to defend itself against a toxic drug effect. In this event, the distribution of the drug is information that the body "feeds back" to its regulators of absorption and metabolism to, in effect, reduce drug quantity.

However, including all the possible feedback loops would strangle this discussion so we review the drug experience and factors influencing it as if everything proceeds linearly. We chart the path as outlined in Table 4-1. For each of the "steps" included in Table 4-1 there may be two or more factors to consider. By the end of the first part of this chapter you will begin to understand the great complexity of how humans experience drug effects.

Distribution
Drugs are distributed, or transported, by the blood to their site(s) of action in the body.

Metabolism
The process by which the body breaks down matter into more simple components and waste.

HOW MUCH DRUG?

You know from Chapter 1 that the effect of a drug depends most fundamentally on how much of the drug is taken. A science about drugs relies on a standard way to determine drug quantities. Thus the questions: How do pharmacologists compute drug dose? How is that quantity communicated? A drug's dose is computed according to a person's body weight because, in general, the same quantity of a drug causes less of an effect on a heavier person. Calculating dose according to body weight assures that a drug is administered in equivalent strengths to people of different body weights. The first step is to determine the desired dose, expressed in milligrams of the drug per kilogram (mg/kg) of body weight. The next step is to weigh the person and record the weight in kilograms. With these two quantities the amount of drug required for the desired dose is easily determined. For example, if the desired dose is .08 mg/kg and the subject weighs 80kg, the necessary amount is $.08 \times 80 = 6.4$ mg of the drug (Leavitt, 1982).

ONCE MEASURED, HOW IS A DRUG DOSE TAKEN?

In pharmacology, the route of drug administration refers to how a drug is taken.[1] The route of drug administration can strongly influence the effects of a drug. The four principal routes of drug administration are oral, subcutaneous, intramuscular, and intravenous, here listed in reverse order of how rapidly drug absorption occurs. Oral administration is generally associated with slower rates of absorption and intravenous with the fastest rates. Another common way that drugs can be absorbed is through the body's mucous membranes.

[1] Our discussion of routes of drug administration draws heavily from Benet and Sheiner (1985) and Jacobs and Fehr (1987).

Oral Route

Oral administration, or swallowing, is the route that you probably are most familiar with. Orally-taken drugs generally are in the form of pills, capsules, powders, or liquids. Numerous examples include the variety of headache medicines, cough syrups, cold remedies, and so on available at any drug store. That such accessible medications are virtually always prepared for oral administration is a result of a major feature of this route: It usually is the safest, most convenient, and most economical of the four major routes.

When drugs are swallowed, they pass through the stomach and are absorbed primarily through the small intestine. This travel course has several consequences for the speed with which a drug can register its effect physically as well as how much effect is registered. A major factor in determining the effect is how much food is in the digestive tract when the drug is taken. The presence of food delays stomach emptying and may dilute the concentration of a drug. The result: delayed absorption and a decrease in the maximum drug level achieved. Perhaps people most commonly notice this result when they compare drinking alcohol after eating a full meal to drinking on an empty stomach. Another point about oral administration is that food may encapsulate the drug so that it is passed out of the body in the feces. Finally, taking a drug orally, even without the complications of food in the stomach, causes the drug to be absorbed into the blood slower than with other routes.

So, the plusses of oral administration—relative safety, convenience, and economy—must be balanced against considerations of speed of absorption and the maximum drug effect that can be reached with a particular drug dose. With some drugs, such as heroin, the stomach acids used for digestion actually break down the drug to some degree before it is absorbed into the blood. Once in the blood the chemically altered drug is passed through the liver before reaching the brain. Because the liver is the major site of the metabolizing of most drugs, only a fraction of the drug dose actually reaches the brain. The outcome is a very diminished drug effect.

Taking Drugs by Injection

The remaining three major routes of drug administration involve injecting drugs into the body using a needle and syringe. When drugs are taken this way they typically are **dissolved** or **suspended** in some solution before injection. The routes for administration when injecting drugs are: subcutaneous, intramuscular, and intravenous.

Subcutaneous   This route involves injecting the drug under the skin. It is the easiest of the injection routes to use, because the target site of the needle is just below the skin surface. Many beginning drug abusers take their drugs subcutaneously. This route may also be preferred medically for drugs

Dissolved
A drug is dissolved by converting it from solid to liquid by mixing the drug with a liquid.

Suspended
A drug is suspended in solution if its particles are dispersed in solution but not dissolved in it.

that are not irritating to body tissue, because of the route's relatively slow (but faster than oral) and constant absorption rate. In fact, the solution the drug is administered in may be selected to adjust the drug's absorption rate. Two reasons for not taking a drug subcutaneously are when the drug irritates body tissue, or if large volumes of solution must be taken in order to introduce enough drug to achieve the desired effect.

Intramuscular The name of this route means within the muscle. Intramuscular injection requires a deeper penetration than the subcutaneous method but is associated with a faster absorption rate when the drug is prepared in a water solution and there is a good rate of blood flow at the site of administration. Absorption rates may differ, depending on what muscle group the drug is injected into. Absorption rate can also be modulated by the type of solution that the drug is prepared in for administration. Drug abusers who take their drugs by injection might prefer the intramuscular to the subcutaneous route because it is possible to inject the drug through clothing.

One disadvantage of intramuscular injection is that it can result in localized (at the site of injection) pain. Furthermore, when drugs are administered intramuscularly by a person who is not formally trained to do so, the risk of infection from irritating drugs and tissue damage is high.

Intravenous Intravenous means into the veins, and because of that most of the problems in absorption are averted. A common street term for the route is mainlining. The drug is injected, in solution, directly into the veins. The effects can be immediate. As a result, intravenous administration is valuable for emergency medical situations, and doses can be precisely adjusted according to the person's response. In addition, irritating drugs can be taken intravenously (as opposed to, say, subcutaneously or intramuscularly) because blood vessel walls are relatively insensitive and the drug is further diluted by blood.

The apparent advantages of intravenous administration raise the question of why this is not the preferred route for prescribed medications. A major reason is that the intravenous route is the one most highly associated with complications, because large quantities of the drug very quickly can reach their site of action. Another point to consider: if a drug is repeatedly administered intravenously, maintenance of a healthy vein is necessary. In general, intravenous injection is associated with such risk that administration must be done slowly and with careful monitoring of a person's response.

Those who regularly take heroin, amphetamine, or other drugs intravenously are called "hard core addicts". These users take drugs intravenously because they want immediate and powerful drug effects. However, the risks of taking a drug intravenously, coupled with the assault that such drug taking has on the body, usually take a toll on a person. Drug-induced deaths,

intentional or not, are an ever-present danger among addicts and other nonmedical drug users who take their drugs intravenously.

A general consideration in taking drugs by injection To prevent diseases such as AIDS, hepatitis, or tetanus, drugs must be injected using sterile needles and solutions. When any of the three injecting routes are used, the body's natural protection from microorganisms, such as skin and mucous membranes, are bypassed. Therefore, dirty needles or nonsterile solutions may carry illness-inducing microorganisms that the body cannot "screen out." This is why, for instance, street drug abusers are increasingly contracting AIDS. In this respect, nonsterile needles are a major culprit, and several cities in the United States, most notably New York, have started "needle exchange" (dirty for sterile) programs available free-of-charge to drug abusers.

Figure 4–1 Intravenous drug injection is associated with rapid drug effects, making it the preferred route of many addicts. Intravenous injection of drugs also is dangerous because large quantities of a drug can reach the site(s) of action so quickly.

Thinking about Routes of Drug Administration

While reading about these routes of drug administration, think of them as ways devised for getting drugs into the body. Each has its own pros and cons for any particular drug. As a result, no route is inherently better than any other. Rather, determining the preferred route depends on the drug administered, the goals of administration, and the advantages and disadvantages of using a particular route, with a particular drug, under particular circumstances. Table 4-2 is a summary, based on our discussion, of general considerations in using the four major routes of drug administration.

Absorption of Drugs Through the Mucous Membranes

A number of drugs may be absorbed through the body's mucous membranes. Drugs that are soluble in fat can be absorbed relatively quickly by

Table 4-2

General Considerations in Using the Four Major Routes of Drug Administration

Route	Considerations
Oral	-Safest, most convenient, most economical of the four routes -Presence of food in the stomach retards absorption or may diminish the amount of drug absorbed -Associated with the slowest absorption rate of the four major routes -Stomach acids may break down some drugs, resulting in reduced drug effect
Subcutaneous	-Easiest of the three injection routes to use -Associated with absorption rates faster than oral administration but slower than intramuscular and intravenous routes -Preferred for medical use of drugs that are not irritating to body tissue, because of its relatively slow but constant absorption rate with sustained drug effects -When a drug irritates body tissue or when large volumes of solution must be used for taking the drug, the subcutaneous route should not be used
Intramuscular	-Requires deeper penetration of injection than subcutaneous but results in a faster absorption rate with proper preparation of solution and an injection site with good blood flow -May be painful at the injection site -Use of this route by medically untrained people is associated with a high risk of infection from irritating drugs and tissue damage
Intravenous	-Considered the fastest absorption rate of the four routes -Because the resulting drug effects can be immediate, this route is valuable for emergency medical needs -Doses can be adjusted precisely according to the person's response, because of immediacy of drug effects -Better than subcutaneous or intramuscular routes for taking irritating drugs, because blood vessel walls are relatively insensitive and the blood further dilutes the drug -Danger exists in the potential for large quantities of a drug to reach their site of action -Repeated use of this route requires maintenance of a healthy vein -A drug dose must be administered gradually and the person's response monitored carefully to prevent serious complications

this method because membranes are thinner than skin and have a greater supply of blood. Furthermore, membranes lack a protein present in skin that reduces its permeability. The major ways of absorbing drugs through the mucous membranes include inhalation, under the tongue (sublingually), and sniffing or snorting.

Inhalation   When drugs can be changed into a gaseous state they may be absorbed through the lung's membranes by inhalation. For such drugs, inhalation results in fast (faster than subcutaneous or intramuscular injection) and effective absorption. A class of drugs called inhalants, including substances such as benzine, gasoline, tolulene, paint thinner, and lighter fluid, are commonly abused. Tobacco and other substances such as marijuana and cocaine **freebase** or crack may be smoked. The frequency of tobacco smoking puts inhalation among the five (along with the four major routes) most commonly used routes of drug administration.

Sublingual   With this route a drug tablet is placed under the tongue and dissolves in saliva. Nitroglycerin, which is taken for treatment of angina pectoris (heart pain), usually is taken sublingually. Nicotine taken in the form of chewing tobacco or "dipping" snuff is being absorbed through the mouth's mucous membranes. The sublingual route results in faster and more efficient drug absorption than oral administration. It also is preferred to oral administration for drugs that irritate the stomach and cause vomiting. Almost any drug with the right chemical properties may be taken in pill form and absorbed sublingually. However, the sublingual route is used less frequently than might be expected because of the unpleasant taste of many of these drugs.

Sniffing   In this route a drug in powdered form is absorbed through the mucous membranes of the nose and sinus cavities. Examples of drugs commonly absorbed this way include cocaine, heroin, and powdered tobacco snuff. When a drug is fat soluble, sniffing is a rapid and effective way to absorb it. However, if a drug is irritating and disrupts blood flow it can cause damage if sniffed. An example that has been cited recently is the damage cocaine sniffing causes to the nasal septum and lining of the nose.

Freebase
A substance may be separated, or "freed," from its salt base. The separated form of the substance is thus called "freebase".

Summary of Routes of Drug Administration

How a drug gets into a person's body is but one factor that influences his or her drug experience, but it is an important one. Again, in thinking about routes of administration, remember there are different ways of getting a drug with certain chemical properties into the body in order to achieve certain desired effects with the fewest possible undesired effects. Table 4-3 is a summary of the routes of administration typically used with a number of drugs taken for medical or nonmedical reasons.

DRUG ABSORPTION AND DISTRIBUTION

Having entered the body, a drug is absorbed into the blood and distributed to its site(s) of action. Drug distribution simply means transportation to a

Table 4-3

List of Drugs and Drug Classes Used for Medical or Nonmedical Reasons and the Ways They Are Most Often Administered

Drug	Route
Alcohol	Oral
Amphetamines	Oral; intravenous (preferred for the chronic, high dose abuser); sniffed by occasional or new users
Barbiturates	Oral; rectal (through the mucous membrane of the rectum); subcutaneous; intramuscular; intravenous
Benzodiazepines	Most common is oral; some of these drugs may be administered intravenously or intramuscularly
Caffeine	Most common is oral; medically, occasionally by injection for mild stimulant properties; abusers have injected caffeine intravenously
Cannabis	Almost all routes have been used, but the most common is by smoking (inhalation)
Cocaine	Cocaine hydrochloride is taken through the nasal or other mucous membranes, such as those of the mouth, vagina, and rectum. Also taken intravenously. Cocaine freebase is volatile and, therefore, is most often vaporized in a freebase pipe and inhaled into the lungs
Heroin	Most commonly dissolved in water and injected subcutaneously, intramuscularly, or intravenously. May be inhaled by smoking or sniffed
Nicotine	Inhaled by smoking (cigarettes), nicotine in cigar or pipe smoke mainly absorbed across membranes of the mouth and upper respiratory tract. Also may be absorbed through membranes of the mouth (chewing tobacco) and nose (snuff)
LSD (Lysergic Acid Diethylamide)	Oral; inhalation; the three injection routes
PCP (Phencyclidine)	Oral; sniffed; inhalation by smoking (sprinkled on marijuana, parsley, tobacco or other smokable substance); intravenous injection

given site. Of course, once a drug enters a person's body, its presence and effects do not last forever. A drug effect may be terminated by a redistribution of the drug away from its site of action. However, in most cases, drugs eventually are metabolized by the liver and excreted through the kidneys (Leavitt, 1982).

However, the drug's exit from the body may not be the end of the drug experience. The elimination of a drug from the body often is associated with changes that are opposite to those that were caused by the drug. For example, the euphoria and high energy that typically are induced by cocaine and amphetamines turn to lethargy and depression as the drugs end their course. Such opposite (sometimes called rebound) effects are important because of their influence on drug use patterns. For example, in the case of cocaine, the downside drug effect of depression is sometimes so unpleasant that the user feels a strong need to take more cocaine in order to stop the bad feelings. Similarly, when coming down from a dose of alcohol, people often feel sleepy and somewhat depressive, so they may try to recapture the more euphoric mood associated with just starting to drink by starting again.

THE FIRST FOUR STEPS TO THE DRUG EXPERIENCE

So far we have gone through the first four steps of Table 4-1, which primarily involve chemical and physical mechanisms in producing the drug effect. These mechanisms are most commonly thought of when studying drug effects in less complex nonhuman animals, such as mice. But several sets of other factors must be examined before we can adequately account for drug effects in humans, and they are represented in steps seven and eight of Table 4-1.

CHARACTERISTICS OF THE USER

The many differences among people probably account for most of the differences in their reactions to a given dose of a drug. We present only the major factors in this section, because more extended discussion would preclude presentation of anything else in this book. Roughly, we can divide the characteristics into two types: physical/biological and psychological.

Physical/Biological Characteristics of the User

Inherited differences in reactions to drugs   Genetically-based differences dictate how people react to some drugs. One example, as mentioned in Chapter 1, is a person's initial sensitivity to a drug. In fact, much research is devoted to discovering the role genetics plays in causing the various psychoactive substance use disorders (Chapter 1). Alcohol dependence in particular has received much attention from scientists, many of whom believe that inherited differences in how alcohol is experienced (as a result of action in the brain) and metabolized may play a major role in developing alcohol dependence.

Gender   Sex makes a difference, too—a specified dose of a drug administered to a man and a woman generally has greater effects on the woman. This is due to the higher percentage of body fat in women than in men, which results in the drug remaining active in women longer than it does in men. Regarding alcohol absorption, this gender difference may be partially explained by a recent finding that women show lower levels of a certain stomach enzyme that helps break down alcohol before it is released into the bloodstream. We discuss this new finding more in Chapter 7.

Weight   Earlier we showed that body weight is part of the formula for computing drug dose. This is because the concentration of a drug in the blood depends on how much blood and other body fluids are in the body. These fluids dilute an absorbed drug. Simply, a heavier person has more blood and other fluids; a given quantity of drug is less concentrated than in a lighter person, resulting in a lesser drug effect in the heavier person.

Age   Age can influence drug effects if the user is very young or old. Children are more sensitive to drugs because enzyme systems that metabolize drugs may not be fully developed. As a result, the drug stays active longer. In the elderly, these same enzyme systems may be impaired, with the same effect of increased duration of drug action.

Tolerance   Tolerance to a drug is thought to be biologically based but modifiable by learning. We consider tolerance mainly a characteristic of the drug user, because the type of tolerance of major interest, protracted tolerance, depends on a person's individual history of using a drug on repeated occasions. Furthermore, different people develop tolerance at different rates.

Simply from the associated terms we introduced in Chapter 1, you may have recognized the complexity of the concept of tolerance. If so, you are correct—the phenomenon is complicated indeed. First, tolerance may develop to some of the effects of a drug but not to others. With the barbiturates, for example, tolerance develops rapidly to the sleep-inducing and pleasantly intoxicating (e.g., euphoria) effects of these drugs. However, tolerance does not develop as readily to the impaired motor coordination and slowed reaction-time effects of the barbiturates. And, tolerance to the anticonvulsant effect of phenobarbital, a barbiturate, does not seem to occur at all (Jacobs & Fehr, 1987). Another example is the amphetamine drugs. Tolerance to their appetite suppressant and euphoric effects may develop rapidly. However, the **psychosis**-like effects of amphetamines are not subject to tolerance.

Psychosis
A severe mental disorder. Symptoms include disorganized thinking and bizarre behavior.

Explanations of tolerance   We have shown that people differ in how rapidly they develop tolerance to a drug effect, and that tolerance may develop to different effects of a drug at different rates, including at no rate at all (zero tolerance). Also, for some drug effects, "reverse tolerance," or increased sensitivity to the effects, develops. For example, some evidence indicates that reverse tolerance develops to cocaine's anesthetic and anti-convulsant effects. Much time has been spent in arriving at an explanation of drug tolerance, because tolerance can strongly affect patterns of drug use by altering the drug effects experienced by the user.

Cell adaptation theory One explanation for tolerance was proposed almost 50 years ago; called the adaptation-homeostasis hypothesis (Cicero, 1980), it assumes that a drug's action occurs on specific cells in the central nervous system (CNS). Because of the plasticity of the CNS, the cells become "adapted" to the presence of the drug with repeated exposure to it. The adaptation allows the cells to maintain normal functioning at a given drug dose. As a result, more drug is required to disrupt cell functioning. This required increase is called tolerance.

Drug compensatory reactions and learning The cell-adaptation and other neurobiological theories of tolerance all have some scientific support, especially more recently, but still cannot account for all the facets of tolerance that have been observed. One facet in particular suggests that tolerance to a given drug effect may be in part learned. Imagine that two people who are "theoretically equal in all ways" (no two people ever really are) take a particular dose of a drug on ten occasions. Person A takes the drug every time under the same conditions, while person B takes the drug under different conditions every time. For example, the room where B takes the drug may vary, the color of the drug tablets may change, and so forth. Then on the eleventh occasion, tolerance for some effect of the drug at the specified dose is measured in A and B under the conditions in which A took the drug ten previous times. Who would show a greater degree of tolerance? The cell adaptation hypothesis would predict equal tolerance for A and B. Yet numerous studies of humans and other animals indicate A would show the greater degree of tolerance (Hinson, 1985). Such findings have led to the idea that tolerance may be modified by learning.

To understand this idea you need to know about compensatory reactions. When an event, such as a drug, disrupts the body's **homeostasis,** sometimes the body counteracts the disruption with a reflex-like response. In this case the counter-reaction is an effect opposite to the drug effect. For example, you drink three beers that are absorbed and distributed in your body. By the time you feel the effects of those beers, your body is working to counteract them, which means to direct you back to the sober state. This aspect of compensatory reactions tells you that when you take a drug, two major actions are biologically triggered: one is "toward" a drug effect and the other is away from it.

One more part of compensatory reactions occurs with repeated use of a given dose of a drug: the body's movement "toward" a drug effect is less-

Homeostasis
A state of equilibrium or balance. Systems at homeostasis are stable; when homeostasis is disrupted, the system operates to restore homeostasis.

ened, and the move away is greater. Thus, we have the makings of an explanation of tolerance, based on an "opposing process" hypothesis about how the body reacts to drugs at the cellular level. It is easy to see how the hypothesis got its name. It also is interesting to note that a general theory of motivation was proposed over 15 years ago and based on an opposing process idea (Solomon & Corbit, 1974).

So where does learning come in? Although the role of experience is clarified, that does not explain why person A shows more tolerance than B on the eleventh drug taking. The final part of the explanation is in classical conditioning.[2] The cues associated with drug taking, such as where it is taken, who is there, and what colors the pills are, are "conditioned stimuli" that become associated with drug actions and compensatory reactions. Over repeated occasions of pairing drug taking and drug–taking cues, just presenting the drug-taking cues alone will elicit a drug compensatory reaction. This indicates drug compensatory reactions, one hypothesis of what underlies tolerance, build in strength with repeated pairings with the same environment. They seem to be tied to the specific drug–taking context. Therefore, the "sum" of the drug effect and counter effect observed when a person takes a drug depends on how often the same drug–taking conditions have occurred in the past. The higher the number of pairings, the larger the compensatory reaction, and the smaller the observed drug effect. That is why A shows more tolerance than B—the drug–taking event never changed for A, so conditioning or learning in that context was stronger for A than B, who changed contexts every time.

Final note on tolerance   Tolerance to a drug effect can be reversed. In this regard, a period of abstaining from a drug increases the user's sensitivity to drug effects he or she may have become highly tolerant to in the past. This, for example, has resulted in the deaths by overdose of some heroin abusers who have resumed heroin use after a relatively long time of not using the drug. When use was resumed they failed to take into account the loss of tolerance that resulted from the long period of abstinence.

Another point about tolerance concerns its reacquisition. Often, resumption of use of a drug after a long period of abstinence from it results in the reacquisition of tolerance at a rate faster than it was first developed (Kalant, LeBlanc, & Gibbins, 1971).

---

[2]Classical conditioning is a type of learning in which, by repeated pairing, a second stimulus elicits a response similar to that elicited without prior learning by another stimulus. For example, a puff of air, a type of stimulus, blown at the eye elicits an eye blink. If, say, a buzzer, which normally does not elicit an eye blink, repeatedly follows by about a half second an air puff directed at the eye, at some point presenting the buzzer alone will elicit an eye blink. We then would say that classical conditioning has occurred: the buzzer now elicits a reaction it did not before the repeated pairing with the puff of air.

CONTEMPORARY ISSUE BOX 4-1
Tolerance and DUI Laws

There have been major changes in the attitudes and behaviors in United States politicians and other citizens about the availability of alcohol and its legal and social consequences. For example, the legal drinking age in most of the United States is now 21 for all alcoholic beverages, compared to recent years when many states had lowered legal drinking ages to 18 or 19. Attitudes also have changed regarding driving under the influence (DUI) of alcohol (and other drugs) laws. These laws pertain to an established blood alcohol level. In most states an individual is declared legally intoxicated with a level of .10%. Arrest and conviction for driving at this level of intoxication are now associated with far harsher penalties than before, especially for repeat offenders. The main reasons behind this change is compelling: consistently for years about 50% of the traffic fatalities in the U.S. have involved alcohol.

Why was the blood alcohol level of .10% chosen? Several reasons are usually cited, but a central one is that driving skills of the average person are greatly impaired at that level. Now that you know something about tolerance to a drug, what do you think of the "average driver" approach to the DUI law? Do you see any value in the argument that arrest should be based on behavioral (especially driving skills) impairment of the driver at a given blood alcohol level, whether it is above or below .10%? What do you see as the health, social, and political consequences of this stance?

How Do the User's Psychological Characteristics Contribute to the Drug Experience?

This question most often is studied in research on personality and drug use. Indeed, psychopharmacologists have paid much attention to drug users' personalities. Not surprisingly, how peoples' personalities affect their drug experiences is not easy to answer. The first obstacle still is in defining personality, although for years many have tried. One definition consistent with the approach to drug use taken in this book is that personality is the field of psychology that explains "how the parts of a person come together to produce total behavioral outcomes" (Klinger, 1983, p. 30, cited in Cox, 1985).

Because personality factors are a central part of Chapter 14, we do not dwell on them here. However, we do highlight the points necessary to give you an idea of why these factors are important for understanding the drug experience.

Drugs, personality, and stress reduction   Stress reduction has long been viewed as a major reason why people drink and use drugs, especially people who become drug or alcohol abusers. In this respect, Sher (1987) has developed the "stress response dampening" (SRD) model of alcohol and other drug use. Alcohol and other drugs such as the barbiturates are seen as having anxiety-reducing effects and, therefore, are of reinforcing value when used in situations in which a person feels stress. People who experience such effects, therefore, are more likely than others to use drugs when they are stressed. Of interest here is that individuals vary in the SRD effects of alcohol they experience according to their personality characteristics. For example, Sher and Levenson (1982) showed that people characterized as aggressive, impulsive, and extraverted were more sensitive to alcohol's SRD effects. Notably, studies have shown that those people who became alcohol dependent tended to exhibit these characteristics before they experienced problems with alcohol.

Placebos and placebo effects   We mentioned in Chapter 1 the idea of giving a person a chemically inert substance that has no biological action. If you tell him or her at the same time you are administering a specific drug, then you have given that person a placebo. The placebo effect is the response to the placebo. (There are also "drug antagonistic" placebo responses, which are thought to be based in the body's compensatory reactions discussed earlier.) Estimates of the influences of placebos vary, but a concensus indicates at least 30% of people will show placebo effects in a given situation.

The placebo effect probably has been studied most extensively in medical treatment. Apparently, many medical disorders are responsive to placebos. Pfefferbaum (1977) listed 24 different diseases for which up to 62% of the afflicted patients studied had responded to placebos. Symptoms such as pain, headache, and angina, which are reactions to physical processes, seem particularly reactive to placebos. Other symptoms that involve subjective responses, such as anxiety and depression, also are especially responsive to placebos. Additional symptoms of the autonomic nervous system, including hypertension, migraine, and nausea, respond to placebos as well.

When drugs are used nonmedically the placebo effect also seems to be powerful. This has been demonstrated in experiments on alcohol and marijuana use, with alcohol studied the most extensively. Conclusions from this research indicate that what a person expects alcohol to "do" for him or her (for example, cause more aggressive behavior) seems to be associated with what the person experiences when given an alcohol placebo. This implies that when drinking alcohol at home, a party, or a bar, what a person expects will happen during that drinking occasion strongly influences what actually will be experienced. The influence of expectancies seems most powerful when a moderate dose of alcohol is drunk and the behaviors in question are social and psychological, such as mood, aggression, anxiety, and sexual arousal (Adesso, 1985; Hull & Bond, 1986).

SETTING FACTORS AND THE DRUG EXPERIENCE

A relatively recent discovery that is generally accepted is that the drug effects people experience are strongly influenced by environmental (setting) factors (see also Chapter 14). The "environment" is an extremely broad term, and its study ranges from the level of government laws about alcohol and drug availability (Chapter 2) to the people and places in the immediate drug use setting (McCarty, 1985).

Setting factors seem to be particularly important in the effects of alcohol, marijuana, and hallucinogenic drugs. A demonstration of this point with alcohol was conducted by Pliner and Cappell (1974). In this study, men and women drank moderate amounts of alcohol alone or with others. When subjects drank alone they mostly reported experiencing physical changes, like fuzzy thinking, sleepiness, and dizziness. In contrast, subjects who drank the same amount of alcohol with others said their mood changed to feeling friendly and more pleasant. Because subjects who drank an alcohol placebo beverage reported no changes whether drinking alone or with others, the number of people you drink with seems to affect how you interpret the physiological changes that alcohol induces.

DRUG INTERACTIONS AND THE DRUG EXPERIENCE

In our discussion we have tried to walk you through the steps "leading to" the drug experience as if traveling a straight line. We have already mentioned that such a linear approach is used only for simplification. Another simplifying feature of the discussion is our assumption that the person is taking only one drug at a time. However, often it is necessary to consider the action of two or more drugs when explaining a person's drug experience. After all, a person could take multiple drugs at the same time, or take one drug before another has totally cleared his or her body. The extremes of this often are seen in polydrug abuse, which we illustrated in Chapter 1. Multiple drug use is also a problem in prescribing medications, because patients often are taking more than one drug at a time for medical reasons.

How Does Multiple Drug Use Affect the Drug Experience?

This question technically refers to the interactive effects of two or more drugs that are introduced into the body. Two major outcomes of drug com-

Summation
The summative effect of combining two or more drugs is the addition of the effects of each of the drugs in question.

Potentiation
The potentiating effect of combining two or more drugs is greater than the sum of the effects of each of the drugs in question.

binations are **summation** and **potentiation.** In summation, the combined effects of multiple drugs are simply their respective effects added together. So, Effect (Drug A + Drug B) = Effect Drug A + Effect Drug B. In potentiation, however, the total is greater than the sum of the parts. When one drug potentiates another, combining them produces an effect that is greater than their simple additive effects. Therefore, in this case, Effect (Drug C + Drug B) > Effect Drug C + Effect Drug D.

Drug potentiation must be considered in both medical and nonmedical drug use. When a physician prescribes medication he or she must know what other drugs the patient is using. First, the effects of one drug could cancel the therapeutic effects of another. Second, the prescribed medication could have detrimental or even lethal effects in the presence of other compounds. In this respect, an increasingly common practice is for pharmacies to have computerized profiles of the medications their customers have been prescribed. Such information allows the pharmacist to inform customers how newly prescribed medications interact with other medications the person is taking and what precautions should be followed to avoid harmful combined drug effects. This backup system to physician advice is valuable to all patients but probably of most help in treating the elderly, who frequently take more than one prescribed medication at a time.

The danger of harmful interactive drug effects also is present in nonmedical drug use, the most common problem being the potentiating effects of alcohol and other central nervous system depressants (see Chapters 7 and 8). For example, alcohol and the barbiturates may be lethal in their potentiation of each drug's sedative effects. As we noted earlier, this drug combination has caused many intentional and accidental deaths.

REPRESENTING DRUG EFFECTS: THE DOSE-RESPONSE CURVE

Knowing the size or magnitude of an effect for a range of drug doses is important. Earlier we saw that drug effects differ according to drug doses. Because representing the different effects a drug can have over a number of doses can become complicated quickly, a tool that would represent such information as clearly and efficiently as possible would be quite useful. In pharmacology, this tool is the dose-response curve, a standard way of representing drug effects resulting from taking different drug doses. This curve is a representation of some effect according to a dose of the drug. For example, several groups of people may drink different doses of alcohol and at a given point be asked to report their degree of relaxation. If the average reports of relaxation for each group were then plotted, we would have a dose-response curve.

Figure 4-2 is a prototypic dose-response curve. The vertical axis of the graph, which we have labeled ''effect size,'' represents the change we are interested in recording. In psychopharmacology these changes usually are

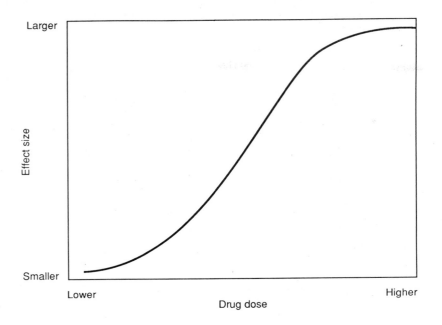

Figure 4–2 A typical dose-response curve.

reported in some generally accepted method of measuring mood, behavior, or nervous system function. Examples might include memory task performance, ratings of mood, or some measure of physiological arousal such as heart rate. On the vertical axis of the graph, the size of some effect is represented. Generally, the effect is depicted as going from smaller to larger. On the graph's horizontal axis the range of doses under investigation is represented, from smaller doses to larger ones. (Often the logarithm of the drug dose is represented on the horizontal axis.) Typically a minimum of three doses are studied. Creating the curve then is simply a matter of plotting the effect, however measured, for the individuals who have received a given dose of the drug under evaluation. Usually, different groups of subjects each receive a given dose, or the same subjects receive all the doses studied in an experiment lasting a number of days. In either case the average effect of each dose is plotted. When the effect is plotted for each dose investigated, the resultant graph represents effect **"as a function of"** drug dose.

Figure 4-2 shows that the effects of this hypothetical substance are not constant across different drug doses. Rather, the S-shape (sigmoid) of the curve reflects that an accurate description of this drug's effects requires specification of a dose. For instance, the hypothetical drug in Figure 4-2 produces greater effects as the dose increases. However, a limit exists; there is a plateau in the graph for the highest doses. This means that increasing the dose beyond a given level does not yield increased effects. Therefore,

As a function of
A term expressing causality. In graphing functional relationships between two variables, changes in one variable (in this case, drug effect) resulting from changes in another (in this case, drug dose) are represented.

the question is not what effects does Drug "X" have, but rather what is the effect of Drug "X" at a specified dose.

Variations and Extensions of the Basic Dose-Response Curve

Biphasic drug effects   Not all the effects of any drug may look like Figure 4-2 when plotted for a range of doses. One variant is a biphasic drug effect. This means an effect of a drug may go in one direction, say increase, as dose goes up, but then the effect changes direction (decreases) as the dose continues to go up. A biphasic drug effect is represented in Figure 4-3. As illustrated, the drug effect increases in size as the drug dose increases to the moderate range. However, as the dose continues to increase, the curve changes direction to represent the decrease in drug effect with higher drug doses. In this example, the size of the effect essentially returns to close to the lowest drug doses. Heart rate is an effect that has been reported to be biphasic for both alcohol and marijuana (Blum, 1984).

Different curves for different effects   Any drug may cause many different effects that can be measured. For each of these effects, a dose-response curve can be plotted. Many of the curves look alike, and they usually are similar to that represented in Figure 4-2. However, some of the dose-response curves for a given drug could look quite different, depending on

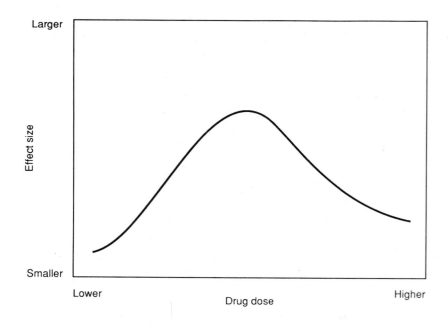

Figure 4-3 Dose-response curve for a biphasic drug effect.

what effects are being compared. This brings out a major point: The dose-response curve for a drug depends on the effect being measured. This is illustrated in Figure 4-4, which shows how college women in laboratory studies perceive their sexual arousal (one effect) and a physiological measure of their sexual arousal (a second effect) at lower to moderate doses of alcohol. Figure 4-4 looks a bit different from the other dose-reponse curves we have depicted because we have changed how effect is represented (vertical axis) to accommodate a negative drug effect. As the figure shows, the college women perceived that their sexual arousal increased with increasing doses of alcohol, at least up to moderate doses (very high doses have not been studied). However, physiological measures of the women's sexual arousal show decreases as dose increased (Abel, 1985).

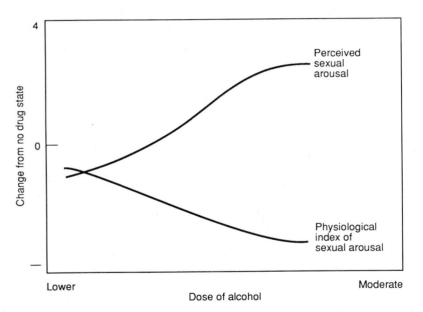

Figure 4-4 Dose-response curves for perceived sexual arousal and a physiological measure of sexual arousal in college women after drinking low to moderate doses of alcohol.

The Dose-Response Curve and Its Slope, Drug Maximal Effect, and Drug Potency

Pharmacologists have a few terms they use to more specifically describe a drug's action. These are illustrated in Figure 4-5, which shows the dose-reponse curves for two hypothetical drugs, A and B. The first feature of the curves is the slope, which refers to steepness. This aspect of the curve reflects the amount of latitude there is in drug dose before a stronger effect is reached. Slope can have very practical implications in prescribing drugs

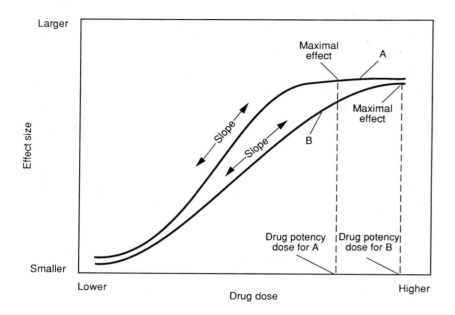

Figure 4–5 The dose-response curves for two hypothetical drugs, A and B—the terms slope, maximal effect, and potency, which are used to further describe a drug's effects, are illustrated on the curves. (Adapted from information in Ross & Gilman 1985)

therapeutically or in considering potentially life-endangering effects of drugs taken nonmedically. Examples of the latter are the sedating effect of the barbiturates or of the effects that occur when taking a benzodiazepine drug and alcohol together. In Figure 4-5, curve A has a steeper slope than curve B, so as the curves rise to a plateau, a given dose of A yields a larger effect.

Maximal effect
The most intense, or peak, level of a drug effect.

Drug potency
The dose of a drug that yields its maximal effect.

Two other terms illustrated in Figure 4-5 are a drug's **maximal effect** and **drug potency.** Maximal effect is defined by finding the peak of the dose-response curve for a given effect. In Figure 4-5, that peak is where the curves plateau. Drugs A and B are drawn to show two drugs with the same maximal effect. The last concept we have included in Figure 4-5 is drug potency, the dose of a drug that yields its maximal effect. On the dose-response curve a line extending from the point of maximal effect down to the horizontal axis gives the dose called the drug's potency for an effect (Ross & Gilman, 1985).

A Drug's Effective and Lethal Doses

The last two terms we define to describe a drug's effect are its effective and lethal doses. Both terms arise from observing the considerable variabil-

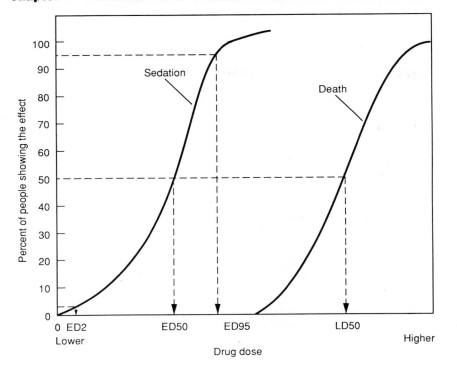

Figure 4–6 The dose-response curves for two of a hypothetical drug's effects, sedation and death—the curves are used to compute three effective doses for sedation and the drug's LD-50. (Adapted from information in Ross & Gilman, 1985)

ity in individuals' reactions to a dose of a drug. As a result, testing one person does not accurately show a drug's effect at a given dose. Rather, an effect is viewed in relative terms, or in the proportions of groups of people showing an effect at a specified dose.

Figure 4-6 shows the dose-response curves for two effects of a hypothetical drug. One difference in Figure 4-6 from the previous dose-response curves we have presented is that the precentage of individuals showing an effect is represented on the vertical axis, rather than the effect size. This slight change allows for the illustration of effective and lethal doses. With these terms, an effect is specified, and then the drug dose associated with different percentages of people experiencing the effect is found.

The **effective dose** (ED) is the percentage of individuals who show a given effect of a drug at a given dose. Another way of expressing this is: the dose at which a given percentage of individuals show a given effect of a drug. The ED is found on a dose-response curve by extending a horizontal line from the vertical axis at a given percentage to the relevant effect curve

Effective dose
The percentage of individuals who show a given effect of a drug at a given dose.

and from there dropping a vertical line to the drug dose axis. That point represents the ED for a given percent. The ED 50 is a standard term pharmacologists use, and the ED 50 for sedation for the hypothetical drug in Figure 4-6 is illustrated there. This means 50% of the people receiving that amount of the drug will experience sedation. Of course, the ED for any percent can be found in the same way. Two others are shown in Figure 4-6.

Lethal dose
The percentage of individuals who are killed by a given dose of a drug within a specified time.

The **lethal dose** (LD) of a drug is a special case of effective dose. As the name implies, in lethal dose the effect of interest is death, and the LD is the percentage of nonhumans (human subjects are not used in experiments to determine the lethal doses of drugs) that die at a given dose of a drug within a specified time. A standard referent in pharmacology is a drug's LD-50, which is the dose at which 50 percent of the animals administered a given dose of a drug died within a stated time. The LD-50 of our hypothetical drug is illustrated on the curve on the right in Figure 4-6.

Relationship between a drug's effective and lethal doses   A drug's EDs and LDs are of more than casual interest. Of particular importance for a city's health officials, for example, is the difference between a drug's ED and LD. When the difference is small, much more danger of accidental suicide exists for a person who is using drugs for nonmedical reasons. For some drugs such as caffeine or marijuana, the ED-LD difference is large. However, other drugs pose more of a problem. Accidental deaths due to heart damage from a dose of cocaine are referred to in one Comtemporary Issue Box in Chapter 1. Alcohol is another example. A 150-pound, relatively nontolerant drinker typically would report feeling relaxed after drinking about two drinks in an hour on an empty stomach. However, the LD 50 for alcohol would be reached if that same person drank about a fifth (25.3 oz) of whiskey in an hour. Such drinking occurs more often than you might think and has been responsible for the serious injuries or deaths that have occurred in fraternity hazings (initiation rites). Furthermore, when potentiating drugs are combined, such as alcohol and the barbiturates, the resulting ED and LD are pushed even closer and the danger higher.

Side effects
Effects of a drug other than those of central interest. Used most often in reference to the other–than–therapeutic effects of medications, such as the side effect of drowsiness for antihistamines. Note that what are considered a drug's side effects depends on what specifically the drug is being used for.

Therapeutic index
A measure of a drug's utility in medical care, it is computed as a ratio, (LD 50/ED 50).

A final point: the ED-LD difference is also important when a drug is administered by physicians for medical reasons. In medicine the goal is to find a drug that can be given in a dose that is therapeutic (that is, effective) for all patients, has no **"side effects"**, and that is not lethal. Accordingly, the **therapeutic index** has been derived. It is the ratio (LD 50/ED 50) for a given drug. Here, the ED of interest is the alleviation of the symptoms of some disease or injury. You can see that the larger a drug's therapeutic index, the more useful the drug is in medical treatment. Another point is that steeper dose response curves tend to have smaller therapeutic indices. The therapeutic index gives physicians a quick idea of the benefits of prescribing a drug as part of a specific treatment.

SUMMARY OF THE DRUG EXPERIENCE

With our review of the major contributors to a drug's effects or, more broadly, the drug experience, you should be starting to appreciate the complexity of human drug use. The pharmacological action of the drug ingested combines with a range of biological, psychological, and environmental factors to produce what people feel or think, or how they act, when they take a drug. The relative strength of any of these factors depends on the drug in question and the strength of any of the other factors. This makes predicting and understanding the drug experience a tough, complicated, but fascinating job. Many scientists are engaged in research on drugs, both in an effort to understand the actions of drugs already known and to create new drugs for medical use.

TWO BASICS OF PSYCHOPHARMACOLOGY RESEARCH: THE USE OF ANIMALS AND THE PLACEBO CONTROL

Subjects of Pharmacology Research: What Do Animals Have To Do with Humans?

Much has been learned about drug effects in humans from research on animals other than humans. Yet the relevance of findings about drugs based on testing of animals is frequently questioned. A more technical way to ask this question is: how **generalizable** to humans are findings based on animals? The answer is that, for the study of a variety of drug phenomena, generalizability from animals to humans is remarkably good. For example, Johansen and Uhlenhauth (1978) commented on the similarity among different species of animals, including humans, in the effects of factors such as drug dose, the individuals's drug use and environmental histories, and the presence and interaction of other drugs in the body.

Generalizability
The degree to which a research finding from one setting or group of people (or other species) can be applied to others.

It is highly fortunate that what we learn about drugs in animal studies can be used to learn more about human drug use and effects. Such research has vastly increased our knowledge about human drug use and effects without unduly risking human health. Furthermore, some **causal relationships** between drugs and functioning in parts of the human body, such as the brain, never could have been established with certainty without animal studies.

Causal relationship
A causal relationship exists between variables if changes in a second variable are caused by changes in a first variable.

Keep in mind that, in science, generalizability is always an "empirical question." That is, we cannot safely assume that what we find in one experimental setting automatically applies to the next. Rather, we do a second experiment, varying some essential factor about the individual or the setting, to see if what was found in the first experiment applies to the second one, too.

CONTEMPORARY ISSUE BOX 4-2
Animal Rights and Animal Research

Research with non-human subjects became a highly controversial issue during the past decade. Animal rights activists have sought to ban or disrupt research at many different laboratories. Activists charge that animal research has little or no value in human affairs and that researchers are unnecessarily cruel to animals.

With regard to the first point, it is clear that animals have contributed greatly to modern medicine in general, and to our understanding of drugs and behavior in particular. Drugs used to treat or prevent rabies, smallpox, polio, diphtheria, rickets, beriberi, diabetes, tetanus, schizophrenia, anxiety, thyroid disorders, arthritis, and leprosy are some notable examples of treatments made possible by animal research. Virtually all the techniques of modern surgery, treatment of disease with antibiotic drugs, and drug treatments for pain owe their developments to animal research. However, some of the studies that led to these developments involved exposing animals to pain or distress, and practically all of these studies involved sacrificing animals' lives to improve human welfare.

Serious ethical issues are raised by the assumption that human welfare is paramount. Those who defend animal rights argue that animals have rights equivalent to those of humans. If this position is taken, then most animal research would have to be viewed as unethical, but so would the practices of killing animals for food, or destroying their habitat for human cities. With regard to research, the dilemma is that if animal research is discontinued, we would lose important tools in the effort to improve our ability to treat and prevent diseases like cancer, heart disease, AIDS, mental disorders, and drug addiction.

To ensure that animal welfare is given high priority in animal laboratories, the federal government and professional organizations have placed animal research under tight regulations. For example, all animal research at institutions receiving federal funding must be reviewed by the Institutional Animal Care and Use Committee, or IACUC. Members of the IACUC must include a veterinarian and non-scientists who are not affiliated with the institution. The research must conform to accepted ethical standards and all possible steps to minimize animals' discomfort must be taken. The IACUC makes unannounced site visits to the laboratory and, if regulations are not followed, can shut down the project. Thus, measures are being taken to assure that when animals are used in research, they are treated as humanely as possible, and that the research is justifiable.

The Placebo Control

A **control group** or control condition is a referent scientists usually build into their experiments to tell if the drug they are investigating is really causing an effect. In psychopharmacology a very important kind of control condition is the **placebo control.** The idea that such a control is essential to determining the pharmacological part of a drug's effect arose long ago, when placebo effects were discovered. We discussed earlier in this chapter how powerful placebo effects can be. In many experiments, the effects of a particular compound can be specified only by comparing results of a tested group, half of whom actually receive a drug, and half of whom receive a placebo. Sometimes all the experimental participants are told they may or may not receive the real drug and then half really get the drug and half do not. In either case, neither the experimenter nor the subject knows whether the drug or placebo is being administered. This "double blind" method is used so that biases from the experimenter or subject, according to their respective feelings about the drug or experimental situation in general, are less likely to affect the results of the study. Using a placebo control **group design** can get complicated, as you can imagine. However, the work is viewed by many as essential to learning how drugs affect people. The idea is that the placebo control allows the experimenter to say with confidence what influence the chemical action of a drug has to do with the way a person reacts upon taking it. The reasoning is that if the measured effect in the "real drug" group is greater than in the "fake drug" group, then the chemical action of the drug must be responsible for the effect.

Control group
In an experiment, the control group is the reference or comparison group. The control group does not receive the experimental manipulation or intervention that is being tested.

Placebo control
A type of control originating in drug research. Placebo subjects are of the same makeup and are treated the same as a group of subjects who receive a drug, except that placebo subjects receive a chemically inactive substance.

Group design
A type of experimental design in which groups (as compared to individual cases) of subjects are compared to establish experimental findings.

CONTEMPORARY ISSUE BOX 4-3.
Ethics of the Placebo Control

Because of the powerful and pervasive influence of placebos, a placebo control generally is accepted as part of good design in drug experiments. Despite the intuitive appeal of using placebos in drug research and in physicians' prescription of drugs in treatment, the use of placebos with human subjects or patients raises difficult ethical questions. The reason is that using placebos involves deceiving subjects or patients about what is going to happen to them.

As with any experimental procedure involving deception, the question is whether the deception is worth the cost of deceiving the experimental participant. The answer would be "yes" if (a) what could be discovered is considered to be valuable, (b) deceiving the individual does not cause him or her unduly serious or irreparable damage or injury, and (c) no reasonable alternative exists to find the answer without using deception.

In drug research the general assumption that a placebo control is essential to answering questions about drug effects may not necessarily be true. In this regard, previous research may show that placebo effects are not significant for certain drug effects. One example is alcohol and cognitive and motor task performance. For studies of such alcohol effects, therefore, including a placebo control may not be necessary. Another possibility is that placebo effects may only be important at certain ranges of drug dose but not at others. In studies of some drugs, placebo effects may outpunch drug effects at low or moderate drug doses but not at higher ones. The researcher concerned only with the effects of a drug at the higher doses may not need to include a placebo control group in the experiment.

Summary

We have presented a few of the fundamentals of research in pharmacology. Much more is involved in learning the full complexities of pharmacology research methods, but these are the basics. You also now have a basis for understanding the last section of this chapter, which concerns how a new drug is developed according to guidelines established by the United States government. All of what we have discussed so far in this chapter enters into drug development.

Of course, this text mostly concerns nonmedical drug use, and, drugs often are developed illegally for nonmedical use, as discussed in later chapters. Yet our emphasis in this book on nonmedical drug use should not be seen as underplaying the importance of drugs developed legally for medical reasons. First, many of these drugs are, in fact, used in a manner not prescribed by a physician. Second, medical drug use is far more prevalent than nonmedical use among adults. A final point is that legal drug development and distribution make up a major economic force in the United States. For these reasons your knowledge about drugs and human behavior would not be complete without knowing how legal drugs are developed.

HOW ARE NEW DRUGS DISCOVERED, DEVELOPED, AND DISTRIBUTED?

The "Discovery"

The "discovery" of new drugs generally occurs in one of three ways (Baldessarini, 1985): the rediscovery of folk usages of various naturally occurring products; the accidental observation of an unexpected drug effect; or

CONTEMPORARY ISSUE BOX 4-4
Searching for the Therapeutic Drug with Zero Abuse Potential

Inventing chemical compounds that can help treat specific physical or psychiatric problems without having undesirable physical effects on a person is hard enough. Add to this the requirements that the compound also not have psychoactive effects such that the patient may start to abuse the drug or take it outside the boundaries of medical prescription, and the drug developer's task becomes formidable indeed. Yet this is exactly the problem that drug companies battle.

Over the years there have been successes and failures. For example, antianxiety medications have high abuse potential (examples are the benzodiazepine drugs), but very recently a few drugs have been developed that seem to have treatment value without the abuse potential. Medications to help people sleep have less abuse potential than the sleeping pills of the past, which were from the barbiturate family of drugs. But use of such "sedative-hypnotic" drugs is still fraught with abuse potential. A chronic problem for drug makers is pain killers. For years efforts have focused on making a pain-killing compound that is as effective as morphine, an opiate drug, but without its high abuse potential.

Drug companies spend much time and money searching for therapeutic drugs that are less likely to be abused. When a likely compound is found, it is first tested with an animal self-administration procedure. Using techniques developed by Schuster and his associates (e.g., Thompson & Schuster, 1964), it has been discovered that many animals (rats and monkeys are most frequently used) learn to self-administer drugs of abuse. The procedure involves preparing the animal with an intravenous catheter and placing it in a chamber where, if the animal presses the lever, a pump delivers a fixed amount of drug into the animal's bloodstream. In effect, the animal is asked whether it likes the drug. If the drug is one of the drugs of abuse like heroin or cocaine, the answer is yes. Animals readily acquire responses that are reinforced by opiate or stimulant drugs. In fact, most drugs with abuse potential in humans are self-administered by animals. Interesting exceptions are LSD and related hallucinogens (Young & Herling, 1986).

If the drug has been shown to be safe and is not self-administered by animals, studies are done in which people are given the compound. Then they are asked to report the effects they are experiencing from the drug, the likelihood of taking it again for pleasure, and the cost they would pay for it on the street. The subjects are paid for their help in the study (see Henningfield, Lukas, & Bigelow, 1986).

Data such as these are used by drug companies in deciding whether to market a drug and, if marketed, the recommended dosage. The federal government uses the data in its decision to approve a drug for commercial use.

Drug companies undertake this work and expense for several reasons. For one, they must provide abuse potential information as part of drug approval requirements. Another reason is quality of care for patients: the therapeutic drug with lower abuse potential is a better drug from a medical viewpoint. And it is profitable. If a therapeutically powerful drug could be created that has little or no abuse potential, it would have a decided advantage over its competitors. Physicians also would likely prescribe such a drug more freely.

the synthesizing of known or new compounds. Despite many advances in psychopharmacology, the first two occurrences account for the majority of new drugs.

No matter how a drug's potential usefulness is discovered, the procedures for testing and marketing them are fairly standard. In the United States, these guidelines are detailed by the Food and Drug Administration (FDA). The typical stages are shown in Table 4-4.

Table 4-4
Stages in the Development and Licensing of a Drug

1. Belief that a particular agent has clinical value
2. Animal studies
3. Experimental studies with healthy volunteers
4. Experimental studies with clinical patients, rigorously conducted
5. Broader clinical trials
6. Licensing and marketing approval
7. After-marketing evaluation of clinical use, particularly short-term and long-term effects

How is a Discovered Drug Developed?

Following the belief that a new drug can be of therapeutic value, a series of studies on the effects of the drug in animals is initiated. These studies are important for several reasons. First, the domains of the drug's actions can be specified overall and according to dose-response relationships. In addition, scientists try to identify delayed effects of the drug and effects attributable to extended use over time. The degree to which increasing doses are tolerated, as well as the drug's toxicity level, also can be established. This process may appear straightforward but actually can be lengthy and tedious. Spiegel and Aebi (1981) estimate that this phase of testing the new drug on animals takes an average of four years.

The next step is to administer the drug, initially in small doses, to healthy human volunteers and to examine the drug's actions and effects. These tests usually are conducted by the pharmaceutical company studying the drug in hopes of developing a marketable product. Assuming some consistent results with these volunteers, the number of subjects involved generally ranges from 80-200 (Tyrer, 1982). Not until this phase is completed are patients administered the drug. At first only a very small number of patients are involved, and rigorous controls are used. These patients generally are experiencing an illness that, according to data gathered in animal and healthy volunteer subjects, could be treated or alleviated through use of the drug. The researcher develops a trial protocol (Spiegel & Aebi, 1981) that outlines the following central phases: description of the drug (chemistry, toxicity, etc., based on the animal studies), patient selection (which patients with what illnesses or symptoms will be included), identification of doses to be investigated, experimental design (who administers the drug? Are placebos to be included? Is the person making ratings aware of the drug or dose administered?), criteria to be studied (identifying the measures through which drug effects will be assessed), documentation and report writing, and identification of procedures for emergency situations.

If the above goes smoothly and the drug seems to have utility, then the trials with patients are broadened. Frequently this involves drug administration with similar patients at several clinical sites (e.g., hospital, medical centers), and as many as 1000 patients might be included as participants.

CONTEMPORARY ISSUE BOX 4-5
Awaiting Drug Approval

The time between preliminary indications of a drug's usefulness and its final approval for prescription use is a long and rigorous process. Valid reasons exist for the lengthy process, primarily to ensure the drug's effectiveness and to study possible side effects. However, the time can seem interminable to the person who now suffers from a fatal disease that in a few years may be treatable with the new drug.

A current case in point is the ongoing testing of potential drug treatments for the acquired immune deficiency syndrome, better known as AIDS. This syndrome, first identified in the early 1980s, rapidly grew from being an isolated clinical oddity to near epidemic proportions within a five-year period. Although researchers quickly were able to identify and trace the actions of AIDS virus, efforts to develop a vaccine to combat it have not progressed at the same quick pace. That is not to say AIDS-fighting drugs are not being tested. Indeed, several drugs are being looked at in various types of trials, but they are not available for general distribution to physicians treating AIDS patients.

This has produced a major debate between research clinicians and AIDS patients. The majority of those who suffer from AIDS die within three years of first seeking medical treatment. Given this rapid course and the severity of the symptoms, different groups have applied great pressure to use potential anti-AIDS drugs before they have been fully studied. Scientists argue that the distribution of a drug not fully tested would be shortsighted and potentially dangerous for the person. On the other hand, some patients argue that using a drug with AIDS-fighting potential is preferable to no treatment, and that they should be allowed to take the risk if they so choose. In fact, in 1987 the FDA eased its regulations in order to expedite commercial use of the drug AZT, which then seemed to be the only hope for slowing the advance of AIDS in some patients. If you were a top FDA administrator, would you have approved this decision? Why? Another question concerns the allowable profits for a drug company that has patent rights on the most effective single treatment for a deadly disease such as AIDS. Should the company be allowed to make as much money as it can, or should price restrictions be imposed so the therapeutic drug is available to anyone who needs it, not only those who can afford it?

How is a Developed Drug Distributed and Marketed?

Once all of these steps have been taken, and the FDA has reviewed the data, the drug will be licensed and the pharmaceutical company will begin marketing the drug. However, the evaluation does not end here, as clinical researchers continue to monitor the effectiveness of the drug and the appearance of any unforeseen side effects associated with its use.

Chemical name
The name given to a drug that represents its chemical structure.

Brand name
The commercial name given to a drug by its manufacturer.

Generic name
The general name given to a drug that is shorter (and easier for most people to say) than its chemical name.

Drugs are designated in different ways once they reach commercial status. First is the **chemical name** of a drug, which is technical and allows chemists to reproduce the drug's structure. The chemical name indicates the drug's structural formula. The manufacturer of the drug also gives it a **brand name** or trademark. This is the name of a drug most people would know, because it is the commercial name for the drug the manufacturer uses exclusively until its sole rights to market the drug expire. The brand name says nothing about the drug's chemical structure. Finally, drugs also are given a **generic** name, which is a general name for a drug that is shorter than its chemical name. Like its trade name, a drug's generic name tells nothing about its chemical structure.

To give you one example, we will cite the three names of Valium (brand name). The generic name of this drug is diazepam, and its chemical name is 7-chloro-1, 3-dihydro-1 methyl-5-phenyl-2H-1, 4-benzodiazepine -2-one.

Current controversy about generic drugs   Generic drugs are in a whirl of controversy because they have made an impressive dent in the brand name drug market. When a drug is approved, the source of its invention, usually a drug company, is granted sole rights to marketing the drug for seventeen years. After that, generic drug companies can sell their versions of the same compound so long as they use the generic rather than the brand name. The dent that generics are making in the drug market is significant. An article in the New York Times in July, 1987, noted that from 1981 to 1986 generic drug sales tripled, to $5.1 billion. This was 23% of the $21 billion prescription drug market for 1986. For example, the patent for Inderal, a medication for treating high blood pressure, expired in 1984. In 1984 sales for Inderal were $294 million. In 1986 sales dropped to $185 million, probably because when Inderal's patent expired, twenty competing generic versions became available.

Not surprisingly, the drug companies that are awarded patents do not appreciate the generic drug onslaught. Generic drugs are a threat because they generally are sold at a considerably cheaper price than are their brand name counterparts. Brand name drug companies have been trying to fight back by claiming that generics may be unsafe for patients and by offering incentives to physicians for prescribing brand name medications. Furthermore, in late 1989, because of improprieties discovered in the generic drug manufacturing process, the federal government launched an investigation of the top thirty generic drugs. The investigation concerned whether the drugs matched the chemical formula they were purported to, and whether manufacturing procedures were as they are supposed to be. So far no unsafe generic drugs have been discovered.

In spite of recent problems, generics are probably here to stay, even with the closer scrutiny. Their use is supported by both consumer groups and the American Medical Association.

SUMMARY

- The basic principles of pharmacology emerge in discussing what contributes to the drug experience.

- Drug dose is computed according to the recipient's body weights. A standard way of expressing dose is by milligrams of drug per kilogram of body weight.

- Five routes of drug administration are discussed in detail: oral, subcutaneous, intramuscular, intravenous, and through the mucous membranes. A route of administration is selected according to the drug taken and the goals and circumstances of administration.

- The route of drug administration affects the drug experience primarily through the rate of drug absorption and the amount of drug absorbed.

- Once they enter the body, drugs are absorbed into the blood and distributed to their site(s) of action. The body also works to metabolize and excrete drugs that enter it.

- Physical or biological characteristics of the drug user affect the drug experience. Some important characteristics are inherited differences in reactions to a drug, gender, body weight, age, and tolerance to a drug.

- Tolerance may be a physiological process modified by learning. Learning occurs through principles of classical conditioning and relates to the body's compensatory or counter reactions that occur when its homeostasis is disturbed.

- An individual's personality also affects the drug experience. Personality, beliefs, expectations, attitudes, and other thoughts about a drug influence the placebo effect.

- The setting in which a drug is used represents another group of factors that contribute to the drug experience.

- When two or more drugs are present in the body at the same time, their combined effect may be summative or potentiating.

- Pharmacologists use the dose-response curve as a standard way to represent graphically the size of an effect according to the dose of a drug taken. The prototypical dose-response curve has an "S" shape, but variations depend on the effects studied.

- Three concepts derived from a dose-response curve offer valuable information about a drug's action: slope of the curve, drug maximal effect, and drug potency.

- Two other important features of a drug's actions are its effective dose and lethal dose. The relationship between these two doses is essential information for medical and nonmedical drug use.

- Much of the knowledge we have today in psychopharmacology is the result of experiments with nonhuman animals. What research on nonhuman animals says about the human drug experience still is debated.

- A part of pharmacology research that has been a standard for years is the placebo control condition.

- Knowledge of factors influencing the drug experience helps you understand the ways a new legal drug is discovered, developed, and distributed.

- Once a drug is commercially available it is given a chemical name, a brand name, and a generic name.

- Generic drugs have caused some controversy in the United States, because their increasing popularity is significantly affecting the profit margins of the major drug companies. The safety of generic drugs has been questioned but so far no claims of unsafe generics have been proven.

References

Abel, E.L. (1985). *Psychoactive drugs and sex*. New York: Plenum Press.

Adesso, V.J. (1985). Cognitive factors in alcohol and drug use. In M. Galizio & S.A. Maisto (Eds.), *Determinants of substance abuse* (pp 179–208). New York: Plenum Press.

Baldessarini, R.J. (1985). *Chemotherapy in psychiatry: Principles and practice* (Revised Edition). Cambridge, MA: Harvard University Press.

Benet, L.Z., & Sheiner, L.B. (1985). Pharmacokinetics: The dynamics of drug absorption, distribution, and elimination. In G.G. Gilman, L.S. Goodman, T.W. Rall, & F. Murod (Eds.), *Goodman and Gilman's The pharmacological basis of therapeutics* (pp. 3–34). New York: Macmillan Publishing Co.

Blum, K. (1984). *Handbook of abusable drugs*. New York: Gardner Press, Inc.

Cicero, T.J. (1980). Alcohol self-administration, tolerance, and withdrawal in humans and animals: Theoretical and methodological issues. In H. Rigter & J. Crabbe, Jr. (Eds.), *Alcohol tolerance and dependence* (pp. 1–51). Amsterdam: Elsevier/North-Holland Biomedical Press.

Cox, W.M. (1985). Personality correlates of substance abuse. In M. Galizio & S.A. Maisto (Eds.), *Determinants of substance abuse* (pp. 209–246). New York: Plenum Press.

Henningfield, J.E., Lukas, S.E., & Bigelow, G.E. (1986). Human studies of drugs as reinforcers. In S.R. Goldberg and I.P. Stolerman (Eds.), *Behavioral analysis of drug dependence* (pp. 69–122). Orlando: Academic Press.

Hinson, R.E. (1985). Individual differences in tolerance and relapse: A Pavlovian conditioning perspective. In M. Galizio & S.A. Maisto (Eds.), *Determinants of substance abuse* (pp. 101–124). New York: Plenum Press.

Hull, J.G., & Bond, C.F. (1986). Social and behavioral consequences of alcohol consumption and expectancy: A meta-analysis. *Psychological Bulletin, 99,* 347–368.

Jacobs, M.R., & Fehr, K. O'B. (1987). *Drugs and drug abuse* (Second Edition). Toronto: Addiction Research Foundation.

Johanson, C.E., & Uhlenhuth, E.H. (1978). Drug self-administration in humans. In NA Krasnegor (Ed)., *Self-administration of abused substances: Methods for study* (NIDA Research Monograph 20) (pp. 68–87). Washington, DC: US Government Printing Office.

Kalant, H., LeBlanc, A.E., & Gibbins, R.J. (1971). Tolerance to, and dependence on, some nonopiate psychotropic drugs. *Pharmacological Reviews, 23,* 135–191.

Leavitt, F. (1982). *Drugs and behavior* (Second Edition). New York: John Wiley & Sons.

McCarty, D.C. (1985). Environmental factors in substance abuse. In M. Galizio & S.A. Maisto (Eds.), *Determinants of substance abuse* (pp. 247–282). New York: Plenum Press.

Pfefferbaum, A. (1977). The placebo. In J.D. Barchas, P.A. Berger, R.D. Ciaranello, & G.R. Elliott (Eds.), *Psychopharmacology: From theory to practice* (pp. 493–503). New York: Oxford University Press.

Pliner, P., & Cappell, H. (1974). Modification of affective consequences of alcohol: A comparison of social and solitary drinking. *Journal of Abnormal Psychology, 83,* 418–425.

Ross, E.M., & Gilman, A.G. (1985). Pharmacodynamics: Mechanisms of drug action and the relationship between drug concentration and effect. In G.G. Gilman, L.S. Goodman, T.W. Rall, & F. Murod (Eds.), *Goodman and Gilman's The pharmacological basis of therapeutics* (Seventh Edition) (pp 35–48). New York: Macmillan Publishing Co.

Sher, K.J. (1987). Stress response dampening. In H.T. Blane & K.E. Leonard (Eds.), *Psychological theories of drinking and alcoholism* (pp. 227–271). New York: The Guilford Press.

Sher, K.J., & Levenson, R.W. (1982). Risk for alcoholism and individual differences in the stress-dampening effect of alcohol. *Journal of Abnormal Psychology, 91,* 350–368.

Solomon R.L., & Corbit, J.D. (1974). An opponent-process theory of motivation: I. Temporal dynamics of affect. *Psychological Review, 81,* 119–145.

Spiegel, R., & Aebi, H. (1981). *Psychopharmacology.* New York: John Wiley & Sons.

Thompson, T. & Schuster, C.R. (1964). Morphine self-administration, food-reinforced, and avoidance behaviors in rhesus monkeys. *Psychopharmacologia, 5,* 87–94.

Tyrer, P.J. (1982). Evaluation of psychotropic drugs. In P.J. Tyrer (Ed.), *Drugs in psychiatric practice.* London: Butterworths.

Young, A.M. & Herling, S. (1986). Drugs as reinforcers: Studies in laboratory animals. In S.R. Goldberg and I.P. Stolerman (Eds.), *Behavioral analysis of drug dependence* (pp. 9-68). Orlando: Academic Press.

5 MAJOR STIMULANTS: COCAINE AND THE AMPHETAMINES

A number of drugs used for recreational as well as medical purposes can induce stimulation of the central nervous system and so are referred to as stimulants. We separate these into two groups according to potency. Cocaine and the amphetamines, the major stimulants, are treated in this chapter, and the minor stimulants such as caffeine and nicotine (somewhat questionably classified as stimulants) are dealt with in Chapter 6. We first consider the history of major stimulant use and discuss the effects of cocaine and the amphetamines as we review their history. Then we return to a more detailed treatment of the pharmacology of these stimulants.

THE COCA LEAF

Our story begins high in the Andes Mountains of Peru and Bolivia where grows a low-growing shrub called the coca bush or coca tree (Erythroxylum coca). From the leaves of this plant comes the powerful stimulant, cocaine. The use of this drug is truly ancient. For centuries the native inhabitants of this region of South America, including the Inca peoples and their descendents, have engaged in the practice of chewing the coca leaf. Although no one knows when this practice began, archeological evidence suggests several thousand years ago (Siegel, 1985). The coca leaf had important religious significance to the Inca people but was used for medicinal and work-related purposes as well. When the Spanish *conquistadores* encountered the Incas during the sixteenth century, they were at first disturbed by the religious use of coca which was, of course, inconsistent with Catholicism. But after conquering the Inca, the Spanish permitted and actually encouraged the use of coca because they believed it helped them to work harder and longer. The Spanish ultimately came to control Inca access to the coca leaf by using it as a form of payment and levying taxes to be paid in coca leaves. The Spanish considered chewing coca a vice, and neither used coca themselves nor encouraged its use among other Europeans (see Grinspoon & Bakalar, 1976; Kennedy, 1985).

Thus, until the 1800s the coca plant was relatively unknown in Europe. Then European naturalists began to explore Peru, experimented with coca, and soon strange and often conflicting tales began to circulate about coca. Some, such as the German naturalist Edward Poeppig, viewed coca as deadly: "The practice of chewing the leaf is attendant with the most pernicious consequences, producing an intoxication like that of opium. As indulgence is repeated the appetite for it increases and the power of resistance diminishes until at last death relieves the miserable victim" (quoted by Kennedy, 1985, p. 55). Others, such as the Italian biologist Mantegazza who chewed coca while in Peru, were more positive: "I sneered at poor mortals condemned to live in this valley while I, carried on the wings of two coca leaves, went flying through the spaces of 77,438 worlds, each more splendid than the one before" (quoted by Mortimer, 1901, p. 137).

Figure 5–1 Indigenous families tend coca bush terraces.

Neither of these quotes represents a very accurate depiction of the effects of chewing the coca leaf. However, of the two, apparently Mantegazza's was more compelling, because nearly every historical reference attributes the rise of scientific interest in coca to his praise. This scientific interest led to the increased availability of the coca leaf in laboratories and in the 1850s European chemists were able to isolate the far more potent active agent in the leaf, which they called cocaine. The extraction of cocaine from the leaf led to a whole new era in the history of stimulant drug use. This is because of the greater potency of cocaine (a single coca leaf contains only a tiny amount of cocaine), and because cocaine seems to produce different and more intense effects when taken through intravenous injection or intranasal absorption (sniffing or snorting), methods of administration made possible only by the extraction of cocaine from the leaf. Presumably the more rapid delivery of large amounts of cocaine to the brain is responsible for the relatively more intense actions of cocaine when it is injected (Siegel, 1985).

EARLY USE OF COCAINE

The next chapter in the history of cocaine is fascinating because it involves a young physician working in Vienna who was looking for some medical breakthrough to make his mark. Though he is now best known for other contributions, Sigmund Freud was first recognized for his writings on cocaine. Freud obtained a sample of cocaine in 1884 and after taking it a few times, felt he had come across a miracle drug. In his first major publication, "On Coca," he advocated cocaine as a local anesthetic and as a treatment for depression, indigestion, asthma, various neuroses, syphilis and drug addiction and alcoholism. Freud also thought cocaine was an aphrodisiac (Freud, in Byck, 1974).

Only one of these therapeutic uses has turned out to be valid, and that is the use of cocaine as a local anesthetic. When cocaine makes direct contact with peripheral neurons, it prevents neural firing, which has the effect of "numbing" the area. This action is quite unlike cocaine's effects on the central nervous system. Cocaine was the first of the local anesthetics and revolutionized surgery. Now, of course, related "caine" drugs such as procaine and xylocaine are more frequently used, but because cocaine also constricts blood vessels, it is still used for surgery on areas such as the face because it reduces bleeding as well as pain.

Freud was mistaken in his early suggestions about cocaine, and he helped launch a major period of cocaine abuse. Ironically, one of the first indications of what was to come was observed in one of Freud's friends, Ernst von Fleischl. Fleischl suffered from chronic pain and had become a morphine addict. Freud prescribed cocaine and Fleischl began to consume larger and larger doses of it. Although doing quite well at abstaining from morphine, Fleischl eventually was consuming a gram of cocaine daily. Not only had Fleischl become the first European cocaine addict, but he began to show bizarre symptoms that we now recognize as characteristic of cocaine overdose. These symptoms included paranoid delusions, which are often seen in paranoid schizophrenia, and a feeling of itching called the **formication syndrome,** which is described as something like insects or snakes crawling on the skin. Today these symptoms are recognized as caused by cocaine overdose, but Fleischl was the first reported of many to experience these effects.

Formication syndrome
Symptoms of itching and feeling as if insects were crawling on skin caused by cocaine and amphetamine.

Surprised by the disastrous effects of cocaine on Fleischl, Freud's later writings on cocaine were not quite so enthusiastic, but the damage had been done. The cocaine epidemic of the eighties was on—the 1880s that is! Not only was cocaine prescribed by physicians, but it also was readily available in patent medicines that could be obtained without prescription such as Mariani's Coca Wine, a best-seller in Europe, and yes, in Coca-Cola. Coca-Cola's early advertising described its contents as containing the "tonic and nerve stimulant properties of the coca plant—back when it *was* the real thing! Cocaine was popularized in music and literature as well. The famous fictional detective Sherlock Holmes was depicted by author Arthur Conan Doyle as using cocaine to give him energy and aid his powers of deductive reasoning. Robert Louis Stevenson apparently wrote the Jekyll and Hyde story while taking cocaine treatments for tuberculosis, and others who provided testimonials to the value of cocaine include Thomas Edison, Jules Verne, Emile Zola, Henrik Ibsen, the Czar of Russia, and President Ulysses Grant (Grinspoon & Bakalar, 1976).

An advertisement from another coca product, Metcalf's Wine of Coca, again illustrates how cocaine became so popular:

> Public Speakers, Singers, and Actors have found wine of coca to be a valuable tonic to the vocal cords. Athletes, Pedestrians, and Base Ball Players have found by practical experience that a steady course of coca taken both before and after any trial of strength or endurance will impart energy to every movement, and prevent fatigue. Elderly people have found it a reliable aphrodisiac superior to any other drug (Siegel, 1985, p. 206).

It isn't hard to understand how cocaine became popular with this kind of publicity, and with so many people using cocaine, casualties began to emerge. Soon many users of cocaine began to discover firsthand the hazards of cocaine use, and with cocaine psychosis, overdose death, and severe dependence becoming major problems, popular sentiment against cocaine began to rise (Allen, 1987). One of the most influential works that changed ideas about cocaine was an article that described the case of Annie C. Meyers, who had been a successful businesswoman and a "well-balanced Christian woman" before becoming a "cocaine fiend." The depth of addiction to cocaine was well-described by Meyers who, upon finally running out of money for cocaine, recounted: "I deliberately took a pair of shears and pried loose a tooth that was filled with gold. I then extracted the tooth, smashed it up, and the gold went to the nearest pawnshop (the blood streaming down my face and drenching my clothes) where I sold it for 80 cents" (quoted in Kennedy, 1985, p. 93). Thus, beliefs and attitudes about cocaine began to change. In addition to dramatic accounts of addiction to cocaine, reports of violent acts committed under the influence of the drug led to a dramatic swing of public opinion culminating in the control of cocaine under the 1914 Harrison Narcotic Act. Although the Harrison Act was primarily designed to control opiates such as morphine and heroin, cocaine's inclusion as a dangerous drug was no accident.

THE AMPHETAMINES

Use of cocaine in America declined during the years following the Harrison Act, but a new stimulant was soon to enter the scene: the amphetamines. The amphetamines are a class of drugs first synthesized in the late nineteenth century that include amphetamine, dextro-amphetamine, and methamphet-amine (see Table 5-1). Although amphetamines had been available for research for many years, the first medical applications were developed in the 1920s. Amphetamines were at one time considered to be useful as a treatment for cold and sinus symptoms (the original inhalers contained Ben-zedrine—amphetamine), obesity, narcolepsy (a disease in which the patient uncontrollably falls asleep), and paradoxically, treatment of **hyperactive children** (see Contemporary Issue Box 5-1). Amphetamines are rarely used for any of these purposes today, and a major reason for the decline in medical use is their high abuse potential. These drugs were used for their stimulant properties by soldiers on both sides during World War II. After the war amphetamine abuse reached epidemic proportions in Japan, Sweden and other parts of Europe, yet was not recognized as a dangerous drug in America until the 1960s. Ironically, amphetamines became a major problem in America when physicians began to prescribe methamphetamine as a treatment for heroin addiction. Like Freud's cocaine treatment of morphine addiction, this treatment backfired, resulting in an explosion of amphetamine abuse, particularly on the West Coast during the early 1960s (Brecher, 1972).

Hyperactive children
Disorder of childhood involving restlessness, inability to be attentive, and disruptive behavior. Today referred to as "attention-deficit disorder."

CONTEMPORARY ISSUE BOX 5-1
Stimulant Drugs and Hyperactive Children

Some children just can't sit still! This can be a problem, especially in the classroom. Historically, when this type of problem became serious and interfered with the child's ability to live at home or perform at school the child was labeled as suffering from "minimal brain damage" (minimal because none was detectible) or "hyperactivity." Today such a child is labeled as suffering from "Attention Deficit Disorder" or ADD. Typical symptoms include inattention, impulsivity, and hyperactivity in a child of otherwise normal intelligence. In 1937 a physician named Charles Bradley discovered what appeared to be an extraordinary paradox: hyperactive children were calmed by a dose of the stimulant drug amphetamine. Since then many millions of ADD children have been treated with stimulant drugs. In the 1970s when amphetamine abuse led to a stigma associated with these drugs, other stimulants became preferred. Now methylphenidate (Ritalin) and pemoline (Cylert) are the most common pharmacological treatments for ADD. However, the effects of these are virtually identical to those of amphetamines. Because of the apparently paradoxical nature of the effects of stimulant drugs on ADD children, they are often assumed to be biologically different from normal children. But studies have shown that stimulants affect both normal and ADD children in about the same way: they increase alertness and attention span. Actually, these drugs have pretty much this effect in adults as well. So the "paradox" may not be real (Rapoport, Buchsbaum, Zahn, Weingartner, Ludlow, & Mikkelsen, 1978).

One thing is certain: stimulant drugs do improve ADD children's performance. However, there are costs. Stimulant drugs suppress normal height and weight increases. Often the children will go on a "growth spurt" during the summer if they are taken off the drug (Safer, Allen & Barr, 1975). Other adverse effects are less well documented, but given the data we have reviewed on stimulants, there is some reason for concern. Do the benefits of stimulant treatment for ADD children outweigh the risks? That remains a controversial issue.

The use of injected amphetamine resulted in a pattern of abuse reminiscent of the cocaine problems seen at the turn of the century and again today. The user experiences a brief but intense "flash" or "rush" immediately after the drug is injected. The strongly pleasurable feeling produced following amphetamine or cocaine injection is often described as orgasmic in nature, but because it lasts only a few minutes, the person is soon craving a return to the heights of pleasure even though the level of the drug in their body remains quite high. A series of injections often follows; the user becomes more and more stimulated but has difficulty obtaining a rush quite as good as the first. Because both cocaine and amphetamines suppress appetite and prevent sleep, persons may go for days without sleep, eating very little, and administering dose after dose. In the 1960s a person who engaged in this pattern of use came to be called a "speed freak." When speed freaks burst on the drug scene, it became clear that amphetamine shares virtually all of the effects of cocaine. For example, when dose levels of amphetamine get large enough, the user develops formication symptoms (called speed bugs or crank bugs by users) and paranoid delusions. Thus, a psychosis is not produced only by cocaine: amphetamines can cause an almost identical phenomenon. Here is a description from the San Francisco street scene of the late 1960s of a speed freak:

> "He is a very nice person, and extremely generous; however when he gets all jacked up and he is wired (stimulated with speed) . . . then he is in trouble. Because pretty quick he's got a shot gun . . . I've seen him out in front of . . . the freeway entrance herding the hitch-hikers away because he's paranoid of them. At four o'clock in the afternoon with a full length shot gun, he's screaming 'move on, you can't stand there, move on.' That's just the way he gets." (Brecher, 1972, p. 287).

Stimulant psychosis Paranoid delusions and disorientation resembling the symptoms of paranoid schizophrenia caused by prolonged use or overdose of cocaine and/or an amphetamine.

So the paranoid psychosis produced by cocaine and amphetamine overdose should probably be called **"stimulant psychosis."** By the late 1960s the word was out on the street—"Speed kills!" What was referred to in this slogan was not just death by overdose. Amphetamine overdose deaths did occur, but they were relatively rare. Far more common was the development of a paranoid state that often led to acts of violence. In addition, after a long binge of amphetamine abuse the user may crash (sleep for an extended period), and then awaken deeply depressed. The depression could last for days and is now recognized as a common withdrawal symptom after heavy use of either amphetamine or cocaine. The depression often leads the user back to drugs to try to get "up" again, and the cycle is repeated. Eventually the user's physical and mental health deteriorates badly unless he or she can break out of the cycle.

Table 5-1
Major Stimulants

Generic Names	Brand Names	Slang Terms
Stimulants:		
Cocaine		Coke, Snow, Freebase, T, Crack
Amphetamine	Benzedrine	Bennies, White Crounes
Dextroamphetamine	Dexedrine, Biphetamine	Black beauties, Cadillacs, Dexies
Methamphetamine	Methedrine, Desoxyn	Speed, Crank, Ice
Methylephenidate	Ritalin	
Phenmetrazine	Preludin	Bam

As the word spread about the hazards of amphetamine abuse, users tried to obtain other stimulants they thought might be safer. For example, a compound related to the amphetamines called phenmetrazine ("Bam" on the street—see Table 5-1) had a run of popularity in the 1970s, but soon it was recognized that it, too, produced all the adverse effects of the amphetamines. By the middle of that decade a different trend was clear: a "new" stimulant drug was on the scene, an "organic" or "natural" drug—surely there could be nothing wrong with . . . cocaine?

COCAINE EPIDEMIC II

It has been said that those who do not know history are condemned to repeat it, and with cocaine that certainly seems to be true. Why did cocaine re-emerge as a stimulant of choice? One reason is that in the early seventies cocaine was fairly difficult to obtain and was quite expensive. It became glamorized as the drug of movie stars and pro athletes (who were among the few who could afford to buy it), and thus acquired a reputation as the "champagne" of the stimulants. Most users during this period experimented with low doses, taken intranasally, and thus rarely encountered the problems associated with intravenous use. Occasional exceptions were encountered: one of the first of many athletes to admit a major cocaine problem was former Dallas Cowboy linebacker Hollywood Henderson who in 1978 acknowledged he had acquired a $1000–a–day habit. But this type of cocaine casualty was relatively rare. Cocaine was believed to be a fairly innocuous drug. To give you a feeling of the times, Ashley (1975) concluded in a popular press book that cocaine was "not an addictive, especially dangerous drug" (p. 186), and argued that it should be legalized.

Unquestionably the contemporary view is that cocaine is, in fact, a very dangerous drug. Today Ashley's comments seem hopelessly naive because we have seen too many people die of cocaine overdose and have witnessed the struggles of many famous personalities trying to recover from cocaine dependence. What happened to bring about this change? One factor has been the increased availability of lower cost cocaine. This has led to changing patterns of use, with more people regularly using the drug in high doses. Another critical factor has been the practice of smoking freebase cocaine, or crack. Although freebasing cocaine has been a problem since at least the late 1970s, **crack** burst upon the national scene in 1986.

Crack
A freebase cocaine produced by mixing cocaine salt with baking soda and water. The solution is then heated resulting in brittle sheets of cocaine that are "cracked" into small, smokable chunks or "rocks."

CONTEMPORARY ISSUE BOX 5-2
The Impact of Crack

Since the introduction of crack cocaine to America's streets in 1986, the drug scene has changed tremendously. Cocaine was a glamour drug in the 1970s and early 1980s, more associated with movie stars and Hollywood than youth gangs and ghettos. But the introduction of inexpensive and highly addictive crack has changed the image and demographics of cocaine. Crack has become one of the major problems of inner city America with a huge impact on crime in cities like Detroit, Los Angeles, Miami, New York, and Washington, D.C. to name a few. Consider this sampling of Washington Post news items from 1988 compiled by Cole (1989):

- A young ballplayer who idolizes Bias swallows six chunks of crack and dies.

- A mother who is reportedly a heavy crack user is charged with strangling to death her children aged three and eight.

- In the drug-laden public-housing project called Paradise Manor, five men are arrested; police confiscate thirty-seven rocks of crack and an arsenal of automatic and semiautomatic weapons.

· In March thirty-three people die of drugs, almost half of them from lethal doses of cocaine.

· In April sixty-five percent of all persons appearing in D.C. Superior Court on criminal charges test positive for cocaine use (Cole, 1989, p. 62).

· Similarly, *Newsweek* (1989a) reported that crack was the major factor responsible for a sharp rise in inner city murders. The magazine reported that more than fifty per cent of the homicides committed in New York involve drugs. Gangs such as the notorious "Bloods" and "Crips" of Los Angeles have infiltrated many other cities and vie with one another and with other groups (some from Jamaica, others from Colombia and other Latin American countries) to gain control of the crack market. These highly organized criminal elements pose a major threat to police and civilians alike. Unlike the traditional notion of the small drug dealer, gang-members possess high-tech weapons (such as

Gangs control sales of crack in many urban areas.

Uzi machine guns, AK-47 rifles, and bulletproof vests). Increasingly police are confronting such gangs. For example, as recently as early 1985, New York police had not reported a single crack arrest, but in the first ten months of 1988, they made 19,074 (Newsweek, 1988).

· In August 1989 the "war" on drugs became even hotter as the Colombian government's crackdown on the cocaine cartel began to draw reprisals. More than 2000 murders were reported during the first six months of 1989 in the city of Medellin, the home of the cocaine cartel. Hundreds of judges and court employees have been assassinated, and in the fall of 1989 more than 500 judges resigned in anticipation of more killings (Newsweek, 1989b). Thus, the advent of crack along with the violence associated with it has dramatically changed our ideas about cocaine from the trendy mild stimulant of the 1970s to one of the deadliest and most dangerous of drugs today.

To understand the impact of crack, we must first focus on the importance of the method of cocaine administration. When cocaine is obtained by chewing the leaf, small amounts are gradually absorbed producing a mild stimulant action, little or no rush, and limited withdrawal "crash." When taken intranasally the effects can be more intense, but because cocaine causes constriction of blood vessels in the nose when taken by that route, absorption is slowed. By the way, it is this vasoconstriction that can cause problems with inflammation and tissue damage of the mucous membranes of the nose in chronic intranasal users. Overdose deaths, psychosis, and dependence are all possible as a consequence of intranasal cocaine but are less common than with injected cocaine. But, when cocaine is smoked, it is absorbed very rapidly and completely in lung tissue and produces an intense high of very short duration followed by a severe crash. Because the cocaine salt is broken down at high temperatures, in order to smoke cocaine it must be separated from the salt base to create freebase. The common method of "freeing the base" involved a highly flammable substance, ether. Many people were badly burned by failing to handle the ether properly. The comedian Richard Pryor developed a popular routine in which he spoofs the very severe burns he received in a freebase accident. However, freebase cocaine can be produced more simply by dissolving the cocaine salt in an alkaline solution (for example, baking soda). After filtering, a hard rock-like substance called crack is formed that has a low melting point and thus can be heated and the fumes inhaled. This results in rapid delivery of high potency cocaine to the brain with an intense "rush" as powerful as intravenous injection of cocaine (Perez-Reyes et al., 1982). The euphoria is quite brief and within 10-20 minutes users often crash and begin to crave another hit. Perez-Reyes found more craving following cocaine smoking than after injection.

Figure 5–2
Crack is a smokable form of cocaine.

Crack is cheaper and less dangerous to produce than freebase, so dealers became attracted to it. Also it is so potent it can be sold in small chunks or rocks for $10-$20, and so it is relatively affordable. Because it produces such strong cravings and dependence a large market for crack developed almost overnight. In the spring of 1986 national magazines such as *Newsweek* and *Time* and television media reported that crack had emerged as a national crisis. By June 1986 estimates indicated that more than one million Americans had tried crack (Kirsch, 1986). When athletes Len Bias and Don Rodgers died in the same week of cocaine overdose, a new era of cocaine consciousness had begun. Cocaine can kill, especially when smoked. Paranoid reactions to the drug are on the rise, and dependence on cocaine has itself become a major drug problem. Actually cocaine deaths and emergencies have been rising for some time. According to NIDA statistics more than 46,000 cocaine-related admissions to hospital emergency rooms occurred in 1987, up dramatically from 37,000 in 1986 and from 10,000 in 1985, 3000 in 1981, and almost none in the early 1970s. New York City alone reported 7457 hospital admissions in 1988 for cocaine. An increasingly large percentage of these emergencies involves crack (over 40% in New York in 1988). The publicity about the dangers of crack has been impossi-

Figure 5–3 Len Bias and John Belushi: cocaine casualities.

ble to avoid during the past few years. So why are people still smoking crack? Consider this seductive and sinister description from a cocaine smoker:

"Imagine you are on an island and offshore about a dozen yards is this orange-pink haze that is glowing and extremely enticing. So you walk out into that cold, dark water and you swim a ways to get near that glow and you're out on the edge of it and it feels so good and so warm, but it moves away a little. So you swim out into deeper water and this time you get even closer to the center and it is so incredibly seductive. But now it's moving a little faster out into the ocean and you swim harder trying to keep up and you're getting farther and farther away from shore. That's how with the first few tokes you feel pretty good and then with a deep toke you are near the center and it's so exhilarating but you come down and keep wanting more. Pretty soon you are way the hell out in the cold black ocean and you're faced with keeping up swimming harder toward that warm, wonderful, glowing haze just out of reach or turning back and swimming miles back to shore in that dark, cold water" (Kirsch, 1986, p. 49).

How extensive has the abuse of crack and other forms of cocaine become? NIDA survey data suggest that more than twenty-one million Americans have used cocaine, six million are current users (have used during the month prior to the survey), and up to one million are compulsive users (Barnes, 1988). Among high school seniors, more than 8% reported having tried cocaine in 1988—down from 10% in 1987, and 13% in 1985 and 1986 (see Chapter 1). Despite this trend, cocaine use and problems caused by cocaine remain extensive in the U.S. In addition, evidence indicates that methamphetamine is returning to popularity among illicit drug users both in an injectable form called "crank," and in a new smokable form referred to as "ice" (see Contemporary Issue Box 5-3).

CONTEMPORARY ISSUE BOX 5-3
A New Ice Age?

Considering the widespread awareness of the dangers of cocaine, you might think stimulant drug use would be on the decline. And it might be. But, there is word of a "new" stimulant on the street called "ice," "crystal," "crank," or "speed." But this new drug isn't so new after all. It's methamphetamine or one of the other amphetamine drugs. Will another generation discover the "speed freak" phenomenon? Particularly dangerous is the new smokable form of methamphetamine called ice. Ice is similar in many respects to crack cocaine. It seems to share with crack the capacity to induce rapid addiction, violence, and psychotic behavior. But, unlike the short duration of action associated with crack, the ice high lasts from four to fourteen hours. Ice may represent a problem even more severe than crack during the 1990s.

PHARMACOKINETICS OF STIMULANTS

Stimulant drugs may be administered and absorbed in a variety of ways, and the intensity and duration of action varies accordingly. Cocaine, the amphetamines, and amphetamine-like stimulants (methylphenidate, phenmetrazine) are readily absorbed after oral administration, but the onset of drug action is slower and the peak effect somewhat less than with other methods.

Both cocaine and the amphetamines are commonly administered intranasally and absorption properties are similar to those associated with oral administration (Jones, 1987). In contrast to oral or intranasal routes, which require 10-15 minutes for drug action to begin, intravenous injection of stimulants results in intense effects within 30 seconds. When cocaine is smoked in the form of crack or freebase, the onset of action is even faster (Jones, 1987).

One important difference between cocaine and the amphetamines is in their duration of action. Cocaine is metabolized quite rapidly with most of its effects dissipating between 20-80 minutes after administration. Cocaine or its metabolites are detectable in human urine for two to three days after administration (Hawks & Chiang, 1986). Amphetamines are much longer acting with effects that persist from four to twelve hours, and they or their metabolites are also detectible in urine for two to three days (Goodman, Goodman & Gilman, 1980; Hawks & Chiang, 1986).

MECHANISM OF STIMULANT ACTION

As noted in Chapter 3, stimulant drugs such as cocaine and the amphetamines are thought to affect the brain primarily through complex actions on monoamine neurotransmitters: dopamine, norepinephrine, and serotonin. For example, both cocaine and the amphetamines block reuptake of norepinephrine and dopamine (Koob & Bloom, 1988). In addition, the amphetamines appear to stimulate the release of norepinephrine and dopamine into the synapse (Ellinwood, 1980), and although the evidence is less clear, cocaine may also stimulate release of transmitters (Gold, Dackis, Pottash, Extein, & Washton, 1986). Cocaine also blocks reuptake of serotonin (Jones, 1984). Thus, the initial effect of stimulants is to produce a storm of activity in neural pathways that are sensitive to the monoamine transmitters. However, because of this increased activity, and particularly because reuptake is blocked so that enzymes break down the neurotransmitters, the long-term effects of stimulant use involve depletion of monoamines. If you remember that low levels of monoamines are linked to clinical depression (see Chapter 3), then you have the basis of a current theory of why the aftereffects of heavy cocaine use involve depression (Dackis & Gold, 1985; Gold et al., 1986). In order to explain this hypothesis, we must turn briefly to data from the animal laboratory.

It has been known for a long time that animals will work to obtain cocaine. Rats and monkeys given a choice between making responses that produce cocaine or other rewards will choose cocaine over other drugs or even over food to the extent that, given unlimited access to cocaine, 90% will die (Aigner & Balster, 1978; Bozarth & Wise, 1985). The powerful reinforcing properties of cocaine (and presumably the amphetamines as well) stem from its action on dopamine-containing neurons in the brain's pleasure

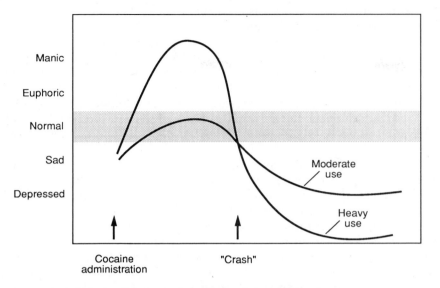

Figure 5-4 Relationship between cocaine dose and mood.

pathways (Goeders, Dworkin, & Smith, 1986; Wise, 1984—see Chapter 3). Thus, cocaine use may involve a kind of chemical shortcut to the pleasure or reward systems of the brain. However, because in the long run a depletion of dopamine (along with other transmitters important in depression) occurs, the cocaine user may then find that his or her ability to experience normal pleasure is diminished. This is consistent with the depression and lack of joy that is so common during cocaine withdrawal it is known as the "cocaine blues." Figure 5-4 illustrates the relationship between mood and cocaine after moderate and heavy use. The peak at the left shows the mood elevation that occurs upon cocaine administration; the valley at right depicts the consequent depression. The depression of mood is greater following heavy use. Note that these general observations seem to hold for amount of use in a single session and for longer term use. However, the depressive abstinence syndrome is thought to be stronger and of greater duration in those who have been abusing the drug for an extended period.

ACUTE EFFECTS AT LOW AND MODERATE DOSES

Stimulant drugs produce a number of physiological effects that are observable outside the brain. We discuss the effects of cocaine and amphetamines together because, for all practical purposes, their measurable effects are identical. Although users often claim to notice subjective differences between stimulants, under controlled laboratory conditions even experienced stimulant users cannot discriminate among the effects of cocaine, amphetamines, and methylphenidate (Fischman, 1984).

Stimulants provide the classic examples of sympathomimetic drugs. That is, they act to stimulate or mimic activity in the sympathetic branch of the autonomic nervous system. Thus, many of their physiological effects are the same as those seen during emotional arousal: heart rate is up, blood pressure is up, respiratory rate is up, and sweating increases; meanwhile, blood flow decreases to the viscera and extremities but increases to the large muscle groups and the brain. Finally, body temperature is elevated and pupils are dilated.

Anorectic effects
Causing one to lose appetite—suppression of eating.

Cocaine and amphetamine also produce appetite suppressant or **anorectic effects.** People simply do not feel hunger after taking these drugs. It is anorectic effects that were sought when amphetamines and phenmetrazine (Preludin) were prescribed as diet pills. Although patients definitely ate less and lost weight on diet pills, doses had to be escalated to maintain loss, and when patients went off the drugs they typically regained the weight. Thus, the benefits of diet pills were outweighed by the risk of dependence and other side effects, and this approach to the treatment of obesity is considered questionable at best (Gilman et. al, 1980; Kramer & Pinco, 1973).

Moderate doses of cocaine and amphetamines also produce a sense of elation and mood elevation. Individuals show increased talkativeness and sociability (Griffiths, Stitzer, Corker, Bigelow, & Liebson, 1977; Higgins & Stitzer, 1988). Alertness and arousal are increased, and marked insomnia often develops. These drugs also enhance performance on a wide variety of tasks involving physical endurance, such as running and swimming, and they increase physical strength. Laties and Weiss (1981) concluded in a review of the literature on amphetamines and sports that amphetamines confer a small but significant edge to the athlete. Consider the effects, shown in Figure 5-5, of methamphetamine on performance on a stationary bicycle machine. Note that a control injection does little to reverse the effects of fatigue on rate of cycling, but that a methamphetamine (Methedrine) injection administered at the three-hour point produces a large improvement that is sustained for several hours. Although the data on cocaine are scantier, it appears to have the same effects but is limited by its short duration of action (Grinspoon & Bakalar, 1976). The expected, and to some extent real, enhancement of performance is probably one reason cocaine abuse has been so prevalent among athletes in recent years. Ironically, when former Maryland basketball coach Lefty Driesell, now coaching at James Madison University, made this very point at a conference on drugs in June 1987, he was sharply criticized. But in fact he was arguing for the need for drug testing in sports—if stimulants provide an edge, even a small one, athletes will be tempted to use them.

Because stimulants increase resistance to fatigue and boredom they have often been used to aid studying, resulting in the amphetamine-induced "all-nighter." Several problems occur with this type of stimulant use. One is that

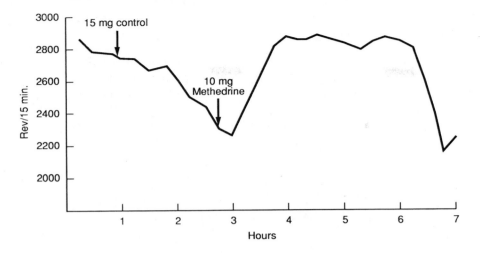

Figure 5–5 Performance on bicycle machine after control and methamphetamine injections (from Laties and Weiss, 1981).

information learned under the influence of a drug is best recalled when the individual is in that same drug-induced state. This phenomenon is called **state-dependent learning** and it is true of a number of drugs other than stimulants (Overton, 1985). Now we are **not** suggesting that students should take the test "high" if they study high. Rather, the phenomenon of state-dependent learning suggests there will be problems in learning information when under the influence of a drug because the ability to retrieve the information will not be as good when sober. Furthermore, experimental evidence shows that stimulants actually may impair learning ability (Fischman, 1984). Figure 5-6 shows increased errors produced by cocaine in a learning task. Note that the effects are dose- and time-dependent and that the effects of injections of 32 mg are far greater than even the highest intranasal dose (96 mg). Considerable anecdotal evidence shows that stimulants may impair complex reasoning performance. Consider the case of William Halstead. Halstead became known as the father of modern surgery for his pioneering work at the turn of the century. But later in his career, while studying the anesthetic properties of cocaine, he became probably the first American to become addicted to the drug. At one point during his cocaine dependency he published an article in the *New York Medical Journal* that begins with the following sentence:

> Neither indifferent as to which of how many possibilities may best explain nor yet quite at a loss to comprehend, why surgeons have, and that so many, quite without discredit, could have exhibited scarcely any interest in what, as a local anaesthetic, had been supposed, if not declared, by most so very sure to prove, especially to them, attractive, still I do not think that this circumstance, or some sense

State-dependent learning Learning under the influence of a drug is best recalled when in the same "state."

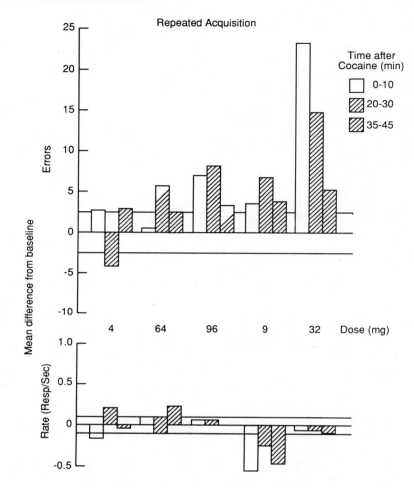

Figure 5–6 Effects of cocaine on learning new behavior patterns. Data collected during each pre-drug, repeated-acquisition task were averaged across subjects; the mean is used as the baseline score. Change from baseline is shown for number of errors and response rate during each of the three 10-minute post-drug tests. Cocaine was inhaled at doses of 4, 64, 96 mg, and 32 mg was injected intravenously. S indicates an intravenous saline injection (from Fischman, 1984).

of obligation to rescue fragmentary reputation for surgeons rather than the belief that an opportunity existed for assisting others to an appreciable extent, induced me, several months ago, to write on the subject in hand the greater part of a somewhat comprehensive paper, which poor health disinclined me to complete (quoted in Grinspoon & Bakalar, 1976, p. 32).

Given the apparent effects of cocaine on Halstead's writing style, it is frightening to imagine how his surgery was going! So the notion that cocaine enhances intellectual performance appears to be a myth.

Another notion about cocaine (and the amphetamines) that appears to be largely mythical is their ability to enhance sexual prowess. Although this has not been well studied, surveys suggest that while some report enhancement of sexual feelings and performance with stimulants, most do not. Many men report impotence with stimulants and women frequently describe a decline in sexual interest, but most report no effects (Abel, 1985).

ACUTE EFFECTS AT HIGH DOSES

As we noted earlier, when high doses of stimulant drugs are taken a characteristic psychotic state emerges. This state can be produced in normal volunteers in a laboratory setting by amphetamines, cocaine, phenmetrazine, (Preludin) or methylphenidate (Ritalin) (Davis & Schlemmer, 1980). Such psychotic reactions are currently a serious problem with high–dose use of crack cocaine. Paranoid delusions are the most common symptom of stimulant psychosis, but a second symptom commonly noted is compulsive, stereotyped behavior like rocking, hair-pulling, chain-smoking, or "fiddling with things." Other symptoms may include hallucinations and, as noted earlier, formication. Interestingly, stimulant psychosis can be successfully treated with chlorpromazine (Thorazine) or other drugs used in the treatment of schizophrenia (Davis & Schlemmer, 1980).

Of course, accompanying high doses of cocaine or amphetamines is always the risk of overdose death. Specifying the dose that places the user at risk is difficult. With cocaine in particular, when we speak of low to moderate doses, we refer to 15-60 mgs (a typical "line" contains 10-20 mgs). But cocaine overdose deaths have been reported in cases of individuals who were given as little as 20 mgs as a local anesthetic, apparently because they suffered from a rare deficiency in the enzyme that breaks down cocaine in the blood and liver (Weiss & Mirin, 1987). Such cases would certainly be exceptional, and generally much higher doses are taken before experiencing either stimulant psychosis or death.

A number of cocaine overdose deaths have occurred during the past few years—more than 500 in 1985—but for many people the deaths of athletes Len Bias and Don Rodgers and comedian John Belushi stand out as remarkable illustrations that cocaine can kill. Stimulants can kill in a number of ways:

1. Cocaine can cause convulsions or seizures that may result in respiratory collapse.
2. Cocaine produces a direct action on cardiac nerves, which may cause irregular beating of the heart (arrhythmia). If severe enough this may lead to fibrillation—the heartbeat flutters but does not pump blood through the system.
3. Cocaine may produce coronary artery spasm leading to impaired blood

flow to the cardiac muscle. This results in myocardial infarction (heart attack) and may cause permanent cardiac damage even if not fatal.

4. Cocaine may cause a cerebral artery to burst because of high blood pressure, which may produce a stroke.

These are the most likely reasons for a cocaine overdose death, but which of these particular factors is responsible is rarely certain (Cregler & Mark, 1986; Mittleman & Wetli, 1984; Weiss & Mirin, 1987).

An additional risk occurs when stimulant drugs are taken during pregnancy. Studies of women using cocaine during pregnancy have shown higher rates of spontaneous abortion, fetal death, and premature labor and birth. Infants born of cocaine-using women had lower birth weights and lengths, and were more likely to die during infancy (Chasnoff, 1987; Ryan, Ehrlich, & Finnegan, 1987).

EFFECTS OF CHRONIC ADMINISTRATION

Tolerance

When stimulants are taken regularly over a long period (chronic use), several additional problems and issues arise. One issue involves the development of tolerance for the drug, and in the case of the stimulants, this turns out to be fairly complex. First, acute tolerance develops for cocaine. That is, the effects obtained from the first administration of the drug are not produced by a second administration shortly after, unless a higher dose is used. This is described by a freebase user as follows:

> "You can do enough freebase to kill you and not realize it because the base numbs your lungs and you can keep sucking it in. After that first hit, you spend the rest of the night trying for that same rush. You keep hoping the next hit will do it, and you add more to the pipe and breathe in deeper, but it's never the same and I mean *never* the same. Nothing compares to that first hit" (quoted by Kirsch, 1986, p. 49).

Acute tolerance to the physiological (heart rate increase) and subjective effects of cocaine also has been demonstrated in humans in laboratory settings (Fischman, Schuster, Javaid, Hatano & Davis, 1985). This acute tolerance dissipates rapidly too, usually within twenty-four hours. But, studies of the development of long-term, protracted tolerance to cocaine and amphetamines have not yielded consistent findings. Some studies have shown clear development of tolerance to various stimulant effects. For example tolerance to the hyperthermic (body temperature increasing) effects of amphetamine develops gradually (Caldwell, Croft, & Sever, 1980). However, other studies have shown the development of what might be termed **reverse tolerance** or sensitization following repeated administration. In these cases, lower doses were sufficient to produce a given effect (Jones, 1984; Post,

Reverse Tolerance Sometimes called sensitization, this is when increased sensitivity develops after chronic use of a drug.

1977). This is particularly true for the convulsant effects of cocaine where the ability of the drug to produce seizures appears to be enhanced by repeated use, a phenomenon called **"kindling."** Kindling may be of significance when overdose death occurs at relatively low doses of cocaine (Jones, 1984). In any case, the occurrence of reverse or regular tolerance may depend on various complex aspects of the response being studied (Hoffman, Branch, & Sizemore, 1987).

Kindling
Repeated exposure to a stimulus may lower the brain's threshold for seizures. This effect, which is produced by electrical stimulation or by cocaine, is called kindling.

Dependence

Although the abstinence syndrome associated with cocaine (or amphetamines) does not involve life-threatening physical symptoms, it is real and compelling. The primary symptoms include depression, social withdrawal, craving, tremors, and sleeping disturbances (Jones, 1984). The temptation to resume use of the drug is described by many as overpowering. Gawin and Kleber (1986) note three distinct phases of cocaine withdrawal. First comes what they call the "crash", approximately three days of intense craving and deep depression. Second, a period of one to ten weeks ensues during which the person continues to feel intense cravings and experiences moderate depression and an inability to experience normal pleasure. Finally, considerable improvement occurs in the third phase, but for nine months or more the person may continue to experience periods of depression and intermittent craving. This may be related to a long-term depletion of monoamine transmitters. Obviously, not all persons who experiment with cocaine develop a dependence pattern and not all who use the drug regularly even over a period of years experience these severe abstinence phenomena (Siegel, 1984). But for those who do, cocaine dependence can be a living nightmare. In addition to the risk of lethal overdose, stimulant psychosis and severe depression, cocaine smokers often report chest pains related to lung or heart damage, and even intranasal users frequently report insomnia, chronic fatigue, severe headaches, nasal and sinus infections, and seizures (Washton, 1987). Because the unpleasant abstinence symptoms are so long-lasting, many cocaine users relapse back to heavy use even after months of abstinence. A variety of new approaches are now being tried to help treat the cocaine-dependent individual. In addition to more traditional approaches to drug treatment (see Chapter 15), some therapists are now using antidepressant drugs to help the cocaine user through the abstinence depression, and new drugs that may reduce craving for cocaine, such as amantadine and buprenorphine are under study (Gawin et al., 1989; Waldrop, 1989). In addition, special self-help groups have developed for cocaine dependency (for example, Cocaine Anonymous). A national hotline has been established for individuals to get information on cocaine and treatment facilities: 1-800-COCAINE (Washton, 1987). Despite the absence of life-threatening physical withdrawal symptoms, cocaine is as hard an addiction to break as any.

SUMMARY

- Cocaine comes from the leaves of the coca bush, and the practice of chewing coca leaves by South American Indians goes back many centuries. Cocaine was introduced to Europe by the Spanish, and when the process necessary to separate cocaine from the leaf was developed in the nineteenth century a major epidemic of cocaine abuse swept the world.

- Amphetamines are synthetic stimulant drugs discovered in the 1920s. They became major drugs of abuse as well, but their popularity waned somewhat in the 1970s and 1980s as cocaine returned to favor.

- Cocaine became one of the most frequently abused drugs in the 1980s with the introduction of an inexpensive smokable form—crack.

- The effects of cocaine and the amphetamines are virtually identical except that cocaine is metabolized very rapidly and thus has a short duration of action (20-80 minutes), while amphetamine effects are more prolonged (four-twelve hours).

- Both cocaine and amphetamines act through the monoamine neurotransmitter systems, particularly by enhancing dopaminergic activity. This action in the brain's pleasure center may account for the highly addictive nature of cocaine.

- Both cocaine and amphetamines are sympathomimetic drugs that increase heart rate, blood pressure, respiratory rate, and cause pupil dilation.

- Other effects of stimulants include anorectic effects, increased alertness and arousal, mood elevation, and at low doses, enhanced performance on a variety of tasks.

- High doses of cocaine or amphetamines may produce a paranoid state called stimulant psychosis or death through overdose.

- Dependence may develop after chronic use of cocaine or amphetamines. The abstinence syndrome is characterized primarily by depression and craving with few measurable physiological effects. Thus, a drug that does not cause severe physical withdrawal symptoms can still be highly addictive.

References

Abel, E.L. (1985). *Psychoactive drugs and sex*. New York: Plenum Press.

Aigner, T.G. & Balster, R.L. (1978). Choice behavior in Rhesus monkeys: Cocaine versus food. *Science, 201,* 534–535.

Allen, D.F. (1987). History of cocaine. In D.F. Allen (Ed.), *The cocaine crisis,* (pp. 7–15) New York: Plenum Press.

Ashley, R. (1975). *Cocaine: its history, uses, and effects*. New York: Warner.

Barnes, D.M. (1988). Drugs: Running the numbers. *Science, 240,* 1729–1731.

Bozarth, M.A. & Wise, R.A. (1985). Toxicity associated with long-term intravenous heroin and cocaine self-administration in the rat. *Journal of the American Medical Association, 254,* 81–83.

Brecher, E.M. (1972). *Licit and illicit drugs*. Boston: Little, Brown and Company.

Byck, R. (Ed.) (1974). *Cocaine papers by Sigmund Freud*. New York: Stonehill Publishing Company.

Caldwell, J., Croft, J.E. & Sever, P.S. (1980). Tolerance to the amphetamines: An examination of possible mechanisms. In J. Caldwell & S.J. Mule (Eds.) *Amphetamines and Related Stimulants: Chemical, Biological, Clinical and Sociological Aspects* (pp. 131–146). Boca Raton, Florida: CRC Press.

Chasnoff, I.J. (1987). Cocaine and methadone exposed infants: A comparison. In L.S. Harris (Ed.) *Problems of drug dependence: 1986*. Research Monograph 76, (p. 278). National Institute on Drug Abuse, Washington, D.C.

Cole, L. (1989). Prisoners of crack. *Rolling Stone, 545,* 61–74.

Cregler, L.L. & Mark, H. (1986). Cardiovascular dangers of cocaine abuse. *The American Journal of Cardiology, 57,* 1185–1186.

Dackis, C.A. & Gold, M.S. (1985). New concepts in cocaine addiction: the dopamine depletion hypothesis. *Neuroscience and Biobehavioral Reviews, 9,* 469–477.

Davis, J.M. & Schlemmer, R.F. (1980). The amphetamine psychosis. In J. Caldwell & S.J. Mule (Eds.) *Amphetamines and related stimulants: Chemical, biological, clinical, and sociological aspects* (pp. 161–174). Boca Raton, Florida: CRC Press.

Ellinwood, E.H. (1980). Neuropharmacology of amphetamines and related stimulants. In J. Caldwell & S.J. Mule (Eds.) *Amphetamines and related stimulants: Chemical, biological, clinical, and sociological aspects* (pp. 69–84). Boca Raton, Florida: CRC Press.

Fischman, M.W. (1984). The behavioral pharmacology of cocaine in humans. In J. Grabowski (Ed.) *Cocaine: Pharmacology, effects and treatment of abuse.* Research Monograph 50, National Institute on Drug Abuse, Washington, D.C.

Fischman, M.W., Schuster, C.R., Javaid, J., Hatano, Y. & Davis, J. (1985). Acute tolerance development to the cardiovascular and subjective effects of cocaine. *Journal of Pharmacology and Experimental Therapeutics, 235,* 677–682.

Gawin, F.H. & Kleber, H.D. (1986). Abstinence symptomatology and psychiatric diagnosis in cocaine abusers. *Archives of General Psychiatry, 43,* 107–113.

Gawin, F.H. Morgan, C. Kosten, T.R. & Kleber, H.D. (1989). Double-blind evaluation of the effect of acute amantadine on cocaine craving. *Psychopharmacology, 97,* 402–403.

Goeders, N.E., Dworkin, S.I. & Smith, J.E. (1986). Neuropharmacological assessment of cocaine self-administration into the medial prefrontal cortex. *Pharmacology, Biochemistry, and Behavior, 24,* 1429–1440.

Gold, M.S., Dackis, C.A., Pottash, A.L.C., Extein, I., & Washton, A. (1986). Cocaine update: from bench to bedside. *Controversies in alcoholism and substance abuse,* (pp. 35–59). The Haworth Press.

Gilman, A.G., Goodman, L.S. & Gilman, A. (Eds). (1980). *Goodman and Gilman's the pharmacological basis of therepeutics.* Sixth Edition, New York: MacMillan Publishing Company.

Griffiths, R.R., Stitzer, M., Corker, K., Bigelow, G. & Liebson, I. (1977). Drug-produced changes in human social behavior: Facilitation by d-amphetamine. *Pharmacology, Biochemistry, and Behavior, 7,* 365–372.

Grinspoon, L. & Bakalar, J.B. (1976). *Cocaine: A drug and its social evolution.* New York: Basic Books Inc.

Hawks, R.L. & Chiang, C.N. (1986). *Urine testing for drugs of abuse.* Research Monograph 73, National Institute on Drug Abuse, Washington, D.C.

Higgins, S.T. & Stitzer, M.L. (1988) Time allocation in a concurrent schedule of social interaction and monetary reinforcement: effects of d-amphetamine. *Pharmacology, Biochemistry, and Behavior, 31,* 227–231.

Hoffman, S.H., Branch, M.N. & Sizemore, G.M. (1987). Cocaine tolerance: Acute versus chronic effects as dependent upon fixed-ratio size. *Journal of the Experimental Analysis of Behavior, 47,* 363–376.

Jones, R.T. (1984). The pharmacology of cocaine. In J. Grabowski (Ed.) *Cocaine: Pharmacology, effects and treatment of abuse.* Research Monograph 50, (pp. 34–53). National Institute on Drug Abuse, Washington, D.C.

Jones, R.T. (1987). The psychopharmacology of cocaine. In A.M. Washton & M.S. Gold (Eds.) *Cocaine: a Clinician's Handbook* (pp. 55–72). New York: Guilford Press.

Kennedy, J. (1985). *Coca exotica.* Cranbury, NJ: Associated University Presses, Inc.

Kirsch, M.M. (1986). *Designer drugs.* Minneapolis: CompCare Publications.

Koob, G.F. & Bloom, F.E. (1988). Cellular and molecular mechanisms of drug dependence. *Science, 242,* 715–723.

Kramer, J.C. & Pinco, R.G. (1973). Amphetamine use and misuse: A medicolegal view. In D.E. Smith & D.R. Wesson (Eds.) *Uppers and downers* (pp. 9–22). Englewood Cliffs, New Jersey: Prentice-Hall Inc.

Laties, V.G. & Weiss, B. (1981). The amphetamine margin in sports. *Federation Proceedings, 40,* 2689–2692.

Mittleman, R.E. & Wetli, C.V. (1984). Death caused by recreational cocaine use. *Journal of the American Medical Association, 252,* 1889–1893.

Mortimer, W.G. (1901). *Peru: History of Coca "the divine plant" of the Incas.* New York: J.H. Vail.

Newsweek (1988). Crack. November 28, pp. 64–79.

Newsweek (1989a). A tide of drug killing. January 16, pp. 44–45.

Newsweek (1989b). Anarchy in Colombia. September 11, pp. 30–34.

Overton, D.A. (1985). Contextual stimulus effects of drugs and internal states. In P.D. Balsam & A. Tomie (Eds.) *Context and learning* (pp. 357–384). Hillsdale, New Jersey: Lawrence Erlbaum Associates.

Perez-Reyes, M., DiGuiseppi, S., & Ondrusek, G. (1982). Freebase cocaine smoking. *Clinical Pharmacology and Therapeutics, 32,* 459–465.

Post, R.M. (1977). Progressive changes in behavior and seizures following chronic cocaine administration: Relationship to kindling and psychosis. In E.H. Ellinwood & M.M. Kilbey (Eds.) *Cocaine and Other Stimulants,* (pp. 353–372). New York: Plenum.

Rapoport, J.L., Buchsbaum, M.S., Zahn, T.P., Weingartner, H. Luclow, C., Mikkelson, E.J. (1978). Dextroamphetamine: Cognitive and behavioral effects in normal prepubertal boys. *Science, 199,* 560–563.

Ryan, L., Ehrlich, S., & Finnegan, L.P. (1987). Cocaine abuse in pregnancy: Effects on the fetus and newborn. In L.S. Harris (Ed.) *Problems of drug dependence: 1986,* Research Monograph 76 (p. 280). National Institute on Drug Abuse, Washington, D.C.

Safer, D.J., Allen, R.P. & Barr, E. (1975). Growth rebound after termination of stimulant drugs. *Journal of Pediatrics, 86,* 113–116.

Siegel, R.K. (1984). Changing patterns of cocaine use: Longitudinal observations, consequences and treatment. In J. Grabowski (Ed.) *Cocaine: Pharmacology, effects, and treatment of abuse,* Research Monograph 50, (pp. 92–110). National Institute on Drug Abuse, Washington, D.C.

Siegel, R.K. (1985). New patterns of cocaine use: changing doses and routes. In N.J. Kozel & E.H. Adams (Eds.) *Cocaine use in America: Epidemiological and clinical perspectives.* NIDA Research Monograph 61, pp. 204–220.

Waldrop, M.M. (1989). NIDA aims to fight drugs with drugs. *Science, 245,* 1443–1444.

Washton, A.M. (1987). Cocaine: Drug epidemic of the '80's. In D.F. Allen (Ed.) *The cocaine crisis.* (pp. 45–64). New York: Plenum Press.

Weiss, R.D. & Mirin, S.M. (1987). *Cocaine.* Washington, D.C: American Psychiatric Press, Inc.

Wise, R.A. (1984). Neural mechanisms of the reinforcing action of cocaine. In J. Grabowski (Ed.) *Cocaine: Pharmacology, effects, and treatment of abuse.* Research Monograph 50 (pp. 15–33). National Institute on Drug Abuse, Washington, D.C.

6 THE MINOR STIMULANTS

In this chapter we focus on a class of drugs called the minor stimulants. Most of the chapter is devoted to nicotine and caffeine, which are classified as stimulants because of their action in the body. It is understated somewhat to call these drugs "minor" because of the numbers of people who use them and, in the case of nicotine, because of the consequences of their use. We also briefly discuss drugs very similar to caffeine, which are classified as methylxanthines.

The discussion of nicotine and caffeine follows the format used for the review of other major drug classes in this book. We begin with the history of use of the drug and the current prevalence of its use and associated problems. Next, we cover the mechanisms of its pharmacological action, as well as medical and psychotherapeutic uses. This is followed by a review of the physical, psychological, and social effects of use. In the case of nicotine, we describe the professional services available to help individuals stop smoking.

NICOTINE

Background

Nicotine occurs naturally from one source: the leafy, green tobacco plant. The plant belongs to the genus Nicotiana and has sixty species. Only two of these can be used for smoking and other human consumption, *Nicotiana rustica* and *Nicotiana tabacum*. The latter species provides all of the tobaccos typically consumed in the United States, including burley, oriental, and cigar tobaccos. Different types of tobacco result mostly from differences in cultivation and processing. In this regard, tobacco leaves are harvested when still green and then undergo curing and fermentation. The tobacco then is converted into the commercial products—cigarettes, cigars, snuff, chewing tobacco, and pipe tobacco (Blum, 1984).

Tobacco has many constituents, but nicotine is singled out as having the broadest and most immediate pharmacological action. Nicotine is extremely toxic, with only 60 mg needed to kill humans. When tobacco is burned the smoke has a small portion of nicotine, which the body metabolizes to a nontoxic substance. The main reason humans consume tobacco is for the effects caused by the nicotine.

The tobacco products meant for smoking—in the form of cigarettes, cigars, or pipes—are generally familiar. Not as familiar are the forms of smokeless tobacco, which include snuff and chewing tobacco (Gritz, Ksir, & McCarthy, 1985). Snuff is powdered tobacco that is mixed with salts, moisture, oils, flavorings, and other additives. It is marketed in two forms, dry and moist. Chewing tobacco is marketed in loose leaf form, pressed as a rectangle called a plug, or in a twist or roll. As with snuff, aroma and flavoring agents are added to chewing tobacco. A quid (piece) of tobacco can

Figure 6–1 These harvested tobacco plants await conversion to commercial products such as cigarettes and chewing tobacco.

either be chewed or held between the cheek and gum. "Dipping" is holding a pinch of moist snuff in the same place. In Europe, snuff is most commonly taken dry and intranasally.

HISTORY OF TOBACCO USE[1]

The West Discovers Tobacco

In the late fifteenth century Columbus and other explorers found Indians in the New World smoking dried tobacco leaves. The pleasant effects of nicotine caught on like fire, and smoking quickly became popular among the

[1]This section on the history of tobacco use is taken from Brecher (1972), Stewart (1967), and Blum (1984).

Europeans. They brought home seeds of the tobacco plant and spread them to other parts of the world on their ventures. In these early years the Spanish held a monopoly on the world tobacco market because *Nicotiana tabacum* is indigenous to South America. However, the English took a piece of the business when John Rolfe's *Nicotiana tabacum* crop flourished in the colony of Virginia.

At first, only the wealthy could afford tobacco. For example, in England tobacco was worth its weight in silver, and people paid that price. However, by the early seventeenth century tobacco use had become widespread, and even the poor could afford it. In 1614 London had about 7000 tobacco shops. By the middle of that century tobacco use had spread through central Europe, and signs of the addictive nature of the drug were evident. For example, African natives would trade land, livestock, and slaves for tobacco because of nicotine's unending addictive demands.

Not everybody regarded tobacco in the highest terms. In the middle 1600s, Popes Urban VIII and Innocent X issued papal bulls against tobacco use, but clergy and laymen alike continued to smoke. In 1633 in Constantinople, the Sultan Murad IV paid surprise visits to his men in combat during war. If the soldiers were caught smoking the good sultan punished them by quartering, hanging, beheading, and worse. Yet the soldiers continued to smoke. The Russian czar in 1634 also prohibited smoking. He punished his offending subjects by slitting their nostrils and other consequences that might impede their smoking. But the Russians did not give up tobacco.

The Japanese were given tobacco by Portuguese seamen in 1542. Like their western counterparts, the Japanese took to smoking quickly—so quickly that by 1603 an edict against smoking already had been issued by the Emperor. But the Japanese did not stop. In 1639 smoking had become so established in Japan that a person was offered a smoke with a ceremonial cup of tea. "From these days until today . . . no country that has ever learned to use tobacco has given up the practice" (Brecher, 1972, p. 213). No substance has replaced tobacco in people's hearts, minds, and bodies. When tobacco smokers discovered the pleasures of smoking marijuana or opium, these drugs did not displace tobacco. They merely were smoked in addition to it.

Tobacco as Panacea

From the time Columbus and his colleagues discovered tobacco use among the Native Americans until about 1860, the tobacco plant was accepted widely as having medical therapeutic value. Probably tobacco reached its peak of recognition as a medicinal herb at the beginning of the seventeenth century, even though at the same time King James I of England published his skepticisms about tobacco's curative powers. The king admonished that using tobacco for pleasure was morally wrong. To give you

Table 6–1

Uses for Tobacco as Medical Treatment Agent, 1492–1853

□ Application externally in various forms (such as ashes, hot leaves, balm, lotion, mush, oil, many more) for pain due to internal or external disorders and for skin diseases or injuries of any kind

□ Introduced into all openings of the head to treat diseases of the ears (such as smoke blown into), eyes (juice to cleanse), mouth (such as small ball chewed) and nose (such as snuff blown up nose of patient by physician)

□ Introduced into the mouth to reach other organs, such as the lungs (such as smoke introduced directly by the physician), the stomach (such as through juice, boiled or uncooked), and the teeth (such as use of ashes to clean)

□ Introduced into the nostrils to reach lungs (such as inhaled odor of snuff powder)

□ Introduced into the intestinal canal (such as smoke or tobacco enema)

□ Introduced into the vagina by injection

Note: This table was adapted from Stewart (1967), Appendix 5.

an idea of how its reputation exceeded its critics' influence, Table 6–1 lists some of the ways tobacco has been used medically. During the 350 years the table covers, some people believed it was literally possible to breathe life into another, as long as that breath carried tobacco smoke. Tobacco was esteemed at one time as a panacea weed.

From Panacea to Panned

The concept of tobacco as a therapeutic agent took a serious blow in 1828 when two Frenchmen, L. Posselt and F.A. Reimann, isolated nicotine. The chemical was named after a man name Nicot, who was the French ambassador to Portugal and who conducted exacting experiments with tobacco as a medicinal herb. He published his purported successes worldwide. The isolation of nicotine was damaging to its medical reputation because the toxic and addictive properties of the compound began to be understood.

During the years 1830–1860 the use of tobacco for medicine and pleasure in the United States was subject to a stream of attacks by clergymen, educators, and some physicians. This also occurred in Europe. Sometimes the ills attributed to tobacco were not based in medical science. For example, **delirium tremens** (DTs), perverted sexuality, impotency, and insanity all were attributed to tobacco. In 1849 Dr. R.T. Trall denounced the medical use of tobacco and illustrated his argument by describing a case of tobacco addiction. By the middle of the nineteenth century tobacco had all but vanished from the United States *Pharmacopoeia,* and the dangers of tobacco as a drug were well-known. As the United States prepared for a civil war in 1860, the use of tobacco as a medical agent had virtually ended. But people continued to use tobacco for pleasure.

Delirium tremens (DTs) Symptom of alcohol withdrawal syndrome characterized by severe agitation, confusion, and disorientation. Terrifying hallucinations and delusions also may be present.

PREVALENCE OF TOBACCO USE

History shows that tobacco's popularity can resist even the most severe obstacles. Until recently, trends in United States tobacco consumption, at least of cigarettes, clearly reflected this. Cigarette smoking is by far the most common way to use tobacco. Six of every seven pounds of tobacco grown in the United States are used for making cigarettes, and the other pound is used for making pipe and cigar tobaccos and smokeless tobacco products (U.S. Department of Health and Human Services (USDHHS), 1987). Furthermore, cigarette smoking demands the most attention because it is the most toxic way to smoke tobacco, followed in order by cigar and pipe smoking (Blum, 1984).

Smoking Among United States Adults

The United States federal government has conducted a number of surveys of smoking among American adults. A summary of these data from 1955 to 1983 for men and women is presented in Figure 6–2. The data show that, overall, the prevalence of current smokers is at its lowest level since 1955. Men have shown a steady decline since the early 1960s, and women are now heading back down toward their 1955 rate. The data also show the percentage of former smokers has increased at the same time. This implies that one reason for the reduced number of current smokers is an increase in the rates of people who have quit smoking. It is probably no coincidence that the peak of current smoking among American adults was in 1963, and that the prevalence began to fall after that year. In 1964 the United States Public Health Service's *Smoking and Health: Report of the Advisory Committee to the Surgeon General* was published. It detailed the health hazards of cigarette smoking in a way then unprecedented in scope and persuasion. As good as the smoking prevalence data are from a health perspective, however, there is little room for complacency. In 1982, 55 million United States tobacco users smoked 623 billion cigarettes, which is about 6.2 trillion doses of nicotine (Jones, 1987). Most of these smokers say they want to quit, but nicotine's addictive properties make quitting seemingly impossible. Obviously, it is not, as we see in Figure 6–2. Data indicate 95% of the smokers who quit do so on their own. These self-quitters are thought to have been "lighter" (usually defined as fewer than 25 cigarettes a day) smokers.

Smoking Among United States Adolescents

Besides an increase in percentages of smoking quitters, another reason for decreased prevalence of current smokers is a lower rate of smoking initiation among adolescents. Figure 6–3 shows the percentage of high school seniors from 1975 to 1986 who said they were daily users of at least one cigarette. The data in Figure 6–3 were collected in the High School Seniors

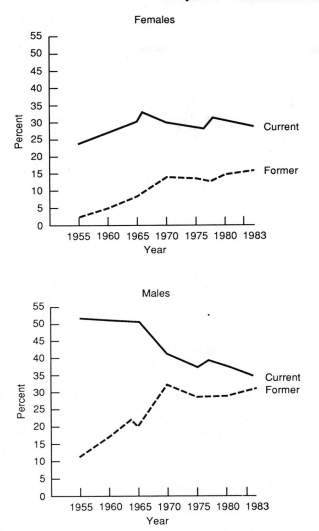

Figure 6–2 The prevalence of former and current smokers is shown for men and women aged twenty and older, 1955 to 1983 (from Shopland and Brown, 1985, p.6.).

surveys cited in Chapter 1. Figure 6–3 shows the highest rates of consumption occurred for young men in 1976 (about 27.5%) and for young women in 1977 (about 30%). After 1975 women have outpaced men in rates of daily cigarette use and have maintained that lead. Rates of daily use generally have declined since the peak years for both sexes. In 1986 about 16.5% of the men were smoking daily, compared to about 19.5% of the women.

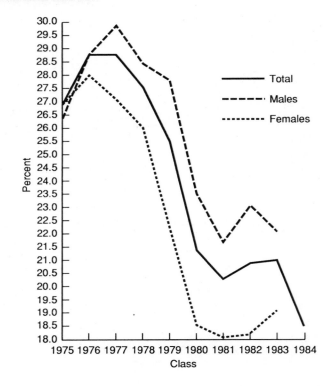

Figure 6–3 This graph shows the percentage of high school seniors who reported daily use of at least one cigarette in the past thirty days, from 1975 to 1986 (from Shopland and Brown, 1985, p. 7, and extended from Johnston, O'Malley, and Bachman, 1987. Published with permission from the Society of Behavioral Medicine.)

Who Is More Likely to Smoke?

Merely citing overall prevalence rates for smoking is a little misleading, because prevalence differs in different classifications of the population of United States adults. For example, in 1983 the National Center for Health Statistics included in its Health Interview Survey current smoking for individuals 18 and older (USDHHS, 1987). The rates of current smoking varied in both men and women according to such factors as income, marital status, education, race, and occupation. For example, black men who are separated or divorced, make under $5000 a year, have some high school education, and work blue collar jobs or are in a service profession are most likely to be current smokers. The profile for the women "most likely to smoke" is similar. That people who earn less than $5000 a year are willing to spend about 10% of their income on cigarettes says something about nicotine's physically addicting properties.

Other differences in the prevalence of cigarette smoking pertain to populations who received mental health services. For example, smoking rates among adults receiving outpatient psychiatric services are almost double those for comparable individuals not receiving such services (Hughes, Hatsukami, Mitchell, & Dahlgren, 1986). Another study showed that the prevalence of heavy smoking among Canadians twenty-five to sixty-four years old in treatment for alcohol problems to be more than double the rate for controls among men (46.9% vs. 18.1%) and more than triple the rate among women (33.8% vs. 10.3%) (Kozlowski, Jelinek, & Pope, 1986).

Per Capita Cigarette Use Has Not Declined as Steadily as Smoking Prevalence

Consistent with the trends in smoking prevalence, the per capita annual cigarette consumption among those 18 years and older has declined steadily from its 1963 peak. However, the decline has not been as steady as we saw for current smoking prevalence. There are two reasons for this. Among people who still smoke, a greater proportion of them are heavier smokers than the proportions in previous years. In addition, the cigarette has changed. Currently, more than 90% of smokers in the United States use filtered cigarettes, compared to less than 60% in 1963, and less than 2% in 1952. Tar content has been reduced in today's cigarette by two–thirds, and nicotine content by one-half, compared to the cigarettes of 1954 (Shopland & Brown, 1985). Because of lower nicotine content, smokers today tend to smoke more cigarettes than did smokers in earlier years.

SMOKELESS TOBACCO PRODUCTS AND YOUTH

For years there has been a steady drop in the prevalence of current use of smokeless tobacco products (and in pipe and cigar smoking, too). The exception to this is the increase in the past five years in the use of moist snuff. For comparison, the last national survey data on the use of smokeless tobacco products among adults 21 years of age and older showed a prevalence of 1.3% in women and 2.5% in men for use of snuff, and .6% and 4.9% for use of chewing tobacco in women and men, respectively. Compared to cigarette consumption, these rates were low. However, a few local studies suggest the recent increase in the use of smokeless tobacco is centered in young males. For example, among students in grades 7–12, there was a 20–25% prevalence of snuff or chewing tobacco use among boys, and there were higher rates with increasing age. In one study of students in junior high school in Wyoming, 24.5% of the boys and 1.2% of the girls were current users of smokeless tobacco. Among the boys who said that someone in their family chewed tobacco, 45.1% reported use of smokeless tobacco products (Gritz, Ksir, & McCarthy, 1985).

Why the Increase?

It is not clear why there has been an increase in the use of smokeless tobacco products among youth. One possibility is that young people have a positive image of people who use such products, and such perceptions may relate to actual use. Chassin, Presson, Sherman, and Margolis (1988) looked at this possibility in their questionnaire study of 429 Arizona high school students (average age = 15.5 years). Almost 60% of the students were girls, and at least monthly use of smokeless tobacco was reported by about 20% of the boys and 1% of the girls. The study involved the students' perceptions of a slide presentation of a peer model who was dressed as an athlete, cowboy, or "average boy," and who had either a cigarette, can of smokeless tobacco, or bag of corn chips in his hand. The image of athlete and cowboy were used because these are the associations that the tobacco industry has used in its advertisements of smokeless tobacco products. Combining the way the model was presented with what product he was holding created nine different experimental slides, and each subject saw only one slide.

The results showed, first, that relative to nonuse both types of tobacco use were associated with greater phoniness, rebellion, unhappiness, bravery, toughness, drug use, and alcohol use. On these ratings the two types of tobacco products did not differ, but they did on others. For example, compared to smokers, smokeless tobacco users were seen as better at school-work, getting along better with their families, and as healthier. Smokeless tobacco users and nonusers were not perceived differently on these characteristics. Another important finding was that about 44% of the girls' and 52% of the boys' images of the boy they most admired most closely were reflected in the ratings given to the smokeless tobacco user model. The smoker model was admired least frequently. Finally, the boy–most–admired ratings were correlated positively with the subjects' own use of tobacco products: Girls who smoked were more likely to rate the smokeless tobacco user as most admired, as were boys who used smokeless tobacco products.

These survey data suggest one reason young people are using smokeless tobacco products is that they have associated positive social characteristics with such use. Smokeless tobacco use also is viewed as not damaging to health, but these perceptions about health consequences are inaccurate.

CONSEQUENCES OF CHRONIC TOBACCO USE

Cigarette smoking is the largest preventable cause of cardiovascular disease and cancer (Abrams & Wilson, 1986). An average of fifteen years are cut from smokers' lives because of these two diseases, and about 300,000 American smokers suffer premature deaths every year (Schelling, 1986). For comparison, overdose deaths due to heroin in 1977 numbered 1750, and 1400 for overdose of barbiturates (Blum, 1984). The economic costs the United States society suffers due to smokers' illnesses were estimated to be about $22 billion, with men accounting for about 60% of the costs.

What Kills in Cigarette Smoke?

Cigarette smoking damages health because of the constituents of tobacco smoke. The three culprits are tar, nicotine, and carbon monoxide, and cigarette smokers face continual exposure to them for years. For example, a two-pack-a-day smoker could be seen 13.4 hours a day with cigarette in hand, mouth, or ash tray, taking about 400 puffs, and inhaling as much as 1000 mg of tar. Carbon monoxide appears to facilitate many of the disease processes associated with smoking. This is due to carbon monoxide's advantage over oxygen in binding to hemoglobin, which carries oxygen from the lungs to the tissues in the body. Exposure even to small amounts of carbon monoxide reduces the amount of hemoglobin available for binding to oxygen and causes deprivation of oxygen to the body's tissues. The brain and heart are especially vulnerable to this action of carbon monoxide, since these systems depend on aerobic respiration for proper functioning (Blum, 1984).

Most of the cancer-causing substances in smoke are in tar, which is the material remaining after cigarette smoke is passed through a filter. Nicotine also has been traced as a source of heart attacks and the onset of cancer (USDHHS, 1987). A cigarette typically contains about 6–8 mg of nicotine (cigars yield 15 to more than 40 mg). When cigarettes are smoked and inhaled, about 10% of the nicotine is absorbed, compared to 2.5% to 5% as much when smoke is drawn into the mouth and then exhaled. That virtually all cigarette smokers inhale is one reason other than sheer numbers that cigarette as opposed to cigar or pipe smoking has been traced as the major cause of diseases related to tobacco use.

SURGEON GENERAL'S WARNING: Quitting Smoking Now Greatly Reduces Serious Risks to Your Health.	SURGEON GENERAL'S WARNING: Smoking By Pregnant Women May Result in Fetal Injury, Premature Birth, And Low Birth Weight.
SURGEON GENERAL'S WARNING: Smoking Causes Lung Cancer, Heart Disease, Emphysema. And May Complicate Pregnancy.	SURGEON GENERAL'S WARNING: Cigarette Smoke Contains Carbon Monoxide

Figure 6–4 Four warnings that must appear on cigarette packages, according to a 1985 federal law. One warning per package appears, with each message rotated every three months. The contents of the messages are based on the *Reports of the Surgeon General on the Health Consequences of Smoking.*

More Statistics on Chronic Tobacco Use and Health[2]

More than convincing evidence exists that the chronic (over a longer time, as opposed to "acute," which means immediate) effects of tobacco use are not healthy to the human body. For example, insurance companies have compiled data on differences in survival rates for men smokers from age 35 to 75. These 1980 data show that, by age 55, 10% of the smokers are dead compared to 4% of the nonsmokers. At age 65 the differences widen to 28% and 10%, respectively. And by age 75 the difference is twofold, 50% and 25%.

What Diseases Are Linked to Cigarette Smoking?

As we noted, cigarette smoking kills because it facilitates the development of coronary heart disease (170,000 deaths a year caused by smoking), cancer (130,000 deaths), and chronic obstructive lung disease (50,000 deaths). Heart disease is the single major killer in the United States, and people who smoke are nearly at twice the risk to contract it compared to nonsmokers. Cancers of the larynx, oral cavity, esophagus, bladder, pancreas, and kidney are associated with cigarette smoking. So associated that 30% of all cancer deaths are caused by it, as are 80% to 90% of all lung cancer deaths. Finally, 80% to 90% of chronic obstructive lung disease, such as emphysema, is caused by smoking. Fortunately, the risk of contracting these diseases falls with time away from cigarettes. If the smoker can manage to abstain for ten years, his or her good health will be at the same risk as someone who has never smoked at all (USDHHS, 1987).

Cigarette Smoking and Women

Many of the statistics on cigarette smoking and health in the United States were based on men who began the habit in a large way after World War I. Twenty years or so later more women took up the habit after World War II, and it was discovered that they began to fall prey to similar health damages. Special risks threaten women who smoke, especially if they are pregnant. Smoking is associated with spontaneous abortion, preterm births, low-weight babies, and fetal and infant deaths. Even if the infant is born healthy, risk is present if his or her mother smokes. During nursing nicotine is present in the mother's milk.

Other Tobacco Products and Health

We have spent considerable space on the hazards of cigarette smoking. This is not to say use of other tobacco products is risk-free. Pipe and cigar

[2]Much of the data presented in this section are from the US Department of Health and Human Services (1987). *Smoking, tobacco, and health: A fact book.* Rockville, MD.

smokers have higher death rates than do nonsmokers, but the differences are not as large as the comparisons we cited for cigarette smokers. Users of snuff and of other types of smokeless tobacco are more likely to get oral cancer and other types of noncancerous oral disease.

Passive Smoking

It once was thought cigarette smokers were harming only themselves. However, we know now that if you merely stay in the vicinity of people smoking, then you will absorb nicotine, carbon monoxide, and other elements of tobacco smoke, although in lesser amounts than if you were actually smoking. Heavy exposure to tobacco smoke may be the equivalent of smoking one to two cigarettes a day (USDHHS, 1987).

Many people find tobacco smoke very unpleasant and irritating. Furthermore, tobacco smoke may exacerbate any symptoms of asthma, bronchitis,

Figure 6–5 The health message of this 1930s advertisement stands in stark contrast to current thinking.

or allergies that a person may have. For children whose parents smoke there is particular risk. These children are more likely than children whose parents do not smoke to have bronchitis and pneumonia, as well as some impairment in pulmonary function (Bonham & Wilson, 1981). Consequences such as these to children and adults are the reasons for recent restrictions, to the dismay of some people, on smoking in public places.

CONTEMPORARY ISSUE BOX 6–1
Cigarette Smoking and Death: Who's Responsible?

Lexington, a rural county seat in Mississippi, attracted uncharacteristic attention in January, 1988 because of a legal battle there. The case concerned a carpenter's family (plaintiff) and the American Tobacco Company. The carpenter had died in 1987 of cancer at age fifty after smoking two packs of Pall Malls a day for thirty-five years. His family argued the smoking caused the premature death and was suing the tobacco company for $2 million in compensatory damages and $15 million in punitive damages. The reason? The company was selling a product that was not fit for consumption.

As late as early 1988 more than three hundred similar cases had been filed in the courts. The tobacco companies had not lost a case yet, because juries saw cigarette smoking as voluntary or self-determined behavior. Then, in June of 1988 a New Jersey jury awarded the husband of a woman who died at age fifty-eight of lung cancer $400,000 in damages to be paid by two tobacco companies. This judgment was the first instance of any tobacco company paying damages because of the death of a user of its products. Yet, the companies were not devastated, because the jury still felt the smoker was 80% responsible. The companies were held as 20% responsible, through their failure to warn consumers of smoking risks and misrepresentation (about health and smoking) in advertisements that appeared before 1966. In January 1990, that landmark decision was overturned by an appeals court, which ruled that whether the plaintiff had seen or believed the pre-1966 advertisements had not been proven. Despite the apparent setback, antismoking advocates interpret the appeals ruling as a victory—they reason that the ruling has defined broader claims that can be considered in future suits against tobacco companies.

Obviously, there is a lot at stake for both parties: The plaintiffs stand to gain their monetary damages, and the tobacco companies stand to lose a fortune if precedent is set in any one case holding them mostly or totally responsible for smokers' health damage. If it were up to you, which side would you support?

PHARMACOLOGY OF NICOTINE

Sites of Action

Nicotine's effects are highly complex because the drug has action on a number of sites in the body. This complexity is increased by the fact that nicotine has both stimulant and depressant phases of action. It appears that the final response to nicotine is the sum of several of its different and opposing effects (Taylor, 1985). One example is nicotine's effect on heart rate. It can either stimulate or depress heart rate, dependent on its excitation or paralysis of sympathetic or parasympathetic cardiac ganglia. Nicotine's actions on still other sites also combine to influence its effect on heart rate.

Absorption, Distribution, Metabolism, and Excretion

Absorption Nicotine can be absorbed through most of the body's membranes. The drug is rapidly absorbed **through the skin,** the oral, buccal (the cheeks or mouth cavity), and nasal mucosa, the gastrointestinal tract, and the lungs (Russell, 1976). Russell related a story to illustrate how readily nicotine can be absorbed. A florist was using a pesticide spray containing nicotine, and by accident soaked the seat of his pants with it. In only fifteen minutes the florist had **nicotine poisoning** and had to be hospitalized for four days. When he recovered and was dressing to return home, the florist put on the same pants, which still had some nicotine on them. He was readmitted to the hospital an hour later with nicotine poisoning.

Nicotine absorption depends on both the site of absorption and how the nicotine is delivered. Nicotine is most readily absorbed from the lungs, which makes inhaling cigarette smoke an efficient way to get a dose of nicotine. Nicotine is not as readily absorbed through the oral, buccal, or nasal mucosa. The nicotine in cigar or pipe smoke, for example, is not as readily absorbed as that in cigarettes because people usually do not inhale cigars or pipes. As a result, the nicotine is absorbed through the mouth. When nicotine is taken by using snuff or by chewing tobacco, it is absorbed through the mucosa of the nose and the mouth, respectively.

How nicotine is delivered also affects absorption for a few reasons. One is the acidity of the medium (for example smoke) of delivery. The more alkaline (basic) the medium, the easier the absorption. Cigar and pipe smoke are more basic than cigarette smoke, which compensates to some extent for the difference between the mouth and lungs in ease of absorption. Time of contact of the nicotine-containing substance with the absorption site also is important. The more contact, the greater the amount of nicotine absorbed. For example, the use of snuff and chewing tobacco allows considerable time for nicotine absorption at the nose and mouth (Blum, 1984).

Absorption through the skin
When a drug is absorbed through the skin it is called transdermal absorption.

Nicotine poisoning
A consequence of nicotine overdose, characterized by palpitations, dizziness, sweating, nausea, or vomiting.

Distribution   After nicotine is absorbed it is distributed by the blood to a number of sites of pharmacological action. When a cigarette is inhaled, nicotine reaches the brain from the lungs within seven seconds. By comparison, it takes fourteen seconds for blood to flow from the arm to the brain, which would be the typical route for intravenous injection. Therefore, in delivery of nicotine brain levels rise rapidly and then decline just as quickly as the drug is distributed to other parts of the body. The effects of nicotine can be observed rapidly, as its distribution half-life is only eight minutes. The speed that absorption and distribution occur is one reason smokers tend to reach for a cigarette so soon after they have finished their last one. The average smoker of a typical cigarette manufactured in the United States absorbs about one mg of nicotine for each cigarette that he or she smokes.

Metabolism and excretion   The major organ responsible for metabolizing nicotine is the liver. The lungs and the kidneys also play a part in the body's chemical breakdown of nicotine. Metabolism of a drug generally results in conversion to compounds that are more soluble in water and therefore more easily eliminated in the urine, which is the major way nicotine is excreted from the body. About 10% to 20% of nicotine also is eliminated unchanged through the urinary tract (Blum, 1984). Less important vehicles of eliminating nicotine and its metabolites are saliva, sweat, and the milk of lactating women (Jones, 1987; Russell, 1976).

Figure 6–6 is a graph of the average levels of nicotine in the blood of a cigarette smoker over the course of a full day. The level of nicotine in the blood rises during the course of the 16-hour part of the day when people

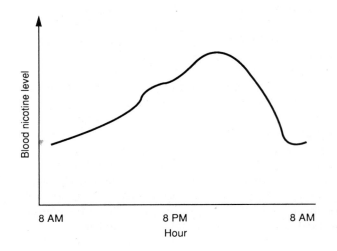

Figure 6–6 This graph shows blood nicotine levels in a typical cigarette smoker over a twenty-four–hour period.

are awake, with a peak around midnight. The level then declines during sleeping hours, but there is a level upon awakening in the morning. This indicates the body of the average daily smoker of cigarettes is continually exposed to nicotine.

TOLERANCE AND DEPENDENCE

Tolerance

First attempts at smoking usually result in palpitations, dizziness, sweating, nausea, or vomiting (Russell, 1976). These are signs of acute nicotine poisoning. However, tolerance to nicotine develops very quickly, even within the time of smoking a cigarette. In this regard, the effects of the nicotine in the initial puffs of the first cigarette of the day are greater than those in the last few puffs of that cigarette (Jones, 1987). The rapid development of tolerance to nicotine also is apparent in the short time it takes some people to reach the status of seasoned smoker. The time from their unpleasant first cigarette to pleasurable smoking of a pack a day or more can be as short as several weeks. Besides tolerance to the effects of nicotine, dispositional tolerance develops. Smokers metabolize the drug more quickly than do nonsmokers (Edwards, 1986).

Physical Dependence

There is no question people can become physically dependent on nicotine. The major criterion for classification of a drug as one that induces physical dependence is what ensues when the drug is taken away for enough time so that the amount of it in the blood drops considerably or is eliminated. When a consistent set of physical symptoms results, it is said that the drug induces physical dependence. The reverse side of this criterion of physical dependence is that readministration of the drug alleviates any withdrawal symptoms that are present. In 1988 the United States Surgeon General's Office issued a full report with the conclusion that physical dependence on nicotine develops and that the drug is addicting.

Actually, studies have shown for some time that users of nicotine may become physically dependent on it. For example, Hughes, Grist, and Pechacek (1987) collected smokers' reports of the symptoms they experienced twenty-four hours after stopping smoking. The most common report (73% of the smokers) was a craving (a strong desire or urge) for tobacco, followed in order by irritability, anxiety, difficulty concentrating, restlessness, increased appetite, impatience, somatic complaints, and insomnia. A range of what generally would be considered unpleasant symptoms results when the dependent smoker stops smoking.

Once an individual begins smoking cigarettes there is a high likelihood that he or she will become dependent on nicotine. For example, Blum

(1984) noted that among the adolescents who smoke more than 2–3 cigarettes occasionally, about 85% will become dependent on nicotine. In the Hughes study (1987) it was found that of the American adults who smoke, about one-third are dependent on nicotine. Therefore, about one-tenth of adult Americans are nicotine dependent.

Why Is Physical Dependence on Nicotine so Likely?

Several possible reasons explain why the dependence liability of nicotine is high. First, the smoker experiences many rapid drug reinforcements from nicotine daily. For the two-pack-a-day smoker, estimates average 300 nicotine rewards a day, which equals more than 15,000 nicotine shots a year. Another reason is nicotine's quick clearance from the brain, which results in a rapid decrease in nicotine effects that depend on drug action, once the drug level in the body drops. As mentioned earlier, this is a powerful motivator for the smoker, who reinstates nicotine's pleasurable effects by smoking. The seasoned smoker does this to such a degree that he or she is continually exposed to nicotine (see Figure 6–6). One consequence of this pattern is that the smoker does not go into withdrawal symptoms when having to abstain from smoking for a period of hours, for instance while sleeping.

Other reasons for nicotine's dependence liability are its accessibility, and its use still is acceptable in many social settings. Furthermore, nicotine may enhance certain types of task performance (Blum, 1984; Jones, 1987). Together, these aspects of nicotine and its use make clear why smoking and other forms of ingesting nicotine are tough habits to break. As seen in the Hughes study (1987), the most frequently reported withdrawal symptom was nicotine craving. Studies show craving for nicotine continues from weeks to even years after smoking stops (West & Schneider, 1987). This craving is the most commonly reported reason why smokers who stopped smoking return to the habit.

THE MAJOR LURE IN TOBACCO PRODUCTS

It seems that smokers smoke, tobacco chewers chew, and snuffers snuff for the effects of nicotine. This is not a simple matter, however. Giving the impression of a man in awe, Russell (1976) wrote "the actions of nicotine in the body are so complex and multitudinous that there are few other psychoactive drugs about which so much is known, though so little understood. Nicotine reaches and can have an effect on every organ of the body" (p26). More recent literature gives the same message.

West and Russell (1985) cite four major reasons why smokers smoke, based on the findings from questionnaire studies. All of the reasons are pertinent to nicotine: The pleasurable effects of nicotine, modulation (up or down) of arousal level, a reduction of hunger and body weight, and a relief of withdrawal symptoms.

The Pleasurable Effects of Nicotine

Especially for the first cigarette of the day, smokers report a pleasant drug effect from nicotine in tobacco. In controlled studies these effects have been shown to be similar to those of cocaine and amphetamines. The effect also increases with higher doses of nicotine. The importance of tolerance is evident in that nonsmokers do not rate nicotine effects as pleasant, probably because they are not tolerant to some of the negative nicotine effects like nausea. Also of interest—the pleasant nicotine effects tend to be experienced only in the first cigarette of the day, which demonstrates the action of acute tolerance.

Modulation of Arousal

This is probably the most complex action of nicotine, in that the drug seems to have both stimulating and tranquilizing effects. Gilbert (1979) called this nicotine's "paradoxical effect," because the drug generally increases physiological arousal and may decrease the degree or level of emotional experience and behavior.

Modulating up   It has been known for some time that nicotine stimulates both the central and peripheral nervous systems. For example, the peripheral effects documented include increased heart rate, blood pressure, skin conductance, and vasoconstriction. Nicotine also causes an increase in the blood of adrenaline and noradrenaline concentrations, as well as other stress hormones.

The central stimulating effects of nicotine are shown in the manner in which the drug affects task performance. Edwards (1986) described one study in which smokers and nonsmokers alike improved their cognitive task performance, such as short-term memory and concentration, with nicotine. Such improvements remain up to thirty minutes after smoking a cigarette. Data such as these highlight the ripple effects of policies such as the smoking bans that we referred to earlier. Work sites have been the scenes of a proliferation of smoking bans in the last few years. Although there may be health benefits attached to this policy, what happens to the job performance of many employees? If their work involves cognitive or behavioral activity that nicotine affects, then the involuntarily abstaining smokers are likely, along with their supervisors, to notice the employees' work performance is not what it was in pre-ban days.

Modulating down   The sedating physiological effects of nicotine are more complex and seem to depend on dose, the individual, and the situation. It has been found that nicotine has a relaxant effect on skeletal muscles (Jones, 1987). Furthermore, in smaller doses nicotine has a stimulating effect on some measures of central nervous system arousal, such as EEG, but there are depressant effects on the same measures with higher doses. Gilbert's (1979) review showed that the user's personality enters into the picture as well. One study he reported showed that smoking produced cortical arousal in people who were defined as extraverts, but that smoking had an opposite effect in introverts.

Perceived arousal It should be kept in mind that, regardless of the physiological effects of nicotine, the psychological effects of the drug often are a decrease in negative emotional experience and an increase in feelings of tranquility and pleasure. Such drug experiences depend in part on the dose of nicotine taken and the corresponding physiological effects of the drug. However, as with other drugs, history of nicotine use, the setting, and personality of the user interact to produce the experience of nicotine effects. For example, part of the sedating psychological effects of smoking are due to the user's association of successfully coping with stress while ingesting the drug (Abrams & Wilson, 1986). Another factor to consider is the association of nicotine use with pleasant social situations like parties. Many other "secondary" (associated) effects of nicotine use exist and can contribute to the user's perception, at certain times, that the drug has calming effects.

Reduction of Hunger and Body Weight

Some important effects of nicotine on body weight contribute to smoking motivation. First, though the evidence is not consistent, smokers tend to consume fewer calories than do nonsmokers. When a reduction in caloric intake does occur it is probably due to nicotine's effect of increasing blood glucose levels. Other studies indicate that smokers and former smokers tend to weigh less than nonsmokers. In this regard, nicotine increases consumption of oxygen in the body, which results in a higher metabolic rate. Both findings together point to nicotine use as a device for weight control, which is highly reinforcing to some users (Russell, 1976; West & Russell, 1985). And it is well–known that quitting smoking is associated with weight gain, which most people do not find too positive. However, at least part of this gain is due to the body's efforts to get back to normal in its efficiency of using calories. Research indicates that quitters do not necessarily consume more calories compared to their intake when they were active smokers. Whatever the reasons, weight gain following smoking cessation generally is not considered pleasant and often is a reason for returning to smoking (Abrams & Wilson, 1986).

TREATMENT OF CIGARETTE SMOKING

In this last section on nicotine we consider ways to stop tobacco smoking. Note that nicotine is the only drug for which we consider treatment outside of Chapter 15, where we study treatment of other drugs and their misuse. This is because such a large amount has been written on the subject compared to other nonalcohol drugs. Furthermore, treatments for stopping smoking have been at the center of health professionals' and the public's attention, due to the health hazards of smoking.

Model of the Course of Cigarette Smoking

Lichtenstein (1982) presented a useful summary of what has been discovered about smoking and what affects the behavior at different times during the average person's smoking "career." You will recognize some of the smoking determinants from material already presented. Lichtenstein's summary, which he presented in the form of a **stage model,** is shown in Table 6–2. What is considered to play a relatively more important part in smoking varies according to the stage of the smoking career. Starting smoking is viewed primarily as a result of social and psychological incentives or motives. The same types of motives, although different in specific content, are seen as important in stopping smoking. For continuing and resuming cigarette smoking, however, the pharmacological properties of nicotine assume a major role. Resumption of smoking pertains to the problem of **relapse,** which you will see is a major problem in the long–term success of treatments of smoking, and of alcohol and drug use in general.

Stage model
A stage model of behavior usually refers to its development. Stage models are based on the idea that development is marked by discrete steps or "stages," each of which has unique features or characteristics.

Relapse
A term from physical disease, relapse means return to a previous state of illness from one of health. As applied to smoking, it means the smoker resumes smoking after having abstained for some amount of time.

Table 6–2

Model of the Stages of Cigarette Smoking and the Factors that Affect Smoking at Different Times During the Average Person's Smoking "Career"

Starting Smoking	Continuing Smoking	Stopping Smoking	Resuming Smoking
Availability	Pharmacological Effects of Nicotine	Health Consequences	Withdrawal Symptoms
Curiosity		Expense	Stress and Frustration
Rebelliousness	Immediate Positive Consequences of Smoking	Social Support for Not Smoking	Social Pressure
Anticipation of Adulthood			Alcohol Use
Social Confidence		Self–mastery	
Social Pressure	Cues in the Environment	Aesthetics	
Modeling: Peers, Siblings, Parents	Avoidance or Escape of Withdrawal Symptoms	Examples to Others	
Media			

Note: Adapted with permission from Lichtenstein, E., & R. Brown, (1980), Smoking cessation methods: Review and recommendations, In W.R. Miller (Ed.), *The addictive behaviors* (pp 169–206). NY: Pergamon Press, and from the authors. The variables listed in each column of the table are those seen as determinants (factors contributing to) of smoking at a given stage of a smoker's career.

The "stopping" and "resuming" stages of Lichtenstein's (1982) model are most pertinent to the treatment of cigarette smoking. We will examine how the determinants of smoking at these stages have influenced the content of formal treatments and their long-term effectiveness. Before we get to that, however, there is the question of whether formal treatments of cigarette smoking are ever needed.

Are Formal Treatments of Cigarette Smoking Necessary?

Schelling (1986) provided some data to help address this question. He estimates currently that there are 90 million people in the United States who have smoked. Of these, 35 million have quit smoking, and 40–45 million have tried to quit but were unable to. These estimates raise two points: The vast majority of smokers want to quit, and a substantial percentage of them do. How do those who quit do it? We know that most smokers quit on their own (for example Zusy, 1987). It seems that formal treatments for smoking may not be necessary.

However, other information must be considered. Although 95% of smokers quit on their own, they tend to succeed only after multiple attempts. Perhaps you have heard of the comment attributed to Mark Twain: "Quitting smoking is easy; I've done it many times." Indeed, with or without formal treatment, success at stopping smoking is more likely with more previous tries at quitting. In this case, practice may make perfect. Another important statistic which we discuss in more detail in Chapter 15 is the rate of "spontaneous remission." Briefly, this refers to the rate of "cure" (in other words, stopping smoking) during a given time period without any formal treatment. Although data on spontaneous remission are basic to evaluating treatment effectiveness, they unfortunately are extremely hard to collect. For cigarette smoking, Abrams and Wilson (1986) estimated that the rate of spontaneous remission ranges from 3 percent to 14 percent. Formal treatments have to do better than the rate of spontaneous remission in order to prove their worth.

Treatment and the socio–economic costs of smoking Another set of statistics to consider in deciding whether formal treatments of smoking are necessary concern the economic and social costs of cigarette smoking. We alluded to these costs earlier in this chapter. In summary, costs in medical treatment and lost productivity due to smoking patients have done in their lifetimes equaled about $22 billion in 1985. The financial figures do not begin to reflect the human suffering of patients and their families that goes with contracting cancer, heart disease, and other diseases associated with chronic tobacco use. Wynder and Hoffmann (1979) argued that if a smoking treatment resulted in a nicotine abstinence rate of 20% to 25% for one year after treatment ended, then that treatment would be worth its while from both health and economic standpoints.

How Effective Are Treatments of Cigarette Smoking?

Programs for stopping smoking focus on controlling nicotine withdrawal symptoms, breaking the habitual motor behavior involved in smoking, and learning skills to cope with the emotions, thoughts, and situations in which smokers say they use cigarettes to help them. People who stop smoking permanently have learned these skills well, have incentives such as health to abstain, and have help from family, friends, and others who care about them for staying off cigarettes (Abrams & Wilson, 1986; Jones, 1987).

Minimal and full smoking treatment programs   Abrams and Wilson (1986) divided stop smoking programs into two types, minimal and full treatment programs. The major difference between minimal and full programs is the amount of professional contact. Minimal programs do not involve the continual assistance of professionals or organizations and require only specific materials and occasional consultation. In contrast, full treatment programs require ongoing contact with professional staff. Regardless of the type of treatment, the most efficient treatment goal is total abstinence from nicotine. Reduction of smoking to "controlled" amounts does not seem feasible for people who request treatment.

Success in minimal treatment programs   Examples of minimal treatment programs include mass–media advertisements against smoking like those sponsored by the American Cancer Society, self-help books, and brief contacts with a physician in the private office or hospital setting. Results of studies of these types of treatments show quitting rates up to the mid-20% range. These outcomes are significant in view of the low costs and small amount of professional time required for their implementation. That such outcomes are possible should not be too surprising in view of the high percentage of former smokers who quit on their own. However, researchers have also shown minimal treatment programs do not work too well with the heavier, more nicotine–dependent smoker. These individuals are more likely to succeed in more intensive, full treatment programs.

Success in full treatment programs   Most of the data we have on full treatment involve applying techniques to stop the smoking habit and changing how smokers think and feel about smoking as an effective method of gaining pleasure and relieving stress. The smoker usually is taught skills to help him or her handle settings associated with smoking. Such programs are called multicomponent behavioral treatments.

Behavioral treatments for smoking have averaged 15% to 20% abstinence rates at the end of six months to a year, and the best rates reported have been in the 35% to 50% range. While the latter percentages are significant, the problem of resumption of smoking remains. For example, Abrams and Wilson (1986) reported that in 1980 72% of the smokers who had quit relapsed within six months.

Why can't smokers stay off cigarettes?   A major reason smokers have such a problem staying off cigarettes is the craving they experience for nicotine whey they stop smoking. This implies that if nicotine could somehow be used in the treatment of smoking, there would be a better chance of quitting for good. Such a treatment has been developed in the form of chewing gum that contains nicotine (Jarvis, 1983). The use of this gum adds substantially to one–year outcome success rates, especially in combination with behavioral treatment programs. It seems nicotine gum reduces nicotine craving (West & Schneider, 1987), which gives the smoker more opportunity to strengthen ways other than smoking of coping with events and situations of everyday life. Fortunately, few patients have trouble with becoming dependent on the nicotine gum they were prescribed for treatment. Therefore, its use seems safe and effective in dealing with the large problem of physical dependence on nicotine in the treatment of smoking.

CONTEMPORARY ISSUE BOX 6–2
One Doctor's Way to Treat Smoking

A general practitioner physician in Beaver, West Virginia, has adopted an unusual method to help others stop smoking, a method that might be classified as one of our "minimal treatment" programs. This doctor's minimal treatment is no treatment at all: he refuses to give nonemergency medical care to prospective patients who refuse to stop smoking. The doctor's reasoning is that giving these people care only encourages them to continue a lethal habit. For example, previously patients came to the doctor for treatment of severe lung problems. They got better eventually, so much so that they resumed smoking! The doctor also questions the ethics of designating a patient as healthy when he or she is a regular cigarette smoker. He reports that twenty-five of his patients have quit smoking because of his stand against treating their medical problems if they continued their habit.

Although some physicians admire this way of dealing with smokers, some are highly critical of it. What do you think of their arguments against the approach? If doctors can refuse to treat smokers, why shouldn't they be free not to treat people who have other health threatening disorders, such as obesity and alcohol dependence, that seem to be based on voluntary behaviors? Is it ethical for a physican to refuse to treat anybody? If all physicians adopted the antismoker treatment stand, where would the smoker get medical care?

NICOTINE: CONCLUSIONS

Nicotine is a powerfully reinforcing drug to humans and can be quickly addicting. Nicotine does have some "adaptive" acute effects, such as improved sensory and cognitive functioning, but most attention has been paid to the health consequences of chronic nicotine use. As a result, the emphasis today is on how to stop the public from using nicotine in a damaging way. The best way to do this is by continuing the information campaigns that have resulted in a decline of the prevalence of smoking and other use of tobacco in the United States. Along these lines, programs aimed at youth who have not begun to use tobacco are the best bet, because once tobacco use starts it is hard to stop. Tobacco use prevention programs with promise are being developed. However, a major counterforce to prevention programs is tobacco industry advertising. Tobacco companies in the United States spend almost $3 billion a year on advertising compaigns (and tobacco products cannot be advertised on television *or* radio). We discussed the image of smokeless tobacco products among teenagers. For adults as well, advertising strengthens the positive associations that go along with smoking and other tobacco use, and play a large part in making smoking cessation such a hard job.

CONTEMPORARY ISSUE BOX 6–3
The "Smokeless" Cigarette

An alternative "smokeless" cigarette has been developed. Although the manufacturer made no claims of less health risk to the smoker who uses the product, the smokeless cigarette did seem to alleviate some of the problems associated with passive smoking.

The smokeless cigarette first appeared on the market in 1987 with the product "Favor." Favor, however, fell into disfavor quickly because the Federal Drug Administration decided it was a "drug delivery system" and should be regulated accordingly. This means the smokeless cigarette contraption could deliver drugs other than nicotine, such as crack. As such, its regulation would have to be by the Food and Drug Administration instead of the Bureau of Alcohol, Tobacco, and Firearms, which regulates other nicotine products. Favor was then removed from the market and has not been heard of commercially since.

Then in 1988, another smokeless cigarette called "Premier" was test marketed. Premier was not really a cigarette at all, but just looked like one. Instead of burning leaf tobacco as with traditional cigarettes, the smokeless cigarette had a charcoal tip that heated a metal chamber filled with pellets of nicotine that were refined from leaf tobacco. The pellets were mixed with nutmeg for flavoring, and glycerol. When the glycerol was heated it formed an aerosol that the smoker inhaled as "smoke." Leaf tobacco was used in the chamber but only as insulation. The tobacco was never consumed.

Unfortunately for efforts at inventing alternatives to the traditional cigarette, the Premier efforts were also stymied. An essential problem was its bad odor and taste. One writer (a smoker) in *Vogue* magazine likened the odor to that of opening a grave on a warm day. A consumer in one of Premier's test market cities said using the product was similar to smoking a stick of plastic. These are not exactly the words that smokers of traditional cigarettes use to describe their tobacco pleasures.

Other problems arose, too. In January, 1989 the American Medical Association (AMA) argued that Premier should be taken off the market and regulated by the FDA as a drug. In this regard, the AMA thought that similar to Favor, Premier actually is a nicotine delivery system. Moreover, in early 1989, two researchers at the National Institute on Drug Abuse published statements in the AMA's influential *Journal of the American Medical Association* that the Premier apparatus can be used to smoke crack. Of course, this idea alarmed everybody who was trying to put a halt to drug abuse in the United States.

The adversity proved to be too much for Premier, and in March 1989 the manufacturer decided to take it off the test market. The cost was about $325 million in product development and promotion. Although this is a substantial setback, the potential loss to the many people who still smoke would be greater if it caused the tobacco industry to stop trying to create new alternatives to the traditional cigarette.

The direction of the future is toward the expansion of minimal treatments. Such treatments are the best way to capture the widest segment of the population who smoke. For example, new minimal treatments at work sites already have proved to be an effective way to help people to stop smoking. The third area for future research is to continue to refine and strengthen full treatments for the heavy, dependent smoker. The combination of behavioral and pharmacological treatment seems to work best for these individuals. Improvements in their efficacy can be realized, for example, by discovering what combination of treatment components works best for different types of smokers (for example, Hughes, 1986). Finally, there probably always will be a percentage of people who simply do not want to stop smoking. Developing a less hazardous cigarette that such people will use would ease the serious health consequences of chronic tobacco use. The reduced tar and nicotine cigarettes dominating today's market are only part of the answer,

because smokers compensate for the reduction to some degree by smoking
more cigarettes.

CAFFEINE

Background

Caffeine, along with theophylline and theobromine, are three chemically-
related compounds that occur naturally in over sixty species of plants. These
compounds are called the methylxanthines and are classified as alkaloids.
An alkaloid is a compound that is of botanical origin, contains nitrogen, and
is physiologically active (Levenson & Bick, 1977; Syed, 1976). Because of
its overwhelming popularity, we will emphasize caffeine in our discussion.

HISTORY OF CAFFEINE USE

The plants that contain the methylxanthines have been used to make beverages popular with humans since ancient times. Many stories, some mythical, attempt to explain how these beverages were created. For example,
coffee supposedly was discovered in Arabia by a holy man. It seems that
goats in the herd had been jumping around at night instead of sleeping,
apparently because they had been nibbling on the beans of the coffee plant.
The holy man got a brilliant idea that beans from the same plant could help
him endure his long nights of prayer. It was a small next step to the first cup
of coffee (Blum, 1984).

Caffeine is found in some of our most popular beverages and foods,
including coffee, different teas, cola, and chocolate. If you recall from the
section on the history of nicotine use, during the time of Columbus, Europe
knew nothing of these caffeine-containing substances. In fact, the only psychoactive substance that fifteenth–century Europeans did seem to know
about was alcohol. However, this all changed with the ventures of the
explorers and others from Europe. In Arabia, Turkey, and Ethiopia explorers
found coffee. In China they found tea. In West Africa they found the kola
nut. In Mexico and much of Central and South America they found the cacao
plant, which is the source of chocolate. Other sources of teas were discovered in parts of North and South America. The travelers brought their discoveries home to Europe and then spread them across other continents.

As with other drugs, caffeine was not always well received by societies
when it was introduced. For example, when the Mohammedans tried caffeine to stay awake during their long vigils, the orthodox priests were not
pleased with the innovation. However, official punishments and attempts to
kill coffee trees were not enough to stop coffee from becoming as popular
among Arabian Moslems as tea is to the Chinese. Similar negative sanctions

for coffee drinking in Egypt and Europe had as much success as the approach had in Arabia. Today, the production of coffee, the major single source of the world's caffeine consumption, is a multi-billion dollar industry that keeps millions of people in about 60 countries employed (Brecher, 1972; Levenson & Bick, 1977).

PREVALENCE OF CAFFEINE CONSUMPTION

What Are the Sources of Caffeine?

Most people take in their caffeine orally, as is apparent in Table 6–3. This table includes the major sources of caffeine and their concentrations of the drug. Several features about sources of caffeine are highlighted by the table. First, there is a wide range of caffeine products that adults and children consume every day. In one survey of 401 New York state employees only eleven of the respondents said they had consumed no caffeine in the last three days (Weidner & Istvan, 1985). Compounds synthesized to treat different medical problems also contain caffeine, even though the latter drug is not always of direct benefit in alleviating the problem symptoms. Finally, Table 6–3 does not contain another source of caffeine—illicit street drugs (Gilbert, 1984). For example, products that contain caffeine, such as aspirin, frequently are used as filler and thus contaminate cocaine and heroin sold on the street, as discussed in Chapter 5.

Caffeine, nicotine, and alcohol have been seen as having a greater effect on human civilization than have all other nonmedical psychoactive substances combined (Levenson & Bick, 1977). Caffeine stands out among these three power hitters because of the ubiquity of its use around the world and because it is a "cradle to grave drug" (Kenney & Darragh, 1985, p. 278). That is, caffeine commonly is used nonmedically by young children and adults alike, which is true of no other psychoactive substance.

What Are the Prevalence Rates?

Good estimates of the prevalence of caffeine consumption are not easy to get, because there have been few surveys done of the caliber we have cited for other drugs. However, it is fortunate that reasonable estimates of caffeine consumption in different societies can be derived from trade data, such as coffee bean sales, tea leaves exports, and cocoa exports.

Table 6–4 shows per capita beverage and chocolate consumption in the United States in selected years during 1960–1982. These products constitute the sources of virtually all of the average United States caffeine consumption. The major point to be drawn from Table 6–4 is the decline over the years in coffee consumption and the marked increase in the consumption of soft drinks, which almost quadrupled during the time span sampled.

Table 6–3

Sources of Caffeine and Their Concentrations

Source	Concentration
Beverages	
Brewed coffee	100–150 mg/180 ml
Instant coffee	60–80 mg/180 ml
Decaffeinated coffee	3–5 mg/180 ml
Brewed tea	40–100 mg/180 ml
Pepsi Cola	16 mg/240 ml
Coca Cola	26 mg/240 ml
Food	
Milk chocolate	6 mg/oz
Cooking chocolate	35 mg/oz
Prescription Medications	
APCs (aspirin, Phenacetin, and caffeine)	32 mg/tablet
Cafergot	100 mg/tablet
Darvon compound	32 mg/tablet
Fiorinal	40 mg/tablet
Migral	50 mg/tablet
Over-the-Counter Preparations	
Anacin, aspirin compound, Bromo–Seltzer	32 mg/tablet
Cope, Easy–Mens, Empirin compound, Midol	32 mg/tablet
Vanquish	32 mg/tablet
Excedrin	60 mg/tablet
Pre Mens	66 mg/tablet
Bromoquinine	15 mg/tablet
Sinarest	30 mg/tablet
Pristan	30 mg/tablet
NoDoz	100 mg/tablet
ViVarin	100–200 mg/tablet

Note: Adapted with permission from a table in Sawyer, D.A., Julia, H.L., and Turin, A.C. (1982), Caffeine and human behavior: Arousal, anxiety, and performance effects. *Journal of Behavioral Medicine, 5,* 415–439 (Plenum Press); and in Kenny, M., & Darragh, A. (1985), Central effects of caffeine in man, in S.D. Iverson (ed), *Psychopharmacology: Recent advances and future prospects,* pp. 278–288 (Oxford University Press).

Not only did per capita soft drink consumption skyrocket, but prevalence did too. In 1962, 33% of the population drank soft drinks, compared to 53% in 1982 (Gilbert, 1984).

The stability in tea and cocoa consumption is in stark contrast to the changes in soft drink and coffee drinking. Changes in soft drink and coffee use patterns seem to be a result of substituting soft drinks for coffee, especially among younger people. No one knows for sure why this substitution occurred.

The question of most direct interest to us is what do these daily doses of caffeine translate into? Table 6–5 addresses this question. We have included

Table 6–4

Per Capita Beverage and Chocolate Consumption in Selected Years during 1960–1982

	Year						
Source	*1960*	*1965*	*1970*	*1975*	*1977*	*1980*	*1982*
Coffee (kg)	7.2	6.7	6.2	5.6	4.3	4.7	4.6
Tea (kg)	.3	.3	.3	.4	.4	.4	.4
Cocoa (kg)	1.6	1.8	1.8	1.5	1.5	1.5	1.7
Soft drinks* (liters)	45	61	85	103	125	142	149

Note: Amounts of coffee, tea, and cocoa are in kilograms of fresh equivalent, such as green (unroasted) coffee beans, tea leaves, and cocoa beans. Soft drink quantities are in liters of beverage. Table adapted from Gilbert (1984), and published with permission from Alan R. Liss, Inc.
*About 75 percent of the soft drinks sold in the United States contain caffeine.

data on the United States and, for comparison, the world, Canada, and the United Kingdom. The United States per capita caffeine consumption is considerably greater than the world average, but modest compared to that of the United Kingdom. Furthermore, although coffee consumption in the United States has declined in recent years, coffee still is the source of well over half of the United States caffeine consumption.

Table 6–5

Estimates of Caffeine Use for the World, United States, Canada, and the United Kingdom, 1981–1982

		Per Capita Consumption	
	Caffeine Source	*(grams/yr)*	*(milligrams/day)*
World	Coffee	14	38
	Tea	11	30
	Other	1	2
	Total	**26**	**70**
United States	Coffee	46	125
	Tea	13	35
	Soft drinks	13	35
	Cocoa	2	4
	Other	5	12
	Total	**79**	**211**
Canada	Coffee	47	128
	Tea	29	79
	Soft drinks	6	16
	Cocoa	1	3
	Other	5	12
	Total	**88**	**238**
United Kingdom	Coffee	32	84
	Tea	118	320
	Other	15	40
	Total	**165**	**444**

Note: "Other" category includes caffeine in medicines and other sources, such as yerba mate tea. Table adapted from Gilbert (1984), and published with permission from Alan R. Liss, Inc.

TOXIC EFFECTS OF CAFFEINE USE

Because of its widespread use in societies all over the world, caffeine's effects on physical and psychological functioning have long been studied. In this section we consider research on caffeine's toxic effects. Paradoxically, all the research on caffeine's toxic effects has not yet yielded good estimates of the prevalence of such effects. In any case, there are findings of interest about caffeine's acute and chronic effects.

Acute Toxic Effects of Caffeine

Caffeine intoxication, or caffeinism, has received a lot of attention recently by health professionals. An example of a case of caffeinism will give you an idea of the phenomenon (adapted from Greden, 1974, pp. 1090–1091):

> A 27-year-old nurse requested an evaluation at an outpatient medical clinic because of lightheadedness, tremulousness, breathlessness, headache, and irregular heartbeat occurring sporadically about two to three times a day. The symptoms had developed gradually over a three-week period. The nurse said there were no precipitating stresses. The physical exam was within normal limits, except that an electrocardiogram showed premature ventricular contractions.
>
> At her final session with the evaluating internist the nurse was referred to an outpatient psychiatric clinic with the diagnosis of anxiety reaction, probably to fear that her husband would be transferred by the military to be stationed in Viet Nam. However, the nurse did not accept this diagnosis and searched for a dietary cause of her symptoms. After about ten days she had linked her symptoms to coffee consumption. With the recent purchase of a new coffee pot the nurse had been drinking ten to twelve cups of strong black coffee a day—more than 1000 mg of caffeine. She stopped drinking coffee, and within thirty-six hours virtually all of her symptoms disappeared, including the cardiovascular irregularities (Published with permission of American Psychiatric Press, Inc.).

Several points about this case illustration are worth noting. First, the symptoms occurred in the nurse apparently as a result of her consuming more than 1000 mg of caffeine a day. However, as with other caffeine effects, people differ in how much caffeine they can ingest before experiencing symptoms of intoxication. For example, caffeinism has been reported following consumption of as little as 250 mg of caffeine in a day, which is not much more than the average for adults in the United States. Generally, ingesting caffeine at the rate of 600 mg a day greatly increases the chances of developing caffeinism (Kenny & Darragh, 1985).

Consuming more than 1000 mg of caffeine increases the risk of experiencing even more severe toxic symptoms, including muscle twitching, rambling flow of thought and speech, cardiac arrhythmia, periods of inexhaustability, and psychomotor agitation (American Psychiatric Association, 1987). Other symptoms that have been reported are ringing in the ears and seeing flashes of light. The lethal dose of caffeine when it is taken orally is about 10 grams for adults and 100 mg/kg for children (Leonard, Watson, & Mohs, 1987). The adult lethal dose is equal to about 75 cups of coffee, 125 cups of tea, 200 colas, or 100 No Doz tables. Six deaths due to caffeine overdose have been reported.

Chronic Toxic Effects of Caffeine

The chronic toxic effects of caffeine have been studied for major problems, including birth defects, cancer, myocardial infarction, and serum cholesterol level (Abbott, 1986). During the past two decades, different estimates of risk of occurrence of these problems have yielded the general opinion that, in the doses of caffeine that humans consume, there is no increased risk of birth defects, cancer, or myocardial infarction. No clear evidence exists for a causal relationship between caffeine consumption and peptic ulcer (Council on Scientific Affairs, 1984). However, research has shown an association between serum cholesterol levels and quantity of caffeine consumption: as one level goes up, the other one also tends to. This effect seems to apply particularly to women. Level of serum cholesterol is related to atherosclerosis.

Quantity of caffeine consumption also is associated with the occurrence of less major symptoms that are experienced more commonly. Abbott (1986) cited a survey of 4,558 Australians that concerned caffeine ingestion and the occurrence of indigestion, palpitations, tremor, headache and insomnia. Respondents were more likely to report these symptoms the more caffeine they ingested (the average consumption for the sample was 240 mg a day).

Summary of Caffeine Toxicity

The general consensus is that caffeine is a relatively safe drug in the doses that adults in the United States typically consume. For example, the American Medical Association's Council on Scientific Affairs (1984) has recommended against labeling of caffeine products. However, in view of the problem of caffeinism and of the association between the experience of more minor symptoms and caffeine consumption, it has been recommended that caffeine consumption be moderated.

The data on caffeine effects in infants and children are far more sketchy. It is notable that caffeine passes the placental barrier, so pregnant women are cautioned to decrease their caffeine consumption. Relatedly, more studies are needed of caffeine effects in infants under six months old, who metabolize the drug much more slowly than does the rest of the population. In this respect, caffeine sometimes is used to treat **spontaneous sleep apnea** in infants and young children. Recommendations also have been made that caffeine consumption be moderated in children, some of whom consume considerable amounts of the drug from soda and cocoa products.

Spontaneous sleep apnea A sudden cessation of breathing that may occur during sleep in infants.

The long-term effects of caffeine consumption in children have not been specified and are an important topic for future research (Abbott, 1986).

PHARMACOLOGY OF CAFFEINE

Sites of Action, Absorption, and Distribution

Caffeine is rapidly absorbed from the gastrointestinal tract and distributed throughout the body. The drug quickly reaches the brain, as it can pass the blood-brain barrier. The half-life of caffeine in the blood varies widely among people and ranges from about 2½ to 7½ hours (Blum, 1984; Leonard, Watson, & Mohs, 1987). Peak levels of caffeine after taking a dose of it occur in fifteen to forty-five minutes, depending on the source. For example, one study (Marks & Kelly, 1973) involved three healthy men who were given an average of 155 mg of caffeine in the form of Coca Cola, tea, or coffee. The men's plasma levels of caffeine were then charted for two hours. The peak levels of caffeine were higher for tea and coffee and were reached within thirty minutes of ingestion. The peak for Coca Cola was lower than that of the other two beverages and did not occur until about an hour passed. After two hours the plasma caffeine level for the cola was higher than for tea or coffee and still at a level comparable to its peak.

Caffeine primarily acts on the central nervous system, but its distribution throughout the body is shown by its other actions: contraction of striated muscle, including the heart; relaxation of smooth muscle, especially coronary arteries, uterus, and bronchi; diuretic effect on the kidneys; at higher doses, a stimulatory effect on respiration; elevation of basal metabolism; and various endocrine and enzymatic effects (Levenson & Bick, 1977). The range of effects explains the years of concern about the potential toxic effects of chronic caffeine use on major organs and systems in the body.

Metabolism and Excretion

The liver does most of the metabolizing of caffeine. The drug is excreted almost entirely by the kidneys, less than 10% in pure form and the rest in metabolites. Very small proportions of caffeine also are excreted in the feces, saliva, semen, and breast milk. Of interest is the variance among people in caffeine metabolism and clearance from the body. For example, rates of these processes are slower in people who have been using caffeine over a shorter period of time (Leonard, Watson, & Mohs, 1987). Other differences in metabolism and excretion are caused by liver disease (it slows the process), pregnancy (slows), and use of oral contraceptives (slows). On the other hand, if you are a cigarette smoker you metabolize caffeine more quickly. Other therapeutic drugs interact with caffeine to increase or decrease its metabolism and excretion.

TOLERANCE AND DEPENDENCE

Caffeine long was considered a strange drug because of its unorthodox potential for inducing tolerance and physical dependence (Gilbert, 1976). Evidence of a distinct caffeine withdrawal syndrome has been available for some time, but for tolerance the data have been far less clear. The usual picture for drugs is the reverse—they can induce tolerance without dependence, but rarely dependence without tolerance.

Caffeine Withdrawal

The caffeine withdrawal symptom most consistently reported is the headache. Other withdrawal symptoms have been documented in one of a series of studies by Goldstein and his colleagues (Goldstein, Kaizer, & Whitty, 1969). Some of the symptoms of caffeine abstinence their subjects reported were depression, decreased alertness, less contentment and relaxed mood, decreased activity and energy, greater sleepiness and drowsiness, and increased irritability. Currently it is thought that physical dependence to caffeine develops in from six to fifteen days of consuming 600 mg of caffeine or more a day. Withdrawal can range from mild to severe in intensity and begins within twelve to twenty-four hours of cessation of caffeine use. It may last about a week (Griffiths & Woodson, 1988).

Tolerance

The contradictions that abound in the experimental findings about tolerance to caffeine are probably a result of poor research methods, such as not specifying caffeine use patterns in subjects (Curatolo & Robertson, 1987). In general, tolerance to caffeine's effects on renal function, sleep (see below) and other physiological functions probably does develop.

Another reason for the confusion about caffeine tolerance is ignoring what may be differences among people in what is an "acceptable" level of caffeine. Differences between high and low caffeine users in the acute effects of a dose of caffeine in children and adults have been attributed to differences in degree of acquired tolerance. However, some better controlled studies offer another explanation: one reason people are heavier or lighter users is their individual ability to tolerate caffeine. This interpretation is always an alternative in studies that fail to specify long-term patterns of caffeine consumption in the experimental participants. The best way to do this would be to measure caffeine use and effects in the same people over a period of time.

THERAPEUTIC USES OF CAFFEINE

Table 6–3 shows that caffeine is used in a variety of prescription and over-the-counter medications. Therefore, caffeine is very much a part of the med-

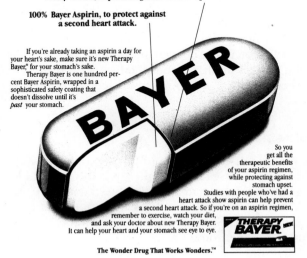

New Therapy Bayer.
State Of The Art,
For Your Heart.

Safety-coated, to protect against stomach upset.

**100% Bayer Aspirin, to protect against
a second heart attack.**

If you're already taking an aspirin a day for
your heart's sake, make sure it's new Therapy
Bayer,* for your stomach's sake.
    Therapy Bayer is one hundred per-
cent Bayer Aspirin, wrapped in a
sophisticated safety coating that
doesn't dissolve until it's
past your stomach.

So you
get all the
therapeutic benefits
of your aspirin regimen,
while protecting against
stomach upset.
Studies with people who've had a
heart attack show aspirin can help prevent
a second heart attack. So if you're on an aspirin regimen,
remember to exercise, watch your diet,
and ask your doctor about new Therapy Bayer.
It can help your heart and your stomach see eye to eye.

THERAPY BAYER NEW

The Wonder Drug That Works Wonders.™

Figure 6–7 Recent research relating the use of aspirin to lowered risk of heart attack has resulted in the increasing numbers of Americans who take aspirin daily upon the advice of their physicians. Caffeine has a major presence in most aspirin products and in many other medications, including over-the-counter and prescribed compounds (see chapter 13 for discussion of the use of aspirin and the risk of heart attack).

ications used to treat a range of ailments. In fact, the other two methylxanthines also have therapeutic value. You can better appreciate this by looking at Table 6–6, which shows xanthine is used to achieve a preferred pharmacological action. The differences among the xanthines in what effect is best produced is based on slight differences in their chemical structure. For example, aminophylline, a cardiac and bronchial dilator that contains theophylline, is used to treat both cardiac and bronchial asthma. Caffeine is the

Table 6–6
Methylxanthine Compounds and Desired Pharmacological Action

Desired Action	*Preferred Compound*
Cerebral stimulation	Caffeine (coffee)
Coronary dilation	Theophylline (tea)
Diuresis	Theobromine (cocoa)
Respiratory stimulant for premature infants	Caffeine

Note: This table is taken from Graham (1978). Products in parentheses are sources of the indicated compound. From *Nutrition Reviews,* 36 (1978):101. Used with permission of the International Life Sciences Institute-Nutrition Foundation.

drug with the most presence, as it is part of a number of remedies for head-aches and colds. Its mild stimulant properties help to counteract some of the side effects of medications for those ailments (Gilbert, 1976). Caffeine also is contained in appetite suppressant medications for its diuretic effects (Snyder & Sklar, 1984).

ACUTE EFFECTS OF CAFFEINE IN HUMANS

We have already referred to some of caffeine's many acute effects in the discussion of caffeine toxicity. For many years caffeine's effects were thought to be a result of the drug's inhibition of the enzyme phosphodiesterase. This enzyme breaks down cyclic AMP. Inhibiting phosphodiesterase results in the increased action of catecholamines, which (as discussed in Chapter 3) are neurotransmitters.

The Adenosine Hypothesis

The phosphodiesterase theory fell out of favor following the realization that caffeine has such action only at doses much higher than the typical one required for pharmacological effects in humans, which is about 200 mg (Snyder & Sklar, 1984). The explanation for caffeine's acute effects most accepted now is the adenosine hypothesis. Adenosine is a chemical that the body produces and is an inhibitory neurotransmitter. Caffeine and the other methylxanthines occupy adenosine receptors and then block the action of that transmitter.

What does this say for caffeine's effects? Table 6–7 provides an answer in listing the contrasting effects of caffeine and adenosine. The chemicals have

Table 6–7

Opposite Pharmacological Effects of Caffeine and Adenosine

Factor	Adenosine	Caffeine
Blood Pressure	Decrease	Increase
Renin (a protein produced in the kidney) release	Decrease	Increase
Catecholamine release	Decrease	Increase
Urine output	Decrease	Increase
CNS activity	Decrease	Increase
Decomposition of Lipids (Lipolysis)	Decrease	Increase
Bronchial tone	Decrease	Increase
Stimulation of the intestines	Decrease	Increase

Note: This table was adapted from Leonard, T.K., Watson, R.R., & Mohs, M.E. (1987): The effects of caffeine on various body systems: A review. Copyright the American Dietetic Association. Reprinted by permission from *Journal of the American Dietetic Association,* Vol. 87: 1048, 1987. Permission to reprint also granted from *Primary Cardiology* 1987; 10:104–110. © 1984, Physicians World Communications Group.

opposite pharmacological effects, which lends credence to the adenosine hypothesis of caffeine effects.

Physiological Effects of Caffeine

Table 6–7 leads directly to listing of caffeine's major physiological effects. These include diuresis, stimulation of the heart, stimulation of the CNS, relaxation of smooth muscles, stimulation of gastric acid, and elevation of free fatty acid and glucose (Graham, 1978). These acute effects are similar to some of the toxic effects of caffeine. Several authors have pointed out that caffeine's toxic effects are extreme versions of the drug's acute effects at lower doses.

Acute Behavioral and Psychological Effects of Caffeine

Mood   The CNS stimulation action of caffeine elevates mood. This was documented in a quote from a will of Dr. William Dunlap, who died in 1848. Dr. Dunlap wrote, "I leave John Caddle a silver teapot, to the end that he may drink tea therefrom to comfort him under the affliction of a slatternly wife" (cited in Gilbert, 1976, p. 77). The acute mood elevating effects of caffeine account for much of the popularity that coffee and tea have as morning wake-up beverages. It also has been speculated that people who are afflicted with significant depression "medicate" themselves by using caffeine products. According to the adenosine hypothesis, caffeine blocks adenosine's inhibition of cells in the brain that underlie alertness and upbeat mood (Konner, 1988).

Caffeine and performance   Caffeine's effects on human task performance are complicated. Table 6–8 gives you a list of some of the major performance effects of caffeine. The table shows that the range of caffeine effects is wide, and many of them are in a stimulation direction. It should be noted that one of the major ways caffeine improves task performance is by decreasing fatigue and increasing vigilance, so that over time performance does not drop below what is typical for a person. Such action is in contrast to an effect that pushes performance above what is normal for a person. In addition, the complexity of caffeine's effects is illustrated in the choice reaction time task. Caffeine impairs the decision making part of the task but improves the motor component. The drug's effects are different even for different components of the same task. You also will note there is some inconsistency in the findings about caffeine effects. This is probably due in part to the different methods experimenters have used. Another reason is that caffeine's effects depend not only on the drug's pharmacological action but also on the dose of the drug, the setting in which it is used, and the personality of the user. This is represented in Table 6–8 by findings such as in verbal test accuracy (the last entry in the table), which caffeine affects

Table 6–8

Caffeine's Acute Effects on Human Performance

Performance Variable	*Effect of Caffeine*
Physical Endurance	
Bicycle ergometer	
-Fixed load	Increases
-Progressive load	No effect
Motor Skills	
Rapidity and accuracy	Decreases, higher doses
	Increases, lower doses
Eye-hand coordination	Decreases
Vigilance	
Visual	
-Night driving analogue	Increases
-Target scanning	
low coffee users	Decreases
high coffee users	No effect
Reaction Time	
Simple reaction time	Decreases (speeds up)
Choice reaction time	
-Decision time	Increases (slows down)
-Motor time	Decreases
Verbal Tests	
Graduate Record Exam Practice Test	
-Speed and accuracy	
extraverts	Increases, with higher doses
introverts	First increases, then decreases, with higher doses
Verbal Test, Time Stress	
Accuracy	
-Extraverts	Increases
-Introverts	Decreases
Verbal Test	
Accuracy	
-Low impulsives	Increases (in the a.m.), decreases (in the p.m.)
-High impulsives	Decreases (in the a.m.), increases (in the p.m.)

Note: Adapted with permission from Sawyer, D.A., Julia, H.L., and Turin, A.C. (1982), Caffeine and human behavior: Arousal, anxiety, and performance effects. *Journal of Behavioral Medicine, 5,* 415–439 (Published by Plenum Press).

according to the personality of the subject ("impulsiveness") and the setting (time of day) (Sawyer, Julia, & Turin, 1982).

Interactions among Caffeine, Nicotine, and Alcohol

We noted that caffeine, nicotine, and alcohol are the psychoactive power hitters. Many people use these three drugs often, and often in combination.

An important question, therefore, is what the interactive effects of these compounds are. It seems, for example, that smokers smoke fewer cigarettes after drinking coffee compared to when they have not had coffee. This effect is stronger for lighter caffeine users. Another effect of nicotine is in excretion of caffeine from the body, which occurs more than 50% faster in smokers than in nonsmokers (Sawyer, Julia, & Turin, 1982).

Alcohol and caffeine interactions have been the subject of scientific investigations for nearly eighty years. As with other data on caffeine effects, this vast research has not greatly clarified the picture. Despite the age-old method of drinking black coffee to emerge from an alcoholic "drunk," caffeine does not seem to antagonize alcohol's CNS depressant effects. So what you get in giving black coffee to somebody who is drunk on alcohol is an energetic drunk. Some experimenters even have found that caffeine increases alcohol-related impairments (Kenney & Darragh, 1985).

Two studies of caffeine, nicotine, and alcohol in combination   A recent study (Lowe, 1988) suggests that everyday forgetting has something to do with the state-dependent effects of caffeine, nicotine, and alcohol in combination. In the first study, twenty-four men and women college undergraduates who were smokers and drinkers were given a moderate dose of vodka and smoked two cigarettes. They were exposed to a list of nineteen items about a route on a map and then had to recall the items in successive tests until they achieved fourteen correct items. On the day of their next session these subjects were randomly assigned to one of four drug conditions: alcohol and nicotine (control condition), alcohol and nicotine placebo, alcohol placebo and nicotine, or alcohol placebo and nicotine placebo. The subjects then were asked to recall as many of the nineteen items that they could from their first experimental session. The results showed no recall decrement (Day 1–Day 2 score) for subjects who had alcohol and nicotine on both days. However, there were significant decreases in recall score for subjects in the other three groups. These "dissociative" or state-dependent effects seemed attributable to alcohol and, to a lesser extent, nicotine.

The next study by Lowe (1988) was the same as the first, except that sixteen undergraduate coffee and alcohol drinkers participated, and caffeine was substituted for nicotine. The results of this study showed state-dependent effects for alcohol and caffeine. Because the major recall decrements occurred in people who had no caffeine the second day, even if they drank alcohol, it seems the state dependence effect mostly was due to caffeine.

CONCLUSIONS ON CAFFEINE

Caffeine is the world's most popular drug, with effects that are complex and varied. Generally, the drug is now thought to be safe at the average levels of consumption, but there is still a lot to learn about caffeine. For example, the long-term effects of caffeine consumption in children is yet to be determined, as well as how or if tolerance develops to specific caffeine effects. Another point is that prevalence data are needed on the occurrence of what we called the "minor" symptoms of caffeine toxicity and, more seriously, of caffeinism. Another question is how caffeine affects people in special populations, such as those who are medically or psychiatrically ill. Hypotheses about use of caffeine to self-medicate depression hints at the importance of this question. Finally, Sawyer, Julia, and Turin (1982) made the excellent point that much of the research on caffeine effects has been done with healthy volunteers who have consumed only well-specified, single doses of caffeine. Little information exists on the cumulative effects, say during one day, of caffeine use on task performance. This is important, because that is the pattern of caffeine use that most people follow. Relatedly, caffeine effects in combination with other commonly used drugs need a lot more attention. Lowe's (1988) findings on state-dependent learning and alcohol, caffeine, and nicotine suggest that important practical questions can be answered by such research.

SUMMARY

- This chapter covers the "minor stimulants"—nicotine, and caffeine and other methylxanthine drugs.

- Nicotine occurs naturally from only one source, the tobacco plant. The major commercial tobacco products are cigarettes, cigars, snuff, chewing tobacco, and pipe tobacco.

- Western Europeans discovered tobacco when they saw Native Americans in the New World smoking dried tobacco leaves. The Europeans seized the idea and spread it throughout Europe and Asia.

- Until about 1860, tobacco was widely believed to have medicinal properties. Nicotine's "medical cover" was blown when it was isolated in 1828 and shown to have addictive properties.

- Cigarette smoking is the most popular way to use tobacco.

- The prevalence of smoking among United States adults is at its lowest level since 1955. A major reduction in the number of current smokers and an increase in the number of former smokers seem related to the United States Surgeon General's 1964 report, and subsequent publications, on the health consequences of cigarette smoking.

- Every year from 1975 to 1986 female high school seniors reported a higher rate of daily cigarette use in the last thirty days than did males.

- Recently the use of moist snuff has increased. The increase seems to be largely because of greater use among young males.

- Cigarette smoking is the largest preventable cause of cardiovascular disease and cancer. Smoking kills because of the smoker's chronic exposure to the carbon monoxide, tar, and nicotine in tobacco smoke.

- In the last twenty-five years women have caught up to men in suffering serious health consequences of smoking.

- Because of the health consequences of active

and passive smoking, there has been a great increase in the banning and restriction of smoking in public places.

· Nicotine's pharmacological action is very complex. It acts on a number of sites in the body and has stimulant and depressant phases of action.

· Nicotine can be absorbed through the skin, the oral, buccal, and nasal mucosa, the gastrointestinal tract, and the lungs.

· By inhalation the nicotine in tobacco smoke reaches the brain in seven seconds. Brain levels thus rise rapidly, but they fall rapidly too, because nicotine is quickly distributed to other sites of action. Nicotine primarily is metabolized in the liver and eliminated mostly in urine.

· Functional tolerance to nicotine's effects is acquired quickly. Dispositional tolerance to nicotine also seems to develop.

· Nicotine induces physical dependence. In 1988 the United States Surgeon General's Office issued a report with the conclusion that nicotine is a physically addicting drug.

· Because of the rapidity of nicotine's absorption, short half-life, and other reasons such as its pleasant acute effects, and acceptability and accessibility of use, nicotine is a drug that leaves the new user very susceptible to developing physical dependence.

· It seems that smokers, even those who say they want to quit, continue to smoke, primarily because of their dependence on nicotine.

· Nicotine use has both stimulant and depressant acute effects. Regardless of the pharmacological action of nicotine, smokers often perceive a decrease in arousal when they smoke.

· Many people who want to quit smoking can do it on their own. Others, thought to be heavier smokers, need the help of formal treatment to quit.

· Smoking treatment programs focus on stopping nicotine withdrawal symptoms, breaking the behavioral or habit part of smoking, and teaching stress reduction skills (smokers say they use the effects of cigarette smoking to help them cope with stressful situations).

· In general, treatment programs can be classified into two types, minimal and full programs. They differ primarily in the amount of contact the smoker has with treatment professionals.

· Quitting smoking is one thing; "staying quit" is another. A high rate of relapse follows smoking treatment.

· A major reason for relapse is that smokers may continue to crave nicotine long after they have stopped smoking. Accordingly, a pharamacologic treatment of smoking has been developed, a nicotine-containing chewing gum. The gum seems to be most effective when used with behavioral treatments.

· Caffeine and other methylxanthine drugs occur natrually in more than sixty species of plants. Caffeine is the world's most popular drug, and humans have used it since ancient times. Many everyday products that children or adults consume contain caffeine.

· In the past twenty-five years or so, per capita rates of coffee consumption apparently have declined. At the same time, the per capita rate of caffeine-containing soft drinks has increased greatly. Tea and cocoa consumption have remained relatively stable during these years. Coffee still is the world's major source of caffeine.

· Caffeine intoxication is called caffeinism. Caffeinism is most likely to occur with doses of 600 mg a day or higher. The symptoms are more severe the higher the dose.

· At the doses humans typically consume, no connection has been proven between caffeine use and major physical problems in adults. However serum cholesterol levels, especially in women, seem to be positively related to caffeine consumption. Caffeine consumption is associated with more minor symptoms such as indigestion, heart palpitations, tremors, headache, and insomnia.

· Caffeine is rapidly absorbed from the gastrointestinal tract and is distributed throughout the body. Its half-life in the blood ranges between 2½ to 7½ hours.

· Because it is distributed bodywide, caffeine has a range of acute effects. The drug is metabolized primarily by the liver and virtually all excreted in the urine.

· Caffeine has an identified withdrawal syndrome, but evidence for tolerance to caffeine is less clear.

· Caffeine's acute effects seem to be due to its blocking of adenosine receptor sites. The effects include diuresis, stimulation of the heart and CNS, relaxation of smooth muscles, stimulation of gastric acid, and elevation of free fatty acid and glucose.

· Because caffeine, alcohol, and nicotine are used by many people in some combination, knowing how each of these drugs interacts with the other two is important.

References

Abbott, P.J. (1986). Caffeine: A toxicological overview. *The Medical Journal of Australia, 145,* 518–521.

Abrams, D.B., & Wilson, G.T. (1986). Habit disorders: Alcohol and tobacco dependence. In A.J. Frances & R.E. Hales (Eds), *American Psychiatric Association Annual Review* (Volume 5) (pp. 606–626). Washington, DC: American Psychiatric Press, Inc.

American Psychiatric Association (1987). *Diagnostic and Statistical Manual* (Third Edition–Revised). Washington, D.C.: Author.

Blum, K. (1984). *Handbook of abusable drugs.* New York: Gardner Press, Inc.

Bonham, G., & Wilson, R. (1981). Children's health in families with cigarette smokers. *American Journal of Public Health, 71,* 290–293.

Brecher, E.M. (1972). *Licit and illicit drugs.* Mount Vernon, NY: Consumers Union.

Chassin, L., Presson, C.C., Sherman, S.J., & Margolis, S. (1988). The social image of smokeless tobacco use in three different types of teenagers. *Addictive Behaviors, 13,* 107–112.

Council on Scientific Affairs (1984). Caffeine labeling. *Journal of the American Medical Association, 252,* 803–806.

Curatolo, P.W., & Robertson, D. (1983). The health consequences of caffeine. *Annals of Internal Medicine, 98,* 641–653.

Edwards, D.D., (1986). Nicotine: A drug of choice? *Science News, 129,* 44–45.

Gilbert, D.G. (1979). Paradoxical tranquilizing and emotion–reducing effects of nicotine. *Psychological Bulletin, 86,* 643–661.

Gilbert, R.M. (1976). Caffeine as a drug of abuse. In R.J. Gibbins, Y. Israel, H. Kalant, R.E. Popham, W. Schmidt, & R.G. Smart, *Research advances in alcohol and drug problems* (Volume 3) (pp. 49–176). New York: John Wiley & Sons.

Gilbert, R.M. (1984). Caffeine consumption. *Progress in Clinical Biological Research, 158,* 185–213.

Goldstein, A.S., Kaizer, S. & Whitby, O. (1969). Psychotropic effects of caffeine in man. IV. Quantitative and qualitative differences associated with habituation to coffee. *Clinical and Pharmacological Therapeutics, 10,* 489–497.

Graham, D.M. (1978). Caffeine: Its identity, dietary sources, intake, and biological effects. *Nutrition Reviews, 36,* 97–102.

Greden, J.F. (1974). Anxiety or caffeinism: A diagnostic dilemma. *American Journal of Psychiatry, 131,* 1089–1092.

Griffiths, R.R. & Woodson, P.P. (1988). Caffeine physical dependence: A review of human and animal laboratory studies. *Psychopharmacology 94*, 437–451.

Gritz, E.R., Ksir, C., & McCarthy, W.J. (1985). Smokeless tobacco use in the United States: Present and future trends. *Annals of Behavioral Medicine, 7*, 24–27.

Hallowell, C. (1987). Ordinary medicines can have extraordinary side effects. *Redbook, 169*, 132–134; 156–157.

Hughes, J.R. (1986). Genetics of smoking: A brief review. *Behavior Therapy, 17*, 335–345.

Hughes, J.R., Grist, S.W., & Pechacek, T.F. (1987). Prevalence of tobacco dependence and withdrawal. *American Journal of Psychiatry, 144*, 205–208.

Hughes, J.R., Hatsukami, D.K., Mitchell, J.E., & Dahlgren, L.A. (1986). Prevalence of smoking among psychiatric outpatients. *American Journal of Psychiatry, 143*, 993–997.

Jarvis, M. (1983). The treatment of cigarette dependence. *British Journal of Addiction, 78*, 125–130.

Johnston, L.D., O'Malley, P.M., & Bachman, J.G. (1987). *National trends in drug use and related factors among American high school students and young adults, 1975–1986.* Rockville, MD: National Institute on Drug Abuse.

Jones, R.T. (1987). Tobacco dependence. In H.Y. Meltzer (Ed.), *Psychopharmacology: The third generation of progress* (pp. 1589–1595). New York: Raven Press.

Kenny, M. & Darragh, A. (1985). Central effects of caffeine in man. In S.D. Iversen (Ed.), *Psychopharmacology: Recent advances and future prospects* (pp. 278–288). Oxford: Oxford University Press.

Konner, M. (1988). Caffeine high. *New York Times Magazine,* January 17, 47–48.

Kozlowski, L.T., Jelinek, L.C., & Pope, M.A. (1986). Cigarette smoking among alcohol abusers: A continuing and neglected problem. *Canadian Journal of Public Health, 77*, 205–207.

Leonard, T.K., Watson, R.R., & Mohs, M.E. (1987). The effects of caffeine in various body systems: A review. *Journal of the American Dietetic Association, 87*, 1048–1053.

Levenson, H.S., & Bick, E.C. (1977). Psychopharmacology of caffeine. In M.E. Jarvik (Ed), *Psychopharmacology in the practice of medicine* (pp. 451–463). New York: Appleton-Century-Crofts.

Lichtenstein, E. (1982). The smoking problem: A behavioral perspective. *Journal of Consulting and Clinical Psychology, 50*, 804–819.

Lowe, G. (1988). State-dependent retrieval effects with social drugs. *British Journal of Addiction, 83,* 99–103.

Marks, V., & Kelly, J.F. (1973). Absorption of caffeine from tea, coffee, and coca cola. *Lancet, 3*, 827.

Russell, M.A.H. (1976). Tobacco smoking and nicotine dependence. In R.J. Gibbins, Y. Israel, H. Kalant, R.E. Popham, W. Schmidt, & R.G. Smart, *Research advances in alcohol and drug problems* (Volume 3) (pp. 1–47). New York: John Wiley & Sons.

Sawyer, D.A., Julia, H.L., & Turin, A.C. (1982). Caffeine and human behavior: Arousal, anxiety, and performance effects. *Journal of Behavioral Medicine, 5,* 415–439.

Schelling, T.C. (1986). Economics and cigarettes. *Preventive Medicine, 15,* 549–560.

Shopland, D.R., & Brown, C. (1985). Changes in cigarette smoking prevalence in the US: 1955 to 1983. *Annals of Behavioral Medicine, 7,* 5–8.

Snyder, S.H., Sklar, P. (1984). Behavioral and molecular actions of caffeine: Focus on adenosine. *Journal of Psychiatric Research, 18,* 91–106.

Stewart, G.C. (1967). A history of the medical use of tobacco. *Medical History, 11,* 228–268.

Syed, I.B. (1976). The effects of caffeine. *Journal of the American Pharmaceutical Association, 16,* 568–572.

Taylor, P. (1985). Ganglionic stimulating and blocking agents. In G.G. Gilman, L.S. Goodman, T.W. Rall, & F. Murod (Eds.), *Goodman and Gilman's The pharmacological basis of therapeutics* (Seventh Edition) (pp. 215–221). New York: Macmillan Publishing Co.

U.S. Department of Health and Human Services (1987). *Smoking, tobacco, and health. A fact book.* Rockville, MD: U.S. Public Health Service.

Weidner, G., & Istvan, J. (1985). Dietary sources of caffeine. *New England Journal of Medicine, 313,* 1421.

West, R.J., & Russell, M.A.H. (1985). Nicotine pharmacology and smoking dependence. In S.D. Iverson (Ed.),

Psychopharmacology: Recent advances and future prospects (pp. 303–314). Oxford: Oxford University Press.

West, R., & Schneider, N. (1987). Craving for cigarettes. *British Journal of Addiction, 82,* 407–415.

Wynder, E.L., & Hoffmann, D. (1979). Tobacco and health. A societal challenge. *The New England Journal of Medicine, 300,* 894–903.

Zusy, A. (1987). For smokers, ways to quit are many, but the goal is elusive. *The New York Times,* July 15, C1, C10.

7 ALCOHOL

In the preceding chapter we said alcohol, nicotine, and caffeine are the most popular psychoactive drugs. By far, of the three, alcohol has been known, manufactured, and used the longest. Most important, this drug has had profound influences on the societies around the world in which it is used. "Alcohol" actually refers to several substances, for example, isopropyl alcohol (rubbing alcohol), methyl alcohol (wood alcohol), and ethanol. Ethanol is the alcohol we drink, and in this book use of the word alcohol means ethanol unless otherwise specified.

In this chapter we give you an overview of the many facets of alcohol use. We begin with information on the major alcoholic beverages, how they are manufactured, and some history about the use of alcohol in human societies. We follow with a discussion of the prevalence of alcohol use and problems in the United States. We also explore more detailed information about alcohol use and patterns of alcohol consumption. With this general background we then examine the pharmacology of alcohol, including site of action, processing of the drug in the human body, and the development of tolerance and dependence. Then we examine the acute and chronic physiological, psychological, and social consequences of alcohol use in humans. The chapter ends with a discussion of the causes of alcohol dependence.

Alcoholic Beverages

Distillation
Process by which the heating of a fermented mixture increases its alcohol content.

Fermentation and distillation   Alcohol virtually always is drunk in the form of the three major classes of alcoholic beverages: beer, wine, and hard liquor (also called distilled spirits). For their manufacture, all these beverages depend upon the process of fermentation and liquor upon the further process of distillation. Fermentation begins when sugar is dissolved in water and exposed to air, which creates the perfect environment for living microorganisms called yeasts. When yeasts are in their perfect environment they multiply rapidly by eating the sugar, which is then converted to ethanol and carbon dioxide by the yeasts' metabolic processes. The carbon dioxide bubbles to the top of the mixture, leaving ethanol. As the number of yeasts grows, so does the percentage of ethanol, as much as 10 to 15 percent. At this highest point the yeasts cease their work. Therefore, fermented beverages will not have an alcohol content higher than 15 percent. Which kind of beverage results from fermentation depends on what sugar-containing substance is used. When grapes are used, the grape juice ferments to form wine. When grains are used, fermentation produces beer.

Distillation was developed to increase the ethanol content of fermented beverages. Distillation first involves heating a fermented mixture. Because alcohol has a lower boiling point than water, the steam emitted through boiling has a higher alcohol content than does the original fermented mixture. The vapor then is condensed through cooling, and the resulting liquid

Figure 7–1 A variety of alcoholic beverages are available to the interested consumer.

is higher in alcohol content than was the original fermented mixture. By repeating this cycle it is possible to raise the alcohol content of a beverage to progressively higher levels.

Expressing the alcohol content of a beverage   In the United States alcohol percentage is denoted by volume. This is straightforward, so that 16 ounces of a beverage that is 50 percent ethanol contains 8 ounces of alcohol. Another way of expressing alcohol content is by weight, which is done

Table 7–1

Major Kinds of Alcoholic Beverages, How They Are Made, and Alcohol Content

Beverage	How Made	Percent Alcohol (by vol.)
Beer (includes lager, ale, malt, stout)	Fermentation of carbohydrate extracted from barley malt (or rice or corn) by cooling with water. Product is boiled with hops, cooled, and fermented. Types of beer vary in malt, hops and alcohol content	Lager = 3–6% others = 4–8%
Wine		
Red (Table wine)	Fermentation of red grapes in skins	
White (Table wine)	Fermentation of skinless grapes	Average 12%
Champagne	Same as white wine, with carbon dioxide	
Fortified (dessert) Wines	Ordinary table wines to which alcohol content raised	Up to 20%
Distilled Spirits		
Brandy	Distilled from any sugar-containing fruit. Probably first to be produced commercially	About 40%
Whiskeys	Grains brewed with water to form a beer of 5–10% alcohol. Beer is distilled and aged in new or used charred oak barrels for two to eight years before blending	40–50%
Bourbon	From corn with rye and malted barley	
Scotch	Malted barley and corn	
Irish whiskey	Corn and malted and unmalted barley	
Rye whiskey	Rye and malted barley	
Other spirits		
Rum	Distilled from fermented molasses, aged about three years	40–75%
Gin	Distilled from any fermentable carbohydrate (barley, potato, corn, wheat, rye), flavored by a second distillation with juniper berries	35–50%
Vodka	Distilled from potato or almost any other carbohydrate source, kept free of flavors	35–50%

Note: Abstracted from Becker, C.E., Roe, R.L., & Scott, R.A. (1975). *Alcohol as a drug*. New York: Medcom Press. Published with permission.

for example in Britain. Alcohol has a specific gravity of about .79, which means a quantity of alcohol weighs .79 of the same amount of water. As a result, a given ratio based on volume contains more alcohol than the same ratio based on weight. A beverage that is a given percentage of alcohol by weight contains about 20% less alcohol than one that is the same percentage of alcohol by volume. So, the alcohol content of a beverage that is 50% alcohol by weight is about 40% alcohol by volume.

Another convention is the designation of alcohol content of a beverage by its **"proof."** Proof is used primarily with distilled spirits and is equal to twice the percentage of alcohol by volume. Accordingly, a beverage that is 43% alcohol by volume is 86 proof. This somewhat indirect way of expressing alcohol content comes from seventeenth century England, where it was determined that a mixture that was 57% alcohol by volume, if poured over gunpowder, would cause its ignition in an open flame. The English still refer to their beverages as "over proof" (>57% alcohol by volume) or "under proof" (<57% alcohol by volume) (Becker, Roe, & Scott, 1975).

Proof
A term used to designate the proportion of alcohol in a beverage, by volume. Proof typically is used in reference to distilled spirits and equals twice the percentage of alcohol.

Types of alcoholic beverages   Table 7–1 is a summary of the essentials about the major types of alcoholic beverages commercially available. Varying the substances forming the base of the beverage and varying the alcohol concentration produce different types of alcoholic beverages.

HISTORY OF ALCOHOL USE

Humans have used alcohol for thousands of years. Keller (1979, p. 2822) reflected this fact in his comment "in the beginning there was alcohol." The first nondistilled alcoholic beverages were made inadvertently, due to natural fermentation. For example, the first wines, which probably were drunk several thousand years ago, were likely made from fruit juice. The juices obtained from most types of fruit are contaminated with microbes, including yeasts, that constitute the flora on the fruit (Rose, 1977). Alcoholic fermentation results when the environmental temperature is right. Authorities believe the first beers were produced in Egypt as long ago as 5000 to 6000 years B.C. Production of the first beers was similar to baking bread. An earthenware vessel filled with barley was placed in the ground until germination occurred. At that point the barley was crushed, made into a dough, and then baked until a crust was formed. This cake of dehydrated dough was soaked in water until fermentation was complete. The resulting product of acid beer was called "boozah." Distilled spirits were the last alcoholic beverages to be produced, but they are by no means recent entries on the scene. The earliest reference to distilled spirits appeared in China at about 1000 B.C. Western Europe apparently does not have record of distilled spirit production and consumption until about 800 A.D.

Since the very early beginnings of its use, alcohol has been a double-edged

Figure 7-2 Eighteenth century Europeans tended to attribute many of their social problems to alcoholic beverages, particularly distilled spirits.

sword to human societies. Alcoholic beverages have played, on the one hand, a part in important social occasions, such as births, religious ceremonies, marriages, and funerals. Such drinking was viewed as not harmful to individuals and as positive to societies. On the other hand, alcohol seemingly always has been consumed in excess by some, with consequent problems to the individual and to the society in which he or she lived. Such social consequences have been the source of repeated condemnations of alcohol by the clergy, prophets, physicians, and philosophers (Keller, 1979).

The two faces of alcohol were seen clearly when distilled spirits hit western Europe. Europeans sang the praises of this drug. For example, a French professor in the thirteenth century dubbed alcohol "aqua vitae," which means "water of life." The Danes expressed the same sentiment with their "akvavit," the Swedes with their "akkevitt." However, European societies also attributed many of their problems to alcoholic beverages, especially distilled spirits. For example, the social problems in eighteenth century England were represented in works of art such as Hogarth's "Gin Lane."

Colonial America adopted alcoholic beverages and many of the drinking customs from western Europe. One story has it the Pilgrims landed at Plymouth Rock because they were out of alcohol. The dualistic nature of alcohol was manifested again in colonial America. The tavern was the center of town politics, business, trade, and pleasure. These Americans drank beer, wine, cider, and distilled spirits in considerable quantities. The practice of drinking was pervasive, as colonial American drinking showed no distinction among time, place, or person. The frequent practice of alcohol consumption coincided with positive attitudes toward it, as alcohol was viewed as fulfilling an array of physical, psychological, and social needs. The importance of alcohol to colonial Americans was represented in language. In 1737 Benjamin Franklin published a "Drinkers Dictionary," which included more than 235 terms to describe the drunkard. Included among these were "Loaded his cart," "Cock ey'd," "Moon-ey'd," "Tipsy," and "He carries too much sail" (Mendelson & Mello, 1985).

With such supporting attitudes and customs, Americans became known as a country of drunkards. In 1790 adult citizens of the young country annually drank six gallons of pure alcohol per capita, and by 1830 per capita consumption had soared to seven gallons of alcohol. The latter computes to almost five alcoholic beverage drinks a day for each adult! With this kind of consumption, the ills of heavy drinking became more and more evident, especially in a society that was moving increasingly toward urbanization and industrialization. Accordingly, some people began to speak out against the ravages of alcohol, again mostly in reference to distilled spirits. The most influential among these critics, and a pillar of the Temperance Movement that was to gain strength in the nineteenth century, was the physician Benjamin Rush. Dr. Rush's 1785 treatise, "Inquiring into the effects of distilled spirits on the human body and mind," delineated the effects of distilled spirits on humans. It also was the basis of the idea that alcoholism is a disease.

In the nineteenth century, America expanded westward, and with that came the rise of the saloon. The word saloon comes from the French word *salon*, which refers to public meeting place and entertainment hall. The saloon did serve a social function to the frontiers-people, but it quickly moved away from a center of civilized interchange to a reflection of the rural community of the American West (Mendelson & Mello, 1985). The first saloons were not exactly pictures of fine carpentry, as they could consist of structures as simple as a tent and a few barrels that made up the bar. The decor was the era's version of macho and might consist of pictures of naked women, famous boxers of the time such as John L. Sullivan, and Custer's Last Stand (Mendelson & Mello, 1985). This decor was in tune with the typical clientele characteristics: aggressive men who were inclined to exploit other men and nature. These explorers, soldiers, Native Americans, trappers, settlers, and cowboys had few of the attachments to family or community that might have helped to limit the occurrence of excessive drinking. Instead, their drinking in the saloon was characterized by the downing of large quantities of whiskey for the purpose of engaging in explosive behavior (Keller, 1979). The whiskey was plentiful and usually wretched—witness names for it such as "extract of scorpions" and "San Juan paralyzer."

Behavior associated with the saloon gave a rebirth to the Temperance Movement, which had been quieted somewhat by the American Civil War. The saloon was the focal scapegoat of the Temperance adherents and was blamed for social ills such as thievery, gambling, prostitution, and political corruption. The Temperance Movement also changed its stand from support of moderate use of nondistilled beverages to total abstinence from alcohol. The captains of industry of the late nineteenth and early twentieth centuries, such as John D. Rockefeller, Andrew Carnegie, and Henry Ford, supported the Temperance Movement. They believed that abstemious employees would be better employees. These industrial giants also gave money to supplement their moral support.

Alcohol Use in the Twentieth Century United States

As World War I approached, the anti-alcohol drive had gained considerable financial, social, and political power. As mentioned in Chapter 2, this drive led to Prohibition and then to passage of the Volstead Act. The short life of Prohibition in the United States is well-known, and it was repealed nationally in 1933. However, part of this action was to leave much to the discretion of the states in regulating the sale and consumption of alcohol. In the stew of local laws that have evolved since, the American ambivalence about the use of alcoholic beverages is apparent. For example, some laws required the windows of drinking establishments be curtained, and others forbade it; some laws forbade women to drink standing at the bar, and others granted women the right to drink standing anywhere that a man could. The laws were consistent in their restriction of youths purchasing alcoholic beverages and in the channeling of alcohol tax revenue to local, state, and federal treasuries (Keller, 1979).

The public ambivalence about alcohol remains. This is reflected in the saying that everybody enjoys a drink, but nobody enjoys a drunk. Still, there has been a general trend in the 1980s toward limitations of alcohol's use through change in social attitudes and tighter governmental controls. However, drinking remains a major part of many social rituals, and many people hail the benefits of moderate alcohol consumption. The negative consequences of excessive alcohol use are probably more apparent than ever because of activists with access to sophisticated communications techniques, yet they and government regulations are far from entirely successful in stopping or limiting alcohol consumption. This seems to be especially true among people who are alcohol dependent. We are still working to learn the greater part of the mystery of how alcohol problems develop, are maintained, and can be prevented and treated.

PREVALENCE AND CORRELATES OF ALCOHOL USE

In this section we consider trends in alcohol use in the general U.S. population. Because we covered data on prevalence of alcohol and other drug use in Chapter 1; we limit this discussion to trends we did not review earlier, including prevalence by specific alcoholic beverages, correlates of alcohol use in the population, and the prevalence of alcohol-related problems.

Trends in Consumption of Alcoholic Beverages in the U.S.

Since 1973 the United States Department of Health and Human Services (USDHHS) has periodically published reports to the United States Congress on alcohol. The sixth of these "Special Reports" appeared in 1987. Among the wealth of information in the report are data on trends over time in the per capita consumption of beer, wine, and distilled spirits from 1935 to 1984. These data are presented in Figure 7–3. In compiling this informa-

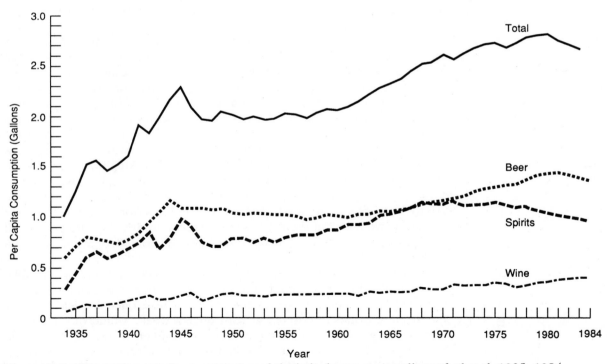

Figure 7–3 Estimated per capita consumption of alcoholic beverages in gallons of ethanol, 1935–1984 (Taken from USDHHS, 1987, p. 2).

tion, the drinking population was defined as all individuals (whether they actually drank alcohol or not) aged fourteen years or older, since fourteen was considered a reasonable estimate for the average age when drinking begins. To arrive at the per capita estimates of alcohol consumption, beverage sales statistics are totaled and then divided by the number of individuals who are included in the drinking population.

Several time-related trends are apparent in Figure 7–3. You can see total consumption rose sharply between 1935 and 1945, although it did not approach what Americans were drinking in 1830. This large increase most likely was due to a return to pre-prohibition levels of consumption. After a decline during the World War II era, total consumption again rose, but only gradually until the early 1980s, when it showed a slight decline. Data for beer and spirits generally show a similar trend, except the per capita consumption of spirits began a decline in the early 1970s. Wine consumption data have shown a steady but very gradual increase from 1935 to 1984.

You can determine from Figure 7–3 that in 1984 each person in the United States aged fourteen years or older drank an average of 2.65 gallons of alcohol. This amount is equivalent to about 50 gallons of beer, 20 gallons of table wine, or more than 4 gallons of distilled spirits. Further, estimates indicate that if alcohol abstainers are excluded and only the actual drinkers are included in the sample, then per capita consumption of ethanol in the United States in 1984 was about 4 gallons.

The data on per capita alcohol consumption tell us how much the "average" drinker in the United States consumes. However, this statistic alone can be deceptive, because the average value masks the large amount of variation in drinking quantity and patterns among Americans. For example, national survey studies have shown consistently that drinking differs according to a number of social and environmental factors, such as residence in an urban versus a rural area, socioeconomic class, and education.

Two factors strongly associated with drinking patterns are sex and age. For example, a 1984 national survey of United States drinking practices and patterns among noninstitutionalized (for example, not living in jails or college dorms) adults eighteen years of age or older showed, first, that younger men (18 to 39 years old) are least likely to be abstainers from alcohol. The same is true for women. Yet there is a sex difference in drinker status across all age groups, as significantly more women abstain from alcohol than do men (Hilton, 1987).

The 1984 survey data further highlight the age-sex drinking pattern relationship regarding those referred to as "frequent heavy drinkers". This category includes people who said they drank at least once a week, and had five or more drinks in one day at least once a week. A total of 18% of the men overall were classified as frequent heavy drinkers. However, the youngest men, those 18 to 29 years old, had the highest proportion in this category (27%), followed by the next youngest group of men, those 30 to 39

CONTEMPORARY ISSUE BOX 7–1
Ends of the Age Spectrum and Drinking

The United States national surveys of drinking patterns and practices have paid relatively little attention to the elderly and no attention to young children. The reason in the case of the elderly probably is that this group has consistently shown a low prevalence of heavy drinking and drinking problems. Young children simply have not been sampled.

The same factors relating to low alcohol consumption and alcohol problems in the elderly recently have been thought to put them at higher risk of negative consequences when they do drink. One factor is an age-related decrease in physical tolerance for alcohol, so that smaller quantities can have considerable effects on an older person. Another factor is that many of the elderly are taking prescribed medications for medical problems that are synergistic with alcohol, again magnifying the effects of a given quantity of it. The higher risk of alcohol problems among the elderly who do drink is receiving a lot more attention than in previous years because of numbers: In 1983 the elderly were 11% of the United States population; in 2025 they are expected to be 17.2%. Along these lines, there is a strong need to learn about the development of drinking patterns and problems among the elderly, and any special needs for treatment of those individuals who do experience problems.

On the other end of the age range, knowledge of young children's drinking is limited at best. However, there has been some research on this age group's knowledge about alcohol and attitudes toward its use. For example, children as young as four years old can identify alcoholic beverages, and six-year-olds show some knowledge of the customs surrounding adult drinking. Unfortunately, much less is known about young children's actual alcohol consumption. There at least seems to be some local and national concern about it. For example, one newspaper report cited the National School Boards Association statement that local school boards were expressing increasing worry about the "spreading alcohol abuse" among children. In this regard, a member of the Westport, Connecticut, Board of Education said that he had seen children as young as eight years old who drank. These and similar observations have alarmed educators and parents. The reason we know so little about the extent of children's drinking is that it is very difficult to study scientifically, say by the survey methods that have been used to study adults' drinking. Can you think of some of the problems you would face if you wanted to research drinking among young children?

years old (21%). In contrast, only 4% of the men who were 60 years of age or older were classified as frequent heavy drinkers.

Significantly fewer women, 5%, than men were overall classified as frequent heavy drinkers. However, proportionately more of the women (7%) who were 18 to 29 or 30 to 39 years old were designated as frequent heavy drinkers. A total of 1% of the women 60 years of age or older were similarly classified.

Prevalence of alcohol-related problems   National surveys of drinking among American adults also have been informative about the prevalence of negative consequences of alcohol consumption. In the 1984 survey, "problematic drinking" and "tangible consequences" (of alcohol use) were measured. Problematic drinking referred to a set of drinking behaviors and associated effects that are not necessarily problems in themselves but may be indicative of alcohol dependence (see Chapter 1 for a definition of dependence). Examples include inability to cut down on drinking, binge drinking, and memory loss associated with drinking. Tangible consequences were specific problems that resulted from drinking, such as problems with spouse, job problems, legal problems, and health problems. To give an idea, the questionnaire item for binge drinking was, "I stayed intoxicated for several days at a time" (The person responds whether that item applies to him or her). An item to measure spouse problems was, "A spouse or someone I lived with threatened to leave me because of my drinking."

The survey data were consistent with earlier studies in showing that age and sex are related to drinking problems. One analysis concerned "moderate level" problem drinkers. "Moderate" was defined by a method of scoring respondents' answers to the problematic drinking and tangible consequences survey items. The results showed, first, that among the drinkers in the sample men had a higher percentage of moderate level problematic drinking and tangible consequences (9% and 14%, respectively) than did women (4% and 6%). However, the men who were 18 to 29 years old had the highest percentages of problematic drinking and tangible consequences, 14% and 20%, respectively. The rates for women in this age group were 6% and 12%. Generally, the percentages for both sexes gradually declined until ages 50 to 59, when they dropped considerably.

In summary, the data on prevalence of drinking patterns and problems show the average United States drinker consumes a considerable amount of alcohol during the course of a year. However, a number of personal, social, and environmental factors are associated with drinking patterns and problems. Among the most important of those are age and sex, as younger men seem to be the heaviest drinkers and have the highest rate of alcohol-related problems. As you might expect, by far the highest rate of moderate level problem drinking is among the frequent heavy drinkers (Hilton, 1987).

MECHANISMS OF ACTION

Alcohol is generally classified as a CNS-depressant drug. Recent research suggests alcohol's depressant effect is partially caused by an increase in neural inhibition through its action on GABA-benzodiazepine receptors. (See Chapter 8.)

Pinpointing a site of action or single mechanism of alcohol effects is difficult because the drug affects cell membranes, all neurochemical systems, and all endrocrine systems (Abel, 1985). However, considerable knowledge exists about how the body absorbs, distributes, metabolizes, and excretes alcohol.

Absorption

Because it provides calories, alcohol is formally classified as a food. However, unlike other foods, alcohol does not have to be digested before the body absorbs it. Nevertheless, alcohol must pass from the stomach to the small intestine in order for rapid absorption to occur. This by far is the most common way humans absorb alcohol. However, if alcohol is vaporized it can be absorbed through the lungs and subcutaneous sites (Ritchie, 1985).

The rate of alcohol absorption can vary widely, depending on individual differences in physiology and on situational factors. This is an important point, because only the alcohol that is absorbed and carried by the blood throughout the body exerts an effect on the drinker. The major factors influencing absorption are those that alter the rate of passing alcohol from the stomach to the intestines. In this regard, the drinker can considerably slow absorption by eating while drinking, since the presence of food in the stomach retards absorption. Milk is especially effective for slowing alcohol absorption. Another factor is the rate an alcoholic beverage is consumed, as faster drinking means faster absorption. Drinks with a higher concentration of alcohol, such as whiskey on the rocks, are absorbed more quickly than those of lower concentration, such as a highball. The food substances in beer slow its absorption. Carbonated beverages are absorbed more quickly than noncarbonated ones, which explains why people may feel a quick kick from a glass of champagne on an empty stomach, which they typically would not feel from drinking a comparable amount of table wine. Given all of these factors, full absorption time for a dose of alcohol can range anywhere from one to six hours (Ritchie, 1985).

Some people exhibit a reflexive action of the body that works to prevent the drinking of high quantities of alcohol. The pylorus, which is the muscular valve separating the stomach from the intestines, shuts when a large quantity of alcohol has been ingested. This action is called **pylorospasm** and prevents whatever is in the stomach from passing to the intestines. As

Pylorospasm
The shutting of the pylorus valve that occurs in some people when very large quantities of alcohol are consumed.

long as alcohol stays in the stomach it will not be absorbed. Therefore, large amounts of alcohol may remain in the stomach unabsorbed when pylorospasm occurs. This mechanism is one of the natural defenses against an individual's becoming a very heavy drinker.

Distribution

After absorption the blood distributes alcohol to all of the body's tissues. Since alcohol is easily dissolved in water, the proportion of water in a tissue determines the concentration of alcohol in it. Blood is about 70% water and, therefore, gets a high concentration of alcohol. Muscle and bone contain smaller percentages of water and have correspondingly smaller percentages of alcohol.

Alcohol primarily affects the CNS, especially the brain. The concentration of alcohol in the brain approximates that in the blood, because of the brain's large blood supply and because alcohol freely passes the blood-brain barrier. Alcohol's LD-50 varies as a function of different factors. The average adult would reach alcohol's LD-50 by drinking about 25 **standard drinks** in an hour or so. A standard drink may be defined as a half an ounce of alcohol, which is about the amount in an ounce of 90- to 100-proof whiskey, 12 ounces of 4% alcohol beer, and four ounces of table wine (12% alcohol).

Standard drink
The alcohol equivalent in a drink of beer, wine, or distilled spirits. A standard drink equals a half ounce of alcohol, which is about the amount in 12 ounces of beer, 4 ounces of table wine, and 1 ounce of 90–100 proof whiskey.

Computation of the BAC   Because all humans have the same proportions of the different tissues and water, it is possible to estimate the concentration of alcohol in the body from its concentration in blood. The BAC, as the name implies, is the amount of alcohol in the bloodstream. It is expressed as a percentage of weight of alcohol per 100 units of blood volume (Sobell & Sobell, 1981). Typically, the ratio is expressed as milligrams (mg) of alcohol per 100 milliliters (ml) of blood. Therefore, one drop of alcohol, about one mg worth, in 1000 drops of blood, about 100 ml, gives a BAC of .01 percent. For your reference, the legal level of intoxication in 47 of the 50 United States is .10 percent; it is .08 percent in Maine, Utah, and Oregon, and in all of Canada. Alcohol's LD-50 is a BAC of .45 percent–.50 percent, although there have been case reports of people surviving BACs up to a little over 1.0 percent (Berild & Hasselbalch, 1981).

You can translate these numbers into an approximation of the number of drinks consumed over time. We emphasize approximation, because, as you saw above, the BAC that is reached depends in part on the different factors influencing absorption. However, knowing approximately what your BAC is at a given time can have practical value.

When a healthy man consumes a standard drink, his BAC is raised by .02 to .03% within forty-five to sixty minutes of drinking. Factors besides dose of alcohol determine the peak BAC that is reached. Total body mass is a major factor, because alcohol is distributed both in muscle and fat. As a result, heavier people will reach a lower BAC than lighter ones after drinking the same amount of alcohol. Another factor is how much of a person's body consists of fat and muscle. Alcohol is soluble in fat, but is even more soluble in water. Everything else equal, a drink will result in a lower BAC for a leaner person than for the drinker with a higher percentage of body fat. This is the reason a woman would tend to reach higher BACs from drinking a given amount of alcohol than would a man of the same body weight: women have a higher percentage of body fat than men do. Also, a recent study suggests women have less of the enzyme alcohol dehydrogenase in their stomachs than do men, preventing women from metabolizing as much of a dose of alcohol in their stomachs. This results in more alcohol entering a woman's bloodstream and, thus, eventually the brain and other organs (Frezza, di Padora, Pozzato, Terpin, Baraona, & Lieber, 1990). This finding suggests that, for a man and a woman of equal weight, the same amount of alcohol affects the woman more.

Another variable that influences what peak BAC is reached is individual differences in the rate at which the body metabolizes alcohol. These and other reasons are why the following formula for computing BAC gives only an approximation.

In the formula, BAC = blood alcohol content, NSD = number of standard drinks and NHD = number of hours since drinking began.

$$\text{Estimated BAC} = \text{NSD} \times (.03\%) - \text{NHD} \times (.02\%)$$

Based on this formula, therefore, a 160-pound man who drank three 12–ounce beers in an hour will have a BAC of about .07 percent. As you can

Figure 7–4 Blood alcohol concentration as a function of time.

see, the BAC essentially depends on the amount of alcohol that has been consumed and the amount of time it has taken to drink it. Figure 7–4 shows the BAC-time relationship. The figure illustrates that the BAC rises quickly and then more gradually returns to zero after drinking stops. Therefore, time is an important factor in determining BAC. Also notice that time enters into the BAC estimation formula independent of the number of standard drinks. This is because of the manner in which the body metabolizes alcohol. Figure 7–5 is a chart listing estimated BACs for drinkers of a given body weight and gender who have drunk a given amount of alcohol in a given time.

For medical or legal purposes BAC is not estimated by formula but is measured by standardized procedures as precisely as possible. Blood and urine samples are taken frequently for medical and medical–legal reasons to measure BAC. For example, BACs of drivers killed in motor vehicle accidents often are determined by blood samples. A very prominent measurement of BAC is done by breath sample, because of the known ratio (1:2100) between the amount of alcohol in the lungs to the amount in the blood. Gas chromatography methods are used to obtain excellent estimates of BAC, so good they are considered legally admissable evidence. The police departments of many United States cities measure BAC by breath analysis. Gas chromatographic methods are expensive, however, and until recently this prohibited precise measurement of BAC in settings where it would be very useful, such as outpatient alcohol treatment programs. However, substantial improvements in electronic technology have made possible breath testing devices that give good BAC estimates and cost only a few hundred dollars (compared, for example, to about $5000 for a gas chromatograph).

Metabolism and Excretion

More than 90% of the alcohol that is absorbed is metabolized by the body, mainly in the liver. (We saw earlier that the stomach also plays a part in metabolizing alcohol.) The small percentage of alcohol that is not metabolized is excreted in pure form through the kidneys and the lungs. When alcohol is metabolized in the liver, it is broken down to acetaldehyde by the enzyme alcohol dehydrogenase. This step is the basis of using the drug **disulfiram** (trade name Antabuse) in the treatment of alcohol dependence. We will have more to say about this in Chapter 15. Acetaldehyde is then further broken down by **acetate** to carbon dioxide and water. The carbon dioxide is excreted from the body through air exchange in the lungs, and the water is excreted in urine. Unlike other foods, such as proteins and carbohydrates, the rate that alcohol is metabolized is independent of the body's need for the calories it could provide or of the amount of alcohol consumed. The rate of alcohol oxidation is constant and averages about .35 to .40 ounces an hour.

Oxidation is the process by which the energy in foods is released in the form of heat and work. In this respect, alcohol liberates about 75 calories

Disulfiram
A drug that interferes with the metabolism of alcohol so that a person soon feels very ill if he or she drinks while on a regimen of disulfiram. The drug may be used as part of a treatment program for alcohol dependence.

Acetate
An ester of acetic acid that is a by-product in the metabolism of alcohol.

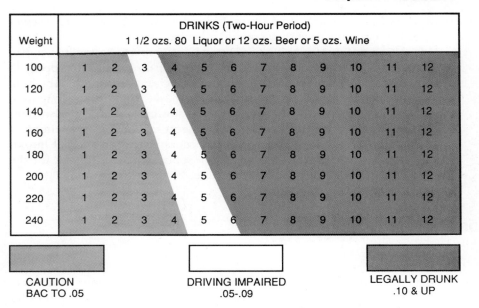

Weight	DRINKS (Two-Hour Period) 1 1/2 ozs. 80 Liquor or 12 ozs. Beer or 5 ozs. Wine											
100	1	2	3	4	5	6	7	8	9	10	11	12
120	1	2	3	4	5	6	7	8	9	10	11	12
140	1	2	3	4	5	6	7	8	9	10	11	12
160	1	2	3	4	5	6	7	8	9	10	11	12
180	1	2	3	4	5	6	7	8	9	10	11	12
200	1	2	3	4	5	6	7	8	9	10	11	12
220	1	2	3	4	5	6	7	8	9	10	11	12
240	1	2	3	4	5	6	7	8	9	10	11	12

CAUTION
BAC TO .05

DRIVING IMPAIRED
.05-.09

LEGALLY DRUNK
.10 & UP

Figures are averages. Alcohol effects may vary with each individual.

KNOW YOUR LEGAL LIMIT

In Texas that means .10% of Blood Alcohol Content. If you are going to drive, don't drink more than two 12 oz. beers or two 1 oz. drinks or two 5 oz. glasses of wine in an hour. Another drink and you will have passed your legal limit. In any case, if you've been drinking at all, be careful!

CONOZCA SU LÍMITE LEGAL

En Tejas este seía , 10% de cantidad de alcohol en la sangre. Si Ud. piensa manejar, no tome más de 2 cervezas de 12 onzas o 2 copas de licor de una onza, o 2 vasos de vino de 5 onzas en una hora. Una bebida más y Ud. se habrá pasado de su limite legal. De todos modos, si Ud. ha estado tomando. !tenga cuidado!

**Tarrant Council on Alcoholism & Drug Abuse
(817) 332-6329**

Figure 7–5 This chart can be used to approximate your blood alcohol concentration as a function of number of drinks, time, and your body weight.

in each half ounce. Therefore, one standard drink of whiskey has about 75 calories, because the calories in distilled spirits are only from alcohol content. However, beverages such as beer provide calories from foods such as proteins and carbohydrates as well as alcohol. A reqular 12-oz 4% alcohol beer has about 150 calories, and a comparable amount of the commercial light beers has anywhere from 95 to 135 calories. Light beers have fewer calories primarily because they contain less alcohol.

Alcohol is notorious for being unaffected by attempts to hasten its removal from the body. Efforts such as vigorous exercise do nothing to speed up alcohol oxidation, except to the extent that exercise takes time and the individual does not drink while exercising. As noted in Chapter 6, the long-used intoxication "remedy" of black coffee, as a source of caffeine, also does nothing to hasten sobering up. However, because caffeine is a stimulant drug the individual may interpret such effects as decreased alcohol intoxication. In fact, little can be done to hasten sobriety except to wait for the liver to do its work in its own constant time.

TOLERANCE AND DEPENDENCE

Tolerance

Regular use of alcohol results to some degree in dispositional tolerance. Therefore, the drinker must consume greater quantities of alcohol in order to maintain a certain BAC. Dispositional tolerance can be reversed with a period of abstinence from alcohol.

Functional tolerance has a greater practical influence than does dispositional tolerance in altering how alcohol affects you with repeated use. There are both acute and protracted tolerances to alcohol. Because of acute tolerance, at a given BAC there are greater alcohol effects when the BAC curve is rising than there are at that same BAC on the descending limb of the curve. For example, at a BAC of .10% as it is ascending, an individual may show considerably impaired performance on tasks related to driving. However, if the BAC peaks at, say, .15% and then hits .10% as it is falling, the individual's performance on those same driving-related tasks would be improved and perhaps even approach the level of performance shown at a BAC of .00%. Of course, such improvement would make no difference to the police. A BAC of .10% is legally drunk, regardless of what direction the BAC is heading when it is measured. Acute tolerance is illustrated in Figure 7–6.

As with dispositional tolerance, the development of protracted tolerance requires that the individual drink greater amounts of alcohol in order to achieve an effect once achieved with less alcohol. Because protracted functional tolerance far outpaces dispositional tolerance, the person becomes more susceptible to serious health and other consequences of heavy alcohol consumption. For example, a person may drink high quantities of alcohol to achieve a mood change once reached with much less alcohol. But the BAC does not behave in the same way. Drinking high quantities of alcohol still will result in a high BAC. With higher BACs the body is more vulnerable to suffering alcohol's toxic effects, which we will review shortly. Similarly, a chronic heavy drinker may not feel drunk or even impaired at BACs greater

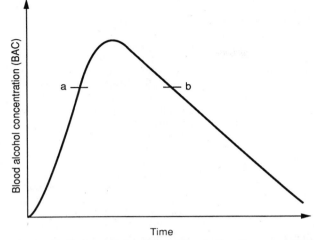

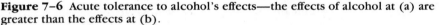

Figure 7–6 Acute tolerance to alcohol's effects—the effects of alcohol at (a) are greater than the effects at (b).

than .10%, but he or she still is defined legally as drunk. Such a designation leaves a person liable to arrests for drunk driving and other alcohol-related charges.

There is cross tolerance between alcohol and the other depressant (for example barbiturates) drugs, including the benzodiazepines (such as Valium, Librium). As a result, an individual who has developed protracted tolerance to alcohol will also have tolerance to, for example, Valium—without ever having taken Valium. Alcohol also shows cross-dependence to these drugs.

Physical Dependence

With chronic, abusive drinking some individuals develop physical dependence on alcohol. Symptoms of physical dependence can be severe and, if not treated professionally, may result in the individual's death. For example, of the estimated 19,587 deaths in 1980 attributable to alcohol, 4350 (or 22%) of them were due to alcohol withdrawal syndrome (USDHHS, 1987). The symptoms of alcohol withdrawal have been classified into three phases, based on their average time of onset after drinking is stopped.

The three phases of alcohol withdrawal are outlined in Table 7–2. As you can see, a wide range of symptoms can appear and are associated with time of onset after drinking cessation, although there is some overlap among the symptoms in the different phases. You should note that not all people who are physically dependent on alcohol experience all three phases of symptoms. For example, Phase 2 symptoms probably appear least frequently, and

Table 7–2

Symptoms of the Alcohol Withdrawal Syndrome in Three Phases

Phase	Onset	Symptoms
1	As soon as a few hours after drinking stopped; BACs may still be >.00 percent.	Tremulousness (shakes), profuse perspiration, weakness, alcohol- and other drug-seeking. Also may include agitation, headache, anorexia, nausea and vomiting, abdominal cramps, high heart rate, and exaggerated and rapid reflexes. Visual and auditory hallucinations may follow in increased intensity. Hallucinations may also occur when the individual is severely intoxicated (called acute alcoholic hallucinosis).
2	When occurs, it is within 24 hours of drinking cessation.	Grand mal seizures, ranging from one seizure to continuous severe seizure activity with little or no interruption.
3	About >30 hours after drinking cessation. Most protracted phase, may last 3–4 days. Commonly called delirium tremens (DTs).	Severe agitation, often appearance of confusion and disorientation. Almost continual activity. Very high body temperature and abnormally rapid heart beat. Terrifying hallucinations, may be visual, auditory, or tactile. Latter most often felt as bugs or little animals crawling on the skin. Hallucinations are accompanied by delusions, with high potential for violent behavior without medical management. Deaths during DTs still occur due to high fever, cardiovascular collapse, or traumatic injury.
End of withdrawal course	About 5–7 days after drinking stopped.	Exhaustion and severe dehydration.

Note: This table is based on information in Jacobs and Fehr (1987) and Wolfe and Victor (1971).

individuals may go from Phase 1 to Phase 3 symptoms. Another important point: withdrawal symptoms may appear when the BAC is falling but still at a fairly high level, such as .15%. The BAC needs not to have fallen all the way to zero for withdrawal to begin. Before its management by use of drugs associated with cross dependence with alcohol, alcohol withdrawal often ended in death. More recently less severe alcohol withdrawal has been managed without the use of drugs (**"social detoxification"**) or with drugs in an outpatient setting.

The following account, based on a case described in the DSM-III *Case book* (Spitzer, Skodol, Gibbon, & Williams, 1981, pp. 104–105), gives a good depiction of an individual experiencing alcohol withdrawal.

Social detoxification
Treatment of alcohol withdrawal without the use of medication.

> The patient was a 43-year-old divorced carpenter. His sister reported that the patient had been drinking more than a fifth of cheap wine every day for the past five years. The patient also had not eaten well, maybe only one meal a day, and had relied on wine as his main source of nourishment. The patient stopped drinking three days ago, and the morning after he, awoke with his hands shaking so badly that he could barely light a cigarette. He also had a feeling of inner panic that made sleep almost impossible. A neighbor called the patient's sister in concern because he was not making any sense and seemed as if he could not take care of himself.
>
> When he was examined at the hospital the patient alternated between superficial, chatty warmth and apprehension. He went back and forth from recognizing the doctor to thinking he was the patient's brother. Twice during the interview the patient called the doctor by his brother's name and asked him when he had arrived, apparently losing track of the interview. When the patient is at rest he shows a gross tremor and picks "bugs" off the bedsheets. The patient has no **orientation to time** and thinks that he is in the parking lot of a supermarket. The patient says that he is fighting against his feeling that the world is about to end in a holocaust. The patient is startled every few minutes, from what he says are sounds and sights of fiery car crashes. These perceptions apparently are retriggered by sounds of rolling carts in the hall. Memory testing is not possible because the patient's attention shifts too rapidly. (Published with permission of American Psychiatric Press.)

Orientation to time
Awareness of temporal specification, such as time of day, the day of the week, or the year. Orientation to time is one of the functions assessed in a psychiatric exam.

THERAPEUTIC USES

Alcohol might have been thought to be the panacea for all of life's ills, but we now know its medical value is probably outdistanced by its social value (Ritchie, 1985). In fact, there was hint of this knowledge some time ago, based on a remedy for treating colds taken from an old English book: At first inkling of a cold, hang your hat on the bedpost, drink from a bottle of good whiskey until two hats appear, and then get into bed and stay there. The therapeutic value of alcohol in this case was in keeping the cold victim in bed.

However, alcohol is an ingredient in several legitimate medical products and does have limited direct therapeutic utility (Jacobs & Fehr, 1987). Because alcohol is an excellent solvent, small amounts are combined with other ingredients in making cough syrups and other products taken orally. Furthermore, alcohol is an ingredient in mouthwashes and shaving lotions. If the individuals like them, alcoholic beverages may be recommended in moderate amounts to convalescent or elderly patients to be taken before meals to stimulate appetite and digestion. Finally, dehydrated alcohol may be injected close to nerves or sympathetic ganglia to relieve chronic pain that may occur, for example, in inoperable cancer (Ritchie, 1985).

EFFECTS OF ALCOHOL

In this section we review both the acute and chronic effects of alcohol consumption. We first go over alcohol's many acute physiological, sensory-motor ("sensorimotor"), and psychological effects. We also discuss several topics of special societal concern related to alcohol's acute effects, including aggression, sexual behavior, and driving.

One point about alcohol's acute effects is that alcohol generally acts on the body as a depressant, and its acute effects are proportional to the magnitude of the BAC. Simply put, as the BAC increases, acute effects increase in number and intensity. However, how humans experience degree of **intoxication** and behave under different doses of alcohol often are modified by psychological and situational factors as well as alcohol dose and tolerance to this drug. For some behaviors these nondrug factors may even be more powerful determinants than drug factors of alcohol's acute effects.

Intoxication
A transient state of physical and psychological disruption due to the presence of a toxic substance, such as alcohol, in the CNS.

Acute Effects of Alcohol

Physiological effects   Alcohol has several physiological effects occurring at lower doses.[1] For example, alcohol inhibits the secretion of the antidiuretic hormone, which causes increased urination. The effect happens when the BAC is rising but not when it is falling. Alcohol also is a peripheral dilator and causes the skin to feel warm and turn red. A number of authors have cautioned against using alcoholic beverages in cold environments in order to warm up. This advice is counterintuitive to many drinkers, since they experience the warmth that occurs with peripheral dilation and know of the St. Bernard and its keg of brandy rescuing victims in snow-covered mountains. However, alcohol's dilating effect on peripheral blood vessels causes some loss of body heat, and it was thought that such action would ultimately cause decreased protection against the cold. It turns out the problem is not a serious one, as experimental studies have shown alcohol does not significantly tilt the balance of the body's regulation of its temperature in cold environments.

An acute alcohol effect with wide practical application is that it increases gastric secretion, which is one basis for the American cocktail hour. The increase in gastric secretion stimulates the appetite. Unfortunately, at high

---

[1]Much of the discussion of alcohol's acute effects is based on Becker, Roe, and Scott (1975), Jacobs and Fehr (1987), McKim (1986), and Sobell and Sobell (1981).

doses alcohol harms the stomach mucosa and causes gastric distress. Nausea and vomiting may occur at BACs over .15%. Another physiological effect of alcohol when taken in high doses and when the BAC increases rapidly is a release of corticosteroids, which is part of the body's general reaction to stress. In this case the stressor is a high dose of alcohol, which is toxic to the body.

An important acute effect of alcohol is disruption of sleep patterns. Even at lower doses alcohol suppresses **REM sleep,** which is the stage of the sleep cycle when most dreaming occurs (REM stands for "rapid eye movements," which characterize this stage of sleep). When the dose is low, the REM suppression tends to occur only in the first half of the night, but in the second half REM time rebounds and increases. At larger doses of alcohol REM is suppressed throughout the night.

Alcohol impairs memory. Its acute effects are on short-term memory, and when high BACs are reached rapidly a **blackout** may occur. Blackouts are an individual's amnesia about events when drinking even though there was no loss of consciousness. For example, a person who had a lot to drink the night before may wake up and have absolutely no recollection of where he or she parked the car. Blackouts are thought to result from a failure in transfer of information in **short-term memory** to **long-term memory.** There also are grayouts, in which an individual can partially recall events occurring in full consciousness during a drinking occasion or can recall the events only with prompting. Grayouts probably reflect state-dependent learning. Blackouts and grayouts do not happen consistently in the same individuals with a given dose of alcohol, and the factors specifically determining their occurrence have not been identified.

Every drinker probably has had at least one somewhat delayed consequence of an episode of overindulgence, the hangover. Hangovers may be thought of as a minor withdrawal syndrome, because they are the body's readjustment to a nonalcohol state. Hangovers begin to appear about four to twelve hours after the peak BAC is reached and generally are not seen as a pleasant alcohol effect. Symptoms may include headache, dizziness, nausea, vomiting, increased heart rate, fatigue, and thirst. Furthermore, although the BAC is zero, hangovers are associated with a reduced ability to perform the complex skills required to drive a motor vehicle (Franck, 1983).

Remedies galore have been sought for cure of the hangover. Perhaps the one heard most often is "hair of the dog that bit you," and in this case the dog is alcohol. It is true alcohol will erase its own hangover symptoms, just as drinking stops alcohol withdrawal symptoms. However, this solution is far from perfect, because all that is being accomplished is postponing the inevitable. Of course, a real danger in using alcohol in this way is that it is courting a pattern of frequent, heavy drinking, because alcohol is used to remove an unpleasant effect of drinking in high quantities. An ample number of studies have shown this effect to be highly reinforcing to humans and other animals alike. The only dependable and safe cure for hangover is time.

REM sleep
Acronym for "rapid eye movements," which are associated with dream activity and are one stage in a cycle of sleep.

Blackout
A person's amnesia about events while drinking even though there is no loss of consciousness.

Short-term memory
Memory for recent events. Short-term memory generally is thought to differ from long-term memory in several important ways.

Long-term memory
Memory for remote events. According to one theory of memory, information enters long-term memory through short-term memory.

DRUG USE AND MISUSE

CONTEMPORARY ISSUE BOX 7–2
The Hangover's Many Cures

Besides the "hair of the dog that bit you," several other supposed hangover cures have made the circuit among drinkers. Here are some of them, as listed by Carroll and Miller (1986).

1. Take megadoses of vitamins, so your body will have the strength to ward off the hangover.
2. Take tranquilizers.
3. Inhale pure oxygen to quicken the body's oxidation of alcohol.
4. Exercise.
5. Eat a big breakfast.
6. Drink a repulsive concoction, so the digusting taste will help you to forget the hangover.
7. Ignore your hangover.
8. Stay in bed and lie still.

Some of these purported remedies sound as though they were created by people desperately suffering from hangovers. None of them has a basis in medical science or practice. Hangovers are "cured" in only two ways: time, or not getting too intoxicated in the first place.

MAO inhibitors
Drugs used to treat depressions that inhibit the activity of the enzyme monoamine oxidase, which degrades the neurotransmitters of norepinephrine and serotonin.

In discussing alcohol's acute effects it is important to re-emphasize that it interacts synergistically with other CNS depressants. The point is worth repeating because of the dangerous effects of mixing alcohol and barbiturates, a common method of intended and unintended suicides. Alcohol and the benzodiazepines do not have the degree of suicide potential that alcohol and the barbiturates have, but there can be serious decrements in performance of skills essential to survival, such as driving a car or staying awake while driving a car. Similarly, marijuana and alcohol are frequently consumed on the same occasion, and there seem to be synergistic effects of these two drugs on skills related to driving (for example, Perez-Reyes, Hicks, Bumberry, Jeffcoat, & Cook, 1988). Antihistamines, which are available over-the-counter, also combine synergistically with alcohol. Another point about combining alcohol with other drugs: alcohol decreases the effects of certain prescribed medications, such as antibiotics, anticonvulsants, anticoagulants, and **monoamine oxidase inhibitors.**

Alcohol causes slight respiratory depression at lower doses, but this effect does not reach dangerous levels in healthy people unless very high doses are consumed. Higher doses also are associated with induction of sleep, stupor, and in extremely high doses, coma. In the overdose range of consumption, cardiovascular depression can occur. We earlier noted that a dose of alcohol can be lethal (LD-50 = BAC of .45–.50%), due to dysfunction of the more primitive areas of the brain controlling breathing and heartbeat.

Sensorimotor effects   At moderate (.05%) to higher BACs alcohol has several different acute effects on the senses. Vision decreases in acuity, and taste and smell are not as sensitive. Pain sensitivity decreases when the BAC is in the .08 to .10% range. Simple reaction time begins to slow significantly at a BAC of .10%. An example of a simple reaction time task is to press a key as quickly as possible when a single light on a panel shines. In complex reaction time, subjects are required to integrate two or more stimuli and then respond to them as quickly as possible. An example is to press a key when a white and red light shines but not to press it when only the white light shines. Complex reaction time may be impaired for both speed and accuracy at BACs of .05 percent or even lower.

Alcohol strongly affects body sway, which is measured by asking the subject to stand steady with his or her eyes closed. The body's deviation from a "steady state" is then recorded. At a BAC of .06% body sway is impaired by about 40%. At a high BAC, we see alcohol's effect on body sway manifested as staggering and, eventually, as an inability to walk independently at all. The sensitivity of body sway to alcohol is the source of the "walk a straight line" test police use to decide whether a suspect is drunk. Alcohol's influence on body sway is due to its effects on balance controls in the inner ear. This also is the reason why the room may spin when the party goer lies down and closes his or her eyes to sleep after a night of heavy drinking.

Alcohol impairs psychomotor skills. In tasks designed to measure these skills, subjects are required to make controlled muscular movements to adjust or position a machine or some mechanism on an experimental apparatus in response to changes in speed or direction of a moving object (for example Levine, Kramer, & Levine, 1975, p. 288). A common example is the pursuit rotor task, in which the subject must keep a stylus on a target that moves circularly on an automated disk.

Psychomotor task performance on the average shows deterioration at BACs of about .03% and higher (Levine and others, 1975). These tasks commonly require relatively fine motor dexterity. At high BACs, .15% or more, there is clear abnormality in gross motor functions, like standing or walking. At these levels, alcohol has impaired the brain centers responsible for motor activity and balance to such a degree that the neural messages are not being sent to the muscles.

Alcohol and Driving Ability

Sensorimotor skills constitute a major part of driving ability. During the early 1980s there was an enormous increase in public awareness of drinking and driving a motor vehicle. Probably most influential in opening the public's eyes and ears about drunk driving were citizens' organizations such as Mothers Against Drunk Driving (MADD) and Students Against Drunk Driving (SADD). These movements contributed to and were strengthened by the more conservative attitudes toward alcohol and drug use that marked the 1980s in the United States. Part of this whole trend has been increased enforcement of stricter legal penalties for driving under the influence (DUI) of alcohol (or other drugs). One example, in over half of the United States, is mandatory jail sentences. Jail may be a consequence even for a first DUI offense.

The center of attention about the dangers of alcohol use has been motor vehicles, particularly cars. There is ample cause for concern. Motor vehicle crashes are the most common nonnatural cause of death in the United States (USDHHS, 1987). Alcohol is implicated as a causal factor in traffic fatalities, but statistics are not conclusive, because we have only correlational studies. The argument for alcohol as cause is strengthened, however, by data on the relationship between relative risk of involvement in a traffic accident and

Figure 7-7 Motor vehicle accidents are the single most common nonnatural cause of death in the United States.

BAC. At a BAC of .05% the risk is about twice the likelihood than when the BAC is zero. At a BAC of .10%, the risk triples from that at a BAC of zero. At a BAC of .15% it is about seven times, and at a BAC of .20%, the risk balloons to more than twenty times (Harvard, 1977).

The case for alcohol as a causal factor in traffic fatalities becomes even more solid with experimental data on how alcohol affects performance on tasks requiring psychomotor skills and an integration of sensory information. An example, called a "divided attention" task, would be combining the pursuit rotor and complex reaction time tasks into one experimental task. Subjects would be required to keep the stylus on target (pursuit rotor) while they are simultaneously responding to the two light stimuli on a panel (complex reaction time). Driving a car requires the same motor control and sensory integration abilities that would be necessary to complete such a divided attention task. Alcohol impairs performance on divided attention tasks at BACs of .05% or lower. In fact, this is one basis of the recommendation of several groups, such as the American College of Emergency Physicians, the Associates for the Advancement of Emergency Medicine, and the American Medical Association, that the legal level of intoxication be uniform across the United States at a BAC of .05%. Currently, in some states, arrest is possible at BACs between .05% and .10% for "driving while impaired."

Alcohol seems to be, therefore, a primary factor raising the risk of involvement in fatal and nonfatal motor vehicle accidents. Other factors interact with alcohol to affect risk, and two of the more important ones are gender and age. Young drivers are far more likely to be involved in alcohol-related accidents. For example, one study showed that in 1980 eighteen year-olds constituted 2.2% of the driver population and drove 2% of the total number of miles traveled. Yet they were involved in 5.5% of the alcohol–related accidents. By comparison, 45–54 year-olds drove nine times as many miles as the eighteen-year-olds but had only one and one–third as many alcohol-related accidents. It also appears young people are put at increased risk for alcohol-related fatal accidents at lower BACs than are older drivers. In a study comparing five different age groups of drivers involved in fatal motor vehicle accidents, 16–19-year olds were measured as having a much lower BAC than did drivers in the older age groups. One explanation for this finding is that younger people have less experience in both drinking and driving (USDHHS, 1987). This means driving is not as well-learned a skill in younger people and is more likely to be disrupted at a given BAC. Furthermore, younger people would tend to show less protracted tolerance in general at a given BAC because of their shorter period of use of alcoholic beverages.

Young males (≤ 25 years old) seem to be the group most likely to be intoxicated, driving, and in traffic accidents. This is consistent with our review earlier of survey data that showed that young men are the ones most likely to drink heavily (five or more drinks) on an occasion. Data published in 1983 show that 38% of the young men drivers who were involved in fatal accidents had a BAC of .10% or higher, compared to 30% for all other age and gender groups (USDHHS, 1987). Young men are more likely to be legally intoxicated and the drivers in fatal accidents because of their tendency to drink heavily on occasion, and because they drive a relatively higher percentage of miles on weekend nights, when all drivers are most likely to be intoxicated.

In summary, motor vehicle accidents continue to be an extremely serious problem in the United States, and alcohol seems to play a major part in them. It appears that continued vigilance both by law enforcement personnel and by citizens groups such as MADD are essential for sustained progress on the drunk driving problem. The driver's perception that DUI arrest and conviction are highly likely consequences for driving while legally intoxicated is particularly important for stemming the DUI problem (USDHHS, 1987). A major part of prevention efforts (Chapter 16) aimed at adolescents and young adults also must continue to be repeated as reminders about the facts and dangers in driving under the influence of alcohol or other drugs.

Psychological effects   Alcohol combines with other factors to change emotion and mood. Different people report a range of psychological effects at a given BAC, and the same drinker may report different effects at a BAC on different occasions. The influences of nondrug factors, particularly situational and cognitive variables (for example expectancies and attitudes), are perhaps most powerful in this domain. The person's mood state before he or she started to drink also is an important factor.

At lower BACs, drinkers report feeling elated and friendly when the BAC is rising, but when it is falling common reports are anger and fatigue. Other reports when the BAC is rising have been expansiveness, joviality, relaxation, and self-confidence. The importance of nondrug factors is accented in the finding that during the ascending phase of these same BACs other subjects have reported feeling hostile, depressed, and withdrawn. When BACs go above .10%, drinkers commonly become more labile, as the drinker may abruptly change from friendly to hostile. Often the level of frustration tolerance is lowered.

Alcohol's effects on thinking and perception are less influenced by nondrug factors and more by BAC. Alcohol significantly impairs short–term memory at BACs over .05%. At a BAC of .05% the ability to estimate time is impaired. Drinkers seem to overestimate time passage at a BAC of .05%. So, they might estimate a time passage of eight minutes to be twelve minutes. The ability to estimate distance (depth perception) also is disrupted at lower BACs, as are attention and concentration. At higher BACs these cognitive effects are intensified and are compounded by more disorganized thinking.

Alcohol and behavior   Among alcohol's effects, those that affect interpersonal behavior are of great social interest. As the word implies, "interpersonal'' means between people. The interpersonal behaviors of sex and aggression in combination with alcohol have garnered the greatest interest and concern.

Alcohol and aggression The United States government keeps detailed records on the occurrence of different categories of crimes and the factors associated with their occurrence. Studies show that when people commit violent crimes, they tend to be under the influence of alcohol (see Contemporary Issue Box 1–2). Violent crimes include murder or attempted murder, manslaughter, rape or sexual assault, robbery, assault, and others, such as kidnapping, purse snatching, hit-and-run driving, and child abuse. These findings also hold for Canada and Western Europe (Collins, 1981). The co-occurrence of alcohol use and violent crime is especially prevalent among young adult (ages 18 to 30) men, who have a relatively high rate of both heavy drinking and criminal activity. Another problem of national concern is physical abuse of spouses (predominantly husbands abusing wives), and alcohol has been estimated to be involved (offender or victim) in 25 to 50% of spouse abuse incidents (Collins, Guess, Williams, & Hamilton, 1980).

National statistics not only show associations between alcohol and violence toward others, but also violence toward the self. For example, suicide is one of the three leading causes of death (the other two are homicide and accidental death) among males 15 to 34 years old and one of the ten leading causes of death among all persons 34–54 years old. In one study of 3400 violent deaths in which the victims' BACs were tested, suicide was determined as the cause of death, and 35% of these suicides had been drinking when they took their lives (USDHHS, 1987).

National attention also has been directed at alcohol and behavior at baseball and other professional sports playing areas and at fraternities. In both cases aggressive behavior has been the focus, and alcohol has been singled out as a major culprit. One example is the fans' rowdy reactions during an April, 1988 game at Cincinnati's Riverfront Stadium, when an umpire made a call unfavorable to the home team Reds. Alcohol was viewed by league officials to be at the heart of the "deterioration" of the situation. This and similar events have led many major league baseball teams to adopt restricted alcohol sales (primarily beer) policies, and even to have alcohol-free sections in the stands, similar to smoke-free areas in public places. Alcohol also has been identified as a major problem in the behavior of members of fraternities on college campuses. For example, misconduct and violence against property and persons that some fraternities are known for have been highly correlated with the occurrence of popular frat functions such as beer bashes.

The consistency of the co-occurrence of drinking and violent behavior tempt the conclusion that alcohol causes such behavior. However, data such as government statistics are only descriptive and correlational and cannot be the bases of valid causal statements about alcohol and aggression. Nevertheless, the adult drinking public believes alcohol does indeed cause aggression. A consistent finding in many studies of beliefs about the effects of alcohol is that it increases power and aggression (Brown, Christiansen, & Goldman, 1987). Perhaps these beliefs underlie officials' statements that alcohol causes disorderly conduct at ballparks and fraternities.

CONTEMPORARY ISSUE BOX 7–3
The Balanced Placebo Design

Because of placebo effects (see Chapter 4) experimental studies of drug effects in humans and other animals always include a placebo control group. In studies of alcohol effects in humans, this group involves telling subjects they are drinking an alcoholic beverage when, in fact, they are not given one. Instead they are given a nonalcoholic drink resembling the alcoholic beverage in every way except alcohol content. So, in the traditional placebo group design everybody in two groups of subjects is told he or she will drink an alcoholic beverage, but only one group's beverage actually contains alcohol. Studies following this design have varied in their success of making the alcoholic and placebo beverages indistinguishable on cues such as taste and smell and, therefore, in the validity of their findings. How do you think failure to make the alcohol and placebo beverages indiscriminable would affect the interpretation of results of a study?

A significant advance in studying drug effects on human behavior was made over 25 years ago in what has been named the balanced placebo design (BPD). The design has helped a lot to advance knowledge about alcohol and aggression and sex, among other human behaviors. The BPD involves adding two groups to the traditional two-group placebo group design. The subjects in each of the two additional groups are told they will not receive a drug, and in one group they get the drug and in the other they do not. Therefore, comparisons are possible with a group of subjects who believe they are not getting, and do not get, a drug (sober control group). It also is possible to make comparisons with a group of subjects who believe they are not receiving a drug but do really get one. The advance that the design offers is that we can separate a pure drug effect, an "expectancy" (about drug actions) effect, and their interaction Under the best conditions of control the traditional placebo design provides a comparison only of drug versus expectancy conditions, which permits conclusions about drug action. The BPD seems much better suited than the traditional placebo design for studying the complexity of drugs and human behavior.

Table 7–3
Balanced Placebo Designs

<table>
<tr><td rowspan="8">Beverage Told</td><td></td><td colspan="2" align="center">*Beverage Received*</td></tr>
<tr><td></td><td align="center">*Alcohol*</td><td align="center">*Placebo*</td></tr>
<tr><td>Alcohol</td><td align="center">Group 1</td><td align="center">2</td></tr>
<tr><td>Placebo</td><td align="center">3</td><td align="center">4</td></tr>
</table>

Outline of the balanced placebo design in studying alcohol effects. The traditional placebo design includes groups 1 and 2 only.

Of course, aggressive behavior is a highly significant social concern, and it is important to find the reasons for the association between drinking and the occurrence of violent behavior. A traditional explanation is disinhibition theory, which was first proposed in the early twentieth century. This theory holds that alcohol releases behavior normally inhibited by society, such as aggression and sex, as a result of its depressant action on the brain. Essentially, the theory suggests that whatever anxieties about the social consequences of behavior such as aggression that we have learned vanish as a result of alcohol's pharmacological action. So, people who have been drinking should be more aggressive than people who have not.

Controlled laboratory experiments involving human subjects do not support the disinhibition theory, however. Some studies have shown a correlation between alcohol and aggression that has been discovered in epidemiological studies. However, this was not a simple matter of alcohol's pharmacological action, as disinhibition theory predicts. Rather, alcohol combines with situational factors, such as social pressure and threat of retaliation (Adesso, 1985). Furthermore, drinkers' expectancies about alcohol and aggression also seem to contribute to aggression, sometimes considerably more than actually drinking alcohol does.

It seems, therefore, that alcohol does not simply cause aggression, despite the beliefs of some public officials and the general population. Instead, aggression is a complex social behavior affected by the characteristics of the aggressor and situational factors, only one of which is alcohol consumption. Theories about aggression must accommodate this complexity to be useful.

Alcohol and sex For almost 500 years Shakespeare probably has been the author most frequently cited on the acute effects of alcohol on human sexual response. The specific reference is from *Macbeth,* Act 2, Scene 2: "It (alcohol) provokes and unprovokes; it provokes the desire, but it takes away from the performance." It turns out that the results of recent experimental studies are in part consistent with Shakespeare's observations.

Alcohol and sexual response in men and women has been a favorite subject of writers for thousands of years. Much of the writing has been like Shakespeare's comments, based on informal personal observations. As regards male sexual response, the folklore leads to dose-dependent conclusions. Alcohol has been thought to be an aphrodisiac in men at lower doses but an impediment to sexual performance at higher doses. An example is a quote of the Greek poet Euenas, from the fifth century B.C.

> The best measure of wine is neither much nor very little;
> For 'tis the cause of either grief or madness.
> Then too, 'tis most suited for the bridal chamber and love.
> And if it breathe too fiercely, it puts love to flight.
> And plunges men in a sleep, neighbor to death.

(Quoted by Abel, 1985).

There have been efforts at systematic study of human sexual response to a dose of alcohol, but only in the past fifteen years or so has it been possible to do well-controlled research on this topic. The significant breakthroughs have been the invention of the penile strain gauge to measure penile erectile response and the photoplethysmograph to measure vaginal blood volume and pressure. These advances have paved the way to experimental study of human sexual response and alcohol.

Experimental studies of men have consistently shown that, at BACs between .05% and .10%, alcohol pharmacologically retards sexual arousal. When the BAC climbs over .10%, erection and ejaculatory competence are inhibited or eliminated. Importantly, these findings have been repeated in samples of nonproblem drinker college students and in alcoholics. Alcohol does not stimulate men's libido, especially at moderate or higher BACs.

At lower BACs alcohol effects are not as dominant. It appears that cognitive factors, such as expectancies about alcohol effects, may work to increase men's libido. Indeed, studies of alcohol expectancies suggest the drinking public generally believes alcohol enhances sexual experience (Brown and others, 1987). Consistent with this finding, balanced placebo design (see Contemporary Issue Box 7–3) studies suggest men's sexual arousal is increased when they believe they are drinking a dose of alcohol that brings them to a BAC less than .05%. Alcohol itself, however, has no effect on measured arousal at such BACs, which coincides with many other studies of the pharmacology of alcohol (Abel, 1985). Another characteristic of the drinker that seems to affect his sexual arousal at BACs below .05% is personality. One study showed increased sexual response was especially evident in subjects who thought they were drinking alcohol and who scored high on a measure of guilt about sex (Lang, Searles, Lauerman, & Adesso, 1980).

A reasonable conclusion about the acute effects of alcohol on male sexual response is that, similar to aggression, the disinhibition theory falls far short of explaining the information that is available. Rather, social and psychological factors seem to be important determinants of sexual response in men at low BACs and often work to increase libido. However, the pharmacology of alcohol begins to dominate at BACs greater than .05% and causes a decrease in arousal and sexual competence.

The folklore about the acute effects of alcohol on sexual behavior in women is that it promotes promiscuity. For example, Chaucer wrote in his "The Wife of Bath's Tale":

> After wine, I think mostly of venue for just
> as it's true that cold engenders hail a liquor
> mouth must have a liquorous tail. Women
> have no defense against wine as lechers know
> from experience.

Previous nonexperimental studies, as well as studies of alcohol expectancies that we cited earlier, suggest that alcohol increases sexual arousal in women and that women believe alcohol has that effect. The recent experimental evidence is that, as in men, women's physiological sexual response decreases with increasing alcohol dose. However, unlike men, women continue to perceive increased sexual arousal and sexual pleasure even as the

Table 7-4

Typical Acute Effects of Alcohol Associated with Different Ascending Blood Alcohol Concentrations (BACs)

BAC (%)	Effects
.01–.02	Slight changes in feeling; sense of warmth and well-being.
.03–.04	Feelings of relaxation, slight exhilaration, happiness. Skin may flush, mild impairment in motor skills.
.05–.06	Effects become more noticeable. More exaggerated changes in emotion, impaired judgment, and lowered inhibitions. Coordination may be altered.
.08–.09	Reaction time increased, muscle coordination impaired. Sensory feelings of numbness in cheeks, lips, and extremities. Further impairment in judgment.
.10	Definite deterioration in motor coordination and reaction time. Person may stagger and slow speech. Legal level of intoxication in 47 of 50 United States.
.15	Major impairment in balance and movement. Large increase in reaction time. Large impairment in judgment and perception.
.20	Difficulty staying awake; substantial reduction of motor and sensory capabilities; slurred speech, double vision, difficulty standing or walking without assistance.
.30	Confusion and stupor. Difficulty comprehending what is going on; possible loss of consciousness (passing out).
.40	Typically unconsciousness; sweatiness and clamminess of the skin. Alcohol has become an anesthetic.
.45–.50	Circulatory and respiratory functions may become totally depressed. LD-50 in humans.

physiological indexes of their response and arousal are declining. It seems Shakespeare's observation most clearly applies to women, even though he was referring to men. It also is important not to conclude that the disinhibition theory accounts for the data on alcohol effects in women. Despite their perceived increased sexual arousal when they drink, whether women act on such perception depends on characteristics in the drinking setting and what the drinker has learned is acceptable sexual behavior in that setting. Therefore, again, a theory about the acute effects of alcohol on women's sexual behavior should incorporate social and psychological factors as well as the pharmacology of alcohol.

EFFECTS OF CHRONIC, HEAVY DRINKING

Chronic, heavy use of alcohol may have numerous physiological and psychological effects. All of the effects involve increased dysfunction, and some may be fatal. Some chronic alcohol effects are caused directly by alcohol's toxicity to the body, such as damage to the liver. Other effects are indirectly related to long-term abusive drinking. For example, Wernicke's disease, which involves impaired cognitive functioning, is caused by nutritional deficiencies that tend to occur in people dependent on alcohol (Jacobs & Fehr, 1987).

Chronic, heavy drinking is difficult to define precisely. Suffice it to say that many of alcohol's long-term effects take years to become evident. And, heavy drinkers vary greatly in their susceptibility to alcohol-related impairments.

A standard for what is heavy, or at least "unsafe" drinking, has been proposed. However, long-term drinking of a given quantity of alcohol affects different drinkers in different ways, both in number and severity of symptoms. Nevertheless, it is useful to have a guide to what is a "safe" level of alcohol consumption for the average drinker. The Addiction Research Foundation in Toronto, Canada, addressed this question in a pamphlet called "Know the Score." It seems that beyond two drinks a day the average drinker is risking his or her good health. An average of five to six drinks a day was called "hazardous," seven to eight drinks a day "harmful," and nine or more drinks a day "extremely dangerous."

Table 7-5 includes the major effects of chronic heavy drinking on body systems. As you can see in the table, alcohol can be highly toxic to the human body and cause extensive damage to it in a variety of ways. Two prominent body systems that alcohol harms are the brain and the liver. We will look at alcohol's chronic effects on these systems in more detail. Alcohol's chronic effects extend to human sexual functioning, which has to do with alcohol's altering the functioning of the hypothalamic-pituitary-gonadal endocrine axis and the fetal alcohol syndrome (FAS).

Table 7–5

The Effects of Chronic, Heavy Drinking on Body Systems

System	Effects
Central Nervous System	Specific and general impairment in cognitive functioning
Liver	Minor, reversible (with abstinence) damage to irreversible, sometimes fatal damage
Cardiovascular	Increased mortality from coronary heart disease, and increased risk for cardiovascular diseases in general; alcohol-induced wasting of the heart muscle (alcohol cardiomyopathy)
Endocrine	Affects secretion of hormones in different hormone hierarchies, or "axes." Examples are hypothalamic-pituitary-adrenal axis, and the hypothalamic-pituitary-gonadal axis
Immune System	Increased susceptibility to several infectious diseases
Gastrointestinal	Causes gastritis and increases risk of pancreatitis
Multiple	Increased risk of contracting the following cancers: oral cavity, tongue, pharynx, larynx, esophagus, stomach, liver, lung, pancreas, colon, rectum

Note: The information in this table is based on USDHHS (1987) and Jacobs and Fehr (1987).

Alcohol and Brain Functioning

The acute effects of alcohol on memory and other cognitive functioning are manifest at moderate BACs and are reversible. However, alcohol affects these same functions in the long-term in some people if it is drunk long enough and heavily enough. Such chronic effects occur in degrees of severity, evidenced as mildly impaired performance on **neuropsychological tests** to severe, irreversible brain structural and functional damage shown as severe memory impairment in Korsakoff's syndrome (Parsons, 1986).

The average alcohol–dependent individual who has been studied, when abstinent from alcohol or other psychoactive drugs, performs more poorly than nonalcoholic control groups on tests of abstracting, problem solving, memory, learning, and perceptual-motor speed. Recent reviews have shown about 60% of the individuals who have been tested show such impairments, which suggests that characteristics of the drinkers also influence their vulnerability to alcohol's effects on brain function. A major one is the individual's drinking history. While the evidence is mixed, in general the longer a person drinks and the higher the quantity that is consumed, the greater the impairment in cognitive functioning.

Fortunately, with long-term abstinence from alcohol most alcohol-related neuropsychological impairment once evident can be virtually reversed, with only mild deficits left compared to control subjects. This conclusion is based on studies that involved following subjects' test performance during

Neuropsychological Tests Formal ways of measuring behavioral functions that may be impaired by brain lesions.

periods of abstinence lasting from one month to five years (Parsons, 1986; Parsons & Leber, 1982). The reversibility of the cognitive dysfunctions is not due to the regeneration of neurons, which does not happen. Rather, recent studies suggest that many changes in the brain as recorded in imaging techniques such as the CAT scan and associated with cognitive impairments among alcohol dependent subjects are due to factors other than loss of brain neurons (Mello, 1987).

Wernicke-Korsakoff Syndrome This severe CNS disorder is the result of combining extreme nutritional deficiency, specifically Vitamin B_1, or thiamine, and chronic heavy drinking. Basically there are two diseases. Wernicke's disease is characterized by confusion, loss of memory, staggering gait, and an inability to focus the eye (Sobell & Sobell, 1981; USDHHS, 1987). In the absence of permanent brain damage, Wernicke's disease is reversible by giving the patient Vitamin B_1.

Korsakoff's syndrome may have a nutritional component to it but is most directly due to alcohol. It is associated with damage to brain structure and most affects memory. In this regard, there are serious impairments in short-term memory and learning. Because of these dysfunctions there often is considerable confusion and **confabulation.** There also is a lesser degree of impairment in memory for events in longer-term memory. The following case, based on one discussed in the DSM-III Case Book (Spitzer, et al., 1981, pp. 56–57), gives a good illustration of some of the major symptoms of Korsakoff's syndrome.

Confabulation
A fabrication about events, when asked questions concerning them, because of our inability to recall.

The patient was a 40-year-old man who in the interview claimed to be an accountant. He said that he had some business troubles and had come to the hospital to get help. His story was coherent, but there was a lack of consistency and details to it. As regards his hospitalization, the patient said that he had been in for only a few days but a few minutes later he said several weeks. He could not recall his doctor's name.

Formal testing showed that the patient could not recall the names of three objects that he had seen five minutes earlier, or repeat a story that was told to him. However, the patient could perform simple calculations, define words and concepts, and find similarities and differences among objects and concepts. The patient's medical record showed that he had a long history of alcohol dependence and had been living in a nursing home for the last three years until he was admitted to the hospital a week ago. He was admitted after several incidents of his wandering from the nursing home and being returned there by police. (Published with permission of American Psychiatric Press.)

Alcohol and the Liver

As the major metabolic site of alcohol the liver is highly vulnerable to alcohol's toxic effects. The damage that alcohol can cause to the liver occurs in three ways: fatty liver, alcohol hepatitis, and cirrhosis. Fatty liver is characterized by fat accumulating in the liver and is the earliest, most benign effect of alcohol's effects on the liver. This condition is reversible with abstinence from alcohol, and there is no evidence that it is a precurser of cirrhosis. Alcohol hepatitis is more serious and involves the inflammation and death of liver cells. Often jaundice occurs because of the accumulation of bile. This condition is reversible with abstinence and medical treatment, but can cause death if it is severe enough and not treated. Liver hepatitis can be caused by means other than heavy drinking. Evidence of such drinking must be obtained in order to diagnose alcohol hepatitis.

The most serious and life-threatening of alcohol's liver assaults is cirrhosis. Alcohol dependence is the leading cause of cirrhosis, which in turn is the ninth leading cause of death in the United States (USDHHS, 1987). Drinking must be prodigious and long-term for someone to develop cirrhosis. For example, one survey showed that people with alcohol dependence who developed cirrhosis drank an average of thirteen drinks a day for about twenty years! It did not matter what beverage form alcohol was consumed in. It should be noted that only a small minority of individuals who are alcohol-dependent develop cirrhosis—about 10%.

For those who do get cirrhosis, the condition is not reversible, and only half are still alive five years after the initial diagnosis is made. Cirrhosis is a chronic inflammatory disease of the liver involving cell death and the formation of scar tissue. It may or may not be preceded by alcohol hepatitis. Death results from cirrhosis because the liver fails to metabolize various toxins, such as ammonia, and these toxins accumulate in the body.

Alcohol and Sexual Functioning

Both men and women suffer impaired sexual functioning as a result of chronic, heavy drinking. In men, such drinking affects the male sex hormones, reflexive responses of the nervous system relating to sexual performance, and sperm production. First, there often is gynecomastia (formation of breasts in men), which is a result of alcohol's altering the balance of the female sex hormone, estrogen, and the male sex hormone, testosterone. The shifting in balance is due to alcohol's damage to the liver and resorption of estrogens into the blood. Another result of changing the balance in the sex hormones is a loss in sexual desire. Along with a loss in desire is a drop in sexual performance, manifested as ejaculatory incompetence and impotence. These latter effects are due to alcohol's inhibition of reflexive responses in the nervous system. Finally, chronic heavy drinking may result in hypogonadism and eventual sterility. There is also some possibility that sperm production is so impaired that defective offspring could be conceived (Abel, 1985; Mello, 1987).

As in most areas of alcohol effects, we know a lot less about chronic alcohol effects on sexual functioning in women. The little scientific information available suggests alcohol dependence in women is associated with dysfunction of the ovaries, disruption of the luteal phase of fertilization, and amenorrhea (cessation of the menstrual period) (Mello, 1987). A household survey suggests that a woman does not have to be diagnosed as having alcohol dependence to experience impaired sexual function related to alcohol use. The survey of more than nine hundred women living in households showed a positive correlation between alcohol consumption and the occurrence of different menstrual disorders (Wilsnack, Klassen, & Wilsnack, 1984).

Fetal Alcohol Syndrome

In this section we discuss a chronic alcohol effect that does not focus on a specific body system or on the drinker. Rather, it focuses on the fetus and what alcohol consumption may do to it if its mother drinks during pregnancy. A characteristic set of symptoms appearing in some newborns of mothers who drink during pregnancy has become known as the Fetal Alcohol Syndrome (FAS). The FAS actually has been written about since the time of Aristotle but only recently has it received the attention of scientists. Since 1973 the literature on it has grown geometrically.

The FAS refers to gross physical deformities that were identified in eleven very young children who had severely alcohol-dependent mothers who drank during pregnancy. These deformities were described in a 1973 clin-

Figure 7–8 This child was diagnosed as fetal alcohol syndrome affected.

ical report and include the following: small eyes and small eye openings, drooping eyelids, underdeveloped midface, skin folds across the inner corners of the eyes (which were abnormal in this sample of eleven white children), underdevelopment of the depression above the upper lip, and a small head circumference. Furthermore, abnormal creases in the palm were reported, along with abnormalities in the joints. Some of the children had cardiac defects, benign tumors consisting of dilated blood vessels, and minor ear abnormalities. A ten-year follow-up of these children showed low-normal to severely retarded intellectual functioning, physical deformities similar to those originally reported, and the development of additional physical problems.

Current estimates are that abnormalities in the fetus related to alcohol occur in one to three of every one thousand live births (Mello, 1987; USDHHS, 1987). It is clear that FAS occurs much less often than does abusive drinking by women during pregnancy. A few recent large surveys suggest there are several factors that together greatly increase the risk of FAS. These are a higher percentage of drinking days during pregnancy, a higher likelihood of having alcohol dependence, a higher number of previous births, and being black. If none of these four variables is present in heavy drinking women, the risk of FAS is less than 2%. When all four are present, the risk is over 85% (USDHHS, 1987).

We should raise two important points before ending this brief discussion of FAS. What part of the occurrence of FAS is due directly to alcohol has not been determined. It is a difficult problem to solve, because when other drugs are taken during pregnancy they also may harm the fetus in ways similar to alcohol. A survey reported in 1988 showed a high rate of illegal drug use among pregnant women (Brody, 1988). Furthermore, no "safe" alcohol use rule during pregnancy has been discovered, and the best advice still is the most conservative: If you are pregnant, do not use alcohol or other drugs.

Moderate Drinking and Health

As we expect you are convinced at this point, long-term, heavy use of alcohol could seriously damage the body. But what about long-term abstinence from alcohol and long-term lighter drinking? In the last ten years or so, over twenty studies have been reported that suggest the moderate drinkers turn out the healthiest, followed by the abstainers, and dead last are the heavy topers. "Health" is measured by risk of cardiovascular disease and mortality (Knupfer, 1987).

The surprise here, of course, is that drinking can be healthy. The first question is, what is "moderate"? Generally, it has been defined as one to three drinks a day. How could such drinking possibly aid health? One hypothesis is that light alcohol consumption increases the production of high density lipoproteins (HDLs), which take damaging cholesterol away

from artery walls. Alcohol could have this effect by its effect on the liver—
it increases the activity of the liver, and the liver produces the protein that
envelops HDL particles.

Many experts have concluded that moderate drinking could improve
health. However, in what may be somewhat of a letdown to drinkers, the
conclusions about moderate alcohol use and health recently have been
questioned. One reason is how the relevant studies have been done. A big
question is whether many "light/moderate daily drinkers" exist. In this
respect, most light drinkers do not drink every day, and most people who
drink every day do not drink lightly. Another major point is that more than
twice as many of the people who were classified as abstainers in the studies
were poor as compared to wealthy. It is well-known that people with low
incomes have worse health (Knupfer, 1987). A final question concerns alcohol's biological action. In order to have the beneficial effects on health that
have been attributed to it, alcohol would have to be associated with stimulated production of a different type (HDL-2) of HDL than it does. For example, jogging stimulates production of HDL-2 (Bennett, 1988).

It seems safe to conclude that the moderate drinking-health hypothesis
stands on a much weaker foundation than typically is thought. If you drink,
you should not be telling yourself you are drinking to be healthier. If you
want cardiovascular health you probably should try aerobic exercise
instead.

ALCOHOL DEPENDENCE: HOW DOES IT DEVELOP?

In this chapter you have seen that many adults drink, and that a minority of
them drink heavily. Some of the heavy drinkers develop problems with alcohol to different degrees. When they do, the effects on themselves, their families, and their society are devastating. Accordingly, this question has pre-
occupied many for many years: How does alcohol dependence develop, or,
what is its etiology? In this last section we briefly present what approaches
to the question have been taken and describe the current thinking.

Traditional Approaches to Etiology

Until very recently researchers and clinicians alike usually sought a single-
factor explanation of what causes alcohol dependence. Theories frequently
outpaced data to evaluate them and could be classified as biological, psychological, and sociological.

Biological approaches have waxed and waned in popularity over the years
(Roebuck & Kessler, 1972). Such theories hold the common premise that
there is a physiological or structural anomaly that causes the individual to

become alcohol-dependent. Earlier single-factor biological approaches, which have not received experimental support, have included hypotheses that the source of the structural deficit was metabolic, glandular, due to body chemistry, or due to an allergic condition. The most prevalent position among United States treatment providers is that alcohol dependence is a physical disease (see Contemporary Issue Box 7–4). Although the source of the disease process is not specified, disease model adherents use the process of a physical disease, such as a fever, as an analogy in order to understand alcohol dependence. As a result, the disease model is classified as a biological model.

Biological explanations of alcohol dependence have regained popularity among scientists because of the findings suggesting there is a genetic predisposition at least to some "types" of alcohol dependence (Schuckit, 1987). The evidence comes primarily from family, twin, and adoption studies. In summary, family studies show that sons and daughters of alcohol-dependent parents are four times more likely to develop the disorder themselves, relative to people whose parents are not alcohol dependent. In addition, studies of twins show there is greater likelihood that both members of identical twin pairs have alcohol dependence ("concordance") than is the likelihood of concordance in fraternal twins. The significance of this finding is that identical twins are genetic matches, whereas members of fraternal twin pairs have 50% of their genes in common. Another finding pertains to adopted children of alcohol-dependent parents. These studies show that the development of alcohol problems in the offspring is far more influenced by having an alcoholic parent than by the foster home environment. This conclusion is especially strong for males. Based on this body of research, the argument for a biological predisposition to alcohol dependence has gained considerable strength.

Psychological and sociological explanations Psychological explanations of etiology have centered on finding the "alcoholic personality," which means a psychological trait or set of traits that predispose someone to become alcohol-dependent. Failure to find such a high risk profile has not been due to lack of trying, as evidenced by the number of publications on the topic. However, some recent, well-designed studies have suggested that presence of an "antisocial personality" (the personality identified with convicted criminals, as one group) and ego weakness, which is manifested by impulsivity, intensity of mood, unstable self-esteem, and alternating dependence on and independence from others, could be psychological factors that predispose to alcohol dependence (Donovan, 1986).

Sociological models of etiology were proposed partly in response to the failure to discover the unique alcoholic personality. The models are supported by findings of cross cultural differences in drinking patterns (MacAndrew & Edgerton, 1969), as well as the demographic factors that you have seen are correlated with drinking patterns and problems. Studies that take them into account have shown consistently that sociological factors help to explain the development of alcohol dependence.

Interactional Approaches to Etiology

Although there are bright spots in each type of single factor explanation, each alone ultimately fails to explain how alcohol dependence develops. For example, a minority of children of alcoholic parents become alcohol-dependent themselves. What happens to the rest? A set of psychological characteristics may be associated with developing alcohol dependence, but those same characteristics could be correlated with other outcomes. Demographic factors are correlated with drinking problems, but the factors themselves are often associated with biological and psychological variables too. It seems single factor researchers design their studies so one type of factor, say psychological, is emphasized and other types are underplayed or not represented at all. Indeed, the fact that there are seeds of support for each type of approach, but not strong support for any one alone, suggests that multiple types of factors influence the development of alcohol dependence. At least among scientists this is the most current thinking: Alcohol, as well as drug dependence, is caused and maintained by a combination of biological, psychological, and sociological factors (for example, Galizio & Maisto, 1985). The jargon way of saying this is that these three sets of factors "interact" in causing and maintaining alcohol dependence.

What this means in practice is that scientists and practitioners alike cannot hope to understand alcohol dependence unless they consider together all the types of influencing variables. A good example is some of the exciting research that has been done with nonalcohol dependent sons of alcoholics. One finding is from electrophysiological studies of the brain that show preadolescent sons of alcoholics may have a deficit that is expressed as a lesser ability to focus on stimuli in the environment. This difference from boys who do not have alcohol dependent parents is presumably inherited and cannot be a consequence of the subject's own drinking. In theory, such a deficit could increase the risk of developing alcohol dependence because of, say, a decreased ability to discriminate degree of intoxication when drinking moderately. Additionally, discrimination deficits could affect performance of various cognitive tasks and how the individual relates to other people (Schuckit, 1987). Whether risk actually is translated into alcohol dependence, however, depends in large part on how the environment (say, the family and school systems) "reacts" to any deficit in discrimination.

Saying that multiple factors interact to cause alcohol dependence is, after all, only an extension of the theme that human experience and behavior under the influence of drugs can be understood only by considering multiple types of factors in combination. The research suggests that the same thinking should be applied to understanding alcohol dependence.

CONTEMPORARY ISSUE BOX 7–4
Is Alcohol Dependence a Disease?

Periodically, controversy flares over whether alcohol dependence is a disease. It happened again in 1988, following a Supreme Court decision denying two veterans an extension of their Veterans Administration (VA) education benefits and because of the legal defense of a previous official in the Reagan administration, Michael Deaver. These events coincided with publication of a book by University of California philosopher Herbert Fingarette challenging the position that alcohol dependence is a disease.

Disease can be defined broadly, but in the strict medical sense it refers to a clearly identified, physical process that is pathological. A critical feature of the definition is that once a disease is contracted, the afflicted individual has no control, or is not responsible, for the disease running its course. Typically, when alcohol dependence is called a disease the traditional medical model of disease is the referent.

Treatment providers and other citizens fought long and hard in the early twentieth century to get alcohol dependence acknowledged as a disease in order to take "treatment" of alcohol dependence out of the legal system and into the medical profession. The campaign has been more than successful. In 1957 the American Medical Association formally recognized alcohol dependence as a disease and still does. Other professional organizations that do include the American Hospital Association, American Academy of Pediatrics, American Dental Association, American College Health Association, American Chiropractic Association, the United States Congress, and the United States Surgeon General. Moreover, a 1987 Gallup poll revealed that almost 90 percent of the American public believe alcohol dependence is a disease.

The controversy is whether the symptoms we call alcohol dependence are not more accurately thought of as a result of behavior that is learned and voluntary rather than as a manifestation of some disease process. The question is based on research and clinical findings over the last 25 years (see Chapter 15) that have sparked much discussion in scientific journals and that are the foundation of Fingarette's book.

The question is not just an academic one. It has large implications for how alcohol-dependent people are given treatment, for one thing. In this respect, the dominant position among United States treatment professionals, as well as Alcoholics Anonymous, is that alcohol dependence is a disease. It also has great legal ramifications. The two veterans argued unsuccessfully that they should have an extension of the time to take advantage of their benefits because they were "afflicted" with alcoholism within the usual benefit period. The gist of their argument was that because alcoholism is a disease they should not be punished for having something they have no control over. The VA instead asserted alcoholism is the result of "willful misconduct." Similarly, Michael Deaver's lawyers tried to argue that what seemed to be misstatements of fact before a grand jury about illegal lobbying activities were due not to deceit but to a clouding of memory produced by Deaver's alcoholism.

With these cases as examples you can imagine what the ripple effects could be in all aspects of life with adherence to a strict disease model position that alcohol dependence is the result of a biological disease process.

SUMMARY

· Alcohol virtually always is drunk in the form of three major classes of alcoholic beverages, which are beer, wine, and hard liquor (also called distilled spirits).

· Alcoholic beverages are produced through fermentation and distillation.

· The alcohol content of a beverage may be expressed by volume or by weight.

· The proof of an alcoholic beverage refers to its percentage of alcohol content.

· People have used alcohol for thousands of years, but societies always have viewed alcoholic beverages as mixed blessings.

· In the United States, per capita consumption of beer and whiskey decreased immediately after World War II, then gradually increased until the early 1970s for spirits and the early 1980s for beer, when the trends reversed themselves. Wine consumption has increased slowly but steadily during the years 1935 to 1984.

· Social and environmental factors, such as urban vs. rural residence, sex, age, socioeconomic class, and education, are associated with alcohol consumption rates. The same is true, particularly sex and age, for the prevalence of alcohol-related problems.

· Alcohol is classified as a CNS-depressant drug. Its depressant effects are due to its action on the GABA-benzodiazepine receptors.

· Alcohol is a food primarily absorbed from the small intestine. The rate of alcohol absorption can vary widely according to a number of physiological and situational factors.

· Following its absorption alcohol is distributed to all of the body's tissues. Blood gets an especially high concentration of alcohol.

· Alcohol primarily affects the CNS, particularly the brain. The LD-50 for alcohol is a BAC of .45 to .50%.

· It is possible to get an approximation of current BAC by using a simple equation that includes alcohol dose and time. Other factors that influence BAC are percentage of body fat, gender, and rate of alcohol metabolization.

· Breath analysis is a very practical, precise way of measuring the BAC.

· The body metabolizes over 90% of the alcohol it absorbs, primarily in the liver.

· The liver metabolizes alcohol at a constant rate of about .4 ounces of alcohol an hour, and little can be done to quicken the pace.

· Alcohol use leads to some degree of dispositional tolerance and, more importantly, to both acute and protracted functional tolerance.

· Chronic, heavy use of alcohol can lead to physical dependence on it. The alcohol withdrawal syndrome is a serious medical problem that can result in death if not treated properly.

· Alcohol has few direct medical uses, but is an ingredient of several legitimate medical products.

· Alcohol's acute action is evident in a wide variety of physiological, sensorimotor, and behavioral effects. In general, as the BAC increases, acute effects increase in number and intensity. However, how humans experience degree of intoxication and behave under different doses of alcohol are modified by psychological and situational factors as well as alcohol dose and tolerance to this drug.

· Sensorimotor skills, which alcohol impairs, make up a major part of driving motor vehicles.

· Alcohol seems to be a major contributor to fatal and nonfatal automobile accidents. Gender and age combine with alcohol to influence risk of involvement in an automobile accident.

· Stemming the drunk driving problem seems to be a matter of sustained attention and action by law enforcement and citizens' action groups. Drivers' perceptions that arrest and conviction are likely consequences of drunk driving also are important.

· Alcohol and sex and aggression are major topics of social interest and concern. To understand alcohol's association with aggressive behavior it is necessary to take into account characteristics of the aggressor and situational factors, only one of which is alcohol.

· Alcohol's effects on sexual behavior are similarly complex. It is necessary to know the physiological basis of alcohol's effect on

sexual function, as well as include situational and psychological factors, in order to explain alcohol's effects on sexual behavior.

· Histories of chronic, heavy drinking are associated with damage to most of the body's organs and systems. Two of the most prominent ones are the liver and the brain.

· A chronic effect of alcohol is impairment in memory and other cognitive functions. Some of these effects are virtually all reversible with abstinence from alcohol. However, when there is structural damage to the brain, as in Korsakoff's syndrome, the effects are permanent.

· As the major metabolic site of alcohol, the liver is vulnerable to the chronic effect of heavy alcohol use. Three liver disorders that are attributable to drinking are fatty liver, alcohol hepatitis, and cirrhosis. The first two disorders are reversible with abstinence; cirrhosis, a leading killer in the United States, is not.

· Chronic, heavy drinking is associated with impaired sexual functioning in both men and women.

· A mother's drinking during pregnancy may result in fetal alcohol syndrome (FAS) in the newborn child. The FAS consists of gross physical deformities that are identifiable at birth. FAS is associated with continued physical problems, as well as subaverage intellectual functioning, later in childhood.

· The idea that moderate alcohol consumption is associated with lowered risk of cardiovascular disease and mortality is not as well founded as once thought.

· The development of alcohol dependence remains an unsolved problem. It does seem that "single cause" theories are inadequate to explain the etiology of alcohol dependence. Instead, it is necessary to incorporate biological, psychological, and sociological factors.

References

Abel, E.L. (1985). *Psychoactive drugs and sex.* New York: Plenum Press.

Adesso, V.J. (1985). Cognitive factors in alcohol and drug use. In M. Galizio and S.A. Maisto (Eds.), *Determinants of substance abuse* (pp. 179–208). New York: Plenum Press.

American Psychiatric Association (1981). *DSM-III Case book.* Washington, D.C.: Author.

Becker, C.E., Roe, R.L., & Scott, R.A. (1975). *Alcohol as a drug.* New York: Medcom Press.

Bennett, W.I. (1988). The Drink-a-day lore. *The New York Times Magazine,* January 10, 55–56.

Berild, D., & Hasselbalch, H. (1981). Survival after a blood alcohol of 1127 mg/dl. *The Lancet, 2* (8242), 363.

Brody, J.E. (1988). Widespread abuse of drugs by pregnant women is found. *The New York Times, CXXXVII,* pp. A–1; C–13.

Brown, B.A., Christiansen, B.A., & Goldman, M.S. (1987). The Alcohol Expectancy Questionnaire: An instrument for the assessment of adolescent and adult alcohol expectancies. *Journal of Studies on Alcohol, 48,* 483–491.

Carroll, L.C., and Miller, D. (1986). *Health: The science of human adaptation* (Fourth Edition), Dubuque, IA: Wm. C. Brown.

Collins, J.J., Jr. (Ed.) (1981). *Alcohol use and criminal behavior: An empirical, theoretical, and methodological overview.* New York: Guilford Press.

Collins, J.J., Guess, L.L., Williams, J.R., & Hamilton, C.J. (1980). *A research agenda to address the relationship between alcohol consumption and assaultive criminal behavior.* Final report submitted to the U.S. National Institute of Justice (Grant No. 78-NI-AX-0112).

Donovan, J.M. (1986). An etiologic model of alcoholism. *The American Journal of Psychiatry, 143,* 1–11.

Franck, P.H. (1983). 'If you drink, don't drive' motto now applies to hangovers as well. *Journal of the American Medical Association, 250,* 1657–1658.

Frezza, M., di Padova, C., Pozzato, G., Terpin, M., Baraona, E., & Lieber, C.S. (1990). High blood alcohol levels in women: The role of decreased gastric alcohol dehydrogenase activity and first pass metabolism. *The New England Journal of Medicine, 322,* 95–99.

Galizio, M., & Maisto, S.A. (Eds.) (1985). *Determinants of substance abuse.* New York: Plenum Press.

Greenberg, L.A. (1958). Intoxication and alcoholism: Physiological factors. *Annals of the New York Academy of Political and Social Science, 315,* 22–30.

Harvard, J.D.J. (1977). Alcohol and road accidents. In G. Edwards & M. Grant (Eds.), *Alcoholism: New knowledge and responses* (pp. 251–263). London: Croon Helm.

Hilton, M.E. (1988). Trends in U.S. drinking patterns: Further evidence from the past 20 years. *British Journal of Addiction, 83,* 269–278.

Jacobs, M.R., & Fehr, K. O'B. (1987). *Drugs and drug abuse: A reference text* (Second Edition). Toronto, Canada: Addiction Research Foundation.

Keller, M. (1979). A historical overview of alcohol and alcoholism. *Cancer Research, 39,* 2822–2829.

Knupfer, G. (1987). Drinking for health: The daily light drinker fiction. *British Journal of Addiction, 82,* 547–555.

Lang, A.R., Searles, J., Lauerman, R., & Adesso, V. (1980). Expectancy, alcohol, and sex guilt as determinants of interest in and reaction to sexual stimuli. *Journal of Abnormal Psychology, 60,* 285–293.

Levine, J.M., Kramer, G. G., and Levine, E.N. (1975). Effects of alcohol on human performance: An integration of research findings based on an abilities classification. *Journal of Applied Psychology, 89,* 644–653.

MacAndrew, C., & Edgerton, R.B. (1969). *Drunken comportment.* Chicago: Adline.

McKim, W.A. (1986). *Drugs and behavior.* Englewood Cliffs, NJ: Prentice Hall.

Mendelson, J.H., & Mello, N.K. (1985). *Alcohol: Use and abuse in America.* Boston: Little, Brown, & Co.

Mello, N.K. (1987). Alcohol abuse and alcoholism: 1978–1987. In H.Y. Meltzer (Ed.), *Psychopharmacology: The third generation of progress* (pp. 1515–1520). New York: Raven Press.

Parsons, O.A. (1986). Alcoholics' neuropsychological impairment: Current findings and conclusions. *Annals of Behavioral Medicine, 8,* 13–19.

Parsons, O.A., & Leber, W.R. (1982). Alcohol, cognitive dysfunction, and brain damage. In National Institute on Alcohol Abuse and Alcoholism, *Alcohol and health* (Monograph 2) (pp. 213–256). Rockville, MD: NIAAA.

Perez-Reyes, M., Hicks, R.E., Bumberry, J., Jeffcoat, A.R., & Cook, C.E. (1988). Interaction between marijuana and ethanol: Effect on psychomotor performance. *Alcoholism: Clinical and Experimental Research, 12,* 268–276.

Ritchie, J.M. (1985). The aliphatic alcohols. In G.G. Gilman, L.S. Goodman, T.W. Rall, & F. Murod (Eds.), *Goodman and Gilman's The pharmacological basis of therapeutics* (Seventh Edition) (pp. 372–386). New York: Macmillan Publishing Co.

Roebuck, J.B., Kessler, R.G. (1972). *The etiology of alcoholism.* Springfield, IL: Charles Thomas.

Rose, A.H. (1977). History and scientific basis of alcoholic beverage production. In A.H. Rose (Ed.), *Alcoholic beverages* (pp. 1–41). New York: Academic Press.

Schuckit, M.A. (1987). Biology of risk of alcoholism. In H.Y. Meltzer (Ed.), *Psychopharmacology: The third generation of progress* (pp. 1527–1533). New York: Raven Press.

Sobell, M.B., & Sobell, L.C. (1981). *Alcohol abuse curriculum guide for psychology faculty* (Prepublication manuscript). Rockville, MD: U.S. Department of Health and Human Services.

Spitzer, R.L., Skodol, A.E., Gibbon, M., & Williams, J.B.W. (1981). *DSM–III casebook.* Washington, D.C.: American Psychiatric Association.

U.S. Department of Health and Human Services (USDHHS) (1987). *Alcohol and health.* Rockville, MD: Author.

Wilsnack, S.C., Klassen, A.D., & Wilsnack, R.W. (1984). Drinking and reproductive dysfunction among women in a 1981 national survey. *Alcoholism: Clinical and Experimental Research, 8,* 451–458.

Wolfe, S.M., & Victor, M. (1971). The physiological basis of the alcohol withdrawal syndrome. In N.K. Mello and J.H. Mendelson (Eds.), *Recent advances in studies of alcoholism* (pp. 188–189). Washington, D.C.: U.S. Government Printing Office.

8 DEPRESSANTS

Although alcohol is the prototype depressant drug (see Chapter 7), a host of other drugs can depress the central nervous system and behavior. These include a variety of different chemical agents, but especially the barbiturates, the benzodiazepines, a number of non-barbiturate sedatives, and the general anesthetics (see Table 8–1). These drugs are often classified according to their most common medical uses, but such a classification can be misleading. For example, benzodiazepines such as diazepam (Valium) and chlordiazepoxide (Librium) are often labeled as **anxiolytic** (anti-anxiety) drugs. Although moderate doses of these compounds do indeed relieve anxiety and are widely used for this purpose, in larger doses benzodiazepines produce **sedative-hypnotic effects** (that is, they induce sleep), and now

Anxiolytic
Anxiety-reducing

Sedative-hypnotic effects
The ability of some drugs to produce a calming effect and induce sleep.

Table 8–1
Representative Depressant Drugs

Generic Name	Brand Name	Slang Name
Hypnotics		
Barbiturates		
Pentobarbital	Nembutal	Yellow jackets
Secobarbital	Seconal	Reds
Amobarbital	Amytal	Blues, Amy's
Phenobarbital	Luminal	
Chloral Hydrate		
Methaqualone	Quaaludes	Ludes
Ethchlorvynol	Placidyl	
Glutethimide	Doriden	
Inhalants		
Halothane	Fluothene	
Chloroform		
Ether		
Nitrous oxide		Laughing gas
Amyl nitrate		Rush, Snappers
Butyl nitrate		Poppers, Locker Room
Toluene products		Glue
Minor Tranquilizers (anxiolytics)		
Benzodiazepines		
Chlordizepoxide	Librium	
Diazepam	Valium	
Flurazepam	Dalmane	
Alprazolam	Xanax	
Lorazepam	Ativan	
Oxazepam	Serax	
Temazepam	Restoril	
Clorazepate	Tranxene	
Nonbarbiturate, Nonbenzodiazepines		
Meprobamate	Equanil	
Hydroxyzine	Vistaril, Atarax	
Ethinamate	Valmid	
Buspirone	BuSpar	

are prescribed widely as sleeping pills. Barbiturates, on the other hand, often are called sleeping pills and can certainly be effective in this regard. In lower doses barbiturates, too, are anxiolytic, and if the dose is high enough these and other depressants can produce surgical anesthesia. All depressant drugs (including alcohol) can relieve anxiety at low dose levels, produce intoxication at a moderate level, induce sedation and sleep at still higher levels, produce **general anesthesia** at very high dose levels, and eventually lead to coma and death. Due to differing potency, duration of action, and safety, some depressants are used for specific purposes more often than others (for example, nitrous oxide is used almost exclusively for anesthesia). The benzodiazepines are currently the most important class of drugs for treatment of anxiety and sleeping disorders.

General anesthesia
The reduction of pain by rendering the subject unconscious.

EARLY HISTORY

Perhaps the first of the depressant compounds other than alcohol to be used was the gas nitrous oxide, discovered by Joseph Priestly and synthesized by Humphrey Davy in 1776. These English scientists were the first to note that inhalation of nitrous oxide produced a short period of intoxication similar to drunkenness. Since the euphoric state produced by nitrous oxide often results in laughter and giggling, it came to be known as laughing gas (Brecher, 1972). Although Davy and others experimented with the gas for recreational purposes, its use in medicine was to be long delayed by one of the most famous stories in the history of medicine.

The story begins in Hartford, Connecticut, in 1845 where a young dentist named Horace Wells attended an exhibition of the effects of laughing gas. People paid admission to sniff nitrous oxide or just to watch others. One of the users apparently tripped and was badly cut during the exhibition, and Wells noticed that he seemed to feel no pain despite the severe injury. As a dentist, Wells immediately realized the possible uses of such a drug. Dentistry and other surgeries were immensely painful during this era due to the lack of anesthetic agents. Wells then experimented with nitrous oxide and discovered that teeth could be pulled without pain. After proclaiming his discovery, Wells was invited to demonstrate his procedure at the Massachusetts General Hospital in Boston. There, before a prestigeous group of physicians, Wells placed a patient under anesthesia. However, Wells had not studied the drug well enough to reliably establish dosages and the patient awakened during surgery screaming in pain. Wells was laughed out of the amphitheater by the skeptical scientists, and the use of nitrous oxide as an anesthesia was set back many years. Today nitrous oxide is widely used in dentistry and some types of surgery.

The next phase in the history of depressants also involved the search for an effective anesthetic. William Morton was a Boston dentist and medical student who was familiar with Wells' blunder, but Morton learned of

Figure 8–1 The first public demonstration of surgical anesthesia by William Morton.

another drug that he believed might be a better choice as an anesthetic: ether. Ether is a highly flammable liquid that vaporizes at room temperature. When the fumes are inhaled, they produce a state of intoxication. After conducting some initial experiments with ether, Morton asked permission to demonstrate its use as a general anesthetic. In 1846, just a year after Wells' failure, Morton gave his demonstration at Massachusetts General Hospital. A large crowd gathered to observe and possibly to laugh at the brash young student who claimed to have developed a method for eliminating surgical pain. Smith, Cooperman and Wollman (1980) describe the events that followed:

> Everyone was ready and waiting, including the strong men to hold down the struggling patient, but Morton did not appear. Fifteen minutes passed, and the surgeon, becoming impatient, took his scalpel and turning to the gallery said, "As Dr. Morton has not arrived I presume he is otherwise engaged." While the audience smiled and the patient cringed, the surgeon turned to make his incision. Just then Morton entered . . . [the surgeon] said "Well, sir, your patient is ready." Surrounded by a silent and unsympathetic audience, Morton went quietly to work. After a few minutes of ether inhalation, the patient was unconscious, whereupon Morton looked up and said "Dr. Warren, *your* patient is ready." The operation was begun. The patient showed no sign of pain, yet he was alive and breathing. The strong men were not needed. When the operation was completed, Dr. Warren turned to the astonished audience and made the famous statement "Gentlemen, this is no humbug" (pp. 258–259).

CONTEMPORARY ISSUE BOX 8–1
From Glue to Poppers—Inhalant Abuse

Many volatile solvents have the capacity to produce a brief euphoria when inhaled. The first reports of inhalant abuse date to the 1950s with accounts of gasoline and glue sniffing. Today dozens of products are being inhaled, including paint, lacquer thinners, cleaning fluids, typewriter correction fluid, nail polish remover, aerosols, and many others. Existing data clearly link chronic inhalation of solvents with a variety of medical problems including brain damage (Sharp & Brehm, 1977). Some related products worth special mention are amyl and butyl nitrate. Amyl nitrate dilates coronary arteries when inhaled and thus is prescribed to angina patients in the form of ampules that must be crushed or popped before inhalation—hence the slang name "poppers" or "snappers." The drug also dilates cerebral arteries, which produces a brief period of euphoria and dizziness. Similar effects are produced by butyl nitrate, which is sold over the counter under brand names like "Locker Room" and "Rush." These drugs have been widely used for recreational purposes. Their use has been particularly widespread in the gay community. Both gay and heterosexual users report that "poppers" inhaled just before orgasm prolong the orgasm. A number of side effects have been noted from these drugs including headache, tachycardia, eye problems, and rare sudden deaths (Bruckner & Peterson, 1977).

Morton had just accomplished the first public demonstration of surgical anesthesia and had revolutionized the practice of surgery. The use of ether as an anesthetic quickly became widespread, and it is still occasionally used today along with newer anesthetics such as halothane, related gases, and barbiturates.

BARBITURATES

History and Development

A number of depressant drugs were introduced in the nineteenth century including chloroform, chloral hydrate, and paraldehyde, but the next truly significant development was the introduction of the barbiturates in 1862. The first barbiturate was developed in that year in the Bayer laboratories in Munich, Germany. Barbiturate compounds are synthesized using, among

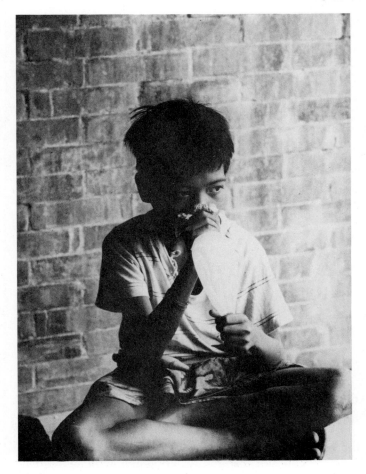

Figure 8–2 Child sniffing glue.

other things, chemicals found in urine, and some say Bayer gave the drugs their name to honor a woman named Barbara who provided the urine samples (Barbara's urates?). Others claim the name came from the fact that the discovery took place on St. Barbara's day (Dundee & McIlroy, 1982). We may never know, but regardless of how they were named the class of depressant drugs called barbiturates now includes more than 2000 different compounds (although only about fifty are currently available in the United States). Because so many barbiturates have been developed custom dictates that both generic and brand names of these drugs end with the suffix "-al." A few representative barbiturates are listed in Table 8–1. The effects of these various barbiturates are generally similar, differing primarily in potency and duration of action. Thus, pentobarbital and secobarbital are considered potent and short-acting (duration of action two to four hours), while amo-barbital is intermediate (six to eight hours) and phenobarbital longer-acting (eight to ten hours). Barbiturates, similar to benzodiazepines, are thought to act by influencing inhibitory neurotransmission, a mechanism of action we discuss later in this chapter.

Barbiturates were first introduced into general medical practice in 1903 when barbital was marketed under the brand name of Veronal. They soon became popular as a treatment for anxiety and as the first "sleeping pills" (Brecher, 1972). Use of barbiturates continued to increase until the 1960s, but has declined markedly in the years since. There are a number of reasons for the rise and fall of barbiturate use. Of the various afflictions experienced by people in the twentieth century, sleeping disorders and anxiety problems are among the most common. Thus, any drug offering relief from anxiety or promising sleep to the insomniac has potential for tremendous popularity and commercial success. The barbiturates do have the capacity to induce sleep and to relieve anxiety, and this accounts for their ascendance. However, there are a number of problems with barbiturate use discussed below that were unknown to consumers and physicians at first. These led to the decline of barbiturate use in the past twenty years.

Physiological and Psychological Effects of Barbiturates

All of the barbiturates possess the properties of central nervous system depressants. Thus, in moderate doses they produce a drunken euphoric state. Similar to alcohol, barbiturates may produce a loss of motor coordination, a staggering gait, and slurred speech. Loss of emotional control and behavioral disinhibition are also characteristic effects. Sedation and sleep are produced by increased doses, and higher doses produce surgical anesthesia. Physiological effects include respiratory depression, which is responsible for most of the overdose deaths associated with barbiturates. In addition, some depression of heart rate, blood pressure, and gastrointestinal activity is noted at higher doses. Also, barbiturates interact with an important liver enzyme (cytochrome p-450), and may thus interfere with liver function.

Medical Uses of Barbiturates

As noted above, the barbiturates once were used extensively as sedative–hypnotic drugs, but except for certain specialized uses they now have been replaced by the safer benzodiazepines. Short-acting barbiturates still are used to produce anesthesia. Other current uses include emergency treatment of convulsions and prevention of seizures in certain types of epilepsy (Harvey, 1985).

Tolerance, Dependence, and Adverse Effects of Barbiturates

One major reason for the movement away from medical use of barbiturates involves tolerance and dependence. Tolerance develops fairly rapidly to many of the effects of the barbiturates. Thus, while a given dose may be effective at inducing sleep for a while, if the drug is used regularly the patient soon may require a higher dose in order to sleep. If doses escalate too much and regular use persists, the patient will experience an abstinence syndrome when he or she attempts to withdraw from barbiturates. The symptoms of the barbiturate withdrawal syndrome are essentially similar to those of alcohol—shakes, perspiration, confusion, and in some cases full-blown delirium tremens (DT's) (see Chapter 7, Table 7–2)—but convulsions and seizures are more likely to occur in barbiturate withdrawal (Harvey, 1985). As with alcohol, the severity of barbiturate withdrawal depends upon the extent of use. Mild symptoms such as **rebound insomnia** (see below) and anxiety may occur after brief use of barbiturates, while life-threatening convulsions occur only after heavier usage.

Many people became dependent on barbiturates even though the drugs were used only under medical supervision. Suppose someone is in crisis, say after the death of a spouse or other loved one. A physician may prescribe a sleeping pill to help the person rest during the crisis. After a few weeks the patient may feel emotionally ready to sleep without the drug—and indeed may be. But the first night he or she attempts to sleep without the barbiturate the person may have a great deal of trouble because one of the features of barbiturate withdrawal is rebound insomnia (Mendelson, 1980). That is, after chronic use of barbiturates, abstinence produces insomnia, even in someone who was untroubled with insomnia previously.

A related problem involves the type of sleep experienced while under the influence of barbiturates and after heavy use of sleeping pills. Barbiturates do induce sleep, but similar to alcohol, they reduce the amount of time spent in the Rapid Eye Movement or REM stage of sleep. This may account in part for the "hungover" feeling some people report after sleeping with the aid of a drug. Although they get enough hours of sleep, it may not be "high quality" sleep. A further problem is that when subjects try to sleep without a pill after taking drugs for several nights, they may experience **REM rebound.** That is, they spend more time in REM than normal. Often accompanying REM rebound are vivid dreams and nightmares with nocturnal awakening. So even if the tired patient is able to get to sleep without drugs during barbiturate withdrawal, he or she may awaken early in the morning and not be able to get back to sleep. There may be other factors involved, but it is clear that once dependence on sleeping pills has developed, considerable time must pass before normal sleep patterns return (Mendelson, 1980). All of these factors make it easy to understand why dependence on drugs such as barbiturates for sleeping so often develops.

Rebound insomnia
Inabiity to sleep produced as a withdrawal symptom associated with some depressant drugs.

REM rebound
An increase in the rapid eye movement or REM stage of sleep when withdrawing from drugs that suppress REM time.

Such dependence is certainly a feature limiting the usefulness of these and other depressants in the treatment of sleep disorders.

An additional problem with the barbiturates is the risk of fatal drug overdose. The lethal dose of many barbiturates is fairly low compared to the effective dose in inducing sleep, and accidental overdoses have been a problem. This is particularly evident when barbiturates are taken in combination with alcohol or other depressant drugs, because these drugs potentiate one another (Harvey, 1980). Barbiturates often were prescribed to persons suffering from depression because sleeping disorders are a common symptom of clinical depression. Because there is a risk that severely depressed patients may attempt suicide, having a prescription for barbiturates could make it more likely the attempt will succeed. Barbiturates have been the lethal drug in many suicides, as noted in Chapter 4, including celebrated cases such as that of Marilyn Monroe.

Barbiturates (particularly the short-acting barbiturates) produce a euphoric state similar to alcohol intoxication. As a result, barbiturates

Figure 8–3 Goodbye, Norma Jean: Marilyn Monroe died of a barbiturate overdose.

became significant recreational drugs on the street during the 1950s and 1960s. An estimated five billion doses of barbiturates entered into the illicit market in 1969 alone (Brecher, 1972)! Clearly, barbiturates were causing some major societal problems, and the quest was on for safer drugs to relieve anxiety and induce sleep.

QUAALUDES AND OTHER NON–BARBITURATE SEDATIVES

Several non-barbiturate sedatives were introduced in the 1950s and 1960s as possible alternatives for the treatment of anxiety and sleep disorders. Meprobamate (Equanil), ethchlorvynol (Placidyl), and glutethimide (Doriden) have all been used in this way, but each seemed to possess the same undesirable properties as the barbiturates. One important candidate as an alternative to barbiturates was methaqualone, first marketed under the brand names Quaalude and Sopor in 1965. Although some thought methaqualone would be much safer because it was not a barbiturate, this did not prove to be true. It quickly became evident that methaqualone was quite toxic at high doses, especially when taken in combination with alcohol. In addition, dependence develops rapidly to methaqualone, with abstinence symptoms similar to those produced by alcohol and barbiturates. Thus, medical enthusiasm for methaqualone was quickly dampened. However, because it produces a pronounced state of ''drunkenness'' and developed a reputation as a sexual enhancer, methaqualone became a major street drug in the 1970s and was sometimes known as ''Disco-biscuits'' or ''Ludes.'' Very little research is available about the true effects of methaqualone on sexuality. Anecdotal data are mixed: some users report a disinhibition they find enhances sexual experience, but others report it interferes with sexual behavior (Abel, 1985). Actually, given the similarity in pharmacology between methaqualone and other depressants such as alcohol, it would be surprising if there were any major differences in the way these drugs affect sexual behavior (see Chapter 7). In any case, the abuse problems with methaqualone and other non-barbiturate sedatives far outweigh their medical benefits, and currently these drugs are rarely used for management of sleep problems or anxiety. In fact, methaqualone has become a Schedule I drug and is no longer produced for medical use. A major reason these drugs and the barbiturates have lost favor has been the widespread acceptance of the benzodiazepines as the treatment of choice in these disorders.

BENZODIAZEPINES

Development of the Benzodiazepines

In the late 1950s, scientists working at Roche Laboratories synthesized a new group of compounds known as the benzodiazepines. Animal tests with these drugs showed sedative, anti-convulsant, and muscle-relaxant effects similar to those of the barbiturates. An additional feature was that they produced a "taming" effect in monkeys. Even more intriguing, these drugs showed very low toxicity: The lethal dose is sufficiently high that it is difficult to achieve. The first of the benzodiazepines, Librium (chlordiazepoxide), was first marketed in 1960, and was closely followed by the introduction of its more potent cousin, Valium (diazepam) in 1963 (see Sternbach, 1983). These two drugs quickly came to dominate the market as treatments for anxiety and insomnia. By the 1970s, they were among the best selling drugs in America with 100 million prescriptions written for benzodiazepines in 1975 alone (Harvey, 1980). Today because of widespread concern about dependence, particularly on Valium, and the over-prescription of these drugs, the use of Valium and Librium is down. However there are a number of new benzodiazepines (see Table 8–1) and these are finding increasing favor such that the overall prescriptions for benzodiazepines are down only slightly. In fact a recent survey revealed four different benzodiazepines (Valium, Dalmane, Ativan, and Tranxene) in the top thirty most prescribed drugs in America (Tallarida, 1984).

Mechanisms of Action

As has been noted, the depressant drugs share many traits. Alcohol, barbiturates, non-barbiturate sedatives, and of course, benzodiazepines all have very similar effects when equated for dose. In addition, cross-tolerance occurs between these drugs. They also potentiate one another. Cross-dependence also occurs between these drugs, because an appropriate dose of any depressant can be used to reduce the withdrawal symptoms produced by any other. In fact, benzodiazepines are commonly used to withdraw alcoholics from alcohol. Thus, substantial evidence indicates a common mechanism of action for depressant drugs (Breese, Frye, Vogel, Mann–Koepke, & Mueller, 1983).

By the 1970s, evidence had begun to accumulate that GABA, the brain's major inhibitory neurotransmitter, might provide the common link (Costa, Guidotti, & Mao, 1975; Ticku, Burch & Davis, 1983). The problem arose when there was no direct evidence that any of the depressant drugs bound to the GABA receptor site. Then, in 1977, two independent laboratories reported the discovery of binding sites for benzodiazepines (Mohler & Okada, 1977; Squires & Braestrup, 1977), and it was subsequently shown that although specific to benzodiazepines, these receptors are part of what is now called the GABA-benzodiazepine receptor complex (Costa, Corda, Epstein, Forchetti & Guidotti, 1983). Apparently, the normal neural inhibition produced by GABA is greatly enhanced when there is activity at the benzodiazepine receptor. In addition, a third receptor in the system has been identified that responds to barbiturates (Olsen, Leeb-Lundberg, Snowman, & Stephenson, 1982). It appears both barbiturates and benzodiazepines act by enhancing neural inhibition in the GABA system, although they act at different receptor sites.

Another recent and exciting discovery has been the development of new drugs that are antagonists at the benzodiazepine receptor. These drugs block or reverse the effects of Valium or other benzodiazepines, but may themselves produce effects. However, the effects of these antagonists (or inverse agonists, as they are called by some) are to produce convulsions and anxiety—effects just opposite those of benzodiazepine agonists such as Valium. For example, Dorow, Horowski, Paschelke, Amin and Braestrup (1983) working with a compound known as FG-7142, noted it produced panic attacks and terror in three humans who were administered the drug. Research with animals seems to confirm FG-7142 produces fear or anxiety (File, Pellow, & Braestrup, 1985). It is now hoped research on this and related compounds may reveal important secrets about the neurochemistry of anxiety. After all, these benzodiazepine receptors must be in our brains for a reason, and it seems unlikely they were waiting in mammalian brains for the discovery of benzodiazepines. More likely, benzodiazepines (or their antagonists) are mimicking some natural neurotransmitter regulating fear and anxiety.

An additional and somewhat unexpected development already has come from the study of benzodiazepine antagonists. A recently developed benzodiazepine antagonist called RO 15-4513 reverses some of the effects of alcohol in rats. Suzdak and others (1986) showed RO 15-4513 reversed the motor impairment and other psychological effects of alcohol in rats—essentially causing these intoxicated rodents to sober up. Although more recent studies have shown RO 15-4513 does not antagonize all effects of alcohol (Lister & Nutt, 1987; Poling and others, 1988), research with this compound suggests at least some of alcohol's actions may be mediated by the GABA-benzodiazepine receptor complex.

Table 8–2
Kinetic Classification of Benzodiazepines

Type	Half–Life (hours)
Long Half–Life	
Flurazepam (Dalmane)	40–250
Diazepam (Valium)	30–200
Intermediate Half–Life	
Alprazolam (Xanax)	6–20
Lorazepam (Ativan)	10–20
Oxazepam (Serax)	5–15
Short Half–Life	
Triazolam (Halcion)	1.5–5

When taken orally, benzodiazepines generally are absorbed slowly and have a long duration of action. Considerable variability exists in duration of action however, and this accounts for different uses for and effects of the different benzodiazepines. Table 8–2 shows the half–life for some of the widely used benzodiazepines. The longer acting benzodiazepines such as Valium are considered most useful when it is desirable to maintain the patient at a constant level of drug over an extended period, for example when an individual is suffering from an anxiety reaction. The short- and moderate-duration benzodiazepines are more useful for treating insomnia when it is desirable to have the drug effects wear off by morning.

Psychotherapeutic Uses for Benzodiazepines

A number of reasons exist for the commercial success of the benzodiazepines. First, they are effective at relieving anxiety and inducing sleep. In fact, it is sometimes claimed benzodiazepines are uniquely effective as anxiolytic agents. It is true they relieve anxiety in animal studies and in humans at doses that do not produce motor impairment (ataxia) or pronounced sedation. In animals anxiolytic action is tested by determining the ability of a drug to increase rates of punished responding. Animals (typically rats) are trained to press a lever to produce food or water reinforcement. Then, during some periods, lever-pressing is punished by electric shock. During other periods no shock is delivered. Normally, rats will show decreased rates of lever-pressing in the punished component. When benzodiazepines are given to animals trained with such procedures, the rates of lever-pressing in the punished component go up almost to baseline levels at doses that do not affect the unpunished component. The clinical efficacy of various benzodiazepines measured in humans is correlated closely with these anti-punishment actions, and for this reason the facilitation of punished responding is viewed as an excellent animal model of human anxiety. In fact, novel anxiolytic drugs have been discovered on the basis of anti-punishment effects on this animal model. While other depressant drugs also show anti-punishment effects, none is as selective in this regard as benzodiazepines. This is one reason for considering benzodiazepines as possessing some unique anxiolytic actions.

The potent anxiolytic actions of benzodiazepines occur at doses producing few serious side effects. Although drowsiness may occur when taking benzodiazepines, it is less of a problem than was true of other depressant drugs. Because the lethal dose is so high, suicide and accidental overdose is far less of a problem with benzodiazepines than with other depressant drugs. However, benzodiazepines do interact to potentiate alcohol and other depressant drugs, and fatal overdoses are not uncommon with such drug combinations (see Contemporary Issue Box 8–2). So benzodiazepines, although not nearly as toxic as depressants such as barbiturates or methaqualone, are not without overdose risk.

CONTEMPORARY ISSUE BOX 8–2
Depressant Drugs and Potentiation

All of the depressant drugs reviewed to this point tend to potentiate one another (Chapter 4). That is, the effects of the drugs when combined are greater than would be expected from the individual doses considered alone. Such effects are among the most dangerous aspects of drug use. The vast majority of drug overdose deaths are due not to overdose of a single

Figure 8–4 Elvis Presley died of a combination of depressant drugs.

drug—but rather to smaller doses of more than one drug taken in lethal combination. Alcohol, barbiturates, non-barbiturate sedatives, (Quaaludes, meprobamate) and benzodiazepines all interact with one another to produce additive effects. They interact with heroin and other opiate drugs to produce additive effects as well. Many deaths attributed to heroin overdose actually involve heroin taken in combination with alcohol or other depressant drugs (see Chapter 10), and the largest number of drug overdose deaths in America every year involves alcohol taken in combination with other depressants, according to the National Institute on Drug Abuse. Such a combination of depressants killed Elvis Presley and it kills thousands of others every year.

A further problem with additive effects involves cases in which lower doses are consumed. Consider a young woman who is given a prescription for Valium to help her weather a family crisis. Suppose after taking her Valium she goes out with some friends for dinner and has a couple of beers. Perhaps under normal conditions she could tolerate this much alcohol without impairment, but taken in combination with the Valium, she may find herself quite intoxicated. If she attempts to drive home after such a drug combination, the loss of motor coordination may prove fatal. Combinations of alcohol with another depressant are thought to be responsible for many highway deaths above and beyond alcohol alone (O'Hanlon & De Gier, 1986). Never combine depressant drugs with alcohol or one another.

Tolerance, Dependence, and Abuse of Benzodiazepines

Tolerance develops to benzodiazepines, and there is cross–tolerance between them and other depressants. However, tolerance to benzodiazepines develops slowly, and fairly high doses are needed for tolerance to develop. The abstinence syndrome associated with benzodiazepine withdrawal is encountered infrequently because heavy use of benzodiazepines is necessary for withdrawal symptoms to occur. When it does occur, it is similar to that of alcohol and barbiturates, but not nearly as severe. Most benzodiazepines are very long–acting drugs with half–lives of more than a day and active metabolites persisting still longer (Greenblatt, Shader, Abernethy, Ochs, Divoll, & Sellers, 1982). Thus, abstinence symptoms may not appear for several days or even more than a week, and may persist for up to four weeks. The main symptoms are rebound insomnia, anxiety, tremors, sweating, and occasionally more serious problems such as seizures (Lader & Pederson, 1983). One of the problems in interpreting benzodiazepine withdrawal is differentiating abstinence symptoms from symptoms the drug was suppressing when it was present. For example, a great deal of controversy about Valium was stirred by the autobiographical book and movie *I'm Dancing as Fast as I Can* by Barbara Gordon (1979). Gordon was a successful professional who was maintained by her psychiatrist on very high doses of Valium. When she decided to quit Valium, her physician told her to simply stop taking the drug, rather than tapering her off the drug. This was certainly a poor decision. Gordon describes her withdrawal symptoms vividly:

"... By early afternoon I began to feel a creeping sense of anxiety. But it was different from my usual bouts of terror. It felt like little jolts of electricity, as if charged pins and needles were shooting through my body. My breathing became rapid and I began to perspire.

... My scalp started to burn as if I had hot coals under my hair. Then I began to experience funny little twitches, spasms, a jerk of a leg, a flying arm, tiny tremors that soon turned into convulsions" (p. 51).

She was unable to leave her own house, much less work. Her relationships with her lover and other friends deteriorated, and eventually she required hospitalization for several months. Nevertheless, her symptoms persisted even beyond this time. Thus, the novel is a moving description of anxiety disorder, although perhaps not a very typical description of Valium withdrawal. As we noted, although there are some very persistent withdrawal symptoms (Smith & Wesson, 1983), it is difficult to differentiate long-lasting withdrawal from the reemergence of previous anxiety symptoms. Thus, Barbara Gordon's experience may illustrate a case where the severity of her symptoms was revealed only when the drug, which had masked them, was removed.

Benzodiazepines do turn up on the street but far less frequently than barbiturates or methaqualone did in their day. In general, the potential for abuse of benzodiazepines is considerd to be less than that for other depressants (Cappell, Sellers, & Busto, 1986). Laboratory animals will self administer benzodiazepines, but they are only moderately potent reinforcers and are less preferred than barbiturates (Griffiths & Ator, 1980; Griffiths, Lukas, Bradford, Brady, & Snell, 1981). Griffiths and his associates also have investigated benzodiazepine self-administration in human volunteers with histories of sedative abuse. In double-blind laboratory studies these researchers have shown humans will self-administer benzodiazepines, and prefer them to placebo, but similar to non-humans, prefer barbiturates (Griffiths, Bigelow, Liebson, & Kaliszak, 1980). When different benzodiazepines were compared, it was shown that the more potent drugs with a rapid onset of action, such as Valium, were preferred to less potent compounds with slower onset of action such as oxazepam (Griffiths, McLeod, Bigelow, Liebson, Roache, & Nowowieski, 1984; Griffiths, Mcleod, Bigelow, Leibson, & Roache, 1984).

Tolerance, dependence, and abuse are associated with the benzodiazepines, but the problems produced are far milder than those connected with other depressant drugs. However, over the years a number of other problems associated with benzodiazepine use have emerged.

DRUG USE AND MISUSE

Adverse Effects of Benzodiazepines

As with other depressants, the main adverse effects of benzodiazepines involve drowsiness and motor impairment. Although even these side effects are rare with benzodiazepines alone (see Cappel, Sellers, & Busto, 1986 for a review), they may become particularly problematic when benzodiazepines are taken, as often they are, in combination with alcohol or other depressant drugs (see Box 8–2).

Anterograde amnesia
Loss or limitation of the ability to form new memories.

A problem more recently recognized indicates benzodiazepines may interfere with the storage of memories, a phenomenon called **anterograde amnesia.** Thus, when an individual is wakened by a phone call from sleep induced by benzodiazepines, he or she may fail to remember the events discussed during the call. The drug may be present in sufficient dose the next morning such that the patient forgets what he or she had for breakfast or what was read in the morning paper. These are examples of benzodiazepine-induced amnesia, and evidence is mounting that it is a common problem particularly with some of the newer benzodiazepines such as triazolam (Halcion) and alprazolam (Xanax) (Scharf, Saskin, & Fletcher, 1987). This type of effect is not unique to benzodiazepines. After all alcohol is known to produce the more dramatic memory loss of the blackout (see Chapter 7). Barbiturates and methaqualone also produce blackouts, suggesting that some type of memory deficit may be characteristic of any depressant drug.

Other adverse effects are occasionally reported with benzodiazepines, especially after chronic use, but despite the high frequency of use of these drugs, reports of toxicity are extraordinarily rare (Cappell, Sellers, & Busto, 1986). Nonetheless there is considerable interest in newly developed non-benzodiazepine anti-anxiety drugs that may be effective with even fewer side effects, such as buspirone (BuSpar—see Contemporary Issue Box 8–3).

CONTEMPORARY ISSUE BOX 8–3
BuSpar—A New Drug for Anxiety

We have noted in the text that all of the drugs used to treat anxiety disorders cause side effects of some sort. Thus, the search for safer anti-anxiety drugs has been a major goal of psychopharmacology. Recently a new drug was brought to the market by Bristol–Myers called "BuSpar" (generic name, buspirone). Buspirone's chemical structure and activity is very different from any of the traditional anxiolytic drugs but, in spite of the differences, it appears to relieve anxiety symptoms much like the benzodiazepines. No withdrawal symptoms have been reported following chronic use of buspirone, and it is considered to have very low abuse potential. For example, animals will not self-administer buspirone, and humans report no intoxication or euphoria after taking it. Virtually no sedation or motor impairment has been shown during buspirone treatment, and it does not produce synergistic effects with alcohol or other depressant drugs. Simply put, buspirone seems to relieve anxiety without producing any of the undesirable side effects of the other anxiolytic drugs. Buspirone is a new drug, and more research is needed to determine whether it really works as well as the benzodiazepines, and whether it may produce side effects that have yet to be determined. We still do not know exactly what is responsible for buspirone's anxiolytic actions. However, the recent increase in prescriptions for BuSpar suggests we may be entering a new era in the treatment of anxiety disorders (see Taylor and others 1985 for a review).

USE AND ABUSE OF DEPRESSANT DRUGS

Over the years a host of different depressant drugs have been used and abused in American society and around the world. Currently the benzodiazepines have become the drugs of choice in the treatment of insomnia and anxiety disorders. There is no doubt these drugs relieve an enormous amount of the human suffering associated with these ailments. There also is no doubt the benzodiazepines do so with far less toxicity and risk of dependence than their predecessors, the barbiturates and other sedatives. But there is considerable debate about the wisdom of benzodiazepine treatment as the *sole* treatment for anxiety disorders, especially as a chronic or long-term treatment. Most benzodiazepines are prescribed not by psychiatrists whose specialty is the treatment of psychological disorders, but instead by general practitioners who have no special training in such matters. Thus, tranquilizers may be used to treat the symptoms of anxiety disorders, but do not really help the patient learn to cope with problems. Taking a sleeping pill may help you sleep on the nights you take one, but pills do not make one's relationship with one's spouse any better, or improve one's job situation, or change any of the stressors that may be causing the insomnia in the first place. In fact, a hidden danger occurs when the use of drugs masks these symptoms and allows the person to function under less than optimal environmental conditions. Whether and when this is a desirable state of affairs may be a value judgment, but we believe it is tremendously important for potential consumers of benzodiazepines (according to statistics that include most of us) to recognize these drugs do not *cure* anxiety or affect its causes, but merely mask these symptoms. When symptom control is considered appropriate as a goal by the physician and patient these drugs can do a great deal of good.

SUMMARY

· All depressant drugs (including alcohol) produce similar effects. At low doses they relieve anxiety, while at moderate doses they induce sleep, and at higher doses produce general anesthesia, and eventually, coma and death.

· The first depressants to be discovered were drugs used for general anesthesia such as nitrous oxide and ether. Modern surgery would not be possible without this development.

· The development of the barbiturate drugs led to use of depressants as sleeping pills and to treat anxiety symptoms and epilepsy.

· Limitations in the use of barbiturates became apparent when a number of adverse effects of barbiturate use were discovered. These include rapid development of tolerance, severe withdrawal symptoms, high risk of overdose, and high abuse potential.

· A number of barbiturate-like compounds have been developed (such as methaqualone or Quaaludes), but these possess the same undesirable effects as the barbiturates.

· The discovery of benzodiazepines revolutionized the medical use of depressant drugs because they relieve anxiety with fewer side effects than previous depressants.

· Benzodiazepines and other depressant drugs are believed to act at the GABA receptor site in the central nervous system.

· The anxiolytic effects of benzodiazepines are more selective than those of other depressants because they relieve anxiety at doses that produce minimal sedation and motor impairment.

· Although less problematic than barbiturates, tolerance and dependence may develop for benzodiazepines and withdrawal symptoms may occur.

References

Abel, E.L. (1985). *Psychoactive drugs and sex,* New York: Plenum Press.

Brecher, E.M. (1972). *Licit and illicit drugs.,* Boston: Little, Brown and Company.

Breese, G.R., Frye, G.D., Vogel, R.A., Mann Keopke, K. & Mueller, R.A. (1983). Comparisons of behavioral and biochemical effects of ethanol and chlordiazepoxide. In L. Pohorecky and J. Brick (Eds.) *Stress and Alcohol Use* (pp. 261–278). Amsterdam: Elsevier.

Bruckner, J.V. & Peterson R.G. (1977). Review of the aliphatic and aromatic hydrocarbons. In C.W. Sharp and M.L. Brehm (Eds.) *Review of inhalants: Euphoria to dysfunction,* Research Monograph No. 15 (pp. 124–163). National Institute of Drug Abuse, Washington, D.C.

Cappell, H.D., Sellers, E.M. & Busto, U. (1986). Benzodiazepines as drugs of abuse and dependence. In H.D. Cappell, F.B. Glaser, Y. Israel, H. Kalant, W. Schmidt, E.M. Sellers & R.C. Smart (Eds.) *Research advances in alcohol and drug problems.* Vol. 9 (pp. 53–126). New York: Plenum Press.

Costa, E., Corda, M.G., Epstein, B., Forchetti, C. & Guidotti, A. (1983). GABA-benzodiazepine interactions. In E. Costa (Ed.) *The benzodiazepines: From molecular biology to clinical practice,* (pp. 117–136). New York: Raven Press.

Costa, E., Guidotti, A., & Mao, C.C. (1975). Evidence for involvement of GABA in the action of benzodiazepines. Studies on rat cerebellum. In E. Costa and P. Greengard (Eds.) *Mechanism of action of benzodiazepines* (pp. 113–130). New York: Raven Press.

Dorow, R., Horowski, R., Paschelke, G., Amin, M. & Braestrup, C. (1983). Severe anxiety induced by FG 7142, a beta–carboline ligand for benzodiazepine receptors. *Lancet, 2,* 98–99.

Dundee, J.W. & McIlroy, P.D. (1982). A history of the barbiturates. *Anesthesiology, 37,* 726–734.

File, S.E., Pellow, S., & Braestrup, C. Effects of the beta–carboline, FG 7142 in the social interaction test of anxiety and the holeboard: Correlations between behaviour and plasma concentrations. *Pharmacology, Biochemistry, and Behavior, 22,* 941–944.

Gordon, B. *I'm dancing as fast as I can.* New York: Bantam Books, Inc.

Greenblatt, D.J., Shader, R.I., Abernethy, D.R., Ochs, H.R., Divoll, M. & Sellers, E.M. (1982). Benzodiazepines and the challenge of pharmacokinetic taxonomy. In E. Usdin, P. Skolnick, J.F. Tallman, D. Greenblatt, and S.M. Paul (Ed.) *Pharmacology of benzodiazepines* (pp. 257–270). London: MacMillan Press.

Griffiths, R.R., & Ator, N. (1980). Benzodiazepine self–administration in animals and humans: a comprehensive literature review. In S.I. Szara and J. Ludford (Eds.), *Benzodiazepines: A review of research results,* Research Monograph No. 33 (pp. 22–36). National Institute of Drug Abuse, Washington, D.C.

Griffiths, R.R., Bigelow, G.E., Liebson, I., & Kaliszak, J.E. (1980). Drug preference in humans: Double-blind choice comparison of pentobarbital, diazepam, and placebo. *Journal of Pharmacology and Experimental Therapeutics, 215,* 649–661.

Griffiths, R.R., Lukas, S.E., Bradford, L.D., Brady, J.V., & Snell, J.D. (1981). Self-injection of barbiturates and benzodiazepines in baboons. *Psychopharmacology, 74,* 101–109.

Griffiths, R.R., McLeod, E.R., Bigelow, G.E., Liebson, I.A. & Roache, J.D. (1984). Relative abuse liability of diazepam and oxazepam: Behavior and subjective dose effects. *Psychopharmacology, 84,* 147–154.

Griffiths, R.R., McLeod, E.R., Bigelow, G.E., Liebson, I.A., Roache, J.D., & Nowowieski, P. (1984). Comparison of diazepam and oxazepam: Preference liking and extent of abuse. *Journal of Pharmacology and Experimental Therapeutics, 229,* 501–508.

Harvey, S.C. (1980). Hypnotics and sedatives. In A.G. Gilman, L.S. Goodman, and A. Gilman (Eds.) *Goodman and Gilman's The pharmacological basis of therapeutics,* 6th ed. (pp. 339–379). London: MacMillan.

Harvey, S.C. (1985). Hypnotics and sedatives. In A.G. Gilman, L.S. Goodman, and A. Gilman (Eds.) *Goodman and Gilman's The pharmacological basis of therapeutics,* 7th ed. (pp. 339–371). London: Macmillan.

Lader, M. (1983). Benzodiazepine withdrawal states. In M.R. Trimble (Ed.) *Benzodiazepines Divided: A multidisciplinary review* (pp. 17–32). New York: John Wiley and Sons.

Lister, R.G. & Nutt, D.J. (1987). Is RO 15-4513 a specific alcohol antagonist? *Trends in neuroscience, 10,* 223–225.

Mendelson, W.B. (1980). *The use and misuse of sleeping pills: A clinical guide.* New York: Plenum Press.

Moehler, H. & Okada, T. (1977). Benzodiazepine receptor: Demonstration in the central nervous system. *Science, 198,* 849–851.

O'Hanlon, J.F. & de Gier, J.J. (1986). *Drugs and driving.* London: Taylor & Francis.

Olsen, R.W., Leeb-Lundberg, F., Snowman, A. & Stephenson, F.A. (1982). Barbiturate interactions with the benzodiazepine-GABA receptor complex in mammalian brain. In E. Usdin, P. Skolnick, J.F. Tallman, D. Greenblatt, and S.M. Paul (Eds.) *Pharmacology of benzodiazepines,* (pp. 155–164). London: MacMillan.

Poling, A., Schlinger, H. & Blakely, E. (1988). Failure of the partial inverse benzodiazepine agonist RO 15-4513 to block the lethal effects of ethanol in rats. *Pharmacology, biochemistry and behavior, 31,* 945–948.

Scharf, M.B., Saskin, P. & Fletcher, K. (1977). Benzodiazepine-induced amnesia: Clinical and laboratory findings. *Journal of Clinical Psychiatry Monographs, 5,* 14–17.

Sharp, C.W. & Brehm, M.L. (1977). *Review of the inhalants: Euphoria to dysfunction,* Research Monograph 15, National Institute of Drug Abuse, Washington, D.C.

Shepard, R.A. (1986). Neurotransmitters, anxiety and benzodiazepines: A behavioral review. *Neuroscience and biobehavioral reviews, 10,* 449–461.

Smith, D.E. & Wesson, D.R. (1983). Benzodiazepine dependency syndromes. *The Journal of Psychoactive Drugs, 15,* 85–96.

Smith, T.C., Cooperman, L.H. & Wollman, H. (1980). The therapeutic gases. In A.G. Gilman, L.S. Goodman, & A. Gilman (Eds.) *Goodman and Gilman's The pharmacological basis of therapeutics,* 6th ed., (pp. 321–338). London: MacMillan.

Squires, R.F. & Braestrup, C. (1977). Benzodiazepine receptors in rat brain. *Nature, 266,* 732–734.

Sternbach, L.H. (1983). The discovery of CNS active 1,4-benzodiazepines. In E. Costa (Ed.) *The benzodiazepines: From molecular biology to clinical practice* (pp. 1–6). New York: Raven Press.

Suzdak, P.D., Glowa, J.R., Crawley, J.N., Schwartz, R.D., Skolnick, P. & Paul, S.M. (1986). A selective imidazobenzodiazepine antagonist of ethanol in the rat. *Science, 234,* 1243–1247.

Tallarida, R.J. (1984). *The top 200—1984: The most widely prescribed drugs in America.* Philadelphia: W.B. Saunders.

Taylor, D.P., Eison, M.S., Riblet, L.A. & Vandermaelen, C.P. (1985). Pharmacological and clinical effects of buspirone. *Pharmacology, Biochemistry and Behavior, 23,* 687–694.

Ticku, M.K., Burch, T.P. & Davis, W.C. (1983). The interactions of ethanol with the benzodiazepine-GABA receptor-ionophore complex. *Pharmacology, biochemistry, and behavior, 18,* 15–18.

9 PSYCHIATRIC DRUGS

Psychoactive substances have been used to treat mental illnesses for centuries. In fact, many of the substances described in this text, such as alcohol, cannabis, and opium, have at one time or another been used as treatments for mental illness. In some cases the motivation to administer psychopharmacological agents to the mentally ill has simply been to subdue them. More typically today these medications are intended to provide persons with some relief and ideally with the opportunity to function better within their environments.

The development, testing, and distribution of psychotherapeutic drugs, as described in Chapter 4, is today a major worldwide industry. In the United States alone more than 200 million prescriptions are processed yearly for the lawful use of psychotherapeutics, including, for example, tranquilizers, antidepressants, stimulants, and sedative-hypnotics. In any given year, approximately 10 to 15 percent of the general population is given a prescription for some psychoactive drug, usually an antianxiety agent.

In the present chapter, we provide an overview of the use of psychiatric drugs in this country. Following a brief historical overview, we discuss some epidemiological features of what are called **psychotropic** drugs. The term psychotropic describes those drugs which have a special or unique effect on the mind or mental functioning. Mechanisms of drug action are discussed, and an overview of the four major classes of psychiatric drugs provided: antipsychotics, antidepressants, antianxiety agents, and antimanic or mood stabilizing drugs. We supplement this material with case examples so you have a feeling for the problems or disorders these drugs are intended to relieve.

Psychotropic
Any substance that exerts a special or unique action on psychological functioning.

HISTORICAL OVERVIEW

The roots of psychopharmacology began in the nineteenth century, when a science of chemistry was developing (Siegel, 1977), and the field has undergone an immense amount of growth since, especially during the twentieth century. The actual coining in 1920 of the term *psychopharmacology* is attributed to Macht, an American pharmacist (Caldwell, 1970).

Prior to 1950: The Pre-Chlorpromazine Era

In the nineteenth century, society had very little understanding of mental illness. Although as early as the 1800s several compendia of treatments and psychopharmacological agents existed (especially in England, France, and Germany) for mental illnesses, the proposed remedies were mostly speculative and without scientific support. Many of the approaches used were actually quite cruel, including bloodletting, hot irons, flogging, revolving chairs, starvation, and sneezing powder (Spiegel & Abel, 1983). Nevertheless, this period was marked by the efforts of some to attempt to understand and treat, or in some cases "cleanse," those with mental illness. The efforts of Emil Kraepelin, Phillip Pinel, and J. E. Esquirol were particularly noteworthy. These scientists were involved in the development of a classification system of mental illnesses. They believed that a scientific understanding and categorizing of mental illnesses was a prerequisite to the identification of effective treatments.

One of the more systematically studied drugs in this period was cannabis. In the 1840s, the French physician Jacques-Joseph Moreau de Tours was working at a mental hospital in Paris. He theorized that treatment should "substitute symptoms of mental illness with similar but controllable drug-induced symptoms" (Caldwell, 1978, p. 16). Moreau used cannabis and

Figure 9–1 Early psychiatric hospitals did not have the advantage of psychiatric drugs to treat mentally ill patients. These two drawings depict mentally ill patients during the early 1800s.

Manic
Relating to mania, a mood disturbance which typically includes hyperactivity, agitation, excessive elation, and pressured speech.

Narcoleptic
A state characterized by brief but uncontrollable episodes of sleep.

Neuroses
Generally describes any non–psychotic emotional disturbance, pain, or discomfort beyond what is appropriate in the conditions of one's life.

Psychosurgery
Surgery which entails the cutting of fibers connecting particular parts of the brain or the removal or destruction of areas of brain tissue with the goal of modifying severe behavioral or emotional disturbances.

found gaiety and euphoria to be among its effects. He decided to give cannabis to two depressed hospital patients to see if it would produce similar results in them. These patients did indeed respond to the cannabis, appearing happy and becoming talkative. Moreau also found **manic** patients given the cannabis subsequently calmed down and relaxed. Unfortunately, the effects of the cannabis tended to be temporary.

The first half of the twentieth century was characterized by further attempts to use drugs and other therapies to treat mental illness. For example, tests on the effectiveness of giving amphetamines to depressed and **narcoleptic** patients were conducted, and carbon dioxide inhalation procedures were used in the treatment of illnesses referred to as the psychoses and the **neuroses.** Also used in the treatment of psychosis were antihistamines, insulin shock, and **psychosurgery.** Electroshock therapy was used in treating severe depression (a procedure still used today). Finally, in 1949, an Australian physician named John Cade discovered that the alkali metal lithium successfully moderated manic conditions; lithium remains a mainstay in the treatment of mania and manic-depressive illness today.

Despite the many efforts, the collective impact of these advances on the treatment of mental illness was modest at best. In fact, the total positive impact of this progress pales in comparison to the successes experienced in the use later of another drug, chlorpromazine. To the extent psychopharmacology is defined as the use of psychotropic medications to restore and maintain some degree of mental health, then the true coming of age for psychopharmacology was in Paris in 1951.

After 1950: The Age of Chlorpromazine

The roots of chlorpromazine as a psychiatric medication extend to its initial use in general surgery. It was synthesized by Paul Charpentier in 1950. Chlorpromazine was used as an anesthesia: it decreased patients' anxiety associated with surgical preparations and prevented shock during surgery. This work in surgery was conducted primarily by Henri Laborit, and it was his observation of chlorpromazine's calming effects that led him to suggest its potential use in psychiatry. This application was initially tried at Val-de-Grace, a military hospital in Paris. Agitated psychotic patients appeared calm following administration of chlorpromazine. In addition, the patients' thoughts appeared to become less chaotic, and the patients were less excitable. Notably, the patients did not exhibit any loss in consciousness. Instead, they showed a disinterested and detached demeanor, or what Deniker (1983) has called "the syndrome of psychomotor indifference" (p. 166).

The effect the introduction of chlorpromazine had for the field of psychiatry and mental health was profound. As described by Caldwell (1978):

By May 1953, the atmosphere in the disturbed wards of mental hospitals in Paris was transformed: straightjackets, psychohydraulic packs and noise were things of the past! Once more, Paris psychiatrists who long ago unchained the chained, became pioneers in liberating their patients, this time from inner torments too, and with a drug: (chlorpromazine). It accomplished the pharmacologic revolution of psychiatry—then and there (p. 30).

Word of the successful use of chlorpromazine spread rapidly, and its adoption spread throughout Europe and to the United States and the rest of the world. The effects following introduction of chlorpromazine in the United States were just as dramatic. Since 1955, the number of hospitalized psychiatric patients in the United States has lowered significantly. In 1955 the figure was 600,000, and today there are approximately 150,000 hospitalized psychiatric patients, despite an overall increase in the general population (Baldessarini, 1985). Of course, other factors have contributed to today's lower figure (for example, the development of other psychotropic drugs and the movement toward deinstitutionalizing psychiatric patients), but the starting point was chlorpromazine.

The decades following the introduction of chlorpromazine witnessed much growth in the field of psychopharmacology. The next major event was the 1954 introduction of reserpine. This drug, similar to chlorpromazine, was originally used in the treatment of another medical disorder (arterial hypertension), and the physicians using the drug noted symptoms of indifference in their patients. Because of this effect, reserpine was given to psychiatric patients. The drug yielded positive effects overall, but its action often took several weeks to be apparent (see Deniker, 1983), and patients using the medication often appeared depressed. Thus, reserpine never achieved the popularity of chlorpromazine.

Other advances in the field included progress in antianxiety (or anxiolytic) medications, such as meprobamate (which also was used as a muscle relaxant), and in antidepressant medications, such as monoamine oxidase inhibitors (MAOIs) and tricyclic antidepressants (these will be described in more detail later). Another drug receiving renewed attention was LSD. Because of the psychotic-like effects produced by LSD, efforts were made to use LSD-created effects as a model for studying psychoses. Researchers used LSD to create a "model psychosis" to study (to date with limited success) possible etiological factors contributing to mental illness. It also enabled them to treat the LSD-created symptoms with psychiatric drugs.

In retrospect, the 1950s were a frontier period for psychopharmacology. Much growth was experienced, and advances in the field continue to be made (although none with quite the impact and significance of chlorpromazine, which remains widely used today). These advances have also had a profound effect on the face of mental illness today. As noted, psychopharmacology contributed to decreases in the numbers of hospitalized psychiatric patients. Unfortunately, there has been a downside to this deinstitutionalization. It had been expected that a variety of outpatient psychiatry services would be available to serve the needs of the discharged chronically mentally ill, and that has not been the case (Flynn, 1985). One result is that a number of patients once under psychiatric care are now without such services. It also has been argued that this is one of the factors contributing to the increased incidence of homeless people, many of whom suffer from psychiatric illnesses.

EPIDEMIOLOGY OF PRESCRIPTION DRUG USE AND ABUSE

It is estimated that approximately 15 percent of the United States population (around one in seven persons) experience some form of mental disorder in any given year (Klerman, 1983). Most of these persons are experiencing symptoms associated with one of three problems: anxiety states, depression and affective disorder, or alcohol-related dysfunction. In addition, it is estimated an additional 15 percent of the population seeks clinical services for various symptoms (for example, stress, depression, anxiety) that cut into their life-functioning effectiveness, even though they may not meet the diagnostic criteria for a particular disorder. These mental health difficulties taken together account for around 15 percent of the total health care expenditures yearly in this country.

The symptoms associated with mental health disorders frequently are treated through the use of prescription medications. Each year 10 to 15 percent of the general population receives a prescription for some psychotropic drug, usually an antianxiety agent. (Antidepressant and antipsychotic medications account for a small fraction of the total number of prescriptions provided.) And considerable relief is reported: national surveys described by Klerman (1983) suggest approximately three-fourths of patients receiving these medications report some degree of symptomatic relief. A listing of the more commonly prescribed psychiatric drugs is provided in Table 9–1.

Table 9–1
Most Commonly Prescribed Psychotropic Medications

Brand Name	Disorder Treated
Valium	Anxiety Disorders
Ativan	Anxiety Disorders
Xanax	Anxiety Disorders
Tranxene	Anxiety Disorders
Mellaril	Psychotic Disorders; Severe Depression
Haldol	Psychotic Disorders
Prozac	Depression
Elavil	Depression
Triavil	Severe Anxiety/Depression Disorders; Some Psychotic Disorders
Atarax	Anxiety Disorders

Note: Based in part on 1984 brand name prescriptions as dispensed in U.S. pharmacies. The above list includes psychotropic medications (in order of use) in the top one hundred most prescribed drugs, as identified in Simon & Silverman (1986).

Many of the most commonly prescribed drugs are benzodiazepines, minor tranquilizers used in the treatment of anxiety and tension.

There are several important findings about the people who use psychotropic medications. One is that the prevalence of psychiatric medication use is about twice as high among women as among men. A second trend is for psychotropic drug use to increase with age, a tendency seen more dramatically among men. Additionally, greater use of psychotropics is found among those who live alone, those with more education, and those with higher income levels (Wells, Kamberg, Brook, Camp, & Rogers, 1985).

While most psychiatric medications are used as prescribed, the nonprescribed use and abuse of psychiatric drugs is a significant problem. Abuse of prescription drugs can take many forms, ranging from patients who exceed recommended dosages to the street sale of pharmaceuticals (Weiss & Greenfield, 1986). Prescription drugs sold on the street are diverted from legal distribution through thefts from drug stores or pharmaceutical companies, the pilfering of supplies by hospital or clinic employees, and the altering or forging of prescriptions. Estimates indicate that prescriptions for one and a half billion drug dosage units are written each year in the United States, and that several hundred million of these units are diverted to street or other illicit use (OSMJ, 1986). The consequences of prescription drug abuse are immense. Consider the following, as reviewed by Weiss and Greenfield (1986):

- Prescription drug abuse accounts for more injuries and deaths than those attributable to all other illegal substances combined.
- Prescription drugs are a factor in 60 percent of all drug-related emergency room cases.
- Prescription drugs are involved in 70 percent of all drug-related deaths.

The drugs most often abused or misused are depressants and stimulants. While people of all age groups have been known to misuse prescription drugs, it is an especially notable problem among the elderly. The elderly use approximately a third of the drugs taken yearly in the United States, yet account for only 10 to 15 percent of the population (see Ellor & Kurz, 1982). It is not uncommon to see the elderly use prescribed medications in combination with each other, with over-the-counter drugs (see Chapter 13), or with alcohol. (The use of multiple prescription drugs is not always intentional, because doctors sometimes provide prescriptions to the elderly without being aware of other prescription medications they already are using.)

Over the years both legislative and medical association efforts have been implemented to monitor and control the availability and access to prescribed medications. Most legal guidelines are consolidated within the Comprehensive Drug Abuse Prevention and Control Act of 1970 and the Controlled Substances Act of 1971 (see Chapter 2). In particular these acts mandate explicit procedures for the distribution and dispensing of prescription medications. Most psychotropic medications are under federal control and require a prescription for use.

Several information gathering networks have been established to monitor the distribution and use (legal and otherwise) of drugs overall, including psychotropic drugs. Two of these, the Client-Oriented Data Acquisition Process (CODAP) and the Drug Abuse Warning Network (DAWN), are operated under federal supervision. CODAP entails the collection of information on drug use among persons entering drug abuse treatment programs. DAWN uses reports from emergency rooms and medical examiners' offices to produce yearly statistics on morbidity and mortality associated with drug use. Both of these systems permit a monitoring of trends in drug use and consequences. The usefulness of this information, of course, is a direct function of the accuracy with which the original data are gathered in the field.

Another system, focused more on prescription drug abuse, is the Prescription Abuse Data Synthesis (PADS). It was developed by the American Medical Association and operates at the state level. PADS serves to identify the ways in which prescription drug diversions occur. The program also yields information on which prescription drugs are most in demand for illicit use in which states.

Before leaving the discussion on prescription drug abuse, it should be noted that a variety of over-the-counter substances with psychoactive properties are also subject to abuse. These include, for example, nonprescription hypnotics which contain antihistamines, nonprescription cold and allergy products, laxatives, nonprescription stimulants, and diet pills. These are described in more detail in Chapter 13.

MECHANISMS OF ACTION

As you recall from Chapter 3, our thoughts, emotions, and behavior can be reduced to the actions of neurons or nerve cells, which in turn are largely dependent on the chemical reactions central to communication between neurons. According to a physical/medical model, mental illness is a consequence of dysfunctional brain chemistry, and this serves as the basis of drug treatments in psychiatry. Therefore, psychiatric medications are designed to operate on these dysfunctional nerve cell communications so that specific biological changes occur.

Remember, neurotransmitter action entails the chemical transmission of messages between nerve cells in the central nervous system and the receptors throughout the system. Psychotropic drugs can modify virtually any stage of synaptic action, but generally affect three main processes: transmitter-receptor binding, reuptake of transmitters, and the manufacture of receptors (Lickey & Gordon, 1983). In each case, the mode of functioning of the nerve cell is changed.

When taken orally (as most psychiatric medications are), the drug is absorbed in the gastrointestinal tract and modified in the liver before being transported in the bloodstream. When administered IV or IM, direct transport in the bloodstream occurs. Drug distribution occurs primarily through the water phase of blood plasma, and the drug's arrival at the intended site(s) of action will vary as a function of the blood flow within the organ and the rate at which the drug can cross the lipoprotein membrane (Boulenger & Lader, 1982; Lader, 1976). The drug arrives fairly rapidly at those organs richly blood perfused, such as the heart, brain, and liver (Poling, 1986). Drugs not bound to plasma protein cross the lipoprotein membranes with most ease and progress toward the intended sites of action. Most psychiatric medications are highly lipid-soluble and thus diffuse fairly easily through the gastrointestinal wall, the blood-brain barrier, and cell membranes (Potter, Bertilsson, & Sjoquist, 1981). Medications can enter the brain via blood transport. The drug arrives at its final sites by passing from small arteries to the capillaries, and then through the capillary walls to the extracellular fluid (Lader, 1976). It is in the extracellular fluid that the drug diffuses and impacts on the cells it affects. The biological action of the drug occurs during this tissue penetration and localization.

As we noted, orally administered medications are processed through the liver before being transported in the bloodstream to sites of action. This is referred to as hepatic "first pass" metabolism, or presystemic metabolism, and drugs can vary significantly in the extent to which they are metabolized in the liver before even reaching systemic circulation. (For example, it has been found that about 80 percent of an oral dose of chlorpromazine is metabolized in the first pass in the liver, leaving about 20 percent to exert the intended drug action.) The resultant metabolites can be inactive or active, and if active either therapeutic or toxic (Potter and others, 1981). In some cases the metabolites can be more active than the originally administered drug (as in the case of chloral hydrate, a sleeping medication).

Drug elimination involves metabolic and excretory processes. Drug metabolism occurs most commonly in the liver through oxidation. Less prevalent metabolic processes include reduction and hydrolysis. Excretion of most psychotropic drugs occurs primarily through the kidneys.

CLASSES OF DRUGS AND THEIR ACTIONS

Psychiatric drugs, similar to other drugs, can be classified along a variety of dimensions, such as chemical structure, clinical actions, or sites of action (see Chapter 1). However, the most common classification used in psychiatry, and the one we will use, is by therapeutic usage. This classification yields four basic categories: antipsychotics, antidepressants, antianxiety agents, and antimanic medication (specifically lithium). In the following sections we will describe representative psychotropics within each of these classifications.

Antipsychotics

As you will recall, the introduction of antipsychotic medications in the 1950s represented a major turning point in the treatment of psychiatric disorders, especially schizophrenia. To a lesser extent, these drugs also have been used in the treatment of mania, **agitated depressions,** toxic (such as drug-induced) psychoses, emotionally unstable personalities, and psychoses associated with old age. Antipsychotic medications are also known as **neuroleptics** or major tranquilizers (the latter a term used much less frequently now). The term neuroleptic is derived from the Greek meaning ''to clamp the neuron'' (Snyder & Largent, 1989). Antipsychotics is the term more commonly used in the United States, with neuroleptics used in Europe. The terms are used interchangeably in this discussion. The major antipsychotic drugs are listed in Table 9–2.

The basic—but oversimplified—notion regarding antipsychotic medications is that they primarily affect the reticular activating system, the limbic system, and the hypothalamus. The effects on the reticular activating system generally moderate spontaneous activity and decrease the patient's reactivity to stimuli. The action within the limbic system serves to moderate or blunt emotional arousal. These actions are thought to produce the drug's dramatic effects on schizophrenic or agitated behavioral patterns. Because of these effects, antipsychotics remain the major approach to the drug treatment of schizophrenia. Below is a case example of clinical **paranoid schizophrenia.** The case is taken, with slight modification, from the DSM-III-R *Case Book* (Spitzer, Gibbon, Skodol, Williams, & First, 1989).

Mr. Simpson is a forty-four-year-old, single, unemployed, white man brought into the emergency room by the police for striking an elderly woman in his apartment building. Mr. Simpson had been continuously ill since the age of twenty-two. During his first year of law school, he gradually became more and more convinced that his classmates were making fun of him. He noticed that they would snort and sneeze whenever he entered the classroom. When a girl he was dating

Agitated depression
Depressed mood accompanied by a state of tension or restlessness. Person shows excessive motor activity, as he or she may, for example, be unable to sit still, pace, wring the hands, or pull at his or her clothes.

Neuroleptic
Tranquilizing drugs used to treat psychoses. Another term for neuroleptic is major tranquilizer.

Paranoid schizophrenia
A type of schizophrenia distinguished by systematic delusions or auditory hallucinations related to one theme.

Table 9–2
Representative Antipsychotic Medications

	Generic Name	Trade Name
Phenothiazines		
	Chlorpromazine	Thorazine
	Prochlorperazine	Compazine
	Trifluoperazine	Stelazine
	Fluphenazine	Prolixin
	Thioridazine	Mellaril
Nonphenothiazines		
	Haloperidol	Haldol
	Thiothixene	Navane
	Loxapine	Loxitane

broke off the relationship with him, he believed that she had been "replaced" by a look-alike. He called the police and asked for their help to solve the "kidnapping." His academic performance in school declined dramatically, and he was asked to leave and seek psychiatric care.

Mr. Simpson got a job as an investment counselor at a bank, which he held for seven months. However, he was getting an increasing number of distracting "signals" from co-workers, and he became more suspicious and withdrawn. It was at this time that he first reported hearing voices. He was eventually fired, and soon thereafter was hospitalized for the first time, at age 24. He has not worked since.

Mr. Simpson has been hospitalized 12 times, the longest stay being eight months. However, in the past five years he has been hospitalized only once, for three weeks. During the hospitalizations he has received various antipsychotic drugs. Although medication has been prescribed on an outpatient basis, he usually stops taking it shortly after leaving the hospital. Aside from twice-yearly lunch meetings with his uncle and his contacts with mental health workers, he is isolated socially. He lives on his own and manages his own financial affairs, including a modest inheritance. He reads the *Wall Street Journal* daily. He cooks and cleans for himself.

Mr. Simpson maintains that his apartment is the center of a large communication system that involves all three major television networks, his neighbors, and apparently hundreds of "actors" in his neighborhood. There are secret cameras in his apartment that carefully monitor all his activities. When he is watching TV, many of his minor actions, such as getting up to go to the bathroom, are soon directly commented on by the announcer. Whenever he goes outside, the "actors" have all been warned to keep him under surveillance. Everyone on the street watches him. His neighbors operate two different "machines"; one is responsible for all of his voices, except the "joker." He is not certain who controls this voice, which "visits" him only occasionally, and is very funny. The other voices, which he hears many times each day, are generated by this machine, which he sometimes thinks is directly run by the neighbor whom he attacked. For example, when he is going over his investments, these "harassing" voices constantly tell him which stocks to buy. The other machine he calls "the dream machine." This machine puts erotic dreams into his head, usually of "black women."

Mr. Simpson describes other unusual experiences. For example, he recently went to a shoe store 30 miles from his house in the hope of getting some shoes that wouldn't be "altered." However, he soon found out that, like the rest of the shoes he buys, special nails had been put into the bottom of the shoes to annoy him. He was amazed that his decision concerning which shoe store to go to must have been known to his "harassers" before he himself knew it, so that they had time to get the altered shoes made up especially for him. He realizes that great effort and "millions of dollars" are involved in keeping him under surveillance. He sometimes thinks this is all part of a large experiment to discover the secret of his "superior intelligence." (Published with permission of American Psychiatric Press, Inc.)

Although several theories address the action of antipsychotics, the predominant theory is the dopamine hypothesis. This theory is based on the observation of amphetamine-induced psychosis, which serves as a pharmacological model of schizophrenic behavior. The symptoms evidenced in this model psychosis are readily ameliorated through the use of neuroleptic drugs. Further, it appears that most amphetamine-induced psychotic behavior is mediated through increased release of dopamine in the brain. Thus, there are two core components to the dopamine theory: (1) Psychosis is induced by increased levels of dopaminergic activity and (2) most antipsychotic drugs block postsynaptic dopamine receptors (Baldessarini, 1985; Hollister, 1983). Unfortunately, it is not certain what leads to this dopaminergic overactivity in the first place.

It is believed that although antipsychotic medications block norepinephrine, serotonin, and acetylcholine, their primary action is as central dopamine antagonists (Niemegeers & Janssen, 1979). That is, these drugs block central dopamine receptors and thus inhibit dopaminergic neurotransmission in the brain. The postsynaptic receptor blockade in the limbic system is thought to produce the reduction in schizophrenic symptoms, although the blockade in the basal ganglia probably results in **extrapyramidal** motor reactions, an unfortunate side effect of neuroleptics.

The preceding represents the predominant beliefs regarding the actions of antipsychotic medications. This thinking, however, probably is best viewed as tentative, because much research is ongoing in an effort to identify the precise mechanisms of action that account for the effects of antipsychotic medications. Nevertheless, while the precise mechanisms underlying the actions of neuroleptics remain to be isolated, current knowledge does point to at least some role for dopamine in the modulation of psychotic behaviors (Snyder & Largent, 1989).

Although the antipsychotics have produced many positive effects in the treatment of mental disorders, their use is not without significant side effects. Antipsychotics also affect the extrapyramidal tract, and these actions produce among the most profound of side effects associated with antipsychotics. Chief among the acute side effects are motor disturbances which taken together give the appearance of a Parkinsonian syndrome. Persons with Parkinson's disease are typified by tremor, blank rigidity, gait and posture changes, and excessive salivation. Extrapyramidal symptoms are the most apparent motor disturbances, primarily **dyskinesia** (disordered movements) and **akinesia** (slowness of movement and underactivity). These symptoms result from the drug's effects on the extrapyramidal system. These are experienced acutely by more than 30 percent of patients receiving antipsychotics (Mackay, 1982). Autonomic side effects of antipsychotics are a result of the drug's actions on the hypothalamus. These side effects of antipsychotics tend to be dose-related: a greater degree of side effects is associated with higher doses of the antipsychotic medication.

The most common side effect associated with long–term use of antipsychotics is another extrapyramidal complication known as **tardive dyskinesia.** Tardive dyskinesia, which typically can be seen after two years or more of antipsychotic drug use, is characterized most often by repetitive involuntary movements of the mouth and tongue (often in the form of lip

Extrapyramidal
Outside the pyramidal tracts, with origin in the basal ganglia.

Dyskinesia
Disordered movements.

Akinesia
Slowness of movement and underactivity.

Tardive dyskinesia
An extrapyramidal complication characterized by involuntary movements of the mouth and tongue, trunk, and extremities. Tardive dyskinesia is a side effect of long–term (two or more years) use of antipsychotic drugs.

smacking), trunk, and extremities. Most cases of tardive dyskinesia are preceded by the Parkinson symptoms described earlier (Hollister, 1977). Some estimates are that up to 40 to 50 percent of patients using antipsychotics exhibit tardive dyskinesia, some symptoms of which are irreversible. The effects are seen more among women than men. Efforts to control or eliminate these effects include reducing the dose of the drug, which sometimes reduces the side effect and still provides some relief from the psychotic symptoms, administering medications designed to treat the side effects symptomatically (for example, benztropine [trade name Cogentin] or trihexyphenidyl [trade name Artane]), or instituting what are called "drug holidays," during which the patient is off medication to provide a physiological break from the use of the drug.

Although great strides have been made in the pharmacological treatment of psychotic disorders, concerted efforts in this area are continuing with several emphases. One focus is on developing neuroleptics providing symptom relief but acting through different mechanisms. The hope is to avoid or minimize the side effects (especially tardive dyskinesia) of current antipsychotic medications. A second emphasis is on developing neuroleptics which not only diminish the obvious symptoms such as hallucinations but also alleviate some less visible symptoms, such as emotional withdrawal. New drugs are being investigated. Some of these new drugs being studied do not appear to exert their effects by blocking dopamine receptors. These issues are discussed in more detail by Snyder and Largent (1989).

CONTEMPORARY ISSUE BOX 9–1
"Wonder Drugs": The Cases of Prozac and Clozaril

Every so often a psychotherapeutic drug enters the marketplace with such fanfare and potential that it is given the label "wonder drug." Sometimes these drugs live up to their early expectations, sometimes they do not.

Two psychiatric medications that have come onto the marketplace in recent years have been placed in the category of "wonder drugs." The first is the antidepressant Prozac (generic name, fluoxetine), and the second is Clozaril (generic name, clozapine), an antipsychotic medication. Both appear to offer great potential for the treatment of psychiatric disorders.

Prozac has received, by far, the greater amount of attention. Introduced in 1987, Prozac was the most prescribed antidepressant medication in the

United States by the early 1990s. One of the major advantages of Prozac is that it appears to have fewer and less severe side effects than many of the currently available antidepressants. (Its actual efficacy in the treatment of depression does not appear to be greater than that of the tricyclics.) Although chemically unrelated to the tricyclic antidepressants, Prozac's mechanisms of action are similar to those of the tricyclics. As such, the drug acts to block neurotransmitter reabsorption. However, while the tricyclics generally bolster the action of serotonin and norepinephrine, Prozac works exclusively on serotonin.

The major attractive feature of Clozaril for the treatment of psychotic and schizophrenic disorders is that it has yielded antipsychotic efficacy among patients who have not responded to other antipsychotics, such as haloperidol. In addition, Clozaril appears to produce a lesser degree of acute extrapyramidal side effects.

Clozaril is a member of the dibenzodiazepine class of drugs and is chemically related to loxapine, another antipsychotic. Clozaril, however, has greater serotonergic, adrenergic, and histaminergic blocking activity, relative to its dopamine-blocking effects. The drug may have its greatest impact among patients who have been chronically hospitalized for psychotic conditions, particularly patients who have been unresponsive to other drugs. But, as with all medications, the side effects must be kept in perspective. The most significant concern with Clozaril is the occasionally seen side effect of agranulocytosis, a destructive condition characterized by severe reductions in the number of granulocytes in the blood. If undetected, agranulocytosis results in death, so a very close monitoring of the patient is required.

The ultimate roles of Prozac in the treatment of depression and of Clozaril in the treatment of psychotic conditions are not yet known. To date, prospects are promising for each drug, but the long-term outcomes remain to be determined.

Antidepressants

Endogenous
Developed from within. When applied to depression, the term means that depressive symptoms seem to be due to genetic factors.

Exogenous
Developed from without. When applied to depression, the term means that depressive symptoms seem to be in reaction to a particular situation or event.

Depression is among the most common psychiatric disorders in the United States. Hollister (1983) estimates 400,000 persons are treated for depression yearly in the United States. Depressions vary in severity, duration, and frequency of occurrence, and the more common symptoms include dysphoric mood and loss of interest and appetite, sleep disturbance, fatigue, withdrawal, thoughts of suicide, and difficulties in concentration. Depressions frequently are classified either as **endogenous,** in which symptoms tend to be chronic and appear associated with genetic constitutional factors, or **exogenous,** in which symptoms are thought to be in reaction or response to a particular situation or event (Cooperrider, 1988). The case below, excerpted from Spitzer and others (1989), is an example of major depression rated as moderately severe.

Connie is a 33-year-old homemaker who separated from her husband 3 months previously. She has a 4-year-old son, Robert.

Connie left her husband, Donald, after a five-year marriage. Violent arguments between them, during which Connie was beaten by her husband, had occurred for the last four years of their marriage, beginning when she became pregnant with Robert. During their final argument, about Connie's buying an expensive tricycle for Robert, her husband had held a loaded gun to Robert's head and threatened to shoot him if she didn't agree to return the tricycle to the store. Connie obtained a court order of protection that prevented Donald from having any contact with her or their son. She took Robert to her parents' apartment, where they are still living.

Connie is an only child, and a high school and secretarial school graduate. She worked as an executive secretary for six years before her marriage and for the first two years after, until Robert's birth. Before her marriage Connie had her own apartment. She was close to her parents, visiting them weekly and speaking to them a couple of times a week. Connie had many friends whom she also saw regularly. She still had several friends from her high school years. In high school she had been a popular cheerleader and a good student. In the office where she had worked as a secretary, she was in charge of organizing office holiday parties and money collections for employee gifts.

During their first year of marriage, Donald became increasingly irritable and critical of Connie. He began to request that Connie stop calling and seeing her friends after work, and refused to allow them or his in-laws to visit their apartment. Connie convinced Donald to try marital therapy, but he refused to continue after the initial two sessions.

Despite her misgivings about Donald's behavior toward her, Connie decided to become pregnant. During the seventh month of the pregnancy, she developed thrombophlebitis and had to stay home in bed. Donald began complaining that their apartment was not clean enough and that Connie was not able to shop for groceries. He never helped Connie with the housework. He refused to allow his mother-in-law to come to the apartment to help. One morning when he couldn't find a clean shirt, he became angry and yelled at Connie. When she suggested that he pick some up from the laundry, he began hitting her with his fists. She left him and went to live with her parents for a week. He expressed remorse for hitting her and agreed to resume marital therapy.

At her parents' and Donald's urging, Connie returned to her apartment. No further violence occurred until after Robert's birth. At that time, Donald began using cocaine every weekend and often became violent when he was high.

In the three months since she left Donald, Connie has become increasingly depressed. Her appetite has been poor, and she has lost ten pounds. She cries a lot and often wakes up at five in the morning, unable to get back to sleep. Ever since she left Donald, he has been calling her at her parents' home and begging her to return to him. One week before her psychiatric evaluation, Connie's parents took her to their general practitioner. Her physical examination was normal, and he referred her for psychiatric treatment.

When seen by a psychiatrist in the outpatient clinic, Connie is pale and thin, dressed in worn-out jeans and dark blue sweater. Her haircut is unstylish, and she appears older than she is. She speaks slowly, describing her depressed mood and lack of energy. She says that her only pleasure is in being with her son. She is able to take care of him physically, but feels guilty because her preoccupation with her own bad feelings prevents her from being able to play with him. She now has no social contacts other than with her parents and her son. She feels worthless and blames herself for her marital problems, saying that if she had been a better wife, maybe Donald would have been able to give up the cocaine. When asked why she stayed with him so long, she explains that her family disapproved of divorce and kept telling her that she should try harder to make her marriage a success. She also thought about what her life would be like trying to take care of her son while working full time and didn't think she could make it. (Published with permission of American Psychiatric Press, Inc.)

Although stimulants once were used as a treatment for depression, their effectiveness was limited, especially among persons with severe depressions. Today stimulants are rarely used for depression (Schlemmer, Ang, & Davis, 1983). Instead, two central classes of antidepressant medications are prescribed; both act in a manner different from stimulants, which produce a euphoria that does not generally occur with the antidepressants (Cooperrider, 1988). The first are tricyclic antidepressants (TCAs), so-called because of their three-ring chemical structure nucleus. In the second class of antidepressions are the monoamine oxidase inhibitors (MAOIs). The TCAs are used much more than the MAOIs in the treatment of depression in the United States; in Europe they are used about equally (Honigfeld & Howard, 1978). Representative antidepressant medications are listed in Table 9–3.

Both the TCAs and MAOIs were available in the late 1950s. As with other psychiatric medications, their potential antidepressant effects were discovered serendipitously. TCAs initially were being investigated as antipsychotic agents, while the MAOIs initially were used in the treatment of tuberculosis.

Table 9–3
Representative Antidepressant Medications

	Generic Name	Trade Name
Tricyclic Antidepressants		
	Imipramine	Tofranil, Antipress
	Amitriptyline	Amitril, Elavil
	Desipramine	Norpramine
	Nortriptyline	Aventyl, Pamelor
	Doxepin	Sinequan
	Protriptyline	Vivactil
	Amoxapine	Asendin
	Trimipramine	Surmontil
MAOIs		
	Tranylcypromine	Parnate
	Isocarboxazid	Marplan
	Phenelzine	Nardil

Note: The most frequently prescribed antidepressant drug is fluoxetine (Prozac) (see Contemporary Issue Box 9–1).

In both cases antidepressant effects were noted by investigators. It was observed, for example, that some tuberculosis patients treated with an MAOI showed an energized state. The TCAs and MAOIs represent the current mainstays of biological treatments for depression.

Before discussing the TCAs and MAOIs in more detail, it is necessary to discuss the postulated biochemical hypotheses for depression. It is believed that depression results from a deficiency in biogenic amines—specifically catecholamines and serotonin—which act as central nervous system neurotransmitters (see Chapter 3). According to the catecholamine hypothesis, depression is a result of a deficiency in catecholamines (particularly norepinephrine) at varied neuron receptor sites in the brain. TCAs are believed to block the uptake of norepinephrine from the synaptic cleft. Thus, there results a greater concentration of norepinephrine in the synaptic cleft, alleviating the hypothesized neurotransmitter deficiency. This TCA-mediated process is thought to occur in the amygdala and reticular formation areas of the midbrain.

The catecholamine theory is derived in large part from observations of the effects of the antipsychotic agent reserpine, discussed earlier in the historical overview. Patients given reserpine often exhibit a depressed appearance. Further, reserpine was found to deplete brain concentrations of norepinephrine. Thus, there was the suggestion that such depletions were causally related to depression.

The serotonin hypothesis, the other central theory regarding antidepressant action, postulates that depression is the result of a deficiency of the neurotransmitter serotonin in the brain stem (Cooperrider, 1988; Kalus, Asnis, & van Praag, 1989). Persons who are depressed have reduced levels of serotonin and chemicals involved in its metabolism in their cerebrospinal fluid. As in the case with the catecholamine norepinephrine, TCAs have been found to prevent the uptake of serotonin (Cooperrider, 1988).

While the TCAs block the uptake of amines, MAOIs prevent the breakdown of the neurotransmitters. As described by Cooperrider (1988), the enzyme monoamine oxidase metabolizes a variety of neurotransmitters, including norepinephrine and serotonin. MAOIs inhibit this degradation process and thus enhance the availability of the transmitter within the neuron. Thus, the actions of the TCAs and MAOIs each are consistent with the hypothesis that decreased brain catecholamine activity causes depression, and that these antidepressants (using different mechanisms) reverse this process by raising catecholamine activity in the brain (McNeal & Cimbolic, 1986).

Taken together, the TCAs and MAOIs each appear to enhance the functional activity of one or more neurotransmitters. But our understanding of the mechanisms remains clouded. One finding contributing to our lack of understanding is that the effects noted above occur within hours, although the therapeutic antidepressant action can take days or weeks to be experienced by the patient. Therefore, current theories regarding the actions of antidepressants probably best are viewed as tentative.

The TCAs and MAOIs are absorbed readily through the gastrointestinal tract. TCAs are administered only rarely through injection, and MAOIs always are taken orally. Following absorption is the development of relatively high concentrations of the drugs in especially the brain, but also in other organs. After absorption, the antidepressant pharmacokinetics resemble those of the antipsychotics, especially chlorpromazine (Baldessarini, 1985). More is known of the absorption and distribution of the TCAs than of the MAOIs, in part because of the difficulty in isolating MAOI metabolites (Tyrer, 1982). Metabolism for each occurs primarily in the liver, with most excreted through the urine.

Despite the rapid absorption of antidepressant medications, one disadvantage (noted above) in their use is that clinical action frequently takes two to three weeks to be apparent in the patient's functioning. Unfortunately, it is during this initial period of use when most of the undesired side effects of antidepressants are experienced, and many patients terminate their use of the antidepressants because they experience the side effects in the absence of rapid symptom relief. The most common side effects of the TCAs are drowsiness and a variety of anticholinergic effects such as dry mouth, constipation and difficulty in urinating, blurred vision, orthostasis (dizziness upon standing up), and tachycardia. The most common side effects of the MAOIs are drowsiness, dry mouth, dizziness, and fatigue. In addition, MAOI use is associated with two other unwanted effects. The first is orthostasis, and the second is impaired sexual functioning. Men may experience impotence and difficulty in ejaculating, and women may report orgasmic inhibition. The use of MAOIs also requires several dietary restrictions. Most significant among these is avoiding substances which contain tyramine, such as most cheeses and some alcoholic beverages. MAOIs and tyramine interact to cause potentially severe hypertensive reactions. Finally, a concern in the use of antidepressants is their potential for lethal use. Overdosing on TCAs can result in coma, respiratory difficulties, and a variety of cardiac problems. Accordingly, the patient's potential for suicide has to be assessed in order to prescribe TCAs safely. MAOIs do not produce intoxicating effects, and overdosing on them is not common.

The therapeutic effects of antidepressants are impressive once the lag time has passed. TCAs in particular show marked alleviation of depressive symptoms. MAOIs also have strong supportive treatment effectiveness rates when compared to placebos, although the positive outcomes are not as dramatic as with the TCAs. Also, MAOIs, when compared directly to TCAs, tend to be not as effective. This has led to a tendency, in the United States at least, for TCAs to be a treatment of choice for most depressions, with MAOIs used when TCAs do not produce desired results.

Antianxiety Drugs

Antianxiety drugs, also known as anxiolytics and tranquilizers, are intended to treat the physiological and psychological symptoms of anxiety.

CONTEMPORARY ISSUE BOX 9–2
Issue: The Right to Refuse Psychiatric Medications

Should a person voluntarily or involuntarily admitted to a psychiatric facility have the opportunity to refuse psychotropic drugs? For many years it was the case that a person hospitalized for psychiatric treatment had little if any say in whether drugs would be administered, based in part on the assumption that they had no expertise in the area of psychiatric medications and that being hospitalized to begin with suggested some impairment in functioning and thus the ability to make decisions.

This issue was addressed in a 1979 case heard in Federal District Court in Massachusetts. The case involved a suit filed several years earlier by seven Boston State Hospital patients to stop the (nonemergency) administration of medications without their first being able to provide their informed consent. Relatedly, the patients claimed the right to refuse medication. The psychiatrists faced a dilemma. On the one hand, they knew by experience certain drugs were able to significantly relieve emotional distress. On the other hand, some of these drugs had unpleasant side effects, and patients understandably might want to avoid these.

The court decided in favor of the patients. It ruled patients should be presumed (whether voluntarily or involuntarily admitted to the hospital) competent to accept or refuse psychotropic medications. The court added that when a patient was not deemed competent, the decision on whether to use medications needed to be made by a court-appointed guardian.

Is this the final word? No, probably not. Other cases are bound to come up, and could yield different rulings. In the late 1960s, for example, doctors in two states were successfully sued for not giving medications to committed patients who refused the drugs (see Gutheil, 1980). Furthermore, the practical implication of the Boston State Hospital case may not arise very often. A study by Appelbaum and Gutheil (1980) noted that the issue of refusing medications by psychiatric patients did not arise often.

It is difficult to provide a complete definition of anxiety, given the wide array of phenomena it encompasses. However, anxiety is frequently experienced as some or all of the following four categories of symptoms: (1) motor tension (for example, shakiness, muscle tension, restlessness), (2) autonomic hyperactivity (for example, sweating, pounding heart, stomach tightness, flushing), (3) apprehensive expectation (such as anxiety, fear, rumination), and (4) vigilance (for example, impatience, hyperattentiveness, insomnia) (APA, 1980). Clinicians frequently speak of two types of anxiety. The first is a trait or characterological anxiety, in that the person seems to experience his or her anxiety practically all the time. The second is a more transient state, called situational anxiety, wherein the anxiety is much greater at some times than at others, when the person may not even feel anxious at all. A related type of anxiety is panic attacks, which are recurrent and unpredictable periods of intense fear and impending doom (APA, 1987). These attacks frequently include sweating, palpitations, dizziness, and difficulty in breathing. It is estimated between 2 and 4 percent of the population have experienced some form of clinically significant anxiety. A case illustration of panic attacks from Spitzer and others (1989), follows.

> Mindy Markowitz is a stylishly dressed, 25-year-old art director who is seeking treatment for "panic attacks" that have occurred with increasing frequency over the past year, often two or three times a day. These attacks begin with a sudden intense wave of "horrible fear" that seems to come out of nowhere, sometimes during the day, sometimes waking her from sleep. She begins to tremble, is nauseated, sweats profusely, feels as though she is gagging, and fears that she will lose control and do something crazy, like run screaming into the street.
>
> Mindy remembers first having attacks like this when she was in high school. She was dating a boy her parents disapproved of, and had to do a lot of "sneaking around" to avoid confrontations with them. At the same time, she was under a lot of pressure as the principal designer of her high school yearbook, and was applying to Ivy League colleges. She remembers that her first panic attack occurred just after the yearbook went to press and she was accepted by Harvard, Yale, and Brown. The attacks lasted only a few minutes, and she would just "sit through them." She was worried enough to mention them to her mother; but because she was otherwise perfectly healthy, she did not seek treatment.
>
> Over the eight years since her first attack, Mindy has had them intermittently, sometimes not for many months, sometimes, as now, several times a day. There have also been extreme variations in the intensity of the attacks, some being so severe and debilitating that she had to take a day off from work.
>
> Apart from her panic attacks and a brief period of depression at 19, when she broke up with a boyfriend, Mindy has always functioned extremely well, in school, at work, and in her social life. She is a lively, friendly person who is respected by her friends and colleagues both for her intelligence and creativity and for her ability to mediate disputes.
>
> Even during the times that she was having frequent, severe attacks, Mindy never limited her activities. She might stay home from work for a day because she was exhausted from multiple attacks, but she never associated the attacks with particular places. (Published with permission of American Psychiatric Press, Inc.)

The antianxiety drugs now more commonly used are listed in Table 9–4. Before the twentieth century, however, the common palliative for anxiety symptoms was drinking alcohol, perhaps the oldest known means of sedation. For much of this century, into the 1950s, anxiety was treated primarily through the use of bromide salts (which were available without prescription) and barbiturates. The latter decreased anxiety symptoms through a generalized and nonspecific depression of all body tissues, but more cru-

Table 9–4
Representative Antianxiety Medications

	Generic Name	Trade Name
Benzodiazepines		
	Chlordiazepoxide	Librium
	Diazepam	Valium
	Alprazolam	Xanax
	Oxazepam	Serax
	Clorazepate	Tranzene
	Temazepam	Restoril
	Flurazepam	Dalmane
	Triazolam	Halcion
	Lorazepam	Ativan
Nonbarbiturate, Nonbenzodiazepines		
	Meprobamate	Equanil
	Hydroxyzine	Vistaril, Atarax
	Ethinamate	Valmid
	Buspirone	BuSpar

cially the central nervous system and the cardiovascular system. By the 1930s scientists were discovering that the use of the bromides had unwanted cumulative effects and could produce toxic delirium (Hollister, 1983). Barbiturates, such as phenobarbital, were used then more frequently as an anxiolytic agent. However, it gradually became clear these drugs were physically addictive, with users developing tolerance and exhibiting a severe withdrawal reaction when drug use ceased. As a result, efforts were directed at developing an anxiolytic medication that would effectively treat the anxiety but not be physically addicting. The first in the desired group of nonbarbiturate sedatives was meprobamate, but again it was found a severe withdrawal syndrome was associated with discontinuing its use after some period of time on the drug.

As mentioned in Chapter 8, the first benzodiazepine was synthesized in the 1950s. This benzodiazepine, chlordiazepoxide (Librium), was made available for distribution in 1960. A number of other benzodiazepines have been made available since that time, and this drug group is the predominant form of medication used for anxiety symptomology. The important advantage of the benzodiazepines is that they effectively treat the anxiety symptoms without overly sedating the patient. An estimated 100 million prescriptions of benzodiazepine drugs at a cost of about $500 million are provided in the United States alone yearly (Baldessarini, 1985).

Benzodiazepines also are used for purposes other than anxiety management. For example, benzodiazepines are frequently used to medically manage withdrawal from alcohol. Alcohol and benzodiazepines have some

CONTEMPORARY ISSUE BOX 9-3
Benzodiazepines: Prescription Caveats

The invention of the benzodiazepine drugs was an advance in the treatment of anxiety and of alcohol withdrawal. The popularity of the benzodiazepines as prescription drugs, however, brought concerns that they were being overprescribed. The major concern was that the benzodiazepine drugs are physically addicting, and that freely prescribing these drugs was solving one problem, for example, severe anxiety, by inducing another, benzodiazepine dependence.

The concern is particularly acute if a physician is treating a person who has a history of alcohol or other drug problems. For example, not too long ago some physicians recommended treating people who were alcohol–dependent with benzodiazepines to relieve emotional distress. It was reasoned that, rather than using alcohol to relieve distress, it would be better to use a benzodiazepine drug. Now that the potential for developing physical dependence on the benzodiazepines is much more widely recognized, few physicians recommend prescribing benzodiazepines to people as substitutes for alcohol.

When treating people who have a history of alcohol or drug dependence there is the added problem of benzodiazepine abuse potential. These drugs have psychoactive properties that are reinforcing and thus are candidates for abuse. For people who have a history of drug or alcohol problems the risk of abuse is higher than in people who have no such history. For example, one study compared the effects of a benzodiazepine drug on alcoholic men who had abstained from alcohol for up to 72 hours to the effects in nonalcoholic men. The study showed that the pharmacokinetics (absorption, distribution, and metabolism) of the drug did not differ in the two groups, but that the alcoholics liked the effects of the drug more. "Liking" the drug was measured with a questionnaire that correlates with drug use liability (Ciraulo, Barnhill, Greenblatt, and others, 1988).

Data such as these sometimes leave the physician in a dilemma. Although few prescribe benzodiazepines to alcoholics as substitutes for alcohol, the drugs may have treatment value for, say, alcoholics who have a major anxiety problem such as panic disorder. It is for such cases that the anxiolytic drug BuSpar has been invented. BuSpar's special feature is that it seems as effective as the benzodiazepines in treating major anxiety problems, but it is not likely to be abused.

The problem in prescribing benzodiazepines accents the general point that the pros and cons of using any drug as part of treatment must be considered carefully. This principle is especially important in drug treatment of people who are or have been alcohol–or drug–dependent.

effects in common so that tapering from alcohol is made easier through the use of benzodiazepines. In addition, benzodiazepines have anticonvulsant properties. Benzodiazepines also are used as an anesthetic for minor procedures such as dental surgery and as a treatment for muscle spasms and seizures.

Mood Stabilizing Drugs

The most specific treatment for the mood disorders of mania and manic-depressive illness is lithium. Mania is a state in which there are pronounced elevations in mood and increased activity. Symptoms of a manic episode typically might include the following: increased talkativeness, flight of ideas or racing thoughts, grandiosity, decreased need for sleep, and excessive involvement in behaviors that can produce negative consequences (such as buying sprees or sexual indiscretions) (APA, 1980). While these symptoms may seem to describe someone who is "happy-go-lucky" or "pleasantly high," their occurrence and severity generally are profound and significantly disrupt the person's functioning. For persons with this disorder, the first manic episode generally occurs in their twenties or thirties, although there are exceptions in both directions. The natural course of an untreated manic episode is generally around a couple of months. Manic attacks generally are a component of what is called bipolar, or manic-depressive, illness; periodic episodes of depression often are experienced by these individuals as well. The following case (Spitzer and others, 1989) illustrates the manic component of bipolar disorder. The case is an example of the development of manic symptoms late in life.

A wealthy, 72-year-old widow is referred by her children, against her will, as they think she has become "senile" since the death of her husband 6 months previously. After the initial bereavement, which was not severe, the patient had resumed an active social life and become a volunteer at local hospitals. The family encouraged this, but over the past three months have become concerned about her going to local bars with some of the hospital staff. The referral was precipitated by her announcing her engagement to a 25-year-old male nurse, to whom she planned to turn over her house and a large amount of money. The patient's three sons, by threat and intimidation, have made her accompany them to this psychiatric evaluation.

Initially in the interview the patient is extremely angry at her sons and the psychiatrist, insisting that they don't understand that for the first time in her life she is doing something for herself. She then suddenly drapes herself over the couch and asks the psychiatrist if she is attractive enough to capture a 25-year-old man. She proceeds to elaborate on her fiance's physique and sexual abilities and describes her life as exciting and fulfilling for the first time. She is overtalkative and repeatedly refuses to allow the psychiatrist to interrupt her with questions. She says that she goes out nightly with her fiance to clubs and bars and that although she does not drink, she thoroughly enjoys the atmosphere. They often go on to an after-hours place and end up breakfasting, going to bed, and making love. After only three or four hours' sleep, she gets up, feeling refreshed, and then goes shopping. She spends about $700 a week on herself and gives her fiance about $500 a week, all of which she can easily afford. (Published with permission of American Psychiatric Press, Inc.)

Lithium is an alkaline metal readily available throughout nature and is found in the form of silicate in such rocks as petalite, lepidolite, and spodumene (Tyrer & Shaw, 1982). Its mood stabilizing properties were discovered in the 1940s. An Australian physician, John Cade, was giving research animals lithium in an attempt to decrease uric acid-induced kidney damage. In the course of his work, he observed a calming effect on the animals and speculated that lithium might be useful in humans as a mood attenuator (Baldessarini, 1985; Sack & De Fraites, 1977). Cade administered lithium to a sample of manic patients and observed positive responses. Subsequent research eventually led to lithium's approval for clinical use in the United States in 1970, although it was in clinical use in Europe several years prior. Although lithium may have some value in treating other psychiatric disorders (such as depression, some schizophrenias, alcoholism, impulsive-aggressive behaviors, and movement disorders), it is approved in the United States only in the treatment of manic episodes and prophylactically to prevent the recurrence of manic episodes. There is strong evidence that lithium is effective with these two indications. Lithium probably is, incidentally, the only drug in psychiatry for which there is effective prophylaxis against disease recurrence (Frieve, 1976; Sack & De Fraites, 1977).

As with the antidepressants discussed earlier, the major biological theory regarding mania concerns the monoamine neurotransmitters. In depression there was a hypothesized underactivity of neurotransmitters, and the hypothesis for mania is that there exists an increased functional activity of the neurotransmitters. Within these hypotheses, the central focus is on catecholamines and serotonin. For mania the theory is that mania results from an overactivity of catecholamine neurotransmitters or an underactivity of serotonin in the brain. However, most of the specific attention concerns the overactivity of catecholamine neurotransmission, and lithium serves to inhibit catecholamine synthesis at the synapse. Importantly, lithium serves to normalize the mood of manic patients, not just offset mania through sedation.

The most common preparations of lithium salts are carbonates (lithium carbonate, or Li_2CO_3), which are prepared in tablet form. In terms of pharmacokinetics, lithium, which is taken orally, is absorbed completely from the gastrointestinal tract (primarily the small intestine) and distributed throughout the system. The lithium is distributed in the body water and is not metabolized. Excretion occurs almost entirely by the kidney, with between 90 and 95 percent eliminated through urine.

Despite its success in the treatment of mania, there are cautions which must be taken into account prior to and during lithium use. Several of these considerations pertain to lithium's therapeutic index, or safety margin. In this regard, the difference between the therapeutic and toxic levels is small.

When the therapeutic range is exceeded, at least several of the following symptoms might be observed: drowsiness, blurred vision, ataxia, confusion, cardiac irregularities, and even seizures and coma. Some deaths have been reported. Thus, lithium use requires close medical supervision. Also, pretreatment medical work-ups are specifically geared toward ruling out cardiovascular problems or renal disease. Cardiac problems are a concern because toxic effects can cause cardiac irregularities which could then exacerbate pre-existing cardiovascular problems. Renal functioning must be satisfactory so that the lithium is efficiently excreted. If it is not, lithium will accumulate in the body. Finally, there are several side effects associated with lithium use, including gastrointestinal problems such as nausea, diarrhea, fine hand tremor, urinary frequency, and dry mouth. However, these side effects often decrease within a period of weeks.

PSYCHOTROPIC DRUGS DURING PREGNANCY

No psychotropic medication is totally safe for use during pregnancy, and all carry FDA warnings regarding use when the patient is pregnant. As a result, a judgment needs to be made between the health of the mother on the one hand, and the risks to the unborn child on the other. The approach most recommended is that psychotropics not be used during pregnancy unless absolutely necessary, and only after nondrug interventions, such as counseling, have been tried first.

There are several reasons why psychotropic drug use during pregnancy is potentially unsafe. Certainly on one level, the risks to the mother are at least the same as when she is not pregnant. However, the risks are increased when one considers the variety of physical changes that occur during pregnancy, including alterations in metabolism and endocrine, renal, and cardiac changes (Kerns & Davis, 1986). These and other changes create an environment in which absorption, distribution, and excretion of the drug can occur. For example, one effect of antipsychotic medication on the mother is lowered blood pressure, which can compromise the placental blood flow to the fetus.

Risks are also faced by the fetus, particularly **teratogenic** effects, long-term effects on neurobehavioral functioning, and direct toxic effects of the drug. Three points should be kept in mind (Kerns & Davis, 1986). First, all classes of psychotropic drugs cross the placenta. Second, drug effects can change the blood flow within the placenta, influencing the transport and nutritive functions of the placenta. Third, the fetus, compared to an adult, has greater cardiac output and a greater proportion of blood flow to the brain. This results in a greater exposure of the drug to the brain.

Teratogenic
Producing abnormalities in the fetus.

The effects of psychotropic drugs on the fetus are not well established. Most of the research has been conducted, for obvious reasons, on animals rather than humans. And the work involving humans, usually follow-up studies on women who used these drugs during pregnancy and their off-spring, is hard to interpret. For example, many of the pregnant women who use psychotropic medications have used more than one drug and many have used other substances as well, such as alcohol or cigarettes. Nevertheless, there are indications that although not well established, various teratogenic, neurobehavioral, and toxic consequences can and do occur when psycho-tropics are used during pregnancy. Perhaps the most widely recognized effect is when lithium is used during the first trimester of pregnancy. Such use is associated with a significant teratogenic risk of cardiovascular system impairment.

SUMMARY

- Psychotropic medications are prescribed in hopes of providing mentally ill persons some relief and ideally with the opportunity to function better within their environments.

- Early efforts to deal with mental illness included a variety of speculative approaches, many of which were cruel. These included bloodletting, hot irons, flogging, and starvation.

- Later on, in the mid-1800s, cannabis was studied as a treatment for depression and mania.

- During the first half of the 1900s, amphetamines were used in the treatment of depression and narcolepsy and carbon dioxide in the treatment of various psychotic and neurotic conditions.

- In 1949, the Australian physician John Cade discovered the benefits of lithium in the treatment of mania, and lithium remains a mainstay in the treatment of that disorder today.

- The greatest advance in psychopharmacology was the use, starting around 1950, of the drug chlorpromazine as an antipsychotic medication. A host of other drugs were introduced in the years following, including antianxiety medications (including meprobamate, a muscle relaxant) and antidepressant medications (including the tricyclic antidepressants and monoamine oxidase inhibitors).

- About 15% of the United States population experience some form of mental disorder in any given year. Most of the persons are experiencing symptoms associated with anxiety, depression, or alcohol abuse.

- More than 200 million prescriptions for the lawful use of psychotherapeutics are written yearly. Approximately 10 to 15% of the general population in any given year are given a prescription for a psychoactive agent, usually an antianxiety agent.

- Psychotropic drug use is more likely among women, older persons, persons living alone, the more educated, and those with higher income levels.

- The illicit use of prescription medications is a serious problem. Prescription drugs are a factor in 60% of all drug-related emergency room cases and 70% of all drug-related deaths. Information gathering networks, such as the Client–Oriented Data Acquisition Process (CODAP) and Drug Abuse Warning Network (DAWN), have been established to monitor the distribution and use (legal and otherwise) of drugs overall, including psychotropic drugs.

- Psychotropic drugs can modify virtually any stage of synaptic action, but generally affect three main processes: transmitter-receptor binding, reuptake of transmitters, and the manufacture of receptors.

- As with other drugs, psychiatric drugs can be classified in different ways. The most common way is by therapeutic use, and there are four major categories: Antipsychotics, antidepressants, antianxiety agents, and mood stabilizing drugs.

- Antipsychotic medications, also known as neuroleptics or major tranquilizers, are used to treat schizophrenia and other disorders, such as mania, agitated depression, toxic psychoses, emotionally unstable personalities, and psychoses associated with old age. These medications primarily affect the reticular activating system, the limbic system, and the hypothalamus.

- The dopamine hypothesis is the most accepted explanation of the action of antipsychotic medications. Two core elements of the dopamine hypothesis are: psychoses are induced by increased levels of dopaminergic activity; most antipsychotic drugs block postsynaptic dopamine receptors.

- Tardive dyskinesia is a major side effect of long-term use of antipsychotic drugs. It is most characterized by repetitive involuntary movements of the mouth and tongue, trunk, and extremities.

- Depression is one of the most common psychiatric disorders in the United States. Depression often is classified as one of two major types, endogenous and exogenous.

- Two major classes of antidepressant medications now are prescribed, trycyclic antidepressants (TCAs) and monoamine oxidase inhibitors (MAOIs). In the United States TCAs are prescribed more frequently than the MAOIs.

- Antidepressant medication treatment of depression follows from the biochemical hypothesis of the disorder. The hypothesis is that depression results from a deficiency in two biogenic amines, catecholamines and serotonin, which act as CNS neurotransmitters.

- Antianxiety drugs also are known as anxiolytics and tranquilizers. They are intended to treat the physiological and psychological symptoms of anxiety. It is estimated that 2 to 4% of the population have experienced some form of clinically significant anxiety.

- A major breakthrough in the psychotropic treatment of anxiety was the invention of the benzodiazepine drugs. These drugs are effective in alleviating anxiety symptoms but they do not overly sedate the patient.

- Because of their clinical utility, the benzodiazepine drugs are an immensely popular treatment choice. However, extreme care must be taken in their use, due to a high potential for abuse and physical dependence liability.

- Lithium is the major drug used in treating the mood disorders of mania and manic-depressive illness. Lithium is the only psychiatric drug that is an effective prophylaxis against disease recurrence.

- Use of lithium is based in the biological theory that mania results from an overactivity of catecholamine neurotransmitters or an underactivity of serotonin in the brain. Lithium inhibits catecholamine synthesis at the synapse and normalizes the mood of manic patients.

- No psychotropic drug is totally safe for use during pregnancy. The best approach is that psychotropic drugs be given to a pregnant woman only when necessary, and when nondrug therapies, such as counseling, have been tried and have failed.

- Psychotropic drug use during pregnancy poses a health risk to the mother and to the fetus. Although the experimental evidence is not solid, the fetus may face various teratogenic, neurobehavioral, and toxic consequences of its mother's use of psychotropic medications during pregnancy.

References

American Psychiatric Association (APA). (1980). *Diagnostic and statistical manual of mental disorders* (3rd Ed.). Washington, D.C.: APA.

APA (1987). *Diagnostic and statistical manual of mental disorders* (3rd Ed.-Rev.). Washington, D.C.: APA.

Appelbaum, P.S., & Gutheil, T.G. (1980). Drug refusal: A study of psychiatric inpatients. *American Journal of Psychiatry, 137,* 340–346.

Baldessarini, R.J. (1985). *Chemotherapy in psychiatry: Principles and practice* (Revised Ed.). Cambridge, MA: Harvard University Press.

Berger, F.M. (1970). Introduction. In W.G. Clark & J. del Giudice (Eds.), *Principles of psychopharmacology* (pp. 3–8). New York: Academic Press.

Bernstein, J.G. (1983). *Handbook of drug therapy in psychiatry.* Boston, John Wright.

Boatman, D.W., & Gagnon, J.P. (1977). The pharmacist as an information source for nonprescription drugs. *Journal of Drug Issues, 7,* 183–193.

Boulenger, J.P., & Lader, M. (1982). Pharmacokinetics and drug metabolism: Basic principles. In P.J. Tyrer (Ed.), *Drugs in psychiatric practice* (pp. 11–30). London: Butterworths.

Brecher, E.M. (1972). *Licit and illicit drugs.* Boston: Little, Brown.

Caldwell, A.E. (1970). *Origins of psychopharmacology—from CPZ to LSD.* Springfield, IL: Thomas.

Caldwell, A.E. (1978). History of psychopharmacology. In W.G. Clark & J. del Giudice (Eds.), *Principles of psychopharmacology* (pp. 9–30) (2nd Ed.). New York: Academic Press.

Carlton, P.L. (1983). *A primer of behavioral pharmacology.* New York: Freeman & Co.

Ciraulo, D.A., Barnhill, J.G., Greenblatt, D.J., Shader, R.I., Ciraulo, A.M., Tarmey, M.F., Molloy, M.A., & Foti, M.E. (1988). Abuse liability and clinical pharmacokinetics of alprazolam in alcoholic men. *Journal of Clinical Psychiatry, 49,* 333–337.

Clarke, F.H. (Ed.). (1973). *How modern medicines are discovered.* Mount Kisco, NY: Futura.

Cooperrider, C. (1988). Antidepressants. In G.W. Lawson & C.A. Cooperrider (Eds.), *Clinical psychopharmacology* (pp. 91–108). Rockville, MD: Aspen Publishers.

Curry, S.H. (1981). Introduction to pharmacokinetics in relation to biological psychiatry. In H.M. van Praag (Ed.), *Handbook of biological psychiatry* (Part 6) (pp. 57–70). New York: Marcel Dekker.

Denber, H.C.B. (1979). *Textbook of clinical psychopharmacology.* New York: Intercontinental Medical Book Corp.

Deniker, P. (1983). Discovery of the clinical use of neuroleptics. In M.J. Parnham & J. Bruinvels (Eds.), *Discoveries in pharmacology (Vol. 1): Psycho- and neuro-pharmacology* (pp. 163–180). New York: Elsevier.

Donlon, P.T., Schaffer, C.B., Erikson, S.E., Pepitone-Arreola-Rockwell, F., & Schaffer, L.C. (1983). *A manual of psychotropic drugs.* Bowie, MD: Robert J. Brady Co.

Ellor, J.R., & Kurz, D.J. (1982). Misuse and abuse of prescription and nonprescription drugs by the elderly. *Nursing Clinics of North America, 17,* 319–330.

Fieve, R.R. (1976). Therapeutic uses of lithium and rubidium. In L.L. Simpson (Ed.), *Drug treatment of mental disorders* (pp. 193–208). New York: Raven Press.

Flynn, K. (1985). The toll of deinstitutionalization. In P.W. Brickner, L.K. Scharer, B. Conanan, A. Elvy, & M. Savarese (Eds.), *Health care of homeless people.* New York: Springer.

Goldfarb, J. (1976). Introduction to pharmacology. In S.D. Glick & J. Goldfarb (Eds.), *Behavioral pharmacology* (pp. 58–84). St. Louis: C.V. Mosby.

Gutheil, T.G. (1980). In search of true freedom: Drug refusal, involuntary medication, and "Rotting with your rights on." *American Journal of Psychiatry, 137,* 327–328.

Hollister, L.E. (1977). Antipsychotic medications and the treatment of schizophrenia. In J.D. Barchas, P.A. Berger, R.D. Ciaranello, & G.R. Elliott (Eds.), *Psychopharmacology* (pp. 121–150). New York: Oxford University Press.

Hollister, L.E. (1983). *Clinical pharmacology of psychotherapeutic drugs* (2nd Ed.). New York: Churchill Livingstone.

Honigfeld, G., & Howard, A. (1978). *Psychiatry drugs* (2nd Ed.). New York: Academic Press.

Hordern, A. (1968). Psychopharmacology: Some historical considerations. In C.R.B. Joyce (Ed.), *Psychopharmacology: Dimensions and perspectives* (pp. 95–148). London: Tavistock.

Jarvik, M.E. (Ed.). (1977). *Psychopharmacology in the practice of medicine.* New York: Appleton-Century-Crofts.

Kalus, O., Asnis, G.M., & van Praag, H.M. (1989). The role of serotonin in depression. *Psychiatric Annals, 19,* 348–353.

Kerns, L.L., & Davis, G.P. (1986). Psychotropic drugs in pregnancy. In I.J. Chasnoff (Ed.), *Drug use in pregnancy: Mother and child* (pp. 81–93). Boston: MTP Press Limited.

Klerman, G.L. (1983). The prevalence and impact of mental illness on society. In R.L. Habig (Ed.), *The brain, biochemistry, and behavior* (pp. 3–28). Washington, D.C.: American Association for Clinical Chemistry.

Kline, N.S. (1970). Monoamine oxidase inhibitors: An unfinished picaresque tale. In F.J. Ayd & B. Blackwell (Eds.), *Discoveries in biological psychiatry* (pp. 194–204). Philadelphia: Lippincott.

Lader, M. (1976). Clinical psychopharmacology. In K. Granville-Grossman (Ed.), *Recent advances in clinical psychiatry* (Vol. 2). Edinburgh: Churchill Livingstone.

Lader, M.H., & Herrington, R.N. (1981). *Handbook of biological psychiatry (Part V): Drug treatment in psychiatry—Psychotropic drugs.* New York: Marcel Dekker.

Leavitt, F. (1974). *Drugs and behavior.* Philadelphia: Saunders.

Lickey, M.E., & Gordon, B. (1983). *Drugs for mental illness.* New York: Freeman & Co.

Mackay A.V.P. (1982). Antischizophrenic drugs. In P.J. Tyrer (Ed.), *Drugs in psychiatric practice.* London: Butterworths.

McNeal, E.T., & Cimbolic, P. (1986). Antidepressants and biochemical theories of depression. *Psychological Bulletin, 99,* 361–374.

Murphy, D.L. (1976). Neuropharmacology of depression. In L.L. Simpson (Ed.), *Drug treatment of mental disorders* (pp. 109–125). New York: Raven Press.

Niemegeers, C.J.E., & Janssen, P.A.J. (1979). A systemic study of the pharmacological activities of dopamine antagonists. *Life Sciences, 24,* 2201–2216.

OSMJ. (1986). PADS: A look at prescription drug abuse. *Ohio State Medical Journal, 82,* 33–38.

Parker, W.A. (1983). Alcohol-containing pharmaceuticals. *American Journal of Drug and Alcohol Abuse, 9,* 195–209.

Parnham, M.J., & Bruinvels, J. (Eds.). (1983). *Discoveries in pharmacology (Vol. 1): Psycho- and neuro-pharmacology.* New York: Elsevier.

Pepper, G.A. (1986). Rational use of OTCs. *Nurse Practitioner, 11,* 75–76.

Poling, A. (1986). *A primer of human behavioral pharmacology.* New York: Plenum Press.

Potter, W.Z., Bertilsson, L., & Sojoqvist, F. (1981). Clinical pharmacokinetics of psychotropic drugs: Fundamental and practical aspects. In H.M. van Praag (Ed.), *Handbook of biological psychiatry* (Part 6) (pp. 71–134). New York: Marcel Dekker.

Sack, R.L., & DeFraites, E. (1977). Lithium and the treatment of mania. In J.D. Barchas, P.A. Berger, R.D. Ciaranello, & G.R. Elliott (Eds.), *Psychopharmacology: From theory to practice.* New York: Oxford University Press.

Schlemmer, R.F., Jr., Ang, L.O., & Davis, J.M. (1983). Amphetamines and related stimulants as antidepressants. In G.D. Burrows, T.R. Norman, & B. Davies (Eds.), *Antidepressants* (pp. 251–266). New York: Elsevier.

Shepherd, M. (1981). *Psychotropic drugs in psychiatry.* New York: Jason Aronson.

Simon, G.I., & Silverman, H.M. (1986). *The pill book* (3rd Ed.). New York: Bantam Books.

Snyder, S.H., & Largent, B.L. (1989). Receptor mechanisms in antipsychotic drug action: Focus on sigma receptors. *Journal of Neuropsychiatry, 1,* 7–15.

Spiegel, R., & Aebi, H. (1981). *Psychopharmacology.* New York: John Wiley & Sons.

Spitzer, R.L., Gibbon, M., Skodol, A.E., Williams, J.B.W., & First, M.B. (1989). *DMS-III-R case book.* Washington, D.C.: American Psychiatric Press, Inc.

Swazey, J.P. (1974). *Chlorpromazine in psychiatry.* Cambridge, MA: MIT Press.

Tyrer, P.J. (1982). Evaluation of psychotropic drugs. In P.J. Tyrer (Ed.), *Drugs in psychiatric practice* (pp. 31–44). London: Butterworths.

Tyrer, P.J. (Ed.). (1982). *Drugs in psychiatric practice*. London: Butterworths.

Tyrer, P.J., & Marsden, C.A. (1982). Classification of psychotropic drugs. In P.J. Tyrer (Ed.), *Drugs in psychiatric practice* (pp. 3–10). London: Butterworths.

Tyrer, S., & Shaw, D.M. (1982). Lithium carbonate. In P.J. Tyrer (Ed.), *Drugs in psychiatric practice*. London: Butterworths.

Weiss, K.J., & Greenfield, D.P. (1986). Prescription drug abuse. *Psychiatric Clinics of North America, 9,* 475–490.

Wells, K.B., Kamberg, C., Brook, R., Camp, P., & Rogers, W. (1985). Health status, sociodemographic factors, and the use of prescribed psychotropic drugs. *Medical Care, 23,* 1295–1306.

10 OPIATES

As indicated in historical overviews in earlier chapters, psychoactive drugs can be two–edged swords in their great potential for improving the human condition on one hand, and their capacity to cause destruction to individuals and society on the other. No group of drugs captures this paradox more dramatically than the class of drugs we call opiates, which includes opium, morphine, heroin, and a number of related compounds. Opiate drugs have been used for many centuries to relieve pain and, when introduced to Europe, were hailed by physicians as a godsend. One of the first European physicians to use opium to relieve pain and suffering in his patients, Thomas Syndenham, wrote in 1680: "Among the remedies which it has pleased Almighty God to give man to relieve his sufferings, none is so universal and so efficacious as opium" (cited in Gay & Way, 1972, p. 47). Even today opiate drugs remain the most potent painkillers available to physicians, yet we now recognize the other edge of the opiate sword—the ability of opiates to produce severe dependence. Heroin is viewed as the prototypic addictive drug and illegal use and traffic in heroin is a major international problem. Thus, many of the concerns in general regarding psychoactive drugs emerge in bold relief in a consideration of opiates.

EARLY HISTORY OF THE OPIATES

Opium
The dried sap produced by the poppy plant.

Opium comes from *Papaver somniferum,* one of the many species of poppy plant. The opium poppy is native to the Middle East in the areas that border the Mediterranean Sea, but it is now cultivated extensively throughout Asia and the Middle East. Contrary to the experiences of Dorothy in *The Wizard of Oz,* however, simply walking through a poppy field will not cause sleep or euphoria. Rather, to experience the active drug effects, special procedures must be followed. The petals fall after the poppy blooms, leaving a round seedpod the size of an egg. If the seed pod is scored lightly with a knife, a milky white sap is secreted. After drying, this sap forms a thick, gummy, brown substance that is called **opium.** Opium effects may be obtained by consuming the substance orally or by smoking it. The use of such crude opium preparations is truly an ancient practice. There is evidence that opium was cultivated and used as long as 6000 years ago by the Sumerian and Assyrian civilizations. The ancient Egyptians had discovered medical uses for opiates 3500 years ago, as documented in the "Therapeutic Papyrus of Thebes" (Scott, 1969). Opium also was used for a variety of medical purposes by the Greek and Roman civilizations. The great Greek physician, Galen (A.D. 130–201) noted the following uses for opium:

"(opium) . . . resists poison and venomous bites, cures chronic headache, vertigo, deafness, epilepsy, apoplexy, dimness of sight, loss of voice, asthma, coughs of all kinds, spitting of blood, tightness of breath, colic, the iliac poison, jaundice, hardness of the spleen, stone, urinary complaints, fevers, dropsies, leprosies, the trou-

Figure 10–1 Opium exudes from incisions of the poppy *Papaver somniferum*.

bles to which women are subject, melancholy and all pestilences'' (Scott, 1969, p. 111).

Although this quote may seem more a testament to the ignorance of medical problems of this age, certainly the remarkable **analgesic** (pain-relieving) properties of opium must have made it at least seem helpful for many disease states. In fact, opiate drugs do have special cough-suppressant and anti-diarrhea properties in addition to their analgesic actions and are used in modern medicine for these purposes.

The use of opium for medical and recreational purposes became widespread among the Islamic peoples of the Middle East. This may have been because the Koran's explicit prohibition of the use of alcohol and some other drugs did not include opiate use (Latimer & Goldberg, 1981). To this day use of opiates is less censored among Muslims than alcohol. Arab traders spread the use of opium to India and China by the ninth century, and it was in China that the practice of smoking opium developed. Dependence on opium was first recognized as a problem in China as well with the first edict

Analgesia
Pain relief produced
without a loss of
consciousness.

against opium issued in 1729. But there were already so many opium addicts in China that the demand remained very high. In spite of the ban on importing opium into China, British ships continued to trade opium grown in India for Chinese tea, and this activity was the basis for the "Opium wars" between China and Great Britain in the middle of the ninteenth century (see Chapter 2).

Opium dependence was a serious problem in China by the beginning of the nineteenth century, but it was not yet seen as such in Europe or America. Although opium was readily available in the form of Laudanum, a beverage containing opium, and various patent medicines, it almost always was taken orally (a practice called opium eating, even though it was really opium drinking) rather than smoked. It was used mostly for medical purposes. There were a number of developments during the century bringing the addictive properties of opiate drugs to the awareness of Western societies. As noted in Chapter 2, opium preparations were readily available and completely legal in nineteenth-century Europe and the United States. It was probably only a matter of time before the pleasurable properties of opium led to widespread use for non-medical reasons. The pleasures of opium were brought to public awareness in a book written by the British poet Thomas de Quincey, *Confessions of an Opium Eater* published in 1822. De Quincey's book praised the effects of opium and included several famous quotes including: ". . . thou hast the keys of Paradise, O just, subtle and mighty opium!" (Scott, 1969, p. 52). Westerners were slow in recognizing that "eating" opium could prove just as addictive as smoking it, but as the use of opium, fueled by tomes such as De Quincey's, became more widespread, so did concern about the drug. By the late 1800s opium use had spread throughout society affecting such noted literary and scientific figures as Elizabeth Barrett Browning, Samuel Coleridge, William Halstead, Walter Scott, and Percy Shelley to name a few. It was becoming recognized that opium dependence was not limited to the Chinese.

Pharmacological developments added to the problems. In 1803 the German pharmacist F. W. Serturner developed the process which allowed the separation of morphine from opium. Morphine is the major active chemical in opium (codeine is another opiate drug found in opium) and is about ten times more potent than crude opium. Serturner experimented with morphine and was so impressed with the blissful, dream-like state it induced that he named the chemical after Morpheus, the Greek god of dreams. Morphine became widely available in the middle 1800s, and with the concomitant development of the hypodermic syringe, injected morphine became a major dependence problem in Europe and the United States. Because of the rapid and potent pain-relieving properties of injectable morphine, it became the treatment of choice during periods of recovery from severe wounds. However withdrawal from the morphine was often more difficult than recovery from the wound. As noted in Chapter 2, morphine dependence was so common among soldiers on both sides during the Civil War in

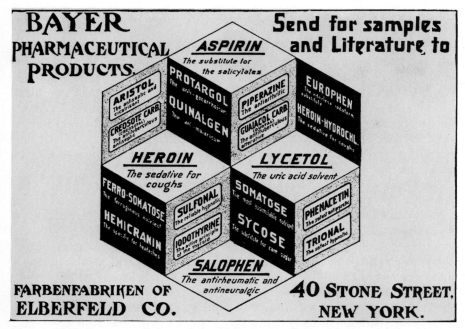

Figure 10–2 Patent medicines of the 19th century frequently contained opiates such as heroin.

America that it was often called "Soldier's Disease." In 1874 British chemist Alder Wright published experiments describing the production of a new chemical compound based on an alteration of morphine: diacetylmorphine. Wright's discovery went unnoticed until 1898 when the great German pharmacologist Heinrich Dreser (who also discovered aspirin—see Chapter 13) rediscovered the compound and noted that it was almost ten times more potent than morphine. Because this new compound was so powerful it was viewed as a new treatment with "heroic" possibilities and was christened **heroin.** Heroin was used immediately as a cough suppressant and pain reliever. Not until many years later was it recognized that heroin was even more likely than morphine to produce dependence.

Heroin
Heroin is produced by chemically processing morphine. It is more potent than morphine, and has become the major opiate drug of abuse.

OPIATE USE IN THE TWENTIETH CENTURY

The growing awareness of the danger and pervasiveness of opiate dependence led to a number of legal changes reviewed in detail in Chapter 2. In the United States these culminated in the 1914 Harrison Act. Of course, the Harrison Act did not eliminate completely non-medical use of opiates and, in fact, marked the origin of drug crime in America. Illegal opiate use meant smuggling of opium and heroin into the country, escalating prices, and a change in the type of person who became or remained addicted to opiates. The Harrison Act placed control of opiate drugs in the hands of physicians, and the determination of whether an addict had a valid medical need for opiates was exclusively the physician's decision. However, several legislative interpretations ruled a physician must not prescribe opiates unless doses could be shown to be decreasing over time (1915), that opiates must not be prescribed to addicts (1917), and in 1924 that heroin might not be prescribed at all (Kramer, 1972). The legitimate channels for obtaining drugs now were blocked for many addicts, so they turned to a growing black market to maintain their addiction.

There have been many changes in opiate use since the Harrison Act. One major change involved the demographics of opiate use. Opiate addiction cut across social classes in the pre-Harrison Act era. A wealthy middle–aged woman was as likely to be an opiate addict as anyone, but she would be addicted to Laudanum purchased at her drug store. When opiates became illegal, their use became focused in large cities where organized crime provided a source. In addition, users tended more and more to be young, poorly-educated persons of lower socio-economic status (Latimer & Goldberg, 1981), which is still the case. Finally, the more potent heroin has come to be the addict's drug of choice. Although there was widespread use of opiates by American GIs during the Vietnam War, that made only a small change in these demographic patterns. As reviewed in Chapter 1, current survey data reveal heroin and other opiate use is relatively infrequent among high school and college students. For example, less than 1% of American high school seniors reported any heroin use during any of the past ten years (Barnes, 1988). Although many different opiate drugs are prescribed for pain today, and certainly some users become dependent upon them, the major opiate problem in the United States today relates to heroin use, and that problem is usually centered in the inner cities.

A huge criminal apparatus for producing and supplying heroin was spawned in the wake of the Harrison Act. Today opium largely is grown in the Middle East (Afghanistan, Pakistan, Iran) or Southeast Asia (Burma, Laos, and Thailand) and processed into heroin in France (the so-called "French connection"), Italy, or Lebanon (Preble & Casey, 1972; White, 1985). Recently Mexico has become a major opium producer. From Europe or Mexico the heroin is smuggled into the United States. Most of the opium grown for legitimate medical purposes is cultivated in India or Australia. Street heroin is adulterated or cut many times as it changes hands on the way from the importer to those who sell to individual users. Heroin remains a large and important source of revenue and helps supply recruits for organized crime. It has been noted that most heroin addicts must get involved in criminal activity in order to support their habit. At first the cost of heroin may apper relatively low to the addict who uses the drug occasionally for "kicks." But in the words of an addict interviewed by Smith and Gay (1972): "It's so good, don't even try it once." Many users find that they take the drug more and more frequently, and since tolerance develops rapidly to heroin and other opiates, higher doses are soon required to produce the desired effect. Soon the cost of maintaining the growing habit virtually forces the addict to engage in criminal activities. Here is another interview with a street addict from San Francisco:

> (Heroin) . . . is the mellowest downer of all. You get none of the side effects of speed and barbs. After you fix, you feel the rush, like an orgasm if it's good dope. Then you float for about four hours; nothing positive, just a normal feeling, nowhere. It's like being half asleep, like watching a movie; nothing gets through to you, you're safe and warm. The big thing is, you don't hurt. You can walk around with rotting teeth and a busted appendix and not feel it. You don't need sex, you don't need food, you don't need people, you don't care. It's like death without permanence, life without pain.
>
> For me, the only hard part is keeping in H, paying my connection, man. I know these rich cats who can get good smack and shoot it for years and nothing happens, but me, you know, it's a hustle to stay alive. I run about a $100, $150–a–day habit, so I have to cop twice that much to keep my fence happy . . . Now me and my partner are into burglary; no strongarm stuff—you feel quiet on dope—just boosting TV sets from houses where we know the people are away. And I do a skin flick once in a while. But it's a hassle, believe me (Luce, 1972, p. 145).

Heroin addiction is a hard way to live for a number of other reasons. Addicts are at great risk for disease and death from AIDS, hepatitis and other needle–borne diseases from sharing contaminated needles (see Box 10–1). Current estimates place the number of heroin addicts in the United States at between 400,000 and 500,000 (Brodsky, 1985), a small number relative to the extent of alcoholism or nicotine dependence. However, risk of over-dose or complications from contaminated street heroin is always present. The National Institute on Drug Abuse (NIDA) estimates heroin overdose is responsible for more than 1000 deaths every year. With the death toll from needle–borne disease, heroin addiction remains a very serious social problem.

CONTEMPORARY ISSUE BOX 10–1
Fatal Attraction: Intravenous Drug Use and AIDS

The National Institute of Drug Abuse estimates 900,000 Americans are regular intravenous (IV) drug users, and that another 200,000 inject drugs at least occasionally (Booth, 1988). The majority of these IV drug users are heroin addicts, but many inject cocaine or methamphetamine. They may be young or old, black or white, male or female, but one thing they have in common is that they are at great risk for developing Acquired Immune Deficiency Syndrome—AIDS. In the early 1980s male homosexuals were the major group at high risk for AIDS, but drug–related AIDS cases have risen so sharply in the past few years that they now account for one–third of all new AIDS cases. The Center for Disease Control in Atlanta recently reported 10,747 or 33.3 percent of the 32,311 AIDS cases newly reported in 1988 occurred among IV drug users, their sex partners, or children born to women in either of those groups. The magnitude of this problem is considerable and likely to get worse. Conservative estimates from New York City are that at least half of the city's 200,000 IV drug users are infected with the human immunodeficiency virus (HIV). As many as 70 percent of the addicts recently tested at the Bellevue (New York) methadone clinic were HIV positive (Booth, 1988).

Moreover, it is not just the users who are involved. Heterosexual spread of the virus is occurring and the babies born of HIV-positive mothers will usually develop AIDS as well. In New York, 60 percent of the female AIDS victims were IV drug users and another 24 percent were sexual partners of IV drug users. As Don Des Jarlais of the New York Division of Substance Abuse Services put it: "If any group is going to serve as the bridge of infection into the heterosexual population it will be the IV drug users" (Booth, 1988).

An ironic aspect of this tragedy is that it is so avoidable. IV drug users are at risk for AIDS only because of the common practice of sharing needles. By using a needle contaminated with the blood of someone with HIV, direct blood to blood transmission occurs, which involves a very high risk of infection. If sterile needles were used, this risk would be eliminated. Health care workers are striving to send the message out to IV drug users that they should avoid sharing needles, or clean them with bleach if sharing is necessary. New York City has even developed a needle exchange, where clean needles are given to users in exchange for dirty ones. However, in most areas in the country, hypodermic syringes are controlled legally and remain difficult for addicts to obtain. In addition, sharing needles has become part of the "culture" for users. IV drug use often occurs in "shooting galleries," places where people gather to inject and enjoy the effects of the drug. A single needle may be used to deliver dozens of injections in such a place, unbeknownst to the users. Unless these practices can be stopped, the desire to use IV drugs will remain a fatal attraction.

The most recent development involving opiate drug use is the disturbing trend in the 1980s for the availability of "designer" heroin. Designer heroin is produced illicitly by chemists who design or develop chemical analogues to heroin. These new compounds are untested, but usually produce effects similar to those of heroin or other opiates. Until recently they had the advantage to the dealer of not being controlled under federal law, because in some cases they are compounds that are new to science. Most of the designer heroin compounds are derivatives of the powerful opioid, fentanyl. The problem with these fentanyl derivatives (often sold on the street as China White) is that they may be ten to one thousand times more potent than heroin. Thus, the risk of overdose death is greater. Numerous overdoses are now being attributed to designer heroin (Kirsch, 1986). Another designer heroin, MPPP or MPTP, is known now to produce brain damage and an associated neurological disorder that closely resembles Parkinson's disease in users (see Chapter 3). Thus designer heroin compounds are often far more dangerous than heroin. As noted in Chapter 2, to control the development and spread of designer drugs, Congress recently has enacted new legislation called the Controlled Substance Analogue Act of 1986.

ABSORPTION, DISTRIBUTION, METABOLISM, AND EXCRETION

Opiate drugs may be taken into the body in a variety of ways. Most are readily absorbed from the gastrointestinal tract, although the effect of a given dose is greater if it is injected intravenously. Most opioids also are absorbed through the nasal mucosa and lungs. Thus, opium often is smoked, and heroin frequently is taken intranasally. Opiates are also absorbed after intramuscular or subcutaneous administration. On the street, for example, heroin may be injected intravenously ("mainlining") or subcutaneously ("skin-popping").

Once in the bloodstream, opioids are distributed throughout the body with accumulations in the kidney, lung, liver, spleen, digestive tract, and muscle as well as the brain. With some opiates, such as morphine, only a small amount penetrates the blood-brain barrier. In fact, the main difference between morphine and the more potent drug, heroin, is that heroin is more lipid-soluble and thus more readily penetrates the blood-brain barrier. Once in the brain, heroin is converted to morphine. So heroin is essentially a more effective package for delivering morphine to the brain than morphine itself.

Most opiate drugs are rapidly metabolized in the liver and excreted by the kidney. Excretion of opiates is fairly rapid, with 90% excretion within a day after taking the drug. However, traces of morphine may remain in urine for two to four days after use (Hawks & Chang, 1986).

MECHANISMS OF OPIATE ACTION

One of the most exciting recent developments in the neurosciences is the discovery of the neural mechanisms of action of opiate drugs in the 1970s.

Research on this topic led to the discovery of a class of brain chemicals called the endorphins, which apparently function as neurotransmitters. It is now believed the effects of heroin, morphine, and other opiate drugs are produced by triggering activity in the brain's endorphin systems. We will review the events leading to these discoveries and consider how these new developments have helped understand the effects of opiate drugs.

One of the first events was the discovery by chemists in the 1960s that making a rather slight change in the morphine molecule resulted in a chemical that did not produce any of the standard opiate drug effects (pain relief, euphoria), but instead reversed or blocked the effects of morphine and other opiate drugs. This compound is called **naloxone (Narcane)** and may be described as an opiate antagonist. When naloxone is given to a patient suffering from an overdose of heroin or morphine, it will reverse completely the effects of those drugs. If naloxone is given to someone who then takes heroin, the heroin has no effect. Obviously naloxone has practical applications in the treatment of opiate overdose, but it also has theoretical implications. Since naloxone's chemical structure is similar to morphine, it seemed to researchers the two drugs might be acting at some common brain receptor site and that morphine's action at that site was blocked by the naloxone. In the early 1970s, two researchers at Johns Hopkins University in Baltimore, Candace Pert and Solomon Snyder, reported they had discovered brain receptors that responded selectively to opiate drugs, and these were dubbed "opiate receptors" (Pert & Snyder, 1973). The existence of opiate receptors was of great interest. One might reasonably wonder why there would be neurons in the brain that responded to such drugs. Did nature somehow intend us to be heroin addicts? Neuroscientists had a different notion: They believed the presence of such receptors must mean there existed natural brain chemicals with morphine-like structure and properties. The search was on for the "brain's own opiates," and in 1975 several such chemicals were discovered (Davis, 1984). Although there appear to be several morphine-like substances found in the brain (beta-endorphin, enkephalin, and dynorphin are the most important compounds), these complex peptide molecules are referred to collectively as endorphins, a contraction of endogenous morphine.

The scientific questions emanating from the discovery of the endorphins have focused on just why the brain is endowed with its own morphine: what do endorphins do? Much of this ongoing work has started with the premise that because opiate drugs apparently mimic endorphin activity by stimulating the opiate or endorphin receptor sites in the brain, then endorphins might share many properties with opiate drugs, such as pain relief and production of pleasure. Probably the most clearly established function of endorphins is as part of a natural pain relief system. Current thinking is that after certain kinds of pain or stress, endorphins are released and analgesia or pain relief occurs (Bolles & Fanselow, 1982; Davis, 1984). This may help explain why under certain circumstances, such as on the battlefield or in

Naloxone (Narcane)
A short-acting opiate antagonist.

athletic events, a person may sustain severe injury, but at least for a time not feel pain. Pain relief produced by acupuncture is probably related to endorphin release, because naloxone can reverse acupuncture-induced analgesia (Han & Terenius, 1982). Because the major action of naloxone is to block the endorphin receptors, naloxone-reversible analgesia is strong evidence that the acupuncture needles are triggering the release of endorphins and relieving pain through this system.

Similarly, vigorous exercise has been shown to result in increased release of endorphins and it is possible that some of the positive effects of exercise on mood, such as the so-called "runner's high," are related to endorphin effects (Farrell & Gustafson, 1986; Steinberg & Sykes, 1985). In fact some researchers seriously have proposed that the "addiction" to exercise some people seem to develop may occur through the same brain mechanisms as heroin addiction (Davis, 1984)! Can we become addicted to our own brain chemicals?

Other functions of endorphins are established less clearly. A link between

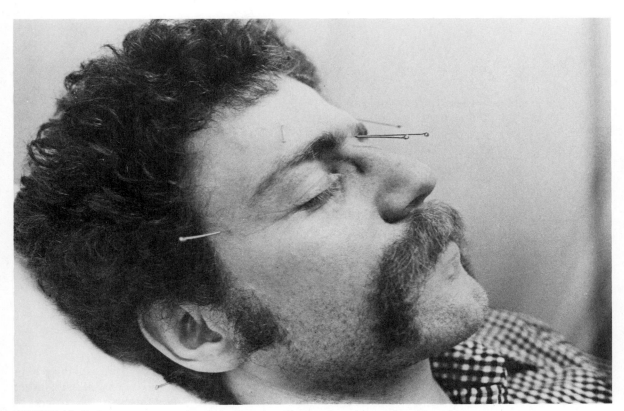

FIGURE 10–3 Acupuncture analgesia is thought to be produced by endorphin release.

Figure 10–4 The thrill of victory or
endorphin release?

endorphins and the experience of pleasure was supported by the intriguing
finding by Belluzi and Stein (1977) that naloxone suppressed behavior
maintained by electrical stimulation of the pleasure area of the brain. If naloxone blockade of the endorphin receptors reduces the responding for stimulation of that center, it suggests that endorphin-release must mediate the
pleasure produced by such stimulation. Although subsequent studies have
not always confirmed the Belluzi and Stein findings, most theorists today
believe endorphins do play some role in the mechanisms of pleasure and
reward (Smith & Lane, 1983; Stolerman, 1985).

TOLERANCE AND DEPENDENCE

Many researchers believe that research on endorphins ultimately may help
us to understand the phenomena of addiction to opiates and perhaps other
drugs as well. One problem with opiate drugs is, of course, that tolerance
develops to many of their effects when they are taken regularly. A related

problem exists after tolerance has developed. Abstinence from opiates produces dramatic and unpleasant withdrawal symptoms (more detail later in
this chapter). There is good reason to believe tolerance and withdrawal
symptoms produced by opiate drugs are related to activity at the endorphin
receptors. One piece of supporting evidence is that naloxone can precipitate withdrawal in opiate dependent subjects (Wei, Loh, & Way, 1973).
Thus, if a heroin addict is administered a dose of naloxone she/he immediately will begin to experience withdrawal symptoms, even if she/he has just
shot up heroin! Another line of evidence comes from studies showing that
if chronic morphine administration always is paired with naloxone, neither
tolerance nor withdrawal symptoms develop (Hendrie, 1985). Thus, activation of the endorphin receptors seems to be involved in some way with
tolerance to and dependence on opiate drugs. There are several theories for
just how this might work, but it is generally agreed that chronic use of opiates must alter the production of endorphins or the number of available
receptor sites, and that these changes are in some way responsible for tolerance and abstinence phenomena (Hendrie, 1985; Wikler, 1980).

MEDICAL USE OF OPIATE DRUGS

The major medical use of opiate drugs is for their analgesic or pain-relieving
effects. As noted above, opiates have been used for this purpose for centuries
and remain the most potent and selective pain-relievers known to medicine.
Unlike the depressant-type anesthetic drugs discussed earlier, opiate analgesics are described as relieving pain without causing unconsciousness.
After receiving moderate doses of opiates, patients remain conscious and
still are able to report painful sensations, but do not suffer from the pain.

Table 10–1
Comparison of the Major Opiate Drugs

Generic Name	Brand Name	Potency	Duration (hrs) of Action
Morphine		1	4–5
Heroin		4	3–4
Hydromorphone	Dilaudid	5	4–5
Codeine		.1	4–6
Oxycodone	Percodan	.75	4–5
Methadone	Dolophine	1	24–48
Meperidine	Demerol	.1	2–4
Propoxyphene	Darvon	.05	6
Fentanyl	Sublimaze	80	1–3
Pentazocine	Talwin	.2	2–3

Note: Potency estimates are presented relative to an effective dose of morphine
(1). Table 10–1 is based in part on Jaffe and Martin (1985).

The other major drugs that possess such analgesic properties are the over-the-counter painkillers: aspirin, acetaminophen, and ibuprofen (see Chapter 13). Table 10–1 shows some of the major opiate drugs used as analgesics, along with their potency and their duration of action. Recall that potency refers to the dose required for a drug to produce a given effect. In Table 10–1, potency is given relative to an effective dose of morphine. For example, heroin has a value of four in Table 10–1. This means that if 8 mg of morphine were required to relieve pain in a given patient, only 2 mg of heroin would be required. In other words, heroin is four times as potent as morphine. Morphine is the prototype opiate analgesic and is the standard by which others are measured. It is used primarily when pain is very severe. As we have noted, although heroin is more potent than morphine, it is not used medically in the United States because it is a Schedule I drug. It is, however, used in other countries (see Contemporary Issue Box 10–2).

CONTEMPORARY ISSUE BOX 10–2
Heroin and Pain Relief

One risk of using opiate drugs for pain relief is addiction. To reduce this risk, less potent opiates are used whenever possible and treatment is as brief as possible. However, when pain is severe and chronic, as with terminal cancer patients, tolerance inevitably develops, and higher doses of more potent drugs must follow if the patient's pain is to be relieved. Ultimately, high doses of morphine may be the only way of relieving the patient's suffering. Eventually even this may not be enough. In Great Britain, physicians then may use the potent opiate, heroin. In fact, a preparation called Brompton's cocktail, composed of heroin and cocaine, is administered sometimes to the terminally ill in Great Britain (Jaffe & Martin, 1985). However, because heroin is a Schedule I drug, it may not be administered by doctors in the United States.

Should physicians in the United States be permitted to administer heroin? One argument against this is that, because of its potency, heroin is more addicting than morphine. However, in the cases of the severe pain of the terminally ill patient, addiction seems somewhat irrelevant. Besides, patients normally are receiving doses of morphine that are high and frequent enough that they certainly are addicted to morphine by the time heroin treatment is begun. Heroin is converted to morphine in the brain, and thus morphine is the active chemical in producing pain relief in both cases (heroin is more potent because it penetrates the blood–brain barrier more efficiently). One could accomplish the same degree of pain relief by giving higher and higher doses of morphine. But terminal cancer patients often become very thin, and with repeated injections may lose tone in their veins. Thus, it may become difficult to administer enough morphine solution to be effective. Here is where the more potent heroin can be of value, because less solution is required. Moving heroin to Schedule II would make it possible for physicians to elect to administer heroin but should not make it any more difficult to control heroin addiction. Yet the move remains controversial, perhaps because it is seen as a softening of the heroin laws. A potential solution may come with the development of more potent opiate drugs that have not yet acquired the stigma associated with heroin.

When pain is less severe, drugs less potent than morphine may be used. Thus, codeine, propoxyphene (Darvon), oxycodone (Percodan), and pentazocine (Talwin) often are prescribed for pain (see Table 10–1). Finally, there are some opiates even more potent than heroin: fentanyl is twenty times as potent. Fentanyl is used primarily to produce anesthesia. In general, opiate drugs are the most potent and effective drugs available to medicine in the treatment of pain. The limitations of their use as analgesics are primarily the tendency of these drugs to produce tolerance and dependence. Tolerance and dependence develop for all these drugs, although some such as pentazocine (Talwin), for example, are thought to possess less abuse liability than others. It is hoped safer analgesic drugs will be developed as more is learned about endorphins and their ability to produce natural analgesia.

There are other medical uses for opiate drugs. Opiates have a constipating effect that can be a problem for addicts but is of value in treating diarrhea. Opiates still are used to treat coughs. The drug most commonly used for this purpose is dextromethorphan, which is a synthetic opiate with no analgesic or addictive properties, but is an effective cough suppressant (Jaffe & Martin, 1985). A final medical use for opiates such as methadone is in the treatment of heroin addicts in withdrawal and in maintenance programs designed to help addicts stay off heroin (see chapter 15).

ACUTE PSYCHOLOGICAL AND PHYSIOLOGICAL EFFECTS OF OPIATES

There are a number of acute effects of opiate drugs in addition to analgesia. Subjective reports of the euphoria produced by opiates include drowsiness, body warmth, and a heavy feeling of the limbs (Jaffe & Martin, 1985). William S. Burroughs describes the feeling in his autobiographical novel *Junky:* "Morphine hits the backs of the legs first, then the back of the neck, a spreading wave of relaxation slackening the muscles away from the bones so that you seem to float without outlines, like lying in warm salt water"

(Burroughs, 1953, p. 7). The pleasure experienced under the influence of opiates seems to interfere with other interests on the part of the user. Burroughs described it as follows: "Junk short circuits sex. The drive to non-sexual sociability comes from the same place sex comes from, so when I have an H(eroin) or M(orphine) shooting habit I am non-sociable. If someone wants to talk, O.K. But there is no drive to get acquainted" (Burroughs, 1953, p. 124). In fact there is good evidence that opiate drugs reduce sexual drive or interest, and in males, often produce impotence (Abel, 1985). Consistent with Burrough's anecdotal reports, laboratory studies also show opiates impair social interactions (Meyer & Mirin, 1975). After smoking opium or taking other opiate drugs, vivid dream-like experiences are often reported. These are the basis for the expression "pipe dreams."

The acute physiological effects of opiate drugs resemble those of depressant drugs, but there are some differences. Like depressants, opiates cause respiratory depression and lowered body temperature, but the effects of opiates on heart rate are complex (Jaffe & Martin, 1985; Mayer, 1987). Nausea and vomiting often occur immediately after taking opiates. Perhaps the most visible sign of opiate drug use is the pupillary constriction caused by opiates. This effect is so pronounced in overdose that "pinpoint pupils" may be used as a diagnostic sign of opiate poisoning. When a high dose of heroin is fatal, the immediate cause is usually respiratory failure. However, the lethal dose of heroin is surprisingly high. As Brecher (1972) has noted, many street overdose victims are found on autopsy to have injected less than would be expected to be lethal. Many of these cases involved not simply an overdose of heroin, but a lethal drug interaction between heroin and alcohol or another depressant drug. Opiates and depressant drugs potentiate one another (Ho & Allen, 1981). This synergy can often be lethal and many of the most publicized "heroin" overdoses actually involve synergy, such as the death of Janis Joplin in 1970:

> The quart bottle of Southern Comfort (whiskey) that she held aloft onstage was at once a symbol of her load, and her way of lightening it. As she emptied the bottle, she grew happier, more radiant and more freaked out . . . Last week on a day that superficially at least seemed to be less lonely than most, Janis Joplin died on the lowest and saddest of notes. Returning to her Hollywood motel room after a late-night recording session and some hard drinking with friends at a nearby bar, she apparently filled a hypodermic needle with heroin and shot it into her left arm. The injection killed her. (*Time* magazine quoted by Brecher, 1972, p. 113).

We now recognize the alcohol was as responsible for her death as was the heroin.

CHRONIC EFFECTS OF OPIATES

The effects are somewhat different when opiate drugs are taken chronically. As noted, tolerance develops to opiates, so the effects are generally dimin-

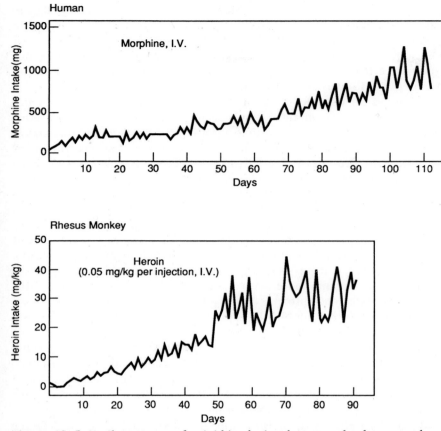

Figure 10–5 Similar patterns of opioid intake in a human and a rhesus monkey under conditions of continuous drug availability. Each graph shows the amount of drug taken over consecutive days. The human data are replotted from an experiment in which a volunteer with a history of drug abuse was permitted to self-regulate his intravenous morphine intake. The animal data are from a study in which lever-press responses by rhesus monkeys produced intravenous injections of heroin (from Elsmore, Fletcher, & Sodetz, unpublished raw data—from Henningfield, Lukas, & Bigelow, 1986).

ished unless the user escalates the dose, which often occurs. Figure 10–5 shows the pattern of opiate intake in a human and a rhesus monkey studied under laboratory conditions of continuous drug availability (Henningfield, Lukas, & Bigelow, 1986). Each graph shows the drug intake plotted over days in the experiment. The human data come from an experiment in which a volunteer with an extensive drug abuse history was studied under laboratory conditions and could regulate his daily intravenous morphine dose. Note the gradual increase in dose chosen by the subject over time. For the first month the subject never administered more than 500 mg/day. By the fourth month, however, he frequently took more than 1000 mg. Also note the bottom panel of Figure 10–5 which reveals a very similar pattern of heroin self-administration by monkeys who could obtain intravenous heroin by pressing a lever. Clearly the emergence of tolerance to the rewarding consequences of opiate drugs is a phenomenon of great generality.

The motives for continued use of opiates over time may change. While repeated use is initially motivated by a desire to re-experience the pleasant rush associated with the drug, addicts report with continued use that taking the drug does not make them nearly as high as before. However, they continue to use the drug in order to avoid the unpleasant symptoms of abstinence. Thus, the processes maintaining heroin use change from positive to negative reinforcement. The withdrawal symptoms associated with opiate dependence may appear after only one to two weeks of chronic use of heroin, morphine, or a synthetic opiate drug. The symptoms become more severe with longer-term use of higher doses. Early indications of withdrawal begin eight to twelve hours after the last dose and include flu-like symptoms such as runny nose, tearing, sweating, irritability, and tremor. As time passes these symptoms become more severe, and others appear, including pupil dilation, anorexia, and piloerection (goosebumps). This last symptom leaves the addict looking a bit like a plucked turkey and may be the basis for the expression "going cold turkey." These symptoms continue to worsen and reach a peak after about forty-eight to seventy-two hours. At this time heart rate and blood pressure are elevated, and the addict experiences severe flu-like symptoms such as nausea, diarrhea, sneezing, excessive sweating, and pain in the bones. In addition, the addict may show spastic movements of the arms and legs which may appear similar to kicking. This is thought to be the basis for the expression "kicking the habit." Other somewhat bizarre symptoms, which apparently indicate a rebound of the addict's sexual system, include spontaneous erection and ejaculation in men and orgasm in women. The loss of fluids and failure of the addict to eat or drink much during withdrawal can leave the addict physically and emotionally drained and occasionally can be fatal (Jaffe & Martin, 1985).

It is worth noting that a suitable dose of any opiate drug (but not depressant drugs) will reverse the abstinence symptoms and restore a feeling of well-being to the addict. Hospital detoxification procedures take advantage of this fact by treating addicts in withdrawal with low doses of a synthetic opiate drug such as methadone. The dose of methadone given is sufficient to reduce the severity of the addict's withdrawal symptoms, but not enough to produce much of a high. Gradually over a period of several weeks the dose of methadone is tapered off, until finally the addict shows no further signs of physical dependence. If physical withdrawal symptoms were the only factors maintaining heroin addiction, detoxification would be a cure. However, after detoxification procedures, there is an estimated relapse rate of 90% within two years after leaving the hospital, and most of these relapses occur during the first six months after detoxification (Hunt & Odoroff, 1962; Wikler, 1980). Thus, returning an addict to the environment in which she/he became addicted is most likely to result in relapse, even if physical withdrawal symptoms are not problems.

That heroin (and other drug) addiction depends on more than just physical withdrawal symptoms is illustrated nicely by the heroin addiction epidemic that failed to occur. During the early 1970s as the Vietnam War was drawing to a close, heroin addiction rates were very high among returning American soldiers, with some estimates as high as 21%. These soldiers were required to go through a detoxification before their return to the United States, but given a 90% relapse rate one would have expected most would return to heroin use after returning home. Thus, an epidemic of heroin addiction in the states was expected. However, follow-up studies showed that very few did relapse (less than 15%), illustrating clearly that environmental and psychosocial factors associated with Vietnam were apparently responsible for the development of the dependence. Upon returning to the United States, Vietnam veterans found heroin far less available. That, added to the change in life style and social environment accompanying their return to the U.S., apparently eased the pressures leading to their initial dependence (Robins, Helzer, & Davis, 1975). However, the radical change in environment from Vietnam to the United States cannot be duplicated in the typical treatment setting. This is one reason it is so difficult to treat heroin addiction, although a number of different types of treatment have been developed. These are reviewed in Chapter 15.

SUMMARY

· Opium is produced from the sap of the poppy plant and it has been used for medicinal purposes for centuries.

· In the nineteenth century the major active agent in opium, morphine, was isolated. More potent than opium, morphine was prized for its analgesic effects, but also became a major addiction problem.

· Heroin was developed as an alternative to morphine, but soon became the addict's drug of choice. While opiate drugs remained important in medicine, after the passage of the 1914 Harrison Act, heroin became a major criminal drug.

· Opiate drugs act in the brain by mimicking endorphins, natural neurotransmitters that are involved in the regulation of pain and pleasure.

· The major medical use for opiate drugs involves the treatment of severe pain.

· Opiates depress respiration, lower body temperature, and cause pupillary constriction. They induce a pleasurable euphoria in addition to pain relief.

· Regular use of opiates results in tolerance and an abstinence syndrome characterized by flu-like symptoms and intense drug craving. However, heroin addiction is more complex than simple avoidance of withdrawal symptoms.

References

Abel, E.L. (1985). *Psychoactive drugs and sex.* New York: Plenum Press.

Barnes, D.M. (1988). Drugs: Running the numbers. *Science, 240,* 1729–1731.

Belluzi, J.D. & Stein, L. (1977). Enkephalin may mediate euphoria and drive-reduction reward. *Nature, 266,* 556–558.

Bolles, R.C. & Fanselow, M.S. (1982). Endorphins and behavior. *Annual Review of Psychology, 33,* 87–101.

Booth, W. (1988). AIDS and drug abuse: No quick fix. *Science, 239,* 717–719.

Brecher, E.M. (1972). *Licit and illicit drugs.* Boston: Little, Brown, and Company.

Brodsky, M.D. (1985). History of heroin prevalence estimation techniques. In B.A. Rouse, N.J. Kozel, & L.G. Richards (Eds.), *Self-report methods of estimating drug use,* Research Monograph No. 57 (pp. 94–103). National Institute of Drug Abuse, Washington, D.C.

Burroughs, W.S. (1953). *Junky.* Middlesex, England: Penguin Books.

Davis, J. (1984). *Endorphins: New waves in brain chemistry.* Garden City, New York: Doubleday and Company.

Farrell, P.A. & Gustafson, A.B. (1986). Exercise stress and endogenous opiates. In N.P. Plotnikoff, R.E. Faith, A.J. Murgo & R.A. Good (Eds.), *Enkephalins and endorphins: Stress and the immune system* (pp. 47–58). New York: Plenum Press.

Gay, G.R. & Way, E.L. (1972). Pharmacology of the opiate narcotics. In D.E. Smith & G.R. Way (Eds.), *It's so good, don't even try it once* (pp. 32–44). Englewood Cliffs, NJ: Prentice Hall.

Han, J.S. and Terenius, L. (1982). Neurochemical basis of acupuncture analgesia. *Annual Review of Pharmacology and Toxicology, 22,* 193–220.

Hawks, R.L. and Chang, C.N. (1986). *Urine testing for drugs of abuse.* Research Monograph No. 73, National Institute on Drug Abuse, Washington, D.C.

Hendrie, C.A. (1985). Opiate dependence and withdrawal: A new synthesis. *Pharmacology, Biochemistry, and Behavior, 23,* 863–870.

Henningfield, J.E., Lukas, S.E., & Bigelow, G.E. (1986). Human studies of drugs as reinforcers. In S.R. Goldberg and I.P. Stolerman (Eds.) *Behavioral analysis of drug dependence* (pp. 69–122). New York: Academic Press.

Ho, A.K.S. & Allen, J.P. (1981). Alcohol and the opiate receptor: Interactions with the endogenous opiates. *Advances in Alcohol & Substance Abuse, 1,* 53–75.

Hunt, G.H. & Odoroff, M.E. (1962). Follow-up study of narcotic drug addicts after hospitalization. *Public Health Reports, 77,* 41–54.

Jaffe, J.H. & Martin, W.R. (1985). Opioid analgesics and antagonists. In A.G. Gilman, L.S. Goodman, & A. Gilman (Eds.) *Goodman and Gilman's The pharmacological basis of therapeutics* (7th ed) (pp. 491–531). New York: Macmillan Publishing Company.

Kirsch, M.M. (1986). *Designer drugs.* Minneapolis: CompCare Publications.

Kramer, J.C. (1972). A brief history of heroin addiction in America. In D.E. Smith & G.R. Gay (Eds.) *It's so good, don't even try it once* (pp. 12–31). Englewood Cliffs, NJ: Prentice Hall.

Latimer, D. & Goldberg, J. (1981). *Flowers in the blood: The story of opium.* New York: Franklin Watts.

Luce, J. (1972). End of the road: A case study. In D.E. Smith and G.R. Gay (Eds.) *It's so good, don't even try it once* (pp. 143–147). Englewood Cliffs, NJ: Prentice Hall.

Mayer, D.J. (1987). The behavioral effects of opiates. In L.L. Iverson, S.D. Iverson & S.H. Snyder (Eds.) *Handbook of Psychopharmacology,* (Volume 19) (pp. 467–530). New York: Plenum Press.

Meyer, R.E. & Mirin, S.M. (1979). *The heroin stimulus: Implications for a theory of addiction.* New York: Plenum Press.

Pert, C. & Snyder, S.H. (1973). Opiate receptor: Demonstration in nervous system tissue. *Science, 179,* 1011–1014.

Preble, E. & Casey, J.J. (1972). Taking care of business: The heroin user's life on the street. In D.E. Smith and G.R. Gay (Eds.) *It's so good, don't even try it once* (pp. 97–118). Englewood Cliffs, NJ: Prentice Hall.

Robins, L.N., Helzer, J.E. & Davis, D.H. (1975). Narcotic use in Southeast Asia and afterward. *Archives of General Psychiatry, 32,* 955–961.

Scott, J.M. (1969). *The white poppy: A history of opium.* New York: Funk & Wagnalls.

Smith, D.E. & Gay, G.R. (1972). *It's so good, don't even try it once.* Englewood Cliffs, NJ: Prentice Hall.

Smith, J.E. & Lane, J.D. (1983). *The neurobiology of opiate reward processes.* Amsterdam: Elsevier Biomedical Press.

Steinberg, H. & Sykes E.A. (1985). Introduction to symposium on endorphins and behavioural processes. Review of literature on endorphins and exercise. *Pharmacology, biochemistry, and behavior, 23,* 857–862.

Stolerman, I.P. (1985). Motivational effects of opioids: Evidence on the role of endorphins in mediating reward or aversion. *Pharmacology, Biochemistry and Behavior, 23,* 877–882.

Wei, E., Loh, H.H. & Way, E.L. (1973). Quantitative aspects of precipitated abstinence in morphine dependent rats. *Journal of Pharmacology and Experimental Therapeutics, 184,* 393–408.

White, P.T. (1985). The poppy. *National Geographic, 167,* 143–188.

11 MARIJUANA

Figure 11-1 The marijuana plant.

Cannabis sativa, more commonly known as marijuana, is a hemp plant that grows freely throughout the world. The cannabis plant most commonly is known today as a potent psychoactive substance, but for many years it was harvested primarily for its fiber. These strong hemp fibers were employed in the production of rope, clothes, and ship sails. Although used for several centuries in other parts of the world for its mind altering properties, it was not until the first third of this century that its psychoactive properties were recognized in the United States. After that, the hemp plant has been more often harvested for its psychoactive effects.

The term *marijuana* is thought to be based on the Portuguese word *mariguango,* which translates as "intoxicant." Marijuana, incidentally, is not the same as hashish, although both are derived from the *cannabis sativa* plant. Marijuana is the leafy top portion of the plant (see Figure 11-1). Hashish is made from the dust of the resin that is produced by the hemp plant to protect it from the sun and heat and maintain hydration. Plants growing in warmer climates will produce greater amounts of the resin, which generally has stronger psychoactive effects.

We begin this chapter with a historical overview of the drug and its use through the centuries. This is followed by a section on the epidemiology of current marijuana use. Next we provide information on absorption, distribution, metabolism, and excretion; mechanisms of action; and tolerance and dependence. Following this is an overview of the medical and psychotherapeutic uses of marijuana. The chapter's final sections concern the physical, psychological, and social/environmental effects of marijuana.

HISTORICAL OVERVIEW

According to Ernest Abel in his book *Marihuana: The First Twelve Thousand Years* (1980), the earliest known evidence of the use of cannabis occurred more than 10,000 years ago during the Stone Age. Archeologists at a Taiwanese site have discovered pots made of fibers presumed to be from the cannabis plant. The earliest known references to the use of cannabis for its pharmacological properties are attributed to Shen Nung about 2800 B.C. Shen Nung was a mythical Chinese emperor and pharmacist who purportedly shared with his subjects knowledge of the medicinal uses of cannabis. It has been speculated cannabis was used in this period in China for its sedative properties, treating pain and illness, countering the influences of evil spirits, and its general psychoactive effects (Abel, 1980; Nahas, 1973).

Cannabis use gradually spread from China to surrounding Asian countries. Of particular note was its adoption in India, where cannabis served a religious function. The *Atharva Veda,* one of the oldest books of Hinduism, includes it as one of the five sacred plants (Aldrich, 1977). This provided the plant with the protection and reverence engendered by cultural or religious acceptance.

The use of cannabis as an intoxicant was not evident outside China and India during these ancient times. Not until much later did cannabis use spread to the Middle East and then later to North Africa. It was during this expansion that hashish was first identified. The use of hashish dates to around the tenth century among the Arabs, and to the eleventh century in Egypt (Abel, 1980).

The use of cannabis for its intoxicating effects appears to have been centered in these parts of the world for an extended period of time. It was not until the nineteenth century that the Western world began to be exposed to cannabis, primarily through written descriptions of the hashish experience. This exposure typically occurred through either medical writings or the popular press. The use of cannabis was introduced to Great Britain primarily by William O'Shaugnessy, an Irish physician. In India he observed the medical applications of cannabis and described them in his writings. Suggestions regarding the use of cannabis were described in France by Dr. Jacques Moreau, a physician who thought it could be used in the treatment of mental illness (Bloomquist, 1971). Subsequently, the use and effects of cannabis were described in much detail in the works of a number of French authors. Perhaps most notable was Theophile Gautier, who was introduced to cannabis by Moreau. Gautier graphically described his initiation into *Le Club des Hachichins* (The Hashish Club), which was centered in 1840s Paris in the exclusive Hotel Pimodan. The hashish consumed was contained in a sweetmeat call Dawamesc. Gautier's descriptions of the drug effects were graphic (some excerpts from his writings are highlighted in Contemporary Issue Box 11–1). His descriptions of the hashish experiences included elements of mystery, intrigue, joy, ecstasy, fear, and terror.

Despite what appeared to some as attractive features of cannabis and hashish, the use of this drug did not immediately become extensive in Europe. In fact, widespread use of cannabis for its psychoactive properties in Europe did not occur until the 1960s when it was reintroduced by, among others, tourists from the United States (Bloomquist, 1971).

CONTEMPORARY ISSUE BOX 11–1
Gautier's Experiences at The Hashish Club

As noted in the main text, Theophile Gautier in the 1840s wrote in graphic detail of his experiences using hashish. Such descriptions are of interest to us today because they provide an opportunity to observe the similarities that exist in the marijuana experience then and now, at least as described by those who write of their experiences.

The hashish used by Gautier and his friends was contained in a sweetmeat (a food rich in sugar, such as candied or crystallized fruit) called Dawamesc, which they ate at the Paris hotel which housed *Le Club des Hachichins* (The Hashish Club). The drug-laced sweetmeat was eaten before dinner. After dinner, sitting in a large drawing room, Gautier described the drug effects as follows:

> After several minutes, my companions had vanished, one after another, leaving no trace other than their shadows on the walls, which were soon absorbed like the brown stains that water makes on sand, fading as they dry.
>
> As I was no longer conscious, from that time on, of what others were doing, you now must be content with a relation of my simple personal impression.
>
> Solitude reigned in the drawing room, which was studded with only a few dubious gleams; all of a sudden, a red flash passed beneath my eyelids, innumerable candles burst into light and I felt bathed in a warm, clear glow. I was indeed in the same place, but it was as different as a sketch is from a

painting: everything was larger, richer, more gorgeous. Reality served as a point of departure for the splendors of the hallucination. (Gautier, 1844; quoted from Solomon, 1966, p. 126)

This period was followed by a state Gautier labelled "fantasia," after which *al-kief* was experienced:

I was in that blessed state induced by hashish which the Orientals call al-kief. I could no longer feel my body; the bonds of matter and spirit were severed; I moved by sheer willpower in an unresisting medium.

Thus I imagine the movement of souls in the world of fragrances to which we shall go after death. A bluish haze, an Elysian light, the reflections of an azure grotto, formed an atmosphere in the room through which I vaguely saw the tremblings of hesitant outlines; an atmosphere at once cool and warm, moist and perfumed, enveloping me like bath water in a sort of enervating sweetness. When I tried to move away, the caressing air made a thousand voluptuous waves about me; a delightful languor gripped my senses and threw me back upon the sofa, where I hung, limp as a discarded garment.

Then I understood the pleasure experienced by the spirits and angels, according to their degree of perfection, when they traverse the ethers and the skies, and how eternity might occupy one in Paradise. (Gautier, 1844; quoted in Solomon, 1966, pp. 130–131)

Al-kief later was replaced by a nighmarish stage in which Gautier felt fear, fury, and aspects of paranoia, then, finally, around five hours after entering The Hashish Club, the drug effects ended:

The dream was at an end.

The hashisheen went off, each in his own direction, like the officers in *Marlborough Goes to War.*

With light steps, I went down the stairs that had caused me so much anguish, and a few moments later I was in my room, in full reality; the last vapors raised by the hashish had vanished. (Gautier, 1844; quoted from Solomon, p. 135)

Cannabis in the New World

The presence of cannabis in the New World dates to 1545, when it was brought to Chile by the Spaniards. In the North American colonies, the cannabis plant was raised for fiber by the Jamestown settlers in Virginia in 1611. Not long after, this hemp product was firmly entrenched as a basic staple crop, and was cultivated by George Washington, among the many others. Cannabis was harvested in New England starting in 1629; it remained a core United States crop until after the Civil War. The center of this hemp production was Kentucky, where it was a major crop product for decades.

Despite its widespread presence, the marijuana plant was relatively unknown as a mind altering substance. However, there was some recognition of its uses beyond the fiber component. Following the lead of European doctors, American physicians used cannabis in the 1800s as a general, all-purpose medication (Nahas, 1973). The most commonly used preparation was Tilden's Extract of Cannabis Indica, an Indian hemp plant produced in East Bengal. By the 1850s marijuana was listed in the *United States Pharmacopeia,* a listing of legitimate therapeutics; it remained listed until 1942. The cannabis extract also was listed in the less select *National Formulary and Dispensatory.*

Cannabis was consumed for recreational purposes only to a limited degree during this period, and descriptions of its psychoactive effects were not common. One notable exception was the publication in 1857 of the book *The Hasheesh Eater.* Written by Fitz Hugh Ludlow, this volume details his cannabis-eating experiences over a four-year period beginning at around age sixteen. Ludlow lived in the town of Poughkeepsie, north of New York City in the Hudson River Valley. He spent much of his time with a friend named Anderson, an **apothecary,** and often engaged in personal experimentation with the varied substances in Anderson's drugstore. One day Anderson pointed out to Ludlow a new arrival: a marijuana extract from Tilden and Co. Ludlow began experimenting with the substance. At first, he experienced no immediate drug effects but after several hours described the onset of effects as follows:

Apothecary
A pharmacist.

> Ha! what means this sudden thrill? A shock, as of some unimagined vital force, shoots without warning through my entire frame, leaping to my fingers' ends, piercing my brain, startling me till I almost spring from my chair.
>
> I could not doubt it. I was in the power of the hasheesh influence (Ludlow, p. 20).

Ludlow continued his experimenting, graphically describing the varied cannabis effects. For example, in a chapter titled "The Kingdom of the Dream," he began by noting:

> The moment that I closed my eyes a vision of celestial glory burst upon me. I stood on the silver strand of a translucent, boundless lake, across whose bosom I seemed to have been just transported. A short way up the beach, a temple, modeled like the Parthenon, lifted its spotless and gleaming columns of alabaster sublimely into a rosy air—like the Parthenon, yet as much excelling it as the godlike ideal of architecture must transcend that ideal realized by man (Ludlow, p. 34).

In his writings, Ludlow also identified two "laws of the hasheesh operation." The first was that "after the completion of any one fantasia has arrived, there almost invariably succeeds a shifting of the action to some other stage entirely different in its surroundings" (pp. 36–37). The second law was that "after the full storm of a vision of intense sublimity has blown past the hasheesh-eater, his next vision is generally of a quiet, relaxing, and recreating nature" (p. 37).

The 1920s marked a wider use of cannabis. Edward M. Brecher, in The Consumers Union Report on *Licit and Illicit Drugs* (1972), attributes this increase in use to alcohol prohibition. He writes, "Not until the Eighteenth

Tea-pad
Historically, a place where people gathered to smoke marijuana. The site could be anywhere from a rented room to a hotel suite.

Amendment and the Volstead Act of 1920 raised the price of alcoholic beverages and made them less convenient to secure and inferior in quality did substantial commercial trade in marijuana for recreational use spring up" (p. 410). In New York City, for example, a number of marijuana "tea-pads" (estimated at more than 500 in Harlem alone) were opened in the early 1920s. These "tea-pads" were generally located in a room or apartment. As described by the 1944 LaGuardia Commission:

> The "tea-pad" is furnished according to the clientele it expects to serve. Usually, each "tea-pad" has comfortable furniture, a radio, victrola or, as in most instances, a rented nickelodeon. The lighting is more or less uniformly dim, with blue predominating. An incense burner is considered part of the furnishings. The walls are frequently decorated with pictures of nude subjects suggestive of perverted sexual practices. The furnishings, as described, are believed to be essential as a setting for those participating in smoking marihuana (p. 10).

The Commission went on to note that:

> The marihuana smoker derives greater satisfaction if he is smoking in the presence of others. His attitude in the "tea-pad" is that of a relaxed individual, free from the anxieties and cares of the realities of life. The "tea-pad" takes on the atmosphere of a very congenial social club. The smoker readily engages in conversation with strangers, discussing freely his pleasant reactions to the drug and philosophizing on subjects pertaining to life in a manner which, at times, appears to be out of keeping with his intellectual level . . . A boisterous, rowdy atmosphere did not prevail and on the rare occasions when there appeared signs indicative of a belligerent attitude on the part of a smoker, he was ejected or forced to become more tolerant and quiescent (p. 10).

The origins of the practice of smoking marijuana in this country in the early part of this century are not clear, but most agree that one of the earliest introductions was through Mexican laborers crossing the border into the United States. The greatest extent of use was found in New Orleans, also in the early 1920s. In fact, New Orleans was a central dispensing arena for marijuana as late as the 1930s. The marijuana could be sent up the Mississippi River to a number of river ports, and then further distributed throughout the country. According to Nahas (1973), marijuana was available in the larger cities by 1930, although its use was primarily limited to black Americans, not infrequently jazz musicians.

Public concern over the use of marijuana was small during this period, with one notable exception. In 1926, a series of articles were printed in two New Orleans newspapers. These articles sensationally "exposed" the "menacing" presence of marijuana, and attributed a number of crimes and heinous acts to use of the drug. Although many of these lurid reports were ridiculous and fabricated, a Louisiana law mandating a maximum penalty of $500 fine and/or six months imprisonment for conviction of possession or sale of marijuana was passed the next year. However, this law had little effect on the sale or use of marijuana in New Orleans, except for a possible moderate increase in the price of a marijuana cigarette (Brecher, 1972).

Despite the fact marijuana had not threatened to enter the mainstream of American life, additional governmental and legal action continued into the next decade. Much of this activity was promoted by Harry J. Anslinger, who in 1932 became director of the Federal Bureau of Narcotics. Anslinger was convinced marijuana represented a major threat to the safety and well-being of the country. He successfully encouraged many states to restrict the trafficking and use of marijuana. In 1930, only sixteen states had statutes prohibiting the use of marijuana; by 1937, virtually all states had such statutes.

Anslinger's efforts culminated in the 1937 passage of the Marijuana Tax Act. The act did not officially ban marijuana. Rather, the bill acknowledged the medicinal uses of marijuana and permitted the prescription of marijuana following payment of a license fee of one dollar per year. However, any other possession or sale of marijuana was strictly outlawed. Punishments for violation could be quite strong: a $2000 fine, five years imprisonment, or both. Anslinger's efforts overall were successful in reducing *legal* dispersement of marijuana, as in the following year only thirty-eight physicians paid the one-dollar license fee to prescribe marijuana (Brecher, 1972). Further, Anslinger's efforts set the stage for progressively stricter penalties for marijuana sale or possession in the ensuing years. Throughout the 1960s judges often had the option of sentencing a user or seller of marijuana to life imprisonment. A second offense of selling marijuana to a minor in Georgia could be punished by death. Since 1970, however, the penalties for marijuana possession and use have been moderated significantly during the gradual decriminalization for possession of small amounts or use of the substance. Whether this trend continues during the ongoing "war on drugs" remains to be seen.

Committee Reports on Marijuana

Several comprehensive reports of the use of marijuana and its effects have appeared during the past century. One of the earliest was the Indian Hemp Drugs Commission Report released in 1894. The committee preparing the report included four British and three Indian commissioners. A second report was the 1933 Panama Canal Zone Military Investigations, which spanned the period 1916–1929.

A third, and one of the most widely-known investigations, was the LaGuardia Committee Report published in 1944. This committee was created by the New York Academy of Medicine at the request of New York City Mayor Fiorello LaGuardia. This study, second in scope only to the Indian Hemp Drugs Commission, was a truly multidisciplinary report. It included coordinated input by physicians, psychologists, pharmacologists, and sociologists. Data were gathered on marijuana use and effects in "tea-pads" as well as in laboratory settings. The general finding of the study was that marijuana use was not particularly harmful to the user or to society at large. The report failed to find evidence for the claim that aggression, violence, and belligerence were common consequences of marijuana smoking. This was not intended to suggest, however, that marijuana did not induce psychoactive effects. A number of individual changes were noted, including in more extreme form "mental confusion and excitement of a delirious nature with periods of laughter and of anxiety" (p. 216).

These report findings were consistent with those of commission reports published earlier. Subsequent reports also have mirrored these basic conclusions. These investigations include the 1968 Baroness Wootton Report from Great Britain, the 1970 Interim Report of the Canadian Government's LeDain Commission, and the First Report of the National Commission on Mental Health and Drug Abuse (titled *Marihuana: A Signal of Misunderstanding*) in 1972. More recent reports in this country, such as the Ninth Report to the United States Congress on Marijuana and Health (1982) and *Drug Abuse and Drug Abuse Research* (1984, the first in a series of triennial reports to Congress), both prepared by the National Institute on Drug Abuse, have likewise not provided markedly discrepant findings, although they are much more cautious in describing non-negative effects of marijuana use.

EPIDEMIOLOGY

Marijuana remains the most frequently used illicit drug in the United States. Its use rose dramatically throughout the 1960s and 1970s. However, steady decreases have been reported in marijuana use since about 1979.

Data gathered as part of a National Institute on Drug Abuse (NIDA) National Household Survey in 1985 revealed that almost 62 million Americans (33% of the population) have used marijuana at least once in their lives. The lifetime (ever used) prevalence rates were 24% for youths (ages 12–17), 60% for young adults (ages 18–25), and 27% for older adults (ages 26+).

These and other data from the survey are shown in Figure 11-2. The first trend to notice is the drop, since the 1979 survey, in lifetime, annual (used in the past year), and current (used in the past thirty days) use for the youth and young adult populations. The greatest changes occurred among young adults. Between 1979 and 1985, lifetime prevalence for the young adult group dropped from 68% to 60%, annual prevalence from 47% to 37%, and current use from 35% to 22%. The findings for older adults (all those older than 25) were different. Annual and current prevalence rates (approximately 10% and 6%, respectively, in 1985) have been relatively stable since 1979. The lifetime prevalence rate for the older adult group is steadily increasing, probably the result of the aging of individuals who had used marijuana in previous years. Preliminary data from a similar household survey conducted in 1988 indicate that these downward trends in marijuana use are continuing. For example, the number of current users of marijuana dropped from 18 million in 1985 to 12 million in 1988 (a decrease of one-

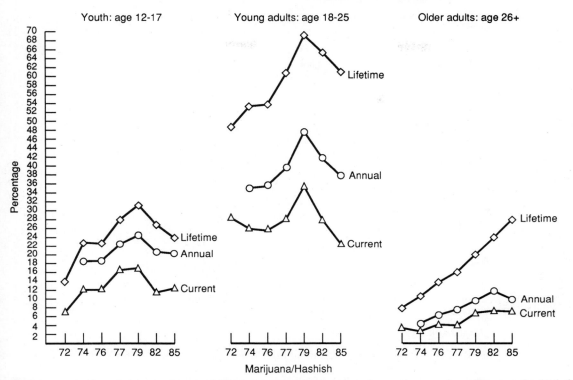

Figure 11–2 Trends in prevalence of lifetime use, annual use, and current use of marijuana or hashish for youths, young adults, and older adults (from National Household Survey on Drug Abuse, 1985, NIDA, Division of Epidemiology and Statistics Analysis, Nov. 1986).

third). Decreases were most notable among youths and young adults; those rates of current use were the lowest since 1972.

Several other findings from the household survey are noteworthy. First, marijuana use showed some variation according to race. The lifetime prevalence rates indicated more whites than blacks or Hispanics have used marijuana at least once, with the exception of older adults, among whom more blacks (21%) than whites (16%) or Hispanics (12%) have tried the drug. Current use of marijuana is highest among blacks in the young and older adult populations. Among youth, the current use rate is highest for whites (13%), followed by Hispanics (10%) and blacks (8%). A second finding is that many marijuana users are using the drug frequently. Among the youth, 23% of the males who reported having tried marijuana have used it at least one hundred times; the comparable rate for females is 10%. Among young adult males, 39% of those who have used marijuana have used it 100 or more times, compared to 24% for female young adults. Finally, the survey revealed that current marijuana users, compared to those not currently using

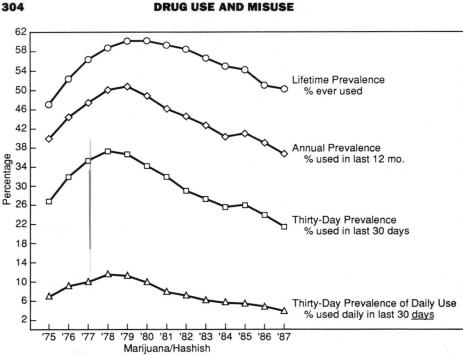

Figure 11–3 Trends in prevalence of marijuana use among high school seniors from 1975 to 1987 (from Johnston, O'Malley, and Bachman, in press).

the substance, are more likely to be current users of other drugs. As an example, at least one-quarter of male and female current young adult marijuana users are also current users of cocaine.

The reasons for the decline in marijuana use have not been specified. However, the decreases probably reflect to some degree economic factors, growing concerns about health and fitness, and concerns over possible negative effects of drug use in general.

The decreases in marijuana use shown in the national household surveys also appear in the annual surveys of high school seniors. As you can see in Figure 11–3, the percentages of seniors ever using, using in the past month or year, or using daily for the past month have all been dropping since about 1979. About one-fifth of the seniors in 1987 used marijuana in the past thirty days, and less than 4% had used it daily for the past month. Indications from the survey among 1988 high school seniors suggest this trend is continuing. Current use declined to 18%, compared to 21% among the 1987 seniors. Daily marijuana use declined from 3.3% in 1987 to 2.7% in 1988. The reasons for the decreases for the high school seniors probably parallel those suggested above for the findings in the household survey.

METHODS OF USE

Marijuana and hashish have been administered in a number of ways in their use as psychoactive agents. For example, they were ingested in India centuries ago in liquid and food form. Further, it has been reported that psychoactive effects of marijuana can be experienced through the chewing of marijuana leaves. However, the most common procedure for ingesting cannabis in this country has been and remains smoking, typically in cigarette (**"joint"**) form. Inhalation through cigarette form is also the most efficient method for absorption of cannabis.

Joint
A hand-rolled marijuana cigarette.

ACTIVE INGREDIENTS

The first chemical analysis of cannabis apparently was performed by Tscheep in 1821 (Mechoulam, 1973). Since then studies have shown cannabis to be a complex plant. More than four hundred individual chemical compounds have been identified in the plant. Approximately sixty of these chemicals, collectively called **cannabinoids,** are unique to the cannabis plant. Continued research will probably identify additional cannabis chemical compounds and cannabinoids.

Despite years of study, not until 1964 was the principal psychoactive agent in cannabis isolated. This substance has been labeled **delta-9-tetrahydrocannabinol,** but is more commonly known as Δ-9-THC or simply THC. The THC compound was first reported by Gaoni and Mechoulam (1964), two researchers working in Israel. Research since 1964 has shown that the Δ-9-THC cannabinoid accounts for the vast majority of known specific pharmacological actions of marijuana. Although THC is the prime psychoactive agent in cannabis, other cannabinoids, such as cannabidiol and cannabinol, can be biologically active and can modify THC effects. However, they tend not to be psychoactive in and of themselves.

Cannabinoids
A general term to describe the more than 60 chemical compounds present in cannabis. One of these cannabinoids is delta-9-tetrahydrocannabinol (better known as THC).

Delta-9-tetrahydrocannabinol
The principal active cannabinoid in marijuana responsible for the experienced psychoactive effects.

Potency of Cannabis

Cannabis exhibits a wide variety of strength. Most of the marijuana grown in the United States has a THC content of about two percent, but the content can vary from near zero percent to as much as 6–8%. Marijuana smoked in the United States today is about five to ten times more potent than that smoked ten years ago (Jones, 1984). Variations in the potency of hashish have also been found. These THC potency values generally range from 5–12%. A third form of cannabis is **hash oil,** a concentrated liquid marijuana extract derived from the cannabis plant using solvents. This oil has been available on the streets for a number of years, and is quite potent relative to the marijuana leaf material or resin. Estimates are that hash oil can contain as much as 60% THC.

Hash oil
A potent distillate of marijuana or hashish. It first appeared in the United States in 1971, and can contain up to 60% THC.

ABSORPTION, DISTRIBUTION, METABOLISM, AND EXCRETION

The absorption of THC depends primarily on the mode of consumption. The most rapid and efficient absorption of marijuana occurs through smoking. This inhalation results in absorption directly through the lungs, and the onset of the THC action begins within minutes. Assessments of blood plasma reveal that peak concentrations occur approximately thirty to sixty minutes later. The drug effects can be experienced for around two to four hours.

Several factors can influence the amount of THC absorbed through smoking. One important variable, of course, is the potency of the cannabis being smoked. Only about half of the THC available in a marijuana cigarette is present in the smoke, and the amount ultimately absorbed into the bloodstream is probably less. Another variable is the amount of time the inhaled smoke is held in the lungs; the longer the smoke is held, the more time for absorption of the THC. Another factor influencing intake is the number of persons sharing the cigarette because more smokers may decrease the amount of marijuana available to any one user.

Oral ingestion of marijuana is much slower and relatively inefficient. The onset of action is longer than when smoked, taking as long as one hour. The marijuana is absorbed primarily through the gastrointestinal tract and peak plasma levels can be delayed for as long as two to three hours following ingestion. An important difference from absorption through smoking is that blood containing orally ingested marijuana goes through the liver before going to the brain. The liver processes or clears much of the THC so that lesser amounts have the opportunity to exert action in the brain. However, the drug effects following oral ingestion can be experienced for longer periods of time, generally four to six hours. It is estimated that the dose needed to create a comparable high when orally ingested is three times greater than that needed when smoking.

Using peak plasma THC levels to assess cannabis effects can be misleading because the psychoactive cannabinoids are highly lipid-soluble; that is, the cannabinoids are lipids, which means almost entirely insoluble in water. The cannabinoids instead are a dark, viscous oil-like substance. Plasma levels of THC decrease rapidly because the THC is deposited in the tissues of various organs, particularly those containing fatty material. Assessments of organs following cannabis ingestion reveal marked concentrations of THC in the brain, lungs, kidneys, and liver. Thus, even when blood levels of THC are zero, the levels of THC in other organs can be substantial. Also, THC is capable of crossing the placental barrier and reaching the fetus.

As noted above, THC is carried through the bloodstream and deposited within various organs. The THC is then over time metabolized to less active products. Although this process occurs primarily in the liver, it can occur in other organs as well. The THC metabolites are excreted slowly and in fairly equal proportions through the feces and urine. Approximately half of the THC is excreted over several days, and the remainder by the end of about a week. However, some metabolites of the THC, a number of which may still be active in the system, can be detected in the body at least thirty days following ingestion of a single dose and, following chronic use, in the urine for several weeks.

The primary psychotropic actions of marijuana occur in the brain and are a result of the drug's effect on neurotransmitters. Much of the research in this area (typically performed with animals) has focused on the effects of marijuana on the chemical transmitter acetylcholine. THC in relatively small doses has been shown to decrease the turnover in acetylcholine, particularly in the hippocampus (Domino, Donelson, & Tuttle, 1978), resulting in a decrease in neurotransmitter activity. In addition, THC facilitates release of the neurotransmitter serotonin. Unfortunately, specification of the drug actions remain speculative, and the question of a specific drug receptor is unanswered.

Tolerance and Dependence

Tolerance to cannabis has been well documented with animal species (for example, Harris, Dewey, & Razdan, 1977). However, the evidence for tolerance to cannabis in humans is less clear, with some studies indicating tolerance and others not. Some of the discrepancies in the studies with humans can be attributed to the dose of marijuana and duration of use being studied. Tolerance is more likely to occur with higher doses used over longer periods of time. This is typically seen in controlled laboratory settings, where the doses and frequencies of use studied are generally much greater than those reported by marijuana users in the general population. The mechanisms by which tolerance occurs are still unknown.

Physical dependence on cannabis is a rare phenomenon. To date, no significant withdrawal syndrome has been identified. There does not seem to be any clustering of withdrawal indicators as has been identified for other substances, such as alcohol or heroin. Jones (1984) has noted that aspects of dependence with heavy sustained use have been described. These aspects generally entail motor symptoms, such as sleep disturbance, nausea, irritability, and restlessness. It has been argued by some that these symptoms are more reflective of a psychological dependence or withdrawal from the use of the drug. Nevertheless, as in the case of tolerance, physical dependence apparently is uncommon. When seen, it has been associated with quite high doses of marijuana taken over extended periods of time, parameters of drug use not typical of marijuana use in this country.

Cannabis has a long history of use for medical and health purposes, with the earliest documentation attributed to Shen Nung in the twenty-eighth century B.C. As we noted earlier, Shen Nung purportedly recommended the use of cannabis to his people for its medicinal benefits. More systematic uses of cannabis as a therapeutic agent did not occur until the 1800s. For example, the Paris physician Jacques Moreau used cannabis in the mid-1800s to treat mental illnesses. (Recall that it was Moreau who supplied the cannabis used by Gautier at *Le Club des Hachichins.*) Much greater legitimization of the medical use of marijuana was provided by Dr. William O'Shaughnessey, the Irish physician who in an 1838 treatise described the use of cannabis for a number of problems, including rheumatism, pain, rabies, convulsions, and cholera.

Cannabis also was used widely in the United States for a number of complaints. It was recognized as a therapeutic drug well into the 1900s. At that time, the cannabis extract was listed for varying periods of time in the *United States Pharmacopeia,* the *National Formulary,* and the United States *Dispensatory.* In the *Dispensatory,* for example, cannabis was recommended for neuralgia, gout, rheumatism, rabies, cholera, convulsions, hysteria, mental depression, delirium tremens, and insanity.

Decline in the medicinal use of cannabis in this century is the result of two factors. The first was the advances made in medicine and the discovery of more specific knowledge regarding various diseases and their treatments. The second factor was the Marijuana Tax Law of 1937. This legislation markedly decreased prescribed medicinal uses of marijuana.

The therapeutic uses of marijuana today are much more circumscribed. For the most part synthetic products (such as Levontradol, Nabilone, and Marinol) that chemically resemble the cannabinoids have been used in current treatment efforts (see Ungerleider & Andrysiak, 1985). These synthetics are used because they provide the active elements of THC in a more stable manner. Synthetics also can provide better solubility.

There are several disorders—especially glaucoma and nausea—for which cannabis is prescribed, and we describe these briefly. More detailed reviews on the medicinal uses of marijuana can be found in Hollister (1984), Institute of Medicine (1982), and Ungerleider and Andrysiak (1985).

Glaucoma

Glaucoma is a generic term used to denote ocular diseases involving increases in intraocular pressure. This pressure damages the optic disc at the junction of the retina and optic nerve and represents the leading cause of blindness in the United States. Over two million Americans over age thirty-five have developed glaucoma, and an estimated 300,000 new cases are diagnosed yearly (Institute of Medicine, 1982). While drug and surgical interventions are available, their effectiveness is variable.

Cannabis has been shown to decrease intraocular pressure, although patients have experienced side effects regardless of whether the cannabis was administered orally, through injection, or by smoking (see Hepler & Frank, 1971; Hepler, Frank, & Ungerleider, 1972; Hepler & Petrus, 1976).

These side effects have included increased heart rate, decreased blood pressure, and psychological effects. Some of these effects dissipate with extended exposure to the cannabis.

The mechanisms through which the cannabis reduces intraocular pressure have not been determined. Cohen and Andrysiak (1982) suggested cannabis dilates the vessels that drain excess fluids from the eyeball. This draining is thought to prevent fluid buildup and the resultant pressure that causes optic nerve damage.

Clinical research on the potential benefits of cannabis as a treatment for glaucoma is continuing, with two emphases. The first is on developing synthetic formulas that reduce side effects. The second emphasis is on modes of application. Particular attention is being given to developing a topical preparation that could be applied directly onto the eye.

Nausea and Vomiting

Cannabis and THC synthetics have been used to counter the nausea and vomiting frequently associated with chemotherapies (and some radiation treatments) for cancer. These side effects, which can last for several hours or even several days, often are not ameliorated by traditional antiemetic medications. Researchers in the 1970s began more systematic study of the antinausea and antiemetic effects of THC (usually administered orally) and results were favorable. This research, incidentally, followed anecdotal reports by chemotherapy patients that their private use of marijuana had reduced the aversive side effects of their treatments.

Positive outcomes have continued to emerge in subsequent research. More recent studies have included the use of THC synthetics, such as Nabilone. The main drawback to the use of cannabis and THC synthetics has been the resultant mental effects, which have been viewed by some patients as uncomfortable and disorienting. Nevertheless, many patients undergoing chemotherapy find the THC side effects an acceptable price for reductions in the chemotherapy side effects. Research in this area perhaps will be enhanced by the 1986 decision by the Drug Enforcement Administration to reclassify synthetic THC as a Schedule II drug, which means some medical value is recognized. The synthetic previously had been classified as a Schedule I drug, meaning it was a prohibited substance with no recognized medical benefit. Marijuana not in synthetic form remains a Schedule I drug.

Other Uses

Cannabis and THC synthetics have been used to a much lesser extent in the treatment of pain, muscle spasticity, convulsant activity, insomnia, hypertension, asthma, and depression. However, the data in support of these uses have been equivocal. More research is needed to identify the utility of cannabis in medical treatment of these and other disorders.

PHYSIOLOGICAL EFFECTS

Although cannabis can produce a number of physiological effects, most of these actions are different for different users, not only in strength or intensity of the effect but also in duration. In general, the acute physiological effects of marijuana in a healthy individual are not dramatic. In fact, the LeDain Commission (1972) reported the "short-term physiological effects of a typical cannabis dose on normal persons are generally quite benign, and are apparently of little clinical significance."

The most commonly experienced effects are cardiovascular. Predominant among these is injection of the conjuctiva, or bloodshot eyes. This effect, a result of vasodilation, is most obvious around one hour after smoking, and it is generally dose-related. Although some cite a concomitant dilation of the pupil, research does not support this claim. It appears more likely the dilation is a consequence of smoking the marijuana in a darkened room. There does, however, tend to be a cannabis-induced sluggish reaction to light.

The second most common cardiovascular effect is an increase in heart rate and pulse rate. Both of these effects are present for around one hour, and each appears to be dose-related. The peak heart rate occurs around twenty minutes after smoking. In addition to these effects, blood pressure tends to become slightly to moderately elevated. No evidence indicates that these effects create any permanent damage within the normal cardiovascular system (Institute of Medicine, 1982).

Another general effect following cannabis use is a generalized decrease in motor activity. The only real exception to this is the loquacious behavior of many following smoking. Some users also report drowsiness. Relatedly, cannabis use also can have a marked effect on sleep stages, tending in part to decrease the total REM sleep achieved. However, this effect typically occurs only with higher doses of cannabis.

A number of other effects have also been reported, but they tend to be minor and/or infrequent, and often variable from person to person. These other effects include (but are not limited to) the following: dry mouth, thirst, fluctuations in respiration and body temperature, hunger or "the munchies" (peaking about two to three hours after smoking), nausea, and headache and/or dizziness.

Longer-Term Effects

Data on the longer-term effects of marijuana are sparse and difficult to interpret. The research that has been conducted has been focused on four central systems: respiratory, cardiovascular, immune, and reproductive.

Respiratory system Little controlled research exists regarding the long-term effects of smoking cannabis. Proper lung functioning seems to be altered as a consequence of smoking cannabis, but much of this impairment, such as airway obstruction, appears to reverse following abstinence from smoking. Marijuana cigarettes contain more tar than tobacco cigarettes. Additionally, cannabis tar contains greater amounts of cancerous agents than does tobacco tar (Jones, 1984). The long-term consequences unfortunately are not known. One difficulty in specifying these effects is that cannabis smokers frequently also smoke cigarettes, and separating the effects of each substance is difficult. Nevertheless, the possibility of irreversible lung damage due to marijuana smoking remains.

Cardiovascular system   The vast majority of cardiovascular effects associated with cannabis smoking were described earlier in this section as short-term (or acute). No evidence shows smoking marijuana to produce deleterious cardiovascular effects among healthy individuals. The acute effects produced (for example, increased heart rate) are, however, potentially dangerous among persons with existing cardiovascular problems, such as abnormal heart functioning or arteriosclerosis.

Immune system   Although some of the research on this topic has been contradictory, apparently cannabis poses no significant threat to the immune system. Although some decreased activity in the immune system may occur, its clinical significance remains questionable.

Reproductive system   Studies using lower animal species and humans suggest cannabis does disrupt the reproductive system in both males and females. For example, chronic marijuana use has been associated with decreases in the number of sperm and sperm motility among men. The potential effects of these disruptions on fertility are difficult to specify (Institute of Medicine, 1982). Frequent use of cannabis by women may produce nonovulatory menstrual cycles, in which menstruation is not preceded by the release of an ovum. As in the case of males, the delayed effects of these disruptions on fertility are not known. In their recent review, Ehrenkranz and Hembree (1986) concluded that disruptions in reproductive function, at least in males, are not obvious, although subtle alterations may be operative.

Of more concern are possible teratogenic effects. The active agents present when marijuana is smoked readily cross the placenta barrier, exposing the fetus to the array of cannabinoids. Although few data are available for humans, it does not appear that major teratogenic or dysmorphogenic effects result. However, this does not mean significant effects cannot occur. Jones (1984), for example, cites tremor, startle responses, and altered visual responses in newborn infants whose mothers used marijuana during pregnancy. The functional impact of these effects has not been determined, in part because it has been difficult to specify the durability of these postpartum effects and because cannabis-using women who are pregnant frequently also smoke tobacco and use alcohol. Nevertheless, the prudent advice at this time is not to use cannabis during pregnancy.

Summary of long-term effects   It appears the majority of effects associated with marijuana use are more acute than chronic, and that longer-term effects tend to be reversible with termination of drug use. However, significant exceptions may occur. The smoking of marijuana may be found to be linked to various respiratory disorders, including cancer. Most of the negative effects found are correlated with higher doses and frequency of use than that described by most cannabis smokers in this country. Nevertheless, these indications are tentative and await confirmation through the conduct of more systematic and controlled research.

PSYCHOLOGICAL EFFECTS

Although cannabis can produce the varied effects previously noted, most marijuana users use the drug in order to experience the psychological effects, some of which users report consistently, and some of which are more idiosyncratic. The psychological effects generally experienced by marijuana users can be divided into three domains: behavioral, cognitive, and emotional.

Some cannabis effects, especially those associated with the "marijuana high" that users describe, are learned. This learning process has been described in detail by Becker (1953, 1963). According to Becker, the first step is mechanical, in which the smoker learns to inhale the smoke and hold it in the lungs to maximize intake and absorption. The second step is to learn to perceive the effects that are created by the cannabis. These effects can be physical as well as psychological. The final step described by Becker is learning to label these effects as pleasant. The existence of this learning process accounts largely for the frequent finding that experienced users are more sensitive to cannabis effects than novice smokers.

Behavioral Effects

The most common behavioral effect is a generalized decrease in psychomotor activity and decrements in some domains of psychomotor performance. These effects appear to be dose-related, with more pronounced changes associated with greater amounts of marijuana taken in. The general decrease in motor activity appears to be pervasive, and the state is described as being associated with feelings of relaxation and tranquility. The only exception to this effect appears to be speech (Paton & Pertwee, 1973), as marijuana use is associated with the presence of rapid or slurred speech, circumstantial talk, and a loquaciousness. These effects in speech often are observed more in the early smoking phase, followed by the more traditional relaxation.

Although relaxation and a sense of well-being are the usual response to cannabis, some users first experience a stage in which they feel excited and restless. However, fairly soon, these users virtually always experience transition into the relaxation stage. Furthermore, despite feeling relaxed, users sometimes also feel the senses are markedly keener. Many users, for example, describe more intense perceptions of touch, vision (especially in perceiving colors), hearing, and smell. However, the research cited to support these reports is not strong. Finally, other research has shown a decreased sensitivity to pain during marijuana intoxication.

Concomitant with the feelings of relaxation and decreased motor activity is a generally subtle impairment in some areas of psychomotor performance.

CONTEMPORARY ISSUE BOX 11–2
Marijuana and Driving Skill

The role of alcohol in motor vehicle accidents and fatalities is well-researched and established, and this has led to specific guidelines on legal limits of blood alcohol concentrations (see Chapter 7). But what about the role of marijuana? Does marijuana impair driving skill, and is it a factor sufficient to initiate remedial action?

The answer to these questions requires a dovetailing of experimental research on the effects of marijuana on skills related to driving behavior, and epidemiological research to assess whether those effects produce actual problems on the roadways. Experimental research has suggested marijuana, especially in high doses, can create impairment in motor skills related to driving, and that this effect is pronounced when a cognitive component is present (for example, making judgments or decisions while involved in the motor task). Does this translate into a greater risk of accident involvement? Epidemiological research provides only some insights, but no final answers. This research has shown that among drivers injured or killed in accidents, just under 10% have THC in their blood (this figure is closer to one-third among young males). However, it must be kept in mind that among these injured drivers 50% also had alcohol in their systems, and among the fatalities this figure rose to 80%. Thus, it may be alcohol is the more important variable in many of these accidents. Also unclear is whether people who use marijuana may be more at risk for accidents because they are willing to take more risks while driving, whether they have been smoking or not.

Taken together, there are indications that marijuana is causally related to an increased risk for motor vehicle accident involvement. Although the final verdict is still out, the best approach probably is for people not to drive after using marijuana.

There do appear to be dose-related dysfunctions in motor coordination, signal detection, and the ability to monitor a moving object. The data on reaction time are not conclusive. Taken together, these findings have implications for driving a motor vehicle after using cannabis. Laboratory studies involving the use of a driving simulator have revealed detrimental effects of marijuana on driving skill. Some of these impairments may be cognitively mediated. Klonoff (1974) found that drivers under the influence of marijuana showed impairment in judgment and concentration along with other general driving skills. Others have suggested that some of the detriments in driving skill may be due to decreased vigilance and thus less awareness of peripheral stimuli. Therefore, it would appear psychomotor impairment can be caused by cannabis, and that this impairment becomes more apparent in tasks where thinking and concentration are necessary.

The influence of marijuana on sexual behavior and functioning is not fully understood, but it appears its effects vary considerably from user to user. Some report that sexual pleasures are more intense and enjoyable when using marijuana, but others describe instead a disinterest in sex. Those who report increased sexual pleasure when smoking probably are responding to the enhanced sensory sensitivity that frequently accompanies marijuana use. The drug itself produces no known specific physiologic response that stimulates sexual drive or performance. However, long-term or heavy use of marijuana has been associated with temporary impotence among men and temporary decreases in sex drive among women.

Cognitive Effects

Two primary cognitive consequences of cannabis intoxication have been documented. The first is impaired short-term memory and the second is the perception that time passes more slowly.

The impairment in short-term memory seen following cannabis use can occur with intake of a fairly low dose. Further, the degree of impairment increases rapidly with the complexity of the memory task. This effect has been observed with various types of stimuli, such as word lists and conversational materials.

The mechanisms of marijuana's effects on memory have not been specified, but several possibilities have been identified by Paton and Pertwee (1973). The first cause simply may be that the user is not motivated to attend to or to retrieve the material presented. Although this hypothesis is plausible, indications suggest subjects in these experiments perceive the tasks administered as a challenge and respond actively to the task demands. A second possibility is that the perceptual changes created by cannabis produce a "curtain of interference" that blocks or hinders intake or retrieval of material. The third hypothesis proposed by Paton and Pertwee (1973) is that marijuana creates a decreased ability to concentrate and attend to the material presented. This mechanism was advocated by Abel (1971) and by

DeLong and Levy (1974). These latter researchers have proposed a model of attentional processes as a central key in understanding the cognitive effects of cannabis. Finally, cannabis drug action may interfere with the neurochemical processes operative in memory and retrieval operations. The exact factor, or set of factors, remains unknown, but it is likely they will in some manner operate in concert to affect short-term memory.

Altered perceptions of the passage of time is the second common cognitive effect of cannabis. This is perhaps best described in statements like "a few minutes seemed to pass like hours" (Paton & Pertwee, 1973). The effect has been noted in both surveys and in the experimental literature. However, the time distortion is not as pronounced in the research reports as it is in more subjective self-reports provided by marijuana users.

Other cognitive effects of marijuana have been reported, but not as consistently as those already described. One effect is that cannabis decreases the ability to attend and concentrate, making the user easily distracted. Many users report that cannabis produces racing thoughts and "flight of ideas," in which various (and sometimes seemingly random) ideas "fly" in and out of mind. Another perception sometimes reported is of enhanced creativity. This especially has been noted by artists such as writers and painters, but no research evidence supports these claims. Finally, some cannabis users describe occasional feelings of "unreality" (see Hollister, Richards, & Gillespie, 1968) and the attachment of increased meaning to events or objects not previously perceived as important.

Emotional Effects

Positive emotional changes following cannabis intake are cited frequently as key motivators to smoke marijuana. A number of alterations in mood can occur; however, there is some uncertainty regarding the extent to which these are direct drug effects. A host of nonpharmacological factors can contribute to the drug effects experienced (Adesso, 1985; Zinberg, 1984). Chief among these non-drug influences are past experiences with cannabis, attitudes about the drug, expectancies regarding the drug use consequences, and the situational context of drug use. These factors, taken in conjunction with the dose of THC absorbed, must be considered in understanding the emotional changes attributed to the drug.

The typical emotional response to cannabis is a carefree and relaxed state. This feeling has been described in various ways; the adjectives commonly used have included euphoric, content, happy, and excited. It frequently includes laughter and loquaciousness, and takes on the character for some of a dream-like state. Most generally, the response is viewed as pleasant and positive. It appears the degree of response is positively correlated with the dose.

It is noteworthy that negative emotional feelings, such as anxiety or dysphoria, are more common than might be expected. Additionally, a variety of somatic consequences have been experienced. Primarily, these include headache, nausea, and muscle tension; less frequently reported are suspiciousness and paranoid ideation.

It has been reported that around a third of marijuana users at least occasionally experience some of these negative effects; however, the effects can be transitory. A user may fluctuate between experiencing these negative feelings and the more positive states described earlier. Also, the negative effects often are reported more by inexperienced cannabis users.

SOCIAL AND ENVIRONMENTAL EFFECTS

Amotivational syndrome
A term used to describe a loss of effectiveness and reduced capacity to accomplish conventional goals as a result of chronic marijuana use.

There are three hypothesized social/environmental consequences of cannabis use which have received attention: the role of marijuana in enhancing interpersonal skills, the effect of cannabis on aggression and violence, and the role of marijuana use in what has been called the **"amotivational syndrome."**

Many young users of marijuana have said they use the drug because it enhances their social skills and allows them to be more competent in social situations. Although insufficient data are available to evaluate it fully, this claim has not been supported by the available research. Rather, what seems to occur is that the user is either (a) more relaxed in the situation and thus perceives less anxiety or (b) interprets his or her behavior differently while under the influence of marijuana. In any event, it does not appear marijuana significantly enhances competence in social situations.

A longstanding claim regarding cannabis use, dating in this country to the 1920s newspaper articles in New Orleans cited above, is that marijuana causes the user to be aggressive and violent. However, the overwhelming conclusion drawn from the available data, including surveys, laboratory investigations, and field studies, is that cannabis use is not causally related to increases in aggression (see Institute of Medicine, 1982; Tinkleberg, 1974). In fact, levels of aggression actually decrease following cannabis use (see also Contemporary Issue Box 1–3).

The third, and perhaps most controversial, social/environmental consequence of cannabis use is the amotivational syndrome. The term was independently used in the late 1960s by McGlothlin and West (1968) and Smith (1968) to describe the clinical observation "that regular marijuana use may contribute to the development of more passive, inward turning, amotivational personality characteristics" (McGlothlin & West, 1968). The list of behaviors proposed as part of the syndrome include apathy, decreased effectiveness, lost ambition, decreased sense of goals, and difficulty in attending and concentrating. Further, based on case reports, the phenomenon was most likely to be seen among younger users who were using marijuana daily or heavily.

CONTEMPORARY ISSUE BOX 11–3
AMP: Another Form of Marijuana

There is seemingly no end to the number of ways in which a drug can be used or abused. Sometimes the effects of a drug will be much more pronounced when taken, for example, intravenously versus orally. Sometimes the way a substance is prepared will have an effect on how and what effects are experienced. One dramatic example of changing the preparation of a psychoactive substance is the drug known as AMP. AMP is marijuana soaked in formaldehyde and dried before being smoked. It is a preparation first described in the clinical literature in 1985 by Ivan Spector, a physician at Baylor College of Medicine in Texas.

According to Spector, who provided case examples of patients seeking treatment following smoking AMP, these users showed some profound psychiatric effects and impairments. Several of them reported they "immediately felt as if a transparent field has been placed between them and their surroundings." Among the symptoms associated with AMP intoxication are a slowed sense of time, memory impairment, disorientation, paranoid thoughts, anxiety, confusion, disordered thought and difficulties in reality testing, and tremor. Physiological components in the response to AMP intake include elevated blood pressure, hypersalivation, tachycardia, and psychomotor excitement.

It may be instructive to describe one of the cases seen by Spector. A 35-year-old woman, called Ms. D., presented for treatment three days after smoking AMP. She felt anxious, was tremulous, was salivating excessively and sweating, and her heartbeat was racing. All of this followed closely the actual AMP smoking. Several hours later she exhibited psychomotor retardation, secluded herself, reported she could not think well and lost all motivation, and described paranoid thoughts. Ms. D. also described hallucinations in which she saw blood on the walls. After three days, many of these complaints disappeared, with the exception of the anxiety and tremulousness. She was treated with an antianxiety medication, and the discomfort cleared within several days.

Ms. D.'s scenario was similar to those of the other AMP users described in the report, and there are two conclusions we can offer. One is that any given drug can be prepared in ways that markedly influence its effect on the user. A second conclusion is that drug users sometimes may be in a situation in which the drug they are using is not quite what they thought it was. Some AMP users have reported they were given AMP by friends who told them it was only marijuana.

Although there does not seem to be much question that the clustering of these characteristics occurs in some marijuana users, the causal influence of cannabis is not clear. Also, there is some debate about just how commonly the syndrome occurs, with some citing it as a fairly infrequent occurrence (NIDA, 1982). In addition, anthropological investigations of heavy cannabis users in other countries generally have not found the presence of the amotivational syndrome (for example, Carter & Doughty, 1976; Comitas, 1976). Further, survey studies do not always find the differences between marijuana users and nonusers that would be expected if marijuana caused this clustering of effects. Also, the amotivational syndrome has been seen in youths who do not use marijuana and is often not seen in other daily users of marijuana. Thus, it would seem that both preexisting personality characteristics as well as some drug effects *together* probably account for the clustering labeled as the amotivational syndrome, when it occurs.

SUMMARY

- The plant *cannabis sativa* is more commonly known as marijuana. It once was harvested primarily for its fiber, but now is most often grown for its psychoactive effects.

- Marijuana is the leafy top portion of the plant, and hashish is the resin produced by the plant to protect it from the sun.

- The use of cannabis for its intoxicating effects appears to have been centered in Asia, the Middle East, and North Africa for an extended period of time before Europe was exposed to these effects in the nineteenth century.

- Cannabis in the New World dates to 1543, when it was brought to Chile by the Spaniards. The cannabis plant was raised in the United States colonies for its fiber.

- Several influential reports have appeared on the use of marijuana and its effects, including the 1894 Indian Hemp Drugs Commission Report and the 1944 LaGuardia Committee Report. Such reports have tended to find marijuana use overall is not particularly harmful to society at large.

- Marijuana is the most frequently used illicit drug in the United States, although there have been steady decreases in the extent of its use over the last decade.

- The most common and efficient procedure for ingesting cannabis is smoking.

- The principal psychoactive agent in cannabis, isolated in 1964, is delta-9-tetrahydro-cannabinol, more commonly known as Δ-9-THC or simply THC.

- The potency of cannabis varies widely. Most of the marijuana grown in the United States has a THC content of around 2%. THC potency values for hashish usually range from 5–12%, and hash oil can contain up to 60% THC.

- The onset of THC action occurs within minutes of inhalation, and peak concentrations occur around thirty to sixty minutes later. The effects usually are experienced for around two to four hours. Most of the THC metabolites are excreted slowly, approximately half within several days and the remainder by the end of about a week. However, some metabolites can be detected in the body for up to and beyond thirty days.

• The main actions of marijuana occur in the brain and are a result of the drug's effect on neurotransmitters.

• Tolerance, when it occurs, is most likely when high doses are used over extended periods of time. Physical dependence on cannabis is rare.

• Cannabis has long been used for medicinal and psychotherapeutic purposes. Today it is mostly used in the treatment of glaucoma and to reduce nausea and vomiting associated with cancer chemotherapies.

• The acute effects of marijuana generally are benign. These effects include blood-shot eyes, increased heart rate and pulse rate, and decreased motor activity.

• Research on long-term effects of marijuana is sparse. Some effects associated with long-term marijuana use appear to be reversible with termination of its use. There may be significant exceptions, such as the possible association between marijuana and lung cancer.

• Psychological effects of cannabis include decreased psychomotor activity, happy feelings and relaxation, impaired short-term memory, and altered time perception.

• Marijuana has not been shown to enhance social skills or to induce aggression or violence.

• The data on an "amotivational syndrome" due to cannabis use are mixed. It appears both preexisting personality characteristics as well as drug effects together account for what has been labeled the amotivational syndrome.

References

Abel, E.L. (1971). Marihuana and memory: Acquisition or retrieval? *Science, 173,* 1038–1040.

Abel, E.L. (1980). Marihuana: *The first twelve thousand years.* New York: Plenum Press.

Adesso, V.J. (1985). Cognitive factors in alcohol and drug use. In: M. Galizio and S.A. Maisto (Eds.), *Determinants of substance abuse: Biological, psychological, and environmental factors* (pp. 179–208). New York: Plenum Press.

Aldrich, M.R. (1977). Tantric cannabis use in India. *Journal of Psychedelic Drugs, 9,* 227–233.

Becker, H.S. (1953). Becoming a marihuana user. *American Journal of Sociology, 59,* 235–242.

Becker, H.S. (1963). *Outsiders: Studies in the sociology of deviance.* New York: Free Press.

Bloomquist, E.R. (1971). *Marijuana: The second trip* (Revised Edition). Beverly Hills, CA: Glencoe Press.

Brecher, E.M. & the Editors of Consumer Reports. (1972). *Licit and illicit drugs.* Boston: Little, Brown, & Co.

Carter, W.E. & Doughty, P.L. (1976). Social and cultural aspects of cannabis use in Costa Rica. *Annals of the New York Academy of Sciences, 282,* 2–16.

Cohen, S. & Andrysiak, T. (1982). *The therapeutic potential of marijuana's components.* Rockville, MD: American Council on Marijuana and Other Psychoactive Drugs.

Comitas, L. (1976). Cannabis and work in Jamaica: A refutation of the amotivational syndrome. *Annals of New York Academy of Science, 282,* 24–32.

DeLong, F.L. and Levy, B.I. (1974). A model of attention describing the cognitive effects of marijuana. In: L.L. Miller (Ed.), *Marijuana: Effects on human behavior* (pp. 103–120). New York: Academic Press.

Domino, E.F., Donelson, A.C., and Tuttle, T. (1978). Effects of 9-tetrahydrocannabinol on regional brain acetylcholine. In D.J. Jenden (Ed.), *Cholinergic mechanisms and psychopharmacology* (pp. 673–678). New York: Plenum Press.

Ehrenkranz, J.R.L., and Hembree, W.C. (1986). Effects of marijuana on male reproductive function. *Psychiatric Annals, 16,* 243–248.

Gaoni, Y. and Mechaulam, R. (1964). Isolation, structure and partial synthesis of an active constituent of hashish. *Journal of the American Chemical Society, 86,* 1646–1647.

Gautier, T. (1844/1966). *Le Club des hachichins*. In: D. Solomon (Ed.), *The marijuana papers* (pp. 121–135). New York: Bobbs–Merrill.

Harris, L.S., Dewey, W.L., and Razdan, R.K. (1977). Cannabis: Its chemistry, pharmacology, and toxicology. In W.R. Martin (Ed.), *Drug addiction II: Amphetamine, psychotogen, and marihuana dependence* (pp. 371–429). New York: Springer-Verlag.

Hepler, R.S. and Frank, I.M. (1971). Marijuana smoking and intraocular pressure. *Journal of the American Medical Association, 217,* 1392.

Hepler, R.S. and Petrus, R.J. (1976). Experiences with administration of marijuana to glaucoma patients. In S. Cohen and R.C. Stillman (Eds.), *The therapeutic aspects of marijuana* (pp. 63–75). New York: Plenum Press.

Hepler, R.S., Frank, I.M. and Ungerleider, J.T. (1972). Pupillary constriction after marijuana smoking. *American Journal of Ophthamology, 74,* 1185–1190.

Hollister, L.E. (1984). Health aspects of cannabis use. In S. Agurell, W.L. Dewey, and R.E. Willette (Eds.), *The cannabinoids: Chemical, pharmacologic, and therapeutic aspects* (pp. 3–20). New York: Academic Press.

Hollister, L.E., Richards, R.K. and Gillespie, H.K. (1968). Comparison of tetrahydrocannabinol and synhexyl in man. *Clinical Pharmacology and Therapeutics, 9,* 783–791.

Institute of Medicine (1982). *Marijuana and health*. Washington, D.C.: National Academy Press.

Johnston, L.D., O'Malley, P.M. and Bachman, J.G. (in press). Illicit drug use, smoking, and drinking by America's high school students, college students, and young adults. Rockville, MD: National Institute on Drug Abuse.

Jones, R.T. (1980). Human effects: An overview. In R.C. Peterson (Ed.), *Marijuana research findings: 1980* (pp. 54–80). Rockville, MD: National Institute on Drug Abuse.

Klonoff, H. (1974). Effects of marijuana on driving in a restricted area and on city streets. In L.L. Miller (Ed.), *Marijuana: Effects on human behavior* (pp. 359–397). New York: Academic Press.

LeDain Commission. (1972). *A report of the Commission of Inquiry into the non-medical use of drugs*. Ottawa: Information Canada.

Ludlow, F.H. (1857/1979). *The hasheesh eater, being passages from the life of a pythagorean*. San Francisco: City Lights Books.

Mayor LaGuardia's Committee on Marihuana. (1944). *The marihuana problem in the City of New York*. Lancaster, PA: Jacques Cattell Press. (Reprinted by Scarecrow Reprint Corporation, Metuchen, NJ, 1983).

McGlothin, W.H. and West, L.J. (1968). The marihuana problem: An overview. *American Journal of Psychiatry, 125,* 370–378.

Mechoulam, R. (1973). Cannabinoid chemistry. In R. Mechoulam (Ed.), *Marijuana: Chemistry, pharmacology, metabolism, and clinical effects* (pp. 2–99). New York: Academic Press.

Miller, J.D. and Cisin, I.H. (1983). *Highlights from the national survey on drug abuse: 1982*. Rockville, MD: National Institute on Drug Abuse.

Nahas, G.G. (1973). *Marihuana—Deceptive weed*. New York: Raven Press.

National Institute on Drug Abuse (NIDA). (1982). *Marijuana and health* (Ninth Annual Report to the U.S. Congress from the Secretary of Health and Human Services). Rockville, MD: NIDA.

National Institute on Drug Abuse (NIDA). (1984). *Drug abuse and drug abuse research*. Rockville, MD: NIDA.

National Institute on Drug Abuse (NIDA). (1986). *Highlights of the 1985 National Household Survey on Drug Abuse*. Rockville, MD: NIDA.

Paton, W.D.M. and Pertwee, R.G. (1973). The actions of cannabis in man. In R. Mechoulam (Ed.), *Marijuana: Chemistry, pharmacology, metabolism, and clinical effects* (pp. 288–333). New York: Academic Press.

Smith, D.E. (1968). Acute and chronic toxicity of marijuana. *Journal of Psychoactive Drugs, 2,* 37–47.

Tinklenberg, J.R. (1974). Marijuana and human aggression. In L.L. Miller (Ed.), *Marijuana: Effects on human behavior* (pp. 339–357). New York: Academic Press.

Ungerleider, J.T. and Andrysiak, T. (1985). Therapeutic issues of marijuana and THC (tetrahydrocannabinol). *International Journal of the Addictions, 20,* 691–699.

Zinberg, N.E. (1984). *Drug, set, and setting*. New Haven: Yale University Press.

12 HALLUCINOGENS

OVERVIEW

One of the most fascinating, but also confusing, classes of drugs is the group called hallucinogens. These drugs are fascinating because they can alter consciousness in profound and bizarre ways. They are, at the same time, confusing because there are so many different drugs that act in a variety of ways as hallucinogens, and because these drugs have been named and classified in many different ways over the years. Originally called "phantastica" by Lewin (1964), hallucinogens have gone through dozens of name changes. Some researchers have used the term "psychotomimetics" because of the belief these drugs mimic the symptoms of functional psychoses such as schizophrenia. This usage is rare today because it is now clear that, although intriguing similarities exist, the effects of hallucinogens differ in a variety of ways (to be considered later) from natural psychosis. During the 1960s, advocates of hallucinogen use referred to them as "psychedelics," a term coined by one of the early LSD experimenters, Humphrey Osmond. Osmond defined psychedelic as "mind-expanding or mind-revealing" (Stevens, 1987), but whether LSD or other hallucinogens actually possess such properties is controversial at best, and we avoid the term for that reason.

The end result is that we are left with the term hallucinogen, but this term too is more than a bit misleading. It does focus attention on hallucinations and other alterations in perception, and indeed the drugs in this category generally do produce sensory disturbances or alterations that can be considered hallucinogenic. However, that is certainly not the only effect these drugs produce. Hallucinogens exert profound effects on mood, thinking processes, and physiological processes as well. Hallucinogens alter nearly all aspects of psychological functioning and the phrase "altered state of consciousness" describes these drugs better than any we have considered.

An additional complexity is that there are more than ninety different species of plants, and many more synthetic agents, that can be used to produce these kinds of effects (Siegel, 1984). In order to simplify this complex group of drugs we divide them on the basis of their effects and mechanisms of action into four different subgroups to be treated separately.

The first, and historically most important group, is referred to as the **serotonergic hallucinogens.** This category includes the synthetic compound lysergic acid diethylamide (LSD) and related drugs, such as **mescaline** (from the peyote cactus) and **psilocybin**, from certain mushrooms. These drugs all produce vivid visual hallucinations and a variety of other effects on consciousness. Recent experiments suggest that, despite differing chemical structures, these drugs also have in common the action of influencing serotonergic transmission in the brain (Jacobs, 1987; Titeler, Lyon, & Glennon, 1988).

The second class of hallucinogens includes **MDA** and **MDMA** (ecstasy), referred to as the **methylated amphetamines.** As the name suggests these drugs are structurally related to amphetamine (as is mescaline), but produce alterations in mood and consciousness with little or no sensory change. They are thought to act like amphetamine and cocaine on dopamine and norepinephrine synapses, although they apparently influence serotonin as well (Commins and others, 1987).

A third class of hallucinogens, called the **anticholinergic hallucinogens,** is less familiar to most people and includes drugs such as atropine and scopolamine found in plants such as the mandrake, henbane, belladonna, and Jimson weed. These drugs produce a dream–like trance in the user from which he/she awakens with little or no memory of the experience. The drugs in this class act on cholinergic synapses of the brain (Grinspoon & Bakalar, 1979).

Anticholinergic hallucinogens
A class of drugs including atropine and scopolamine.

Finally, a fourth class of hallucinogens includes phencyclidine (PCP or angel dust) and the related compound ketamine. These are often referred to as the **dissociative anesthetics** because of their ability to produce surgical anesthesia while the individual remains at least semiconscious. PCP is thought to act through a receptor that influences activity of the excitatory amino acid neurotransmitter, glutamate (Koek, Woods, & Winger, 1988).

Dissociative anesthetic
A class of drugs including PCP and ketamine.

SEROTONERGIC HALLUCINOGENS: LSD AND RELATED COMPOUNDS

Early History

Table 12–1 shows some of the major drugs thought to obtain their hallucinogenic properties by altering serotonin function in the brain. LSD is the prototype hallucinogen of this class, but drugs with effects similar to those of LSD were used long before LSD was synthesized. As you can see in Table 12–1, LSD-like hallucinogens can be found in a wide variety of plants. The hallucinogenic properties of these plants were primarily discovered and used by the Indian peoples of Central and South America (an exception is ibogaine, which was discovered and used by tribal peoples of Africa). The uses to which these hallucinogenic plants were put have been reconstructed by historians and anthropologists and are worth some consideration here.

When the Spanish *conquistadores* began to explore and colonize Mexico and other parts of Central and South America, they encountered new civilizations with customs and religious practices unfamiliar to Europeans. Among these practices was the use of hallucinogen plants in religious ceremonies. One of the earliest documentations of these practices was by Fernando Hernandez, the royal physician to the King of Spain (Stewart, 1987), who in 1577 studied the plants used by the Aztecs and noted the use of peyote cactus (referred to as peyotl), psilocybe mushrooms (called teonanacatl), and morning glory seeds (called ololuiqui). Although each of these plants contains a different drug, all are capable of producing vivid visual hallucinations, and the Indians took the visions produced by them as oracles that could reveal the future and solve other mysteries, help in decision–making, and aid the medicine man or shaman in healing the sick.

Table 12–1

Serotonergic Hallucinogens

Drug	Botanical Source	Area Found	Other Names
Lysergic acid diethylamide (LSD)	Synthetic, but derived from the ergot fungus	Ergot native to Europe	Acid, many others
Ibogaine	Iboga plant: *Tabernanthe iboga*	Africa	—
Psilocybin	Mushrooms of genus *Psilocybe, Conocybe, Panaeolus,* and *Stropharia*	Throughout the world	Teonanacatl
Dimethyltryptamine (DMT)	Virola tree *Virola calophylla* and other species	South America	Yakee, Yopo
Mescaline	Peyote cactus *Lophophora williamsii*	Mexico and Southwest USA	Peyote
Harmaline, Harmine	Ayahuasca vine *Banisteriopsis caapi Banisteriopsis inebrians*	South America	Yage'
Ergine, Isoergine	Morning glory seeds: *Rivea corymbosa Ipomoea violacea*	Throughout the world	Ololuiqui

Figure 12–1 Psilocybin comes from mushrooms such as this Psilocybe cubensis.

Figure 12-2 Mescaline comes from the peyote cactus, Lophophora williamsii.

The hallucinogenic compounds in the morning glory (ergine and isoergine) are similar to, but far less potent than LSD, and besides producing their hallucinogenic effects cause severe nausea and vomiting, a factor that has limited their current use.

The Aztec and Mayan peoples called the psilocybe mushrooms "teonanacatl" which means "flesh of the gods," and as one might guess from that name, the mushrooms were viewed as sacred. Mushroom icons found in Mayan ruins dating back to more than 1000 B.C. suggest the use of the sacred mushroom is an ancient practice (Schultes, 1976). One Spanish writer, de Sahagun in the 1500s, described the use of mushrooms by Aztecs as follows:

> These mushrooms caused them to become intoxicated, to see visions and also to be provoked to lust . . . They ate the mushrooms with honey and when they began to feel excited due to the effect of the mushrooms, the Indians started dancing, while some were singing and others weeping. . . . Some Indians who did not care to sing, sat down in their rooms, remaining there as if to think. Others, however, saw in a vision that they died and thus cried; others saw themselves eaten by a wild beast; others imagined that they were capturing prisoners of war; others that they were rich or that they possessed many slaves; others that they had committed adultery and had their heads crushed for this offense. . . . (quoted by Schlieffer, 1973, p. 19).

This may be the first description of hallucinogenic drug effects capturing the range of experiences different individuals may have after taking the drug. As with the morning glory, use of sacred mushrooms persists in parts of Mexico today with rituals for healing and divination (Schultes, 1976).

Peyote may have been the most widespread hallucinogenic drug in the new world. This is surprising considering the peyote cactus is limited in range to a relatively small area of northern Mexico and southwestern Texas. The Aztecs used peyote in their rituals and de Sahagun noted "Those who eat or drink it see visions either frightful or laughable . . ." (Stewart, 1987, p. 19). Peyote, like ololiuqui and sacred mushrooms, was forbidden to the Indians by the Spaniards, who regarded its use for religious purposes as blasphemous. Thus, the use of all these agents persisted only "underground," and little is known of them before the twentieth century. However, intriguingly, the peyote religion apparently spread widely during the eighteenth and nineteenth centuries, becoming a religion uniting most Indian tribes in western Mexico and the United States.

The southwestern tribes gathered peyote by cutting the cactus at the soil-line, leaving the root intact. The cactus was sliced and dried into hard "buttons." These buttons could be transported great distances without losing their potency, and indeed they found their way to Native American tribes living throughout the west and as far north as Minnesota and Wisconsin. The ritual itself was (and is) almost identical regardless of the tribe studied. The all-night ceremony takes place in a large tepee where the participants sit in a circle around a fire. Peyote buttons are eaten and peyote tea is drunk. Tobacco is smoked in the form of cigarettes or a pipe. The night is spent chanting, singing, and praying, and later on, in discussing and interpreting the peyote-induced visions. The ceremonies still are conducted today by some Native American tribes in the American southwest, much as they were many centuries ago (Stewart, 1987).

In South America a number of different hallucinogenic plants traditionally have been used in much the same way as peyote and psilocybin were to the north. Hallucinogens called harmaline and harmine are found in the bark of the vines *Banisteriopsis caapi* and *B. inebrians.* These plants are known as Ayahuasca or Caapi by natives of the western Amazon area of Brazil, Colombia, Peru, Ecuador, and Bolivia. Local names for the drink made from the bark of these vines are yage', pinde, and dapa. These plants are used in healing ceremonies, initiation rites, and other rituals. They are said by the natives to provide the user with telepathic powers, but there is no scientific support for this claim (Schultes, 1976). Also widely used in South America for their hallucinogenic properties are various species of the Virola tree (*Virola calophylla, V.calophylloidea,* and *V.theiodora*) of Brazil, Colombia, and Venezuela. The bark of these trees is taken as a snuff that contains the potent hallucinogen dimethyltryptamine (DMT). Virola snuff is taken by some Amazon tribes in a funeral ritual in which the powdered bones of the deceased are consumed along with the snuff (Schultes, 1976).

Recent History

Despite the long history of hallucinogenic drug use, these drugs had virtually no impact on mainstream European or American culture until the

1960s when an explosion of hallucinogen use occurred. The history of the
"psychedelic movement" began in Basel, Switzerland, where Albert Hofmann, a chemist working in Sandoz Laboratories, discovered LSD in 1938.
Hofmann was studying derivatives of ergot, a fungus that infests grain and
occasionally caused outbreaks of disease (St. Anthony's Fire) in medieval
Europe when infected bread was eaten. Ergot derivatives have medical use
in the treatment of migraine headache and in effecting uterine contractions
during pregnancy, and this accounted for Sandoz' interest. Hofmann eventually synthesized a number of compounds involving lysergic acid, the
twenty-fifth of which was lysergic acid diethylamide—abbreviated LSD-25
on the bottle. LSD was given several preliminary animal tests and, not showing any commercially interesting properties, was shelved. It stayed
unknown until 1943 when Hofmann decided to re-examine its properties.
During a laboratory experiment, Hofmann apparently spilled a small amount
of LSD on his hand where it was absorbed. Thus Hofmann became the first
person to experience the effects of LSD. He described his experiences as
follows:

> I was forced to interrupt my work in the laboratory in the middle of the afternoon
> and proceed home, being affected by a remarkable restlessness, combined with a
> slight dizziness. At home I lay down and sank into a not unpleasant intoxicated-
> like condition, characterized by an extremely stimulated imagination. In a dream-
> like state, with eyes closed . . . I perceived an uninterrupted stream of fantastic
> pictures, extraordinary shapes with intense, kaleidoscopic play of colors (Hof-
> mann, 1980, p. 15).

Hofmann decided the bizarre experience must have been due to contact
with LSD, and decided to test that hypothesis with an experiment. He reasoned that LSD must be very potent to have produced such effects through
an accidental exposure, and measured out for oral administration 250
micrograms—a minute amount by standards of drugs known at that time.
What Hofmann could not have known is that LSD is *so* potent that this dose
was at least twice as potent as the normal effective dose (25–125
micrograms).

After taking the drug Hofmann noted in his journal: "Beginning dizziness,
feeling of anxiety, visual distortions, symptoms of paralysis, desire to laugh"
(Hofmann, 1980, p. 16). At this point Hofmann was overcome by the drug
and could no longer write. He asked his assistant to escort him home, and
he later wrote the following about his LSD trip:

> On the way home, my condition began to assume threatening forms. Everything
> in my field of vision wavered and was distorted as if seen in a curved mirror . . .
> Finally we arrived at home safe and sound, and I was just barely capable of asking
> my companion to summon our family doctor and request milk from the neighbors
> . . . as a nonspecific antidote for poisoning.
>   My surroundings had now transformed themselves in more terrifying ways.
> Everything in the room spun around, and assumed grotesque, threatening forms.
> They were in continuous motion, animated, as if driven by an inner restlessness.

> The lady next door, whom I scarcely recognized, brought me milk. . . . She was no longer Mrs. R., but rather a malevolent, insidious witch with a colored mask. . . . (Hofmann, 1980, p. 16–17).

Later, as the intensity of the drug effects began to subside, Hofmann reports enjoying the hallucinations and altered thought processes. After he recovered and made his report to Sandoz, many other experiments followed.

Sandoz began to distribute LSD to psychologists and psychiatrists for use as an adjunct to psychotherapy. The theory was that the drug would break down the patient's normal ego defenses, and thus facilitate the psychotherapy process. Psychiatrists were encouraged to try LSD themselves so they would better understand the subjective experience of schizophrenia. The idea was that LSD was psychotomimetic—mimicked psychosis.

By the early 1960s many people had tried LSD, and it was beginning to generate some publicity. One user was movie star Cary Grant, who said in an interview that his LSD psychotherapy changed his whole life and brought him true peace of mind. Another famous user, Henry Luce, head of Time, Inc., said he talked to God under LSD's influence. The British author Aldous Huxley, who earlier had tried peyote and written a book about his experiences (Huxley, 1954), promoted LSD and other hallucinogenic drugs as leading to the next step in human evolution! But the most influential of the early LSD users were Harvard psychologist Timothy Leary and the writer Ken Kesey.

Leary and his Harvard associate Richard Alpert (who later became known as religious writer Baba Ram Dass) had taken LSD and other hallucinogens and become convinced of the psychological and spiritual value of these drugs. What began as legitimate experiments, including work on the possible beneficial effects of hallucinogens on prison inmates, began to look suspiciously like LSD parties involving Harvard faculty, students, and an assortment of celebrities and intellectuals. At some point, Leary had stepped out of his role as a scientist and had become the leader of a social and religious movement. Calling himself "High Priest," Leary claimed LSD was a ticket to a trip to spiritual enlightenment. He exhorted an entire generation to "Turn on. Tune in. Drop out" (Stevens, 1987). Leary left Harvard under duress in 1963, but continued to proselytize for LSD and in fact became a media celebrity. Harassment by law enforcement officials continued to increase Leary's eminence, and he became viewed as something of a martyr, winning new converts as a curious nation heard more and more about the wonders of LSD.

On the west coast, LSD was popularized by Ken Kesey, celebrated author, and his "merry pranksters." Kesey is the author of *One Flew Over the Cuckoo's Nest*. As recounted by Wolfe (1969), Kesey's "acid tests" were large parties where hundreds of people would be "turned on to LSD" in a single night. LSD began to make an impact on the emerging hippie subculture, particularly through the music of groups like the Grateful Dead, Jefferson Airplane, Jimi Hendrix, and others whose music became known as "acid rock.'' Eventually the Beatles became part of the movement and the surreal images of songs such as ''Lucy in the Sky with Diamonds'' had the entire Western world talking about, if not using, LSD. By the late 1960s LSD had become the most controversial drug in the world. As many as two million people had tried LSD in the United States, but the positive statements about LSD had become counterbalanced by increasing negative publicity. LSD was claimed to cause chromosome damage—users were said to be likely to have mutant children. It was said to cause insanity, suicide, acts of violence, and homicidal behavior (Stevens, 1987). All of this controversy led to a decline in LSD use in the 1970s and 1980s, but perhaps equally important was a loss of faith in the LSD mystique, the recognition that spiritual enlightenment produced by LSD was a false hope. As Hunter S. Thompson put it in his chronicle of the era:

> This was the fatal flaw in Tim Leary's trip. He crashed around America selling consciousness expansion without ever giving a thought to the grim meat–hook reali-

Figure 12–3 Ken Kesey and Timothy Leary helped make LSD a household term.

ties that were lying in wait for all the people who took him too seriously. . . . Not that they didn't deserve it: No doubt they all Got What Was Coming To Them. All those pathetically eager acid freaks thought they could buy Peace and Understanding for three bucks a hit. But their loss and failure is ours, too. What Leary took down with him was the central illusion of a whole life-style that he helped to create . . . a generation of permanent cripples, failed seekers, who never understood the essential old-mystic fallacy of the Acid Culture: the desperate assumption that somebody—or at least some *force*—is tending that Light at the end of the tunnel." (Thompson, 1971, pp. 178–179.)

But use of LSD did not vanish, and in fact the 1980s ushered in renewed interest in and use of hallucinogens (Stock, 1986a). Perhaps the publicity surrounding new hallucinogens like MDMA or Ecstasy (discussed later) renewed curiosity about LSD. Stock (1986a) notes the increased availability of high-quality LSD as a possible factor.

In any event, many of the questions that arose about LSD and related hallucinogens during the controversial 1960s have now been well researched, but others are still unanswered.

Mechanisms of Action of LSD-like Drugs

The mechanisms by which LSD and related drugs are capable of producing—in such small doses—such dramatic effects as visual hallucinations and alterations of consciousness remain enigmatic, but there is increasing consensus that an important aspect involves the alteration of activity of brain systems mediated by the neurotransmitter serotonin. The first bit of evidence was suggested by the chemical structures of some of the major hallucinogens. LSD, psilocybin, harmaline, and most of the other drugs in Table 12–1 are classified according to their chemical structure as indolealkylamines (Nichols & Glennon, 1984). That chemical structure is shared by the naturally occurring transmitter serotonin. The structural similarity led to the notion that LSD and related compounds might act by mimicking serotonin, and thus activate serotonin receptors in the brain. This hypothesis has now received considerable support. For example, it has been shown that LSD and the other hallucinogenic indolealkylamines bind to serotonin receptors, and that the potency of serotonin binding correlates strongly with the potency of the drug as a hallucinogen (Glennon, Titeler, & McKenny, 1984; Titeler, Lyon, & Glennon, 1988).

One problem with the above analysis is mescaline. Mescaline's chemical structure is quite different from the others. In fact, mescaline has a structure far more similar to amphetamine than LSD. For this reason, it has often been classified as having a different mechanism than LSD. However, unlike amphetamine (and the methylated amphetamines like MDA—see the following), mescaline produces vivid visual hallucinations virtually identical in form to those of LSD. Further evidence for a common mechanism of action between LSD and mescaline comes from studies on tolerance. Tolerance to all the effects of LSD develops fairly rapidly. The same is true for mescaline. In addition, there is cross-tolerance between LSD, mescaline, and other drugs of this class (Jacobs, 1987). Finally, recent data suggest that mescaline (or perhaps one of mescaline's metabolites) also binds to the serotonin receptor (Appel & Rosencrans, 1984; Davis, 1987; Jacobs, 1987).

As we noted in Chapter 3, serotonin is distributed widely in the brain. This may account for the many and various effects of LSD-like hallucinogens. Serotonin is thought to play an important role in mood, which is consistent with the powerful emotional effects of these drugs. The precise areas of the brain responsible for the hallucinogenic actions of these drugs, however, remain a mystery.

Pharmacokinetics of LSD-like Drugs

As we have noted above, the effects of all of the hallucinogens that act upon serotonin receptors are quite similar. However these drugs differ widely in potency, duration of action, and other pharmacokinetic variables. LSD is the most potent of the class, with oral doses of as little as 25 micrograms producing effects. Street doses range from about 75 to 250 micrograms and are prepared by placing a small amount of LSD solution on paper (blotter) or in a gel (windowpane) or in a tablet (Stock, 1986a). LSD is rapidly absorbed and subjective effects are usually noted within twenty to sixty minutes after consumption. The drug is distributed throughout the body and readily penetrates the blood-brain barrier. The effects of LSD persist for eight to twelve hours, and the drug is rapidly metabolized and eliminated from the body. Even the most sensitive techniques can detect LSD or its metabolites in urine for no more than seventy-two hours after use (Hawks & Chiang, 1986). Although the hallucinogens found in morning glory seeds (ergine and isoergine) are quite similar to LSD, they are far less potent— perhaps 5 to 10% as strong as LSD (Grinspoon & Bakalar, 1979).

Psilocybin normally is taken orally by either eating the mushrooms or drinking a brew containing them. It is difficult to specify doses because the amount of psilocybin varies depending on the species of mushroom, among other things. Typically, 5 to 10 grams of mushrooms are taken, containing 10 to 20 mg of psilocybin. Thus, psilocybin is about 1% as potent as LSD. The duration of action is about four to six hours. As is true of virtually all of the serotonergic hallucinogens, tolerance develops to psilocybin, and it shows cross-tolerance with other members of the family (Grinspoon & Bakalar, 1979).

Mescaline is normally taken by consumption of peyote buttons, as described above. Usually five to twenty buttons are eaten, delivering about 200–800 mg of mescaline. Mescaline is about $\frac{1}{3000}$ as potent as LSD, with 200 mg considered an effective dose. Duration of action is about eight to twelve hours.

Less information is available about the other serotonergic hallucinogens, but most are similar to the above. One noteworthy exception is dimethyl-tryptamine (DMT), which is usually taken by using the bark of the Virola as a snuff or by smoking it. Its effects begin within minutes of use, but persist for only about 30 minutes.

Psychotherapeutic Uses

LSD and the related hallucinogens historically have been thought to have two applications in psychotherapy, but neither is well-accepted today. One notion was that LSD produced a model psychosis, and that the psychotherapist would benefit from having experiences similar to those of the patient. It is true that hallucinations, unusual affective reactions, and loss of reality contact are characteristic of both schizophrenia and hallucinogen experiences. But there also are important differences. For example, the hallucinations experienced under the influence of LSD are primarily visual in nature, while those of schizophrenics are usually auditory (Anderson, 1980). So the subjective experiences of the psychotic are certainly not identical to those of the hallucinogen user. However, an intriguing similarity is that chlorpromazine and the other antipsychotics used in the treatment of schizophrenia are effective antagonists of LSD effects. Thus, hallucinogens may yet provide clues about the biochemistry of mental disorders.

Paradoxically, the other major application of hallucinogens has been as an adjunct to psychotherapy. The general idea was that the therapist would be able to learn important information when the patient was using LSD, and that the patient would be better able to gain insight into his or her condition because LSD could break down ego defenses. Many extravagant claims have been made about the benefits of LSD for mental health and spiritual development, but the use of LSD in psychotherapy gradually has declined. Although one important reason for this was the political climate, another was that most therapists thought the potential risks of LSD outweighed the benefits. In fact, it never has been demonstrated scientifically that the use of LSD is superior to placebo as an adjunct to psychotherapy. Some therapists think these drugs deserve further evaluation as possible psychotherapeutic agents (Grinspoon & Bakalar, 1979, 1983), but the current controversy has shifted to the related drugs MDA and MDMA (see page 336).

Effects of Serotonergic Hallucinogens

The physiological effects of LSD and related hallucinogens are generally similar to those of amphetamine and cocaine. That is, they are sympathomimetic. Thus, the effects include pupil dilation, increased heart rate and blood pressure, increased body temperature, and increased sweating (Grinspoon & Bakalar, 1979).

The psychological effects are more difficult to characterize. Experiences with hallucinogenics are tremendously variable between individuals and, for a single individual, may vary from one experience to the next. Common to all the serotonergic hallucinogens are profound changes in visual perception, although there is some consistency in the types of visual changes that occur. Many were summarized by Albert Hofmann in his account of his first LSD trip described earlier. Hofmann added:

> Kaleidoscopic fantastic images surged in on me, alternating, variegated, opening, and then closing themselves in circles and spirals, exploding in colored fountains, rearranging and hybridizing themselves in constant flux. It was particularly remarkable how every acoustic perception, such as the sound of a door handle or a passing automobile, became transformed into optical perceptions. Every sound generated a vividly changing image, with its own consistent form and color (Hofmann, 1980, p. 19).

The spiral explosions and vortex patterns described by Hofmann have been noted by Siegel (1977) to be among the most common forms in hallucinogenic experiences. Siegel calls them *form constants* because they are reported so frequently. Another form constant noted by Siegel is the lattice pattern—a checkerboard-like pattern that appears in an otherwise plain surface. The experience described by Hofmann of sensing a sound stimulus as a visual one is called **synesthesia,** and it has been reported by others as well. Other visual effects are flashing lights, increased brightness and intensity of colors, the experience of trails or plumes around objects, and the sense of movement in stable objects (for example, the wall breathes or moves rhythmically).

However, there is a good bit more to the "trip" than just a light show. Other perceptions may be altered. Mood is extremely labile, and bizarre cognitive experiences occur (Cohen, 1971). Some examples of such experiences are given in Contemporary Issue Box 12–1. Although the descrip-

Synesthesia
An effect sometimes produced by hallucinogens characterized by the perception of a stimulus in a modality other than the one in which was presented (for example a subject may report "seeing" music).

CONTEMPORARY ISSUE BOX 12–1
Descriptions of Subjective Effects of LSD

Many attempts have been made to describe the effects and experiences produced by LSD. Such accounts are remarkably diverse, often confusing, and sometimes contradictory, yet there are some common features. The following are vivid recollections given by well-known LSD users, illustrating the variety of the experience:

> I looked into the glass of water. In its swirling depths was a vortex which went down the center of the world and the heart of time. . . . A dog barked and its piercing howl might have been all the wolves in Tartary. . . . At one moment I would be a giant in a tiny cupboard, and the next, a dwarf in a huge hall

(Humphrey Osmond on mescaline—quoted by Grinspoon & Bakalar, 1979, p. 100).

I was lying on my back on the floor. Then the room itself vanished and I was sinking, sinking, sinking. From far away I heard very faintly the word "death." I sank faster, turning and falling a million light years from the earth. The word got louder and more insistent. It took shape around me, closing me in.
   "DEATH . . . DEATH . . . DEATH." I thought of the dread in my father's eyes in his final hours. At the last instant before my own death I shouted, "No." Absolute terror, total horror (Lingeman on LSD—quoted by Grinspoon & Bakalar, 1979, p. 112).

Now a series of visions began. The imagery appeared to synchronize with the phonograph music. . . . I envisioned myself at the court of Kubla Khan . . . at a concert being held in an immense auditorium . . . in some futuristic utopia . . . at Versailles . . . at a statue of Lincoln. . . . I felt myself engulfed in a chaotic, turbulent sea. . . . There were a number of small boats tossing on the raging sea . . . [I was] in one of these vessels . . . we came upon a gigantic figure standing waist–deep in the churning waters . . . His facial features were graced by an unforgettable look of compassion, love, and concern. We knew that this was the image of God. We realized that God, too, was caught in the storm (Krippner on psilocybin—quoted by Grinspoon & Bakalar, 1979, pp. 100–101).

tions recounted in the box are quite different, they do reveal some similarities. All are characterized by strong affect, although the nature of the emotional state varies. All involve "magical" thinking and, particularly in the last two, events are fraught with cosmic significance. If the visions are terrifying (as in the second quote) the subject may behave in a psychotic manner—and this is usually referred to as a bad or bum trip. The insights, enlightenments, and beliefs that occur and seem so significant during the trip often turn out to be trivial or false afterwards. For example, subjects are often convinced they possess telepathic or clairvoyant abilities under the influence of the drug, but when tested, these abilities are not present. Nonetheless, it is easy to see how such experiences must have led pre–scientific cultures to attach mystical and religious significance to hallucinogens.

Adverse Effects of Serotonergic Hallucinogens

An important part of the LSD controversy revolves around the adverse effects stemming from its use. One of the major concerns about LSD use involved the claim that it produced chromosome damage—that those who used the drug, male or female, would stand a high risk of having deformed children. This concern was based on a study that found LSD produced chromosome breaks in white blood cells artificially cultured in the laboratory.

The study raised fears that LSD also might damage human gametes (Cohen & Marmillo, 1967). However, breaking chromosomes in white cells in a test tube under high doses of LSD has not been shown to be relevant to *in vivo* conditions. After considerable research into this question, there is no convincing evidence that LSD (or any other serotonergic hallucinogen) increases birth defects in offspring when taken in normal doses. Although in high doses some risk is possible, LSD is no more likely to cause birth defects than aspirin under ordinary circumstances (Grinspoon & Bakalar, 1979; Long, 1972). As with most drugs, however, there is risk of fetal damage if taken by pregnant women (Grinspoon & Bakalar, 1979).

Some of the other adverse effects of LSD and related hallucinogens are more cause for concern. An important problem has been acute panic or paranoid reactions to the drug. These bad trips can leave individuals in an acute psychotic state during which they may harm themselves or others. The frequency of bad trips is difficult to estimate, but was high enough in the 1960s to lead to the widespread development of walk-in crisis centers where victims could be brought for reassurance (talking the subject down), and if necessary, hospital referral. Bad trips appear to be less frequent today perhaps because more is known about how to prevent them. Set and setting are important. For example, one of the few documented LSD-suicides took place after a man was administered LSD without his knowledge in an experiment conducted by the CIA in the 1950s (Grinspoon & Bakalar, 1979). Being exposed to the drug without foreknowledge is apparently quite frightening and disturbing. Individuals seem to be less likely to have bad trips if they are aware and frequently reminded that they are under the influence of a drug. A calm and comfortable setting and low doses of LSD are thought to reduce the frequency of bad trips as well, although bad trips may occur even under the best of circumstances (Brecher, 1972).

Another problem associated with LSD-like hallucinogens is a phenomenon known as the **flashback.** Flashbacks involve a sudden, unexpected re-experience of some aspect of a hallucinogenic trip that occurred weeks, months, or years before. Although, as with bad trips, it is difficult to estimate the frequency of flashbacks, in one study 53.5% of LSD users reported flashbacks (Abraham, 1983). Most subjects did not find these flashbacks to be terribly disturbing, but 12.9% sought clinical help for the problem. Although little is known about the causes of flashbacks, they tend to be precipitated by anxiety, fatigue, marijuana, or sudden changes in the environment such as emergence into darkness (Abraham, 1983).

Flashback
A sudden recurrence of an LSD–like experience.

LSD also has been linked to long-term psychiatric disorders. Perhaps the most publicized and horrifying example is Charles Manson and his "family." The Manson family used LSD heavily, but it is unclear what role, if any, the drug played in the development of their psychopathology and subsequent mass murders. When confronted with a psychotic individual who has used LSD, it is difficult to determine whether LSD caused the psychosis, or whether the person was psychotic to begin with and LSD made the symptoms more flagrant. To complicate matters further, most users of LSD who are diagnosed as psychotic have extensive histories with other drugs as well, and the role these other drugs may have played is rarely certain. It generally is agreed hallucinogens may precipitate or exacerbate psychosis or emotional disturbance in certain vulnerable individuals (Bowers, 1977; Smith & Seymour, 1985).

METHYLATED AMPHETAMINES

Overview

The recent controversy over designer drugs has focused a great deal of attention on the drugs in this category, particularly MDMA, better known as ecstasy. MDMA is one of a group of drugs known as methylated amphetamines because of their chemical structures (there are dozens of drugs in this category, but the more well-known variations are presented in Table 12–2). These drugs are often categorized with the serotonergic hallucinogens, and indeed, their chemical structures resemble that of mescaline. In addition they influence serotonin transmission (but also norepinephrine and dopamine—Commins and others, 1987). DOM not only resembles mescaline in structure, but also produces similar effects, including visual hallucinations. However, the others (MDA, MDMA, DOET) are different from the serotonergic hallucinogens reviewed above in that they produce few or no visual hallucinations. In drug-discrimination studies, laboratory animals identify MDA, MDMA, and DOET with amphetamine and discriminate them from LSD. Similar observations are reported by humans (Boja & Schecter, 1987; Oberlender & Nichols, 1988). The effects of MDA and MDMA seem to be primarily a mild euphoria accompanied by openness and lack of defensiveness. These properties led some psychotherapists to advocate the use of these drugs, particularly MDMA, as an adjunct to therapy. Thus, there is growing sentiment to consider these drugs as belonging to a unique category among hallucinogens. However, on the less positive side, there are new data suggesting these drugs may damage serotonergic neurons (Ricaurte and others, 1985; Schmidt, 1987).

Table 12–2
Methylated Amphetamines

Chemical Name	Abbreviation	Street Names
2,5-dimethoxy-4 methylamphetamine	DOM	STP
3,4-methylenedioxyamphetamine	MDA	Love drug, Mellow Drug of America
3,4-methylenedioxymethamphetamine	MDMA	Ecstasy, XTC, Adam
N-ethyl-3,4-methylenedioxyamphetamine	MDE	Eve

History and Epidemiology

DOM was first reported on the street in the late 1960s, when its potent hallucinogenic effects and very long duration of action (as long as twenty-four hours) led to many bad trips. MDA also surfaced on the street about this time, but it had a better reception. It was referred to as Mellow Drug of America because it is less intense and has fewer perceptual effects than LSD. It also was called the Love drug, because users reported positive feelings toward others and great empathy as part of the experience. Use of MDA declined along with the LSD in the 1970s while MDMA began to increase in popularity, peaking in the mid-1980s. In 1976 it was estimated 10,000 doses of MDMA were used on the street during the year. In 1985 the Drug Enforcement Agency (DEA) estimated 30,000 doses were distributed per month in one Texas city alone (Stock, 1986b). What accounted for this enormous increase? Publicity about the therapeutic benefits of MDMA made it attractive (Sound familiar? Remember Timothy Leary . . .). It did not hurt public relations for the drug to pick up the nickname "ecstasy." Finally, until 1985 MDMA was a legal drug. Although MDA was a Schedule I drug, its close relative MDMA had not been classified under the schedule system. Thus, dealers preferred the low risks associated with the designer drug, ecstasy. However, in the face of the explosive rise in MDMA use, coupled with animal research implicating the drug with brain damage, the Drug Enforcement Agency classified MDMA as Schedule I in 1985 on an emergency basis (Barnes, 1988). As soon as MDMA was controlled, dealers began to distribute DOET, which is a similar drug that also is now controlled by the Designer Drug Act of 1986 (Boja & Schecter, 1987). These decisions have been controversial, because they effectively banned further psychiatric testing of MDMA and related compounds. As of this writing the drug is in a legal limbo: the answers to some of the questions about its therapeutic potential and neurotoxicity will determine where MDMA winds up in our legal system.

Effects of Methylated Amphetamines

The effects of MDMA, MDA, and DOET are similar enough to be discussed together (DOM effects are like those of mescaline or LSD and are not considered further). These drugs are usually taken orally, but can be injected or absorbed intranasally (snorted). They are absorbed rapidly and have a duration of action of about six to eight hours. At effective doses (75–150 mg for MDMA; 50–150 mg for MDA; 1–2 mg for DOET) these drugs produce clear sympathomimetic effects, including increased heart rate, blood pressure, and pupil dilation. Additional physical effects include muscle tension, jaw-clenching (bruxism), appetite suppression, and insomnia—effects remarkably similar to those of amphetamine (David, Hatoum, & Waters, 1987; Grinspoon & Bakalar, 1979). The psychological effects claimed for these drugs are euphoria, increased emotional warmth, lowered defensiveness and increased communicative ability (Barnes, 1988; Kirsch, 1986; Peroutka, 1987). Hallucinations are uncommon or absent at ordinary doses. These properties led some psychiatrists to advocate use of these drugs as an adjunct to psychotherapy, but as yet there is no controlled study supporting the value of MDMA (or any others of this class) in psychotherapy (Kirsch, 1986).

CONTEMPORARY ISSUE BOX 12–2
Trouble With Ecstasy

The research necessary to determine the value of MDMA in psychotherapy may never be done because of recent evidence that the drugs in this family may produce long–term damage of certain brain structures. The report sounding the alarm (Ricaurte and others, 1985) showed that after several administrations of high doses of MDA, rats had a depletion of serotonin apparently caused by degeneration of serotonergic neuron terminals. These effects were apparent as long as two weeks after treatment and Ricaurte and others speculated the effects might prove to be permanent. Similar results now have been reported for MDMA at fairly low doses and in several species including primates (Barnes, 1988; Commins and others, 1987; Johnson and others, 1988). Whether these neurons ever recover from the toxic effects of the drugs is unknown. As noted in Chapter 3, serotonin is a neurotransmitter modulating sleep and is thought to be deficient in depressive disorders. Therefore, depletion of serotonin could lead to serious problems. Whether MDMA and MDA will produce these neurotoxic effects in humans at moderate dose levels is unknown at the present, but until these questions are answered, the psychotherapeutic applications cannot be tested.

ANTICHOLINERGIC HALLUCINOGENS

Atropine
An anticholinergic hallucinogen found in certain plants.

Scopolamine
An anticholinergic hallucinogen found in certain plants.

Atropine and **scopolamine** are drugs that block acetylcholine receptors in the brain. Although used in low doses for medical purposes, these drugs can produce hallucinogenic effects in high doses. They are found in a number of plants known throughout the world and have a long history of use. Hundreds of years B.C., plants containing scopolamine and atropine were used by the ancient Greeks at the oracle of Delphi. In the middle ages such plants were included in the infamous witches' brews. Plants such as belladonna, also called the deadly nightshade *(Atropa belladonna),* mandrake *(Man-*

dragora officinarum), henbane (Hyoscyamus niger) of Europe, and Jimson weed (Datura stramonium), and other plants of the Datura genus from the new world, have been eaten for their hallucinogenic properties (Schultes, 1976). Although these drugs are no longer in use for witchcraft, Datura is allegedly one of the ingredients in Zombie powder in Haiti (Davis, 1988).

Anticholinergic hallucinogens produce a variety of physiological effects, including dry mouth, blurred vision, loss of motor control, and increased heart rate and body temperature. They can be fatal due to respiratory failure at doses only slightly higher than the effective dose (Grinspoon & Bakalar, 1979). The psychological experience appears to be a dream-like trance or stupor. The user appears delirious and confused, but may be able to describe visions if asked. A unique feature of the drugs of this class is that memory of the experience is very poor and subjects may be unable to recall details of any of the experiences. This may be one of the reasons these drugs are rarely seen on the street today.

One additional plant to be discussed in this section is the fly agaric mushroom (Amanita muscaria). Fly agaric contains several different hallucinogenic chemicals, including muscarine, which is a cholinergic agonist, and muscimole, a hallucinogen that may be similar to the LSD-like drugs. Although rarely used today, the mushroom is worth noting because it may represent the earliest form of hallucinogen use. Fly agaric grows through much of Europe and Asia and it may have been the mysterious "Soma" described in the Indian Rig-Veda more than two thousand years ago. The Rig-Veda describes the rather bizarre practice of recycling the drug effect by drinking the urine of the intoxicated individual. Muscimole is the only hallucinogen known that passes through the system into the urine unchanged (Wasson, 1979). The effects of the mushroom are somewhat unique among hallucinogens. Users of the fly agaric typically fall into a stupor for several hours during which they experience visions, and later experience intense euphoria and energy accompanied by visual hallucinations (Wasson, 1979).

DISSOCIATIVE ANESTHETIC HALLUCINOGENS

History

The final class of hallucinogens to be considered is a large group, but only two of its members, **phencyclidine** (PCP, angel dust) and its close analog, **ketamine,** have been used enough to warrant discussion here. PCP was synthesized in 1956, and because it had pronounced tranquilizing effects it was tested as an anesthetic. With animals it produced a general anesthesia that left the animal conscious but not feeling pain, even during surgery. However, in clinical trials with humans, some patients experienced hyperexcitability, delirium, and visual disturbances. Thus, PCP was abandoned for

Phencyclidine
A dissociative anesthetic.

Ketamine
A dissociative anesthetic.

human use, although it was marketed as a veterinary anesthetic and tranquilizer under the brand name Sernyl (Linder, Lerner, & Burns, 1981). Little more was heard about PCP until the late 1960s, when it began to appear as a "rip-off" drug sold under the guise of being THC, MDA, or mescaline. Although PCP got a bad reputation on the street during this time, it emerged in the 1970s as a street drug of preference. Sold under a variety of names, including angel dust, hog, horse tranquilizer, and lovely, it was often taken by sprinkling the powder on a cigarette or joint and smoking it. Although PCP also is effective orally and can be injected, smoking remains the most popular route of administration. By the early 1980s some surveys were finding that more than 20% of America's high school students had tried PCP. Because of the high frequency of dangerous side effects, PCP has become a notorious drug. Although its use has declined in recent years, PCP remains widely available on the street (Kirsch, 1986; Young, Lawson & Gacono, 1987). Although no longer widely used in veterinary medicine, the similar analog, ketamine, is commonly used in animal surgery.

Pharmacokinetics of PCP

PCP's mechanism of action is poorly understood, but appears to involve interaction with receptors for the excitatory amino acid, glutamate (Koek, Woods, & Winger, 1988; Quirion and others, 1987). PCP is absorbed rapidly after smoking or injection with peak blood concentrations noted within five to fifteen minutes after smoking. In contrast, peak concentrations are reached two hours after oral administration. The drug remains in the system unmetabolized for more than two days, and PCP is detectable in urine for several weeks after a single use (Hawks & Chiang, 1986).

Effects of PCP

The effects of PCP are relatively unique. A moderate dose (1–10 mg) produces feelings of euphoria and numbness resembling alcohol intoxication. Speech may be slurred and generally there is motor discoordination. The subject may be catatonic and rigid with a blank stare, or may be aggressive and hyperactive. There is profuse sweating, heart rate and blood pressure may be increased, and there are rapid jerky eye movements called nystagmus (Lindner and others, 1981; Young and others, 1987). Subjects often report blurred vision or double vision, but rarely visual hallucinations. Rather there are changes in perception of body image—distortions of the tactile senses. Consider these descriptions from PCP users:

> It's weirdly hallucinogenic. It makes you go, boy that's steep stairs I have to climb there, that you realized you climb in five minutes you know, and stuff, and it actually feels like you're going to float off the couch and stuff, you know. Your arm is over somewhere. I can remember like crawling down the stairs because the only thing that I trusted was my fingers and my knees. . . .

The most frequent hallucination is that parts of your body are extremely large or extremely small. You can imagine yourself small enough to walk through a keyhole, or you can be lying there and all of a sudden you just hallucinate that your arm is twice the length of your body (from Feldman, Agar, & Beschner, 1979, p. 133).

These effects normally last from four to six hours, but are quite variable and, particularly after high doses, may persist for days or weeks. Overdoses (more than 20 mg) may result in seizures, prolonged coma, and sometimes death from respiratory failure. PCP is extremely likely to produce bad trips. These may occur in 50% to 80% of PCP users (Young, Lawson, & Gacono, 1987).Toxic psychosis produced by PCP is often characterized by paranoia and violence and may persist for several days. Additionally, PCP frequently precipitates long-term psychotic episodes and depressions that last seven to thirty days or more. Talking the subject down from a PCP bad trip generally is unsuccessful. Physical restraint and intensive medical care are often necessary. PCP is far more likely than other hallucinogens to produce medical or psychiatric complications. In many cities, PCP is responsible for more psychiatric emergencies than any other drug, and in some hospitals PCP psychoses exceed schizophrenia and alcoholism as a cause of psychiatric admission (Luisada & Brown, 1976; McCarron, 1986; Young, Lawson and Gacono, 1987).

SUMMARY

· Hallucinogens are a group of drugs with the capacity to alter perceptual, cognitive, and emotional states.

· Hallucinogens may be divided into four classes: serotonergic hallucinogens, the methylated amphetamines, anticholinergic hallucinogens, and dissociative anesthetics.

· Serotonergic hallucinogens include drugs such as LSD, psilocybin, and mescaline. Psilocybin comes from mushrooms of the Psilocybe genus and mescaline from the peyote cactus. These drugs have a long history of use by early Indian peoples for religious purposes.

· LSD is a synthetic compound. Its hallucinogenic properties were discovered by the Swiss chemist Albert Hofmann, but it was made popular by counter-culture figures such as Timothy Leary and Ken Kesey.

· LSD and the other drugs in this class affect serotonergic neurons. They are sympathomimetic drugs as well.

· The psychological effects of these drugs are diverse, but include visual hallucinations, alterations of mood and thought, and dream-like visions.

· Many adverse effects have been linked to LSD and other drugs in this class including acute psychotic reactions (bad trips), flashbacks, and long-term psychological deficits.

· Methylated amphetamines include drugs such as MDA and MDMA (ecstasy). These drugs are sympathomimetic and produce many other effects similar to LSD, but generally do not produce visual hallucinations.

· Anticholinergic hallucinogens include atropine and scopolamine, which are chemicals found in plants such as the deadly nightshade, mandrake, Jimson weed, and henbane. These drugs produce a semi-sleep state characterized by vivid visions and very poor memory for the experience later.

· Phencyclidine (PCP) and ketamine are classified as dissociative anesthetic hallucinogens. They produce a potent intoxication in moderate doses and complete surgical anesthesia with higher doses. Violent psychotic reactions appear to be fairly common with PCP.

References

Abraham, H.D. (1983). Visual phenomenology of the LSD flashback. *Archives of General Psychiatry, 40,* 884–889.

Anderson, E.F. (1980). *Peyote, the divine cactus.* Tucson, Arizona: University of Arizona Press.

Appel, J.B. & Rosecrans, J.A. (1984). Behavioral pharmacology of hallucinogens in animals: Conditioning studies. In B.L. Jacobs (Ed.), *Hallucinogens: Neurochemical, behavioral, and clinical perspectives.* (pp. 77–94). New York: Raven Press.

Barnes, D.M. (1988). New data intensify the agony over ecstasy. *Science, 239,* 864–866.

Boja, J.W. & Schecter, M.D. (1987). Behavioral effects of N-ethyl-3-4-methylenedioxyamphetamine (MDE; "Eve"). *Pharmacology, Biochemistry and Behavior, 28,* 153–156.

Bowers, M.B. (1977). Psychoses precipitated by psychotomimetic drugs: A follow-up study. *Archives of General Psychiatry, 34,* 832–835.

Brecher, E.M. (1972). *Licit and illicit drugs.* Boston: Little, Brown, and Co.

Cohen, M.M. & Marmillo, M.J. (1967). Chromosome damage in human leukocytes induced by lysergic acid diethylamide. *Science, 155,* 1417–1419.

Commins, D.L., Vosmer, G., Virus, R.M., Woolverton, W.L., Schuster, D.R. & Seiden, L.S. (1987). Biochemical and histological evidence that methylenedioxymethylamphetamine (MDMA) is toxic to neurons in the rat brain. *The Journal of Pharmacology and Experimental Therapeutics, 241,* 338–345.

Davis, M. (1987). Mescaline: Excitatory effects on acoustic startle are blocked by serotonin-2 antagonists. *Psychopharmacology, 93,* 286–291.

Davis, W. (1988). *Passage of darkness: The ethnobiology of the Haitian Zombie.* Chapel Hill, North Carolina: University of North Carolina Press.

Davis, W.M., Hatoum, H.T. & Waters, I.W. (1987). Toxicity of MDA (3,4-methylenedioxyamphetamine) considered for relevance to hazards of MDMA (ecstasy) abuse. *Alcohol and Drug Research, 7,* 123–134.

Feldman, H.W., Agar, M.H. & Beschner, G.M. (1979). *Angel dust.* Lexington, Massachusetts: Lexington Books.

Glennon, R.A., Titeler, M., & McKenny, J.D. (1984). Evidence for 5-HT-2 involvement in the mechanism of action of hallucinogenic agents. *Life Science, 35,* 2505–2511.

Grinspoon, L. & Bakalar, J.B. (1979). *Psychedelic drugs reconsidered.* New York: Basic Books.

Grinspoon, L. & Bakalar, J.B. (1983). *Psychedelic reflections.* New York: Human Sciences Press.

Hawks, R.L. & Chiang, C.N. (1986). *Urine testing for drugs of abuse* (NIDA Research Monograph 73). Rockville, Maryland.

Hofmann, A. (1980). *LSD: My problem child.* New York: McGraw-Hill Book Co.

Huxley, A. (1954). *The doors of perception.* New York: Harper.

Jacobs, B.L. (1987). How hallucinogenic drugs work. *American Scientist, 75,* 386–392.

Johnson, M., Letter, A.A., Merchant, K., Hanson, G.R., & Gibb, J.W. (1988). *The Journal of Pharmacology and Experimental Therapeutics, 244,* 977–982.

Kirsch, M.M. (1986). *Designer Drugs,* CompCare Publications: Minneapolis, Minnesota.

Koek, W., Woods, J.H. & Winger, G.D. (1988). MK-801, a proposed noncompetitive antagonist of excitatory amino acid neurotransmission, produces phencyclidine-like behavioral effects in pigeons, rats and rhesus monkeys. *The Journal of Pharmacology and Experimental Therapeutics, 245,* 969–974.

Lewin, L. (1964). *Phantastica—narcotic and stimulating drugs: Their use and abuse.* London: Routledge and Kegan Paul.

Linder, R.L., Lerner, S.E., & Burns, R.S. (1981). *PCP: The devil's dust.* Belmont, California: Wadsworth.

Long, S.Y. (1972). Does LSD induce chromosomal damage and malformations? A review of the literature. *Teratology, 6,* 75–90.

Luisada, P.V. & Brown, B.I. (1976). Clinical management of the phencyclidine psychosis. *Clinical Toxicology, 9,* 539–545.

McCarron, M.M. (1986). Phencycline intoxication. *PharmChem Newsletter, 15-3,* 1–7.

Nichols, D.E. & Glennon, R.A. (1984). Medicinal chemistry and structure-activity relationships of hallucinogens. In B.L. Jacobs (Ed.), *Hallucinogens: Neurochemical, behavioral, and clinical perspectives* (pp. 95–142). New York: Raven Press.

Oberlender, R. & Nichols, D.E. (1988). Drug discrimination studies with MDMA and amphetamine. *Psychopharmacology, 95,* 71–76.

Peroutka, S.J. (1987). Incidence of recreational use of 3,4-methylenedimethoxymethamphetamine (MDMA, "Ecstasy") on an undergraduate campus, *New England Journal of Medicine, 317,* 1542.

Quirion, R., Chicheportiche, R., Contreras, P.C., Johnson, K.M., Lodge, D. Tam, S.W., Woods, J.H., & Zukin, S.R. (1987). Classification and nomenclature of phencyclidine and sigma receptors sites. *Trends in Neurosciences, 10,* 444–446.

Ricaurte, G., Bryan, G., Strauss, L., Seiden, L. & Schuster, C. (1985). Hallucinogenic amphetamine selectively destroys brain serotonin nerve terminals. *Science, 229,* 986–988.

Schmidt, C.J. (1987). Neurotoxicity of the psychedelic amphetamine, methylenedioxymethamphetamine. *The Journal of Pharmacology and Experimental Therapeutics, 240,* 1–7.

Schultes, R.E. (1976). *Hallucinogenic plants.* New York: Golden Press.

Schlieffer, H. (1973). *Sacred narcotic plants of the New World Indians.* New York: Hafner Press.

Siegel, R.K. (1977) Hallucinations. *Scientific American, 237,* 132–140.

Siegel, R.K. (1984). The natural history of hallucinogens. In B.L. Jacobs (Ed.) *Hallucinogens: Neurochemical, behavioral, and clinical perspectives* (pp. 1–19). New York: Raven Press.

Smith, D.E. & Seymour, R.B. (1985). Dream becomes nightmare: Adverse reactions to LSD. *Journal of Psychoactive Drugs, 17,* 297–303.

Stevens, J. (1987). *Storming heaven: LSD and the American dream.* New York: Atlantic Monthly Press.

Stewart, O.C. (1987). *Peyote religion: A history.* Norman, Oklahoma: University of Oklahoma Press.

Stock, S.H. (1986). Synthetic drugs: A history of ups and downs—Part 1. *PharmChem Newsletter, 15-4,* 1–6.

Stock, S.H. (1986). Synthetic drugs: A history of ups and downs—Part 2. *PharmChem Newsletter, 15-5,* 1–6.

Thompson, H.S. (1971). *Fear and loathing in Las Vegas.* New York: Random House.

Titeler, M., Lyon, R.A., & Glennon, R.A. (1988). Radioligand binding evidence implicates the brain 5-HT-2 receptor as a site of action for LSD and phenylisopropylamine hallucinogens. *Psychopharmacology, 94,* 213–216.

Wasson, R.G. (1979). Fly agaric and man. In D.H. Efron, B. Holmstedt, & N.S. Kline (Eds.), *Ethnopharmacologic search for psychoactive drugs.* (pp. 505–514). New York: Raven Press.

Wolfe, T. (1969). *The electric Kool-Aid acid test.* New York: Bantam Books.

Young, T., Lawson, G.W., & Gacono, C.B. (1987). Clinical aspects of phencyclidine (PCP). *The International Journal of the Addictions, 22,* 1–15.

  OTHER PRESCRIPTION
AND OVER-THE-COUNTER
DRUGS

We have discussed the major traditional classes of psychoactive drugs: stimulants, depressants, and hallucinogens. However, there are other drugs of importance with psychoactive properties that do not fit neatly into the categories of earlier chapters. In this chapter we review some of these. We first discuss some significant prescription drugs, including birth control pills and anabolic steroids. Next we consider the wide array of drugs that do not require a prescription to purchase: the over-the-counter drugs. These primarily include analgesics (such as aspirin), antihistamines and other cold and allergy medications, diet pills, and sleeping aids.

OTHER PRESCRIPTION DRUGS

Birth Control Drugs

The first birth control pill became available in the early 1960s, and since that time "the pill" has had a profound impact on our culture. It is probably no accident that the so-called sexual revolution of the late 1960s coincided with the widespread availability of the pill. Today it is estimated that 60 million women worldwide and ten million in the United States use the birth control pill, making it the most widely used form of contraception (Katchadourian, 1989).

The most common form of the birth control pill is the **combination pill** which consists of synthetic forms of two female sex hormones, **progesterone** and **estrogen.** With some forms of the combination pill (multiphasic) the amount of synthetic progesterone or estrogen varies depending on where the woman is in the menstrual cycle. The combination birth control pill works by suppressing ovulation. It is taken daily for twenty-one days, then removed for seven days, during which a period of menstruation should occur. Most birth control pills contain placebo or vitamin pills to be taken during the seven off days to help the woman stay in the habit of taking a pill each day. Used properly the combination pill is the most reliable form of birth control available (other than surgical procedures that are frequently non–reversible) with a failure rate of between 0.5% to 3%, much lower than the alternatives (Katchadourian, 1989—see Table 13–1 and Contemporary Issue Box 13–1). The pill has other advantages over other contraception methods as well. Because it does not require taking precautions just before or after intercourse, it permits more spontaneity than other approaches. A disadvantage of the pill compared to condoms, of course, is that the pill does not prevent the spread of sexually-transmitted disease. In addition, there are a number of side effects of the combination pill.

One of the more serious concerns is the increased risk of blood clots in users of the combination pill. Such blood clots can produce stroke or heart

Combination pill
Birth control pill containing synthetic forms of both female sex hormones: progesterone and estrogen.

Progesterone
(proh-JEST-er-own)
One of the female sex hormones that are involved with the regulation of ovulation and the menstrual cycle.

Estrogen
(ESS-troh-jen)
One of the female sex hormones involved in the regulation of ovulation and the menstrual cycle.

CONTEMPORARY ISSUE BOX 13–1
What Kind of Birth Control Is Best?

Perhaps the question most college women have when reading about the pill is whether it is the best method of contraception. But, it is impossible to evaluate the pill without considering the other available methods. Table 13–1 shows the failure rates for various methods of birth control in typical users. The difference between these various techniques often amount to error in their proper use. Failure is minimized with surgical procedures such as vasectomy. But, in addition to the possible complications of surgery, this procedure may be irreversible. Thus, this procedure is uncommon among young people. Notice that birth control pills are the most effective techniques not requiring surgery. The drawbacks of the pill are the side effects noted in the text. The intra–uterine device (IUD) is also highly effective and is a very popular technique. But the IUD also can produce side effects. The most common are irregular bleeding and pelvic pain. More serious complications are less common but may include greater risk of pelvic inflammatory disease, uterine perforation, and complications if pregnancy should occur when the IUD is in place. There are a variety of "barrier" techniques that are used by women including the diaphragm and the contraceptive sponge. These devices involve blocking the cervical opening and when used with a spermacide produce acceptable failure rates. A disadvantage of these methods is the repeated insertion and removal of the device that some women find problematic.

In the late 1980s the condom gained favor as a method of birth control. The reason is the protection that condoms may provide against sexually transmitted disease. With the current concern about AIDS, condoms should be recommended to most couples. However, unless used properly (and reliably), condoms may have a high failure rate as Table 13–1 shows. As you will also note in Table 13–1, techniques such as withdrawal and rhythm have a common side effect: pregnancy! Then, of course, there is abstinence . . .

---

attacks, and indeed women over forty show an increased risk of heart attack when they take the combination pill. This risk is greatly increased if the woman is also a cigarette smoker. Mood changes, including severe depression, are often reported by women on the pill (it is, after all, a psychoactive drug). Other side effects experienced by some women include high blood

Table 13–1
Comparison of Contraceptive Methods

Method	Failure Rate in Typical Users
Vasectomy	<0.2%
Combination Birth Control Pill	3%
Progestin Only Pill	3%
IUD	6%
Condom	10%
Diaphragm + spermatacide	10%
Condom + spermatacide	5%
Withdrawal	25%
Rhythm, Body Temperature	20–30%
Chance	90%
Abstinence	?

pressure, benign liver tumors, and gall bladder disease, although the risk of these and many other reported side effects is controversial (see Belcastro, 1986, and Crooks & Baur, 1987, for reviews).

In an effort to minimize the side effects due to estrogen, an alternative form of birth control pill has been developed containing only small amounts of synthetic progesterone (progestin). The **progestin pill** is sometimes called the mini–pill. It is thought to work somewhat differently from the combination pill in that it may not always block ovulation. Rather, the major effect of the progestin is to alter the cervical mucus medium in such a way as to block sperm entry. A limitation of the progestin pill is that it is less

Progestin pill
Birth control pill containing only progestin—a synthetic progesterone.

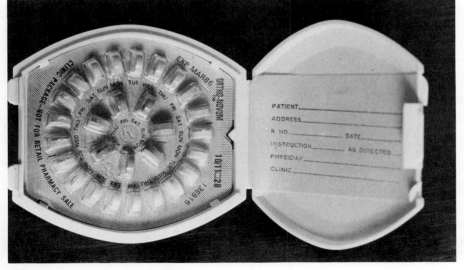

Figure 13–1 Birth control pills.

effective than the combination pill, although it is still more reliable than other reversible methods (see Table 13–1).

When considering the potential side effects of birth control pills and other methods of contraception, it is important to keep things in perspective. Although there are risks associated with use of the pill, they are lower than the risks involved in pregnancy and delivery.

Anabolic Steroids

Anabolic steroids
Tissue-building drugs which produce masculinizing effects as well.

Background   On a sunny September day in Seoul, Korea, the world of sports was changed forever. Ben Johnson ran the 100 meter dash in a time of 9.79 seconds to win the Olympic gold medal and break the world record. Johnson had become the world's fastest human—of all time. Then just two days later, after finding traces of the **anabolic steroid** stanozolol in Johnson's urine sample, he was stripped of his record and his medal and left the games in disgrace. The reverberations in the sports world are still being felt, and perhaps more significantly, Johnson's scandal has opened the eyes of the

Figure 13–2 Ben Johnson won the 100-meter dash in world record time at the 1988 Olympic Games in Seoul, Korea but was stripped of his victory after testing positive for anabolic steroids.

public to a little understood and potentially very dangerous new drug epidemic: steroid abuse.

Anabolic steroids are synthetic drugs resembling the male sex hormone **testosterone.** In addition to its role in determining male sexual characteristics such as facial and chest hair (androgenic or masculinizing effects), testosterone helps build body tissues and repair damaged tissue. Such bodily construction processes are called anabolic effects. These anabolic effects also can be attained by taking synthetic testosterone for certain medical problems, or for improving athletic performance or body-building. The clinical uses for anabolic steroids include treatments for testosterone deficiency, some types of anemia, breast cancer, osteoporosis and arthritis. The efficacy of anabolic steroids in these medical situations is controversial, and the drugs are not extensively used (Colby & Longhurst, 1988). Most commonly, anabolic steroids are obtained illicitly and used for the purpose of body-building or otherwise enhancing athletic performance.

Although most people are becoming aware only recently of the use of anabolic steroids, the drugs, in fact, have been around for a long time. They were first developed in Nazi Germany in the 1930s, allegedly to help create an army of supermen (Marshall, 1988). The first known use of anabolic steroids in athletics is reported to have been by Russian weight-lifters and some female athletes in the early 1950s. By the late 1950s, they were being tested by American athletes as well (Wade, 1972). By the 1968 Olympics, steroids were in widespread use. Consider this testimony given by Harold Connelly, Olympic gold medalist in the hammer throw, before a Senate committee:

> It was not unusual in 1968 to see athletes with their own medical kits, practically a doctor's bag in which they would have syringes and all their various drugs. . . . I know any number of athletes on the 1968 Olympic team who had so much scar tissue and so many puncture holes on their backsides that it was difficult to find a fresh spot to give them a new shot (Hecht, 1985 p. 270).

It was not until 1976 that the International Olympic Committee ruled steroids could not be used by athletes. Urine testing was used to enforce this policy. After that time a great many athletes have tested positive and have been banned from the games, but certainly the Ben Johnson case has been the most notorious.

Estimates on the contemporary use of steroids by athletes vary widely. Olympic hurdler Edwin Moses had this to say about the scene at the 1988 Seoul Olympics: ". . . drug use definitely is rampant. In Seoul we had a community of people ravaged by steroids and other banned substances. My educated guess is that at least 50% of the athletes in the high performance sports such as track and field, cycling, and rowing would be disqualified if they weren't so adept at beating the tests" (Moses, 1988, p. 57). Some estimates place the number of weight-lifters and body-builders who use steroids as high as 90%. Perhaps even more disturbing were the findings of a recent national survey of high school seniors that reported 6.6% of the male stu-

Testosterone
The male sex hormone. Anabolic steroids are basically synthetic versions of testosterone.

dents sampled had taken or were taking steroids. Of those using steroids, just over 47% reported they used them to improve athletic performance, but many (over 26% percent) reported using the drugs for cosmetic benefits (Buckley and others, 1988). Apparently "getting big" has become so important that many young people are willing to take the risk of using steroids to achieve the larger muscles and better definition they believe are associated with these drugs. It appears from the Buckley and others (1988) survey that steroid use is reaching near epidemic proportions, at least among adolescent males. Therefore, we consider in some detail the available data on how steroids work and the side effects that may follow their use.

Actions of anabolic steroids   There are a number of different anabolic steroids including ethylestrenol, methandrostenolone, nandrolone, oxandrolone, ometholone, and stanozolol (brand names Dianabol, Anaver, and Winstrol). These drugs may be taken orally or injected (see Table 13–2). In the Buckley study, 38% of the steroid users reported injecting steroids, while the remainder took the drugs only orally. The metabolization and elimination of steroids is quite variable. Steroids can be detected reliably in urine for between four and fourteen days after use, but there are reports of positive urine tests as long as thirteen months after use of nandrolone (Marshall, 1988).

Table 13–2

Anabolic Steroids (from Keenan, 1988)

Drug	Trade Name	Administration
Ethylestrenol	Maxibolin	oral
Methandrostenolone	Dianabol	oral
Oxandrolone	Anavar	oral
Stanozolol	Winstrol	oral
Nandrolone	Androlone, Durabolin Nandrolin	injection
Methandriol	Anabol, Durabolic, Methabolic, Steribolic	injection

One of the most ironic features of the widespread use of steroids among athletes is that medical researchers have had great difficulty determining whether they produce performance benefits. It is clear that at puberty male testes increase testosterone output resulting in the increase in muscle mass and strength characteristic of males at that age. However, this does not necessarily mean supplemental testosterone would result in further gains in a normal male. There have been a number of studies of the effects of anabolic steroids on weight gain, strength, and performance. Some of these have shown improvement in subjects taking steroids, but others have not (Lamb, 1983). Even in the studies where enhanced performance is shown, the

Figure 13–3 Do they or don't they? Only their pharmacist knows for sure.

effects were generally rather small. Yet athletes persist in believing anabolic steroid regimens (combined with training) increase lean muscle mass, strength, and other measures of performance. Performances such as that of Ben Johnson and physiques such as the ones shown in Figure 13–3 tend to support those claims. Why then have the body–building effects of steroids been so difficult to demonstrate in laboratory studies? Lamb (1983) suggests that the reason is that the doses used in laboratory studies are much lower than those actually used by athletes and body-builders. As Lamb pointed out, researchers are unable to administer higher doses because of the risks it poses to their subjects. Indeed athletes who take high doses of anabolic steroids may be paying a high price for the enhanced performance.

Side effects of anabolic steroids There are a number of physical side effects associated with anabolic steroid use. Perhaps the most commonly reported are acne, balding, and reduced sexual desire. In men, there is often atrophy of the testes and a related decline in sperm count and enlargement of the breasts. It seems ironic but many male steroid users have to take special drugs to prevent breast growth! These effects are usually reversible. In females, there are pronounced masculinizing effects from steroid use, and many of these effects are irreversible. They include growth of facial and chest hair, baldness, deepening of the voice, breast shrinkage, clitoral enlargement, and menstrual irregularities. Another cause for concern is that steroid use often results in changes in cholesterol levels that may increase the risk of heart disease. Damage to liver function is also common and can include an increased risk of liver cancer (Colby & Longhurst, 1988; Hecht, 1985; Keenan, 1988; Lamb, 1983). In addition, when children and adolescents use steroids premature bone fusion can occur, causing stunted growth. Alteration of normal pubertal development is also a risk in young people. Cause for alarm exists in the finding of Buckley and others (1988) that more than 4% of their sample began using steroids at sixteen years of age or younger.

In addition to the physical side effects of steroids, a number of psychological effects of these drugs exist. Most users report a mild euphoria during periods of steroid use, and increased energy levels also are noted. Less desirable are reports of increased irritability and aggressiveness, sometimes leading to violent behavior. Mood swings and even psychotic reactions have been reported. Pope and Katz (1988) reported a study of forty-one bodybuilders and football players who had used steroids. Nine of the subjects (22%) experienced emotional disturbance associated with steroid use, and five (12%) developed psychotic reactions during their steroid regimens. One of the subjects studied deliberately drove a car into a tree at 40 mph. Another described becoming irritated at a driver in front of him who had left his blinker on. At the first stoplight, he jumped out of his car and punched out the other car's windshield!

The use of steroids by athletes will continue as long as athletes believe their competition is using them. Better testing methods are needed, but perhaps more important would be regular tests. The current procedures allow athletes to discontinue the drugs prior to an important event in order to avoid a positive urine test. A hopeful development is the announcement by the United States and Soviet Union in early 1989 that a reciprocal random testing procedure would be developed so potential Olympic athletes from both countries would be subject to random tests at any time. Such procedures could reduce cheating sharply. But what of the thousands of young men (and women) who are *not* Olympic-caliber athletes and who are taking steroids to improve their performance at the high school or college level or just to "get big"? Steroids may represent one of the major drug abuse problems facing the country today, and most drug education programs do not even discuss them. Clearly there is a need to make the public aware of the potential dangers of steroid abuse.

OVER-THE-COUNTER-DRUGS

About Over-The-Counter Drugs

The Federal Food and Drug Administration (FDA) divides drugs into two categories: those requiring a prescription from a physician to purchase (such as the psychiatric drugs discussed in Chapter 9, and the birth control pills and anabolic steroids just described), and those considered safe enough to dispense without a prescription. These drugs are often referred to as over-the-counter (OTC) drugs. The FDA was charged by the 1962 Kefauver-Harris amendment with regulating and reviewing OTC drugs, no small task when you consider there were over 300,000 products on the market! Rather than focus on specific brands, the FDA has organized the ingredients found in these products, and divided them into the categories shown in Table 13–3. As shown a wide range of ailments is treated by OTC drugs. The FDA created panels to study these ingredients and to evaluate them on two major criteria: safety and efficacy. The panel's final reports were presented in 1985; then those drugs authorized as OTC drugs must meet the standard of "Generally Recognized as Safe" or GRAS, and "Generally Recognized as Effective" or GRAE. Drugs not meeting these criteria are removed from OTC products. However, it should be noted that safety and efficacy are relative terms. Some OTC drugs can be hazardous, and some are of very limited efficacy.

Table 13–3
FDA Classification of OTC Drugs

1. Antacids	9. Laxatives	17. Emetics
2. Antidiarrheal products	10. Antiemetics	18. Antiperspirants
3. Sunscreens	11. Vitamin and mineral products	19. Antimicrobials
4. Dandruff products	12. Oral hygiene products	20. Hemorrhoidal products
5. Bronchodilators	13. Analgesics	21. Sedatives and sleep aids
6. Stimulants	14. Antitussives	22. Allergy drugs
7. Cold remedies	15. Eye products	23. Contraceptive products
8. Skin preparations	16. Dental products	24. Weight control products

In addition to reviewing the ingredients of OTC drugs, some of the FDA panels reviewed prescription drugs and, on the grounds that some were relatively safe and effective, recommended they be made available without prescription. The pain reliever ibuprofen and some antihistamines, such as diphenhydramine, are examples of drugs previously available only by prescription. They are available now over the counter.

Of the many categories of drugs noted in Table 13–3 we focus on those with psychoactive properties—analgesics, diet pills, cold and allergy medications, stimulants, and sedatives.

Figure 13–4 Over-the-counter drugs.

Analgesics

In Chapter 10 we discussed the use of opiate drugs in the treatment of pain. But the use of opiates for pain relief is usually reserved for severe cases. Many effective pain-killers are available over the counter. The most widely known and used is aspirin. **Acetylsalicylic acid** (aspirin) is closely related to a chemical found in the bark of the willow and other trees (salicylic acid). Willow bark was used in the treatment of painful conditions and fever by the ancient Greeks and by Native Americans. Salicylic acid was isolated and used as a pain reliever in Europe, but it causes severe stomach distress. It was not until the late nineteenth century that acetylsalicylic acid was synthesized and named aspirin by the Bayer company of Germany. Aspirin has come to be one of the most important drugs known to medicine. It is marketed under the brand names Anacin, Bufferin, and Excedrin to name just a few, and more than ten thousand tons of aspirin are consumed every year (Julien, 1988).

Aspirin is analgesic (produces pain relief without unconsciousness), anti-pyretic (reduces fever), and anti-inflammatory (reduces swelling). It is thought to accomplish these effects by a mechanism quite different from opiate analgesia. Aspirin (and other OTC pain-killers) act by blocking the production and release of **prostaglandins,** chemicals that are released by the body at sites of pain. These chemicals are thought to enhance certain kinds of pain—dull pain and aches, such as headache. Indeed, aspirin is not very effective with sharp pains or with stomach pain. It is however very effective with muscle aches, headaches, and soreness due to inflammation such as arthritis (Grogan, 1987).

Acetylasalicylic acid
(ah-SEAT-ill-sal-iss-ill-ik)
Chemical name for aspirin.

Prostaglandins
(pross-tah-GLAND-inz)
Naturally occuring chemicals blocked by aspirin and related analgesics.

Aspirin is not without some adverse effects though. It causes stomach irritation and bleeding and is contraindicated in persons who have stomach problems. Aspirin may be related to a rare and dangerous disease called Reye syndrome. Reye syndrome occurs only in children treated with aspirin for flu or chickenpox, and involves severe vomiting, disorientation, and sometimes, coma, brain damage, or death. Thus aspirin should be avoided by children with these diseases. Aspirin is also an anticoagulant and may prolong bleeding under certain circumstances. However, this same mechanism may be useful in the prevention of strokes and heart attacks (Steering Committee of the Physicians Health Study Research Group, 1988).

An effective analgesic drug useful for people with stomach problems is **acetaminophen.** This drug, marketed under brand names such as Datril and Tylenol, reduces fever and produces analgesic effects, but does not cause stomach irritation. However, acetaminophen is not a potent anti-inflammatory drug, and in high doses may cause liver problems. It is worth noting that an overdose of acetaminophen is a more serious problem than one with aspirin. Both drugs are leading causes of poisonings in children. As few as ten Extra–Strength Tylenol can be lethal to a child (Grogan, 1987). It is important to keep these and all drugs out of the reach of children.

Acetaminophen
(ah-seat-ah-MIN-ah-fen)
Aspirin-like analgesic.

Finally, the newest OTC pain-killer is **ibuprofen,** which had been exclusively a prescription drug (Motrin) until 1984. Now it is marketed under brand names such as Advil and Nuprin. Ibuprofen has effects similar to aspirin but it is more potent and is already a big seller.

Ibuprofen
(ih-BYOU-proh-fen)
Aspirin-like analgesic.

Appetite Suppressants

We discussed in Chapter 5 the use of amphetamines and related drugs in weight control. There are dozens of OTC preparations taken to suppress appetite. Some are essentially high-fiber or some type of food replacement low in calories. Others (Dexatrim, Appedrine) contain an anorectic drug called **phenylpropanolamine** or PPA (often in combination with caffeine). Often an ingredient in "look-alike" stimulant pills (see Contemporary Issue Box 13–2), PPA has a chemical structure similar to amphetamine. It is only a mild stimulant and does not produce euphoria. It does have anorectic properties, but it has not been demonstrated to be effective in long-term weight control (Grogan, 1987).

Phenylpropanolamine
(feen-ill-proh-pan-OH-lah-meen)
A mild stimulant with decongestant and appetite suppressant properties (PPA).

PPA also serves as a decongestant and is found in OTC cold and allergy medication. PPA also has a number of undesirable side effects, such as elevated blood sugar levels, hypertension, heart palpitations, rapid heart beat, insomnia, headache, nausea, and anxiety. Geraldine Ferraro, who ran for vice president of the United States in 1984, testified on OTC diet pills before the House of Representatives Subcommittee on Health and Long-Term Care (cited in Hallowell, 1987, p. 133). Ferraro, referring to her use of diet pills to lose weight, said:

> I can recall . . . my heart started beating very fast and I cleaned my house as if I was . . . the white tornado . . . I'd be up very early in the morning and I couldn't

CONTEMPORARY ISSUE BOX 13–2
Side Effects from Over-the-Counter Drugs?

OTC drugs are so widely used in our society that most of us do not think of them as drugs. We walk into the supermarket or convenience store and buy cold or pain medication without really recognizing we are buying potent psychoactive drugs. Yet these drugs can produce side effects. There simply is no drug that is completely safe. As noted earlier, even drugs as innocuous as aspirin and acetaminophen can be toxic if taken in overdose levels.

Some OTC drugs may possess abuse potential as well. For example, appetite suppressants such as PPA are potent enough stimulants that they are frequent ingredients (usually along with caffeine) in "look-alike" stimulant preparations. Look-alike drugs are made to closely resemble a controlled substance, usually a prescription amphetamine, but actually contain only OTC products. Such look-alikes often are misrepresented as amphetamine, and sold on the street. These compounds may be taken in high enough doses that dangerous side effects occur.

Finally, some OTC drugs, particularly antihistamines used in cold preparations or sleeping aids cause fatigue and may potentiate the effects of alcohol or other depressant drugs. These sedatives should not be taken in combination with other drugs, and driving should be avoided after exposure to them.

sleep at night . . . I decided I didn't want to become a nervous wreck, so I stopped taking them . . . and immediately . . . the symptoms stopped.

Thus, PPA side effects can cause some relatively severe problems. In view of the limited effectiveness of OTC diet preparations and their potential for causing problems, some criticize the FDA's approval of PPA preparations (such as, Grogan, 1987).

Cold and Allergy Medication

The common cold is common enough that its victims spend 1.3 billion dollars on OTC cold remedies in the United States every year. OTC cold and allergy medications contain a variety of different ingredients. These include analgesics, such as aspirin or acetaminophen, which are of value in reducing aches, pain, and fever. In addition, many OTC cold preparations include PPA because of its decongestant properties. An alternative decongestant is **pseudoephedrine** (Sudafed), which is as effective as PPA but has fewer

Pseudoephedrine
(soo-doh-eff-EHD-rin)
An OTC decongestant.

side effects. Cold remedies also may include expectorants which help to break up phlegm so that it may be coughed up. **Guaifenesin** is the most common expectorant. **Antitussive** agents actually suppress coughing and are often included in cold and cough formulations (dextromethorphan is an example).

Other common ingredients in OTC cold and allergy preparations are **antihistamines.** These compounds actually are more effective in the treatment of hay fever and related allergic reactions. Many allergic symptoms are caused by the release of a naturally occurring chemical called histamine. As the name suggests, antihistamines act by blocking histamine. Commonly used antihistamines include diphenhydramine and chlorpheniramine maleate. However, antihistamines produce a number of side effects limiting their usefulness. Drowsiness and fatigue are probably the most significant. It can be very hard to stay awake after taking antihistamines, and in fact, diphenhydramine is the major ingredient in most OTC sleeping aids. Other side effects include thickening of mucus secretions, blurred vision, dizziness, dry mouth and nose, and sweating (Grogan, 1987).

Guaifenesin
(guay-FEN-eh-sin)
An OTC expectorant.

Antitussives
Cough suppressant drugs.

Antihistamines
Common OTC drugs with decongestant effects.

OTC Stimulants and Sedatives

We already have discussed the ingredients in OTC stimulants. They are basically caffeine and/or PPA. OTC stimulants include popular brands such as No-Doz and Vivarin. They certainly will induce mild central nervous system stimulation, but one No-Doz, for example, contains about as much caffeine as a cup of coffee, so the user should expect about that effect. More information on the side effects of caffeine is in Chapter 6.

As we noted, the major ingredient in OTC sleeping aids is an antihistamine, diphenhydramine. Because fatigue is a common side effect of antihistamines, they sometimes can help people suffering from insomnia. However, other side effects associated with antihistamines (for instance, dry mouth, dizziness, and nausea) may limit their use as sleeping aids. In addition, the problems associated with using prescription sleeping pills may apply to these drugs too, as discussed in Chapter 8.

SUMMARY

- The combination birth control pill consists of synthetic versions of the two female sex hormones, estrogen and progesterone.

- Although highly effective at reducing risk of pregnancy, the birth control pill has been linked to a number of side effects, including increased risk of heart attack and stroke.

- Anabolic steroids are generally synthetic versions of the male sex hormone testosterone, and are used to promote the development of muscle mass and enhance athletic performance.

- Side effects associated with anabolic steroids include masculinizing effects in women, liver real:

damage, acne, hair loss, and emotional disturbance.

- Three major analgesic drugs are available without prescription: aspirin, acetaminophen, and ibuprofen.

- Aspirin relieves pain, reduces fever, and is also anti–inflammatory. Its side effects include stomach irritation and bleeding. The effects of ibuprofen are similar.

- Acetaminophen is also a potent analgesic drug, but it lacks the anti–inflammatory effects of aspirin. However, it also is less likely to cause stomach irritation.

- Phenylpropanolamine (PPA) is a drug used in over-the-counter appetite suppressants and cold preparations.

- Other ingredients of non-prescription cold and allergy medications include pseudoephedrine, guaifenesin, dextromethorphan, and antihistamines.

- The antihistamine compound diphenhydramine also is used as the major ingredient in non-prescription sleeping pills.

References

Belcastro, P.A. (1986). *The birth control book,* Boston: Jones & Bartlett Inc.

Buckley, W.E., Yesalis, C.E., Friedl, K.E., Anderson, W.A., Streit, A.L. & Wright, J.E. (1988). Estimated prevalence of anabolic steroid use among male high school seniors. *Journal of the American Medical Association, 260,* 3441–3445.

Colby, H.D. and Longhurst, P.A. (1988). Fate of anabolic steroids in the body. In J.A. Thomas (Ed.), *Drugs, athletes and physical performance* (pp. 11–30). New York: Plenum Press.

Crooks, R. & Baur, K. (1987). *Our sexuality* (Third Ed.). Menlo Park CA: Benjamin/Cummings Co.

Grogan, F.J. (1987). *The pharmacist's prescription.* New York: Rawson Associates.

Hallowell, C. (1987). Ordinary medicines can have extraordinary side effects. *Redbook, 169,* 132–134; 156–157.

Hecht, A. (1985). *Addictive behavior: Drug and alcohol abuse.* Englewood, CO: Morton Publishing Co.

Katchadourian, H.A. (1989). *Fundamentals of human sexuality* (Fifth ed.). New York: Holt, Rinehart and Winston.

Keenan, E.J. (1988). Anabolic and androgenic steroids. In J.A. Thomas (Ed.), *Drugs, athletes, and physical performance* (pp. 91–103). New York: Plenum Press.

Lamb, D.R. (1983). Anabolic steroids. In M.H. Williams (Ed.), *Ergogenic aids in sport* (pp. 164–182). Champaign, IL: Human Kinetics Publishers.

Marshall, E. (1988). The drug of champions. *Science, 242,* 183–184.

Moses, E. (1988). An athlete's Rx for the drug problem. *Newsweek,* October 10, p. 57.

Pope, H.G. Jr. & Katz, D.L. (1988). Affective and psychotic symptoms associated with anabolic steroid use. *The American Journal of Psychiatry, 145,* 487–490.

Steering Committee of the Physicians' Health Study Research Group (1988). Preliminary report: Findings from the aspirin component of the ongoing Physicians' Health Study. *New England Journal of Medicine, 318,* 262–264.

Wade, N. (1972). Anabolic steroids: Doctors denounce them, but athletes aren't listening. *Science, 176,* 1399–1403.

14 SOCIAL AND PERSONALITY FACTORS IN SUBSTANCE USE

Microenvironmental
Term used to describe environmental factors specific to the immediate drug use context, such as lighting, music, others present, and the like.

Macroenvironmental
Term used to describe environmental factors that are widespread and thus operate on a broad scale, such as culture, urbanization, and legal guidelines regarding drug use.

As you have observed in previous chapters, a number of drugs exist that are used by a variety of individuals for a wide range of reasons. Further, drug use can result in a variety of consequences—some positive, others negative. What is it that contributes to all of this variation? In this chapter we address this question in part by focusing on a number of individual and environmental factors influencing drug use (see Table 14–1). "Individual factors" refer to person-specific factors such as personality style and the person's beliefs about drugs and their effects. Environmental factors—that is, influences in the environment and thus "outside" the individual—will be discussed on two levels. The first level, called the **microenvironment,** includes parts of the immediate environment, such as the drug use setting or context, and who else is present. The second level, called the **macroenvironment,** includes aspects of the environment affecting whole populations of individuals at once. This includes governmental sanctions and guidelines and cultural influences. In this way, you will develop a sense of the factors—some obvious, others not—influencing drug use on several levels.

Table 14–1

Levels of Factors that Can Influence Alcohol and Drug Use Patterns

Individual Factors

Person–specific influences, such as personality and expectations regarding alcohol/drug effects.

Microenvironmental Factors

Influences operating in a specific drug use setting, such as who else is present and type of music being played.

Macroenvironmental Factors

Broad–based influences affecting a number of persons simultaneously, such as cultural teachings, laws regarding drinking age, advertising, and taxation policies.

INDIVIDUAL FACTORS

Individual factors refer to a person's unique characteristics. These characteristics are sometimes referred to as "individual differences." In this section, the focus will be on two important topics within the category of individual factors. The first factors to be considered are personality factors, and the second factors are expectations (or beliefs) regarding drug use and drug use effects.[1]

---

[1]Another individual factor, of course, is the person's genetic make-up. This topic is discussed most frequently in the context of alcohol abuse, where genetic influences have been related to alcoholism (especially among males). This topic was addressed in greater detail in Chapter 7.

Personality Factors

As you may recall from Chapter 4, personality is a term used to represent a cluster of traits or characteristics describing the ways in which an individual thinks, perceives, feels, and acts. These characteristics are thought to be fairly constant, although variations may occur when the person acts in different situations. Nevertheless, personality characteristics are for the most part viewed as enduring.

One frequently heard idea in discussions on drug use and personality is that of the **"addictive personality,"** or in the case of alcoholism, the "alcoholic personality." This refers to the idea a personality structure common to all substance abusers exists. Such a theory has appeal. After all, if abusers of a particular substance were a homogeneous group, it theoretically would be easier to understand or change the drug use patterns of that group. Unfortunately, there are significant individual differences among drug abusers. Further, research has not provided strong support for the "drug abuser personality" hypothesis. One team of researchers concluded in its assessment of this research that "there does not exist a modicum of hope for the notion of an addictive personality" (Pihl & Spiers, 1978, p. 162).

Addictive personality The notion there exists a clustering of traits common to persons who engage in addictive behaviors, such as drug abuse and alcoholism.

Does that mean personality is not a variable of interest in understanding drinking and drug use? Not at all. It means only that personality *alone* does not adequately explain drug use among people. Personality characteristics, however, do play an important role in the process of drug use when those characteristics are viewed in combination with environmental variables (see, for example, Galizio & Maisto, 1985).

An example can be seen in the work of Jessor and his colleagues. These investigators, as part of a larger investigation (see Jessor & Jessor, 1977), were interested in (a) understanding what characteristics discriminated marijuana users from nonusers and (b) determining what characteristics discriminated continuing nonusers from those who later began marijuana use. In their studies (Jessor, 1976; Jessor, Jessor, & Finney, 1973), junior high school and senior high school students were initially surveyed on their drug usage. Measures also were included to assess (1) aspects of personality (for example, values regarding achievement and independence, alienation, attitude toward deviance, religiosity); (2) the ways in which students perceived their environments (for example, compatibility between values of their friends and parents, parental versus friend support, friends' versus parental approval of drug use); and (3) other behavior (for example, church attendance, school grades, engaging in other behaviors viewed as socially deviant).

In the first phase of their project, the investigators compared marijuana users with marijuana nonusers. They found consistent support for the hypothesis that these two groups would differ in all of the principal areas described above. For example, marijuana users were found to value achievement less and independence more than nonusers. Users also were more tolerant of deviance, were less religious, perceived lower rates of compatibility between views of peers and parents, valued peer influence more, and perceived a greater degree of pressure to use drugs and greater peer approval for the drug use. Further, users, relative to the nonusers, were less likely to attend church, more likely to engage in social criticism (for example, protests), and more likely to have engaged in other socially disapproved behaviors. These findings were true for both male and female students.

In the second part of the study, the students were reinterviewed yearly for the next two years. As a result of this follow-up, it was possible to identify which students remained marijuana nonusers and which shifted from nonuser to user status between testings. These two groups were then compared. Not surprisingly, the students who had shifted from nonuser to user status now presented characteristics more similar to those of the marijuana users noted above. For example, those who shifted to use, when compared to those who remained nonusers, described a lower valuation of achievement, greater valuation of independence, less religiosity, greater degree of friend versus parental influence, more peer acceptance of drug use, and more deviant behavior generally. Nonusers, on the other hand, showed a pattern that might be described as more socially conforming or conventional.

The Jessor and Jessor research demonstrates that personality variables, along with other factors, such as peer, familial, and sociocultural influences, together can shed considerable light on some of the processes associated with drug use. This information would not have been derived from looking at only one type of variable. An implication of Jessor and Jessor's work, and one which they emphasize, is that transition to marijuana use can be viewed in the framework of "transition proneness." Thus, the likelihood of shifting toward marijuana use appears to be associated with shifts in attitudes and perceptions that are, relatively speaking, more "nontraditional" or "nonconventional." Such a pattern also has been found in a study on variables influencing onset of drinking among high school students (Jessor & Jessor, 1975).

Before leaving the area of personality factors, note that several longitudinal studies have been conducted to find which traits characterize young men who later became alcoholics. Typically, in these studies a group of people is followed over an extended period of time (in some cases over twenty years, although they may have been contacted only a few times). Those followed up are then divided into two groups—those who became alcoholic and those who did not—and studied to see if they were different in particular ways when they were younger. The logic is that we will be in a better position to prevent alcoholism if we can identify early on those at risk for becoming alcoholic. A listing of several general characteristics found among young men who were later identified as alcoholic is shown in Table 14–2. It should be re-emphasized that the presence of these charcteristics alone does not efficiently predict later alcohol problems among men. Instead,

Table 14–2

A Sampling of Some General Characteristics of Young Men Who Later Became Alcoholic

Nonconforming
Over-confident
Self-centered
Rebellious
Overtly hostile
Impulsive
Talkative and gregarious
Socially aggressive
Overly expressive
Self-indulgent
Low inhibition
Need for personal power

Based on longitudinal studies conducted by Jones (1968), Loper, Kammeier, and Hoffman (1973), and McCord, McCord, & Gudeman (1960), and reviews by Barnes (1979) and Cox (1986). The characteristics listed are relative to groups of individuals who later did not exhibit alcohol problems.

these characteristics in combination with other environmental variables (such as stressful situations, peer influences, family history, and so on) together may increase the likelihood of alcohol abuse.

Much less longitudinal research exists on women who later became alcohol abusers. One study, by Jones (1971), followed a sample of women over an extended period of time and assessed their drinking behavior. Jones found that the women who were the heaviest drinkers had in common a history of social competence and an adeptness at manipulating people. In addition, these heavy drinkers had as adolescents been described as power-oriented, content, and self-indulgent.

Comparable studies, fewer in number, have also been conducted to assess the personalities of drug abusers (predominantly males) before the onset of those problems. Except for drug users' tendency to have been impulsive, adventurous, and socially skilled at an early age (for example, Goldstein & Sappington, 1977), they did not differ considerably from those who did not later become drug users or abusers (see Pihl & Spiers, 1978). Again, personality style in conjunction with environmental influences, such as the peer group, together appear the more likely and powerful determinants of subsequent drug use and abuse.

Drug Expectancies and Beliefs

A second type of individual factor to be considered is what a person expects to achieve or happen when using a drug. This anticipation is referred to as a **drug expectancy.** A person's expectancies are based on

Drug expectancy
What a person expects to occur as a function of drug use.

previous experiences regarding a given psychoactive substance and its effects. These experiences could have been direct (that is, the person has experience in actually using the substance) or indirect (that is, the person has been exposed to the substance and its effects through friends' use, television, advertising, reading, and so on). Expectancies can be an important variable in understanding drug use because these expectations can influence decisions to use a drug.

Most of the research in this area has been conducted on alcohol use. In one early work, by MacAndrew and Edgerton (1969), it was suggested that what people have learned and believe about alcohol is an important determinant in how they conduct themselves while drinking. Thus, what people *expect* to happen when they drink can be an important factor in determining their response to the alcohol consumed. In some cases this may be more influential than alcohol's pharmacological action. Researchers have investigated alcohol-related expectancies by conducting studies (using the balanced placebo design; see Chapters 4 and 7) in which some participants are told they are drinking alcohol but actually receive a nonalcoholic beverage. A summary of such research (Hull & Bond, 1986) shows expectancy effects appear more likely to occur when the behavior being studied is proscribed from free expression. Examples include aggression, sexual arousal, and humor. Thus, it would be predicted that people who believe alcohol fosters aggression or enhances sexual arousal would experience those effects, but largely because they expect that result than because of any specific pharmacological effect of the alcohol.

Expectancies appear to have a considerable effect on the way people respond to other drugs as well. The use of marijuana is a good example. The person who anticipates a relaxed, "mellow" feeling is more likely to experience that result than the person who anxiously anticipates some type of drug-induced "loss of control." In part this relates to the ways the various sensations produced by the marijuana are interpreted or understood by the smoker. The same sensation might be interpreted positively by one user but negatively by another. Many of the discrepancies can be attributed to what the user expected to occur prior to using marijuana.

In summary, we see that drug use can vary as a function of personality and individual beliefs and/or expectancies regarding the effects of the substance. We have also seen the explanatory power of these variables is increased when they are used together with other information, such as setting and other environmental influences. More details on these environmental factors are provided in the next two sections.

MICROENVIRONMENTAL INFLUENCES

We focus first on the immediate environment, or what has been referred to as the microenvironment (or, alternatively, the microsetting). As defined by McCarty (1985), the microenvironment includes the following:

(1) the physical environment, including such influences as size of the room and its location
(2) attributes of the setting, including music, lighting, temperature, wall hangings, cost of drinks, and furnishings
(3) companions or coparticipants, which refer to who else is there and the relationship of those persons to the drinker or drug user
(4) the user's individual characteristics, such as personality and expectations, which he/she brings into the microsetting, and
(5) the interaction among these variables

We highlight the influences of several of these variables, especially setting attributes and the presence and behavior of others in the drinking or drug use environment. These elements play an important part in defining the context for substance abuse.

Setting attributes are most evident in barroom environments. The strongest finding about drinking in a bar is: the longer the time spent in the bar, the greater the amount of alcohol consumed (see McCarty, 1985). As a result, bar owners will make efforts to attract patrons, and keep them around once they are there. "Happy hours," free appetizers, and reduced drink prices are all efforts to initially attract customers. Once there, a number of setting factors come into play which can affect drinking behavior. For example, bartenders and waiters/waitresses encourage drinking by the rate at which they ask if they can provide refills. Lighted signs and posters serve to encourage the consumption of one brand of alcohol over another. Musical entertainment also plays an important role. Babor, Mendelson, Uhly, and Souza (1980) observed drinkers at a tavern on evenings in which a football game was shown on television versus evenings when a "sing-along" piano bar was operated. They found that patrons drank more and spent more time drinking when the piano bar was operating. Further, the pace of the music may be an important setting influence, at least with some forms of music. Bach and Schaffer (1979) studied the drinking rate of patrons listening to country-western music in several western Montana bars. They found patrons drank faster when slower tempo music was being played. On the flip side, slower drinking rates were associated with faster tempo music. McCarty (1985) speculates patrons may find themselves more involved when faster music is playing and as a result are distracted somewhat from drinking.

The type of drinking setting also can influence alcohol consumption and the effects of alcohol. Kalin, McClelland, and Kahn (1965) found male social drinkers were more aggressive, less anxious, and less conscious of time at a fraternity party than at a business discussion group where alcohol was served. Relatedly, Kalin (1972) found drinkers consumed less alcohol at a classroom gathering than at a gathering at a private apartment. In another study, Pliner and Cappell (1974) investigated people drinking alcohol either alone or in a social setting. They found subjects drinking alcohol in a group were more friendly, less unhappy, less bored, and more euphoric

Figure 14–1 What individual and environmental factors do you think are contributing to the behavior of the people in these two drinking settings?

than grouped subjects consuming a placebo (nonalcoholic) beverage. In the case of the placebo beverage, subjects were told they were drinking alcohol but actually received a nonalcoholic beverage. On the other hand, subjects who drank alcohol alone described themselves as thinking less clearly and dizzier than the solitary placebo subjects. Thus, given a moderate dose of alcohol, grouped drinkers seem to describe more affective consequences of alcohol than solitary drinkers, who tend to report their state in terms of physical symptoms.

Other environmental influences can affect drinking behavior and alcohol effects. Rosenbluth, Nathan, and Lawson (1978) observed male and female drinkers at a college tavern. They found that males drank more than females and that more alcohol was consumed in groups than in dyads. The males and the drinkers in groups also consumed their alcohol faster. It is likely that the presence of other drinkers in this setting strongly affected drinking behavior. A large body of research, summarized by Collins and Marlatt (1981), suggests that normal drinkers exposed to a drinking partner who drinks heavily tend to consume more alcohol than when the drinking partner is drinking less. That is, drinkers appear to follow the lead of their drinking partner.

The fact that a person is drinking in a setting also can affect others' perceptions of him or her. Wilson, Perold, and Abrams (1981) found in an experimental situation that when male social drinkers were led to believe that a female accomplice had consumed alcohol before their interaction the males were less anxious than drinkers not given such information. An accomplice works for the experimenter and is unknown to the subject. The female accomplice who ostensibly had consumed alcohol also was rated by the males as more personally attractive and less anxious than when no information was provided about her. Such changes in person perception were also noted by Connors and Sobell (1986). An accomplice who was identified as "intoxicated" and acted accordingly was judged by the subject as more friendly, admirable, and responsive, and less cold and reserved than when the accomplice acted "sober."

These influences appear important among users of other substances as well. The presence of others smoking cigarettes often is implicated in a smoker's decision to light up a cigarette in that situation (Foss, 1973; Glad & Adesso, 1976). Carlin, Bakker, Halpern, and Post (1972) noted that at lower doses of marijuana, smokers viewed others in the setting as more intoxicated than they actually were. To enhance or diminish the degree of reported marijuana intoxication experimenters had an accomplice act "up" or "down." Setting was not as influential at higher doses of marijuana. Studies such as these support an influential 1963 work by Becker, who discussed the "making" of a marijuana user. Becker described this as a sociocultural process in which experienced users essentially "teach" new users what to anticipate, how to interpret the effects, what effects to enjoy, and what effects to ignore.

Taken together, these studies emphasize that parts of what contributes to an experienced or observed drug effect can be found outside the person and in the immediate environment. Indeed, some think these microenvironmental factors are the central determinant of much of the drug experience that drug users describe. Nevertheless, it seems the most useful perspective for

Figure 14-2 A variety of social and setting factors can affect the marijuana experience.

now is that a range of individual and environmental variables interact in determining drug responses. Another, broader domain of environmental factors is described below.

MACROENVIRONMENTAL INFLUENCES

We use the term macroenvironmental to encompass those environmental factors operating on a broad scale. These factors can be divided into the two categories of governmental factors and social factors.

Governmental Factors

There are a number of governmental policies and regulations affecting drug use. One of the most basic influences is the financial cost. In the case of alcohol, for example, taxes are a major determinant in the overall price of alcohol to the consumer. In fact, state and federal taxes (plus various other miscellaneous fees imposed) account for approximately half the price paid for spirits in the United States and about twenty percent of the price for beer and wine (Cook, 1981). The price of alcohol can affect alcohol consumption rates, because alcohol use generally is **price elastic.** This

Price elastic
Refers to the finding for some substances that changes in price are inversely related to the demand for the substance.

CONTEMPORARY ISSUE BOX 14–1
Alcohol Advertising

Did you know the alcohol beverage industry spends over $1 billion yearly on advertising? Such activity represents another environmental influence affecting all of us. How many different forms of alcohol advertising can you think of? A short list would include television and radio commercials, magazine advertisements, billboards, neon signs and posters in bars, and glassware containing the logo of a particular brand. Other examples of advertising include hiring a well-known figure to endorse a brand and arranging for actors in a movie to be seen drinking a particular brand.

Does alcohol advertising work? Does it influence your thinking about drinking? The beverage industry is convinced their efforts to encourage drinking do work. The data are not clear-cut, but it is true that the amounts of money spent on advertising go up yearly. The extent to which advertising directly contributes to drinking, however, is subject to debate. Nevertheless, we are not likely to see any decrease in expenditures for advertising.

A postscript of note is that groups wishing to encourage safe uses of alcohol have been turning more and more to advertising to communicate their messages. These efforts have included public service announcements, commercials, and billboards. The general themes have been avoiding drinking and driving, drinking responsibly when you do drink, and avoiding drinking when pregnant. And even alcohol producers are infusing this message into some of their advertising. One beverage producer, for example, has been communicating the message to "Know when to say when" in many of its advertisements.

means that an increase in price will result in a decrease in demand. This relationship is particularly pronounced for spirits, but does not hold up as strongly for beer (Lau, 1975; Ornstein, 1980). In addition, higher taxes on alcohol are associated with decreased levels of negative consequences of drinking, such as decreases in liver cirrhosis and auto fatality rates (Cook, 1981).

It is more difficult to specify the effect of price on the use and abuse of other drugs. There is not much question supply and demand influence the price of any given drug, but what is not clear is the effect price has on actual drug use rates. You might expect that drugs, similar to spirits, would be price elastic (that is, an increase in cost will decrease demand and usage), but this is not always true. Heroin, for example, is price inelastic, whereby demand appears to remain the same even when price increases (Brecher, 1972).

Governmental policies frequently affect the price of drugs, generally by influencing either the supply of, or demand for, drugs. Efforts to decrease supply do not appear to markedly influence actual drug use or negative consequences of drug use (Phares, 1973), and actually may serve to attract more entrepreneurs to the drug selling "business" (Brecher, 1972). For this reason, some policy makers have focused more on demand for drugs. With this strategy, efforts are geared toward decreasing drug users' desire for the substance. Examples of this include education about the negative effects of drugs and the offering of alternatives to drug abuse. Methadone maintenance programs would be an example of an alternative to drug abuse. Indeed, methadone maintenance programs are one current broad-based governmental intervention designed to decrease drug abuse.

Another pervasive macroenvironmental variable is a legislative restriction on the legal drinking age. Many states in the early 1970s lowered the legal drinking age to eighteen. However, during the late 1970s and into the 1980s, that trend reversed, and most states have reinstated a higher minimum drinking age, in almost all cases twenty-one years. These legislative changes have been in part based on reserarch showing that the lowering of the drinking age in the 1970s was followed by increased alcohol consumption and alcohol-related problems among those eighteen- to twenty-year-olds (Whitehead & Wechsler, 1980) and higher rates of alcohol-related traffic accidents (Douglass, 1980). Although it seems that increasing the minimum drinking age will produce decreases in drinking and alcohol-related problems, it will take longer to determine how long the effect lasts (see Nathan, 1983).

Governments also have acted to regulate alcohol availability by limiting sales to certain days of the week or hours of the day, and by regulating the number and types of sales outlets. Interestingly, there has been little evidence that these measures have had much of an effect on drinking or alcohol problems (Popham, Schmidt, & de Lint, 1976). Also studied has been the influence of selling alcohol through a monopoly or private enterprise system. The authority to regulate the availability of alcohol in the United States was given to the individual states following Prohibition. Today about 60% of the states license private alcohol-related businesses, while the remainder supervise the actual sale of alcohol through the state's alcohol beverage control board. However, no significant effects on drinking have been noted between the two systems (Popham and others, 1976; Simon, 1966).

The use of drugs other than alcohol also is influenced by governmental regulation. The general stance is one of total prohibition. This approach dates back essentially to the 1914 Harrison Narcotic Act. Before the enactment of that legislation, as discussed in Chapter 2, narcotic-prescribing clinics were readily accessible, as were a variety of over-the-counter elixirs whose contents included narcotics. Due to concerns about the addictive properties of these substances, governmental actions moved in the direction of keeping such drugs away from potential users. This stance was and remains controversial. Brecher (1972), among others, has argued that prohibitions on psychoactive substances, as in the case of alcohol prohibition, simply do not work. It has further been argued that these prohibitions serve only to raise the price of the drug and consequently put a greater number of people in a position of needing to steal in order to purchase the drugs.

Another mechanism exists through which governments can exert widespread influence over the use of alcohol and drugs: legislative action that defines abuse of legal substances. For example, statutes exist to define what constitutes appropriate versus inappropriate uses of alcohol. The two most prominent are laws against public intoxication and driving while intoxicated. Guidelines outlining acceptable uses of other drugs are rare because any use of other psychoactive substances (aside from prescribed medications) is already defined as illegal.

Understandably, a number of questions arise any time legislatures address drug prohibition. One of the stickiest issues is where to draw the line between a person's freedom of choice to use a given substance, on the one hand, and the right of society to be protected from potential negative consequences of that drug's use. Consider the case of marijuana. Although it remains classified as a Schedule I drug, a number of states gradually have been reducing restrictions on its possession and use. Notably, marijuana use does not seem to have increased to any signifcant degree as a result (Single, 1981).

Taken together, the host of governmental rules and regulations regarding alcohol and drugs does not seem to have had a major effect on drug use and abuse. The only exceptions to this are pricing policies and restrictions on drinking age. Nevertheless, legislative actions have not served to prevent people from abusing drugs, given the number of persons who have remained addicted to alcohol and drugs. Although it is possible fewer persons are initiating drug use as a result of legal forces, data are not available to evaluate this possibility. Finally, it is not likely that governmental legislation alone will effectively reduce substance abuse. Such an outcome,

Figure 14–3 Advertisements for alcoholic beverages generally are intended to obtain—and maintain—loyalty to a certain brand.

according to Westermeyer (1982), would require "a nation-wide integration of virtually all social institutions: law enforcement, religion, health, education, ethnic enclaves, and special interest groups" (pp. 29–30). Such a coalition is rarely formed on any issue, let alone one as volatile as alcohol and drug use.

Social Factors

The second class of macroenvironmental factors includes social influences. We focus on three such factors in this category: sociocultural, occupational, and geographical.

Research has shown consistently that drug use is closely associated with cultural variables. Societies have historically provided guidelines for accepted uses of psychoactive substances. While such guidelines have contributed to the normative structure of each society, the process, at least in

Western societies, is in considerable flux. The reasons for this are current rapid cultural changes, the introduction of a variety of new drugs, and the apparent tendency for drug use to increase across all populations (see Connors & Tarbox, 1985). Nevertheless, societies continue to play a major role in determining how psychoactive substances are used by their members.

CONTEMPORARY ISSUE BOX 14–2
The Role of Crack in Teenage Crime

While the social environment can influence patterns of cocaine/crack use, such use also has effects on the social environment. One social consequence of the "crack epidemic" is an increase in criminal behavior. This relationship may be particularly apparent among crack-using teenagers, according to a survey of teens in the Miami area (see Laign, 1989).

In this study, 254 teens between the ages of twelve and seventeen were interviewed regarding their criminal behavior during the preceding twelve months. These teenagers were users and/or sellers of crack cocaine. Their responses indicated they had committed over 800 crimes each during that period. Included in these criminal offenses were drug dealing, prostitution, robberies, and burglaries. Even if the teenagers interviewed had exaggerated their responses, the results still suggest a staggering amount of criminal behavior.

According to the survey responders, the main reason for getting involved in crime was to pay for drugs. This is similar to the frequently identified connection between heroin use and crime, described in Chapter 1. The subjects in the present survey also reported they began using drugs before age ten, which was three years before first using crack and three years after first using alcohol. About half (55 percent) were using crack daily.

The report offered several recommendations to communities facing drug-related criminal behavior among youth. It was suggested efforts be made to increase communication between the schools, juvenile courts, and young offenders. A need for more treatment services also was identified. The report noted that communities need to intensify efforts to identify substance abuse among youths early on and to initiate prevention programs as soon as preschool or kindergarten. Finally, the report proposed the ultimate solution of the drug abuse problem (including its associated crime) may entail the resolution of much broader social ills, such as poverty.

Most studies of culture and drug use have concerned alcohol. In the United States, this research has focused predominantly on four ethnic populations: Irish Americans, Jewish Americans, Italian Americans, and Native North Americans. Studies have shown, for example, that Irish Americans and Jewish Americans have quite different drinking patterns and rates of alcohol problems (Bales, 1946; Snyder, 1958; Stivers, 1976). Although a relatively large proportion of Jewish Americans drink alcohol, relatively few experience alcohol-related problems. Among the Irish Americans, on the other hand, drinking is associated with a relatively high rate of alcohol abuse. In attempting to make sense of these variations, sociologists have speculated that differences in cultural guidelines regarding alcohol use are the central mechanism. As noted by Bales (1946), and by others since, the use of alcohol by Jewish Americans has been ingrained within a religious context. Irish Americans, on the other hand, are said to view alcohol more as a "social lubricant," a way of demonstrating solidarity and of coping with life's stressors. The broader point here, and one that has received support (for example, Cahalan, Cisin, & Crossley, 1969; Cahalan & Room, 1974; Kandel & Sudit, 1982; MacAndrew & Edgerton, 1969; Snyder, Palgi, Eldar, & Elian, 1982), is that alcohol is used differently from culture to culture according to how the society defines the designated functions of drinking.

Sociocultural forces influence in similar ways the use of drugs other than alcohol. However, the sociocultural milieu differs. For example, the legal status of the drug affects the number of users and the size of the drug-using culture overall. And, of course, the places and contexts in which the drug is used will be different than in the case of alcohol. Nevertheless, it should not be assumed that the influence of these drug cultures is any less powerful than in the case of alcohol. Drug cultures can be just as influential, if not more so, than they are in the use of alcohol. Recall for example the earlier reference to Becker's (1963) work on the acculturation process inherent in becoming a marijuana user.

A second macroenvironmental factor that can affect substance use and abuse is the occupational or work environment. Most of the research in this area has keyed on identifying occupations with relatively higher rates of alcohol use and alcoholism. Some of the occupations more typically associated with increased rates of alcohol problems are shown in Table 14–3.

You might have presumed that particular job characteristics account for greater degrees of alcohol problems in some occupations, and, indeed, some occupations seem to provide more acceptance of drinking than do others. But this is not always the case. In attempting to account for the finding that some occupations are associated with more drinking than others, Hitz (1973) has offered several possibilities. One hypothesis is that "selective recruitment" is occurring, meaning that heavy drinkers may be more likely to take a position where alcohol is available and/or its use accepted. An example would be bartending. Another hypothesis is that loosely structured or supervised positions may set the stage for more drinking. A third possi-

Table 14–3

**A Sampling of Occupations Associated with
Higher Rates of Problem Drinking or
Alcoholism**

Alcohol beverage industry workers
Army personnel
Bartenders
Unskilled workers
Entertainers
Executives
Journalists
Navy personnel
Offshore fishermen
Offshore oil riggers
Policemen
Salespeople
Seamen
Waiters/Waitresses

Source: Whitehead & Simpkins (1983)

bility is that "certain occupations may for various reasons (geographic isolation, unusual working hours or shifts, particularly esoteric skills required)
form subcultural groups or cliques" (Hitz, 1973, p. 504) that might engen-
der particular patterns of drinking. A fourth possibility is that jobs that are
boring or alienating may lead to increased drinking.

Although alcohol abuse is associated more with some occupations than
others, it is not clear whether the job engenders such drinking or whether
certain individuals are drawn to these occupations. At this point, it appears
both possibilities are operating to some extent. That is, although certain jobs
do seem to attract heavier drinkers, the structural characteristics of any
given position also influence alcohol consumption and alcohol-related
problems.

The final macroenvironmental influence of note is geographic environment. Two features of the environment stand out. The first is region of the
country, and the second is degree of urbanization.

Geographic areas in the United States have long been known to vary in
their rates of alcohol use and alcohol problems. National surveys of American drinking practices (for example, Cahalan and others, 1969; Clark &
Midanik, 1982) have shown that the highest proportions of drinkers in general and of heavy drinkers in particular were found in the New England,
Middle Atlantic, East North Central (for example, Michigan, Wisconsin,
Ohio, Indiana, Illinois), and Pacific regions of the country. Lower proportions were reported for the Southern states and for the Mountain regions. It
is believed these differences reflect regional differences in both urbanization
and economics.

Cahalan and Room (1974) studied survey data on problem drinking among men. In comparing the geographic regions noted above, they found that "drier" regions (areas that tend to have, for example, stronger sentiments in favor of temperance), compared to "wetter" regions (areas with less of such a sentiment), had higher rates of abstainers and lower rates of problematic heavy intake. The two types of regions (drier versus wetter) did not differ in the proportions of drinkers who drank without problems. Of special interest was the finding that the proportion of drinkers experiencing negative consequences related to their alcohol consumption did not differ in the "drier" and "wetter" regions (15% and 13%, respectively). Cahalan and Room note these findings are consistent with the hypothesis "that a given level of intake in the drier regions of the country is associated with a higher level of (negative) consequences . . . than is true in the wetter regions" (p. 176).

Urbanization also influences drinking patterns. The Cahalan and others (1969) national survey found there are fewer abstainers and infrequent drinkers and a greater number of heavy drinkers in highly urbanized areas than in less urbanized areas. Further, the highest prevalence of problem drinking among men in the United States is located in the highly urbanized areas (Cahalan & Room, 1974). Differences between rural and urban areas in problem drinking rates were more pronounced in "drier" regions of the country.

Geographic differences have also been assessed for other drugs, although not as extensively. The general finding has been that in rural areas the prevalence of ever using most drugs (excluding heroin) was about two-thirds the rate for metropolitan areas (NIDA, 1981). However, these differences seem to be declining and may eventually disappear. Finally, differences in drug use in rural versus metropolitan areas were more pronounced in the South and in the North Central regions. Smaller differences were found in the Northeastern and Western regions of the country.

SUMMARY

- There are a variety of individual (that is, person-specific factors) and environmental (influences outside the individual) factors affecting drug use behaviors.

- One individual factor concerns personality characteristics. In this regard, the notion of an "addictive personality" has been proposed to describe those individuals who become dependent on the use of a substance. However, research suggests personality factors *alone* do not adequately explain drug use

among people, but instead appear to play an important role in the process of drug use when those characteristics are viewed in combination with environmental factors.

- Another individual factor concerns drug beliefs and expectancies. This factor refers to what the person expects to achieve or happen when using a drug. Expectancies appear to have a considerable effect on the ways people respond to drugs.

- Environmental factors affecting drug use can be classified into microenvironmental and macroenvironmental influences.

- Microenvironmental influences refer to the immediate environment and include such factors as the physical environment, setting attributes, and others present.

- Macroenvironmental influences, on the other hand, refer to widespread factors acting in a broad-based manner. Examples of macroenvironmental influences are governmental factors, such as taxes on alcohol, legislation defining certain drugs as illicit, drinking-age laws, and social factors, such as culture, geographic region, and degree of urbanization.

- The above personality and environmental factors alone are not sufficient to account for the variety of ways drugs are used and experienced. Instead, it is necessary to study these influences in combination with each other in order to advance our understanding of substance use and abuse.

References

Babor, T.F., Mendelson, J.H., Uhly, B., & Souza, E. (1980). Drinking patterns in experimental and barroom settings. *Journal of Studies on Alcohol, 41,* 635–651.

Bach, P.J., & Schaffer, J.M. (1979). The tempo of country music and the rate of drinking in bars. *Journal of Studies on Alcohol, 40,* 1058–1059.

Barnes, G.E. (1979). The alcoholic personality: A reanalysis of the literature. *Journal of Studies on Alcohol, 40,* 571–634.

Bales, R.F. (1946). Cultural differences in rates of alcoholism. *Quarterly Journal of Studies on Alcoholism, 6,* 480–499.

Becker, H. (1963). *Outsiders.* New York: The Free Press.

Brecher, E.M. (1972). *Licit and illicit drugs.* Boston: Little, Brown.

Cahalan, D., Cisin, I., & Crossley, H.M. (1969). *American drinking practices.* New Brunswick, NJ: Rutgers Center for Alcohol Studies.

Cahalan, D., & Room, R. (1974). *Problem drinking among American men.* New Brunswick, NJ: Rutgers Center for Alcohol Studies.

Carlin, A.S., Bakker, C.B., Halpern, L., & Post, R.D. (1972). Social facilitation of marijuana intoxication: Impact of social set and pharmacological activity. *Journal of Abnormal Psychology, 80,* 132–140.

Clark, W.B., & Midanik, L. (1982). Alcohol use and alcohol problems among U.S. adults: Results of the 1979 national survey. In *Alcohol consumption and related problems* (NIAAA Alcohol and Health Monograph No. 1) (pp. 3–52). Rockville, MD: NIAAA.

Collins, R.L., & Marlatt, G.A. (1981). Social modeling as a determinant of drinking behavior: Implications for prevention and treatment. *Addictive Behaviors, 6,* 233–240.

Connors, G.J., & Sobell, M.B. (1986). Alcohol and drinking environment: Effects on affect and sensations, person perception, and perceived intoxication. *Cognitive Therapy and Research, 10,* 389–402.

Connors, G.J., & Tarbox, A.R. (1985). Macroenvironmental factors as determinants of substance use and abuse. In M. Galizio & S.A. Maisto (Eds.), *Determinants of substance abuse: Biological, psychological and environmental factors* (pp. 283–314). New York: Plenum Press.

Cook, P.J. (1981). The effect of liquor taxes on drinking, cirrhosis, and auto accidents. In M.H. Moore & C.R. Gerstein (Eds.), *Alcohol and public policy: Beyond the shadow of prohibition* (pp. 255–285). Washington, D.C.: National Academy Press.

Cox, W.M. (1986). *The addictive personality.* New York: Chelsea.

Douglass, R.L. (1980). Legal drinking age and traffic casualties: A special case of changing alcohol availability in public health context. In H. Wechsler (Ed.), *Minimum–drinking-age laws* (pp. 93–132). Lexington, MA: D.C. Heath.

Foss, R. (1973). Personality, social influence, and cigarette smoking. *Journal of Health and Social Behavior, 14,* 279–286.

Galizio, M., & Maisto, S.A. (Eds.) (1985). *Determinants of substance abuse: Biological, psychological, and environmental factors.* New York: Plenum Press.

Glad, W., & Adesso, V.J. (1976). The relative importance of socially induced tension and behavioral contagion for smoking behavior. *Journal of Abnormal Psychology, 85,* 119–121.

Goldstein, J.W., & Sappington, J.T. (1977). Personality characteristics of students who became heavy drug users: An MMPI study of an avant garde. *American Journal of Drug and Alcohol Abuse, 4,* 401–412.

Hitz, D. (1973). Drunken sailors and others. *Quarterly Journal of Studies on Alcohol, 34,* 496–505.

Hull, J.G., & Bond, C.F. (1986). Social and behavioral consequences of alcohol consumption: A meta-analysis. *Psychological Bulletin, 99,* 347–360.

Jessor, R. (1976). Predicting time of onset of marijuana use: A developmental study of high school youth. *Journal of Consulting and Clinical Psychology, 44,* 125–134.

Jessor, R., & Jessor, S.L. (1975). Adolescent development and the onset of drinking: A longitudinal study. *Journal of Studies on Alcohol, 36,* 27–51.

Jessor, R., & Jessor, S.L. (1977). *Problem behavior and psychosocial development: A longitudinal study.* New York: Academic Press.

Jessor, R., Jessor, S.L., & Finney, J. (1973). A social psychology of marijuana use: Longitudinal studies of high school and college youth. *Journal of Personality and Social Psychology, 26,* 1–15.

Jones, M.C. (1968). Personality correlates and antecedents of drinking patterns in adult males. *Journal of Consulting and Clinical Psychology, 32,* 2–12

Jones, M.C. (1971). Personality antecedents and correlates of drinking patterns in women. *Journal of Consulting and Clinical Psychology, 36,* 61–69.

Kalin, R. (1972). Social drinking in different settings. In D.C. McClelland, W. Davies, R. Kalin, & E. Wanner (Eds.), *The drinking man* (pp. 21–44). New York: Free Press.

Kalin, R., McClelland, D.C., & Kahn, M. (1965). The effects of male social drinking on fantasy. *Journal of Personality and Social Psychology, 1,* 441–451.

Kandel, D.B., & Sudit, M. (1982). Drinking practices among urban adults in Israel: A cross-cultural comparison. *Journal of Studies on Alcohol, 43,* 1–16.

Laign, J. (1989). Crack fuels youth crime. *U.S. Journal of Drug and Alcohol Dependence, 13* (9), p. 13.

Lau, H.H. (1975). Cost of alcoholic beverages as a determinant of alcohol consumption. In R.J. Gibbons, Y. Israel, H. Kalant, R.E. Popham, W. Schmidt, & R.E. Smart (Eds.), *Research advances in alcohol and drug problems* (Vol. 2) (pp. 211–246). New York: Wiley.

Loper, R.G., Kammeier, M.L., & Hoffman, H. (1973). MMPI characteristics of college freshman males who later became alcoholics. *Journal of Abnormal Psychology, 82,* 159–162.

MacAndrew, C., & Edgerton, R.B. (1969). *Drunken comportment.* Chicago: Aldine.

McCarty, D. (1985). Environmental factors in substance abuse: The microsetting. In M. Galizio & S.A. Maisto (Eds.), *Determinants of substance abuse: Biological, psychological, and environmental factors* (pp. 247–282). New York: Plenum Press.

McCord, W., McCord, J., & Gudeman, J. (1960). *Origins of alcoholism.* Stanford, CA: Stanford University Press.

Nathan, P.E. (1983). Failures in prevention: Why we can't prevent the devastating effect of alcoholism and drug abuse. *American Psychologist, 38,* 459–467.

National Institute on Drug Abuse. (1982). *Drug abuse in rural America.* Washington, D.C.: Department of Health and Human Services.

Ornstein, S.I. (1980). The control of alcohol consumption through price increases. *Journal of Studies on Alcohol, 41,* 807–818.

Phares, D. (1973). The simple economics of heroin and organizing public policy. *Journal of Drug Issues, 3,* 186–200.

Pihl, R.O., & Spiers, P. (1978). Individual characteristics in the etiology of drug abuse. In B.A. Maher (Ed.), *Progress in experimental personality research* (Vol. 8) (pp. 93–195). New York: Academic Press.

Pliner, P., & Cappell, H. (1974). Modification of affective consequences of alcohol: A comparison of social and solitary drinking. *Journal of Abnormal Psychology, 89,* 224–233.

Popham, R.E., Schmidt, W., & de Lint, J. (1976). The effects of legal restraint on drinking. In B. Kissin & H. Begleiter (Eds.), *The biology of alcoholism* (Vol. 4). *Social aspects of alcoholism* (pp. 579–625). New York: Plenum Press.

Robins, L.N., Helzer, J.E., & Davis, D.H. (1975). Narcotic use in Southeast Asia and afterward: An interview study of 898 Vietnam returnees. *Archives of General Psychiatry, 32,* 995–961.

Rosenbluth, J., Nathan, P.E., & Lawson, D.M. (1978). Environmental influences on drinking by college students in a college pub: Behavioral observation in the natural environment. *Addictive Behaviors, 3,* 117–121.

Simon, J.L. (1966). The economic effects of state monopoly of packaged liquor retailing. *Journal of Political Economics, 74,* 188–194.

Single, E.W. (1981). The impact of marijuana decriminalization. In Y. Israel, F.B. Glaser, H. Kalant, R.E. Popham, W. Schmidt, & R.G. Smart (Eds.), *Research advances in alcohol and drug problems* (Vol. 6) (pp. 405–424). New York: Plenum Press.

Snyder, C.R. (1958). *Alcohol and the Jews: A cultural study of drinking and sobriety.* New Haven: Yale Center of Alcohol Studies.

Snyder, C.R., Palgi, P., Eldar, P., & Elian, B. (1982). Alcoholism among the Jews in Israel: A pilot study. *Journal of Studies on Alcohol, 43,* 623–654.

Stivers, R. (1976). *A hair of the dog: Irish drinking and American stereotype.* University Park, PA: Pennsylvania State Press.

Westermeyer, J. (1982). Sociocultural aspects of alcohol and drug use and abuse. In J. Solomon & K.A. Keeley (Eds.), *Perspectives in alcohol and drug abuse* (pp. 15–34). Boston: John Wright.

Whitehead, P.C., & Simpkins, J. (1983). Occupational factors in alcoholism. In B. Kissin & H. Begleiter (Eds.), *The biology of alcoholism* (Vol. 6). *The pathogenesis of alcoholism* (pp. 405–553). New York: Plenum Press.

Whitehead, P.C. & Wechsler, H. (1980). Implications for future research and public policy. In H. Wechsler (Ed.), *Minimum-drinking-age laws* (pp. 177–184). Lexington, MA: D.C. Heath.

Wilson, G.T., Perold, E.A., & Abrams, D.B. (1981). The effects of expectations of self-intoxication and partner's drinking on anxiety in dyadic social interaction. *Cognitive Therapy and Research, 5,* 251–264.

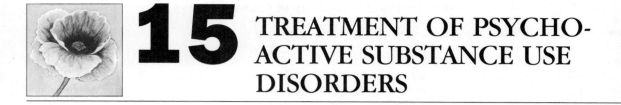

15 TREATMENT OF PSYCHO-ACTIVE SUBSTANCE USE DISORDERS

Now that we have covered the most commonly used psychoactive substances we are ready to address the question, "what is done for people whose use becomes abuse or dependence?"[1] The question pertains to **treatment,** or planned activities designed to change some pattern of behavior(s) of individuals or their families. In this chapter we are concerned with patterns of psychoactive substance use. We emphasize psychological and behavioral treatments (also called interventions), as opposed to medical treatments, although some examples of the latter are discussed.

The chapter begins with models of problem behaviors and their solutions. Thinking about models of behavior problems is important, because views of problem behavior and its resolution have a large effect on how treatments are designed. We discuss the major settings where alcohol and drug treatments are carried out. Within these settings a wide variety of specific treatment types and activities are available. We address the important topics of pharmacotherapy of alcohol and drug dependence and the use of self-help groups. We follow with a summary of what is known about the effectiveness of treatments. Treatment effectiveness is also discussed in a section on treatment goals and matching people to treatments.

Treatment
Planned activities designed to change some pattern of behavior(s) of individuals or their families.

MODELS OF PROBLEM BEHAVIORS AND THEIR SOLUTION

It has been a long-standing and continuing problem in the mental health professions, such as psychiatry, clinical psychology, and social work, that many, often conflicting models and theories exist for the disorders that are treated. A way to organize models would help clinicians and researchers better understand psychological and behavioral problems and how to treat them effectively. Brickman, Rabinowitz, Karuza, Coates, Cohn, and Kidder (1982) provided one approach to organizing models that can be applied to models of alcohol and drug abuse.

Brickman and others (1982) classified four types of models, based on views of whether or not people are responsible for a problem's development and whether or not they are responsible for its solution. Brickman and others called the four models the moral model, the compensatory model,

---

[1]As we reviewed in Chapter 1, there has been considerable controversy about diagnosis and diagnostic terms among clinicians and researchers in the addictive behaviors. In this chapter an attempt has been made to use the DSM-III-R terminology "Psychoactive Substance Use Disorder" as much as seemed feasible. However, frequently that was not possible because of apparent awkwardness of style. More importantly, the language used in the existing literature is not easily translated into DSM-III-R terms. As a result, we often used the common terms "alcohol or drug abuse," or "alcohol or drug problems" to denote a pattern of drug or alcohol use associated with negative consequences for the individual. When physical addiction is pertinent we indicate that by explicitly referring to physical dependence, which is consistent with DSM-III-R terminology.

Table 15–1
Summary of Brickman and Colleagues' (1982) Model Types

		Responsibility for Solving the Problem	
		Person	External Agent
	Person	Moral Model	Enlightenment Model
Responsibility for Developing the Problem			
	External Agent	Compensatory Model	Medical Model

Note: "External agent" refers to a source other than the person, such as public authorities or health professionals.

the medical model, and the enlightenment model. Table 15–1 is a summary of the four types of models.

According to the moral model, people are responsible for both the development and solution of their problems. Therefore, external agents such as public authorities or health professionals see neither obligation nor ability to help people with their problems. Rather, it is up to the person with the problem to use willpower to get back on track. Historically the moral model was applied widely to alcohol and other drug abuse and was the basis of using the legal system (for instance, jail) as the primary way of "treating" persons with these problems.

In the compensatory model people are not blamed for the development of a problem but are seen as responsible for its solution. Accordingly, people have to compensate for handicaps or obstacles resulting from untoward circumstances and events by making extra or special efforts alone or with the help of others. The individual is viewed as responsible for using any of the resources made available by others.

In the medical model, people are not responsible for the development or the solution of a problem. The most obvious application of the medical model is the theory and practice of treating physical illnesses. However, the model generally applies to any problem which is the result of uncontrolled (and uncontrollable) forces. People who are ill are expected to try to get well (if possible), and the proper way to do this is through following the advice of experts, such as physicians, in solving the problem.

The enlightenment model refers to the case in which people are blamed for their problems but are not responsible for their solutions. The model's name is based on the perceived need of experts to educate (enlighten) people about the nature of their problems, and then to do whatever is necessary to solve them. Solving a problem may require that a person submit to strict social controls.

These four categories of models cover the most influential specific models and theories that have been proposed to explain and treat alcohol and drug abuse. In the area of alcohol and other drug abuse, beliefs about those problems still polarize treatment professionals. For example, some of the major controversies have been whether alcohol or drug abuse is a moral or medical problem. Medical model and compensatory model proponents also have had their clashes.

In the next sections when we refer to specific treatment approaches or techniques we connect the approach to one of the Brickman and others (1982) models of behavior.

TREATMENT OF THE PSYCHOACTIVE SUBSTANCE USE DISORDERS

In this section we look at formal treatment of the Psychoactive Substance Use Disorders. The substances to be included in this overview are alcohol and other drugs that are abused. The latter typically refer to the opiates, stimulant drugs, and depressant drugs. We will not, however, include nicotine. We covered treatment of cigarette smoking in Chapter 6, because the research on this topic is so extensive and often is considered separate from research on the treatment of other drug use.

We begin this part of the chapter by describing several approaches to the treatment of the psychoactive substance use disorders and how they relate to the Brickman and others (1982) models of problem development and solution. We consider the effectiveness of a treatment in helping patients meet goals: matching people to specific treatments and specifying the goals for substance use.

Classification of Treatment Settings and Services

Many types of services are offered for treatment of psychoactive substance use disorders but are often referred to with idiosyncratically used terms. One way to achieve some order is to classify the different treatment settings and services into more general categories. We do this in turn for alcohol abuse and drug abuse treatment.

Classification of alcohol abuse treatment settings and services
The settings and services of treatment for alcohol problems could be classified in a number of ways. We use the classification Armor, Polich, and Stambul published in their well-known 1976 Rand Corporation study of alcoholism treatment in the United States.

Armor and others (1976, p. 102) identified the general treatment settings of hospital setting, intermediate setting, and outpatient setting. Within each of these settings specific treatment services are offered. Inpatients in the hospital setting live there for the duration of their treatment, and the organization of patient care is similar to that given to persons hospitalized for physical problems. For example, nurses play a large role in treatment, and

Psychological Treatment
Treatments geared to changing emotions, thoughts, or behavior without the use of medications or other physical or biological means.

much weight is given to the medical aspects of alcohol and other drug problems. In this way the hospital setting follows a medical model of treatment. On the other hand, a good deal of the specific alcohol and drug rehabilitation methods followed in hospital based programs are **psychological** in origin. The emphasis of these non-medical treatment methods is on learning about the self and the environment we live in, how they alter the course of alcohol and drug problem development, and how a person can change both the self and his or her environment to produce desired changes in psychoactive substance use. As such, these treatment techniques follow a compensatory model. Partial hospital care occurs in the hospital setting, but the patient[2] is not in the setting for twenty-four hours a day. Typically, treatment programs of this type are designed for six-to-eight hour schedules, usually in the day time or evening hours. The last type of service in the hospital setting is detoxification, mainly involving the medical management of alcohol withdrawal symptoms. Care mostly consists of the management of medications given to treat withdrawal, although counseling is available, especially referral to additional treatment services.

Milieu Treatment
Treatment in which the organization and structure of a setting are designed to change behavior.

Within the intermediate setting are halfway house services. Halfway houses usually are designed as **milieu treatment** (in milieu treatment the organization and structure of a setting are designed to be therapeutic) settings. These settings are at the patients' residence during treatment. Other treatment services usually available include **counseling, psychotherapy** and a strong orientation toward use of **self-help groups,** usually Alcoholics Anonymous (AA). Alcoholics Anonymous is a self-help program of recovery from alcohol problems. A quarterway house is similar to a halfway house except, as the name implies, it is more structured and allows residents less independence than is accessible to halfway house residents. (Similarly, less structured versions of halfway houses have been called three-quarterway houses.) Finally, the intermediate setting also includes residential care, consisting of living quarters, but little other treatment.

Counseling
In alcohol and drug treatment, counselors are specially trained professionals who perform a variety of treatment activities, including assessment, education, and individual, marital, or family counseling.

The outpatient setting is perhaps the most idiosyncratic of the three Armor and the others (1976) described. Two general distinctions of treatment services are made: individual and group. In individual treatment, the patient works with a professional in a one–to–one relationship. Similarly, "individual" couples or families also may work with a professional in a planned course of treatment. In contrast, group treatment usually involves five to ten individuals joined together in regular sessions and led by a pro-

Psychotherapy
Typically, conversation between a specially trained individual (therapist) and another person (or family) that is intended to change patterns of behavior, thoughts, or feelings in that person.

Self-help group
A therapeutic group in which all members have some identified problem that is the focus of the group's therapeutic activity.

[2]In the treatment of psychiatric disorders, including the addictions, there is inconsistency among professionals in their use of the words "patient" or "client" to refer to individuals presenting for treatment. What underlies this disagreement are beliefs about the utility of a medical model as a guide to understanding the psychiatric disorders. In addition, often what term is chosen depends on the setting of treatment. For example, individuals in hospital inpatient settings are more likely to be referred to as patients compared to persons receiving treatment in outpatient clinics. In this chapter we have used the terms patient and client as synonyms to refer to an individual who is in formal treatment for his or her alcohol or drug problems.

CONTEMPORARY ISSUE BOX 15–1
Inpatient Treatment Programs and the Trend to Outpatient Care

The great increase in awareness of alcohol (and other drug) problems over the last 25 years and an increase in the priority given to treatment of alcoholics have effected both a huge rise in the availability and cost of treatment programs in the United States. The major force behind this was the legislated mandate that health insurance companies reimburse for the treatment of alcoholism. These events spawned numerous inpatient, "for profit" (for example, treatment centers dependent entirely on making a profit to stay in business) alcohol and other drug abuse treatment programs. Typically, the length of stay in these programs, including time for detoxification, has been about 30 days, and costs for such treatment average about $6,000.

The good news is that abundant help is now available and accessible if people want it. The bad news is that accessibility invites users, and businesses and insurance companies are getting tired of spending large sums to help problem employees. Especially important here is the widening agreement among experts that inpatient care is no more effective for most patients than outpatient treatment, which is far cheaper and much less disruptive of patients' lives. Therefore, insurance companies are becoming more stringent about who they allow to receive coverage for inpatient alcohol treatment and are encouraging as an alternative, outpatient services. This trend is likely to continue and strengthen in the future.

fessional. In such treatment, much of what helps group members to change stems from the way group members interact with each other and form relationships. The leader's job is to guide this process and to keep group members on productive tracks of discussion. Groups often are organized around specific themes governing the types of people who join the group and what they discuss. Examples are adults whose parents were alcoholic, and ways to prevent a recurrence (relapse) of alcohol problems once they are treated. Other groups are general and have only the theme of maintaining abstinence from psychoactive substance use. Individual and group alcohol treatment is conducted by a range of workers with mental health training. There are "paraprofessionals," who are people working in direct patient care and not possessing a formal degree. Then there are the professionals who are physicians (typically psychiatrists), clinical psychologists, and social workers.

Paraprofessionals or professionals may have achieved special credentialing in alcoholism or drug counseling. In that case they would be permitted to call themselves Certified Alcoholism (or Drug Abuse) Counselors. In some cases certification in "chemical dependence" counseling is available covering both alcohol and drug abuse treatment.

Classification of drug abuse treatment settings and services
There also is a wide array of treatment services for drug abusers. Allison and Hubbard (1985, p. 1322) noted, "Treatment programs may involve outpatient, residential, or day care and may take place in a hospital, clinic, mental health center, prison, or group home environment. Treatment may be drug-free or use chemical aids. Counseling, job training, physical health care, and a variety of other services may or may not be part of the treatment program. The staff may be highly trained professionals or the program may be of the self-help type."

The traditional classification of drug abuse treatments includes detoxification, methadone maintenance, residential, and outpatient drug-free treatment. Similar to alcohol treatment, the primary goal of detoxification is a medically managed withdrawal from physical dependence on drugs. Managing detoxification often involves the use of medications, but could be drug-free. As with alcohol withdrawal treatment, detoxification services may include some counseling services directed in part at guiding the patient to additional treatment services.

Methadone maintenance programs are based on a medical model of heroin addiction and probably have received the most attention from researchers and the popular press. The attention centers on the conflict in treating dependence on a chemical substance (heroin, an opiate) with another opiate (methadone). Proponents of this approach say that if the heroin addict's craving for heroin is prevented by methadone, he or she will be more likely to break out of the destructive life style associated with drug addiction and then engage in rehabilitation leading to a socially acceptable and productive way of living. The major opposition to methadone treatment is that it perpetuates the individual's dependence on an opiate drug.

Methadone maintenance treatment typically involves administration of a daily, prescribed dose of methadone in order to block the addict's **cravings** for heroin. Usually, methadone maintenance programs are outpatient so that the individual may pursue activities that build to a socially productive life. Furthermore, many programs (and state or federal regulations) require patients to receive some kind of counseling while enrolled in methadone maintenance, and patients are required to adhere to a formal set of rules for continued participation in methadone maintenance treatment.

As you might have guessed, one of the problems with the use of methadone is its potential for abuse. That is, addicts may use their methadone in nonprescribed ways just as they used heroin. One alternative to methadone that combats the problem of potential abuse has been developed. This

Craving
As noted in Chapter 1, a strong or intense desire to use a drug.

Figure 15–1 A treatment group is in progress in a program for drug abuse.

option is **levo-alpha-acetylmethadol** (LAAM), which is similar in pharmacological action to methadone but has longer-lasting effects. The advantage of a longer-lasting methadone substitute is that patients are more likely to comply with the regimen for taking the drug and are less likely to abuse their prescriptions.

Residential treatment is known more commonly as the therapeutic community (TC). Drug TCs are run mostly by ex-addicts, who work as peer counselors and administrators. There is heavy reliance on self-help groups. The TC is a highly structured residential program, especially at the beginning of treatment, and clients gain more responsibilities and independence as they progress through the program by meeting certain requirements. In TCs there also is an emphasis on group counseling and therapy, which often is confrontational. TCs most clearly follow a compensatory model of treatment, according to the Brickman and others (1982) system.

The final drug abuse treatment modality is outpatient-drug-free. Similar to alcohol abuse treatment, outpatient treatment is the most varied of the treatment types and includes a wide range of programs and services. The most

Levo-alpha-acetylmethadol (LAAM)
A drug used in treating heroin addiction that is similar in action to methadone but has longer-lasting effects.

salient features of outpatient treatment are that it is not residential and drugs are not used in treatment. Almost half of the drug abusers in treatment receive their treatment in this setting.

Treatment of Nonopiate Drug Abusers

In general, the classification of drug abuse treatment refers to services that have been available for the treatment of heroin abuse. In this regard, the great expansion in drug abuse treatment services over the last twenty-five years largely was due to public alarm over increasingly widespread use and abuse of heroin, with its highly visible and well-publicized negative social effects. For example, a sharp increase in violent crime in some urban areas, such as the recent experience with crack use, was attributed to heroin use. However, in recent years there has been an increase in the numbers of individuals appearing for drug abuse treatment who primarily abuse drugs other than alcohol or the opiates. For example, in 1977 33.4% of the clients admitted to drug abuse treatment programs were nonopiate abusers, and this proportion had increased to 54.9% by 1980 (USDHHS, 1984). As with the abuse of heroin and alcohol, nonopiate abusers may appear in treatment settings other than those designed specifically to treat the psychoactive substance use disorders. These include hospital emergency rooms, physicians' offices, or general psychiatric treatment settings. In general, little is known about any special problems and characteristics of nonopiate drug abusers that might be important for their treatment.

CONTEMPORARY ISSUE BOX 15–2
What Influences the Expansion of Drug Treatment?

Currently political and social forces are contributing to the increased demand for drug treatment, just as these same forces pushed the growth of treatment of heroin abuse. This recent trend reaffirms the importance of social and political factors in how United States society deals with alcohol and other drug use.

In 1986 the surge in demand for drug treatment, particularly in the residential or inpatient setting, arose from two major sources: crack and AIDS. These worked in a political climate that was strongly in favor of eradicating drugs and drug abuse.

As you saw in Chapter 5, crack is the highly addictive, cheaper form of cocaine. People who start using it are quickly hooked on it, and in the mid-1980s people from a wide range of social classes became addicted to crack. The variety of people affected, along with social consequences such as large increases in drug-related criminal activity and flagrant selling of crack in public places, lighted the public's torch for getting crack abusers off the streets and into treatment. Further, the media devoted much time to the crack epidemic, just as they have to other diseases or medical problems in the past.

The AIDS scare has sent drug abusers, particularly heroin abusers who take their drugs intravenously, to treatment programs to help them stop their drug abuse. The reason: fear of catching the deadly immune disease of AIDS through the use of contaminated needles. The fear of AIDS sent addicts looking to treatment when it is unlikely they otherwise would have done so. Again, the media attention to AIDS and the general public alarm and fears about AIDS supported the increased demands for more drug treatment programs. These two examples show how political and social forces, and not only an actual increase in drug use or in the valuing of a drug-free society, affect the demand for drug and alcohol treatment.

Combinations of treatment settings and services   It is somewhat artificial to describe settings for treatment of the psychoactive substance use disorders in discrete categories, because a treatment episode for many people involves participation in more than one treatment setting. For example, a common course of treatment includes detoxification from alcohol or other drugs and later referral to an inpatient or outpatient treatment program. Or, an individual may begin treatment by completing an inpatient intensive rehabilitation program and then engage in outpatient treatment as part of an **aftercare** plan. Other combinations are possible, each suited to the person's needs.

Aftercare
In alcohol and drug treatment, this term usually refers to therapeutic activities following completion of a formal treatment program.

Diversity of Treatment Techniques

Categories of treatment settings and services can give only an outline of actual treatment activities occurring in drug or alcohol programs. It is difficult to characterize alcohol and drug programs except in the broadest terms. In alcohol or drug treatment programs, what is called individual or group counseling or psychotherapy can refer to many specific activities. They can occur in any of the treatment settings described, with some settings having greater latitude than others. For example, the smallest range of treatment activities is in settings devoted primarily to detoxification. In contrast, outpatient or inpatient treatment programs can include many different activities that are called treatment.

To give an idea of the many treatment activities used, Maisto and Nirenberg (1986) studied the use of treatment procedures in inpatient alcoholism treatment programs funded by the Veterans Administration (VA) (now called the Department of Veterans Affairs). In this study a detailed questionnaire was sent to the directors of the VA alcoholism treatment programs. One survey question concerned patients' use of different treatment "components." The directors' responses to this questionnaire item confirmed the impression that there is great variation in what constitutes treatment of alcohol (and drug) problems. No fewer than forty-eight different program components were reported by at least one of the seventy-two directors. Each component had been used in the last three months by at least some of their patients. Any of the treatment program components could be offered in combination. Again, it should be remembered that Maisto and Nirenberg's study addressed only VA inpatient alcoholism treatment programs. It is possible that if there were more variety in the types of treatment settings sampled, there would have been reports of even greater variety of treatment activities.

ADDITIONAL TOPICS ON THE TREATMENT OF THE PSYCHOACTIVE SUBSTANCE USE DISORDERS

So far we have presented an overview of the approaches and content of treatment of the psychoactive substance use disorders. In this section we look at three topics deserving some elaboration in a discussion of treatment. These topics include (1) pharmacological therapy of alcohol and drug abuse and dependence, (2) the treatment of individuals who consistently abuse more than one substance, with no one substance the dominant or primary substance, and (3) the use of self-help groups in treatment of alcohol and drug problems.

Pharmacological Treatment

Although the discussion of treatment in this chapter has emphasized nonmedical interventions, drugs frequently are used in the treatment of alcohol and drug problems. This practice is known as pharmacotherapy. In discussing pharmacotherapy it is important to distinguish between detoxification and post-detoxification treatment. Detoxification of people who are physically dependent on alcohol or drugs often involves the use of drugs in the medical management of withdrawal, although there are drug-free approaches to detoxification. These latter approaches, as noted in Chapter 7, are called "social detoxification," in which a person's withdrawal is monitored by professional staff in a treatment setting, but no drugs are administered, if at all possible. There is little controversy about using drugs in managing acute withdrawal. However, there are some disagreements over the use of chemicals in treatment activities subsequent to detoxification.

In discussing pharmacotherapy a distinction should be made between the use of medications in management of addiction or of associated psychological symptoms, and the use of "antidrug" drugs. Antidrug drugs are chemicals used to modify the effects a person experiences upon taking his or her drug of choice.

Biological theories of addiction focus on abnormalities or changes in brain chemistry as causes or consequences of alcohol or drug abuse. This implies a correction of the abnormal brain chemistry is essential to alleviating the addiction problem. Although there are such theories of alcohol and drug dependence, implications for pharmacotherapy of these problems generally have not been applied much beyond extensive research with animals. An exception is the use of antidepressant medication, such as **desipramine** in treatment of cocaine abusers (Annis, 1987). Such medications are thought to alter neural transmission in the brain so that the cocaine abuser does not experience the extreme drug cravings and depression that tend to be part of cocaine withdrawal. These reactions seem to be a big reason why people dependent on cocaine have such a hard time stopping its use or staying "straight" if they do manage to stop (also see Chapter 5).

Psychotropic medication may be part of treatment of alcohol or drug abuse when a person has an alcohol or drug problem and another psychiatric disorder. These psychiatric disorders include depression and manic depression, especially among alcoholics. A relationship exists between alcohol or drug abuse and disorders characterized by a high degree of anxiety, and the **personality disorders,** particularly what is commonly called **sociopathy.** The use of psychotropic agents in the treatment of alcohol or drug abuse usually is done on the premise that patients use alcohol and other drugs to **"self-medicate."** This means the individual acts as his or her own physician and self-prescribes alcohol and other drugs to lessen troubling psychological symptoms such as anxiety or depression. When used, psychotropic agents generally are administered in combination with nonmedical techniques in treating the psychoactive substance use disorder.

Considerable controversy still exists over the use of psychotropic agents as part of alcohol or drug treatment services. The primary objection is that the use of drugs in treating a person who abuses drugs is tantamount to inducing a dual (the drug the person entered treatment for and the prescribed drug) dependency (Diesenhaus, 1982). In some cases this opposition is ideological rather than based on scientific evidence, such as in the outright rejection by some drug therapeutic communities of using medication as part of treatment. More objectively, the value of using medication in treating alcohol or drug abuse varies with the purpose of use and the individual being treated.

"Antidrug" drugs   Anti-alcohol drugs have been used for over 40 years and have been the center of much hope, disappointment, and discussion. The use of anti-alcohol drugs as part of treatment for alcohol abuse and dependence still is popular.

Peachey and Annis (1985) reviewed what they called the alcohol-sensitizing drugs, the most popular of which are disulfiram (trademark Antabuse) and carbimide (trademark Temposil). Antabuse has been in use in the United States since 1948. Temposil, on the other hand, is not available in the U.S. and is used less frequently than Antabuse. In any case, use of both

Desipramine
An antidepressant medication.

Personality Disorder
Patterns of behavior that are long-standing, usually recognizable from adolescence or earlier. These behavior patterns are a disorder because they frequently create distress for the person due to their personal or social consequences.

Sociopathy
A type of personality disorder that is characterized by a lack of concern for social obligations or rules, a lack of feelings for others, and a tendency toward violence.

Self-medication
The idea that some people prescribe their own medication, in the form of alcohol or illicit drugs, to alleviate psychological difficulties such as anxiety or depression.

agents in treatment is based on similar assumptions regarding the psychological effects of their chemical action.

The chemical action of alcohol-sensitizing drugs results in an increase in the blood level of acetaldehyde after alcohol consumption (see Chapter 7 on the metabolizing of alcohol). The consequence of the heightened acetaldehyde depends on how much alcohol is drunk. For people on therapeutic doses of disulfiram and carbimide, one or two drinks will produce flushing, tachycardia (excessive rapidity in action of the heart, usually a pulse rate of over 100 per minute), tachypnea (excessively rapid respiration), sensations of warmth, heart palpitations, and shortness of breath. These effects usually last about thirty minutes and are not life threatening. However, if larger quantities of alcohol are consumed, the reaction may include intense palpitations, dyspnea (difficult or labored breathing), nausea, vomiting, and headache, all of which may last more than ninety minutes. In some people this more severe reaction has induced shock, loss of consciousness, or death due to myocardial infarction (Peachey & Annis, 1985, p. 202).

The unpleasant effects of drinking while on a regimen of the alcohol-sensitizing drugs is why such drugs are used in treatment. The assumption is that fear of experiencing the unpleasant effects will deter a person from drinking and will have the concurrent result of building a learned aversion to alcohol based on the imagined negative consequences of drinking. If a person on disulfiram or carbimide tests out the effects of drinking, the same learned aversion will proceed more rapidly because of the addition of experiencing direct, as well as imagined, negative consequences. The learned aversion to alcohol underlies eventual avoidance of it and, with the cessation of drinking, improvements in other areas of functioning such as job and family that often are impaired with abusive drinking patterns.

Alcohol-sensitizing drugs virtually always are used as part of a treatment program that includes other treatment components. In this sense they are regarded as similar to psychotropic medications, as adjuncts to treatment of alcohol problems. When they first were available for treatment, the antialcohol drugs were perceived as magic pills that would revolutionize alcoholism treatment and make it a simple matter of medical management. Unfortunately, these hopes soon were dashed by research findings and an increasing awareness of the complexity of alcohol abuse and dependence.

Use of antidrug drugs in treating opiate and other drug abuse and dependence   An important antidrug drug used to treat opiate dependence is naltrexone, which is an opiate antagonist. Remember from Chapter 1 that an antagonist to a drug is a drug that blocks the effects or chemical action of that drug. Naltrexone has its most common use among patients who have been maintained for long periods on methadone and then choose to become drug-free. The naltrexone helps these people to bridge the gap between methadone maintenance and a drug-free life. It is interesting to compare Antabuse and naltrexone in how they achieve their antidrug effects. As discussed, Antabuse blocks alcohol effects by altering its metabolism. As a result, if alcohol is drunk when a person is on Antabuse, he or she will experience very unpleasant physical effects. Therefore, sufficient quantities of alcohol cannot be consumed to produce its psychoactive effects. Naltrexone, however, can have therapeutic value because it affects neural transmission in such a way that the abused opiate cannot achieve its effect in the brain. The result is that the person loses a major reason for using the opiate, which is the psychoactive effects.

Along these lines, **buprenorphine,** a mixed opiate agonist-antagonist, is a drug that blocks the effects of heroin and has been used in treatment. Buprenorphine has a lower potential for abuse than does methadone. Moreover, recent data showed that rhesus monkeys greatly reduced cocaine self-administration when given buprenorphine compared to saline injections (Mello, Mendelson, Bree, & Lukas, 1989). Since buprenorphine already is known to be safe for human use, the Mello and others study implies that this compound soon may be an effective pharmacotherapy for people addicted both to heroin and cocaine, an increasingly frequent problem.

Buprenorphine
Another drug used in the treatment of opiate addiction, this substance blocks the effects of opiates.

Again, it is worth noting that the prevailing philosophy in using chemical agents in treating opiate addiction is that such treatment be adjunctive to required types of nonmedical treatments that usually constitute the main part of rehabilitation for alcohol or drug problems. Taking away this incentive for using opiates can make it easier, for example, for a person to stay off these drugs when he or she is making the change from methadone maintenance to a drug-free life.

Treatment of the Multiple Substance Abuser

The traditional and common way of viewing treatment implies that someone called an alcohol abuser or alcoholic does not have trouble with or does not abuse other drugs. Similarly, the traditional view gives the impression that people called drug abusers have no patterns of abusive alcohol use. However, it may be a mistake to designate programs as either alcohol treatment or drug treatment.

For example, Sokolow, Welte, Hynes, and Lyons (1981) reported a survey of multiple substance use among patients arriving for treatment at New York State funded alcoholism rehabilitation programs. The total sample of 1340 men and women selected for this study represented wide ranges in age and educational background. Most (57.3%) of the patients were between thirty-one and fifty years old. In addition to their alcohol use, which was their reason for beginning treatment, patients were asked about their licit and illicit use in the past thirty days of minor and major tranquilizers, sedatives, amphetamines, antidepressants, opiates, hallucinogens, marijuana, and cocaine.

Almost half of the patients reported use of at least one of the other than alcohol drugs during the thirty days before their treatment began. About

20% of these patients used combinations of the drugs. The single drug class reported most frequently was the tranquilizers (12.7% of the patients), which is notable because tranquilizers are cross tolerants with alcohol and are the drugs most abused by those identified as alcoholics. We should also note that people identified as drug abusers often abuse alcohol too, according to Carroll, Malloy, and Kenrick (1977).

Studies of multiple substance use have important implications for treatment. As we have said, the very strong tendency has existed to develop programs centered on alcohol treatment or drug treatment, implying major differences in treatment. The differences sometimes became real in practice. Furthermore, some treatment providers strongly object to treating substance misuse other than what has been identified as the patient's primary substance of abuse. Such reactions have been found especially in alcohol programs and restrict treatment, given the prevalence of multiple substance use. In this respect, two points quickly emerge about treatment effects. First, if treatment programs concentrate only on, for example, alcohol use, the abuse of other drugs may result in poorer, shorter lasting **treatment effects** than if the person's substance use patterns were treated in a more unified way. Another point is that people seeking alcohol or drug treatment who are multiple substance abusers may have more severe social, legal, and psychiatric difficulties than those in treatment whose patterns of abuse are limited to single drug categories (Carroll and others, 1977). Beginning treatment with more severe problems predicts poorer functioning following treatment. So, failing to address patterns of multiple substance use because of program philosophy and policy could mean inadequate treatment planning.

Treatment Effects
The result of experiencing a treatment, usually measured in different areas of functioning, such as substance use, family functioning, and vocational functioning.

Treatment of multiple substance abusers relates to more general questions about treatment. One of these is the need to view substance use as part of a person's total pattern of behavior in order to achieve an understanding of drug and alcohol use. Those who take this approach suggest effective treatment planning can occur only if connections are made among all of a person's different problems. Similarly, some clinicians and researchers believe addictive behavior patterns have a lot in common with what causes them, what maintains them, and how they are treated. It is thought these commonalities should underlie treatment programming instead of the traditional emphasis on single addiction patterns. According to this viewpoint, behaviors identified as addictive, including, for example, alcohol and other drug abuse, over-eating, and compulsive gambling, have common factors that may be addressed in "generic" treatment programs to the improvement of any one or more of the problem areas troubling a person. The DSM-III-R recognizes this approach in addressing the psychoactive substance use disorders as a diagnostic class rather than addressing alcohol and other drug diagnoses in a nonintegrated way. Nonetheless, it should be remembered that the properties of the various drugs of abuse vary, as do the characteristics of the users, and there is no guarantee that a program that works well for alcoholics would be successful with heroin addicts.

As mentioned, alcohol and drug treatment programs have not been designed according to a more integrated look at alcohol and drug use. Although some projects examine combined treatment of alcohol and other drug abusers in one program, such efforts have not been accepted widely. Furthermore, a systematic evaluation of the benefits of integrated treatment approaches is not available.

Self-Help Groups

A major part of treatment of the psychoactive substance use disorders is the peer self-help group. According to Emrick, Lassen, and Edwards (1977), members of peer self-help groups perform therapeutic functions, but do not have professional credentials. A member of a peer self-help group could have training pertinent to conducting therapy, but such credentials are not used in performing self-help group functions. Members of these groups all have some identified problem that is the focus of the group's therapeutic activity. This is the basis of using the term "peer self-help," to distinguish from groups in which therapeutic agents (the group leader, for example) are not identified as having the same problems as the clients. Therefore, through the peer self-help group participants both give and receive help with their problems.

Although the peer self-help movement does not use professionally defined methods to help participants with their problems, it does not mean professionals are shunned. In fact, the professional community is welcome to join with the peer self-help group in achieving common goals in helping people alleviate their problems (such as Alcoholics Anonymous, 1972). The reasons are the complementary functions that professionals and the self-help group serve with each other. In practice, professionals working in the treatment of alcohol and drug problems often use the relevant self-help groups (such as Alcoholics Anonymous for alcohol problems and Narcotics Anonymous for other drug problems) when patients are participating in a professionally run rehabilitation program and as part of aftercare planning. Indeed, many alcohol and drug treatment programs are organized around principles of peer self-help groups.

In discussing treatment of the psychoactive substance use disorders it is important to review peer self-help groups because of their popularity and influence. In the treatment of alcoholism and other drug abuse there has been a trend to increase use of peer self-help. Peer self-help also has been a popular treatment of choice for other addictive behaviors: there are Weight Watchers and TOPS (Taking Off Pounds Sensibly) for treatment of obesity, Smokers Anonymous for treatment of cigarette smoking, and Gamblers Anonymous for treatment of compulsive gambling.

In this section we briefly describe the peer self-help movement organized for helping individuals identified as alcoholic—Alcoholics Anonymous (AA). Because of space limitations we cannot describe in detail the self-help groups for the treatment of drug problems. However, one of these groups, called Narcotics Anonymous (NA), is analogous to AA. Information described about AA can be applied readily to NA.

Emrick and others (1977) have called AA the prototypic self-help group, because it is the oldest, established in 1935. It has been the basis for development of other self-help movements for treatments in other problem areas. The AA movement began when an alcoholic surgeon (Dr. Bob) and an alcoholic stockbroker (Bill W.) helped each other to maintain sobriety. They spread from its Ohio origin their idea that alcoholics needed to help each other. Today AA is an international organization. A few alcohol self-help groups such as Alateen and Alanon have been derived from AA. Alateen's purpose is to help teenagers who have an alcoholic parent. Alanon generally is organized for spouses and others close to the alcoholic.

The bases of the AA "program" are self-help recovery through following the Twelve Steps and group participation. The core of AA is the model of recovery outlined in the Twelve Steps, which are listed in Table 15–2. There are a few features of the Twelve Steps important to point out. The first step states AA absolutely dismisses the notion that alcoholics can control their drinking or can ever reach that position. This emphasis on lack of control identifies AA as fitting a medical model, and in fact traditionally AA has

Table 15–2
The Twelve Steps of Alcoholics Anonymous

1. We admitted we were powerless over alcohol—that our lives had become unmanageable.
2. Came to believe that a Power greater than ourselves could restore us to sanity.
3. Made a decision to turn our will and our lives over to the care of God *as we understood Him.*
4. Made a searching and fearless moral inventory of ourselves.
5. Admitted to God, to ourselves, and to another human being the exact nature of our wrongs.
6. Were entirely ready to have God remove all these defects of character.
7. Humbly asked Him to remove our shortcomings.
8. Made a list of all persons we had harmed, and became willing to make amends to them all.
9. Made direct amends to such people wherever possible, except when to do so would injure them or others.
10. Continued to take personal inventory and when we were wrong promptly admitted it.
11. Sought through prayer and meditation to improve our conscious contact with God *as we understood Him* praying only for knowledge of His will for us and the power to carry that out.
12. Having had a spiritual experience as the result of these steps, we tried to carry this message to alcoholics, and to practice these principles in *all* our affairs.

The Twelve Steps reprinted with permission of Alcoholics Anonymous World Services, Inc. Alcoholics Anonymous is a program of recovery from alcoholism. Other self-help programs address other addictions. Any opinions on either the steps or AA are those of the authors.

looked at alcoholism as a disease. The beginning of recovery occurs when the alcoholic admits to himself or herself a powerlessness over alcohol, that without alcohol a return to health is possible and that with it the downward spiral to self-destruction continues. Another point causing much controversy is the frequent reference to God in the Twelve Steps. An immediate reaction to this is that AA is only for alcoholics who accept Western religious beliefs. However, AA takes pains to accent the phrase "God as He is understood," which means each person may interpret "God" or "Higher Power" as he or she wishes. The importance of referring to a Supreme Being is to emphasize that alcoholics have lost control over alcohol and of their lives and must enlist the assistance of a greater power in recovery. A final point is that the Twelve Step recovery program is oriented toward action, both in self-examination and change and in behavior toward others.

The Twelve Steps are a guide designed for people to follow largely by themselves on the road to **recovery.** The Steps are bases of recovery, but there are other parts to the AA program. One of these is group participation. Two major types are discussion meetings and speakers' meetings. In discussion meetings the chairman of the group tells his or her personal history of alcoholism and recovery from it, and then the meeting is opened for members' discussion of alcoholism and related matters. In a speakers' meeting a couple of members recite their personal histories of alcoholism and recovery. In open speakers' meetings, anyone who is interested may attend. Closed meetings are for alcoholics only.

One purpose of group meetings is to aid recovery through peer identification and learning from the experience of others. Building social relationships that do not revolve around alcohol represents an entirely new social life. The importance of forming sober social relationships may be seen in various AA functions such as "Sober Anniversaries" (the first day of a member's current episode of continuous sobriety) and "Sober Dances" (dances without alcohol or drugs).

Other major activities in the AA program are "Twelfth Stepping" and sponsorship. Twelfth Stepping refers to the twelfth of the Twelve Steps and involves members reaching out to other alcoholics in a time of need. Pertinent activities include helping an active alcoholic begin the AA program or helping a current AA member return to sobriety after he or she has begun drinking again. Sponsorship is similar to Twelfth Stepping, but there are important differences. First, sponsorship involves a stable one-to-one relationship between a member with more sobriety (the sponsor) and one with less (the sponsoree). To quote, "the process of sponsorship is this: An alcoholic who has made some progress in the recovery program shares that experience on a continuous, individual basis with another alcoholic who is attempting to attain or maintain sobriety through AA" (Alcoholics Anonymous, 1983, p. 5). Another important difference is that the sponsor helps the person in a variety of ways that may include taking the newer member's "inventory" (looking at what is behind a person's behavior) when asked,

Recovery
In the addictions field, this term means changes back to health in physical, psychological, and social functioning. It generally is believed that recovery is a lifetime process that requires total abstinence from alcohol and nonprescribed drugs.

guiding an individual to AA literature, such as the *Big Book* and *Twelve Steps and Twelve Traditions,* and explaining the AA program to family and others close to the sponsoree. Therefore, the sponsor-sponsoree relationship is in many ways more varied and more enduring than that involved in Twelfth Stepping. AA members view both types of activities as essential to their continued sobriety.

What has been described for AA is directly applicable to Narcotics Anonymous (NA). NA's organization and program of recovery is derived directly from AA's, including the use of the Steps of Recovery Program, group meetings, and the sponsor-sponsoree relationship. As the name implies, NA evolved with concentration on helping people addicted to opiate drugs, usually heroin. However, people who identify their primary problem as addiction to drugs of any type other than alcohol use NA instead of AA.

In summary, the AA program of recovery has been the cornerstone of a self-help movement that has been of value to many and that is reaching increasing numbers of people. It is worth mentioning again that both AA and NA may be, and are, used alone as programs of treatment. However, many members of these organizations began treatment or concurrently are receiving treatment from professional sources.

THE EFFECTIVENESS OF TREATMENT

When we talk about treatment effectiveness, we refer to the relationship between participation in some treatment and achieving a desired level of functioning, or outcome. Therefore, treatment effectiveness centers on if and how treatment participation causes different outcomes. Evaluations of the effectiveness of treatment are called **treatment outcome research.** In this section we discuss the effectiveness of treatments for alcohol and other drug problems.

Treatment Outcome Research
Research designed to show a causal relationship between undergoing a treatment and some physical, psychological, or social change.

Conclusions about Psychoactive Substance Use Disorder Treatment Outcome

Questions about the effectiveness of treatment for alcohol problems have been studied scientifically for more than fifty years. Evaluations of the outcomes of treatments of abuse of drugs other than alcohol seem to have begun far more recently, primarily in the 1960s. Nevertheless, enough data exist to draw some conclusions about both alcohol and other drug abuse treatment outcome. In general, these conclusions have held across the many specific treatment techniques that have been tried and across varied outcome times (most commonly within one year after a treatment episode ends). The verdict is this: no evidence exists that any treatment type(s) or setting(s) is consistently better than others, but staying in any kind of treatment increases the chances for long-term improvement.

It is important to understand what the conclusion about alcohol and drug treatment says and what it does not say. The finding that staying in treatment is beneficial should not be taken lightly. Studies have shown that the amount of money saved in, say, health care and business expenses as a result of improvements in people undergoing treatment is greater than the amount of money the treatment costs. Similarly, research completed by insurance companies, which pay a considerable share of the bills of alcohol and drug treatment, indicate substance abusers (and their families) use significantly fewer health care services after treatment than before. This shows the benefits of alcohol and drug treatment in financial terms; again, the more important, but more difficult to measure, gains in human welfare also are considerable.

What the general conclusions about treatments do not say, however, is what specific treatment techniques or interventions should be applied at a specific time for a specific person. We only know that enrolling in and sticking with a program that passes as formal treatment is better than dropping out of a program. In view of the variety of treatment methods available, this can be very inefficient and sometimes frustrating to the service provider. Consequently, a lot of effort has been devoted to figuring out ways to design or match treatment programs to specific people.

It also is implicit in the conclusions about treatment effectiveness that, because setting of treatment does not seem to make a consistent overall difference in outcomes, it may be best to spend money and time in the future on developing the content of treatment instead of researching further setting (for example, inpatient or outpatient) effects (Miller & Hester, 1986). For example, some settings of treatment are far less expensive than others, and it is sensible from everyone's perspective to use the one that costs less.

In discussing the effectiveness of treatment it is also important to take into account the rate of **spontaneous remission** of the psychoactive substance use disorders. Spontaneous remission refers to the resolution of a problem (in this case, alcohol abuse or drug abuse) without the aid of formal treatment (also see Chapter 6). As you might guess, in order to show a treatment is worth its cost, one thing that must be demonstrated is that it helps significantly beyond the rate of spontaneous remission. This reasoning is sound, but it is extremely difficult to determine just what are the rates of spontaneous remission. In this regard, people who resolve their problems without treatment are the ones with whom clinicians and researchers are least likely to have contact. Professionals instead tend to see people who are referred to a formal treatment setting.

Spontaneous Remission
Resolution of a problem without the help of formal treatment.

Despite this problem, estimates of spontaneous remission have been made for alcohol abuse, mostly through studies of people who have entered a formal treatment program, but who dropped out of it prematurely and could say they received "no treatment." Another method to estimate involves rates of improvement in "no treatment" or similar control groups in treatment outcome studies. The estimates of spontaneous remission of alcohol problems that have been made vary with the definition of remission, the comparison groups used, and the length of the interval during which functioning is measured. Miller and Hester (1980) suggested the spontaneous remission (abstinence or improvement in drinking patterns) in one year for untreated alcohol abusers is 19%, while Emrick (1975) calculated 13% for abstinence and 28% for abstinence plus "improved."

Unfortunately, there are no comparable statistics for problems with drugs other than alcohol. However, for both alcohol and drug problems it seems formal treatment aids improvement in functioning in different areas (for example, substance use, occupational functioning, family functioning) beyond levels that would have been realized without treatment, at least for those people in treatment settings.

Any conclusions about treatment outcome should be specific to the question, "Outcome in what?" In the case of the psychoactive substance use disorders, the major concern is the patient's substance use. Traditionally, substance use was the sole index of outcome or, at least, was talked about often to the exclusion of other areas of functioning that may have been measured. Although substance use can be viewed as an essential variable to measure in alcohol and drug treatment outcome research, it is now becoming generally accepted that complete portrayal of an individual's response to treatment requires assessment in areas of functioning besides alcohol or drug use.

The selection of outcome variables should be determined by what the treatment is supposed to affect and by what model or theory about alcohol or other drug abuse is used. As noted earlier in this chapter, many models and theories of these behaviors have been proposed. However, it is becoming more widely accepted that alcohol and drug use patterns develop and are maintained by a combination of biological, psychological, and environmental factors. What contribution each of these types of factors makes to behavior has not been specified and probably varies in different people. Nevertheless, this multiple variable (multivariate) perspective suggests it is necessary to measure treatment outcome in areas of functioning other than drinking or drug use. A practical reason exists for measuring multiple areas of functioning. Studies have shown, for example, that drinking behavior alone does not necessarily say much about how a person is doing in other parts of his or her life. Therefore, good functioning in drinking outcome does not necessarily mean good functioning in, say, job performance or psychological functioning. The upshot of these findings is that a balanced, representative depiction of how a person is doing after treatment requires assessment in multiple areas of functioning.

Psychoactive Substance Use Outcome Goals

Substance use treatment outcome goals require separate discussion for several reasons. Because the disorder being treated is defined in part by a

CONTEMPORARY ISSUE BOX 15–3
Relapse and the Addictions

It seems impossible to have a discussion about alcohol and drug abuse, as well as other addictive behaviors, without mentioning relapse. Everybody has heard of the alcoholic who seemed to have everything going for him or her during a year's sobriety but then blew it all inexplicably by taking a drink. The same goes for other drug abusers. Beyond these two classes of addiction, we have heard and probably have known perpetual weight cyclers, people who repeatedly go through periods of weight gain and loss, all the while trying to maintain weight control. And for tobacco smokers, Mark Twain summed it up nicely when he said, "Quitting smoking is easy . . . I've done it many times."

In the scholarly literature on alcohol and drug problems a widely-cited article by Hunt, Barnett, and Branch (1971) showed that about 70% of individuals treated for alcohol, tobacco, or heroin abuse in abstinence-oriented programs had returned to their primary substance use by the time they were out of treatment for three months. Such research findings, along with our personal experiences, place treatment for the addictions in not too favorable a light, at least as regards long-term effectiveness. Although there still is a lot to learn to improve our treatments for the addictions, treatment weakness may not be the only problem. Rather, how we study and interpret relapse may be. Any episode of relapse must be viewed in a context of long-term substance use patterns. If we look at relapse outside of this context, a result is that we risk getting a biased view of a relapse and an overly harsh perception of the value of addictions treatment programs.

pattern of substance use, such use naturally is the focus of most treatment providers and consumers. Another reason is the controversy in alcohol treatment about whether moderate (defined in various ways) drinking is a legitimate treatment outcome goal. The controversy involves an assumption of disease models of alcoholism, which implies that lifetime abstinence from alcohol is the fundamental and essential part of recovery in alcoholism. The need for abstinent outcomes is not questioned in the treatment of other drug abuse, however. It is likely abstinence from nonprescribed use of drugs is the only acceptable goal because the drugs are illegal, and society has a strong reaction against illicit drug use.

There are some clinicians who believe a goal of a reduction in drinking quantity, frequency, and problems is a reasonable one for some patients. In this respect, looking at outcomes in black and white terms, such as abstinent or nonabstinent, is thought to cloud the effects of a treatment that could be of true benefit to a person. Also, some experts believe that considering a range of drinking outcomes would attract more people to alcohol treatment who need it, but who shun it because they do not want a goal of lifelong abstinence from alcohol. This is thought to apply especially to people whose alcohol problems are not severe.

Practically, abstinence remains the dominant drinking outcome goal of alcohol treatment for all patients. It is generally recognized that wider application of nonabstinent drinking outcomes awaits additional research for predicting who can sustain nonabstinent and nonproblem drinking outcomes after alcohol treatment.

Assessment and Treatment Matching

Assessment is a major way clinicians develop treatment for psychiatric disorders, and the psychoactive substance use disorders are no exception. The assumption is that good assessment underlies good treatment outcome. When we say assessment in this context we mean use of mostly formal (for example, standard psychological tests), but sometimes informal (for example, casual observation of a patient's behavior on a treatment unit), procedures to measure some aspect of a person's functioning. Assessment of persons appearing for drug and alcohol treatment often is aimed at making diagnoses and can include several different procedures.

Measuring qualities or characteristics of people in order to design treatment means that treatment is tailored to the person. This is the same as matching the treatment to the individual. Patient-by-Treatment matching recently has received a lot of attention in treatment of psychiatric disorders in general. The question raised by Patient-by-Treatment matching is this: Which treatment choices are preferred for different groups of patients to produce the best outcomes?

In alcohol and drug treatment the "matching hypothesis" has been proposed as an explanation of why it has proved difficult, as we saw earlier in this chapter, to demonstrate consistent differences in the effectiveness of different treatments. The explanation is that treatment generally has beneficial effects, but since alcohol and drug abusers show so many differences among themselves, no single treatment approach could be expected to show consistently that it is better than others. The reasoning here is that characteristics of the patient can account for at least as much in how a person does after treatment, if not more so, than the treatment itself. Therefore, those characteristics must be considered in designing treatment(s). In fact, this argument is supported indirectly by the numerous studies that have shown relatively high correlations between characteristics of patients and their functioning after treatment, independent of the treatment the patients received.

It is important to include Patient-by-Treatment matching in any discussion of drug and alcohol treatment effectiveness because it currently is seen as a research priority of relevant federal funding agencies. In the near future, at least, there likely will be continued developments in this research area. Also, the ideas behind Patient-by-Treatment matching have been supported at least implicitly with funding for research on treatment considerations for special populations (for example, blacks and other minorities, women, the elderly). The idea behind singling out special populations in designing alcohol and drug treatment is that "the treatment program must be tailored to incorporate the needs and characteristics of the special population if it is to be effective" (Diesenhaus, 1982, p. 258). Presumably, the social and cultural factors common to identified subgroups influence the development and maintenance of drug and alcohol problems among group members and how they respond to treatment.

In summary, Patient-by-Treatment matching is an intuitively appealing hypothesis to account for the failure to find a generally superior treatment for drug and alcohol problems. The hypothesis goes further to say that looking for such general effects is misguided, because no one treatment could be designed in accordance with the many different characteristics of persons who appear for treatment. Studies of the matching hypothesis have yielded some promising results, but substantially more work is required before matching can be done in a refined way, even in a research setting.

The Effectiveness of Alcoholics Anonymous

With the large and increasing numbers of people using self-help groups for their alcohol and drug problems, it is important to determine how effective such groups are. Almost all of the research on this question concerns AA, and this discussion focuses on that organization.

As important a question as it is, how effective AA is, can be difficult to answer. One reason for the difficulty is the AA emphasis on anonymity of its members. The principle of anonymity is a major part of the "Twelve Traditions" of AA, which are a set of principles or guidelines adopted in 1950 for the operations of AA (Leach & Norris, 1977). The twelfth tradition, Anonymity, "is the spiritual foundation of our traditions, ever reminding us to place principles before personalities." This tradition is strictly adhered to in AA groups and makes outcome research very difficult to do, because it often requires identification of those receiving treatment.

Despite the difficulties associated with the systematic evaluation of AA, some research has been done. Emrick and others (1977) provided an excellent review of this research and concluded (p. 135) the following: (a) of its members who gave AA a "fair trial," a little under one half remain abstinent from alcohol for a year while actively involved in the program; (b) about 30% to 40% of participants remain abstinent during an average of two and a half to four years of membership; (c) about 10% of participants return to drinking early in the program, but then remain abstinent for long periods; and (d) between 60% and 68% of the members improve (in drinking outcome) to some extent (for example, drinking less heavily than before they began AA or not drinking at all) while participating at all. It is notable that, overall, these outcome figures are similar to what you would find if you reviewed the success rates of programs run by professionals.

As in evaluating other kinds of treatment, it may be better to ask for whom and under what conditions is AA effective? There have been a number of studies done on the "for whom" part of this question. For example, Ogborne and Glaser (1981) found AA affiliation was most likely to appeal to white, middle-aged, middle to upper class, socially stable men. Other characteristics included a history of physical dependence on alcohol and of **"loss of control" drinking,** as well as threat of losing a valued life style as a result of drinking. Psychological characteristics clustered such that Ogborne and Glaser speculated on an underlying "structuredness" factor. In this regard, people who have lost control over their drinking; who believe alcoholism is a disease that they cannot control; who tend to perceive the world globally rather than attend to details; and who seem to have high affiliative needs for a group having clear principles and rules, are unstructured, and an organization such as AA can provide the structure that is missing for them.

It appears, therefore, AA is reaching many individuals whose numbers are increasing each year. The best studies available suggest AA's effectiveness is comparable to standard professional treatment for maintaining abstinence from alcohol. Also similar to professional treatment is the finding individuals with certain characteristics do better in AA than do others. This, of course, reflects directly on the importance of matching individuals to treatments for the best outcomes.

Summary and Conclusions about Alcohol and Drug Treatment Effectiveness

In our discussion of treatment we have seen that people with drug or alcohol problems can be helped through either professional or self-help treatment programs. Yet we also saw that the search for treatment(s) generally resulting in better outcomes has been elusive. Rather, it seems that how people do in treatment depends considerably on who they are (for example their personal and social characteristics) and what they want to achieve (for example what outcomes they are considering). Another important factor is what environment those people have to stay sober in outside of treatment. This suggests the idea that a treatment can be imposed on an individual to create desired lasting changes after the treatment has been lifted is misguided. It appears necessary to look at treatment as one event in the life of a person who is trying to change the way he or she uses alcohol or drugs. In addition, the person and the treatment interact in a social context that strongly contributes to the course of change.

Loss-of-control drinking
The idea that once an alcoholic takes a drink of alcohol, he or she cannot stop by volition. Sooner or later, it is thought, the person will drink to a high degree of intoxication.

SUMMARY

- In thinking about treatment of the psychoactive substance use disorders, it is important to know about views of problem behavior that a treatment is based on. We review four models in this chapter: the moral model, the compensatory model, the medical model, and the enlightenment model. The models are based on two factors, responsibility for development of a problem and responsibility for its solution.

- Alcohol treatment services can be classified broadly into three categories of settings: hospital, intermediate, and outpatient. Within each of these settings a wide variety of services may be offered.

- Settings of drug abuse treatment have been defined primarily in relation to treatment of heroin abuse. They include detoxification, methadone maintenance, residential, and outpatient. As with alcohol treatment, a wide variety of treatment services may be offered in a setting.

- Recently there has been an upsurge in the treatment of nonopiate drug abusers. However, treatments primarily geared to drug use other than the opiates have not been well-defined.

- Pharmacological treatment of drug or alcohol problems centers on three areas: management of the addiction, treatment of psychological correlates of drug and alcohol dependence, such as depression or anxiety, and the use of antidrug drugs.

- Treatment of the psychological correlates of substance dependence is based on the idea that people use illicit drugs or alcohol to "self-medicate" their psychological difficulties.

- The major antidrug drug used in the treatment of alcohol dependence in the United States is disulfiram (Antabuse). Naltrexone has been used in treating opiate dependence.

- Treatment providers have found increasing numbers of their patients are multiple substance abusers. This has caused a change in the thinking that drug and alcohol treatment are independent efforts. Rather, there is increasing recognition of the need for settings that can accommodate multiple substance users, and for understanding common aspects of the addictive behaviors.

- The self-help groups Alcoholics Anonymous and Narcotics Anonymous are major resources in helping people with alcohol and drug dependence, respectively.

- Research shows there is no generally superior treatment for alcohol and drug dependence. However, people who stay in treatment do better than those who do not.

- Evaluating a treatment means determining how individuals are doing with their alcohol or drug use and in other areas of their lives. This is a multivariate view of alcohol and drug treatment outcome.

- It has long been standard practice to specify abstinence from alcohol and other drugs as the major outcome goal for alcohol and drug treatment. However, there are some who favor the idea that improvements (reductions) in alcohol use and alcohol problems are reasonable outcome goals for some patients.

- It is becoming widely accepted that treatments may be more effective if they are tailored or matched to patients' characteristics.

- It has proved very difficult to conduct good outcome research on self-help groups. However, what research has been done suggests that, overall, alcohol treatment outcome rates for AA are comparable to those for professionally based treatments. It also seems that people with certain characteristics tend to do better in AA than do others.

References

Alcoholics Anonymous (1972). *If you are a professional A.A. wants to work with you.* New York: A.A. World Services, Inc.

Alcoholics Anonymous (1983). *Questions and answers on sponsorship.* New York: Alcoholics Anonymous World Services, Inc.

Allison, M., & Hubbard, R.L. (1985). Drug abuse treatment process: A review of the literature. *The International Journal of the Addictions, 20,* 1321–1345.

Annis, H.M. (1987). Effective treatment for drug and alcohol problems: What do we know? Invited address presented at the Annual Meeting of the Institute of Medicine, National Academy of Sciences, Washington, D.C., October 21.

Armor, D.J., Polich, J.M., & Stambul, H.B. (1976). *Alcoholism and treatment.* Report prepared for the National Institute on Alcohol Abuse and Alcoholism (R-1739-NIAAA). Santa Monica, CA: Rand Corporation.

Brickman, P., Rabinowitz, V.C., Karuza, Jr., J., Coates, D., Cohn, E., & Kidder, L. (1982). Models of helping and coping. *American Psychologist, 37,* 368–384.

Carroll, J.F.X., Malloy, T.E., & Kenrick, F.M. (1977). Drug abuse by alcoholics and problem drinkers: A literature review and evaluation. *American Journal of Drug and Alcohol Abuse, 4,* 317–341.

Diesenhaus, H. (1982). Current trends in treatment programming for problem drinkers and alcoholics. In USDHHS, *Alcohol and health* (Monograph No. 3) (pp. 219–290). Washington, D.C.: U.S. Government Printing Office.

Emrick, C.D. (1975). A review of the psychologically oriented treatment of alcoholism, II. The relative effectiveness of different treatment approaches and the effectiveness of treatment vs. no treatment. *Journal of Studies on Alcohol, 36,* 88–108.

Emrick, C.D., Lassen, C.L., & Edwards, M.T. (1977). Nonprofessional peers as therapeutic agents. In A.S. Gurman & A.M. Razin (Eds.), *Effective psychotherapy: A handbook of research* (pp. 120–161). New York: Pergamon Press.

Hunt, T., & Meiners, M. (1979). *Guidelines for cost-of-illness studies in the Public Health Service.* Bethesda, MD: Public Health Service Task Force on Cost-of-Illness Studies.

Leach, B., & Norris, J.L. (1977). Factors in the development of Alcoholics Anonymous (AA). In B. Kissin & H. Begleiter (Eds.), *The biology of alcoholism* (Vol. 5) (pp. 441–544). New York: Plenum Press.

Maisto, S.A., & Nirenberg, T.D. (1986). The relationship between assessment and alcohol treatment. Paper presented as part of the Symposium, "The Matching Hypothesis in Alcohol Treatment: Current Status, Future Directions," at the 94th Annual Convention of the American Psychological Association, Washington, D.C., August.

Mello, N.K., Mendelson, J.H., Bree, M.P., & Luckas, S.E. (1989). Buprenorphine suppresses cocaine self-administration by rhesus monkeys. *Science, 245,* 859–862.

Miller, W.R., & Hester, R.K. (1980). Treating the problem drinker: Modern approaches. In W.R. Miller (Ed.), *The addictive behaviors: Treatment of alcoholism, drug abuse, smoking, and obesity* (pp. 11–141). New York: Plenum Press.

Miller, W.R., & Hester, R.K. (1986). Inpatient alcoholism treatment: Who benefits? *American Psychologist, 41,* 794–805.

Ogborne, A.C., & Glaser, F.B. (1981). Characteristics of affiliates of Alcoholics Anonymous. A review of the literature. *Journal of Studies on Alcohol, 42,* 661–675.

Peachey, J.E., & Annis, J. (1985). New strategies for using the alcohol-sensitizing drugs. In C.A. Naranjo & E.M. Sellers (Eds.), *Research advances in new psychopharmacological treatments for alcoholism* (pp. 199–216). Amsterdam: Elsevier Science Publishers B.V.

Sokolow, L., Welte, J., Hynes, G., & Lyons, J. (1981). Multiple substance use by alcoholics. *British Journal of Addiction, 76,* 147–158.

U.S. Department of Health and Human Services (1984). *Drug abuse and drug abuse research.* Washington, D.C.: U.S. Government Printing Office.

16 PREVENTION OF SUBSTANCE MISUSE

The preceding chapters include a great amount of information on alcohol and drugs, their actions and their use and abuse. The last chapter concerned the treatment of problems associated with substance use. This brings us to our final chapter, which focuses on the prevention of substance use problems.

It may seem a bit curious that preventing drug misuse is discussed in the last and not first chapter of a text such as this. After all, you might say, if the focus of society and government were on prevention, might not material on drug misuse be unnecessary? Unfortunately, professionals and funding sources historically have not made prevention a high priority. The reasons for this are not certain, but two possibilities stand out. One is that past prevention efforts have tended to yield at best only modest influences in changing patterns of drug use. A second reason is that current, ongoing substance abuse is dramatically visible, and thus receives a more rapid response in personnel and financial resources. Whether this approach is shortsighted is a question that is often and strongly debated.

Despite the lesser emphasis on prevention than on treatment, most would agree that prevention efforts should—indeed must—be an important component of any comprehensive approach to substance abuse. In this chapter, we first provide an overview of definitions of prevention. The major models of prevention and their implications then will be discussed. We also provide examples of several types of prevention projects and their outcomes. The chapter closes with some comments on the prospects for future work in prevention.

DEFINING PREVENTION

Prevention in this context pertains, broadly, to the avoidance or alleviation of problems associated with substance use. This relatively straightforward proposition opens the door to a variety of potential goals for prevention efforts. For example, the goal of prevention efforts aimed at illegal drug use generally is to stop its occurrence. However, an alternative or additional goal of such activities might be to minimize the effects of any illegal drug use that does occur. As such, the approaches chosen for implementation probably would be different. Therefore, in speaking of prevention, it is important to identify what is being prevented, whether it be onset of use, negative effects on society, health problems, or something else.

Primary prevention
Attempts to avoid substance use or abuse before it has a chance to occur.

Prevention of substance abuse traditionally has been divided into three types of intervention. The first is **primary prevention,** which pertains to the avoidance of substance abuse before it has a chance to occur. For example, one goal of primary prevention would be precluding the initial use of a substance. Never starting to use a drug, it is argued, means that you will not have any problems with it. This thinking in part underlies the ''Just Say

No" advertising effort, initiated during the administration of President Ronald Reagan and used to encourage young persons to turn down invitations to use drugs. Another goal of primary prevention for some substances might be the development of responsible attitudes and/or substance use behaviors. The best example of this would be responsible drinking behaviors. A number of posters and television spots have emphasized the need not to, for example, drive during or after drinking.

Secondary prevention refers to interventions applied when substance use problems already have begun to appear. This type of prevention, then, is analogous to early treatment in that interventions are used when problems are first surfacing. Secondary prevention frequently is used in the legal system response to substance misuse. For example, persons arrested for driving under the influence of alcohol often are referred to alcohol education courses designed to decrease the likelihood of the person drinking and driving again. Similarly, in some parts of the country educational programs are used with youthful offenders first arrested for drug possession. In each case the emphasis is on nipping the problem in the bud, just as it first appears. Central to such efforts, of course, is the early identification of these drug problems.

Secondary prevention
Interventions designed to prevent substance use problems just as the early signs of abuse begin to appear.

The third form of prevention, called **tertiary prevention,** includes interventions used in treating persons who are beyond the early stages of substance abuse or dependence. The goals of tertiary prevention essentially are to terminate use of the substance and thus avoid further deterioration in the person's functioning. As Nirenberg and Miller (1984) noted, tertiary prevention and substance abuse treatment (see Chapter 15) are comparable activities, and prevention efforts are more appropriately viewed as being either primary or secondary in nature. In the remainder of this chapter we will accordingly emphasize primary and secondary prevention activities.

Tertiary prevention
Refers to treatment interventions with persons well beyond the early stages of substance abuse or dependence.

MODELS OF PREVENTION

Over years of much debate and some research, three major prevention models have evolved. In reading about these models, you will notice the philosophy underlying each model has diverse implications for what approaches would be recommended to prevent substance use problems.

Sociocultural Model

The sociocultural, or social science, framework to understanding prevention posits that social norms directly influence the use and abuse of psychoactive substances. This model primarily has been used in efforts to prevent alcohol abuse, although the model also has implications for the prevention of other substance abuse, which we describe later in this section. When

Figures 16–1 and 16–2 Posters are widely used to communicate messages about the dangers of alcohol and drug misuse. Sometimes these posters deal with specific drugs and are directed at specific groups that are at risk for drug use (the poster on the left focuses on inhalants and is directed at Native American youths and young adults). Each of these posters encourages adolescents and young adults to "Say No" to alcohol and drugs. Copies of similar posters are available from the U.S. Office of Substance Abuse Prevention, Box 2345, Rockville, MD, 20852.

applied to drinking behavior, the model, according to Blane (1976), consists of three basic components:

an emphasis on the culture's normative structure

a need to integrate drinking into socially meaningful activities

a focus on providing for the gradual socialization of drinking behavior.

As you can see, prevention efforts derived from this model involve influencing the entire climate of drinking within the culture.

One of the strongest proponents of the sociocultural model is Rupert Wilkinson, who argues that alcohol use can be affected by planned policy measures. Wilkinson (1970) notes identifiable patterns of alcohol consumption exist that correspond to low rates of problematic drinking, and that these patterns can be used as guides for ingraining altered drinking patterns within the culture.

Wilkinson (1970) has identified five proposals worth pursuing to modify drinking patterns culturally. At the forefront is the need to have within the culture a low level of emotionalism about drinking and at the same time a lack of ambivalence about alcohol use. Emotionalism surrounding drinking, according to Wilkinson, merely creates tension and produces an environment in which discussion and change in drinking behavior cannot occur. A more measured and nonreactive approach will have the added benefit of reducing societal ambivalence about drinking and thus provide more clarity about drinking norms.

A second tenet of Wilkinson's sociocultural model is that there must be a distinction between drinking per se and drunkenness. The notion here is that acceptable drinking and unacceptable drinking (drunkenness) both should be clearly defined. Unfortunately, arriving at such definitions is not easy. Wilkinson's third point is that after identifying what drunkenness is, there should be firm taboos on its occurrence.

A fourth and central theme is that drinking should be integrated into a broader social context. That is, alcohol consumption should not be the focus of activity at any given gathering, but instead should be adjunctive to other activities.

Finally, Wilkinson proposes that society should allow the serving of alcohol only when food also is availabe. The belief here is that when food is available, alcohol consumption will not necessarily be the sole focus of activity. Furthermore, food slows the absorption of alcohol and potentially reduces the rate of drunkenness.

Taken together, these proposals designate acceptable and unacceptable forms of drinking, and thus clearly identify desired patterns of responsible drinking. These patterns of drinking then should be integrated into routine family and other social activities. It is noteworthy that the goal of the sociocultural approach is not the cessation of drinking but rather changes in social norms regarding drinking. Therefore, the approach is not a prohibitionist strategy, and some have argued that a fault of the sociocultural approach is that it may encourage drinking.

A major criticism of the sociocultural model is that it may not be widely applicable. Many countries, such as the United States and Canada, have diverse cultures and subcultures, and customs and values that fit one of them may not be amenable to or be accepted by another. A second criticism is that the sociocultural approach, while emphasizing moderate consumption, fails to account for the value and pleasure many people attach to heavier drinking. A third concern with the model is that it assumes attitudinal changes in the culture will result in the desired behavioral changes. However, there is no specification of the mechanisms by which that change will occur, and past research has provided no strong indication that attitudinal change even leads to behavioral change. Finally, it is argued that the sociocultural model does not adequately take into consideration physical problems associated with alcohol consumption (for example, cancers, liver and stomach ailments). In fact, some think that use of the sociocultural model may result in a greater prevalence of such physical problems, even if social problems are eliminated, simply by virtue of widespread use of alcohol (Blane, 1976; Nirenberg & Miller, 1984; Skirrow & Sawka, 1987; Whitehead, 1975).

Despite these concerns, the sociocultural model remains influential in the United States. Indeed, this approach probably is the dominant strategy currently being used (Skirrow & Sawka, 1987). When it is applied, the strategy has a broad scope. Examples of its applications include the advertising and education approaches to the problem of driving after drinking.

The sociocultural model has been applied predominantly in the context of alcohol use problems, but it also has been a cornerstone to many prevention efforts geared toward problems associated with other drug use. As noted earlier, an example would be the "Just Say No" campaign, which encourages people nationwide, but particularly young people, to refuse offers or temptations to use drugs. The only major difference between use of the sociocultural model with drugs as opposed to alcohol is that the former application keys on inculcating in society a norm of no use, as opposed to responsible use.

Distribution of Consumption Model

The second major model of prevention is the distribution of consumption approach. This model has been studied predominantly in the context of prevention or reduction of alcohol problems, although in recent years some effort has been directed at extending it to other drugs (see Skirrow & Sawka, 1987). The model is based on research showing a fairly consistent statistical distribution of alcohol consumption across cultures. The pioneering work in the development of the model was conducted by the French mathematician Sully Ledermann in the 1950s. The model's visibility was enhanced greatly by its endorsement a number of years later for the prevention of alcohol problems by an international group of scholars (Bruun, Edwards, Lumio, Makela, Pan, Popham, Room, Schmidt, Skog, Sulkunen, & Oesterberg, 1975).

There are three central propositions of the distribution of consumption model (Rush & Gliksman, 1986; Schmidt & Popham, 1978). The first is that the proportion of heavy alcohol users in a given population is positively correlated with the mean level of alcohol consumption in that population. This relationship, found in a number of countries, is graphed in Figure 16–3; the number of heavy drinkers in a society increases with the society's per capita consumption. Given this relationship, it is predicted that a decrease in average alcohol consumption within a given culture would be accompanied by a corresponding decrease in the proportion of heavy alcohol consumers.

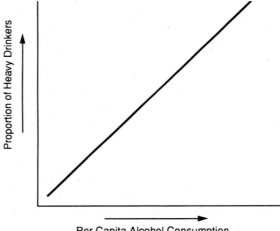

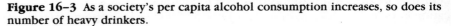

Figure 16–3 As a society's per capita alcohol consumption increases, so does its number of heavy drinkers.

The second proposition of the distribution of consumption model is that heavy alcohol consumption increases the probability of negative alcohol–related consequences, such as mental/emotional, physical, and social problems. Should the population's mean consumption increase, and thus raise the number of heavy drinkers, a corresponding increase in these negative consequences would be anticipated.

Finally, the model's third proposition is that societies should attempt to reduce the negative consequences of alcohol consumption by restricting the availability of alcohol. It is assumed that restricting alcohol availability, especially but not exclusively through procedures designed to raise the price of alcohol relative to disposable income, will lower per capita consumption and correspondingly the damages associated with alcohol use. Other approaches could include limiting the hours that bars and taverns can be open, controlling retail sales of alcohol, and raising the minimum drinking age.

Although it is a well-regarded approach to prevention, the distribution of consumption model has its critics. Some think the model is purely descriptive and does not provide any insights into the reasons people drink or how a person's drinking environment may contribute to drinking behavior. Skog (1985) has addressed this problem in more detail, and noted that sociocultural variables such as the drinking environment actually can be incorporated in the distribution of consumption model. Whitehead (1975) has gone further in his discussion of the ways in which the sociocultural and distribution of consumption models might be used together. Of more concern to critics is that "normal" drinkers in a population may react differently to efforts to reduce or restructure alcohol availability than "heavy" or "alcoholic" drinkers (Nirenberg & Miller, 1984). Again, the concern is that sociocultural and psychological variables are not included in the distribution of consumption model. For example, differences between normal drinkers and alcohol abusers may be crucial in predicting drinking behavior, with alcohol abusers perhaps less likely to respond to price increases and other policies designed to decrease per capita consumption. Relatedly, there may be a point at which these policies on restructuring alcohol use have no benefit. If, for example, the price of alcohol rises too much, the result may be an increase in bootlegging and home production of alcohol and in the mystique surrounding alcohol use (Skirrow & Sawka, 1987). As you can see, the task of reducing per capita consumption is very complex.

Proscriptive Model

This third prevention model is the most basic in principle. It takes a moral stance in addressing substance use problems. The guiding theme is that if there is no use of the substance, there can be no problem. If a person does use the substance, that use is not seen as a societal problem but instead as a product of a person's character flaw. As such, the goals of the proscriptive model are (a) prohibition of availability and (b) abstention from use (Skirrow & Sawka, 1987).

The proscriptive model has been applied to both alcohol and other drug use. The most important application to alcohol use was during Prohibition in the United States from 1921 to 1932. However, the model has been applied more consistently in the context of drug use. There has been for decades a strong proscriptive approach to drug use, generally focused on marijuana and heroin and more recently on cocaine. The proscriptive model in the 1930s and 1940s was most evident in films and newspaper and magazine articles geared toward mass audiences. Sensationalized stories about marijuana-induced crime sprees commonly were found in newspapers, and similar themes are evident in films from that era, such as *Reefer Madness, Assassin of Youth,* and *Marijuana: Weed with Roots in Hell.* Then, as now, the key to such campaigns has been that "good" people do not use drugs (Skirrow & Sawka, 1987).

CONTEMPORARY ISSUE BOX 16–1
Zero Tolerance for Drugs

Among the more recent applications of the proscriptive model of drug abuse prevention has been the "zero tolerance" policy implemented by some states and federal agencies. The theme behind the approach is that there will be no tolerance of any drugs in any amount in any place at any time. The goal of the policy is to attack the "demand side" of the drug abuse problem and thus hold drug users accountable for their role in drug trafficking.

Under the policy, which was prominently reported in the news services in mid-1988, cars, boats, luxury yachts, and other private property were seized when even the smallest amount of a substance was found. During a one-month period in spring of 1988 alone, the Coast Guard confiscated 27 boats. One yacht, the *Ark Royal,* was seized when Coast Guard officials found some marijuana seeds and two stems in a dresser drawer and in a trash can. Another yacht seized in the program was the *Monkey Business,* the vessel upon which presidential hopeful Gary Hart and model Donna Rice had made their well-publicized voyage to a Bahamas island. Coast Guard inspectors found one-twenty-eighth of an ounce of marijuana on the vessel. The two yachts, which frequently were chartered out, were returned to their owners after fines and seizure costs were paid. These, however, were just the more celebrated cases. Smaller amounts of private property, such as cars and luggage, also have been confiscated, and many of these cases remain in the judicial system.

Some government officials think the zero tolerance policy should be expanded. Edwin Meese III, Attorney General of the United States in Ronald Reagan's administration, called for drug testing of all workers across the country, with any positive test findings to result in termination of employment. According to Meese, this zero tolerance policy in drug testing is an "absolute necessity" to reduce drug problems. Meese thinks the fear of losing one's job would be a strong deterrent to drug use. Other observers have noted that constitutional questions surrounding such tests, especially when administered by the government, likely will preclude their widespread use.

Do you think the zero tolerance policy will have an effect on drug use or the overall drug problem? Clearly the Reagan administration thought it would. However, many others are not optimistic. They note that arresting only a small percentage of those using drugs would totally clog the legal system—even if most of them pleaded guilty to the charges! These same observers subscribe more to the approach of focusing on drug producers and drug traffickers.

Although the proscriptive model remains popular with some, it has not resulted in any significant contribution to the prevention of substance abuse problems. It is well-known that Prohibition was less than successful in alleviating problems associated with alcohol use, and other substance use problems also have continued. Perhaps the major difficulty with the model is that it is too simple to tackle a problem that is complex.

CURRENT TOPICS IN PREVENTION

Prevention efforts are being implemented on a number of fronts. In this section we provide an overview of several contemporary topics in primary and secondary prevention. Notice the majority of these prevention activities are derived predominantly from the sociocultural model.

Education and Mass Media Efforts

By far the most common and pervasive approaches to substance misuse prevention have been education and **mass media** efforts. Traditionally, these programs have been geared toward adolescents and young adults, two of the more visible groups at-risk for substance abuse. More recently, there have been efforts to extend these interventions to children.

Mass media
Communications designed for widespread distribution, such as advertisements, films, and printed materials.

The school system has been touted as an ideal setting for providing educational materials on substance use and misuse. Indeed, most states in the United States now require the inclusion of alcohol education in the school curricula, and many schools couple this with educational material on other drugs as well. Unfortunately, these state laws have not been translated in any systematic way into comprehensive instructional programs (Milgram, 1975). In her historical review of alcohol education, Milgram (1976) argues that there are a number of factors that impede the development of effective alcohol education, factors which apply to the provision of drug education as well. As she notes, to be effective, education strategies

. . . must be handled by teachers prepared in the field, have adequate time allotments, use objective and scientific materials, have specific and clear goals, be geared toward the needs of students, and be covered at the grade levels indicated by the needs of the students (Milgram, 1976, p. 12).

It is unfortunate that programs such as these have been exceptions to the rule. To compound these difficulties, teachers often are not trained in alcohol and drug education to begin with, and some are uncomfortable discussing the topic with their students (Milgram, 1976).

CONTEMPORARY ISSUE BOX 16–2
Warning Labels for Alcoholic Beverages

A proposed form of education/mass media intervention directed at preventing alcohol-related problems is the placement of warnings at alcohol sales outlets and on alcoholic beverage containers. The idea behind the proposal is analogous to why labels are placed on cigarette packages.

For years, efforts to pass legislation to require alcohol warning labels had been unsuccessful, despite the endorsement of approximately 100 health and public interest groups. However, such legislation became law in 1989. A bill passed by Congress now requires rotation of the following five warnings on all alcohol beverage containers:

WARNING: The Surgeon General has determined that the consumption of this product, which contains alcohol, during pregnancy can cause mental retardation and other birth defects.

WARNING: Drinking this product, which contains alcohol, impairs your ability to drive a car or operate machinery.

WARNING: This product contains alcohol and is particularly hazardous in combination with some drugs.

WARNING: The consumption of this product, which contains alcohol, can increase the risk of developing hypertension, liver disease and cancer.

WARNING: Alcohol is a drug and may be addictive.

Alcohol producers are less than supportive of labels. They argue that the information on the containers is common knowledge and unlikely to produce changes in drinkers' behavior. More basic, however, to their reservations is the issue of product liability. Some producers fear the use of the labels will open the door to lawsuits for drinkers' previous use of alcohol. On the other hand, argue proponents of the labeling, not placing the labels now, at a time when there is more research in support of the warnings, may result in an even greater number of lawsuits later.

The passage of the national labeling legislation goes beyond policies that already had been in place on a smaller scale in several cities. Since 1983, New York City, Philadelphia, Washington, D.C., and Columbus, Ohio, among others, passed city ordinances requiring posting of a sign where alcohol is sold indicating the relationship between drinking during pregnancy and the incidence of birth defects. And not all alcohol producers are against warning labels. For more than twenty years, Walter Stephen Taylor, a winemaker at Bully Hill Vineyards in upstate New York, has been placing warning labels on his products. He also has testified at Congressional hearings in favor of such labeling.

What happens when alcohol and drug education courses are administered? The results, interestingly, have not been all that promising. The general outcome is that students presented with educational materials do increase their knowledge about the topics covered. However, there has not been much of an indication that patterns of substance use change (Cellucci, 1984; Schaps, DiBartolo, Moskowitz, Palley, & Churgin, 1981). Indeed, in some cases (for example, Engs, 1977; Kalb, 1975; Kinder, 1975; Kinder, Pape, & Walfish, 1980; Stuart, 1974; Williams, DiCicco, & Unterberger, 1968) students receiving the education program have actually been found in the short run to escalate their drug use! However, these findings should be viewed with caution until more systematic research on education programs has been conducted, especially research on the long-term effects of these interventions. Tentatively, though, increased knowledge about alcohol and other drugs does not necessarily translate into modifications in their use.

One factor that may contribute to these discouraging results is the age at which youths receive exposure to the intervention. As a result of data indicating that young children have already begun to form concepts about intoxication, drinking behavior, and alcohol effects (Jahoda & Cramond, 1972), more attention is being placed on educational materials geared toward children in early elementary school. Preparing materials for that level of development may be more successful than trying to modify beliefs at a later age when they are more firmly established. An example is research on smoking beliefs and behavior. Chen and Winder (1986) wanted to determine the best time to apply a smoking intervention program. They surveyed over 500 sixth, ninth, and twelfth graders in a Massachusetts school system. The results showed that students are likely to respond best to a smoking educational program around the sixth grade. There were several reasons for this conclusion. One is that fewer of the sixth graders (6.5%) described themselves as occasional or regular smokers than among the ninth (21%) or twelfth (32%) graders. Sixth graders also reported much less peer pressure to smoke than the ninth or twelfth graders, less knowledge about smoking and its effects, and less familiarity about their parents' attitudes regarding smoking. In addition, there were indications that many of the sixth graders surveyed were planning to smoke within the following five years. Consequently, the use of an education program with these sixth grade students would appear to hold the most promise for engendering attitudes against personal smoking.

A related trend in the area of prevention education has been the use of parents serving as teachers of their children. According to DuPont (1980), a former director of the National Institute on Drug Abuse, "It is ironic that after a decade of parent put-downs that we are today rediscovering that parents, who were written off as ignorant and meddlesome at best and as 'the problem' at worst, are now 'the solution' to drug problems" (p. 2). While this statement might be overstating the point, it does appear that parents can be an important—perhaps crucial—element in prevention activities. Much of this growing emphasis on parents derives from the view that substance use is a family concern. These parent-focused programs seek to enhance family communication about alcohol and other drugs, to have parents model or foster either abstinence or responsible use of accepted substances (generally alcohol), and to encourage abstinence from other substances (Kimmel, 1976). One such program, called "The Power of Positive Parenting," includes a curriculum designed to make parents aware of the profound influence their behavior has on their children's (Richmond, 1977). Children, especially in their preschool years, turn primarily to their parents when looking for models of appropriate behavior. The program aims to make parents aware of the ways they influence their children's beliefs about drugs and to help them determine what constitutes "responsible modeling" of, for example, drinking behavior.

Educational efforts also have been implemented in broader scope using mass media technology. Mass media in this context refers to "communication through television, radio, newspapers, billboards, films, and printed materials designed for widespread distribution" (Hewitt & Blane, 1984, p. 282), although television and radio are the most frequently used vehicles for these messages. Because mass media campaigns often involve frequent presentations of a relatively brief message (for example, a 15-second television spot), developers of these campaigns generally will create a slogan which unites the material within the various spots. Slogans of some recent campaigns include "Just Say No" for drugs and "Know When to Say When" and "Friends Don't Let Friends Drive Drunk" for alcohol. Most of the campaigns in recent years regarding alcohol abuse have focused on decreasing the incidence of driving under the influence.

While research on mass media campaigns has not yielded a clear picture of their effects, it appears the programs do succeed in raising knowledge levels and increasing awareness about the use of drugs (Blane, 1988; Hewitt & Blane, 1984). Of particular note is the finding that campaigns on drunk driving pretty consistently yield changes in knowledge level (for example, knowing the legal definition of intoxication). As with other prevention approaches, attitude change has been found less consistently. There is no evidence, however, that significant changes in patterns of alcohol or drug use are occurring as a function of these mass media strategies. These approaches will more likely be successful if they are directed at particular substance using groups.

Taken together, education and mass media approaches continue to command the majority of resources available for prevention. Their benefits appear to be primarily in the areas of knowledge and, to a lesser extent, attitude change. Their effectiveness is likely to increase as a function of better tailoring of campaign messages and efforts to target these campaigns to particular populations of drug users. And, of course, more work is needed to increase the likelihood that these approaches will result in actual changes in substance use.

Affect-Oriented Programs

Many prevention programs, and particularly those geared toward youth, incorporate what is called an "affective" component. This affective feature typically involves **values clarification** and decision making. Values clarification activities include self-exploration, life-values assessment, and strategies for fulfilling needs that are part of those values (Hewitt, 1982). These programs provide students with general strategies for making life choices and for applying these techniques to situations that involve alcohol or other drugs. The goal of the affect-oriented material overall is to have participants be aware of their own feelings and attitudes regarding drugs, so they can deal effectively with drug use situations according to their individual value structures.

The logic behind the use of an affective component is that thoughts, feelings, attitudes, and values regarding alcohol and drugs can be just as important in drug use situations as knowledge, and perhaps more so. As yet, we do not know the extent to which affect-oriented programs are beneficial. As with educational programs, there has not been much well-designed research on the effects of affect-oriented interventions. The research that has been conducted does suggest, though, that such interventions do help to clarify personal views on substance use.

Values clarification
A frequent component of affect-oriented prevention programs, it typically involves exploration of one's own needs and beliefs regarding drugs.

Workplace Programs

Substance use problems among employees can be costly for employers. The costs can be seen in lost production, accidents, absenteeism, and thefts to support drug habits. As such, it makes sense to some employers to provide the opportunity for early identification and intervention when an employee begins to show impairments due to drug use. Although part of the employer's motivation may be humanitarian, a central incentive frequently is to avoid losses in company productivity.

CONTEMPORARY ISSUE BOX 16–3
Server Interventions

Holding people who serve alcohol to patrons or guests responsible for the patrons' behavior if they become intoxicated is not a new idea. Its roots are in what are referred to as dram shop (an old English term for taverns) laws. These laws, which in various forms are active and being upheld in courts today, have two implications. The first is that servers of alcohol, whether a bartender or the host of a private dinner party, can in some circumstances be held liable for the actions of intoxicated patrons or guests. The second implication, important in the context of prevention, is that servers and hosts can contribute to preventing alcohol-related problems through their decisions not to serve alcohol to persons who are intoxicated. Indeed, the premise of model legislation for a uniform dram shop law is the prevention of alcohol-related injuries, deaths, and other damages (Mosher & Colman, 1986).

This model legislation has been enacted in several states and introduced in a number of others. Part of the legislation identifies several practices that businesses and hosts may be able to use in preventing or limiting their liability in serving alcohol, such as encouraging patrons or guests not to become intoxicated if they consume alcohol, providing nonalcoholic beverages and food, and promoting the use of safe transportation alternatives to preclude the intoxicated drinker from driving home. These guidelines very much are derived from a sociocultural framework of drug misuse in that they seek to prevent alcohol-related problems by modifying the context of the drinking by encouraging safer drinking practices.

One important outcome of the dram shop legislation is that a variety of education and training programs have been developed to help alcohol servers and hosts to detect intoxication and to stop serving alcohol to a person who appears intoxicated. There are indications that these programs can have a positive effect (for example, Geller, Russ, & Delphos, 1987), but there are obstacles to their implementation, especially in business situations. For example, one frustrating experience described working with alcohol servers in Atlantic City, New Jersey, gambling casinos (Nathan, 1984; Nathan & Niaura, 1987). Nathan and his colleagues were asked to provide information on how to detect intoxication among patrons and how to stop serving them drinks (most of which were served free to the patrons if they were at a gambling table). Although servers did acquire these skills, the program eventually broke down because casino owners resisted allowing their servers to cut off intoxicated patrons who still were gambling. Thus, servers were in a true bind. According to Nathan and

Niaura (1987), they would refuse drinks to an intoxicated patron and avoid legal liability, but at the same time they might antagonize their employer if the patron stopped gambling!

There are several potential advantages to worksite prevention programs. One is their service to adults who still are functioning relatively well. As Nathan (1984) notes, they still have their jobs and are more likely to be physically, psychologically, and economically healthy compared to those who already have lost jobs because of their substance abuse. Thus, they may be in a better position to respond to prevention opportunities. Other advantages, according to Nathan (1984), are that the company employees are a captive audience, making it easier to direct prevention-related messages to them. Relatedly, employees do not have to travel outside the company to see or hear these messages. Finally, an employer implementing a program that benefits employees may improve employee morale, thus improving work performance.

One disadvantage to employers of worksite programs is their cost. Despite the possible payoff of enhanced employee functioning, some company executives are skeptical of the effectiveness of prevention programs, or do not think program benefits outweigh program costs. Another problem is employees' concerns about confidentiality. Employees may hesitate to identify themselves as having problems with alcohol or other drugs for fear of being dismissed from their positions. A worksite prevention and intervention program is unlikely to be effective without stringent guidelines to protect the confidentiality of those the program is intended to help.

Prevention and intervention efforts, when they do occur, can take several forms. Primary prevention might include the use of posters and mailings providing educational material on drug problems. Some companies have used films and outside speakers to increase awareness about these problems. These strategies, which generally heighten awareness about substance use and its effects, also are intended to set the stage for employees who are abusing alcohol or drugs to decide to start treatment. This treatment phase represents a second tier of the prevention effort. It can take several forms. Frequently it involves the employee meeting with an on-site counselor. These counselors typically operate through what has been called an employee assistance program, or EAP. The counselor will either work with the employee on the substance use problem in that setting or arrange for the employee to participate in an outside treatment setting (for example, inpatient treatment, sessions with an outside counselor). Either separately or as part of either of these two treatment options, the counselor could encourage the employee to begin attending self-help groups, such as Alcoholics Anonymous or Cocaine Anonymous.

So far worksite programs have not been established too often. Further,

Figure 16–4 Posters such as these have been placed at worksites to encourage workers to participate in employee assistance programs when their lives are being affected by alcohol or drug problems.

when programs are put in place, their effectiveness rarely is evaluated. In addition, most current programs focus on secondary rather than primary prevention (such as, identifying alcohol or drug abusers and arranging for treatment). Nathan (1984), in reviewing worksite programs, noted that "when prevention efforts are undertaken, they are usually a small, ineffective afterthought grafted onto a treatment program" (p. 404). Thus, as with the national scene, prevention efforts in the workplace appear to be a low priority.

Programs for College Students

Abuse of alcohol—whether chronic or sporadic—long has been a problem on college campuses (Kraft, 1984). Studies on collegiate drinking practices have consistently documented a higher prevalence of alcohol use than in the general population (Engs, 1977; Girdano & Girdano, 1976; Penn, 1974), and an apparent increase in the number of alcohol-related problems over the course of the past twenty years. Problems associated with drinking in college students include relationship difficulties, driving under the influence, involvement in arguments or fights, vandalism and other property destruction, and lowered grades. Both male and female drinkers are candidates to experience such problems related to alcohol. Estimates are that up to one-quarter of student drinkers can be considered problem drinkers, in that at least some degree of negative consequence is associated with their use of alcohol (Berkowitz & Perkins, 1986; Saltz & Elandt, 1986).

Colleges have taken various approaches in attempting to curtail problematic uses of alcohol, and we describe two well-known programs. The first, implemented at the University of Massachusetts at Amherst, has a primary prevention focus, and the second, at the University of Washington at Seattle, is a secondary prevention strategy.

The program at the University of Massachusetts was intended as a university-wide strategy "to create a campus environment that encouraged responsible use of beverage alcohol and discouraged irresponsible drinking behaviors" (Kraft, 1984, p. 328). The program was viewed mostly as a primary prevention strategy—that is, to educate people about alcohol use *before* problems arise. The logic behind this approach, as with the educational strategies described earlier, is that knowledge will translate into an ability to avoid alcohol problems. The program included three forms of prevention effort. The first, called extensive educational activity, was used to enhance awareness about alcohol and its use. Information was disseminated by use of posters, radio and newspaper advertisements, and pamphlets. The second form of intervention involved intensive approaches, which included small discussion groups, classes, and workshops on a variety of topics related to alcohol use and abuse. The final form of intervention—community development actions—keyed on the identification of and response to the specific alcohol-related needs of special groups of students, such as Black and Latino students and women. Other community actions included liaison with the management of the local campus pub to arrange for service of food and non-alcoholic beverages, and in-service training workshops for staff members of the university's health services center.

The University of Massachusetts project is an example of a coordinated effort to use a variety of interventions to prevent alcohol problems. In contrast to most projects, where only a unidimensional educational program is used, the Massachusetts program was multifaceted. Subsequent evaluation of the program's effects has been both encouraging and disappointing. On the positive side, it was found that the program, using its variety of approaches, had significant saturation—that is, a large number of the students came into contact with the program components, whether that contact was seeing a program poster, hearing a radio spot on drinking, or attending a workshop on alcohol. There also was evidence of increased awareness and knowledge about drinking. However, as with the majority of programs aimed at modifying knowledge or attitudes regarding alcohol, changes in actual alcohol use or alcohol use problems were not apparent.

The program at the University of Washington has been developed by Alan Marlatt and his colleagues (Baer, Kivlahan, Fromme, & Marlatt, in press; Fromme, Kivlahan, & Marlatt, 1986; Kivlahan, Coppel, Fromme, Williams, & Marlatt, in press). In contrast to the Massachusetts program, Washington's prevention approach focuses on skills training. In this regard, their program includes four central components:

training in blood alcohol level monitoring to acquire knowledge about specific alcohol effects

development of coping skills to use in situations associated with risky or heavy drinking

modifying expectations regarding alcohol use and alcohol effects

development of stress management and other life-management skills

As you can see, the "skills" that the University of Washington program is designed to impart can be used to avoid problematic uses of alcohol.

Results from the University of Washington program have been impressive and encouraging. For example, from before to after the eight-week program, students in the skills training program showed decreases on three measures of alcohol consumption: number of drinks per week, peak blood alcohol level reached per week, and hours per week with a blood alcohol level exceeding .055 percent (recall that a level of .10% is considered legally intoxicated in most of the United States). These decreases were not observed in students who only participated in an assessment phase or who only attended an alcohol education class that emphasized alcohol effects. Most important, the changes observed among the students receiving the skills training program were still evident twelve months after the intervention

(Baer and others, in press). Although it will be important to see if these differences in response to the program continue over longer periods of time, the degree of change maintained through twelve months is impressive.

CLOSING COMMENTS ON PREVENTION

Prevention of alcohol and drug abuse is a topic that almost everyone acknowledges as being central to any coherent response to alcohol and drug problems in this country. Unfortunately, it is an area that has been allocated meager resources, at least in comparison to the monies spent annually in the treatment of alcohol and drug abuse. Although past efforts at prevention, especially education and mass media approaches, have increased relevant knowledge, they have had much less effect on alcohol and drug use. Especially critical in future research on prevention will be the design and evaluation of programs for specific cultural subgroups, the creation of programs geared toward the specific developmental levels of children and teenagers, parental involvement programs, and programs aimed at providing alternatives to alcohol and drug use. However, full exploration of these possibilities requires more resources from state and federal agencies compared to what has been available so far.

SUMMARY

- Most would agree that prevention efforts should be an important component of any comprehensive approach to substance abuse, but professionals and funding sources have not made prevention efforts a high priority.

- Prevention traditionally has been divided into three types of intervention: primary, secondary, and tertiary.

- Primary prevention refers to efforts focused on avoiding substance use or abuse before it occurs.

- Secondary prevention involves early interventions designed to address substance abuse just as problems are beginning to appear.

- Tertiary prevention, which actually is more treatment than prevention, includes intervention used to treat persons beyond the early stages of substance abuse.

- The sociocultural model of prevention, probably the dominant approach applied in the United States, posits that social norms directly influence substance use. Prevention efforts derived from this model involve influencing the entire climate of drinking within a culture.

- Another major prevention model is the distribution of consumption approach, which posits (1) that the proportion of heavy drinkers in a culture is positively related to the mean level of alcohol consumption, (2) that heavier alcohol consumption increases the probability of alcohol problems, and (3) that societies should attempt to reduce the negative consequences of drinking by reducing alcohol consumption across the culture.

- A third model of prevention is the proscriptive approach, which focuses on prohibiting availability of substances and emphasizes abstention from drug use.

· The most common substance abuse prevention interventions have included education and use of mass media. Most states in the United States now require the inclusion of alcohol education in school curricula. Frequently this is coupled with educational materials on other drugs as well.

· Alcohol and drug education courses generally have been shown to increase knowledge levels, but have not been as successful in changing substance use patterns.

· In recent years there has been an increasing use of parents in education prevention programs, especially in prevention programs focused on children.

· Mass media campaigns appear to succeed in raising levels of knowledge and awareness about drugs. Changes in attributes and actual drug use behavior have not been found as consistently.

· Prevention programs are sometimes located at worksites, where the goal is to identify drug abusers and to intervene when drug problems interfere with job performance. These programs, when established, generally concentrate more on secondary than on primary prevention.

· A variety of prevention programs, generally focused on alcohol use, have been established on college campuses.

· The full potential of prevention interventions has not yet been tested. But before this potential can be assessed, more resources from state and federal agencies will be needed.

References

Baer, J.S., Kivlahan, D.R., Fromme, K., & Marlatt, G.A. (in press). Secondary prevention of alcohol abuse with college student populations: A skills-training approach. In G. Howard (Ed.), *Issues in alcohol use and misuse by young adults.* Notre Dame, IN: Notre Dame University Press.

Berkowitz, A.D., & Perkins, H.W. (1986). Problem drinking among college students: A review of recent research. *Journal of American College Health, 35,* 21–28.

Blane, H.T. (1976). Education and the prevention of alcoholism. In B. Kissin & H. Begleiter (Eds.), *The biology of alcoholism (Vol. 4): Social aspects of alcoholism* (pp. 519–578). New York: Plenum.

Blane, H.T. (1988). Research on mass communications and alcohol. *Contemporary Drug Problems, 15,* 7–20.

Bruun, L., Edwards, G., Lumio, M., Makela, K., Pan, L., Popham, R.E., Room, R., Schmidt, W., Skog, O., Sulkunen, P., & Oesterberg, E. (1975). *Alcohol control policies in public health perspective.* Helsinki: Finnish Foundation for Alcohol Studies.

Cellucci, T. (1984). The prevention of alcohol problems: conceptual and methodological issues. In P.M. Miller & T.D. Nirenberg (Eds.), *Prevention of alcohol abuse* (pp. 15–53). New York: Plenum.

Chen, T.T.L., & Winder, A.E. (1986). When is the critical moment to provide smoking education at schools? *Journal of Drug Education, 16,* 121–134.

DuPont, R.L. (1980). The future of primary prevention: Parent Power. *Journal of Drug Education, 10,* 1–5.

Engs, R.C. (1977). Drinking behaviors among college students. *Journal of Studies on Alcohol, 38,* 2144–2156.

Fromme, K., Kivlahan, D.R., & Marlatt, G.A. (1986). Alcohol expectancies, risk identification, and secondary prevention with problem drinkers. *Advances in Behaviour Research and Therapy, 8,* 237–251.

Geller, E.S., Russ, N.W., & Delphos, W.A. (1987). Does server intervention training make a difference? *Alcohol Health and Research World, 11,* 64–69.

Girdano, D.D., & Girdano, D.A. (1976). College drug use—A five-year survey. *Journal of the American College Health Association, 25,* 117–119.

Hewitt, L.E. (1982). Current status of alcohol education programs for youth. In *Special population issues* (Alcohol and Health Monograph No. 4) (pp. 227–260). Rockville, MD: NIAAA.

Hewitt, L.E., & Blane, H.T. (1984). Prevention through mass media communication. In P.M. Miller & T.D. Nirenberg (Eds.), *Prevention of alcohol abuse* (pp. 281–323). New York: Plenum.

Jahoda, G., & Cramond, J. (1972). *Children and alcohol.* London: HMSO.

Kalb, M. (1975). The myth of alcoholism prevention. *Preventive Medicine, 4,* 404–416.

Kimmel, C.K. (1976). A prevention program with punch: The national PTA's Alcohol Education Project. *Journal of School Health, 46,* 208–210.

Kinder, B.N. (1975). Attitudes toward alcohol and drug abuse: II. Experimental data, mass media research, and methodological considerations. *International Journal of the Addictions, 10,* 1035–1054.

Kinder, B.N., Pape, N.E., & Walfish, S. (1980). Drug and alcohol education programs: A review of outcome studies. *International Journal of the Addictions, 15,* 1035–1054.

Kivlahan, D.R., Coppel, D.B., Fromme, K., Williams, E., & Marlatt, G.A. (in press). Secondary prevention of alcohol-related problems in young adults at risk. In K.D. Craig & S.M. Weiss (Eds.), *Prevention and early interventions: Biobehavioral perspectives.* New York: Springer.

Kraft, D.P. (1976). College students and alcohol: The 50 plus 12 project. *Alcohol, Health and Research World,* Summer, 10–14.

Kraft, D.P. (1984). A comprehensive prevention program for college students. In P.M. Miller & T.D. Nirenberg (Eds.), *Prevention of alcohol abuse* (pp. 327–369). New York: Plenum.

Milgram, G. (1975). Current status and problems of alcohol education in the schools. *Journal of School Health, 46,* 317–320.

Milgram, G. (1976). A historical review of alcohol education research and comments. *Journal of Alcohol and Drug Education, 21,* 1–16.

Mosher, J.F., & Colman, V.J. (1986). Prevention research: The model Dram Shop Act of 1985. *Alcohol Health and Research World, 10,* 4–11.

Nathan, P.E. (1984). Alcoholism prevention in the workplace: Three examples. In P.M. Miller & T.D. Nirenberg (Eds.), *Prevention of alcohol abuse* (pp. 387–405). New York: Plenum.

Nathan, P.E., & Niaura, R.S. (1987). Prevention of alcohol problems. In W.M. Cox (Ed.), *Treatment and prevention of alcohol problems: A resource manual* (pp. 333–354). New York: Academic Press.

Nirenberg, T.D., & Miller, P.M. (1984). History and overview of the prevention of alcohol abuse. In P.M. Miller & T.D. Nirenberg (Eds.), *Prevention of alcohol abuse* (pp. 3–14). New York: Plenum.

Oei, T.P.S., & Fea, A. (1987). Smoking prevention program for children: A review. *Journal of Drug Education, 17,* 11–42.

Penn, J.R. (1974). College student life-style and frequency of alcohol usage. *Journal of the American College Health Association, 22,* 220–222.

Richmond, L.B. (1977). Decisions and drinking: A prevention approach. *Alcohol Health and Research World,* Winter, 22–26.

Rush, B., & Gliksman, L. (1986). The distribution of consumption approach to the prevention of alcohol-related damage: An overview of relevant research and current issues. *Advances in Alcohol and Substance Abuse, 5,* 9–32.

Saltz, R., & Elandt, D. (1986). College student drinking studies, 1976–1985. *Contemporary Drug Problems, 13,* 117–159.

Schaps, E., DiBartolo, R., Moskowitz, J., Palley, C.S., & Churgin, S. (1981). A review of 127 drug abuse prevention program evaluations. *Journal of Drug Issues, 9,* 17–43.

Schmidt, W., & Popham, R.E. (1978). The single distribution theory of alcohol consumption. *Journal of Studies on Alcohol, 39,* 400–419.

Skirrow, J., & Sawka, E. (1987). Alcohol and drug abuse prevention strategies: An overview. *Contemporary Drug Problems, 14,* 147–241.

Skog, O.J. (1985). The collectivity of drinking cultures: A theory of the distribution of alcohol consumption. *British Journal of Addiction, 80,* 83–99.

Stuart, R.B. (1974). Teaching facts about drugs: Pushing or preventing. *Journal of Educational Psychology, 66,* 189–201.

Wallack, L.M. (1980). Mass media and drinking, smoking, and drug taking. *Contemporary Drug Problems, 9,* 49–83.

Whitehead, P.C. (1975). Prevention of alcoholism: Divergences and convergences of two approaches. *Addictive Diseases, 7,* 431–443.

Wilkinson, R. (1970). *The prevention of drinking problems: Alcohol control and cultural influences.* New York: Oxford University Press.

Williams, A.F., DiCicco, L., & Unterberger, H. (1968). Philosophy and evaluation of an alcohol education program. *Quarterly Journal of Studies on Alcohol, 29,* 685–702.

APPENDIX

INFORMATION AND TREATMENT RESOURCES

National and Regional Organizations Providing Substance Abuse Information

Al-Anon or Alateen
P.O. Box 182
Madison Square Station
New York, New York 10159-0182

Alcohol and Drug Abuse Education
    Program
U.S. Department of Education
400 Maryland Avenue N.W.
Room 4145, MS6411
Washington, D.C. 20202

Alcohol and Drug Problems Association of
    North America
Hall of States
444 North Capitol Street N.W.
Washington, D.C. 20001

Alcoholics Anonymous
P.O. Box 459
New York, New York 10163

American Alcohol and Drug Information
P.O. Box 10212
Lansing, Michigan 48901-0212

American Council on Alcohol Problems
6955 University Avenue
Des Moines, Iowa 50311

Americans for Non-Smokers Rights
2054 University Avenue
Suite 500
Berkeley, California 94704

Boost Alcohol Consciousness Concerning
    the Health of University Students
(BACCHUS)
c/o Campus Alcohol Information Center
124 Tigert Hall
University of Florida
Gainesville, Florida 32611

Central States Institute of Addictions
Addiction Materials Center
120 W. Huron Street
Chicago, Illinois 60610

Children of Alcoholics Foundation
P.O. Box 4185
Grand Central Station
New York, New York 10163

Citizens for Safe Drivers Against Drunk
    Drivers and Other Chronic Offenders
5632 Connecticut Avenue N.W.
P.O. Box 42018
Washington, D.C. 20015

Co-Dependents Anonymous
P.O. Box 5508
Glendale, Arizona 85312-5508

Distilled Spirits Council of the United States
1250 I Street N.W.
Suite 900
Washington, D.C. 20005

Families in Action National Drug
    Information Center
3845 North Druid Hills Road
Suite 300
Decatur, Georgia 30033

Just Say No Foundation
1777 North California Boulevard
Walnut Creek, California 94596

Licensed Beverage Information Council
425 13th Street N.W.
Suite 1300
Washington, D.C. 20004

Mothers Against Drunk Drivers (MADD)
669 Airport Freeway
Hurst, Texas 76053

Narcotics Anonymous
P.O. Box 9999
Van Nuys, California 91409

National Association for Children of
P.O. Box 421691
San Francisco, California 94142

National Association of Women in
   Alcoholism and Other Drug Dependencies
700 Dimmick Drive
Los Angeles, California 90065

National Clearinghouse on Alcohol and
   Drug Information*
P.O. Box 2345
Rockville, MD 20852

National Black Alcoholism Council
417 South Dearborn Street
Suite 1000
Chicago, Illinois 60605

National Council on Alcoholism
12 West 21st Street
7th Floor
New York, New York 10010

National Organization for the Reform of
   Marijuana Laws
2001 S Street N.W.
Suite 640
Washington, D.C. 20009

Office on Smoking and Health
Technical Information Center
5600 Fishers Lane
Room 116
Rockville, Maryland 20857

Remove Intoxicated Drivers (RID)
P.O. Box 520
Schenectady, New York 12301

Rutgers Center of Alcohol Studies
P.O. Box 969
Piscataway, New Jersey 08854

Stop Teenage Addiction to Tobacco (STAT)
P.O. Box 50039
Palo Alto, California 94303

Students Against Driving Drunk (SADD)
Box 800
Marlboro, Massachusetts 01752

United States Brewers Association, Inc.
1750 K Street N.W.
Washington, D.C. 20006

Up Front Drug Information
5701 Biscayne Boulevard
Suite 602
Miami, Florida 33137

Women for Sobriety, Inc.
Box 618
Quakerstown, Pennsylvania 18951

STATE AND TERRITORIAL LISTING OF ORGANIZATIONS

Alabama

Alabama Department of Mental Health/
   Mental Retardation
P.O. Box 3710
200 Interstate Park Drive
Montgomery, Alabama 36193

Alaska

Alaska Council on Prevention of Alcohol
   and Drug Abuse
7521 Old Seward Highway
Anchorage, Alaska 99518

*The NCADI is the U.S. Federal clearinghouse for information and services on alcohol and other drugs. It is the largest, most comprehensive resource on alcohol and drug information in the world. Most of its materials (for example, pamphlets, booklets, posters, fact sheets, directories, resource lists, and so on) and services are free to the public.

American Samoa

Department of Human Resources
Social Services Division
Government of American Samoa
Pago Pago, American Samoa 96799

Arizona

Office of Community Behavioral Health
Arizona Department of Mental Health
411 North 24th Street
Phoenix, Arizona 85008

Arkansas

Office on Alcohol and Drug Abuse
   Prevention
P.O. Box 1437
400 Donaghey Plaza N.
7th and Main Street
Little Rock, Arkansas 72203-1437

California

State of California
Department of Alcohol and Drug Programs
111 Capitol Mall, Room 250
Sacramento, California 95814-3229

Colorado

Colorado Alcohol and Drug Abuse Division
4210 East 11th Avenue
Denver, Colorado 80220

Connecticut

Connecticut Clearinghouse
334 Farmington Avenue
Plainville, Connecticut 06062

District of Columbia

Washington Area Council on Alcoholism
   and Drug Abuse
1232 M. Street N.W.
Washington, D.C. 20005

Delaware

The Resource Center of the YMCA of
   Delaware
11th and Washington Streets
Wilmington, Delaware 19801

Florida

Florida Alcohol and Drug Abuse Association
1286 North Paul Russell Road
Tallahassee, Florida 32301

Georgia

Department of Human Resources
Division of Mental Health
878 Peachtree Street N.E.
Room 319
Atlanta, Georgia 30309

Guam

Department of Mental Health and
   Substance Abuse
P.O. Box 9400
Tamuning, Guam 96911

Hawaii

Hawaii Substance Abuse Information
   Center
200 North Vineyard Boulevard
Room 603
Honolulu, Hawaii

Idaho

Health Watch Foundation
1076 North Cole Road
Boise, Idaho 83704

Illinois

Prevention Resource Center Library
901 South 2nd Street
Springfield, Illinois 62704

Indiana

Indiana Prevention Resource Center for
   Substance Abuse
840 State Road, 46 Bypass
Room 110
Indiana University
Bloomington, Indiana 47405

Iowa

Iowa Substance Abuse Information Center
Cedar Rapids Public Library
500 First Street S.E.
Cedar Rapids, Iowa 52401

Kansas

Kansas Alcohol and Drug Abuse Services
Department of Social and Rehabilitation
  Services
300 S.W. Oakley
Topeka, Kansas 66606

Kentucky

Drug Information Service for Kentucky
Division of Substance Abuse
275 East Main Street
Frankfort, Kentucky 40621

Louisiana

Bureau of Criminal Justice and Prevention
Office of Prevention and Recovery from
  Alcohol Abuse
2744-B Wooddale Boulevard
Baton Rouge, Louisiana 70805

Maine

Maine Alcohol and Drug Abuse Clearinghouse
Office of Alcoholism and Drug Abuse
  Prevention
State House Station #11
Augusta, Maine 04333

Maryland

Alcohol and Drug Abuse Administration
Department of Health and Mental Hygiene
201 West Preston Street
4th Floor
Baltimore, Maryland 21201

Massachusetts

Massachusetts Information and Referral
  Service
675 Massachusetts Avenue
Cambridge, Massachusetts 02139

Michigan

Michigan Substance Abuse and Traffic Safety
  Information Center
925 East Kalamazoo
Lansing, Michigan 48912

Minnesota

Minnesota Prevention Resource Center
2829 Verndale Avenue
Anoka, Minnesota 55303

Mississippi

Mississippi Department of Mental Health
Division of Alcoholism and Drug Abuse
1101 Robert E. Lee Building
9th Floor
239 N. Lamar Street
Jackson, Mississippi 39207

Missouri

Missouri Division of Alcohol and Drug Abuse
1915 Southridge Drive
Jefferson City, Missouri 65109

Montana

Department of Institutions
Chemical Dependency Bureau
1539 11th Avenue
Helena, Montana 59620

Nebraska

Alcohol and Drug Information
  Clearinghouse
Alcoholism Council of Nebraska
215 Centennial Mall South
Room 412
Lincoln, Nebraska 68508

Nevada

Bureau of Alcohol and Drug Abuse
505 East King Street
Suite 500
Carson City, Nevada 89710

New Hampshire

New Hampshire Office of Alcohol and Drug
  Abuse Prevention
6 Hazen Drive
Concord, New Hampshire 03301

New Jersey

New Jersey Department of Health
Division of Narcotic and Drug Abuse
  Control
129 East Hanover Street
Trenton, New Jersey 08625

New Jersey Division of Alcoholism
Training, Prevention, and Education Unit
129 East Hanover Street
Trenton, New Jersey 08625

New Mexico

Health and Environment Department
Substance Abuse Bureau
1190 St. Francis Drive
Harold Runnles Building, Room 3350
Sante Fe, New Mexico 87504-0968

New York

Prevention/Intervention Group
194 Washington Avenue
Albany, New York 12210

Narcotic and Drug Research, Inc.
Resource Center
11 Beach Street
2nd Floor
New York, New York 10013

North Carolina

North Carolina Alcohol/Drug Resource
   Center
G5
1200 Broad Street
Durham, North Carolina 27705

North Dakota

Division of Alcoholism and Drug Abuse
Department of Human Services
1839 East Capitol Avenue
Bismarck, North Dakota 58501

Ohio

Bureau of Drug Abuse and Bureau on
   Alcohol Abuse and Alcoholism Recovery
170 North High Street
3rd Floor
Columbus, Ohio 43266-0586

Oklahoma

Oklahoma State Department of Mental
   Health
P.O. Box 53277
Oklahoma City, Oklahoma 73152

Oregon

Oregon Drug and Alcohol Information
   Center
235 North Graham
Portland, Oregon 97227

Pennsylvania

Pennsylvania Department of Health
Department of Health Programs
P.O. Box 2773
Harrisburg, Pennsylvania 17105

Puerto Rico

Department of Anti-Addiction Services
Apartado 21414-Rio Piedras Station
Rio Piedras, Puerto Rico 00928-1414

Rhode Island

Rhode Island Division of Substance Abuse
Substance Abuse Administration Building
Cranston, Rhode Island 02920

South Carolina

South Carolina Commission on Alcohol and
   Drug Abuse
The Drug Store Information Clearinghouse
3700 Forest Drive
Suite 300
Columbia, South Carolina 29204

South Dakota

Department of Health
Division of Alcohol and Drug Abuse
523 East Capitol
Joe Foss Building Room 125
Pierre, South Dakota 57501

Tennessee

Division of Alcohol and Drug Abuse Services
Tennessee Department of Mental Health
706 Church Street
4th Floor
Nashville, Tennessee 37216

Texas

Texas Commission on Alcohol and Drug
   Abuse Resource Center
1705 Guadalupe
Austin, Texas 78701-1214

Utah

Division of Substance Abuse
120 North 200 West
4th Floor
P.O. Box 4550
Salt Lake City, Utah 84145-0500

Vermont

Office of Alcohol and Drug Abuse Programs
103 South Main Street
Waterbury, Vermont 05676

Virgin Islands

Division of Mental Health, Alcoholism, and
Drug Dependency
P.O. Box 1117
St. Croix, Virgin Islands 00821

Virginia

Office of Substance Abuse Services
State Department of Mental Health and
Mental Retardation
P.O. Box 1797
109 Governor Street
Richmond, Virginia 23214

Washington

Washington State Substance Abuse
Coalition
14700 Main Street
Bellevue, Washington 98007

West Virginia

Division of Alcohol and Drug Abuse
State Capitol
1800 Westington Street E.
Room 451
Charleston, West Virginia 25305

Wisconsin

Wisconsin Clearinghouse
University of Wisconsin-Madison
1245 East Washington Avenue
Madison, Wisconsin 53701

Wyoming

Division of Community Programs
Office of Substance Abuse
351 Hathaway Building
Cheyenne, Wyoming 82002-0710

SOME PROFESSIONAL JOURNALS FOCUSING ON SUBSTANCE ABUSE TOPICS

These are available at most university and medical school libraries.

Addictive Behaviors
Advances in Alcohol and Substance Abuse
Alcohol
Alcoholism: Clinical and Experimental Research
Alcoholism Treatment Quarterly
American Journal of Drug and Alcohol Abuse
British Journal of Addiction
Contemporary Drug Problems
Drug and Alcohol Dependence
Drugs and Society
International Journal of the Addictions
Journal of Chemical Dependency Treatment
Journal of Drug Educations
Journal of Drug Issues
Journal of Substance Abuse Treatment
Journal of Studies on Alcohol
Pharmacology, Biochemistry and Behavior
Psychology of Addictive Behaviors
Psychopharmacology

GLOSSARY

absorbed   drugs are absorbed, or entered into, the bloodstream (Chapter 4).

absorption through the skin   when a drug is absorbed through the skin it is called transdermal absorption (Chapter 6).

acetaminophen   aspirin-like analgesic (Chapter 13).

acetate   an ester of acetic acid that is a by-product in the metabolism of alcohol (Chapter 7).

acetylcholine   a neurotransmitter found both in the brain and in the parasympathetic branch of the autonomic nervous system (Chapter 3).

acetylsalicylic acid   chemical name for aspirin (Chapter 13).

action potential   the electrical impulse along the axon occurring when a neuron "fires" (Chapter 3).

acute tolerance   a type of functional tolerance occurring within the course of action of a single drug dosage (Chapter 1).

addiction   in reference to drugs, overwhelming involvement with use of a drug, getting an adequate supply of it, and a strong tendency to resume use of it after stopping for a period (Chapter 1).

addictive personality   the notion that there exists a clustering of traits common to persons who engage in addictive behaviors, such as drug abuse and alcoholism (Chapter 14).

aftercare   in alcohol and drug treatment, this term usually refers to therapeutic activities following completion of a formal treatment program (Chapter 15).

agitated depression   depressed mood accompanied by a state of tension or restlessness. Person shows excessive motor activity, as he or she may, for example, be unable to sit still, may pace, wring the hands, or pull at his or her clothes (Chapter 9).

agonist   a substance occupying a neural receptor and causing some change in the conductance of the neuron (Chapter 3).

akinesia   slowness of movement and underactivity (Chapter 9).

Alzheimer's disease   one of the most common forms of senility among the elderly. Alzheimer's disease involves a progressive loss of memory and other cognitive functions (Chapter 3).

amotivational syndrome   a term used to describe a loss of effectiveness and reduced capacity to accomplish conventional goals as a result of chronic marijuana use (Chapter 11).

amphetamine   a central nervous system stimulant whose actions are similar to those of the naturally occurring adrenaline (Chapter 2).

anabolic steroids   tissue-building drugs producing masculinizing effects as well (Chapter 13).

analgesia   pain relief produced without a loss of consciousness (Chapter 10).

anorectic effects   causing one to lose appetite—suppression of eating (Chapter 5).

antagonist   a substance occupying a neural receptor but blocking normal synaptic transmission (Chapter 3).

anterograde amnesia   loss or limitation of the ability to form new memories (Chapter 8).

anticholinergic hallucinogens   a class of drugs including atropine and scopolamine (Chapter 12).

antihistamines   common over-the-counter drugs with decongestant effects (Chapter 13).

antitussives   cough–suppressant drugs (Chapter 13).

anxiolytic   anxiety-reducing effects (Chapter 8).

apothecary   a pharmacist (Chapter 11).

as a function of   a term expressing causality. In graphing functional relationships between two variables, changes in one variable (in this case, drug effect) resulting from changes in another (in this case, drug dose) are represented (Chapter 4).

atropine   an anticholinergic hallucinogen found in certain plants (Chapter 12).

autonomic nervous system   part of the PNS, the autonomic nervous system or ANS has two branches: the sympathetic and parasympathetic (Chapter 3).

avoirdupois   something sold or measured by weight based on the pound of 16 ounces (Chapter 2).

axon   a long cylindrical extension of the cell body of the neuron. The axon contains an electrical charge from the cell body to the axon terminals (Chapter 3).

axon terminal (or terminal button)   enlarged button-like structures occurring at the end of axon branches (Chapter 3).

basal ganglia   forebrain structures important for motor control. The basal ganglia include the caudate nucleus, the putamen, and the globus pallidus (Chapter 3).

beta-blockers   drugs that block beta-adrenergic receptors of the sympathetic system and thus act to relieve high blood pressure (Chapter 3).

blackout   a person's amnesia about events while drinking even though there is no loss of consciousness (Chapter 7).

blood-brain barrier   a term given to the system that "filters" the blood before it can enter the brain (Chapter 3).

brand name   the commercial name given to a drug by its manufacturer (Chapter 4).

budget deficit   in reference to governments, the difference between the amount of money spent and the amount earned in taxes and other revenues (Chapter 1).

buprenorphine another drug used in the treatment of opiate addiction, this substance blocks the effects of opiates (Chapter 15).

cannabinoids a general term to describe the more than 60 chemical compounds present in cannabis. One of these cannabinoids is delta-9-tetrahydrocannabinol (better known as THC), the main psychoactive compound in marijuana (Chapter 11).

cannabis sativa the Indian hemp plant whose resin, flowering tops, leaves, and stem contain the plant's psychoactive substance. The more popular term for the plant is marijuana (Chapter 2).

causal relationship a causal relationship exists between variables if changes in a second variable are due directly to changes in a first variable (Chapter 4).

central nervous system the brain and the spinal cord comprise the central nervous system or CNS (Chapter 3).

cerebellum hindbrain structure important in motor control and coordination (Chapter 3).

chemical name the name given to a drug that represents its chemical structure (Chapter 4).

combination pill birth control pill containing synthetic forms of both female sex hormones: progesterone and estrogen (Chapter 13).

computer axial tomography (CAT) the CAT scan is a technique for developing a three-dimensional X-ray image of the brain (Chapter 3).

confabulation a fabrication about events, when asked questions concerning them, because of an inability to recall. Due to memory deficits, confabulation differs from lying in that the person is not trying to deceive the questioner (Chapter 7).

control in research, control means to be able to account for variables that may affect the results of a study. Control can be accomplished either by statistical procedures or by including different groups in an experiment (Chapter 4).

control group in an experiment, the control group is the reference or comparison group. The control group does not receive the experimental manipulation or intervention whose effect is being tested (Chapter 4).

cortex the cerebral cortex or cortex is the outermost and largest part of the human brain (Chapter 3).

counseling in alcohol and drug treatment, counselors are specially trained professionals who perform a variety of treatment activities, including assessment, education, and individual, marital, or family counseling (Chapter 15).

crack a freebase cocaine produced by mixing cocaine salt with baking soda and water. The solution is then heated, resulting in brittle sheets of cocaine that are "cracked" into small, smokeable chunks or "rocks" (Chapter 5).

craving   a term variously defined in reference to drug use. Typically it refers to a strong or intense desire to use a drug (Chapter 1).

cross dependence   suppression of symptoms of withdrawal from one drug by another drug (Chapter 1).

cross tolerance   tolerance to a drug or drugs never taken that results from protracted tolerance to another drug or drugs (Chapter 1).

delirium tremens (DTs)   symptom of alcohol withdrawal syndrome characterized by severe agitation, confusion, and disorientation. Terrifying hallucinations and delusions also may be present (Chapter 7).

delta-9-tetrahydrocannabinol   the principal active cannabinoid in marijuana responsible for the experienced psychoactive effects (Chapter 11).

dendrite   spiny branch-like structures extending from the cell body of a neuron. Dendrites typically contain numerous receptor sites and are thus important in neural transmission (Chapter 3).

desipramine   an antidepressant medication (Chapter 15).

dispositional tolerance   an increase in the rate of metabolizing a drug as a result of its regular use (Chapter 1).

dissociative anesthetic   a class of drugs including PCP and ketamine (Chapter 12).

dissolved   a drug is dissolved by converting it from solid to liquid by mixing the drug with a liquid (Chapter 4).

distillation   process by which the heating of a fermented mixture increases its alcohol content (Chapter 7).

distribution   drugs are distributed, or transported, by the blood to their site(s) of action in the body (Chapter 4).

disulfiram   a drug interfering with the metabolism of alcohol so that a person soon feels very ill if he or she drinks while on a regimen of disulfiram. The drug may be used as part of a treatment program for alcohol dependence (Chapter 7).

dopamine   a neurotransmitter found in the brain (Chapter 3).

driving while intoxicated   operating a motor vehicle with enough alcohol or other drug in the blood to be legally defined as intoxicated (Chapter 1).

drug   broadly defined as any chemical entity or mixture of entities, not required for the maintenance of health, that alters biological function or structure when administered (Chapter 1).

drug dosage   measure of the quantity of drug consumed (Chapter 1).

drug effect   the action of a drug on the body. Drug effects are measured in different ways (Chapter 1).

drug expectancy   what a person expects to occur as a function of drug use (Chapter 14).

drug potency   the dose of a drug yielding its maximal effect (Chapter 4).

dyskinesia   disordered movements (Chapter 9).

effective dose   the percentage of individuals who show a given effect of a drug at a given dose (Chapter 4).

electroencephalography (EEG) technique used to measure electrical activity in the brain (Chapter 3).

endogenous developed from within. When applied to depression, the term means that depressive symptoms seem to be due to genetic factors (Chapter 9).

endorphins neurotransmitters found in the brain that are mimicked by opiate drugs (Chapter 3).

enzyme breakdown one process by which neurotransmitters are inactivated. Chemicals called enzymes interact with the transmitter molecule and change its structure so that it no longer is capable of occupying receptor sites (Chapter 3).

estrogen one of the female sex hormones involved with the regulation of ovulation and the menstrual cycle (Chapter 13).

exogenous developed from without. When applied to depression, the term means that depressive symptoms seem to be in reaction to a particular situation or event (Chapter 9).

extrapyramidal outside the pyramidal tracts, with origin in the basal ganglia (Chapter 9).

feedback in this context, in a series of events, what happens in a later event alters the ones before it in some way (Chapter 4).

fermentation a combustive process in which yeasts interact with the sugars in plants, such as grapes, grains, and fruits, to produce an enzyme which converts the sugar into alcohol (Chapter 2).

flashback a sudden reoccurrence of an LSD-like experience (Chapter 12).

forebrain a large part of the human brain, the forebrain includes the cerebral cortex, thalamus, hypothalamus, and the limbic system (Chapter 3).

formication syndrome symptoms of itching and feeling as if insects were crawling on skin, caused by cocaine and amphetamine (Chapter 5).

freebase a substance may be separated, or "freed," from its salt base. The separated form of the substance is thus called "freebase" (Chapter 4).

functional tolerance decreased behavioral effects of a drug as a result of its regular use (Chapter 1).

GABA short for gamma-amino-butyric acid, a neurotransmitter found in the brain (Chapter 3).

general anesthesia the reduction of pain by rendering the subject unconscious (Chapter 8).

generalizability the degree to which a research finding from one setting or group of people (or other species) can be applied to others (Chapter 4).

generic name the general name given to a drug that is short (and easier for most people to say) than its chemical name (Chapter 4).

grain as a measure, a unit of weight equal to .0648 of a gram (Chapter 1).

group design a type of experimental design in which groups (as compared to individual cases) of subjects are compared to establish experimental findings (Chapter 4).

guaifenesin   an over-the-counter expectorant (Chapter 13).

hash oil   a potent distillate of marijuana or hashish. It first appeared in the United States in 1971, and can contain up to 60% THC (Chapter 11).

hashish   the resin-covered flowers of the cannabis sativa hemp plant. This part of the plant generally contains a greater concentration of the drug's psychoactive properties (Chapter 2).

heroin   heroin is produced by chemically processing morphine. It is more potent than morphine, and has become the major opiate drug of abuse (Chapter 10).

hindbrain   the lower part of the brain including the medulla, pons, and cerebellum (Chapter 3).

hippocampus   a structure of the limbic system thought to be important in the formation of memories (Chapter 3).

homeostasis   a state of equilibrium or balance. Systems at homeostasis are stable; when homeostasis is disrupted, the system operates to restore homeostasis (Chapter 4).

hyperactive children   disorder of childhood involving restlessness, inability to attend, and disruptive behavior. Today referred to as "attention-deficit disorder" (Chapter 5).

hypothalamus   forebrain structure regulating eating, drinking, and other basic biological drives (Chapter 3).

ibuprofen   aspirin-like analgesic (Chapter 13).

illicit drug use   drug use not in accord with legal restrictions (Chapter 1).

inferior colliculi   midbrain structures controlling sound localization (Chapter 3).

initial sensitivity   the effect of a drug on a person the first time he or she uses it (Chapter 1).

intoxication   a transient state of physical and psychological disruption due to the presence of a toxic substance, such as alcohol, in the CNS (Chapter 7).

intramuscular   a route of drug administration, meaning in the muscle (Chapter 1).

intravenous   a route of drug administration, meaning "into the veins" (Chapter 1).

joint   a hand-rolled marijuana cigarette (Chapter 11).

ketamine   a dissociative anesthetic (Chapter 12).

kindling   repeated exposure to a stimulus may lower the brain's threshold for seizures. This effect, which is produced by electrical stimulation or by cocaine, is called kindling (Chapter 5).

Korsakoff's syndrome   a disorder characterized by memory loss and psychotic behavior related to heavy use of alcohol and malnutrition (Chapter 3).

L-dopa   a chemical precursor of dopamine used in the treatment of Parkinson's disease (Chapter 3).

lethal dose   the percentage of individuals killed by a given dose of a drug within a specified time (Chapter 4).

levo-alpha-acetylmethadol (LAAM)   a drug used in treating heroin addiction; similar in action to methadone, but has longer-lasting effects (Chapter 15).

limbic system   forebrain structures including the amygdala, hippocampus, and others (Chapter 3).

long-term memory   memory for remote events. According to one theory of memory, information enters long-term memory through short-term memory (Chapter 7).

loss-of-control drinking   the idea that once an alcoholic takes a drink of alcohol, he or she cannot stop by volition. Sooner or later, it is thought, the person will drink to a high degree of intoxication (Chapter 15).

macroenvironmental   term used to describe widespread environmental factors operating on a broadly-based scale, such as culture, urbanization, and legal guidelines regarding drug use (Chapter 14).

manic   relating to mania, a mood disturbance which typically includes hyperactivity, agitation, excessive elation, and pressured speech (Chapter 9).

MAO inhibitors   drugs used to treat depressions that inhibit the activity of the enzyme monoamineoxidase, which degrades the neurotransmitters of norepinephrine and serotonin (Chapter 7).

mass media   communications designed for widespread distribution, such as advertisements, films, and printed materials (Chapter 16).

maximal effect   the most intense, or peak, level of a drug effect (Chapter 4).

medial forebrain bundle   pathway that is rewarding when stimulated. Thus it is often referred to as the pleasure center (Chapter 3).

medulla oblongata   the lowest hindbrain structure of the brain, the medulla is important in the regulation of breathing, heart rate, and other basic life functions (Chapter 3).

mescaline   an LSD-like hallucinogen found in the peyote cactus (Chapter 12).

metabolism   the process by which the body breaks down matter into more simple components and waste (Chapter 4).

methylated amphetamines   a class of drugs including MDA and MMDA (ecstasy) (Chapter 12).

microenvironmental   term used to describe environmental factors specific to the immediate drug use context, such as lighting, music, presence of others, and the like (Chapter 14).

midbrain   includes the inferior and superior colliculi (Chapter 3).

milieu treatment   treatment in which the organization and structure of a setting are designed to change behavior (Chapter 15).

monoamine   a class of chemicals characterized by a single amine group. This class includes neurotransmitters: norepinephrine, dopamine, and serotonin (Chapter 3).

morphine   a derivative of opium best known as a potent pain relieving medication (Chapter 2).

mucous membranes   the moist surfaces lining the mouth, nose, eye sockets, throat, rectum, and so forth (Chapter 1).

myelin   a fatty white substance covering the axons of some neurons (Chapter 3).

naloxone (Narcane)   a short-acting opiate antagonist (Chapter 10).

narcoleptic   a state characterized by brief but uncontrollable episodes of sleep (Chapter 9).

narcotic   a central nervous system depressant containing sedative and pain relieving properties (Chapter 2).

neuroleptic   tranquilizing drugs used to treat psychoses. Another term for neuroleptic is major tranquilizer (Chapter 9).

neuromuscular junction   junction between neuron and muscle fibers where release of acetylcholine by neurons causes muscles to contract (Chapter 3).

neuron   the individual nerve cell that is the basic building block of the nervous system (Chapter 3).

neuropsychological tests   formal ways of measuring behavioral functions that may be impaired by brain lesions (Chapter 7).

neuroses   generally describes any non-psychotic emotional disturbance, pain, or discomfort beyond what is appropriate in the conditions of one's life (Chapter 9).

neurotransmitters   chemical substances stored in the axon terminals that are released into the synapse when the neuron fires. Neurotransmitters then influence activity in post-synaptic neurons (Chapter 3).

nicotine poisoning   a consequence of nicotine overdose, characterized by palpitations, dizziness, sweating, nausea, or vomiting (Chapter 6).

norepinephrine   a neurotransmitter found in the brain and involved in activity of the sympathetic branch of the autonomic nervous system (Chapter 3).

nuclear magnetic resonance (NMR)   increasingly referred to as magnetic resonance imaging (MRI), this technique creates a high-resolution, three-dimensional image of the brain (Chapter 3).

opium   the dried sap produced by the poppy plant (Chapter 10).

opium poppy   a plant cultivated for centuries, primarily in Eurasia, for opium, a narcotic which acts as a central nervous system depressant (Chapter 2).

oral   as a route of drug administration, it means taken into the mouth and swallowed (Chapter 1).

orientation to time   awareness of temporal specification, such as time of day, the day of the week, or the year. Orientation to time is one of the functions assessed in a psychiatric exam (Chapter 7).

over-the-counter drugs that can be legally obtained without medical prescription (Chapter 1).

paranoid schizophrenia a type of schizophrenia distinguished by systematic delusions or auditory hallucinations related to one theme (Chapter 9).

parasympathetic branch the branch of the ANS responsible for such activities as lowering heart rate and blood pressure (Chapter 3).

Parkinson's disease a disease primarily afflicting the elderly that involves a progressive deterioration of motor control (Chapter 3).

peripheral nervous system sensory nerves, motor nerves, and the autonomic nervous system comprise the peripheral nervous system or PNS (Chapter 3).

personality disorder patterns of behavior that are long-standing, usually ally recognizable from adolescence or earlier. These behavior patterns are a ''disorder'' because they frequently create distress for the person as a result of their social consequences (Chapter 15).

peyote a cactus plant whose top (a ''button'') is dried and ingested for its hallucinogenic properties (Chapter 2).

pharmacology the scientific study of drugs. It is concerned with all information about the effects of drugs on living systems (Chapter 1).

phenylpropanolamine a mild stimulant with decongestant and appetite suppressant properties (PPA) (Chapter 13).

placebo in pharmacology, refers to a chemically inactive substance (Chapter 1).

placebo control a type of control originating in drug research. Placebo subjects are of the same makeup and are treated exactly the same as a group of subjects who receive a drug, except that placebo subjects receive a chemically inactive substance (Chapter 4).

polydrug use the same person's regular use of more than one drug (Chapter 1).

pons hindbrain structure important in the control of sleep and wakefulness (Chapter 3).

positron emission transaxial tomography (PETT or PET) the PET scan is a technique used to measure activity in selected brain regions (Chapter 3).

potentiation the potentiating effect of combining two or more drugs is greater than the sum of the effects of each of the drugs in question (Chapter 4).

prevalence the general occurrence of an event, usually expressed in terms of percentage of some population. Another common statistic in survey studies is incidence, or the number of first–time occurrences of an event during some time period (Chapter 1).

price elastic refers to the finding for some substances that changes in its price are inversely related to the demand for the substance (Chapter 14).

primary prevention   attempts to avoid substance use or abuse before it has a chance to occur (Chapter 16).

progesterone   one of the female sex hormones involved with the regulation of ovulation and the menstrual cycle (Chapter 13).

progestin pill   birth control pill that contains only progestin—a synthetic progesterone (Chapter 13).

prohibition   the legal forbidding of the sale of a substance, as in the alcohol Prohibition Era in the U.S., 1920–1933 (Chapter 2).

proof   a term used to designate the proportion of alcohol in a beverage, by volume. Proof typically is used in reference to distilled spirits and equals twice the percentage of alcohol (Chapter 7).

prostaglandins   naturally occurring chemicals that are blocked by aspirin and related analgesics (Chapter 13).

protracted tolerance   a type of functional tolerance occurring over the course of two or more drug administrations (Chapter 1).

pseudoephedrine   an over-the-counter decongestant (Chapter 13).

psilocybin   an LSD-like hallucinogen found in some kinds of mushrooms (Chapter 12).

psychoactive   pertaining to effects on mood, thinking, and behavior (Chapter 1).

psychopharmacology   the subarea of pharmacology that concerns the effects of drugs on behavior (Chapter 1).

psychological set   an individual's knowledge, attitudes, expectations, and other thoughts about an object or event, such as a drug (Chapter 1).

psychological treatment   treatments geared to changing emotions, thoughts, or behavior without the use of medications or other physical or biological means (Chapter 15).

psychology   the scientific study of behavior (Chapter 1).

psychosis   a severe mental disorder whose symptoms include disorganized thinking and bizarre behavior (Chapter 4).

psychosurgery   surgery which entails the cutting of fibers connecting particular parts of the brain or the removal or destruction of areas of brain tissue with the goal of modifying severe behavioral or emotional disturbances (Chapter 9).

psychotherapy   typically, conversation between a specially trained individual (therapist) and another person (or family) intended to change patterns of behavior, thoughts, or feelings in that person (Chapter 15).

psychotropic   any substance which exerts a special or unique action on the mind (Chapter 9).

pylorospasm   the shutting of the pylorus value occurring in some people when very large quantities of alcohol are consumed (Chapter 7).

rebound insomnia   inability to sleep produced as a withdrawal symptom associated with some depressant drugs (Chapter 8).

receptor sites   specialized structures located on dendrites and cell bodies for neurons which are activated by neurotransmitters (Chapter 3).

recovery   in the addictions field, this term means changes back to health in physical, psychological, and social functioning. It is generally believed that recovery is a lifetime process requiring total abstinence from alcohol and nonprescribed drugs (Chapter 15).

reinforcing   describing a consequence of a behavior that increases the likelihood it will occur again (Chapter 1).

REM rebound   an increase in the rapid eye movement or REM stage of sleep when withdrawing from drugs that suppress REM time (Chapter 8).

REM sleep   acronym for "rapid eye movements," which are associated with dream activity and are one stage in a cycle of sleep (Chapter 7).

relapse   a term from physical disease, relapse means return to a previous state of illness from one of health. As applied to smoking, it means the smoker resumes smoking after having stayed quit for some amount of time (Chapter 6).

reticular activating system   pathway running through the medulla and pons that regulates alertness and arousal (Chapter 3).

reuptake   another process by which neurotransmitters are inactivated. Neurotransmitter molecules are taken back up into the axon terminal that released them (Chapter 3).

reverse tolerance   sometimes called sensitization, this occurs when increased sensitivity develops after chronic use of a drug (Chapter 5).

route of drug administration   the way drugs enter the body (Chapter 1).

scopolamine   an anticholinergic hallucinogen found in certain plants (Chapter 12).

secondary prevention   interventions designed to prevent substance use problems just as the early signs of abuse begin to appear (Chapter 16).

sedative-hypnotic effects   the ability of some drugs to produce a calming effect and induce sleep (Chapter 8).

self-help group   a therapeutic group in which all members have some identified problem that is the focus of the group's therapeutic activity (Chapter 15).

self-medication   the idea that some people "prescribe" their own medication, in the form of alcohol or illicit drugs, to alleviate psychological difficulties such as anxiety or depression (Chapter 15).

serotonergic hallucinogens   a class of drugs including LSD and drugs with similar effects and mechanisms of action (Chapter 12).

serotonin   a neurotransmitter found in the brain (Chapter 3).

short-term memory   memory for recent events. Short-term memory generally is thought to differ from long-term memory in several important ways (Chapter 7).

side effects   effects of a drug other than those of central interest. Used most often in reference to the other than therapeutic effects of medications, such as the side effect of drowsiness for antihistamines. Note that what are considered a drug's side effects depend on the specific uses of the drugs (Chapter 4).

social detoxification   treatment of alcohol withdrawal without the use of medication (Chapter 7).

sociopathy   a type of personality disorder characterized by a lack of concern for social obligations or rules, a lack of feelings for others, and a tendency toward violence (Chapter 15).

solvent   a substance, usually liquid or gaseous, used to disperse one or more other, frequently intoxicating, substances, as in glue sniffing (Chapter 2).

speakeasy   a slang expression used to describe a saloon operating without a license. The term was used popularly during alcohol prohibition (Chapter 2).

spontaneous remission   resolution of a problem without the help of formal treatment (Chapter 15).

spontaneous sleep apnea   a sudden cessation of breathing that may occur during sleep in infants (Chapter 6).

stage model   a stage model of behavior usually refers to its development. Stage models are based on the idea that development is marked by discrete steps or "stages," each of which has unique features or characteristics (Chapter 6).

standard drink   the alcohol equivalent in a drink of beer, wine, or distilled spirits. A standard drink equals a half-ounce of alcohol, which is about the amount in 12 ounces of beer, 4 ounces of table wine, and 1 ounce of 90–100 proof whiskey (Chapter 7).

state-dependent learning   learning under the influence of a drug is best recalled when in the same "state" (Chapter 5).

statistically different   findings based on samples estimated, by use of statistical tests, to be real and not due to chance fluctuations (Chapter 1).

stimulant psychosis   paranoid delusions and disorientation resembling the symptoms of paranoid schizophrenia caused by prolonged use or overdose of cocaine and amphetamines (Chapter 5).

subcutaneous   a route of drug administration, meaning introduced under the skin (Chapter 1).

substantia nigra   literally, "black substance," this basal ganglia structure is darkly pigmented. The substantia nigra produces dopamine, and damage to this area produces Parkinson's disease (Chapter 3).

summation   the summative effect of combining two or more drugs is the simple addition of the effects of each of the drugs in question (Chapter 4).

superior colliculi   midbrain structures controlling visual localization (Chapter 3).

suspended   a drug is suspended in solution if its particulates are dispersed in solution but not dissolved in it (Chapter 4).

sympathetic branch   branch of the ANS activated during emotional arousal and responsible for such physiological changes as increased heart and respiratory rate, increased blood pressure, and pupil dilation (Chapter 3).

sympathomimetic term applied to drugs such as cocaine and amphetamine which produce the physiological effects of sympathetic activity (Chapter 3).

synapse the junction between neurons (Chapter 3).

syndrome in medicine, a number of symptoms occurring together and characterizing a specific illness or disease (Chapter 1).

synesthesia an effect sometimes produced by hallucinogens characterized by the perception of a stimulus in a modality other than the one in which it was presented (for example, a subject may report ''seeing'' music) (Chapter 12).

tardive dyskinesia an extrapyramidal complication characterized by involuntary movements of the mouth and tongue, trunk, and extremities. Tardive dyskinesia is a side effect of long-term (2 or more years) use of antipsychotic drugs (Chapter 9).

tea-pad a place where people gather to smoke marijuana. The site could be anywhere from a rented room to a hotel suite (Chapter 11).

teratogenic producing abnormalities in the fetus (Chapter 9).

tertiary prevention refers to treatment interventions with persons well beyond the early stages of substance abuse or dependence (Chapter 16).

testosterone the male sex hormone. Anabolic steroids are basically synthetic versions of testosterone (Chapter 13).

thalamus forebrain structure that organizes sensory input (Chapter 3).

therapeutic index a measure of a drug's utility in medical care, it is computed as a ratio (LD 50/ED 50) (Chapter 4).

tolerance generally, a diminished drug effect with its continued use (Chapter 1).

treatment planned activities designed to change some pattern of behavior(s) of individuals or their families (Chapter 15).

treatment effects the result of experiencing a treatment, usually measured in different areas of functioning, such as substance use, family functioning, and vocational functioning (Chapter 15).

treatment outcome research research designed to show the causal relationship between undergoing a treatment and some physical, psychological, or social change (Chapter 15).

values clarification a frequent component of affect-oriented prevention programs; it typically involves exploration of one's needs and beliefs regarding drugs (Chapter 16).

vesicles tiny sacs located in axon terminals that store neurotransmitters (Chapter 3).

withdrawal symptoms a definable illness occurring with a cessation or decrease in use of a drug (Chapter 1).

Subject and Author Index

Pages in italics refer to figures. Pages followed by "t" refer to tables; pages followed by "n" refer to notes.

Acknowledgments of Permission

Chapter 1

pp. 23–25 "Symptoms of Dependence" from American Psychiatric Association: *Diagnostic & Statistical Manual of Mental Disorders, Third Edition. Revised.* Washington, D.C. American Psychiatric Association.

Chapter 2

Table 2–1, p. 45; adapted from Blum, K., *Handbook of Abusable Drugs;* Gardner Press, Inc.

Table 2–2, p. 46; adapted from Cohen, S., *The Substance Abuse Program,* Tables V–2, V–6, pp. 370–372; Haworth Press (1981).

Chapter 3

Figure 3–3, p. 56; from Bardo & Risner (1985) chapter in Galizio/Maisto *Determinants of Substance Abuse,* p. 74, Plenum Press, Inc.

Figure 3–5, p. 62; from figure 3.9, p. 76 of *Biological Psychology* by Kimble, Daniel P., copyright 1988 by Holt, Rinehart and Winston, Inc., reprinted by permission of the publisher.

Figure 3–6, p. 63; from figure 3.11, p. 78 of *Biological Psychology* by Kimble, Daniel P., copyright 1988 by Holt, Rinehart and Winston, Inc., reprinted by permission of the publisher.

Chapter 5

pp. 120–121 adapted from Goodman & Gilman, *Pharmacological Basis of Therapeutics, Sixth Edition,* Macmillan Publishing Group. Also from Goldberg & Stolevan *Behavioral Analysis of Drug Dependence;* Academic Press.

p. 123 adapted from Laties & Weiss *Federation Proceedings,* 1981, Vol. 40, # 12, p. 2690, Fig. 2.

Chapter 6

Figure 6–2, p. 137; Shopland, D.R. & Brown, C (1985). Current trends in smoking control. *Annals of Behavioral Medicine,* Vol. 7, 5–8, (Figs. 1 & 2).

Table 6–2, p. 151; Adapted with permission from Lichenstein, E., and Bram, R. (1980) Smoking Cessation Methods: Review & Recommendations from W.R. Miller (ed), The addictive behaviors (pp. 169–206). NY: Pergamon Press, and from the authors.

Table 6–3, p. 159; Sawyer, D.A., Julia, H.L. & Turin, A.C. (1982), Caffeine & human behavior: arousal, anxiety & performance effects. *Journal of Behavioral Medicine,* 5, 415–439. (Plenum Press); and also from Kenny, M., and Darragh, A. (1985). Central effects of caffeine in man, in S.D. Iverson (ed), Psychopharmacology: Recent advances and future prospects, pp. 278–288. (Oxford Univ. Press).

Table 6–4, 6–5, p. 160; Tables adapted from Gilbert (1984) and published with permission from Alan R. Liss, Inc.

Table 6–6, p. 165; Adapted from Graham (1978); from Nutrition Reviews, 36 (1978): 101. Used with permission of the International Life Sciences Institute—Nutrition Foundation.

Figure 6–7, p. 165; Advertisement reproduced with permission of Glenbrook Laboratories.

Table 6–7, p. 166; Leonard, T.K., Watson, R.R. and Mohs, M.E. (1987): The effects of caffeine on various body systems: A review. Copyright the American Dietetic Association. Reprinted by permission from Journal of the American Dietetic Assn., Vol. 87: 1048, (1987). Permission to reprint also granted from Primary Cardiology 1987; 10: 104–110, 1984 Physicians World Communications Group.

Table 6–8, p. 168; Sawyer, D.A., Julia, H.L., and Turin, A.C. (1982). Caffeine and human behavior: arousal, anxiety and performance effects. Journal of Behavioral Medicine, 5, 415–439 (published by Plenum Press).

Chapter 7
p. 178; abstracted from Becker, C.E., Roe, R.L., Scott, R.A. (1975). Alcohol as a drug. New York: Medcom Press.

p. 210; Case based on one discussed in the DSM-111 Case Book (Spitzer, et al., 1981. pp. 56–57) American Psychiatric Press.

Chapter 9
pp. 252–253, 257–258, 262, 265–266; DSM-III-R Casebook (1989) Washington D.C., American Psychiatric Press, Inc.

Chapter 11
pp. 297–298; Reprinted with permission of MacMillan Publishing Co., from Gautier, T. *The Hashish Club,* (1844) from Solomon, D. *The Marihuana Papers.* pp. 126, 130–131, 135 (1966).

Chapter 14
Figure 14–3, p. 372; Photo by Susan Pierce, copyright Holt, Rinehart and Winston, Inc. (1990).

Table 14–3, p. 375; Adapted from Table 17 (pp. 478–479) of Whitehead/Simpkins chapter in Kissin/Begleiter *Biology of Alcoholism* V. 6 (1983) Plenum Press.

Chapter 15
Table 15–2, p. 396; Reprinted with permission of Alcohol Anonymous World Services, Inc.